Third edition

Fast Guide to
Propellerhead
REASON

Debbie Poyser, Derek Johnson
and Hollin Jones

D1286739

PC Publishing

PC Publishing
Keeper's House
Merton
Thetford
Norfolk IP25 6QH
UK

Tel +44 1953 889900
Fax +44 1953 889901
email info@pc-publishing.com
web site http://www.pc-publishing.com

First published 2003
Second edition 2005
Third edition 2007

© Debbie Poyser and Derek Johnson

ISBN 10 1 870775 27 9
ISBN 13 978 1 870775 27 4

British Library Cataloguing in Publication Data
A catalogue record for this book is available from the British Library

Printed and bound in Great Britain by Biddles, Kings Lynn, Norfolk

Contents

Acknowledgments

We would like to thank the following people for their help while this book was being written: Niels Larsen (unfailingly fast, efficient and insightful when we had questions during the first edition of this book); Ernst Nathorst-Böos; All at Midiman UK; Peter Gaydos, known better in the Reason community as Pegasus; and Phil Chapman of PC Publishing for his patience!

Hollin Jones would like to thank Phil Chapman, Neil Worley and Kevin Steel, all for totally different yet equally musical reasons.

Introducing Reason

Welcome to The Fast Guide to Propellerhead Reason

Congratulations on choosing Propellerhead's Reason software. In the few years it's been around, Reason has established itself as the electronic music-making software of choice for many thousands of serious musicians who want to make their tracks in an intuitive environment that encourages them to think like creative artists and producers, rather than mathematicians. They appreciate the friendly, 'studio-identical' look of Reason, its excellent sound quality, its literally unlimited sound-creation options, elegant ease of use, and the way it caters for how electronic musicians like to work.

As hi-tech music journalists and musicians ourselves, we have seen a lot of music and audio programs over the years – going back to the early Atari music years. But as soon as we got the chance to try Reason, we realised it stood out from the rest of the pack as something unique and very special. It was music software that didn't feel like software.

Reason has given rise to a dedicated user community and is contantly attracting newcomers eager to discover how best to use this exciting tool. This book helps both the new user and the more experienced Reason musician to explore fully the nooks and crannies of the Reason studio, as well as introducing projects and techniques that exploit its capabilities. Though the book is not specifically aimed at expert Reason users (if you're an expert, you probably don't really need an instructional book!), there are nevertheless ideas and techniques in here that such people could benefit from. And as well as this book, don't forget the excellent Propellerhead Getting Started and Operation manuals, and the continuing support on Propellerhead's web site.

One important thing for newcomers to bear in mind is that they should expect it to take a while before they are really proficient in using every aspect of Reason to the full. It is an entire studio in a computer, after all, and no-one expects to be able to use everything in a studio, expertly, overnight.

So please enjoy reading the book, trying out the ideas, and – most importantly – getting the best from the musical phenomenon that is Reason.

What is Reason?

Reason is literally a self-contained electronic music studio/lab emulated in software. It contains all the necessary components required for playing and creating synthesizer sounds, drum kits and patterns; importing, playing and

Info

Which version?

This book takes account of the new features added to Reason by V3, but it is also suitable for users of earlier versions since the basic ways in which Reason operates have changed little since V1.

1

manipulating samples and sampled loops; sequencing and editing complete compositions (using both track-based and pattern-based methods); applying effects treatments and signal processing to sounds and tracks; and, finally, mixing the whole into a stereo audio file – a finished product.

There are a few things that Reason won't currently do, the main one being audio recording. The only way to get audio (in the form of commercial samples or audio samples you have created yourself) into the program is to import it into Reason's sample playback modules. There is at present no 'tape-recorder'-style method of recording digital audio directly into the program, as there is with the mainstream MIDI / Audio sequencing applications such as Cubase SX or Logic Pro. This makes the program perhaps less suitable, when used alone, for conventional song-based projects than for predominantly electronic instrumental work. However, there are certainly ways to bring, say, vocal performances into Reason to work alongside your electronic backing tracks, and the program can be used efficiently in tandem with all major sequencing platforms, so that the advantages of both approaches can be gained.

Who can use Reason?

Anyone who has a suitable computer, whether Mac or PC. The program will be almost instantly comfortable in use for those who have experience of studio hardware and analogue or virtual analogue synths. However, it is so friendly in its approach that it should hold few fears for even the complete beginner.

Neither is musical style necessarily a barrier to using Reason. While it is arguably best suited to electronica and modern dance music, it is sonically open ended and can be used for most musical genres – excepting, perhaps, the predominantly acoustic-based styles.

Brief overview

Reason appears to the user as a 19-inch studio rack, complete with graphic mounting bolts. What to put into the rack, choosing from a set of instrument and studio 'devices' is entirely up to you, with two exceptions.

First, at the top of the rack will always be the 'Hardware Interface'. This device allows you to direct any incoming MIDI signals to various parts of the rack (for example, sending information from a MIDI hardware control surface to a Reason synth), and to direct audio out of the program. The sounds you'll produce with Reason will be sent to either the built-in sound-reproducing circuitry in your computer, or to any installed audio hardware such as a soundcard. From this point, you can decide whether to listen to Reason's output on headphones or send it to a pair of speakers.

The other device that is always present in the rack is at the bottom, and it's the Transport. Here you'll find the tape machine-style play, stop, fast-wind and record controls needed for Reason's sequencer and synchronised device playback, as well as information displays relating to various aspects of the program's operation.

Apart from these two modules, the rack is yours to fill as you like, with as many of each module as required (and a different set for every Song, if desired), as long as your computer is powerful enough to provide the processing power for them. Here is what you can choose from:

Rack with h/w interface + transport

The SubTractor analogue-style synthesizer

A polyphonic synth module that emulates the interface of a vintage knob-driven synth and takes its name from the fact that the analogue style of sound-making is known as 'Subtractive'. It's a well-specified instrument with which you should be able to create a wide range of sounds, from thumping bass timbres, through impressive pads to cutting leads – anything, in short, which a genuine analogue synth could create. In addition, because this is software and the designers can thus be as generous as they like with features, SubTractor has more options than the average analogue synth and even allows you to create very digital-sounding timbres. Sounds can be made with SubTractor even by those with no knowledge of how analogue synthesis works – just move knobs and press switches until you hear something you like – but some basic analogue theory, as provided in the SubTractor chapter, will be valuable.

SubTractor

The Malström Graintable synthesizer

Debuted in Reason V2, this cutting-edge synth introduces a new synthesis system – graintable synthesis, Propellerhead's hybrid of 'granular' and 'wavetable' systems, processed by analogue-style filters. The result is a powerful synth that is rather different from standard analogue and allows the creation of a huge variety of different and dramatic timbres, from the weirdly atmospheric to the gritty and edgy. Malström is also unique amongst Reason instrument devices in having an audio input, allowing any other Reason audio to be processed by its signal path – sound design heaven!

Malström

The Redrum drum computer

This is Reason's equivalent to a hardware drum machine, with a design and operating method that borrows much from classic pre-MIDI drumboxes, most notably the fashionable TR808 and TR909 from Roland. Programming is via

ReDrum

a pattern-based, 'step-time' method that encourages hands-on experimentation and requires little or nothing in the way of conventional drumming skills. Drum hits for each of 10 voices are simply placed on a 16-step grid, with instant audible feedback of the result, and may be moved and deleted at will until the desired effect is achieved. Each drum voice is a sample; many are provided with the program, and others can be imported. Drum kits may thus be built up from any sounds in any combination. And that's not all, as every sample can also be extensively manipulated by its own set of basic synthesis parameters.

The NN-19 sampler

As mentioned earlier, NN-19 doesn't actually sample, but is rather a sample playback module, for samples provided with Reason and for others that you can import. Samples can be found on the Internet, taken from commercial sample CDs, or recorded yourself.

Though it doesn't sample, NN-19 is a very decent sample-playback module, with comprehensive multisample mapping powers, plus synthesis parameters almost the equal of the Subtractor module – and similar to those you may have come across in expensive studio hardware samplers. The NN-19, NN-XT advanced sampler and the Dr:rex ReCycle loop player are important to Reason's ability to change and adapt to different musical styles, as they allow sounds specifically suited to different genres to be brought into the program.

NN-19

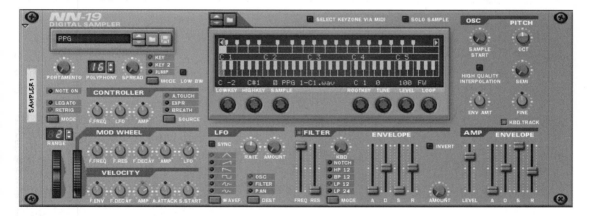

The NN-XT sampler

The NN-XT expands on what is possible with the NN-19 in many ways – and not just in size! The NN-XT offers lots of extra facilities, one of the most important being the abilty to create patches with 'layers', allowing multisamples with much greater expressive potential to be created. The NN-XT's synthesis engine has also been enhanced over that of the NN-19, and each sample you load can have its own individual synthesis settings – a great advance. Add separate audio outputs and a brilliant graphic interface, and you have a sample device as sophisticated and powerful as you'll ever need.

Info

How do I put all this together?

Assuming you have the program installed and ready to go (see Chapter 2 for some help with this), you can start by going to the Tutorials in Chapter 3, to create a rack and then make a simple track with some of the devices.

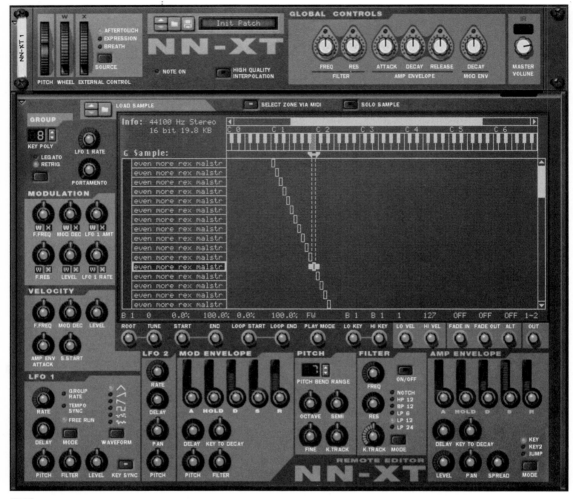

NN-XT

The Dr:rex loop player

Dr:rex exists to allow the playback and manipulation of sampled loops that have been processed using Propellerheads' popular ReCycle software. However, you don't need to own ReCycle in order to use Dr:rex, since ReCycle-treated loops can be found on the Internet and in commercial sample collections. Many are also included in Reason's sound banks.

The advantages of ReCycled loops are considerable: once a loop has been processed through this software, its pitch and tempo become freely changeable, facilitating the matching of loops of any base pitch or tempo to songs of any other pitch or tempo. Almost anything can fit with almost anything else, which obviously saves huge amounts of time and trouble for the producer of heavily sample-based music. If you do own ReCycle, of course, you'll have that much more flexibility for using loops of your choice within Reason. But since Dr:rex has its own synthesis facilities and allows you to change the

playback order of loops, even loops gleaned from other sources can be modified and made more individual to you.

Dr:rex

Combinator

The Combinator is a fascinating new module. More of a tool than an instrument, it is essentially a container into which you can place any number of
other modules, at least as many as your computer will support. It's like a rack
within a rack, and allows you to build complex chains of effects and instruments which can be saved and recalled, and placed directly into a project. Of
course you've always been able to create chains like this, but until now you
had to save them as a Reason project, then open and modify the project to
use your pre-built setup. The Combinator is self-contained, so any multi-
instrument, effects chain or performance patch you create can be inserted
directly into any project, multiple times.

Modules within a Combi can be freely patched, and you can even drop a
whole ReMix in there to create a huge sub-mix, which is then fed through a
stereo output into the main mixer. Another trick up the Combinator's sleeve is
its programmer window which lets you split and layer all the devices within the
Combi - perfect for creating performance patches. You could for example easily create a bass in the left hand, piano in the middle and synth at the top, each

The Combinator

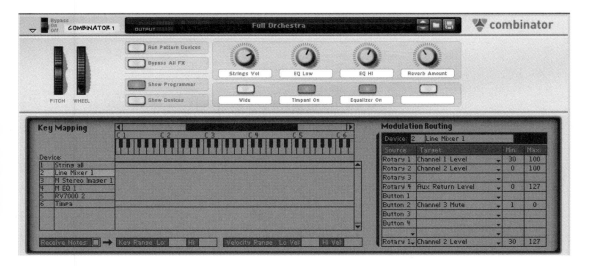

running through separate effects, all within the Combi. It's also able to run pattern devices, so you can trigger drum or Matrix patterns from within it.

What the Combinator provides is an amazing new way to use the great modules that Reason already offers. And if you're not into building your own Combis yet, there are some fantastic ones supplied in the Factory Sound Bank.

The Matrix Pattern sequencer

The Matrix emulates the oldest type of electronic music sequencer, the step sequencer. It does not record what you play in a tape-recorder fashion, like most modern software sequencers, but instead requires you to manually enter each note you would like to hear played back, on a grid which has up to 32 separate note-slots, or steps. Step sequencers are capable of producing effects of enormous complexity, and allowing patterns to be created that could not be played by a human performer. They're also well suited to producing bass lines, arpeggios, and repeating motifs. One of the most enjoyable aspects of step sequencing is that it can be done almost randomly and doesn't require any playing skill.

Matrix

The ReMix mixer

Every studio needs that central point through which signals are pulled together, balanced, equalised and processed to make a proper mix. Reason is no exception, with its easy-to-use ReMix rack mixer. The difference with the ReMix is that the sometimes confusing signal routing that would have to be done by hand in the real world can often be completed invisibly and automatically for you by the software itself. ReMix mixers can also be chained

Mixer

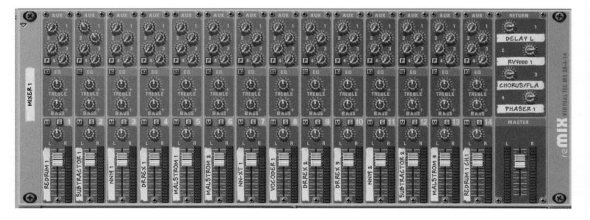

together, to make a mixer as big as you need for your session. And when it comes to mixing down, ReMix can be automated very easily, recreating every move you require.

Line mixer 6:2

New in V3, the Line mixer is a simple six-channel mixer with its own Aux send, pan and level controls for each channel. It's particularly useful in a Combi, because very often you need to sub-mix a number of modules before they are sent to the Combinator's stereo inputs. A ReMix is overkill, but a stripped-down Line mixer is perfect. It's also handy to use in the rack for audio and CV routing and splitting signals as well as creating an effects chain for a particular module before it passes to the main mixer, adding another layer of flexibility.

Line Mixer 6:2

The effects

Until V2, Reason effects and processors comprised a set of eight easy to use and processor-efficient devices. As of V2.5, sophisticated reverb and distortion processors were added, plus a simple 'unison' processor. V3 adds the MClass mastering effects, plus the Combinator provides a great new way to use all the effects in new ways. The collection as a whole will provide you with reverb, delay, chorus, flange or phase, a spot of filtering, some distortion, compression or EQ or even full mastering. Effects and processors are also chainable in all sorts of weird and wonderful ways, to create more sophisticated effect treatments and unheard-of multi-effects configurations. You can get pretty strange with Reason's sound-making devices, but if weird is your thing, don't neglect the effects.

Effects

MClass effects

New in Reason 3, the MClass mastering suite of effects addresses one lingering doubt about previous versions of Reason - the overall sound and volume of mixdowns. There's an equalizer, stereo imager, compressor and maximizer, all of which can be applied to the output stage of a mix (between the mixer and the Hardware Interface) to give the whole sound a more polished, professional quality. Some of the modules have the same basic function as existing modules, like the EQ and compressor, but here they have been specially created to add sparkle to a whole mix. Of course you can still use them individually as insert or send effects if you like. They work particularly well inside a Combi, which simplifies the cabling in your projects.

It's worth reading up about some of the principles at work in the MClass effects so that you better understand what you're doing to the signal, and how to tweak it. The presets supplied with Reason are actually a great starting point and it's quite likely that you won't have to change them very much at all. You can get a good idea of how much they are boosting your sound by temporarily switching them off and witnessing the sudden change as the punch and clarity drops out!

MClass Effects

The ReBirth Input Machine

Users of Propellerhead's cult ReBirth RB338 Techno Microcomposer software are encouraged to bring their ReBirth projects and sounds into Reason, integrating its approach via the ReBirth Input Machine (RIM). The easy-to-use RIM exists only to direct the audio signals from ReBirth's two TB303 Bassline synth emulations and its virtual TR808 and 909 drum machines into Reason, where they can be mixed and effected alongside Reason audio.

ReBirth Input

ReBirth discontinued

Rebirth was discontinued in 2005 but is still available as a free download for registered users from www.rebirthmuseum.com. There's also a free ReFill for download which contains all the sounds from Rebirth, plus a few more! Version 2.0.1 is the last ever version of Rebirth, and still works on Windows 95, 98, NT, Me and XP as well as Mac OS9. It is not compatible with the newest, Intel-based Macs. There was never a native OS X version, and running it under Classic was impractical at best.

The BV512 Vocoder

A vocoder, as Propellerhead see it, is much more than just a way to super-impose synth textures on voice or vocal performances. It takes the idea further, allowing any sound to take on the pitch and timbral characteristics of almost any other. The device itself is hard to categorise: where it feels like an effects processor in one context, it feels like an instrument in another. As a processor, it offers a mode where it functions as a flexible bank of fixed frequency filters, for precise and dynamic (if desired) equalisation.

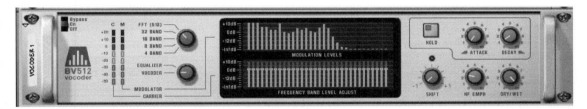

Spider Audio and Spider CV mergers/splitters

One simple module available in many realworld analogue modular synths is a 'mult'; this simply allows one gate or control voltage signal to be sent to one or more (multiple) destinations. In Reason, such a feature allows one Matrix sequencer to easily 'play' two or more Subtractor synths. Propellerhead have gone the extra mile, of course: the Spider CV module also allows gate and CV merging, and a separate Spider is dedicated to splitting or merging audio. The last was a left-field release that has many mundane and specialised uses.

The sequencer

The multitrack main sequencer is the hub of music-making activities in Reason: even if you haven't chosen to record musical performances into the sequencer, instead using the Pattern-based devices for your sequencing, you'll almost certainly want to automate knob tweaks, Pattern changes, mixer levels and other parameters, and edit controller data – all done via the approachable sequencer.

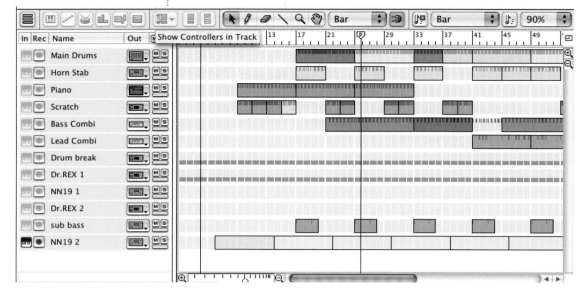

Main sequencer

If you've used one of the major computer-based sequencers before, the stripped-down approach of the Reason sequencer will hold no fears for you, and may even feel refreshingly clean and straightforward. The flip side for the most experienced sequencer users is that they may miss certain sophisticated features of other sequencer platforms. Fortunately, thanks to Propellerhead's ReWire technology, Reason runs alongside other ReWire-compatible music applications, so the best of both worlds is available. In version 3, numerous enhancements have been made to Reason's sequencer.

The cable system

Reason devices are connected together in the same way they would be in the real world: by cables, which you can see at the rear of the rack by hitting the Tab key. You can either leave it to Reason to make the most logical connections it can in any given situation, or connect cables between devices yourself – or use a combination of both systems.

Addendum for the Third Edition

As up-to-date users will have noted from the above summary, this book now covers all the devices and features found in V3 of Reason. Propellerhead's approach of addition and refinement rather than wholesale change is good news for everyone because it means that the transition between versions is much more gentle than with some other software. Someone who had only ever used Reason V1 for example would have little difficulty in adjusting to

V3, as many of the basic principles are the same.

Where versions 2 and 2.5 added some major new modules, the changes in V3 are more workflow-oriented. Even the new modules – Combinator, Line Mixer and MClass effects – are tools rather than instruments. Elsewhere, Reason's functionality is extended with the Remote system for live performance, as well as a much-improved browser and new sound banks.

Many of the screenshots in the book are taken on Mac OS X, but this is of no particular significance since the program is functionally identical on a Mac or on Windows. There are minor differences in some areas like the installation procedure and windowing system, but these make no real difference to the way you use the program.

Installation and setting up

What do I need to make music with Reason?

Because Reason is so self-contained, you need only a few things to get up and running: at the most basic, a computer (Mac or PC); a soundcard or other audio hardware (all Macs and many PCs have in-built audio hardware); a pair of headphones or monitors and some means of powering them; and of course the software. Most people will also want to add a MIDI interface and a MIDI keyboard for inputting notes (though Reason can actually be used without these if absolutely necessary). You may be able to combine the last two by buying a keyboard that has some way of interfacing with your computer already built in. Users still running Mac OS9.x and a version of Reason prior to v3 will also require OMS (Open Music System) for MIDI operation.

In general, the most flexible MIDI setup is a keyboard and a separate multi-port MIDI interface. MIDI interfaces are available with from one to eight or more MIDI ports; a 2-to 4-port interface would be a good bet for use with Reason, making it easy to connect a hardware MIDI controller box as well as your MIDI keyboard, should you want one at some point. See Chapter 16 for more on remote control.

All current Macs and PCs use USB (Universal Serial Buss) for connecting to peripherals, and if you have a computer with USB you'll need a USB-compatible MIDI interface. Such interfaces are widespread, with many affordable options (look at M-Audio, Roland, Yamaha, MOTU and Steinberg). Alternatively, you could use one of the many USB MIDI keyboards on the market, without the need for a separate MIDI interface, via a single cable from the USB port of the computer to that of the keyboard. M-Audio, Roland and Evolution, for example all make suitable keyboards of this type. However, you may then be back to a single MIDI port, which is not so flexible.

There's one more USB issue, which arises if your computer only has one USB socket. If this is the case, you may well need to use a hub, which provides several USB outputs from one input. It just so happens that Griffin Technologies amongst others produces the Audio Hub, a four-port USB hub designed for USB audio recording and playback and developed in response to problems some musicians have experienced with general-purpose hubs. Generally, computers have several USB ports.

If you have an older serial-equipped computer, things are different and you will need a serial MIDI interface (which will probably be an older model), or perhaps to add a USB PCI card (with USB sockets) to your computer so that you can use one of the more readily available USB interfaces.

Some computer sound/audio cards have MIDI interfacing built in, as do some computer digital audio systems, such Digidesign's project studio systems, Digi 002 and the Mbox. These studio-quality systems are especially appropriate if you plan to use audio recording software as well as Reason, which is quite likely. Buying the best audio hardware you can afford will also improve the Reason sound you hear while you work.

There is probably no real need to buy a keyboard with a synth built in, as Reason has all the sounds you will need, and if Reason is your only music software it can't transmit MIDI data anyway, so if you're starting from scratch you might prefer to look for controller keyboards, which make no sound of their own but are perfect for note and MIDI controller input. They will probably also be cheaper than a new synth. Some models are incredibly small and light, suitable for Reason use anywhere, especially with a laptop.

Some kind of monitoring system so that you can hear what Reason is producing will also be necessary. This could be as simple as a pair of headphones connected to the audio output of your Mac or your PC soundcard. However, you'll certainly want to attach a pair of speakers at some point, and again you

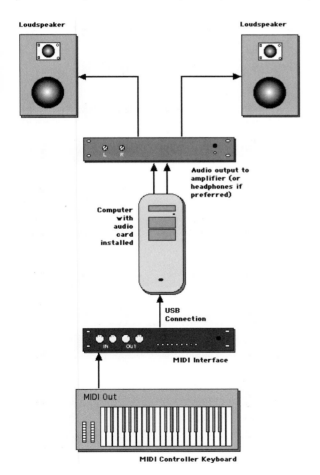

A basic MIDI setup for running Reason. If your keyboard has USB MIDI interfacing built in, simply omit the MIDI interface in the diagram.

Loudspeaker

Loudspeaker

Audio output to amplifier (or headphones if preferred)

Computer with audio card installed

USB Connection

MIDI Interface

IN   OUT

MIDI Out

MIDI Controller Keyboard

should aim for the best you can afford. A decent full-range studio monitoring system is the ideal. Look for names like Genelec, Event, Mackie, Dynaudio Acoustics, and Tannoy.

Reason V3 minimum system requirements

PC

- Intel Pentium III processor or better, running at 600MHz or faster.
- 256 Megabytes of RAM.
- A CD-ROM drive.
- Windows 2000, XP or later
- 800x600 or larger screen resolution
- A 16-bit Windows-compatible audio card, preferably with an ASIO or DirectX driver. Microsoft DirectX (only if the card supports it).
- A MIDI interface and MIDI keyboard.

Mac

- G4, G5 or Intel-based Mac
- 256 Megabytes of RAM.
- A CD-ROM drive.
- Mac OS X 10.2 or later, 10.3 or later strongly recommended
- 800x600 or larger screen resolution
- A MIDI interface and MIDI keyboard.

These are minimum specs; you will be able to use more devices if you have plenty of RAM and a fast processor. Having said this, Reason runs well (with fewer devices) even on fairly modest processors.

Users of Reason v2.5 or earlier may be running Mac OS 9, in which case OMS (Open Music System) 2. x or later must be installed. Reason 3 won't run on OS 9, and new Macs haven't booted into the older operating system for a number of years now.

Owners of new Intel-based Macs should note that Reason v3.0.5 is a Universal Binary and so will run natively on both G4 / G5 and Intel systems.

Installing Reason

Installation instructions are provided on the packaging of the Reason program CDs and in the Getting Started guide that comes with the software, but we'll run through the process quickly here.

- Place the Reason program CD in your CD-ROM drive.
- The installer will boot automatically for PC users.
- Otherwise, double-click on the disc icon to see its contents or right click on the CD icon and select 'Explore' (Windows users).
- Double-click on the 'Install Reason' icon. (Mac users can choose between installers for Mac OS9 and OSX depending on which OS they're using.)
- Follow the on-screen instructions.

You'll be prompted to install the Factory Sound Bank and Orkester Sound

Bank that come with Reason. As of v3 you are not able to choose not to install them, as it's assumed you will want to use some of the excellent sounds and patches that they contain. You will also be prompted to insert them at various points in the future for authorization purposes, so hang on to them. The banks take up just over 1GB of space, which won't trouble large, modern hard drives.

Soundcard drivers

Before you launch Reason for the first time, you should make sure you have taken care of one further step; this is optional for Mac users without sound-cards installed but necessary for people who have a soundcard or external audio hardware (such as an integrated MIDI/audio interface unit) that they wish to use, whether they're using a Mac or a PC. You need to install the latest driver (a small piece of software) for your soundcard. It's important that you get the right kind of driver for your card, as latency could be a problem for you otherwise. Many FireWire and PCI interfaces require drivers, although a growing new generation of USB2 audio interfaces are "class compliant", and work simply by plugging them in.

Mac

Macs have audio hardware built in, and no special driver is needed to access this. However, if you're using a soundcard or other audio hardware with a Mac running OS 9.x, it will have to adhere to the ASIO standard. This driver should be placed in the 'ASIO Drivers' folder in the main Reason folder. All modern cards have Mac OS X CoreAudio drivers, and will be compatible with Reason running on that platform. Always check for the latest driver version from the manufacturer's website.

PC

The situation differs for PC users; they too can use ASIO drivers if their cards have one – in fact, this is the option recommended by Propellerhead and definitely preferable. However, Reason will also work with soundcards that are compatible with Microsoft's DirectX audio protocol. As a last resort, if your card doesn't have access to ASIO or DirectX drivers, Reason will communicate with cards using Windows MME (Multi Media Extensions), though this option is reported to result in real-time playback problems and latency issues.

Launching Reason for the first time

When you first launch the program to use it, you will be presented with an on-screen authorisation form. Find your Product Authorization Card from the Reason software package and enter the relevant details from it – the most important being the long serial number. (You'll also be asked if you want to register your software with Propellerhead, which is recommended, but you don't have to do this right now; you can do it on-line at any time, or snail-mail the registration card.) The program will also prompt you to insert the Soundbank CD-ROMs (even if you have already installed the sound banks on your computer), as a security measure.

The next thing you'll see is the Preferences dialogue box, which should automatically appear, along with a default 'rack'. Note that while you should make some basic settings now (so that you can play Reason and hear its output), you can change these preferences at any time without even needing to reboot the software.

When you have the Preferences dialogue box on screen, you first need to make some audio settings, to tell Reason what type of audio hardware in your computer it should address: click on the dropdown menu and select the Audio Preferences page. The options you see next to 'Audio Card' will depend on whether you're using a Mac or a PC, and on what audio hardware you have connected.

PC

Next to 'Audio Card Driver', you should be able to select a driver for the soundcard/audio hardware you have installed in/attached to your PC. If there is an ASIO driver, select that; if not, the next best is a Direct Sound driver. If you don't have either of these, use the MME driver.

Mac OS 9.x for Reason v2.5 or earlier

Mac users with no extra audio hardware installed (other than that built into the Mac) will see only an 'SM (Sound Manager) built-in' option, which means that the software will use Apple's Sound Manager system extension to communicate with your Mac's built-in audio hardware.

If you have a soundcard/audio hardware installed in/attached to your Mac and have placed its driver in the Reason ASIO folder, it should appear in the Audio Card pop-up.

Mac OS X

The audio driver you choose for Mac OS X should be selected by name from the pop-up list; 'Built-in Audio' is the option for using the Mac's own audio hardware. Third party audio hardware, if installed properly, will appear in the pop-up list; simply select the audio output you require.

Other Audio settings will depend on your card. With 'Master Tune', you'll be able to set a tuning offset (+/-100 cents around a central A-440Hz tuning reference), which is handy if you find yourself trying to work with or sync to an audio source which can't be tuned (analogue tape or real musicians!). Be warned, though, that changing the Master Tune setting will have a detrimental effect on any samples you might have loaded into your Song: they'll all play faster or slower, with a resulting change in pitch. This will be particularly noticeable with any loops that you might have loaded into NN19 or NNXT; there may be gaps or overlaps between consecutive triggerings of the samples.

You may also be able to choose a sample rate (44.1kHz or 48kHz), and Windows and Mac OSX users may have a buffer size/output latency control. All users will see a quoted value for latency for the currently selected audio device. Also common to all systems is a Latency Compensation parameter, which is used to make allowances for any delays that may occur between Reason and another MIDI application when they're running together via MIDI Clock.

Other options, such as output channels beyond a basic stereo pair (Reason can handle up to 64 audio outputs, if available), digital clock source and so on, may or may not be available, depending on your card. If you've an ASIO-compatible card installed, there will also be a button for launching the card's ASIO Control Panel; again, the options available here will depend on your card. See your soundcard's documentation for details.

Info

Latency

Latency is the term used to describe the delay between pressing a key on your MIDI keyboard and the corresponding sound being produced by your software. There is always some latency, because the MIDI instruction has to pass into the computer, the software has to generate a sound in response to the MIDI data, and that sound has to then pass out of the computer via the audio hardware. This all takes a finite amount of time, but if your audio hardware and its driver are efficient, the delay should be so small that it's not noticeable – anything below 12 milliseconds (mS) is usable and shouldn't make it awkward for you to play Reason sounds from the keyboard. As latency gets larger, the delay between pressing a key and hearing the sound gets longer, and eventually it's not possible to play naturally.

The latency you experience depends to a large extent on your audio hardware and its drivers, plus, to a certain extent, your computer's operating system and internal buss speeds. With some soundcards you will be able to adjust latency, but bear in mind that producing a lower latency figure places heavier demands on your computer. For example, if you have a PC running Windows with DirectSound or MME audio drivers, you will be able to alter the output latency value, but if you go too far and set the latency too low for your system, you'll experience clicks, pops, and possibly sound breaking up during playback, as the computer struggles to produce the latency figure you've asked for and do everything else it has to do too. You'll then have to adjust latency back in the other direction until you reach a satisfactory compromise. If you're a PC user, there are one or two tweaks you can make to help reduce latency; the best place to find out about these is the discussion forums at Reasonstation (www.reasonstation.net) and the Propellerhead web site (www.propellerheads.se). In fact, anyone who has problems of any kind with Reason can take advantage of the wealth of knowledge and experience of other users at these very active and useful forums.

Setting Up MIDI

Configuring the Open Music System (OMS) on OS 9.x Macs

(Note – this applies only to Reason v2.5 and earlier.) Before making MIDI settings inside Reason, it will be necessary for Mac users running Mac OS9.x to set up OMS, the routing system that facilitates communication between your MIDI keyboard and Reason (and other MIDI software).

Install OMS

OMS is supplied with Reason. The installer application, 'OMS 2.3.8', is included on the Reason program disk, with full installation details provided in a supplied PDF manual. Simply double-click on the installer application and

Info

Mac Virtual Memory

If you're using Mac OS 9.x, you must disable Virtual Memory in order to run Reason, and the majority of other MIDI and audio software. You'll find the switch in the Memory control panel accessible from the Apple Menu. Mac OS X, which the majority of Mac users will be running, manages virtual memory automatically and presents no problems at all to Reason.

Info

In Audio Preferences, you may be able to set a playback sample rate lower than the more usual 44.1 and 48kHz options. While this will have an effect on the audio quality you hear, it may also allow you to play back a Reason Song that your computer otherwise refuses to play, as it reduces the system impact. This is much less of a problem on more recent, more powerful computers.

follow the instructions. All OMS's various components will be installed in the correct place on your hard drive. It may also be necessary to further install OMS MIDI drivers for your MIDI interface, or USB-equipped keyboard, in the OMS folder in your Mac's system folder. If you plan to route MIDI between non-ReWire-compatible programs on your computer, you'll need to install OMS's IAC (Inter Application Communication) driver. Make the choice in OMS's custom installation option.

Set up OMS

Once OMS and any required drivers have been installed, it's time to set up OMS to talk to your MIDI equipment. If you're using a MIDI interface connected to your Mac, whether multi-port or a simple 1-In/1-Out device, make sure it's attached to your Mac and that your MIDI gear is attached to it.

Launch the OMS Setup application; this leads you through a logical series of steps that automatically locate any MIDI gear attached to your computer, or MIDI interface, and create a 'studio set up' document. This appears on screen as a window filled with a graphic list of what's been detected.

If you're lucky and your equipment is listed in OMS's database, this will be the end of the process: you'll see named graphic representations of your gear in the list. If there are any question marks next to detected MIDI devices, you'll need to customise the entries yourself. In general, this simply means naming the entry, and perhaps telling OMS which MIDI channels a given device transmits over and responds to, plus a couple of other parameters.

Now, use the 'Save and Make Current' option in the File menu to make this setup the one that OMS, and OMS-compatible applications, recognise. From now on, your attached MIDI devices will appear in Reason's MIDI Preferences dialogue box so you can set which one will control Reason.

Mac OS X MIDI configuration

In Mac OS X, MIDI functionality is built into the system – no OMS required. You may need to install drivers for your USB MIDI interface, or USB-equipped MIDI keyboard, though for some simple devices even this step may not be necessary. Consult the documentation included with your interface. Mac OS X MIDI functionality is customised in the Audio MIDI Setup utility (found in the Utilities folder, in the Applications folder, unless you moved it!).

PC MIDI configuration

MIDI configuration of Reason on a PC should be simply a matter of deciding which MIDI Inputs are assigned to which Reason ports. The backbone of MIDI routing from your interface to any MIDI software installed on your computer should have been automatically handled by the installation of your interface's drivers. Consult the documentation included with your interface.

Reason MIDI settings

Now it's time to tell Reason what external MIDI devices will be playing or controlling it, by making some MIDI Preferences settings.

Launch Reason and choose the MIDI page in the Preferences dialogue (under the Edit menu, or the Reason menu in Mac OSX). Here you select which MIDI instrument you'll be using to record performances into the tracks of Reason's main sequencer. Your attached MIDI instrument or instruments, or ports on your MIDI interface, should appear in the 'Port' pop-up. Choose the one you want to use for playing and recording into Reason. Also set the MIDI channel on which your instrument will be transmitting data to Reason here. (The MIDI instrument must be set to transmit on this channel too.)

Next, choose the Advanced MIDI Preferences page if you intend to play sounds from Reason devices via an external hardware sequencer, or another piece of MIDI software installed on your computer. Here you can route MIDI data coming from up to four external devices to four internal Reason buses. (See the chapter on using Reason with other software and instruments for more.)

The Advanced MIDI prefs also set up whether you'll be remotely controlling Reason's on-screen knobs and sliders from an external MIDI device (such as a hardware fader box – see the automation chapter), and from where Reason will derive MIDI clock if it's being synchronised to external hardware or software (again, see the 'Reason + others' chapter).

Reason and Mac OS X drivers

Don't forget that using Reason with OS X is not just a case of installing the OS X version on a computer that's running OS X. You will also have to make sure your MIDI interface and audio hardware is compatible with the version of OS X you are running. M-Audio interfaces for example are quite picky about which driver version you're running with which OS revision. Owners of new Intel-based Macs should check with the relevant manufacturer that Universal Binary drivers are available before buying. In most cases, they will be.

Reason and laptops

The idea of running Reason on a laptop has really taken off – laptop processors no longer lag behind desktop machines as they used to. It's perfectly possible to buy a PC laptop, for example, that offers exactly the same performance in CPU terms as a desktop PC. Apple's PowerBooks and especially the new MacBooks and MacBook Pros with their dual core CPUs are blazingly fast and are more than capable of running heavy Reason projects. There's also no longer the price difference that once existed between Macs and decent PC systems.

Not only are many Reason musicians using a laptop in preference to a desktop computer, giving themselves the ability to compose anywhere and on the move, they're taking their laptops on stage – often in groups – and creating a Reason live experience. The new collaborative Remote system is geared specifically towards several people controlling a Reason project from a single laptop. Here are some of the considerations if you're thinking about using a portable yourself.

All modern laptops should be able to run Reason happily, and you can now get very small, portable peripherals – MIDI interfaces, audio hardware and MIDI keyboards – which are ideal for mobile use. Look for names such

---

Info

Saving and backing up

It almost goes without saying that your Reason projects need to be backed up. They should exist in at least two places – saving Songs and Patches to only one drive is asking for trouble. The best plan is have a second, dedicated backup drive (not just a partition on your main drive) apart from the one your Songs and Patches are normally recorded to. You could also backup to CD or DVD, if you have a burner – most current computers have such a drive built in. You could also backup to Flash media or even an iPod. Back up at the end of each session if possible. You also need to maintain your recording and backup drives – even more so if you're recording audio (via another application) to hard disk. Buy a drive-maintenance application such as Norton Utilities or Disk Warrior and run it regularly.

Info

Reason without a MIDI keyboard

There are a couple of utilities that turn the computer keyboard into a MIDI input device, thus allowing you to use Reason without a MIDI keyboard. These may be useful when you first get started, or if you're on the move with Reason on a laptop and would like to compose without dragging a keyboard around.

as M-Audio, Steinberg, Roland/Edirol, Evolution and Novation. As with desktop machines, look for the fastest processor you can afford, as much RAM as possible, and a large hard drive.

- Reason MIDI Board 1.1 (PC): A colourful Czech utility designed specifically for Reason which provides nine octaves of control, key volume and pitch shift. Works with Windows 98/NT/2000/Me/XP. Surf over to http://www.slunecnice.cz/product/Reason-MIDI-Board/ for a free download.
- Bome's Mouse Keyboard (PC): You can find Bome's Mouse Keyboard at www.bome.com/midi/keyboard/. This little program allows both computer keyboard and mouse to be used as input devices for Reason's sequencer, and has a few other nice features. The web site also offers a basic tutorial on using it with Reason.
- Sweet Little Piano (PC): Costs around US$15 and can be purchased online from www.ronimusic.com/sweet_pi.htm.
- MidiKeys (Mac): Available from http://www.manyetas.com/creed/midikeys.html, this handy little program provides a miniature onscreen keyboard which is visible to your sequencer software as a MIDI source, playable via mouse or keyboard.
- v.m.k (Mac): Another lightweight MIDI input program, available for free from http://www.fredrikolofsson.com/pages/code-apps.html.

With a utility such as MidiKeys or Bome's Mouse Keyboard for making the computer keyboard into a MIDI input device, you could even use Reason without a MIDI keyboard – ultimate portability if you're running it on a laptop.

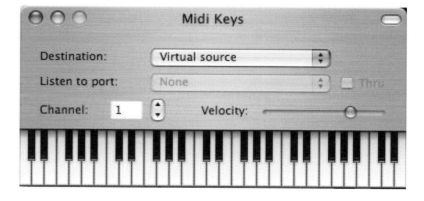

Quickstart tutorials

T his chapter aims to give you some hands-on experience of using Reason devices before you read up on the detail in the individual device chapters.

During Reason installation, a Tutorial song (Tutorial Song.rns) should have been saved to your hard drive. The Quick Tutorial chapter in your Reason Getting Started manual will take you through it. You should have a go with that tutorial before starting on the ones in this chapter, as it's very useful and gives you some hands-on practice with Reason devices. When you've worked through the Propellerhead tutorial, you can move on to the ones below.

This chapter is divided into three tutorials:

* Create a rack
* Create a Song
* Experiment with the tutorial Song

It will take a while to go through these steps, but if you do you will find yourself familiar with many of the basic procedures you need to write your own music with Reason. There are other ways of doing some of the actions you'll be asked you to do, but things have been kept as simple as possible for these tutorials. Various concepts will be touched upon only in as much detail as needed at this point, but you will find explanations of all device features in their relevant chapters elsewhere in the book, so don't panic!

Before going any further, make sure you have made the Reason MIDI settings explained in Chapter 2, so that your MIDI keyboard acts as the input device for the Reason sequencer.

Create a rack

* Launch Reason.
* Under the Edit menu (Reason Menu in Mac OS X), choose 'Preferences'.
* In the Preferences dialogue, General section, under Default Song, click the 'Empty Rack' button. Close the Preferences dialogue.
* Under the File menu, choose new, or use Apple/Control-N, to open a New Song, which at this stage will be the empty rack. Only the Hardware Interface is at the top, and the main sequencer and transport bar at the bottom.
* Older versions of Reason: Open the 'Empty Rack.rns' song in the Template Songs folder inside your Reason folder, or select all the devices

in the current rack ('Select all devices' under the Edit menu) and choose 'Delete device' from the Edit menu, to start with an empty rack. Save any Song first, if you do the latter.

Note that later on, when you're more experienced with Reason, you can create a rack with your favourite device configuration and settings and save it as your default Song, then set it in Preferences to open when you launch the program. For now, it's best to have an empty rack.

The empty rack.

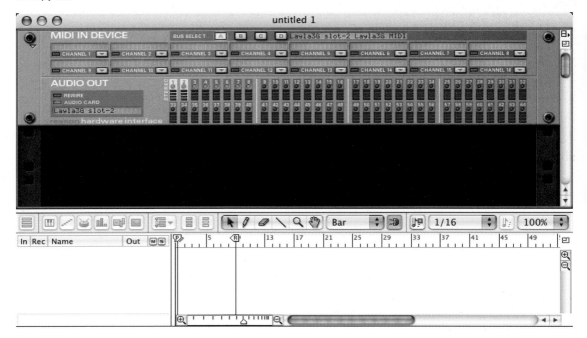

Create a mixer

Go to the Create menu in the menu bar and select Mixer 14:2. This fixes a ReMix mixer into the rack and automatically connects it to the hardware interface so that audio can be routed out of your computer. It's a good idea to start every new rack with a mixer, as every new device created will then automatically be connected to the mixer for you.

Create some instruments

- Select Dr:rex from the Create menu. Its stereo output is automatically connected to input channel 1 of the mixer, and its name appears on the scribble strip next to the channel 1 fader.
- Select ReDrum from the Create menu. Now its stereo output is automatically connected to channel 2 of the mixer, and its name appears on the corresponding scribble strip, as above.
- Select another Dr:rex from the Create menu. It should be automatically connected to channel 3 on the mixer.

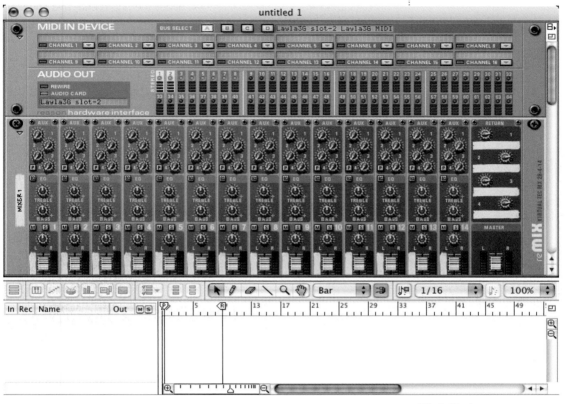

untitled 1

Add a ReMix mixer.

- Select SubTractor from the Create menu. Its mono output is connected automatically to mixer channel 4. Note that the mixer's inputs can be either mono or stereo according to the device connected. You don't have to do anything, as Reason chooses automatically for you.
- Select Matrix from the Create menu. This adds a Matrix Analogue Pattern Sequencer to the rack, which should be automatically linked to the SubTractor for triggering the SubTractor's sounds. Because the Matrix doesn't generate its own sounds, but only triggers those made by another device, it doesn't need a connection to the audio Mixer, and Reason doesn't create one.
- Select NN-19 from the Create menu. This adds a sampler device to the rack. Its stereo output is automatically connected to mixer channel 5. Though the sampler will be triggered from the main sequencer in this tutorial example (just as the SubTractor will be triggered from the Matrix sequencer we've just created), there's no need to highlight the sequencer before creating the sampler, as every device added to the rack automatically makes its own track in the main sequencer. Drag the top edge of the main sequencer window to make it larger so you can see the tracks which have been added so far as you've created devices. The sequencer can also be 'broken off' from the rack display in V2 by choosing 'Detach Sequencer Window' from the Windows menu.

Create some effects

- Select the Mixer by clicking within it.
- Now select DDL1 Digital Delay Line from the Create menu. Because the Mixer was highlighted, the Delay is connected to it in a 'send-return' loop.
- Add a reverb effect by clicking in the mixer again and selecting RV7 Digital Reverb from the Create menu. The names of the effects appear in scribble strips under the 'Return' knobs on the right of the mixer.

Part of the full rack. Some of the devices have been 'folded' by clicking the small arrow on the far left of their front panels, just for the purposes of this picture.

Devices can be moved anywhere in the rack (by clicking and dragging with your mouse) and will retain their original connections to other devices, until you change them yourself.

View the back of the rack

Hit the Tab key on your computer keyboard. The whole rack will instantly swing around so that you can see the rear panels of the devices, and all the cable connections Reason has made for you so far. Hit Tab to swing the rack back to the front.

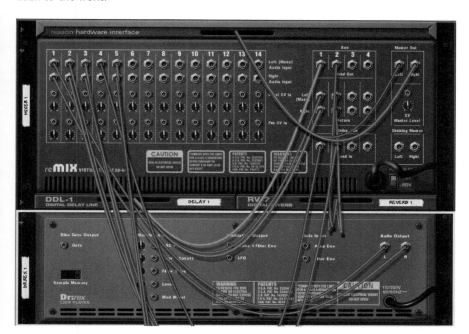

The back of the rack, with cable connections.

Save the rack

Although there's no music in it yet, this collection of devices is saved as a Song file, with the suffix 'rns'. It's just as well to save before going any further.

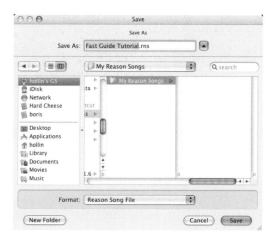

• Go to the File menu and select 'Save As'.
• The Save dialogue box that appears gives you an option to create a New folder. Select that option and name your folder 'My Reason Songs', or something similar. You could save all your projects to this folder in the future.
• Name the Song 'Fast Guide Tutorial', and save it. Adding a date to a file name can help you keep track of your work, especially if you do more than one version of a given Song. Note that when you want to save changes made to a Song that you've already named, you can use Apple/Control-S, as you would in normal computer use. This will overwrite the previous version, so be sure this is

Saving the Song via the 'Save As' dialogue.

The 'Details' section of the Browser

what you want before you do it. It's advisable to get into the habit of saving your work every time you make a significant change that you'd like to keep.

Create a Song

We're going to create a simple short track featuring a Dr:rex drum loop and a Dr:rex instrument loop; some added ReDrum rhythm parts; a bassline programmed in the Matrix, triggering a SubTractor sound; and finally a sampled sound played into the main sequencer.

Load Dr:rex loops

- Go to the first Dr:rex and click on the Folder button next to the file name display in the top left, or click on the file name display itself and select 'Open Browser' from the pop-up menu that appears. You can also use Apple/Control-B on the computer keyboard. Whichever way you choose, the REX File Browser dialogue should then open.
- Double-click on 'Reason Factory Sound Bank' in the Locations list, then Music Loops > Variable Tempo > Downtempo Loops. Scroll through the list in that folder and double-click on 090_VinylRhodes. Its name should appear in the Dr:rex file name display and a waveform should be loaded into the device's main display.

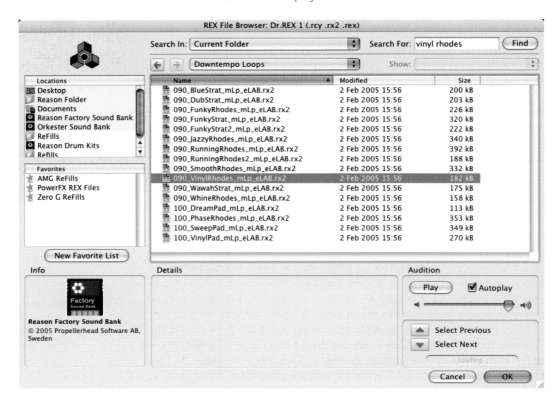

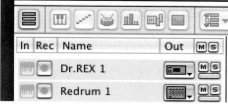

Left
The REX loop in the Dr:rex waveform display.

Above
Select the Dr:rex sequencer track.

- Scroll down to the main sequencer at the bottom of the rack. Click in the track list on the Dr:rex name, to highlight the track.
- Go back to the Dr:rex device (it should be right in front of you, as you have clicked its sequencer track). Click on the 'To Track' button above the waveform display. This action inserts all the notes required to trigger the Dr:rex loop into the sequencer track.
- Find the second Dr:rex device. Follow the procedure above to load loop Hse_08_Armand_135, from the House Folder inside the Dr:rex Drum Loops folder of the Factory Sound Banks. Scroll to its track in the sequencer (Dr:rex 2), click on it, then return to the second Dr:rex and click 'To Track', as above.
- Go to the Transport bar at the bottom of the rack and set the Song tempo to 100 in the Tempo display. Drag the figures in the display or use the arrow buttons.
- Click the Play button in the Transport, or hit the Space bar on your computer, to hear the loops play back together. Hit the Space bar again to stop playback.

Set Song tempo in the Transport bar.

Program some extra drum parts in ReDrum

The ReDrum drum machine uses the pattern style of programming.

- Locate ReDrum in the rack and click in it to select it. Now choose a drum kit so that you can hear what you are programming. Use Apple/Control-B, to open the Patch Browser. Locate the ReDrum Drum Kits folder in the Reason Factory Sound Banks folder, and choose Chemical Kit 02 from the Chemical Kits folder. This automatically assigns a set of drum sounds to ReDrum's 10 drum channels.

The Steps display and Resolution knob.

The drum pattern is programmed using the row of 16 square Step buttons (which correspond to steps in a ReDrum pattern) along the bottom of the device. When a button is lit, it means that a drum sound has been programmed to play on that step of the pattern. For this example, different 'dynamic' levels (varying their volume to create more realism) are not being used for the drum parts; using dynamics is explained in the ReDrum chapter.

Make sure the Step display is set to 16 (it has a range of 1-64). If it is not, use the up and down arrows to make it show 16. Also check that the resolution knob is set to 1/16, meaning that the pattern will be made up of 16th notes.

A ReDrum drum
sound channel.
Click the Select
button to program
a part for that
channel with the
Step buttons.

Above right
The bass drum part.

The tambourine part.

The high conga part.

The low conga part.

The hi-hat part.

The ReDrum Run button. Click on this to
play back the ReDrum pattern alone. To
play all device parts at the same time,
use the Play button in the Transport, or
the Space bar on the computer
keyboard.

- First, we'll enter the bass drum hits. Select drum channel 1, which contains a bass drum sound, by clicking on the SELECT label at the bottom of the channel, which will then light.
- The pads will now program only the bass drum. Click on the pads shown in the screen below. If you click on the wrong pad, click it again to switch it off.

- Now click the SELECT label at the bottom of drum channel 4. It should light up, meaning that channel 4's sound, a tambourine, will now be programmed by the pads. Click the pads shown below.

- Select channel 6 (high conga), as above, and click the pads below

- Switch to channel 7 (low conga) and program hits on the pads shown below.

- Select channel 8 (hi-hat) and program the pads below.

- Now click on the ReDrum's RUN button to hear all five sounds play together in the finished drum part. Click RUN again to stop playback.

Choose a bass sound from SubTractor

In a moment we'll create a bass line with the Matrix. But first, let's choose a sound to play it with. SubTractor has a default sound (Init Patch) which is there when the device is created, but we need a specific bass timbre.

- Scroll the rack, using the right-hand scroll arrows or scroll bar, until SubTractor is conveniently positioned on screen, and click in it to select it. Alternatively, click in the main sequencer's track list on the track

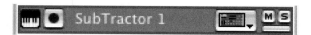

The SubTractor track in the sequencer, ready to accept MIDI input, as shown by the MIDI plug icon.

assigned to the SubTractor, which automatically places it before you, and ensure it's selected (highlighted).

- Open the Patch Browser and locate the 'Reason Factory Sound Bank'. Then go SubTractor Patches > Bass > Sub bass 2. Double-click on the file name to load the Patch into SubTractor. Its name should appear in the Patch display.
- If you'd like to play the sound, go down to the sequencer and click in the keyboard icon to the left of the SubTractor track name. it lights up, signifying that the track can accept MIDI input (notes played from your MIDI keyboard). Play a few notes to hear the bass sound.

Create the bass line with the Matrix

- Go to the Matrix. In the Steps display to the top right, make sure the number displayed is 16. This is the number of steps for the pattern. (A pattern can have any number of steps between 1 and 32.)
- The Resolution knob below the Steps display should already be set to 1/16 (which means that each step of the pattern is equal to a 16th-note). If it is not, move the knob pointer with your mouse until it is. (Pattern resolution can be set anywhere between a half note and a 128th note.) Given that a 4/4 bar contains 16 16th notes, our pattern is one bar long.
- The programming grid will allow you to enter notes over up to five octaves, via the five-way 'Octave' transposition switch to the left of the keyboard display. Set this switch to 1. This selects the Matrix's lowest octave of notes, since we are programming a bass part.
- Now, copying the figure below, click in the upper part of the central grid display to place the notes of the tune. Each column of small rectangular boxes, left to right, is one step. Top to bottom, each box represents a note, and when it is clicked it fills in red. When you click in a note box, a ghosted line runs from your selected note to the keyboard graphic on the left, so you always know what note is being selected. If you click in the wrong box on a given step, just clicking in the correct box for that step moves the red fill and fixes the mistake.
- When you've input all the notes for the bass line in the main grid, it's time to tell the notes when to play and for how long – give them some

The Matrix Steps display and Resolution knob.

The 'Octave' five-way transposition switch, keyboard graphic and 'Tie' button.

The grid display with bass line note pattern in the top part of the grid and the Gate events in the lower strip. The grid is only half full because our pattern is 16 steps long and the grid can display up to 32 steps.

rhythm. Look at the bottom part of the Matrix's main grid: if you click in one of the larger spaces here, you'll find that your mouse pointer makes a vertical bar, the height of which you can change by moving the mouse up and down. This vertical bar does two things: it tells the note on that step to play (it 'triggers' the note), and it tells the note how loud it should be. The higher the bar, the louder the note (or the higher its 'velocity' level). No note will sound if it doesn't have a trigger (called a 'Gate' event) directly below it.

- Click in the same spaces as you see filled in the lower strip of Figure 3.22, to create Gates for the notes in the tune. To make the thick bars in the screen, click on the 'Tie' button at bottom left before creating the bar. 'Tied' bars are twice as fat, and last twice as long as the other triggers. Wherever such a 'fat' Gate event is placed next to another event, the adjacent notes will run into each other and the tune will sound more 'legato', or smooth.

Using Tie is an easy way to introduce rhythmic variation and interest into your Matrix sequences. However, remember that you need to switch 'Tie' off again to return to making 'thin' staccato Gate events. It may be useful to use the keyboard shortcut if you're entering a mix of different types of Gate: holding down shift while creating the event toggles between short (thin) and long (fat) events.

This sub-bass sound may distort if it is too loud, so try to keep the Gates similar to what you see in the screen. If you click in the wrong space, just drag the height of the bar back downwards with your mouse and the event will disappear, or use Apple/Control-Z to Undo.

- You'll notice that not every step in the pattern has a Gate event. Don't worry about this at this stage.
- Play the bass pattern by clicking on the Matrix Run button. Stop it by clicking the button again. If you use the transport's Play button, or the computer keyboard Space bar, the REX loops, the drum pattern and the bass line will play back together.

Add a main sequencer part

The final component of the piece is a simple two-note synth part, recorded into the main sequencer and played with an NN19 sampler Patch. This NN19 part will be played in by you from your MIDI keyboard, rather than being entered with mouse clicks on the screen, as with the Matrix and ReDrum parts we have programmed so far.

- Locate the main sequencer. Click in the track list under the 'In' column of the 'NN19 - 1' track to make the keyboard icon appear.
- Locate the NN19 sampler in the rack. (Because you've just selected its track in the main sequencer, it should be right in front of you.)
- Open the Patch Browser, then go Reason Factory Sound Bank > NN19 Sampler Patches folder > Synth & Keyboard folder > 'Synpad'. Double click on the Patch name. This synth pad sound is now assigned to NN19. You should be able to press a key on your keyboard and hear the sound.

The Synpad Patch loaded
into NN19.

The playback Loop area in the Transport
bar. When you're recording with a playback
loop, the Loop button must be lit.

- Ensure that the sequencer is set to loop, by checking to see that the 'Loop' button in the Transport bar is switched on (lit). It should already be engaged if you started from the 'Empty Rack' default Song. The default 'loop' in the sequencer should be four bars long, which you can see, in the Ruler above the main sequencer window, by the position of the Left and Right markers.
- Now set Reason's input quantizing, to automatically correct the timing of every note you play. Select this by clicking the 'Quantize Notes During Recording' button above the main sequencer display. In the pop-up to the right of that button, choose 1/2 note. See the accompanying screen.
- If you'd like to have a steady quarter note click as an additional timing reference, engage the Click button in the Transport bar, then click the Play button in the Transport (or hit the Space bar) to start playback (the cursor should start to move across the sequencer display). Adjust the level of the resulting audio click with the knob beneath the Click button, if necessary. Click the Stop button in the Transport a couple of times (or press the the Return key twice) to stop playback and return to the start of the Song.
- Now click the red Record button in the Transport, followed by the Play button. (Alternatively, press Apple/Control-Return, then hit the Space bar.)

Click the 'Quantize Notes During Recording' button in the sequencer Toolbar to have the timing of your playing tightened up as you play. Choose 1/2 quantize 'resolution' for this example.

The Click button provides a timing metronome. The Level knob adjusts its volume.

The sequencer Transport controls. Click the Red 'record' button, then the 'arrow' Play button to engage recording mode.

- Recording starts immediately, but you might like to let the loop go around once to give yourself a count-in. When you're ready, play the 'D' and then the 'C' above middle 'C' on your keyboard for two beats each, repeating for the length of the loop. You will have played each note four times when you've done this. See the notes to play in the screen below – the keyboard graphic on the left may help.
- When you've finished recording, click the Stop button in the Transport, or press the Return key, two or three times, to stop and return to zero. Click the Play button or hit the Space bar to see how you did. (Disengage the Click button first if you don't want to hear the audio click during playback.) If you did anything wrong, use Apple/Control-Z to Undo and try again. (We'll discuss actually editing recorded notes in the sequencer chapter.)

This is what it should look like in the sequencer when you've played the 'D' and 'C' notes on your keyboard. Notice the Left and Right markers in the 'Ruler' defining the four-bar playback loop.

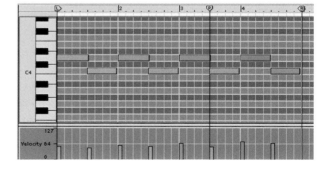

Adjust delay and reverb levels on mixer channel 1 using the Aux 1 and 2 knobs.

Click the mixer channel 1 Solo (S) button to hear channel 1 (Dr:rex) in isolation. Now you can better appreciate the effect of the delay and reverb applied to it.

Add reverb and delay effects

- Locate the mixer. Dr:rex 1 should already be assigned to mixer channel 1. Find the red auxiliary send knobs in the Aux section at the top of channel 1. You may remember that we placed delay and reverb effects in the rack earlier, and their effects levels are controlled by the auxiliary send knobs.
- Turn the aux 1 knob (delay send level) so that its pointer is at about 12 o'clock. Turn the aux 2 knob (reverb send level) to about 11 o'clock. (Altering controls is not as with real-world knobs; click and hold on the control, then drag upwards to increase the value and downwards to decrease it. Don't try to move controls in an arc as you would with physical knobs.)
- Now click the small S (Solo) button above the channel fader in channel 1, and start playback of the tune again. The Dr:rex Rhodes piano loop should play back alone. You'll notice that the loop sounds a lot more lively, as the reverb puts some 'space' around the dry sound, and the delay introduces a feeling of added complexity because of the rhythmic repeats it adds. Click the Solo button again to bring back the rest of the tracks.
- Turn up the aux 1 and 2 knobs on mixer channel 5, to which the NN19 playing the synth pad is routed – again, you'll hear more space and interest added to the sound if you 'Solo' it and play it back.

Play the parts back together

- Click the mixer Solo buttons on channel 1 and/or 5 off.
- Now click Play on the Transport bar, or hit the Space bar on the computer keyboard, to hear all the parts you've recorded playing back together. If you like, record some extra parts with the same or different devices, following the instructions given earlier.

Balance levels and alter pan positions at the mixer.

Balance levels and change pan positions with the mixer

How do you feel about the relative levels of the parts? They may need balancing against each other, and this is done with the mixer. The level faders on each channel adjust the volume of each instrument. Just grab the fader cap and drag the fader up or down to change an individual channel's level in the 'mix'. The Master fader, on the far right of the mixer, changes the overall level for the whole stereo mix, so you can use it to adjust how loudly Reason plays back through your headphones or over your speaker system.

Also try changing the 'pan' position of the different channels, with the pan 'pots' above each channel, making their parts play back further to the left or right in the stereo image.

Experimenting with the tutorial song

Change overall song tempo

Locate the 'Tempo' display in the Transport bar, and change the tempo of the Song as it plays back, by clicking on the up and down buttons next to the tempo value, or dragging in the display itself.

Mute and Solo tracks

- Locate the mixer in the rack.
- Play the Song back by clicking the Play button in the Transport bar or hitting the Space bar.
- As it plays back, click the Mute buttons on channels 1 and 5. The Dr:rex Rhodes piano loop and the NN19 synth pad sound drop out of the mix. Click the Mute buttons again to bring them back.
- Now click the Solo button on channel 2. Only the ReDrum pattern plays back. Click the Solo button again to bring the other parts back. Now do the same with channel 3. Carry on muting and soloing if you like.

Try REX loop transposing

- Locate Dr:rex 1 (playing the Rhodes piano loop). Notice the small keyboard graphic under the waveform in the central display. This is the Transpose Keyboard.
- Start playback of the Song. As it plays, click the highest note on the Transpose Keyboard. The REX loop is transposed up an octave.
- Now click the lowest note on the Transpose Keyboard. The loop is shifted down an octave. Click the 'C' in the middle of the Transpose Keyboard to take the loop back to its original pitch. This real-time transposing can be automated to make it a permanent part of a Song. See the Dr:rex chapter for more.

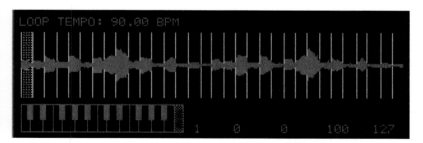

The Dr:rex waveform display with the Transpose Keyboard at the bottom. Transpose REX loops in real time by clicking the keys. The top key and bottom key transpose an octave up or down.

Explore Matrix note resolution

- Locate Matrix 1 in the rack.
- Click on its Run button to play the bass line. While it's playing, grab the Resolution knob and change its setting from 1/16 to 1/8.
- You'll notice that the bass line immediately seems to run at half speed. What's actually happening is that the note value of each step has been doubled, so that each step is held for twice as long – eighth notes instead of 16th notes. Move the knob around again to 1/4 and the part seems to run even more slowly, because every note is now held for twice as long again.

Move the knob right around to 1/32 and the bass part runs very fast, because each note is a short 32nd note. Reset the knob to 1/16.

Try real-time Matrix transposing

Try transposing the bass line in real time. Click on the Matrix Run button to make it play, then press Apple/Control U. The line now plays one semitone higher. Use the same key press again to transpose the bass up a further semitone. To transpose down in real time, use Apple/Control-D.

If you keep transposing like this, eventually you can't go any higher or lower; all the notes in your pattern will be transposed to a very high or very low C! (You will lose your pattern if this happens, unless you have recently done a Save.) However, if you bear in mind that the Matrix has a five-octave range, you shouldn't get into too much trouble. If in doubt, save under a different name before experimenting.

Understand Matrix 'Gates'

Remove some of the Matrix bassline Gates, in the lower Gate strip, to see how this affects the rhythm of the part.

You'll remember that after you entered notes into the Matrix, you also had to add 'Gates' in the area below the note grid, so that the required notes would sound.

To understand better how these work, try taking away some of the Gate bars. Just randomly grab one with the mouse and drag its level down to nothing. Do this with several. Then play the bassline back by hitting the Run button. You'll quickly hear how important Gates are. When you've tried this, use Undo (Apple/Control-Z) repeatedly to return to the original rhythm. (Note that this facility only 'undoes' up to 10 steps.)

Clicking the Patch name display brings up a menu giving the kits in the current folder, plus the 'Open Browser' option if you want to open other folders. You can also use the arrow keys beneath the ReDrum display to step through the kits in a folder.

Change drum kits in ReDrum

- Locate ReDrum in the rack. Click its Run button to make the drum pattern play.
- Click on the Patch name display to the bottom left of the device. In the pop-up menu that appears, choose Chemical Kit 03.drp. Immediately, your drum pattern will be played by that kit. Work through the kits in that list, listening to them playing your drum pattern. If you like, select the Open Browser option from the pop-up and then the ReDrum Drum Kit folder. Work through any of the themed folders selecting different kits in turn and hearing how they can give a drum pattern radically different 'feels'.

Open browser...

Chemical Kit 01.drp
Chemical Kit 02.drp
Chemical Kit 03.drp
Chemical Kit 04.drp
Chemical Kit 05.drp
Chemical Kit 06.drp
Chemical Kit 07.drp
Chemical Kit 08.drp
Chemical Kit 09.drp
Chemical Kit 10.drp

Play ReDrum sounds from your keyboard

Just as you played an NN19 sampler string sound from your attached MIDI keyboard, you can play the ReDrum drum sounds.

- Go to the main sequencer. Click next to 'ReDrum 1' in the 'In' column to the left of the track name list. The keyboard icon should appear, indicating that ReDrum is ready to accept MIDI data from your keyboard.
- On a typical 61-note keyboard, ReDrum sound 1, which is usually a bass (or kick) drum, is mapped to the bottom C, with sounds 2-10 being mapped to successive semitones thereafter. Find where the sounds are mapped on your keyboard and press keyboard keys to trigger them.
- If you prefer to compose drum parts from the keyboard in this fashion, you can use ReDrum as a drum sound module and record your drum part into the main sequencer – but that'll be covered later!

Use the 'Shuffle' facility

- Locate the ReDrum in the rack. Click its Run button to play the drum pattern. Now engage the Shuffle button next to the Resolution knob.
- In the Transport bar, turn the Pattern Shuffle knob on the far right to a value of about 90 (keep the mouse pointer over the knob to summon a Tool Tip with the knob value). You should hear a noticeable difference in how the pattern plays back. This is because the Shuffle facility introduces a more syncopated 'triplet' feel, adding 'swing'.

The Shuffle knob in the Transport sets how much shuffle feel will be applied to the pattern playing back in Matrix or ReDrum. Click the Shuffle button on the device too, or the knob will have no effect.

Try out SubTractor's controls

- Go to the main sequencer. Click next to 'SubTractor 1' in the 'In' column to the left of the track name list, to make the keyboard icon light up.
- Locate the SubTractor in the rack (because you've just selected it in the sequencer, it should automatically have been placed before you). Under the Edit menu, choose 'Initialize Patch'. This loads the basic SubTractor starter Patch, so you can hear the changes we're about to make more clearly.
- Press a key on your keyboard and hold it down. With your mouse, operate the 'Bend' (pitch-bend) wheel at the bottom left of the SubTractor, and hear how it bends the pitch of the sound up or down according to the direction of movement.
- You can do the same with the pitch-bend wheel on your MIDI keyboard, and if you do, that will move the one on-screen too. This is because moving the pitch-bend wheel on your attached keyboard sends a pitch-bend MIDI 'controller' message to SubTractor, which makes it move its pitch-bend wheel in response.
- Now press and hold a key on your keyboard and try operating the SubTractor Mod (modulation) wheel. Hear the sound change as you move the wheel.
- Because the mod wheel can be assigned to control one of five different aspects of a sound, applying modulation can create different effects with different sounds, according to how a given sound has been programmed. Just as with the pitch-bend wheel, moving the mod wheel on your

The SubTractor pitch-bend and modulation wheels.

keyboard also moves the mod wheel on screen, because the on-screen wheel is responding to a modulation controller message sent from your keyboard when you moved its mod wheel.

Feel free to play around with the knobs and sliders on the SubTractor and notice their effects as you play notes from the keyboard; SubTractor's controls will be discussed further in its own chapter. If you want to restore SubTractor to its previous state before you experimented with the controls, just re-select the original Sub Bass 2 Patch from the pop-up list that appears when you click the Patch-name display. To change to a different sound, use the same Patch selection method we've been using throughout the tutorials.

You can do the same kind of experimentation with the controls of the NN19 sampler. Just make sure the keyboard icon is lit to the left of the sampler's name in the main sequencer track list. This will mean that you can play the NN19 sounds from your MIDI keyboard.

Change the reverb type

- Locate the mixer in the rack. In channel 5, click the 'S' (Solo) button.
- Press the play button in the transport control to set the sequence playing. Notice that you only hear the part being played by NN19, rather than the whole sequence, because the NN19 channel in the mixer is 'solo'ed'.
- Locate the RV7 reverb. We're going to change the type of reverb being applied to the sound, by clicking the up/down arrow buttons next to the reverb-name display. In order to hear the reverb effect properly, you might first want to switch the DDL1 delay to 'Bypass', so that you no longer hear the delay effect it is producing. Do this by moving the three-way switch in the top left corner of the DDL1 to the 'Bypass' position.
- Return to the RV7 reverb and click the up arrow repeatedly to step through the reverb types (or Algorithms) and hear how they change the sound. Larger spaces have longer 'decay' times (that is, the time it takes for the sound to die away). If you like, move the RV7's knobs to see what effect they have on the reverb. See the effects chapter for more.

Change reverb type by clicking and dragging on the name display or clicking the up/down arrow buttons. The three-way switch on the left of the effect devices allows you to 'bypass' their effect.

Basic Reason operations

T here are a number of basic operations and features that are common to most of the Reason devices. In this chapter, these operations and features are discussed so that there will be no need to repeat them in every device-specific chapter hereafter.

The menus

File menu
Offers operations related to storing and retrieving Songs; importing and exporting MIDI files and exporting audio files; provides a list of the last eight Songs that have been open (similar to the 'Recent Documents' option in some popular word processors); and allows you to Quit the program.

Edit menu
Offers all editing options for a given device (or the sequencer), when that device or sequencer is selected. Options change according to device selected. Also access the important Preferences settings (MacOS 9.x and Windows) via this menu, or the Reason menu in OS X.

Create menu
For the creation of new devices and sequencer tracks.

Options menu
Miscellaneous operations related to MIDI, synchronisation, surface locking, remote control, and rack toggling/cable viewing.

Windows menu
Provides a list of currently open Songs, from which Songs can be selected; offers an option for detaching/re-attaching the sequencer window; and for PCs features a set of window viewing options. For Mac OSX, a Minimize document option is also available.

Help or Contacts menu
Provides a list of web links to allow you to access content and help at the Propellerhead web site if your computer is connected to the Internet. For PC users, this is the Help menu and additionally offers access to an online Help system. The Help menu option in MacOS 9.x is not supported.

Reason menu (OS X)
About Reason, Preferences, and a Quit option.

About Songs

Creating a new Song
The Song is the format in which compositions using the Reason devices are saved. Songs may also be used to store particular device setups.

Launch Reason and press Apple/Control-N or select 'New' from the File menu to start a Song. If this is the first time you are creating a new Song, or you have not yet made a custom Default Song, you'll get the Built-In Default Song, which is a Reason demo. In general Preferences, under the Edit menu, you can choose whether an Empty Rack, this Built-in Song, or the custom Default Song of your choice (see below) will open when you launch Reason and/or start a New Song.

Note that it is usually best to begin any new rack by creating a ReMix mixer device. If you don't, the first sound-making device you create will be automatically connected to the hardware interface, and you will be able to hear the device when you play your keyboard, but the next device created won't be automatically connected to anything, and you won't be able to hear it. You could manually connect this device to the hardware interface yourself, but it's generally best to just begin with a mixer, as mixer inputs are all automatically routed to the hardware interface. Then you will always be able to play and hear devices as soon as you have routed MIDI input to them via the sequencer.

In General Preferences, you can set which Song will open when you launch Reason or begin a new project.

Loading a Song
Select 'Open' from the File menu, or use Apple/Control-O. You'll be presented with the Browser, allowing you to navigate to where your Songs are stored. Alternatively, double-click on the Song's file-name from anywhere on the hard drive to open it and Reason at the same time.

You may notice that you can have several Reason Songs loaded at the same time. This ability becomes useful if you want to play live with Reason, probably running the program on a laptop, as it allows you to start the next Song playing when the previous one has only just finished, eliminating loading time between Songs. However, in general it's probably best not to leave a Song other than the one you are working on open, as there is an impact on CPU 'overhead' and RAM.

Setting a personal default Song
Setting a default Song can save you a lot of time in the long run, as you can include favourite devices and settings that you will not then have to think about when you start a new project.

Start a New Song, as above, and include in it the devices and settings of your choice (see below for some suggestions). Now save the Song to your hard drive. Choose general Preferences from the Edit menu. Click on the

'Custom' button, then on the folder icon at the right. Navigate to the Song you have chosen as your default. Its name will appear next to 'Custom'. Since V2, the default Song does not have to be called 'Default song.rns', as it did in previous versions of Reason, but note that if you move the Song you've chosen as a default (if you put it in a different folder, say), Reason will not be able to find and load it automatically.

So what should be in your default Song? Here are some ideas (see the relevant chapters for more on each device):

- Start with a mixer and a favourite set of devices. Some basic effects – certainly reverb and delay – should be ready-patched into the mixer aux loops. Synths/samplers should be connected to Matrix Pattern Sequencers where desired, and if you use ReDrum, pre-load a favourite starting kit.
- Load favourite 'basic' Patches into one or several devices. Our default Song has an electric piano Patch loaded into a SubTractor. If you do this, enable the keyboard icon on the sequencer track assigned to your favourite 'playing' device. We have the icon in the SubTractor sequencer track, so that the electric piano is playable from the instant the program has launched.
- Set up the sequencer size so that you can see all the device track names and have tracks displayed at a comfortable level for getting a good overview. Since V2, you can tear off the sequencer as a separate window and save that in your default Song, if that's how you will prefer to work.
- Make sequencer tracks for any devices that do not automatically get one, such as the mixer, ready for automation, and your effects if you tend to automate them.
- If you have a MIDI controller box, make some basic 'MIDI Remote Mapping' assignments of the sort that you will use a lot – for example, simple synth tweaks such as filter cutoff frequency, resonance, and so on, and mixer control assignments such as levels and pans. Make them part of the default Song and you'll have them on every project. (See the automation/remote control chapter for more.)
- Fold the Hardware Interface (more on 'folding' in a moment), since you won't usually be needing to change its settings.

Saving Songs

There are three different Song formats. Songs (which have a .rns or .rps file suffix) include all the devices that you've assigned to a Reason rack, all the inter-connections between those devices, the Patches and samples that are referenced and played by the devices, and everything you have recorded into the step and main sequencers, including automation data.

Standard Song Files

The standard Song file has the suffix .rns, but comes in two variants. The first is the type that you'll normally save while working, and doesn't actually contain any samples that you've assigned to ReDrum, NN19 or Dr:rex, but instead has pointers to where the samples can be located on your hard drive. To save this type of Song, just use 'Save As' under the File menu.

The second kind of .rns file (there is no way, visually, to tell the two types apart) creates a transportable, 'self-contained' Song, which includes samples that have been assigned to the relevant modules. Thus this type of Song can be moved to another computer (perhaps for swapping work with a friend or collaborator), with the assurance that it will play back precisely as you intend. Save a self-contained Song as follows:

The Song Self-Contain Settings dialogue.

- Select the 'Song Self-Contain Settings' option from the File menu. The window that pops up displays a list of sample-based devices, plus the samples they require.
- Tick the box next to each sample if you would like it to be included in the self-contained Song (click the 'Check All' button if you'd like all listed samples included).
- If you now use the 'Save' or 'Save As' function in the file menu, the saved Song will have all required samples embedded within it.

Be aware that samples that are part of a 'ReFill' (see elsewhere in this chapter), such as the Factory Sound Bank ReFill that came with your software, cannot be saved with a self-contained Song. Such Songs will only play back correctly on another computer that also has the same ReFill installed. Most Reason users will have the factory ReFill installed, but not necessarily any third-party ReFills that you may have acquired.

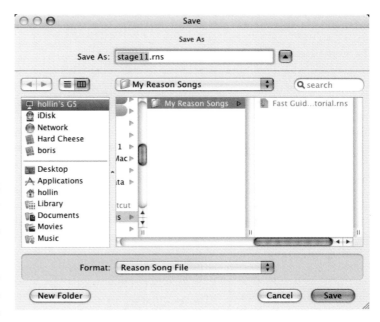

The standard 'Save As' dialogue.

A self-contained Song can be 'un-self-contained', and any constituent samples extracted and filed away on your hard drive; use the Song Self-Contain Settings option again, unchecking the samples you'd like to extract and clicking 'OK'. Any samples that Reason can't already find in its database will cause a dialogue box to pop up, asking you where you'd like to save the sample.

The expanded Create menu in Reason 3

Sequencer Track
Create Device by Browsing Patches...
Combinator
Mixer 14:2
Line Mixer 6:2
SubTractor Analog Synthesizer
Malstrom Graintable Synthesizer
NN19 Digital Sampler
NN-XT Advanced Sampler
Dr.REX Loop Player
Redrum Drum Computer
MClass Mastering Suite Combi
MClass Equalizer
MClass Stereo Imager
MClass Compressor
MClass Maximizer
RV7000 Advanced Reverb
Scream 4 Distortion
BV512 Digital Vocoder
RV-7 Digital Reverb
DDL-1 Digital Delay Line
D-11 Foldback Distortion
ECF-42 Envelope Controlled Filter
CF-101 Chorus/Flanger
PH-90 Phaser
UN-16 Unison
COMP-01 Compressor/Limiter
PEQ-2 Two Band Parametric EQ
Spider Audio Merger & Splitter
Spider CV Merger & Splitter
Matrix Pattern Sequencer
ReBirth Input Machine

Published Song Files

The third Song format is the so-called 'published' Song, with a .rps suffix. This includes samples (this time, you don't get to choose which ones go with the Song) and is saved in a 'read only' format designed for distributing your Reason work via the Internet, and to prevent anyone who downloads one of your Songs in this format from saving any changes to it, extracting any samples from it, or using the cut/copy and paste operations. However, it should be pointed out that it is suspected that the .rps format is not 100 percent secure in this respect, due to the activities of 'hackers'.

To save a Song in .rps format, select the 'Publish Song' option from the File menu. Once again, any components in your Song that come from a ReFill will not be saved when you publish the Song – whoever downloads your published Song will need the same ReFills as you to hear the Song properly. Obviously, you will be OK using sounds from the Factory ReFill, as other Reason users should have this.

File extenions like .rps or .rns are added automatically on Windows and OS X as files are saved. Modern operating systems are less fussy about whether a suffix is visible or not. If a file refuses to open and you know it's a .rns file, try manually adding the suffix to re-establish the link to the Reason application.

Optimising Songs

Bear in mind that Songs using lots of samples require more RAM to load. You should find that SubTractor-based Songs load with much less RAM requirement. For greatest efficiency, only have one Song at a time open, don't run other applications at the same time unless you need to, and don't use stereo samples where mono ones will do. In addition, don't leave devices in your rack if they are not being used.

Sequencer tracks

Every time a new sound-making device is created, a new track is automatically created for it in the main sequencer. Devices that do not make a sound in themselves (such as mixers and effects) do not automatically get a sequencer track. However, you can easily create one for such a device (or, indeed, any device) yourself. See the sequencer chapter for more.

A sequencer track, generated automatically when a device is created.

Device Operations

Creating devices

Launch the program. Go to the Create menu and select the device you want to make, or right-click in the rack to bring up a context menu giving a list of the device options, and choose one.

Selecting devices

Click on the device to make a coloured highlight box appear around it. That device can now be programmed, copied, and so on.

Deleting devices

Select the device and choose 'Delete Device' from the Edit menu or a Context menu, or use Apple/Control-backspace from the computer keyboard. If you hit the backspace key when a device is selected, you will also be asked if you want to delete the device. Finally, when you choose to delete a sequencer track, you will be given an option to delete the device it is assigned to (or you may keep the device and delete only the track).

Moving/re-ordering devices

Click on the device and drag to another place in the rack. A coloured 'ghost' box appears around the device, and as you drag over other devices they acquire a coloured line along their left-hand edge. If you then 'drop' over the device that has the coloured line at that moment, the device you are moving will be re-positioned immediately above that device. Rear-panel connections remain intact.

Cutting/Copying/Pasting devices

Select the device, use Cut or Copy from the Edit menu or a Context menu, select another device in the rack, and use Paste from the Edit or Context menu. The cut or copied device is pasted immediately below the newly selected device. Using Shift-Paste causes Reason to attempt automatic connection of the device. Note that you can direct the automatic routing to some extent, by clicking on another device before Shift-pasting. For example, if you have cut or copied a Matrix sequencer and there are two sound source devices in the rack not already connected to a Pattern device, clicking on one of the sound sources causes the Matrix to be connected to that when you Shift-paste. If you don't click before Shift-pasting the Matrix, Reason will connect to the nearest available sound-source device.

You may copy or cut several devices at a time, by Shift-clicking on them all and proceeding as above. Their interconnections will generally be preserved after pasting.

Copying a device (or duplicating it – see below) will also copy its currently selected Patch and any edits, all Patterns, and/or all samples. Cut, Copy and Paste device operations can also be done between Songs. Have both Songs open and proceed as above. This is ideal if you would like to use a set of Matrix or ReDrum patterns, for example, as the basis for a new Song. Using Combinator presets as the basis for new tracks is a good technique too.

Duplicating devices

Copy and Paste the device, or Option/Control-drag the device to a new place in the rack. Using Shift at the same time (Option/Control-Shift-drag) causes Reason to attempt to automatically route the duplicated device.

Naming devices

Each device has a 'scribble strip', that looks like a piece of tape, somewhere on its front panel. When a device is created, it is automatically named by Reason and given a number – for example, the first Dr:rex you create is labelled 'Dr:rex 1', the next one 'Dr:rex 2', and so on. You can change the

An effect device 'scribble-strip'.

device names yourself by clicking on the strip and typing a new name into the pop-up. The name will always end up in upper-case and can be up to 16 characters long. It's a good ideas to name your devices for what they are doing in your track – for example, a SubTractor synth producing a bass line could be called 'Bass SubTractor' or something similar.

Device names are automatically duplicated on the scribble-strip next to the mixer channel the device has been assigned to. Note that in the case of devices being processed by 'chains' of insert effects, the mixer input channel scribble strip always shows the name of the last effect in the chain, rather than the name of the device being processed by the chain. You might thus wish to name the last effect in the chain so that it reflects the name of the device – 'NN19 flange', for example.

Device names also have a relationship with the corresponding sequencer track name. See the sequencer chapter for details of the latter.

Folding devices

Just click the arrow to fold the device.

If you don't need access to the controls of a device in your rack, you can 'fold' the device, to make the rack more manageable and allow you to see more devices at one time. Folding collapses the device panel down to a slender '1U' (one unit) rackmount appearance and is done by clicking the small arrow at the top left of the device. To unfold the device, click the arrow again. Option/Alt-clicking folds/ unfolds every device in the rack.

Navigating the rack

One way to get around the rack is via the standard scroll bars or arrows.

There are several ways to get around the rack:
- Use the scroll bar on the right-hand edge of the rack, or the up/down arrows at the bottom of the scroll bar.
- Use the up/down arrow keys on the computer keyboard to step through devices one at a time.
- Use the page up/down keys on the computer keyboard to step through the rack one screenful of devices at a time.
- Use the 'Home' and 'End' keys on the computer keyboard to go to the top or bottom of the rack. If you always begin a rack with a mixer, using the 'Home' key is a fast way to get to the mixer.
- Summon a device Context menu by Control/right mouse-clicking in a device. The 'Go To' list in the menu will take you to any device the selected device is connected to.
- If you're in the sequencer, clicking a device's track (as long as the device is assigned to the track) scrolls the rack automatically to place the device before you.
- Using the scroll wheel on a mouse.

Keyboard shortcuts

There are lots of keyboard shortcuts to help you use Reason more efficiently and help you avoid depending too heavily on the mouse. The specific short-cuts that apply to each device are listed near the start of each device chapter; they and others are referred to throughout the book, where appropriate. (The Reason electronic documentation also provides a collated list of short-cuts.) Mac and PC equivalents are given, in the order Mac/PC – for example, Apple/Control-C for 'Copy'. This book uses 'Apple' instead of the more correct 'Command', because most Mac users use this terminology (and the key has an Apple symbol on it anyway).

Toggle rack

The Tab key swings the whole Reason rack around so that you can see the fantastically detailed back panels and the cables that connect the different devices. You can also make manual cable connections here. (More about that shortly.) Hit Tab again to return to the front of the rack.

About cables

Connection cables, which you may see at the rear of the rack, come in several varieties and are colour-coded to indicate their function.

- *Shades of red* = Audio cables that go device-to-mixer or device-to-Hardware Interface
- *Shades of green* = Effect interconnects
- *Shades of yellow* = CV/Gate cables

Connecting

Cable connections at the rear of the rack are usually made automatically by Reason when a device is created. The logic of some of these connections is discussed in the ReMix chapter. However, if you want to make some connections yourself (as you might very well do for many sorts of custom routing), there are two ways. Use the Tab key to get to the back of the rack and:

- Click on the cable you wish to reconnect elsewhere, or click and hold on a socket to create a new cable, and drag to the destination socket. Release the mouse button.
- Click and hold on a socket to summon a pop-up menu from which you can select a destination for the cable. For example, clicking on the audio output of a sound-making device brings up a choice of all audio inputs for devices in the rack – including mixer inputs, any available effect device input, the Malström audio input, and the Hardware Interface inputs. If you were to click on a Matrix CV output, you would get a list of all CV and Gate inputs available in the rack.

You can alternatively ask Reason to automatically route a device that has no connections, by choosing 'Auto Route Device' from the Edit menu.

Disconnecting

Click and drag the cable out of the socket and release the mouse button. The cable disappears. Alternatively, select 'Disconnect

Clicking on a SubTractor audio output brought up this list of available inputs to connect it to.

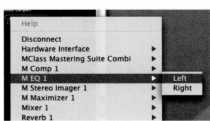

Device' from the pop-up that appears when you click on the socket. There is also a 'Disconnect Device' option in the Edit Menu; if you use this, all a device's connections will be disconnected.

Hiding/showing

You may not always want to see the cables at the back of the rack, as they can make quite a 'soup' if you have a busy rack and can obscure sockets you need to see. Hide cables by using Apple/Control-L (toggles between hidden and shown) or un-checking 'Show Cables' from the Options menu. Note that if you have the cables hidden, you can still see which are connected to something because sockets that are in use have a coloured centre (coloured according to cable type).

Leave the mouse pointer over the socket and a Tool Tip will appear to tell you what the socket is connected to – so you can still know what's going on even if you have cables hidden. (The Tool Tip will still do the same job even if cables are showing.)

Cable animation

It's fun to see the cables swing about when you Tab the rack to the back, but hardly necessary. Disabling cable animation, in general Preferences under the Edit menu, saves a bit of CPU overhead.

Context menus

Context menus are available at the click of a mouse (right mouse button for PCs, Control-click or right-click for Macs) to provide useful options and operations tailored to whatever you're doing within Reason. Because they pop up wherever your mouse happens to be and usually duplicate the editing operations available from the main menu bar, they can save you a lot of 'mousing around'.

A sequencer Context menu in v3

- *Device Context Menus:* Clicking anywhere in a device (make sure it's an empty area of the panel) brings up a menu offering editing commands specific to that device; for example, cut, copy, paste and shift Pattern in the case of Pattern-based devices.
- *Parameter Context Menus:* Clicking on a device control brings up a menu offering items for creating or editing remote-control assignments. This type of menu also offers an 'Edit Automation' option that may be used to access automation creation and editing for that control.
- *Empty Rack Context Menus:* This type of menu, available when you click in an empty area of the rack, offers a Create option for creating new devices, and a Paste Device item for any copied or cut device.
- *Sequencer Context Menus:* The content of this type of menu depends on where you click within the sequencer, and on whether you click on an event. Functions available include create sequencer track, change events, cut, copy, delete, and quantise notes.

Making device parameter settings

- Knobs: Parameter changing on-screen can be appear to be counter-intuitive to newcomers to music software. You can't move the knob in exactly the same way as you would with a real-world example, trying to re-create the arc of a real knob move. The basic action you need is to click on a knob, hold the mouse button down, and move the mouse pointer up to turn the knob right (increasing the parameter value) and down to turn it left (reducing the value). Once you understand that, moving Reason on-screen knobs is easy.

Though all knobs are moved left or right in order to change a parameter's value, in fact there are two sorts of knob. The most common increments a parameter from a value of 0 to 127 as it moves left to right; the other variety has a bipolar travel, and moves left or right from a central – 12 o'clock – position. Bipolar controls are used for parameters such as pan, and those, like mixer EQ cut/boost, which provide positive or negative offsets, and have a red LED at 12 o'clock that flashes when an offset has been applied. Bipolar parameters have a range of –64–0–63.

- *Sliders:* Grab with the mouse and move up or down, within a parameter range of 0-127.
- *Buttons:* Click to select on or off state.
- *Multi-mode selectors:* Continuous clicking on Mode buttons cycles through a range of three or more options, such as the five filter types of SubTractor's Filter 1. The list of options, above the switch, is bulleted with LEDs; the choices can also be made by clicking directly on the relevant LED rather than cycling through the options.
- *Value displays:* Most of these are numeric LED displays (the exception is the RV6 Digital Reverb algorithm display, which shows an algorithm name). Change values by clicking on the value itself and dragging up or down (changes values rapidly), or by clicking on the up/down arrows next to the display. The second option provides fine control for parameters with large value ranges, such as the millisecond delay time on the DDL1 Digital Delay.

Most parameters tend to change in increments of two value steps during normal operation. However, this can be overridden by holding down the computer keyboard Shift key during a parameter change, engaging 'fine' control that gives you access to all parameter value steps.

The types of controls you'll find in Reason: left to right, value displays with 'spin' arrows, LED button (labelled Ring Mod in this picture), two normal parameters knobs, two sliders, and a multi-mode selector.

Note that any parameter can be returned to its default value for the Patch as saved, by Apple/Control-clicking it. This can be a very handy option if you've gone too far in editing a SubTractor Patch, say, and can't return to a previous state by using the 10-stage Undo function.

Don't forget that you can assign on-screen controls to be altered by hardware controls, for hands-on use of Reason. See the automation/remote control chapter for more.

A Tool Tip.

Tool Tips

As first mentioned in the tutorial section of this book, if your mouse pointer
hovers over a device's control for more than a second or two, a Tool Tip will
appear. The red Tool Tip label tells you the name of the control and its currently set value. At the rear of the rack, Tool Tips also tell you where a given
socket is connected, if at all. You can turn off Tool Tips in the general
Preferences page (under the Edit menu), if you like, but there's probably no
need to, as they only appear when your mouse has been stationary for a few
moments and therefore don't interfere with rapid operation of the software.

About Patches and Samples

Reason sound-making devices, and two of the effects devices, can load
Patches (suitably named) and/or single samples via the Browser, and can
save also Patches. The exception is Dr:rex, which loads only REX loops (.rx2,
.rcy or .rex), via the Browser, and whose settings can only be saved as part
of a Song. The different Patch types are as follows:

- *SubTractor (.zyp) and Malström (.xwv) Patches:* These synth Patches
  comprise the settings of all front-panel controls. Samples and sampler
  Patches can't be loaded into these devices.
- *NN19 (.smp) and NNXT (.sxt) Patches:* These comprise pointers to the
  collection of samples that make up the Patch, how those samples are
  arranged across a MIDI keyboard, and the settings of all front-panel
  controls. Both Patches and single samples can be loaded into these
  devices. Synth Patches cannot be loaded, and though NNXT can load
  NN19 patches the opposite is not true.
- *RV7000 (.RV7) and Scream 4 (.SM4) Patches:* These effect device
  patches contain the settings for all all the front panel controls.
- *ReDrum (.drp) Patches:* These comprise pointers to the collection of
  samples that makes up a 'kit', plus the settings of all front-panel
  controls. Both Patches and single samples can be loaded into ReDrum.
  Synth Patches cannot be loaded.
- *.cmb patches:* These are native to the Combinator and contain all the
  information concerning any devices, routing and Matrix data contained
  within a Combi.

Except for the Combinator, no inter-device routing settings, back-panel connections, remote assignments or automation data are saved as part of a Patch, nor
are ReDrum Patterns. All these things must be saved as part of a Song if you
require their recall later. In fact, due to the way that it's easy to copy bits of the
Reason rack from Song to Song, collections of favourite routings could be saved
as virtual libraries. Or more conveniently, as .cmb Combinator patches.

Loading Samples

Samples are loaded via the Sample Browser buttons in NN19, NNXT and
ReDrum. It can be confusing that the Sample Browser and the Patch Browser
both have an icon that looks like a folder. It may help to remember that the
Patch Browser is always located next to the main Patch Name display of the

Left
The Sample Browser button (folder icon) on NNXT.

Right
The Patch Browser button (also has a folder icon!) on NNXT. Patch Browsers are always right by a Patch name display.

device and always sits between the Patch Save floppy disk icon and a pair of Patch increment/decrement arrow buttons. Also, if you have Tool Tips active, leaving the mouse pointer over the folder icon will soon tell you which Browser it accesses. To load a sample:

- Click on a Sample Browser button to access the Browser window. This is new in Reason 3 and allows you to move to different locations and folders on your hard drive. Navigate to the folder where your samples are stored, or to the factory sample folders. You can now preview any sample by selecting it in the Browser, then double-clicking on the required filename will load it into the device.

The Sample Browser window.

- Alternatively, choose 'Browse Samples' from a device Context menu. This opens the Sample Browser.
- In ReDrum, you can also click on the sample name display in each voice channel and select 'Open Browser' from the pop-up menu that appears. This, again, opens the Sample Browser.

Once you have loaded a sample, clicking the arrow keys next to the Sample Browser button takes you through the contents of the current bank of samples, one at a time. All sample devices since V2 will load AIFFs, WAVs, Sound-Fonts, and individual slices from REX loops.

Loading Patches

The Patch Browser and Sample Browser use the same window, but each by default is set to display either patches or samples. Four methods are available for loading Patches. Either:

- Click on the Patch Browser button next to the Patch-name display to bring up the Patch Browser dialogue. Navigate to the required folder and double-click on the Patch name.
- Click on the Patch name display itself and select 'Open Browser' from the pop-up menu that appears. This, again, opens the Patch Browser.
- Choose 'Browse Patches' from a device Context menu.
- If you've already done one of the previous operations (and thus have a

Info

In V3 you can preview any combi, patch, sample or effect straight from the Browser without having to load it into the rack first. Simply select it and play.

bank of Patches open), you can alternatively scroll through the Patches in the currently-selected bank using the up/down buttons next to the Patch-name display.

The Patch Browser.

The data Location and Favorites windows.

Up to Reason V 2.5, when the Patch or Sample Browser is open and you need to navigate to the Reason factory sound bank, you may find it helpful to click on the 'Find all ReFills' magnifying-glass button at the top right of the Browser window. This automatically locates all ReFills (ReFills being collections of Reason sounds) on your hard drive. When you have just installed Reason, only the factory ReFill will be available, but you may add third-party Patch and sample ReFill collections later, and this is an easy way to access them all.

Info

Patch/sample folder appears to be empty?

Note that when you open a Browser for a given device, you will only be given access to files which that particular device can load. This may result in you sometimes thinking that the file folders are empty when they are not. For example, if you have a SubTractor selected and you attempt to browse a folder of samples, the folder will appear to be empty. The samples are actually still there – you just can't get at them via SubTractor. This is one of the most common mistakes made by new Reason users, and apparently the cause of many tech-support calls. The 'Show' menu in the Browser can toggle the filtered view on and off, although Reason is now pretty good at guessing what file type you're after. In Reason V 3 you can bypass this problem by selecting 'Create device by selecting patches'.

Saving Patches

Saving new Patches that you have created, or edited factory Patches that you want to re-name and save elsewhere is a simple matter of clicking on the 'floppy disk' icon alongside the device's Patch-name display. A standard Save window then allows you to navigate through the contents of your hard drive and choose a folder in which to save the Patch.

Name the Patch, and click 'Save'. When you have navigated once to your preferred Patch location, the device in question will remember that path and open that folder automatically when you save a Patch.

Info

Copying Patches

Copy Patch data from one device to another like device by selecting the source device, choosing 'Copy Patch' from the Edit menu or the device

Context menu, selecting the destination device in the same or another open Song, and choosing 'Paste Patch' from the Edit or Context menu.

Database Folders (in Reason 2.5 and earlier only)

When you have begun building libraries of your own Patches, Songs and samples, you will be able to take advantage of a useful shortcut called Database Folders.

At the top right of the Patch, Sample or Song Browser dialogue is a row of four blue folder buttons. These are handy automatic references to any folder on any hard drive (fixed or removable) that's accessible to your computer, and can be set up to refer to your own Patch folders.

The Database Folders.

The folders are customised in the Sound Locations Preferences (find Preferences under the 'Edit' menu, then select Sound Locations from the Page pop-up). Here you may define four sound and Patch-search paths, which are then used by the Patch Browser.

Customise the Database Folders by setting up search paths for your sounds in Sound Locations Preferences.

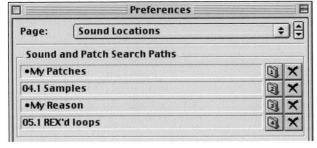

Click on one of the numbered blue folder icons and you will be presented with a standard file-selector window. From here, navigate to the required Patch folder and select it by clicking on the 'Choose' button. The numbered icon will now always automatically locate the Patch folder that has been

Info

Why it's good to save Patches

If for some reason you save a Song in which you've created some new synth or sampler Patches, or a new ReDrum kit, and haven't saved the edited Patches because you forgot or were in a hurry, don't worry: any edits you made are saved with the Song and will remain exactly as you left them when you saved the Song. But if you don't save the Patches separately, it will be harder to re-use them later in other Songs – you might not even remember which Song that great Patch was in – so saving Patches is a good habit to get into. Fortunately, you can save Patches at any time.

Info

Saving as Song instead of Patch

It's possible, using Reason's comprehensive control and audio-routing facilities, to interconnect devices to a very complex degree that rivals the classic hardware modular synthesizers. Unfortunately, none of these connections are saved in standard device Patches. However, if you create a rack that produces a particular sound that you feel you'd like to use again, simply save it as a Song: all connections will be saved, for re-use at any time. Just highlight all the devices that are interconnected (using Shift-click), use Copy Device from the Edit or Context Menus and paste into a new Song; all you'll have to do is make an audio connection to the new Song's mixer, and perhaps create a sequencer track or tracks. This is also easy to do using the Combinator. See its chapter for more.

assigned to it. You might find it useful to have one Database Folder that always points at your central sample collection on your computer's hard drive, plus another Database Folder that accesses your device Patches.

Missing sounds

As mentioned above, you might tend to keep all your samples in one folder, referenced by a Reason Database link (prior to v3) so that it can always find the samples that NN19 and ReDrum need. However, it's sometimes necessary to re-organise that folder, and once any samples have been moved, Reason won't find them the next time it looks for them.

The Missing Sounds dialogue.

A 'Missing Sounds' window will pop up, telling you that 'Some sounds could not be found', and giving you some options for what to do next. Generally, if you haven't renamed any of the samples in question, simply clicking on the 'Search & Proceed' button will tell Reason to search your hard drive for missing sample files, and reload them. Now save the Patch and the Song so that the problem won't happen again.

If you've re-named one of the samples that Reason can't locate, you can use the manual search function to find it. Click on the 'Open Dialog...' button in the Missing Sounds window, which brings up a standard file selector, allowing you to manually search your hard drive for the missing file or files.

Info

Automatic sync

Reason Pattern devices and REX loops played by the Dr:rex device, always play in sync with the main Reason sequencer, without you having to do anything.

The new Browser

In Reason 3, the Browser got a big overhaul, making it much faster and easier to work with. With ever-growing sound libraries, finding and managing patches, loops and samples becomes more important than ever, so the Props obliged with a greatly expanded new tool to improve workflow and productivity. The Browser is now integrated so the one window lets you do all your file management. No longer is it dependent on what you're searching for. Here is the lowdown on the new features and how they help you.

Search

This is a huge improvement over the old system. What you get now is much more like a conventional Windows or Mac OS search window, with different parameters and criteria. The Search In box lets you specify the whole hard drive (can take a while), User Locations (set by you) or Current Folder (may be restrictive). In the Search For box you enter any keywords, and the Show menu filters what is displayed by type. Now, if for example you want a piano sound but have many over different modules, you no longer have to search all NN19 patches, then all NNXT patches and so on. Just search for 'piano'

The new and much-improved search tools in Reason 3

and choose to Show All Instruments. Alternatively, if you have navigated from a Combinator and know you want a Combi, choose Show Combinator Patches. The menu changes based on which device you have navigated from. If you choose Create > Create Device by Browsing Patches, you can't filter results by specific instrument type, just by show instruments or show effects. The back and forward buttons and context menu let you see what folder you're in relative to the root of the drive, and navigate backwards or forwards quickly. If you look in the All Instrument / All Effect Patches folders on the Factory Sound Bank you get a handy list of every sound grouped by type, not module. This is a good way to find a type of sound regardless of what format the patch is in.

Tip

If you try to search a whole hard drive, the search will take ages. Try to practice good file management and keep things organised. Searching specific folders is far quicker than whole drives.

Sort by instrument type, not module type.

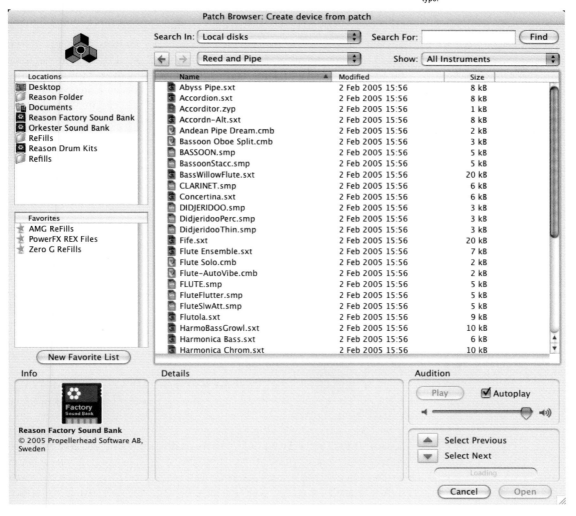

The new location shortcuts in Reason 3

Try out sounds and effects directly from the Browser

A breakdown of the contents of a patch or Combi in the Browser

Locations and Favorites

These are like the Database Folders from prior to V3, but more flexible. To add folders or ReFills to the Locations shortcut box, navigate to them in the main window and just drop them in. This is a great way of keeping groups of samples or ReFills together for quick access. In the Favorites list, you can click the button to create a new list, name it and then drop patches or REX loops from the main window into it. You can't drop folders or ReFills into it – use the Locations box for that. To remove either a Location or a Favorites list, select it and hit backspace.

Audition

It makes sense to leave the Autoplay function on, as it tends to save a lot of time when you're trawling through material. Lower the volume slider to halfway to avoid any nasty surprises from loud samples! You can manually play files using the play button, and cycle through a list using the Previous and Next buttons. The Loading bar tells you when Reason is pre-loading a larger multisample or Combi into memory for you to hear. The best thing about the new Browser is that when you preview any patch or effect, it is actually loaded in the background. You can see Reason doing this if you watch. But it is only kept if you click OK. The best part is that everything can be auditioned. If you select a patch, you can play it from your keyboard while still in the Browser. If you're previewing an effect from an effect module, you

can hear the sound processed before you commit to using it. If the effect is attached to an instrument and you are previewing the effect, any notes you play on the MIDI keyboard, even while in the Browser, will pass through the effect and show you how it's going to sound. So there's no more loading, deciding and deleting, which speeds up your workflow a lot.

Details

This displays information about the patches or files you're previewing, including a splash from the manufacturer if it's a ReFill. It's of most interest for Combis, as it shows the contents of the Combi before you load it.

About ReFills

ReFill is the term for a collection of sounds and samples ready-prepared in the correct formats for Reason devices.

The Factory ReFill

Reason now ships with two free ReFills – the Factory Sound Bank, the quality 24-bit orchestral sample library that is Orkester, and the classic electric keyboard collection ElectroMechanical is available to download for registered users. Between them, these ReFills offer well over 1GB of free synth and sampler patches, drum sounds and kits, instrumental and loop samples and REX loops (the last processed with Propellerhead's Recycle software for easy manipulation).

The factory ReFills are installed when you install Reason so that you have constant access to its sounds. You can, of course, install further ReFills at any time, even if you chose not to when you installed Reason itself. See Chapter 2 for installation details. Note that you can only open the sounds in a ReFill from inside Reason itself, and not from the desktop. ReFill is a closed format – you can't 'unpick' it.

Third-party ReFills

Additional ReFills, both commercial and free (often created by other users) are available. See Appendix 1 for lists of places to find them. Be aware that any sound bank in the ReFill format cannot have its constituent sounds and samples extracted from the ReFill.

Making your own ReFills

It is also possible to make your own ReFills, either for convenience and to save space (samples in a ReFill are around 50% smaller than normal AIFF or WAV audio files), to share with friends, or even, perhaps, to sell or share via the Internet.

To this end, Propellerhead have created a simple application called ReFill Packer, that comes with comprehensive documentation. With this, you organise the Patches for devices that you'd like to 'pack', plus samples and REX loops, follow the simple on-screen prompts and create a ReFill. It's best to follow the documentation's advice and arrange Patches and samples for related devices in separate folders – SubTractor Patches, NN19 Samples and so on – within a single overall folder. You can supply a bit of descriptive text, a splash image, web link and so on, all of which will be saved with the ReFill and appear in Browser windows when elements are loaded.

ReFill Packer isn't included on the Reason program disk, and has to be downloaded from Propellerhead's web site. Note that you will need the latest version of ReFill Packer to create ReFills that include material from the latest Reason devices.

Undo

Almost all actions in Reason can be Undone, with Undo extending back 10 steps – that is, you will be able to Undo your last 10 actions (going back-

ReFill Packer.

wards 10, 9, 8, 7, and so on) by using the Undo operation 10 times. You can select Undo from the Edit menu, or use the familiar key combination Apple/Control-Z . There is also the option to Redo an Undone action. You can find an in-depth explanation of the rules that govern the Undo process in the Reason 'Getting Started' manual, if you feel you need one.

The Hardware Interface

Fixed permanently to the top of the Reason rack, the Hardware Interface has two jobs: to route audio out of the program and to route MIDI inwards. It has a limited set of controls and is divided into two – the upper 'MIDI In Device' section, and the lower 'Audio Out' section.

The Hardware Interface.

Audio routing

When it comes to audio, the HI lets you route up to 64 channels of Reason audio to a compatible piece of audio software on the same computer, or to the outside world via your audio hardware – this last option would allow you to mix your Reason Song via whatever hardware mixing and processing tools you own. The audio side of the Interface is configured as 64 numbered virtual jack sockets at the rear and 64 bargraph level meters at the front; you will see activity in these meters if audio is being directed out of Reason. There's also an indication of what audio driver you're currently using in a virtual LCD display. In addition, each bargraph has a green LED above it which lights when the corresponding audio channel is active.

A word about terminology: you'll see the HI's audio channels referred to as 'inputs'; this is quite correct, as you connect audio outputs from Reason devices to its jack sockets. The Interface then routes the audio onwards.

When you first launch Reason, two of the 64 inputs will be active – channels 1 and 2, which are highlighted and additionally labelled 'Stereo'. This pair is set to route Reason's stereo output mix to the main stereo out of your audio hardware. When you create your first ReMix in an empty Reason rack, its stereo output will be routed to the the HI's first two inputs, corresponding to this main stereo out.

The audio inputs on the Hardware Interface's rear panel. When you make a ReMix, its stereo output is automatcially connected to the first two inputs on the Interface. How many of the remaining sockets you will be able to use to route audio out of Reason depends on a number of factors.

Exactly how many of the remaining audio socket/level meter pairs you'll be able to use will be down to your audio hardware. For example, if you have an 8-channel audio card, you'll be given the option to activate any or all of its channels within Audio Preferences. If you enable them all, the first eight inputs of the Hardware Interface will be active – the green LEDs above their bargraphs will light. The audio out of any Reason device routed to these inputs will now be routed to the equivalent output of your audio card. If your card has digital interfacing as part of its outputs, Reason audio will be routable here too. If it's in the list of potential Active Channels in Audio Prefs, you can route audio to it!

Reason, as you may know, is a ReWire-compatible application that can route its audio, using the ReWire protocol, to compatible applications. It does this via the Hardware Interface. When Reason is launched as a ReWire 2 slave, all 64 inputs of the Interface will be active, and it's up to you to link Reason device outputs to Hardware Interface inputs for routing to the master software (the program Reason is being ReWired to). If the master ReWire application isn't yet compatible with ReWire 2, there will be fewer audio channels available, and the Hardware Interface will reflect this in only making active as many input channels as are available. The use of ReWire is covered in more detail in the chapter dealing with Reason and other software and hardware.

The Audio Input section of the Hardware Interface is rounded off with a virtual LCD which indicates your currently-selected soundcard, and whether Reason is currently a ReWire slave or not.

MIDI routing via the Hardware Interface

Some of you may never actually need to use the 'MIDI In Device' portion of the Hardware Interface – for example, you won't need it if all you want from a MIDI connection is a way to route your MIDI keyboard to the sequencer, for playing or recording one device at a time. This is set up via the basic MIDI Preferences, as explained in Chapter 2.

The four MIDI input buses available via the 'MIDI In' section of the Hardware Interface. The 'LCD' shows where MIDI input is coming from for whichever bus has been selected (select a bus by clicking one of the A-D buttons).

However, if you plan to use some of the more advanced 'layered device' performance tips discussed later in the book, the Hardware Interface will come into play. You'll also need more MIDI input flexibility if you aim to control Reason, as a 'sound module', from a non ReWire-compatible sequencer on the same computer, from another computer entirely, or from a hardware sequencer. Reason provides this flexibility via four extra MIDI buses, A-D, the MIDI input sources for which are set up in Advanced MIDI Preferences. The four buses can be seen in the 'MIDI In Device' section of the Hardware Interface. Their use is best explained by example.

Imagine you want to control Reason sounds from an external hardware sequencer. Some way of routing its MIDI input into Reason is thus required. If you connect the sequencer's MIDI Output to a MIDI Input on your MIDI interface, you can set this input in Reason's Advanced MIDI Preferences as the 'external control' Bus A. The sequencer's MIDI input then enters Reason via Bus A of the Hardware Interface, and can be seen in the Bus A LCD display if Bus A is selected by clicking on its button.

Not only is it possible to route a MIDI input into Reason as explained above, it is also possible to define which MIDI channel of that input will play which device in the Reason rack. This is done via the 16 Channel LCDs, which each have a pop-up menu button. When a bus is selected, all the Channel displays refer to that bus, and you may use a Channel pop-up to select a device in the rack. The chosen MIDI bus and channel now control that device, and the device name is seen in the Channel LCD. (When MIDI data comes into the input, a red LED lights on active channels.) Given that there are four buses in total, you could control up to 64 Reason MIDI devices externally!

It's worth reiterating at this point that both audio and MIDI are 'unidirectional' within Reason: audio can go out but not come in, and MIDI can come in but not go out.

High Quality Interpolation

All Reason's sample-based devices have a 'High Quality Interpolation' button; when engaged this engages a 'more advanced' interpolation algorithm, which results in better audio quality. Propellerhead note that HQI is particularly effective when a sample has significant high-frequency content – a bright sound. The drawback is that this option does require extra processing power (except in the case of Apple G4, and later, computers). In any case, the audible results may be undetectable or not at all obvious. Try it and have a listen. On a modern computer it's unlikely to cause any performance problems.

Low Bandwidth

Dr:rex, Subtractor and NN19 each have a switch labelled 'Low BW'. This engages a low-bandwidth mode that uses less computer power but reproduces less of the high-frequency content of a sound. Again, the effect of this switch isn't always obvious, especially on bass sounds or samples that have been filtered to eliminate much of their HF content. If you can hear no difference, engaging the switch does save some processing power, so it may be a valuable option when running a busy session on an older computer.

The High-Quality Interpolation and Low BW switches.

The CV and Gate control system

When Reason was being developed, its programmers needed a way for the user to visualise the control (as distinct from audio) interconnections between devices. A number of solutions were explored, but the one arrived at has produced one of Reason's most powerful features: its CV and Gate control system.

CV and Gate history

Overall, Reason's studio 'paradigm' harks back to the 'classic' electronic music studios that were prevalent before the introduction, in the early '80s, of MIDI (the Musical Instrument Digital Interface that is used to connect together and control hardware instruments and equipment in the modern studio). Many would argue that this was the heyday of pure electronic music, where synthesis was analogue rather than digital, and instruments were connected using 'CV and Gate'.

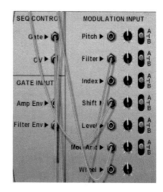

The CV/Gate system in action.

In classical electronic terms, CVs – Control Voltages – were used for the dynamic control of parameters. Depending on the exact voltage sent, a CV determined the pitch an oscillator would play at, and also (for example) created the continuous signal which, when patched correctly, changed a filter's cutoff frequency over time. Gates – AKA triggers – were mainly used to tell a note when to play, by 'firing' envelope generators; to use an analogy with MIDI, Gates created the 'Note On' message, while CVs determined the pitch of the note.

How it works in Reason

This is broadly how the Reason CV/Gate system works too, but one big difference is that in the hardware world CV outputs can't usually be connected to Gate Inputs (and vice versa), while in Reason they can, and this sometimes produces an interesting sonic result. Another difference is that Reason Gate signals, as well as providing 'Note On' information, also provide 'velocity' information which can be used to control prameters such as amplitude – loudness – in many Reason devices.

Beyond simply governing pitch, duration and velocity response, CVs and Gates can be used for complex 'modulation' of devices, creating vast sonic potential. The possibilities are discussed in device chapters to come and some of them are summarised in a chart given in Chapter 21. The interconnections possible with Reason are really only approached in the hardware world by (expensive) modular synth systems, in which each component of the electronic sound-making process (such as oscillators, filters and envelope generators) is 'discrete', often contained in a separate module, and must be connected to others via audio and control cabling, just like the Reason devices.

Although, strictly speaking, Reason isn't a MIDI application per se, in practice MIDI can obviously be used to record into it and control it. MIDI doesn't really interact with the CV and Gate system, but in a way is layered on top of it, providing even more real-time control of Reason's devices.

Other Preferences settings

The settings in the General page of Reason Preferences (under the Edit menu) not discussed so far are as follows:

- Mouse Knob Range: Choose 'Precise' or 'Very Precise' here and you'll be able to adjust on-screen controls with much more precision, since the mouse will have to be dragged further to get the same result as when using the 'Normal' setting.
- CPU Usage Limit: Though Reason has been economically designed in terms of the demands it places on your computer, it'll still require more in terms of CPU overhead than the average word processor. The more devices in the Reason rack, the more computer power is required, and the less available to graphics handling and general 'responsiveness' of the program. The CPU Usage Limit lets you take control of the situation to a certain extent; if you find mouse handling and screen redraws unacceptbly sluggish when you build a large rack, you can set this parameter to a lower percentage. Then Reason will only use that percentage of CPU resources for audio, leaving the rest for other aspects of the program. There are six choices between 70 and 95%, or no limit.
- Use High Resolution Samples: Reason has always been able to load samples in a wide range of rates, and 16- or 24-bit resolution, though all samples prior to V2 were converted to 16-bit internally. Since V2, you

General Preferences.

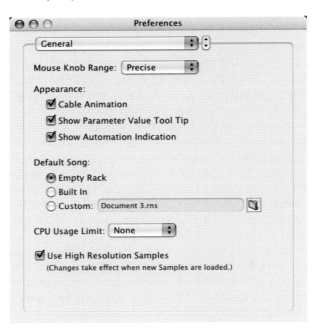

can use 24-bit samples in full 24-bit resolution throughout. Un-check 'Use High Resolution Samples' to make Reason convert 24-bit samples to 16-bit. This is a useful option if your computer is struggling or your audio card doesn't support 24-bit.

Remote setup

All MIDI communication in Reason is now handled by a protocol called Remote, which is a system for easily mapping control surfaces and devices to the various buttons, knobs and sliders on Reason's modules. Some people might just be using a single MIDI keyboard and playing notes, but Remote supports multiple controller devices at once. Most USB MIDI keyboards nowadays have some realtime controls on them. Some even have a full set of assignable knobs and sliders – others still are dedicated control surfaces with no keys but an array of knobs and buttons. The idea is to give you more hands-on control over Reason's many 'tweakable' parameters, which makes the experience of making music much more spontaneous and organic. The idea is tighter integration between hardware and software, and a more seam-less overall experience. The genius is that Reason automatically maps the controls on your hardware to the most commonly used controls on whichev-er device you select. So for example if you are using a MIDI keyboard to tweak synth parameters on a Subtractor but then switch focus to a NN19, the controls are instantly reassigned for you to the most useful parameters on the NN19. The same applies to any module, including effect modules and the mixers. By default, all control surfaces will follow the focus of the master keyboard, unless you lock them to a device. If you have several devices con-nected, you may find that some controls are mapped to the same parame-ters. This isn't a conflict, so don't worry about it!

Setting up

Under the Preferences dialogue in Reason 3 is a new option – Control Surfaces and Keyboards. When starting Reason 3 for the first time you're prompted to set up at least one MIDI device to play the system with. If your device is one of the many supported natively by Reason (check the props website for a full list) then it will be picked up automatically by Remote. If it's not you can try the Auto-detect button to make Reason re-scan the computer for devices.

Auto-detect surfaces

Auto-detect Surfaces

If nothing is picked up, which will happen if you have a standard MIDI key-board, you can click the Add button and choose from a list of preset devices, if you have one. Usefully, there's additional info in these windows about spe-cial quirks and characteristics of the various devices that you need to know when setting them up. You should also be able to rename the device here and set its MIDI in and out ports.

If the device you have doesn't appear in any of the lists – and there are many MIDI keyboards which won't – you can click on the Find button in the Add window. From the Manufacturer menu, choose 'Other', and then what type of controller it is. If you are running MIDI in through a MIDI interface rather than a USB controller, you'll almost certainly have to use the Add and

Setting up a specific control surface

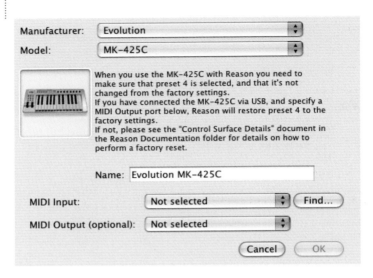

| Manufacturer: | Evolution |
| Model: | MK-425C |

When you use the MK-425C with Reason you need to make sure that preset 4 is selected, and that it's not changed from the factory settings.
If you have connected the MK-425C via USB, and specify a MIDI Output port below, Reason will restore preset 4 to the factory settings.
If not, please see the "Control Surface Details" document in the Reason Documentation folder for details on how to perform a factory reset.

Name: Evolution MK-425C

MIDI Input: Not selected   Find...

MIDI Output (optional):   Not selected

Cancel   OK

Find option. The window explains what types of controllers exist and you should pick the one that sounds most like yours.

Basic MIDI Keyboard

Select this is you have a MIDI keyboard without programmable knobs, buttons or faders. This is used for playing only (including performance controllers such as pitch bend, mod wheel) - you can't adjust Reason device parameters with this type of control surface.

MIDI Controller

Select this if you have a MIDI controller with programmable knobs, buttons or faders (but without keyboard). You need to set up your control surface so that the controllers send the correct MIDI CC messages, depending on which Reason device you want to control - check out the MIDI Implementation Chart in the Reason Documentation folder. If your control surface has templates or presets for different Reason 2.5 devices, these can be used.

MIDI Keyboard with Controls

Select this is you have a MIDI keyboard with programmable knobs, buttons or faders. Again, you need to set your controllers to send the right MIDI CCs. This is the type of MIDI keyboard that is in most common use.

If your MIDI interface doesn't appear in the MIDI input menu, press the Find button, then press a key on the keyboard. Reason should pick it up and you can choose it and press OK. If Reason still isn't finding your device, you should check that it's working and connected properly, and transmitting MIDI on the correct channel.

If you create a Basic MIDI Keyboard or MIDI keyboard with controls, Reason will automatically make it the 'Master Keyboard'. This is the device which sends MIDI note data to the sequencer, and you can only have one device specified as the Master Keyboard, and it can't be locked to a Reason device, as it needs to be able to switch MIDI focus in the sequencer. You can't record note data into

Different types of keyboard can be set up for different remote control results

the sequencer for more than one module at a time, so any device other than the master keyboard is used for controlling rather than 'playing' in the conventional sense. Although additional keyboards will be able to play the notes of whichever device has MIDI focus (the device the master keyboard is playing), if you lock a keyboard to a device it loses the ability to play notes and is used for controlling knobs and sliders only.

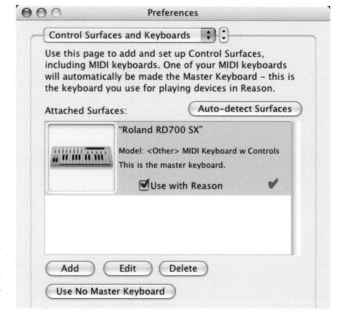

Above: MIDI learn

Right: Managing a list of attached MIDI devices

The device you have set up will have a 'Use with Reason' checkbox. When you connect further devices you can uncheck this box so that although Reason sees the devices, it won't use them. This is in case you have those devices set up for other programs and don't want Reason interfering. You can edit or delete devices at any time using the relevant buttons.

To add a further input device, repeat the above procedure. You can add as many as you like, although after a while you will start to run out of MIDI or USB ports to connect any more devices!

Additional devices can be turned on or
off

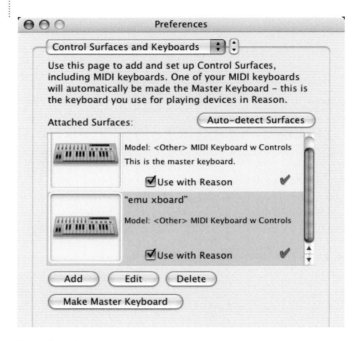

Example setups

1   MIDI keyboard with controls. The most likely and simplest setup,
    whereby you have a single MIDI keyboard with some realtime controllers.
    You can switch what you play easily by changing MIDI focus – selecting
    the keyboard icon for different devices in the sequencer.
2   Basic MIDI keyboard plus a controller. A more complex setup with a
    notes-only keyboard used to play and record notes into the sequencer,
    and a control surface following the master keyboard – and so having its
    controls re-focused every time you select a new module, or locked to a
    completely different device to the master keyboard.
3   MIDI keyboard with controls plus additional controllers. A more complex
    setup, providing a great deal of control for several performers at once.
    The keyboard plays the modules but the other controllers are locked to
    devices like the mixer or other Combinators or instruments, meaning you
    can control much of the rack without using a mouse. This is ideal for live
    performance.

Mapping variations

As there are often more parameters on a device than there are controls on a
control surface, there are standard mapping variations available for most
devices. When selecting a standard mapping variation, a new set of parameters is mapped to the controls on your control surface for a selected Reason
device. For example, if you have a control surface with 12 rotary knobs routed to a Subtractor, the knobs may control oscillator parameters by default.
Selecting variation 2 may make the knobs control the filter settings, variation
3 may control LFOs and so on. For devices that support keyboard shortcuts,
you switch between mapping variations using [Command] + [Option] (Mac)

/ [Ctrl] + [Alt] (Windows) and the numerical keys [1] to [10] (not the numer-ical keypad), where [1] selects the default standard mapping.

See the chapter on automation and remote control for more on the prac-tical uses of Remote.

Some basic FAQs

How do I record into a sequencer track?

First, ensure your computer system and any MIDI input device are set up properly, as explained in Chapter 2. Then you need to make sure you have the keyboard icon lit by the device track name in the sequencer (click in the 'In' column). Now click the red Record and then the Play button in the Transport bar. You should now be able to record. See the Tutorials chapter and the sequencer chapter for step-by-step sequence recording instructions.

Can I record to multiple tracks in the Reason sequencer simultaneously?

This is not possible; only one track can be active for recording at one time. On the otehr hand, controller (automation) information can be recorded on multiple tracks at once, using thh Remote system or using the mouse during recording playback.

How can I make a drum pattern?

Programme in step fashion in ReDrum, or play the part into the main sequencer from your MIDI keyboard (probably in several passes). You could alternatively use a sampled drum loop in Dr:rex or one of the samplers as the rhythmic basis for your track.

What should I use to create a bassline?

Programme in step-fashion in a Matrix linked to a Reason synth or sampler, by clicking in a grid; or play a part, with a Reason synth or sampler sound, into the main sequencer from a MIDI keyboard. You could also draw in notes on the note display in the main sequencer, but this is rather fiddly.

How can I edit a MIDI part recorded into the main sequencer?

Enter the sequencer's Edit View, where you can delete notes, cut, copy and paste, and so on. You can also quantise in either sequencer View (Arrange or Edit), to tighten up timing.

How can I sketch out the structure of a Song?

Use copy and paste in the Arrange View of the main sequencer to arrange parts that you have recorded into the sequencer ('Group' sections that you want to move or copy, so that they can be edited as a single entity). In the case of the Matrix and ReDrum, record Pattern chains in the sequencer so that Patterns change where you want them to. Convert individual Patterns or whole chains to notes in the main sequencer if you would like to have all your data in the same place when arranging the Song.

How can I bring parts in and out of the mix?

You can do this either with your sequencer arrangement, deleting sections on different tracks where you don't want the part to play; or automate mixer channel mutes for sections where you don't want specific parts to play; or, with Pattern-based devices, automate Pattern mutes.

Can I add real-time knob tweaks to a synth sound, drum part or sample?

Yes – record the movements of the device's knobs into its track of the main sequencer, as automation data. Using a MIDI keyboard with knobs and sliders helps greatly here.

Can I use a hardware MIDI control surface with Reason?

Absolutely – see the automation and remote control chapter.

Is it possible to sync LFOs to Song tempo?

Click the Sync button on LFO-equipped devices in Reason V2 and higher; use the Matrix to simulate an LFO in earlier versions.

Could I use Reason without a MIDI keyboard?

You're much better off with a keyboard, but you can just about use Reason without. Program parts by mouse-clicking in the Matrix and ReDrum, use the audition feature in most devices to hear sounds without triggering from a keyboard, and see Chapter 2 for details of utilities that change the computer keyboard into a MIDI input device. If you're working mostly with REX loops, a MIDI keyboard becomes less vital.

How do I import a MIDI File?

In the main sequencer, use the 'Import MIDI File' command in the File menu.

Can I save my Reason work as a MIDI File?

Yes. Make sure all your Song data is in the main sequencer (see Matrix and ReDrum chapters) and choose 'Export MIDI File' from the File menu.

How do you import a WAV, AIFF or Soundfont?

Load into NN19, NNXT or ReDrum via the Sample Browser (for individual samples from within a SoundFont; use NNXT or NN19's Patch Browser for entire SoundFonts). In pre-V2 Reason, you can't load Soundfonts.

Can I load other sample formats?

Not directly. They will need to be converted with a suitable utility. For example, Propellerhead's own ReLoad program makes is easy to convert samples and programs from Akai S1000 and S3000-format media to something that can be loaded by the NN19 and NN-XT sample playback devices. ReLoad is a free download for registered Reason users, and is available for MacOS X and Windows XP.

Can the Reason samplers do 'timestretching'?

No. When you transpose the pitch of a sample in NN19 or NNXT, its length and speed are affected too. You'll need to do any timestretching in an external application or use REX loops in Dr:rex. These can, in effect, be altered in pitch without affecting duration/speed, and altered in duration/speed without affecting pitch, though timestretching isn't used for the process.

Can I edit samples in Reason?

Not in a conventional sense, though in NNXT you can set them to start and end at specific points and also set an internal loop. For proper sample editing you'll need an external audio-editing application. There are many available, and some are even free.

Can I record audio into Reason?

No. Again, you'll need to use an external sequencing or audio recording/editing application and import the audio, as WAV or AIFF data, into a Reason sample-based device.

How can I get a vocal performance into a Reason Song?

You can load vocal snippets into one of the samplers or ReDrum; for a conventional song, cut the vocal performance into chunks as long as possible in an external audio editing application (excluding long pauses), save as WAV or AIFF and load into a sample-based device for triggering in appropriate places in the Reason Song. Or run Reason in sync with a MIDI + Audio sequencer into which the vocal performance has been recorded.

Does Reason create REX files?

No, it only plays them back and allows you to manipulate them. To make REX files you'll need Propellerhead's ReCycle. Songs, or sections of Songs, can be saved as AIFF or WAV files though.

Can I add plug-in effects to Reason tracks?

Not actually inside Reason, as it doesn't support plug-ins. Use ReWire to route the tracks to a ReWire-compatible audio application, running on the same computer, that does.

Can I play Reason devices from external sequencers?

Yes. This works via either the MIDI buses in the Hardware Interface or via ReWire. See the chapter on using Reason with other software and instruments for more.

Can I control external synths and samplers with Reason sequencer devices?

This is not possible, as Reason doesn't have MIDI output. But if you run Reason in sync with another sequencer that will control hardware instruments, you can get Reason devices and hardware synths/samplers playing in the same Song, in effect. The data recorded into Reason's sequencer can be saved as a Standard MIDI File, so in a long-winded way, a Reason performance can be played by external sounds.

How can I change tempo in the middle of a Song?

Reason does not support tempo changes (as in a tempo map). You'll have to sync the Reason Song to another sequencer that does allow tempo changes. As Reason is always the 'slave' in these situations, the Reason tempo will change in line with the sync'd application's tempo. If you're really keen, don't mind taking some trouble and can't sync to another application, see the sequencer chapter for a way of faking tempo changes inside Reason. But it's not pretty!

The ReMix mixer

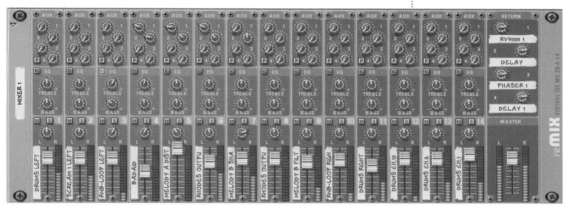

Like the other devices in the Reason rack, the ReMix mixer has been created to work and behave almost exactly like its real-world, hardware equivalents. It's a device you're sure to use a lot when producing tracks in Reason, being the centre for most of the audio connections in the rack, as well as the focal point when it comes to mixing down a composition into its final stereo form. And as ReMix controls can be fully automated, with all automation data being editable in the main sequencer, there's really no excuse for not producing exactly the mix you're after.

One of the neatest things about the way the ReMix has been implemented is that it saves the user a lot of the manual connection time that would be necessary with a real mixer, by offering logical automatic connections. This is ideal for beginners, and very handy even for the experienced. Of course, every automatic connection can be overridden manually, and manual connections can be made from the very start if preferred.

Info

Keyboard shortcuts

Apple/Control-click any control
Restores default value
(centres pans)

Shift-click-hold on control
Access fine adjustment

Mixer basics

At the most basic level, a mixer simply combines two or more audio signals and provides facilities for independent adjustment of their levels, or volumes. Metering is usually provided so that the user has visual feedback of the signal level going through each mixer 'channel'. It is also possible to decide where in the left-right stereo 'image' a signal is placed, by means of the pan (for panoramic) control, enabling a satisfying spread of sounds to be built up. Most mixers also offer tone controls, or equalisation (EQ) in each channel; at their simplest these will offer the means to boost or reduce the treble and bass content of each signal, to improve and tailor sounds and make them work better with other sounds.

An important part of mixing is temporarily removing signals from the mix, to change the arrangement of a track and create sections with different balances of instruments, and this is facilitated by Mute buttons on each channel, which basically silence that channel for as long as they are engaged. The opposite of the Mute button is the Solo button, which mutes all channels except the one being 'solo'd', so that the solo'd channel plays alone. The Solo button is often used to isolate a part from the mix so that it can be refined without distraction: tweak the EQ parameters, effects settings, and so on. Yet another important function of a mixer is providing easy access to effects, such as reverb. Effects may be connected to the mixer such that every sound source also connected to the mixer can have a share of their processing, via a 'send/return' system.

After the mixer has played its part in allowing a balanced and exciting sound picture to be created, it is then used to combine the many signals that make up the track into just two channels – a stereo mix. Because real-time mixing can be a complex and demanding business (especially on a computer, with just a mouse between you and the mixer controls!), we have automation. This allows you to make progressive changes in mix parameters and have these changes recorded. You can then make additional changes, recording these too, until every mix parameter that you want altered during the course of the track has been automated. With the help of a fader- or knob-equipped MIDI hardware controller, computer mixing can also become much more of an intuitive, hands-on experience.

Guided tour

Input channels

The ReMix is a 14-channel device, each channel having an identical range of features, and each capable of accepting mono or stereo signals. Once you understand one 'channel strip', you understand them all.

Level fader and bargraph level meter

The fader provides volume control for the channel. Three-colour (green, amber, red) metering graphically displays the level of signal going through the channel. The 'Scribble Strip' label alongside the fader automatically changes to reflect the name of the device connected to that channel.

Pan control

Sets the position of the channel's signal in the left-right stereo image. If a stereo signal is coming through the channel, the Pan Pot changes to function as a balance control for the two sides of the stereo signal.

Mute and Solo buttons

Click the Mute button to silence the channel's output. Click again to unmute it. Click the Solo button and the output of that channel is 'singled out', muting other channels at the same time. The Solo function is a true 'solo in place', which means that not only do you hear the solo'd sound, but also any effects that have been applied to it. You can solo several channels at the

Channel strip

Fader/meter

Pan

Mute/solo

same time. To mute channels that have been solo'd in this situation, click their Solo button again, rather than the Mute button.

The EQ Controls & EQ Enable Switch

Provides simple two-band (treble and bass) tone control over signals going through ReMix channels. Each band offers up to 24dB of cut or boost, with the treble band centred on 12kHz, and the bass centred on 80Hz.

The switch at top left brings channel equalisation in and out of the signal path. If you don't need EQ, switching it out saves a little CPU power.

EQ

Aux sends

The Auxiliary Send System

Used to control the amount of signal, in mono or stereo, sent from a mixer channel to up to four effects processors. Aux 4 has a switch, labelled 'P', for selecting pre-fader, rather than the more usual post-fader, operation.

The Master Section

This is where the other channels are combined to a stereo output. From top:

Aux returns and Master fader/meter

- *Auxiliary return knobs:* Control how much of each effect device's output is added to the stereo mix. The scribble strips next to the knobs automatically change to reflect the names of the effect devices connected to the mixer.
- *Stereo Master fader and bargraph meters:* The fader sets the overall level of the stereo mix and is used to create a fade at the end of a Song, if required.

The rear panel

The back panel of the ReMix device is almost as busy as the front – but it's just as easily broken down. Each of the 14 input channels has the same collection of connections.

Rear panel

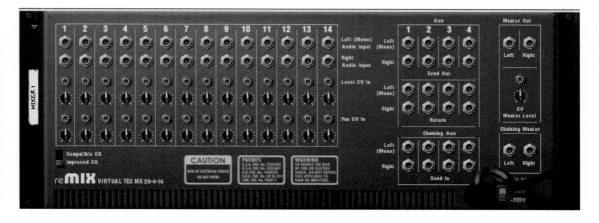

Left/Right audio input jack sockets

The audio outputs of sound-making devices are connected to these sockets to route them into the mixer. Use just the left jack for a mono device, such as SubTractor or a single mono ReDrum drum voice. (If you connect a mono device to the right input, all you'll hear is audio panned hard right.)

Level CV Input, with trim control

Allows any CV source in the rack to modulate (alter or control) a channel's level (see Chapter 4 for more on the CV and Gate system), with the trim control determining how strong the effect is. Though this facility could provide an alternative way to automate level changes, its main purpose is to allow you to create special effects, such as tremolo (explained later in this chapter).

Pan CV Input with trim control

Allows any CV source in the rack to 'modulate' (alter or control) a channel's pan position. The trim control determines how strong the effect is. Again, this facility is more of an aid in the creation of special effects, such as auto-pan, than a subsitute for Reason's automation system.

Rear-panel channel connections

Aux Send Section

Four stereo pairs of *Aux send* sockets for the four effects that can be connected to the mixer send/return system. Cables are connected between these sockets and the inputs of the desired effects devices. To feed a mono effect, or work with an effect in mono, just connect the left socket to a device's input.

Eight *Aux Return sockets* (a stereo pair for each effect device attached to the sends). This is where the outputs of effect devices are returned to the mixer.

Four pairs of stereo *Aux Chaining In* sockets for linking the send system of one mixer to another, so that both mixers can share one set of send effects. ReDrum effects sends can also be 'Chained In' to a ReMix; in this case, just the left sockets of the Chaining In Pair would be used, since ReDrum's effect sends are mono only.

Rear aux section

Master Section

Stereo Master Output, usually used for sending the stereo mix from a ReMix to the hardware interface, and thence to other software or hardware, or your monitoring system. However, effects can be connected between this output and the hardware interface, if you want to apply some processing to an entire mix. See the effects chapter for more. This output could also be routed to a 'Chaining Input' or ordinary input channel of another mixer (see next entry).

Rear master section

Master Chaining Inputs, used for connecting the master output of another ReMix, so that the mix level of both can be controlled from one Master fader.

Master Level CV Input and trim control, allowing Master level to be automated or modulated by another device.

The EQ response switch, located at the lower left of the back panel, is not labelled as such, but offers quick access to the ReMix's original EQ response and the new, improved response introduced in V2.5. Default is 'Compatible EQ', and this will be used by songs created with earlier versions of

Reason. The 'Improved EQ' setting produces a much smoother sound, resulting in EQ that's less likely to unbalance the overall sound of a mix or an individual channel's audio.

The EQ response switch

ReMix automatic connections

When you begin a new Song, it makes a lot of sense to always make a ReMix mixer the first device in your rack. (Of course, if you make a default Song, there will be a mixer in that – see Chapter 4 for some default Song guidelines.) If you do this, Reason will automatically connect subsequent devices to the mixer for you, in the most sensible way it can. It will also automatically connect the stereo output of the ReMix to the first available pair of inputs on the Hardware Interface device, which in turn sends the stereo mix to your computer's audio hardware (and thence to whatever system you use for listening).

As an example of automatic mixer connections, if you began with an empty rack and first created a ReMix and then a SubTractor synth, you would find that the synth's audio output had automatically been patched by Reason to the mono input of ReMix channel 1 – see the figure below. SubTractor is a mono device, so the mixer senses this and gives it a mono input on the mixer.

Info

Hands-on ReMix

You can get some basic experience of using ReMix – employing effects via the Send/Return system, changing levels and pan positions, and muting and soloing tracks – by going through the tutorials in Chapter 3.

Reason's automatic connections between the hardware interface, a ReMix mixer (first device created) and a SubTractor synth (second device created).

If you then created an NN-19 sampler, its stereo audio output would be automatically patched to the input of ReMix channel 2. As NN-19 is a stereo

<table><tr><td></td></tr></table>

Info

Avoiding automatic connections

If you want to do some or all of your signal routing manually, holding down Shift while creating a device creates it with no automatic connections at all. This is good for learning how all the connections work, as you won't get any untoward ones that might confuse you. You can disconnect a device that's already been connected by selecting 'Disconnect device' from the Edit menu or a contextual menu.

Info

Unwanted connections

Be careful which devices you have selected (highlighted) in the rack when you create new devices, as it's possible to create automatic connections you may not have wanted.

device, the mixer gives it a stereo channel. Each sound-making device added would be patched to a subsequent channel of the mixer. Note that it will save you processing power to connect a device playing material in mono (say, a sampler playing a mono sample) to ReMix in mono, rather than stereo just because it has a stereo output. Manual patching is discussed shortly.

Automatic connections with a second mixer

When all 14 channels of the mixer are full, any extra sound-making devices created can't be patched automatically. However, if you create another mixer, any sound-making devices created after that are automatically patched to the channels of the second mixer, in the same way as with the first. In addition, the mixers are automatically 'bussed' together, via rear-panel connections, so that they will work in tandem. The master fader on the first ReMix then controls the overall stereo mix produced by both mixers.

You can continue in this way, adding mixers and devices as needed, for as long as your computer can stand it!

A second mixer is automatically connected to the first, via the Chaining Master inputs and outputs, and the Aux chaining sockets.

Automatic effects connections

The first four effects devices that you create will also be connected to your mixer automatically – patched into its four aux send/return 'loops', so the aux sends on each mixer channel can have the use of the effects.

Any effects devices created thereafter cannot be automatically connected (unless you delete an existing effect device), the four aux loops being in use. Even if you add a second mixer to the rack, extra effects will not be automatically patched to that, because the aux sends of the second mixer have been automatically 'bussed' to the first, via the Aux chaining sockets, so that the second mixer has access to the first mixer's effects processors, as shown in Figure 5.3.

In effect, when you make a second mixer and use the automatic connections you're making a bigger mixer that still has just the four effect sends. (Note that if you connect mixers manually there is no requirement to bus aux sends of different mixers together. Each mixer can instead link its own four sends to its own collection of four effects. See the section on using several mixers, later in this chapter.)

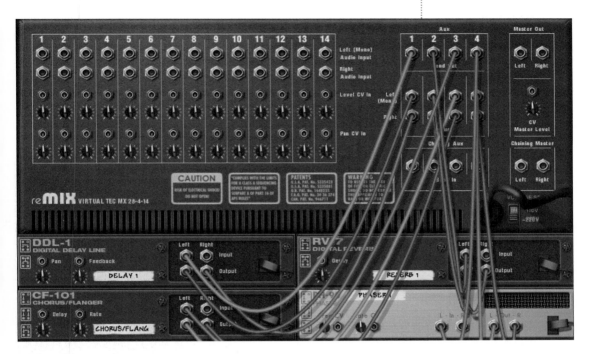

'Insert' effects

Even if there was no way around the 'bussing' together of mixer aux systems (which there is) you wouldn't be confined forever to only four effects per mixer, because effects can also be connected 'in line' with sound sources – the output of the sound source connected to the input of the effect. It's called an 'insert' effect. This can be done in an automatic fashion, too. To create automatic 'insert' effect patching:

- Select a sound-making device by clicking in it.
- Create an effects device.
- The effects device will automatically be connected in-line with the selected sound-making device.

In the figure overleaf, the delay has been automatically connected in-line between the SubTractor and the mixer.

If the sound-making device has already been automatically connected to the mixer, Reason will interrupt that connection for you and plug the output of the sound-making device into the effect device's input, and the effect device's output into the mixer input that was previously occupied by the sound-maker. Simply put, it places the effects device between the sound-maker and the mixer.

The ins and outs of the first four effect devices created, at the bottom of the picture, have been automatically connected to the four aux/send return loops of the ReMix.

Info

Auto-Route Device

If, for some reason, you would like an automatic connection to the mixer where one has not been made, you can click in the device to be connected to the mixer and select 'Auto-Route

An 'insert' effect connection between a delay device and a SubTractor synth, where the delay processes only the synth. The output of the delay is auto-connected to the input of a mixer channel. This configuration is the alternative to using effects in mixer send/return loops.

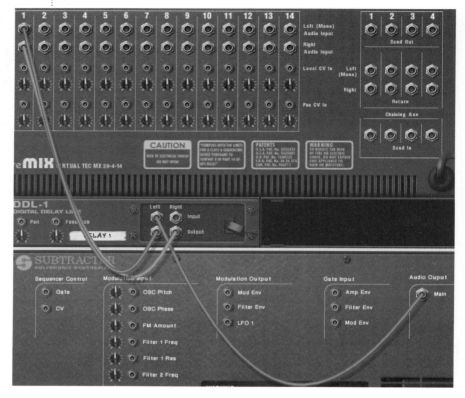

Manual connections

Any automatic connection made by Reason (or, for that matter, any connection made by you!) can be changed by swinging the rack around and manually patching the cables. You may also create devices with no automatic connections and make your own connections manually from the start. Note that you'll only be allowed to complete connections that 'make sense': ie. an audio output can only be sent to an audio input, and vice versa. Input-to-input or output-to-output connections are not possible. See Chapter 4 for how to manually make and break connections.

Why override the automatic connections?

There are many occasions when you may need to create custom routings. As an example, if you've created a lot of sound-making devices and find they are not logically arranged across the mixer channels, you might want to swap them between the channels, perhaps grouping several SubTractors on adjacent channels, for example. If you're working with multiple mixers, especially if using each mixer as a 'subgroup' during mixing, you will also want manual control over device audio routing. (See the section later in this chapter on using multiple mixers.)

Manually patching ReDrum sounds to mixer channels

Another time when manual connections are required is if you want to route individual drum sounds out of the ReDrum device and give each its own mixer channel for greater control and further processing. This type of connection can't be done automatically. If you have a ReDrum in your rack, you might like to try the following for a bit of manual patching practice.

Drag a cable from the ReDrum channel audio output...

- With the ReDrum highlighted, a kit loaded and a pattern programmed (see the ReDrum chapter for more) swing the rack around to the back by pressing the Tab key.
- Click on the top socket in ReDrum channel 1 on the rear panel. This is the audio output for channel 1. It highlights in red, and a red cable appears, which you can drag anywhere.
- Drag it to a free channel on the back of the ReMix mixer and plug it into the top socket (audio input) of that channel. You've now connected ReDrum channel 1 to a mixer input.
- Swing the rack around again and set the ReDrum pattern playing. You should see level meter activity for the overall ReDrum channel in the ReMix mixer and also for whichever ReMix channel you used to patch in ReDrum sound channel 1. Mute the overall ReDrum mixer channel with the channel Mute button and you will still hear the sound assigned to ReDrum's channel 1 playing back through the mixer. Now you can give it its own effects treatment and EQ settings. All ReDrum's separate sounds can be brought to their own mixer channels in this way.

... and plug into a ReMix channel input. The ReDrum voice on channel 1 is removed from the ReDrum stereo mix and now has separate access to the mixer channel's facilities.

More on the Auxiliary Send/Return System

The aux send/return, or effects loop, system is a way of connecting effects to the mixer and sharing their processing between as many mixer channels as you like. As you've already seen, up to four effects devices can be connected to the ReMix mixer at one time. Each channel can be treated with variable amounts of any or all of those effects.

The Send Controls

Which effects a given channel is processed by is determined by the settings of the Aux Send knobs in each channel. What the Aux Send actually does is tap off some signal from that going through the mixer channel and literally 'send' it off to an effects device. How much signal is sent to the effect (and therefore how 'effected' the signal sounds) is set by the Aux Send knob. Sending more signal to the effect device results in more effect being apparent to the listener.

As an example of the use of the Aux Sends, if a reverb was connected to Aux 1, a delay was connected to Aux 2, a chorus to 3 and a phaser to 4, you might apply those effects as follows:

- On mixer channel 1, a vocal sample, only reverb is required, so the Aux 1 knob is turned to the right until the reverb level sounds right. The other three knobs are left in the zero position.
- On mixer channel 2, an electric piano sample, a little delay and quite a lot of phase might be appropriate, so the Aux 2 and Aux 4 knobs are used to set the levels of these effects. The other two knobs are left at the zero position.
- On channel 3 there's a drum loop that just needs some delay, so a little is added with the Aux 2 knob.

Tip

Panning

Think about your sound picture when setting mixer pan positions. The rhythm section and bass should generally be panned centre to anchor the track. It's also wise to keep the main hook-line or melody of the track central – as if it was a lead vocal. (Of course, it may be a lead vocal!). Some people like to pan similar parts hard left and right so that they don't interfere with each other and can be heard as separate. You can also set up a 'call and response' feel between parts with panning. Alternate certain parts left to right to add interest, or pan a sweeping pad slowly across the stereo image. You can approach panning as if you had a band, with each separate part being a player on a stage, with their own position on that stage.

Info

Post-Fade or Pre-fade Aux Sends?

On the ReMix, three of the aux sends are what is known as 'post fade'. The signal path of ReMix starts at the channel fader and goes through the rest of the channel from there. This means that the aux sends occur in the signal path after the channel level fader, and that as the level of the channel's signal is pulled down with the fader, so is the level of signal being sent to the effects device (and hence the perceived level of the effect). The level of signal and the level of effect thus decrease (and increase) in proportion to each other.

In addition, Aux 4 has an option to be switched to pre-fader operation. This is something one would expect in a hardware mixer (and typically is used for setting up monitor mixes in that situation), but here could have two applications. First, to create the particular sound of this kind of send – bringing the channel fader down doesn't reduce the amount of signal sent via the aux send's signal path – which might be preferable when using a reverse reverb algorithm in the RV7000 reverb device; and second, to provide an independent feed to the BV512 Vocoder device from audio that's being balanced as part of a Reason mix.

• On channel 4 there's a rhythm guitar sample that would benefit from some chorus and a little reverb, so the Aux 1 and 3 controls are used to set these.

… And so on. You can see from this how it's possible to use four Aux Sends to treat a lot of sound sources with quite different combinations of effects.

The Return Controls

We've dealt with the 'send' bit of the system. How about the 'return' bit?

The Aux Return knobs are located in the Master section of the mixer and simply govern the level of effected signals being returned to the mixer from the effects devices. If there were no effects returns, the signals could not come back to the mixer after having been sent to the effects devices, and you wouldn't hear any effected signals at all. What the Aux Return knob for each effect does is set how much of that effect is going to be present in the mix overall.

As an example, imagine you had set the Aux Send knob on a mixer channel so that a lot of reverb was apparent – so that the signal was practically swamped in reverb. However, you then set a very low level of reverb coming back to the mixer with the equivalent Aux Return knob in the Master section. The result would still be a lot of reverb on the signal in question, but the reverb would be heard very quietly in the mix, regardless of how loud the signal itself was. This is one way of using a lot of reverb, but in a subtle fashion, so that the signal is not drowned.

How should the effects and processors be used?

Not all of the effect/processing devices should really be used via the send/return system, which is designed primarily for the delay-based effect devices (delay, reverb, chorus, phaser) rather than processors (compressor, EQ, filter and distortion). This is because the processors are designed to process an entire signal, instead of just processing part of it and allowing you to set a balance between the wet (effected) and dry (un-effected) portions of the signal, as do the true effects.

Most people would concede, for example, that there is little point in using a compressor in a send/return loop, since when you want to compress something you need to compress the entire signal. If you have the 'dry' (uncompressed) portion of the signal still hanging about, you still have the same problems – such as uncontrolled signal peaks that may have made you use the compressor in the first place.

Processors are normally used via mixer 'insert' points, which apply to just one channel and process the entire signal going through that channel. ReMix doesn't have inserts, but Reason's patching system is flexible, and instead you can put processors 'in line' with the devices that need them (see 'Automatic Effects Connections', earlier in the chapter, and the effects chapter). This method, just like an insert point, processes just the device in question, and processes its entire signal. (Of course, you can also use effects in-line like this if you want to; in this case the 'Wet/Dry' control on the effect sets the mix of dry and effected signal.)

You may notice that in the Reason documentation Propellerhead recommend using the Phaser as an 'insert' effect (and therefore patched in-line, like a processor). This makes sense, given the design of the Phaser and the way in which phase is often applied to instruments, but phase can neverthe-less also be used in the send/return system. In fact, though the usual 'rules' around which effects/processors can be used in the send/return system and which should be inserts have been established through years of studio prac-tice, they can be bent (and broken) if that's what you want.

Mixer levels

Setting mixer levels is largely a matter of common sense. However, since the margins beyond which distortion occurs are not quite as wide with digital sys-tems – which Reason is – as they are with analogue, and you certainly don't want digital distortion on your mixes, here are a few guidelines.

- *Watch the Clipping LED:* You should always keep an eye on the 'Audio Out Clipping' LED below the CPU activity meter in the transport bar, which shows if too much level is going to the Hardware Interface, with possible distortion as a consequence. Pull down the Master level fader on your main ReMix mixer to prevent this LED from lighting. Also keep an ear out for any audible clicks or distortion. You may hear distortion without the LED flashing, and the LED may flash when you can't hear distortion, so stay aware. The LED should not be on continuously. Aim for no more than the occasional flash.
- *Master and Channel Levels:* Should any distortion or untoward LED-flashing occur, your first move should probably be to take ReMix's master fader down a bit. If the Master meter is spending too much time in the red (topmost) section, you should definitely turn it down – let it just flash into the red (which looks more like orange), and you should be OK. If this doesn't solve the problem, have a look at the meters for each of the mixer channels; if any of these are blasting red, turn them down a bit, and rebalance your mix accordingly.
- *EQ or Filter settings:* There may be occasions where the mix, when levels have been adjusted, lacks energy or is just too quiet. This might mean that the cause of the distortion of overloading wasn't level per se but rather an inappropriately-EQ'd sound – too much bass, say – or perhaps one that has overcooked filter settings on one of the sound-making devices. High filter resonance values can cause rather unpredictable sonic results. If you suspect EQ might be the problem, adjust the EQ knobs on the mixer or any PEQ2 device you may be using. If the filter might be at fault, edit the relevant device's filter to smooth out the sound. Occasionally, a sound may peak erratically due to how it responds to velocity. Listen to the mix and notice where the problems occur, and then consider changing the velocity value for a given note in the Matrix or main sequencer, whichever applies.
- *Use compression:* You can also protect against distortion and increase the apparent level and energy of signals, without causing yourself problems, by using compressors, on individual channels (in line between the sound source and its input channel) and on the stereo mix (in line between the master output and the Hardware Interface). In fact, lots of musicians wouldn't consider creating a mix without some compression.

Tip

Dynamic mixing

When you're mixing, don't assume that once you've set a level for a part, it has to stay the same all the way through the track. One neat technique is to allow new parts to come in at quite a high level, then inch the fader back down again once the ear has noticed the part. When the part has been 'pointed out' to the listener in this way, they will be able to pick it out even when its level is reduced to allow the next new part to shine. By reducing parts in level when they've 'made their point', you'll also be de-cluttering your mix and maintaining light and shade and dynamics.

AUDIO OUT CLIPPING

The Audio Out Clipping LED.

Info

Visible Clipping

If you have audio editing software installed on your computer, you can see the effects of the digital clipping which may be happening when the Audio Out clipping LED lights. Simply save a section of a Reason song that has a small amount, or a lot, of clipping (as indicated by the flashing of the Clipping LED), using the 'Export Loop as Audio File' option in the File menu. Load the resulting file into your audio editor: clipping and digital distortion will be obvious by the visibly flattened peaks in the waveform. You might not hear this as distortion or clicks, but the clipping is there nonetheless.

Here's what clipping looks like. This clipped audio from Reason is displayed in the D-Sound Pro shareware audio editor.

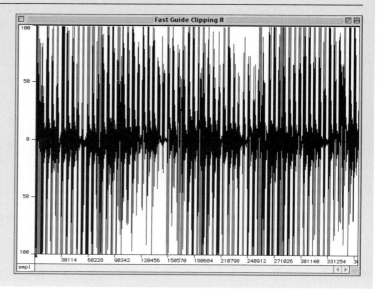

Tip

Getting Maximum Levels

If you find yourself regularly pushing the mixer's faders to the top of their travel, and have nowhere to go to get the balance of levels you want, check the output level of each device in your rack. Each has an output level control and you should make sure this is at its full value. The mixer's faders will probably now have to be pulled down to avoid distortion, giving you loads more room to manoeuvre. Be sure to also check the volume controls on your sound card and any external hardware.

Info

Mono aux sends

Before V2.5, even though the main channels of the ReMix can work in both stereo and mono, the aux sends were mono. This meant that even if a stereo signal was passing through a channel, it would be 'summed' to mono before being sent out to an effects device via the send/return system. But since the effects devices that are meant to be used via the send/return system – broadly, the delay-based effects – do not operate in 'true' stereo anyway (which would entail processing each 'side' of a stereo signal separately) without a little creative thought, this has no detrimental effect on the sound in the end. And if you're still using a pre-V2.5 Reason, you won't have any of the true-stereo processors that were introduced with that upgrade.

Using ReMixes as 'submixers'

As mentioned earlier, a second mixer is automatically 'bussed' to the first mixer that you placed in your Reason rack, subsequently-created mixers are bussed to the second, and so on. Any number of mixers can be linked in this way – where the aux sends and stereo master out of a new mixer are linked to the Chaining Aux and Chaining Master inputs of the mixer above it – with no impact on audio quality.

Extending the use of chained mixers lets you use concepts that pertain to real-world mixing situations, such as Submixing. Submixing on a hardware mixer lets you set up and balance the levels and pan positions of, typically, related instruments – the individual drums and cymbals of a drum kit, for example – and route them via internal mix bussing to a pair of 'subgroup' or 'submix' channels. Thus, no matter how big the drum kit you're mixing, once you've set the mix of its component parts, changing its overall level in the full track mix only requires you to move two faders; similarly, muting or soloing the whole drum mix requires just the press of two buttons.

Submixing can be achieved in Reason by chaining ReMix devices, although really basic sub-mixing is also possible with the Spider Audio device.

Dedicate a mixer to handling related audio, and route the stereo 'submix' of that audio to the main mixer. A fairly typical application might be, as with the example above, to route individual ReDrum voices, or the outputs from several ReDrums, to one mixer. This drum submix could also include any rhythm loops being played by Dr:Rex, and/or any percussive material being played by NN19. You could also add your main bass sound to the drum-heavy submix, to provide a true 'rhythm section'. All these related sounds can be balanced, and their stereo mix passed to your main mixer's 'chaining' input, or even one of its input channels.

Another submix could be made up of any vocal samples or speech snippets that might be part of your track. We often cut song-length vocals (lead and harmonies) that have been recorded in other applications into snippets, and load them into NN19 or Dr:rex for triggering as part of the final track; submixing the vocals via one mixer (we use a lot of harmonies) makes it easier to balance the vocal mix, and makes a potentially tricky mix situation much more manageable.

Giving each submixer its own send effects

One advantage that chained ReMixes in Reason have over the submixing facilities of real-world mixers is that each of the submixers can, if desired, have its own set of four send effects – you don't have to buss chained mixers' effect sends to those on the main mixer. It might suit you to have a different set of effects available to the drum or vocal submixes mentioned above than will be applied to the whole mix, and Reason gives you this flexibility. If the subsidiary mixer has already been automatically connected to the main mixer:

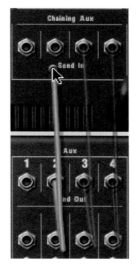

Break the connections between the second mixer's Aux Send outputs and the first mixer's Chaining Aux inputs, to free the second mixer's aux sends and allow it to have its own set of four effects.

- Flip to the back panel of the rack with the Tab key.
- Disconnect the cables connecting the submixer's sends to the Chaining Aux inputs on the main mixer. (Leave alone, for now, the routing of the submixer's Master stereo output to the main mixer's Chaining Master input. We'll discuss an alternative to this in a moment.)
- With the submixer selected, any newly created effects will be automatically connected to its auxiliary send/return loops.

'Solo' with chained submixers – and how to make it work

There is one area where chained mixers in Reason don't function quite as you might hope: solo. For example, if you solo a channel on any mixer in a chain, only the other channels on that mixer will mute. Channels on chained mixers stay unmuted, and the channel you want to solo is not, therefore, truly solo'd.

Tip

Processing submixes for sonic control

Separating complex mixes into submixes on separate ReMix mixers makes sense in many ways. Not only can you focus on getting related parts of the mix really working well together and simplify the making of the final mix, you can also process each submix with its own compression and/or other 'in-line' effects, to give it a homogenous feel. This is especially useful with rhythm-section submixes, where the same compression setting can help everything to 'sit' well and sound really solid. Working in this way does not prevent you, of course, from processing the individual drums in a submix separately if you want to.

There is no complete remedy for this problem, though there is a half-solution. Instead of using the Chaining Master connections to create the link between mixers, route the submixer's stereo outs to actual input channels of the main mixer. Now when you solo a channel on the main mixer (automatically muting the other channels at the same time), the input to which the submixer has been routed will mute, in effect muting the whole submix. This method allows solo to work properly on the main mixer.

Connecting the stereo Master output of the second mixer to an input channel of the first, instead of connecting the mixers via the Chaining Master sockets. This has various benefits, including improved Solo operation.

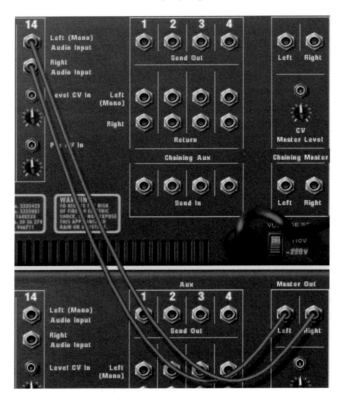

However, you still won't be able to solo quite so easily on any chained submixers. To solo a channel on the submixer in this situation:

- Solo the channel in question on the submixer.
- Then solo the channel to which the submixer has been routed on the main mixer.

It's two mouse-clicks rather than one, but it works – and it's better than the many mouse-clicks you'd need to manually mute all the other channels to get the same effect.

This idea is good if you're solo-ing in order to tweak a sound while it plays back, or tailor EQ or effects treatment with the sound in isolation. However, if you want to Solo parts in real time during a mix, the two-stage process is not as spontaneous as just clicking one Solo button, and it may not be fast enough to get the effect you want. It will almost certainly be best to draw in the necessary Solo on/off events in the controller lane of the main sequencer. See the sequencer chapter for more.

As you'll surmise from this explanation, complete submixes can be muted or solo'd if they're routed to main mixer input channels, using the main mixer channels' mute and solo switches. If you have created a set of submixes on separate mixers, each connected to the main mixer via an input channel, you can mute and solo these submixes to your heart's content on the main mixer.

Potential Mute/Solo problems

There is one problem that arises when you patch a submixer sharing the main mixer's effects (via Chained Auxes) into an input channel of the main mixer. A similar problem arises with the ReDrum, when you're sharing two of ReMix's send/return effects with ReDrum's two effects sends (again, via the Chaining Aux inputs).

If you mute the main ReMix channel to which the submixer or ReDrum device has been routed, you'll still hear the effect return – a faint 'ghost' of the signal being effected – even though the channel signal has been muted. You can avoid the problem in the case of chained mixers, by not using the Chaining Aux inputs, and instead setting up separate effects for the submixer, but you can't really avoid it with ReDrum's effect sends. You could route drum sounds instead to their own mixer channel, via the ReDrum individual outs, and effect them there, not using ReDrum's effect sends at all; alternatively, during a mixdown, automate the turning down of the problem aux send controls.

There's also an opposite issue: imagine you solo the channel on your main ReMix to which a ReDrum or a submixer, sharing the main mixer's effects, has been routed. Soloing the channel results in everything else on the main mixer being muted – including the effect sends. And since these effect sends are connected to either the ReDrum or the submixer (via the Chaining Aux connections), their effect sends are muted too. The result, in this particular set of circumstances, is that the solo-d channel will have no effects. Again, the way around it for the submixer is to give it its own effects and not connect via the Chaining Aux sockets. There's really no tidy way around it for the ReDrum, other than not using the ReDrum send/return system, as explained above.

Neither of these situations are problems or bugs per se, but just side-effects of the way mixers work. Neither ReDrum or a submixer is actually part of the main ReMix, so individual voice or channel sends on the slaved devices shouldn't be expected to behave as if they were.

Summary: three ways you can connect mixers together

- *Simple daisy-chaining:* See Figure 5.2. Master stereo output and Aux send outputs of second mixer to Chaining Master Inputs and Chaining Aux Inputs of main mixer. Subsequent mixers chained in the same way to previous mixer in the chain. This system is the one used when automatic connections are made. It allows all mixers access to the one set of four aux effects assigned to the first (main) mixer and the level of all mixers to be controlled by the master fader of the main mixer. The relative levels of the daisy-chained mixers are controlled by their own master faders.
- *Each mixer with own send effects:* See Figure 5.9. Master stereo output of second mixer to Chaining Master Input of main mixer. Aux send outputs not connected. Subsequent mixers chained in the same way to

> ### Tip
>
> **Stereo width enhancement**
>
> Delay one channel of the mixer's master stereo output, using a DDL1 delay, by up to 20mS, to create a wider stereo image on a mix. Full instructions are given in the effects chapter.

Tip

Live muting of multiple mixer channels

It may be frustrating to some Reason users that there's no immediate way to mute several ReMix channels at the same time in a 'live' context (obviously, if you're recording you can automate or draw as many simultaneous mutes as you like in the controller lanes of the sequencer). Reason doesn't have subgrouping, which some other software (and real mixers) offer, to allow several related mixer channels to be muted with one button-push, but you can get a similar effect in two different ways. First, if you've grouped related mixes of audio on their own ReMixes (using these ReMixes as submixers and connecting them to the main mixer via its input channels, as explained elsewhere in this chapter), each ReMix is really a subgroup. You can mute each subgroup – thereby muting several channels at a time – simply by muting the channel it's connected to in the main mixer.

previous mixer in the chain. This system allows each mixer to have its own set of send effects, but still means that the level of all mixers is controlled by the master fader of the main mixer. The relative levels of the daisy-chained mixers are controlled by their own master faders.

- *Mixers connected via input channels only:* See Figure 5.10. Master stereo output of each submixer connected to an input channel of the main mixer.No Master or Aux Chaining connections at all. This method is more like a 'star' system of connection. Every mixer can have its own set of send effects. Each submix becomes a channel on the main mixer, with its level controlled by a channel fader on the main mixer. The overall level of the entire mix is controlled by the master fader on the main mixer. Connecting in this way means that the submixes can be treated with the effects assigned to the main mixer (as well as their own effects) and it adds more flexibility in muting and soloing (see 'Solo with chained mixers' section).

Methods 1 and 2 can be modified by connecting just some of the Chaining Aux sends between submixer and main mixer, allowing a combination of the send effects of the main mixer and the send effects of the second mixer to be used on the second.

The second idea is to assign ReMix mutes to keys on your keyboard (see the automation and remote control chapter) for live mixing. Then you can mute as many mixer channels simultaneously as you can press down keyboard keys.

The Final Mix

There are several options for creating final stereo mixes of your tracks. You can:

1 Simply record a mix to your hard drive, using the Export options in the File menu. From here, it can be transferred to a playback medium, such as CD, at your leisure. (You could, alternatively, Export separate tracks or submixes for importing and reassembling in another application.)

2 Record a mix from Reason direct to a stereo master recorder, such as DAT or Minidisc, or even CD, via the Hardware Interface and your soundcard's outputs.

3 Send individual channels or submixes out to a hardware mixer via the Hardware Interface, or via ReWire to the mixer of another sequencer, and do the final mix to stereo there. This could offer the benefit of hardware outboard processors in the case of the hardware mixer and plug-in processing in the case of the sequencer.

1 Exporting (recording) a mix to disk

After the arrangement of a track is complete, effects treatments have been set up, automation recorded, and any master compression and EQ applied:

- Set the end point marker in the sequencer where you would like the mix to finish. Make sure you don't cut off any reverb tails or delay echoes by setting the end point too soon.

- Choose 'Export Song as Audio File' from the File menu. A file window pops up, and you can give your mix a name (it defaults to the name you've given the Reason song), and choose a location in which to save the file. Choose

Set the End marker in the sequencer to define the length of the Song to be Exported.

AIFF or WAV format for the
final audio file. Enable 'Add
Extension to File Name' if
you're running a PC.

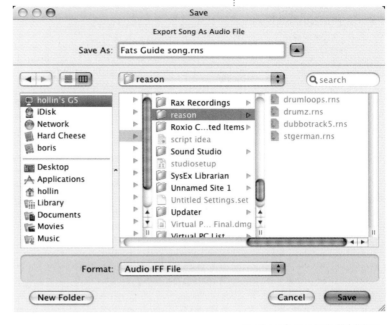

- Click 'Save'. The Export
Audio Settings window pops
up: choose a sample rate
(11025, 22050, 32000,
44100, 48000 or
96000Hz) and a bit depth
(16- or 24-bit) for the mix.
It's unlikely that you will want
anything less than 44100Hz
(44.1kHz) at 16-bit, which is
the current CD standard.
Think carefully before
choosing 24-bit and 96kHz,
unless you have a definite
reason for wanting these
options. (One reason might
be that you intend to carry
out mastering processes on

The 'Export Song as Audio File' dialogue.

the stereo mix, using a dedicated mastering software package that
accepts high bit- and sample-rate files.) Not only will the resulting file be
larger than a 44.1kHz/16-bit file, but if you later want to write the mix to
an audio CD, your CD-burning software may not be able to convert the
24-bit file properly to 16-bit.
- Click 'Export' to save the file. The process is around four times faster
than real time and depends on the complexity of the project and speed
of your computer.

Note that only audio routed to the main stereo inputs of the Hardware
Interface is included in the bounce. Any audio routed to the other outputs is
removed from the mix.

The 'Export Audio Settings' dialogue.

To dither, or not?
The Dither option, new in v3, assists with sample rate conversion when you
export an audio file. If you are exporting to a lower bit resolution (i.e. from
24 bits to 16 bits), you should activate the Dither checkbox. As digital audio
is converted between bit depths, errors occur which can affect sound quality. DIthering helps to reduce any negative effects on the quality of the sound.

Exporting (recording) individual tracks to disk
You may want to export the tracks of a Reason composition individually to
your hard drive, for reassembling as a multitrack performance in another
program, where you intend to further process and mix into stereo. This is a
good option if your other audio program isn't ReWire compatible and you'd
like to use its effects and other tools. To do this:

- Follow the instructions for exporting the whole file, above, but in the mixer mute every track except the first one you want to export. The Export process will then send out only that track. Be sure to give the file a name that will mean something comprehensible when you import it into the other application!
- Now mute that track and unmute the next one you want to export – and so on.
- Import the files into the application of your choice, following the instructions that came with that application.

If you use this process, note that any master mix compression you have set up will probably behave differently when you have muted all but one of the mix tracks, and it may no longer be doing what you want it to do. It may be best to disable master mix compression in this situation and add dynamics processing in the other application you are exporting to. Also, you may want to disable any effects that are connected to the send/return loops of your mixer(s), since you probably won't want to have the effects fixed as part of the individual audio files. However, you will probably want to leave in place any insert effects that form an important part of a device's final sound.

Reason exports audio tracks only in stereo, so if any should really be mono you'll want to split the stereo file into two. In Cubase SX, you'd use the 'Export Audio Mixdown' option to split the file and and re-import one 'side' of it . You may well find something similar in your own sequencer. Alternatively, use an audio editor.

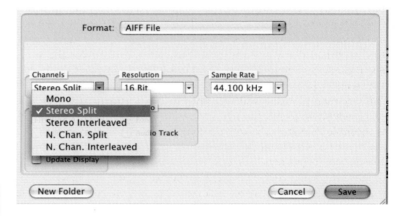

Info

Exporting Loops

As well as 'Export Song as Audio File', the File menu also offers an option to 'Export Loop as Audio File'. If you choose this, the operation for Exporting a Song is carried out for the audio located between the currently selected locator points in your Reason song. This facility is particularly useful if you plan to export sections of a Song as audio to another audio application – verses, choruses, breakdowns, alternative mixes and so on – or to use Reason for more creative purposes, as a treatment tool for processing and then exporting audio.

Another issue that will arise when you load individual tracks from Reason into another application is that all Reason audio is exported as stereo audio files. This is generally what you want when exporting Songs or loops, and may often be what's needed when bouncing drum parts, pad parts and so on.

But there may be times when you'd like to export in mono: for example, SubTractor is a mono device (unless you're treating it with stereo effects), but its exported file will still be stereo. To return it to mono, you need some way of splitting the stereo file into its left/right components and discarding one file. Most sample editing software will allow you to do this, and it may also be possible to do the job in your audio sequencer.

In Cubase VST or SX, you would highlight the Reason audio file in the Arrange window and choose 'Export Audio Tracks' from the File Menu. Select 'Selected Parts', and 'Stereo Split', and make any other relevant settings, as outlined in the Cubase manual. Choose a destination, and the 'interleaved' stereo audio file becomes separate left and right files, each of which is strictly mono. Discard the unwanted file and re-import the desired mono file into Cubase, perhaps renaming it appropriately first.

As another example, Digidesign's Pro Tools LE tends to automatically split audio into two separate files. Again you'll be able to discard one of them and use just the mono file that remains, by dragging it from the Audio Regions list to a new track.

You can also export a loop as audio and re-import that into NN19 or NNXT (or Dr:rex, if you have access to ReCycle) for further work – potentially very useful on under-powered computers, as you will save on the devices and effects that were used to create the imported audio. As with any Export operation, make sure you account for delays or reverb tails that might go on longer than the loop section itself, by making the loop long enough so that they are not cut off abruptly.

2 Recording a mix from Reason to a mastering machine

You may have a DAT machine, stand-alone CD Recorder, MiniDisc recorder or cassette deck that you'd like to directly record Reason mixes to.

If the audio interface that you use with your Mac or PC has a digital output, and the mastering machine of your choice has a digital input, it's obviously best to make the connection between them. Finalising a mix is thus a matter of putting the recorder into record mode, playing back the Reason song and stopping the record process once the Song is done. Most digital recorders, especially domestic ones, don't have a level control for use when recording digitally, so you won't even have to set up record levels: if the mix you've created in Reason doesn't cause the 'Audio Out Clipping' LED to flash, the recording probably won't overload on the mastering machine. But it might be advisable to run through once with the recorder in standby, in case its record-level meters tell you a different story.

If you don't have a digital output on your audio card, or wish to record your Reason mix to analogue cassette or another analogue medium, you'll need to make the audio connection via the computer audio hardware's main analogue stereo output and the recording machine's analogue input. In this case, you will have to set up recording levels in the recorder.

However you record it, what goes to tape or disk is the stereo output of the main mixer in your Reason rack, the one that's routed – either automatically or by you – to the main stereo input of the Hardware Interface.

3 Routing device outputs or submixes outside Reason

You don't have to use the ReMix to create a final mix. As discussed in the chapter on using Reason with other software and instruments, individual devices or submixes from within the Reason rack can be routed, via the Hardware Interface and Propellerhead's ReWire protocol, to another audio application, to take advantage of the other application's mixing and processing facilities.

The Hardware Interface is also the central point for routing the audio from individual devices (or, again, submixers) to the outputs of the audio interface installed on your computer, and so to the outside world. Here, Reason audio may be mixed and processed via a hardware mixer and hardware effects processors. The number of channels of audio you can send out will be limited, obviously, by the number of outputs on your audio card. Note that the audio path is not two-way: unlike conventional MIDI + Audio sequencing packages, there is no way to bring audio back into Reason once it's been sent out. The issues around routing Reason audio externally are also covered in the 'Reason + others' chapter.

Mix Automation and remote control

It's very easy to automate the controls of the ReMix, so that you can manage even very complex mixes effortlessly. Automation becomes even more relevant if you're making extensive use of submixing, as explained elsewhere in this chapter. Automation is covered fully elsewhere in the book, but here's an explanation of the basics of recording your ReMix actions as automation data.

- Create a sequencer track for the ReMix (as you may know, mixers do not automatically have a sequencer track created for them). The fastest way is via a contextual menu: Control/right mouse-click in the ReMix and from the pop-up that appears, select 'Create sequencer track for ReMix'. A new track will appear in the sequencer track list.
- Click in the 'In' column to the left of the sequencer track name to make the keyboard icon appear. The track is now ready to accept data.
- Click the red Record button, then the Play button in the Transport bar (or use Apple/Control-Return then the Space bar) to play back the Song in Record mode.
- Make the required movements with the mixer controls as the Song plays back. The mix can be completed in several passes, automating different controls each time. Automation data may also be drawn into the controller lanes in the main sequencer. See the sequencer chapter and the automation/remote control chapter for full details.

If you prefer hands-on mixing, you can assign a MIDI hardware controller to alter ReMix controls. Even if you don't have a remote fader box, you can assign MIDI keyboard notes to control on/off mixer functions, and if you use a keyboard with a few assignable rotary controls or faders, these can also be assigned to ReMix parameters. Again, see the automation/remote control chapter for more. It's also possible to lock a control surface to the ReMix using the Remote system via the Options > Surface Locking menu item. See the chapters on automation and Remote for more on this.

ReMix and the CV/Gate system

Mixer tremolo and auto-panning

Because some ReMix parameters are controllable by the CV system, the ReMix mixer can be more than just a device for routing audio around.

For example, modulating the level of a mixer channel with the LFO of another device allows a very effective tremolo to be added to the signal of that channel. (Have a look at the SubTractor chapter if you're not sure what

LFOs are, and how they can modulate, or affect, audio signals.)

You might wonder why you want to do this when it's quite straightforward to create a tremolo effect in most sound-making devices. Well, for a start the LFO may well be doing another job in a device's patch. Though SubTractor has a second LFO, with an option to route it directly to level, NN-19 and Dr:rex don't. Also, though both NN-19 and Dr:rex allow you to route their single LFO to level – manually, using the CV sockets on their back panels – the LFO rate and waveform set for the current patch may not be compatible with the tremolo effect you want to make. So it's good to have an alternative CV routing option. In addition, there are no level – or pan – modulation options within ReDrum, so the technique outlined below adds a little more sonic variety to ReDrum's output.

• Create a SubTractor, NN-19 or Dr:rex device, holding down Shift while creating it, to leave its audio unconnected to the mixer. This device is being made only for modulation purposes (it won't make any audible sounds), so it needs no audio connections.
• Now patch the LFO Modulation Output socket on the device's rear panel to the Level CV Input on a mixer channel. The LFO runs continuously, even if the device producing it isn't being played, so you now have LFO-controlled level, for standard tremolo effects, on that mixer channel, once a signal is passing through it. You can even change the speed and waveform of the LFO from the front panel of the device producing the effect. You can choose to have the LFO's speed sync'd to the Song's tempo, by clicking the 'Sync' button on the sound-makingdevice (in V2), or leave it free-running, so that you can creato pseudo-polyrhythmic effects, since the 'tremolo' won't necessarily be in sync with the song.
• Control the depth of the tremolo effect with the Level CV Input Trim pot.

Follow the instructions above, substituting the mixer channel's Pan CV input for the Level CV input, to achieve instant auto-panning effects. Automating pan in this way gives you access to subtle slow panning effects, or mad, fast jumping back and forth. So if you were wondering why there wasn't an auto-pan device among Reason's effects, it's because you can do the job in other ways.

The Line Mixer 6:2

This handy addition to Reason 3 is a simple six stereo channel mixer with an independent Aux send loop. It's basically a stripped-down version of the main ReMix, designed more for submixes than controlling entire projects. For each of its six channels it has separate level, mute, solo, pan, pan CV and aux send controls as well as a master gain knob and aux return control. These all work

Line Mixer

in the same way as a ReMix and by default the stereo outputs of a Line Mixer are routed to the next available channel on the ReMix, although you can of course manually patch them anywhere you want, including the Hardware Interface.

Here are some typical uses for a Line Mixer:

- Inserted first into a Combinator, all subsequent devices are routed through it, making it easy to submix the devices before they leave the Combi. If you don't use a mixer of some kind here, only the first instrument you create will be heard. You can also use the aux loop to treat all the devices independently of the main mixer's aux sends.
- When using a Spider audio splitter, a Line Mixer can be useful in providing greater routing flexibility without the unneccesary extra features of a ReMix.
- In very simple projects you nay not need a full ReMix - use a Line Mixer as your main mixer instead.
- If you're routing channels through to a ReWire application or out to external audio hardware, using a Line Mixer gives you more options for flexible sending and grouping of channels, and processing through effects.
- Add another aux send to the main mixer without having to create a whole ReMix.

The SubTractor synth

The SubTractor should be comfortable and familiar in use for anyone who has worked with analogue or virtual analogue synths, or even S+S (Sample + Synthesis) instruments, as it uses a very traditional way of creating sounds, called 'Subtractive' synthesis. As analogue-style synths go, SubTractor is very well specified; indeed, as well as the usual analogue array of waveform generating and modifying tools it offers additional features that a real analogue synth would not have, and can be used to create a wide variety of sounds. More experienced users will even be able to approach fully 'modular' synth techniques by using the Gate and CV interfacing system, as discussed later in this chapter.

To anyone not used to analogue-style synthesis, the SubTractor front panel will probably look like a confusing jumble of controls and labels at first sight. However, it is quite logically organised, and once you have a grasp of the basics it becomes clear that every knob, slider and switch has a defined and usually audible function. Even if you initially do not know what these functions are, the beauty of a 'knob-driven' synth is that even beginners will find it easy to create their own sounds, by tweaking controls until something good comes out.

A brief guided tour

This quick run-through of the SubTractor front panel will get you acquainted with the basic function of each of the sections. The detail will be filled in later in the chapter.

The Patch Load/Save area

Patch Load/Save

Access SubTractor synth Patches stored on any drive attached to your computer, and save your own edited Patches.

The Oscillators

Oscillators

The heart of SubTractor's sound-making engine, producing the waveforms that are the raw material for any Patch.

The Filters

Tailor the timbral character of your sounds, by modifying the harmonic content of the oscillator waveforms.

Filters

The Envelope Generators

Create a shape for your sounds with the Amplitude Envelope, deciding how their level (volume) will develop over time. Give the filter dynamism with the Filter Envelope, and create even more interest in your Patches by controlling synth parameters with the Modulation Envelope.

Left: EGs

Below: Play Parameters

The Play Parameters

Make the velocity of your playing introduce extra character into sounds, by setting it to alter any of these parameters.

The LFOs

The key to complex, cyclical modulation, adding change and movement.

The LFOs

PB/Mod wheels

Key mode/portamento

Level

The Pitch Bend & Modulation Wheels

These on-screen performance controllers mirror the movements of your MIDI keyboard's wheels, or can be moved on screen with the mouse.

Polyphony Control

Set how many notes the SubTractor will be able to play simultaneously, from 1-99.

Polyphony

External Modulation Routing Area

Route MIDI controller data from keyboards, breath controllers and even other sequencers, to alter SubTractor parameters.

Key Mode & Portamento Section

Make Patches respond exactly to your playing style and get the performance feel you want.

The Level Control

Governs the output level (volume) of the SubTractor. It's usually best to have this control set to full and set the level of the SubTractor relative to the other devices in the rack with the level fader on the Sub's mixer channel.

External Mod

SubTractor basics

Depending on how you use Reason, an array of SubTractor synths (perhaps augmented with a Malström or two) could form the core of your compositions, or you might alternatively just use one or two SubTractors to embellish mainly sample-driven tracks.

Although SubTractor is up to 99-note polyphonic (can play up to 99 notes at the same time), it is not multitimbral – ie. it doesn't produce more than one sound at a time, so you'll need a SubTractor device for each musical task – for example, one for a bassline, one for an arpeggio-style accent pattern – and so on. You can write parts for the synth in the Matrix Pattern sequencer, or play SubTractor 'live' from your keyboard into Reason's main sequencer.

Info

Analogue Synthesis

Obviously, SubTractor is not actually an analogue synth, as its sounds are generated digitally by software running on a computer. However, it is designed to behave in a very similar fashion to true analogue, and has an interface which closely emulates classic analogue instruments. An in-depth exploration of analogue synthesis, which is a pretty big subject, is beyond the scope of this book, but beginners will get enough synthesis background to help them make the most of SubTractor from the detailed descriptions of the SubTractor controls and features in this chapter. The Reason Operation Manual is also very well written and helpful. If you want to know more about analogue synthesis, have a look at our suggested reading list in Appendix 3.

Get going with SubTractor

Loading and Saving Patches

Follow the usual procedure as outlined in Chapter 4, Basic Operations and Features.

Play a Patch

To play a SubTractor Patch from your keyboard:

- Go to the main sequencer and find the SubTractor track created by Reason.
- Click in the 'In'column to the left of the track name. A MIDI plug icon should appear.
- You should now be able to play the Patch from your keyboard.

Tutorial

Create a synth bass sound

Before we get into examining the controls and features of SubTractor in depth, here's a quick exercise in Patch programming to get you going if you're not familar with sound creation using analogue synths. Beginners should perhaps read the Tutorials chapter, and perhaps go through the steps there, before focusing on SubTractor. By the way, if you're not asked to change a parameter, leave it in the state it was for the 'Init Patch' with which all the tutorials start.

1 Open the program and create a basic rack:

- Launch Reason. Begin with an empty rack, as explained in the first step of Chapter 3, Tutorials.
- Create a ReMix mixer, then a SubTractor synth, using the Create menu or a contextual menu. When the SubTractor is created, it contains a basic 'Init Patch', whose name shows in the Patch Name display. This is the starting point for programming any new Patch. You can select the Init Patch, for a set of neutral parameter values, any time you want to create a new sound, by choosing Initialize Patch from the Edit menu.

Tip
Programming control

You may find it helpful, when programming the exact values given in the tutorials in this chapter, to access fine control of knobs and sliders by holding down Shift when moving them. You will also need to let the mouse pointer hover over the control to allow a Tool Tip giving its current value to appear.

Starting rack.

2 Choose an Oscillator 1 waveform and add Phase Modulation:
- Select the square waveform in the Osc 1 panel, by clicking the 'up' arrow next to the waveform display once.
- Select '3' in the Oct display to the right, by clicking its 'down' arrow once. This sets the pitch of the oscillator an octave lower, as we're making a bass sound.
- Click the Mode button to make the LED next to the 'x' light up, or click the LED next to the 'x'. This sets the Phase Offset Modulation mode to 'multiply' – more on this later.
- Turn the Phase knob to around 12 o'clock (a value of 70; leave your mouse pointer over the knob for a few moments to cause a 'Tool Tip' to appear, giving the current value of the control). This applies Phase Offset Modulation, creating a richer and more cutting effect.

Oscillator 1 settings

3 Choose an Oscillator 2 waveform and add Phase Modulation:

Oscillator 2 settings

- Turn on Osc 2 by clicking on the small LED switch next to its name, and again set a square waveform in the waveform display.
- Make an octave setting of '2' in the Oct display. This sets the pitch of Osc 2 to an even lower register than Osc 1, giving the bass sound more depth.
- Set the mode switch to 'x', as above.
- Turn the Phase knob to a value of 50.

4 Set Filter Frequency and Resonance:

Filter 1 settings.

- Move to the Filter 1 section.
- Click the Type button until the LED next to 'LP24' lights up. This sets a Low-Pass filter type for the sound.
- Set the Freq slider to near the bottom of its travel (a value of 12). This makes the filter's 'cutoff frequency' low, filtering out most high frequencies for a deep, bassy sound.
- Set the Res slider to a value of 45. This adds some resonance to the sound, emphasising the frequencies around the filter cutoff point and adding 'bite'.
- Set the Kbd knob to a value of 40. This sets 'keyboard tracking' for the filter, regulating how it will change its sound across the keyboard range.

5 Create a Filter Envelope:

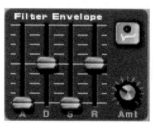
Filter Envelope settings.

- Move to the Filter Envelope section. Set the sliders to A=0, D=66, S=0, and R=66.
- Set the Amt knob to about 10 o'clock (40). This sets how much effect the envelope will have upon the filter's action.

6 Create an Amplitude Envelope:

Amplitude Envelope settings.

- Move to the Amp Envelope section and set the sliders to A=0, D =80, S=0, R=66. This envelope sets how the sound's level (amplitude) will develop over time. You'll notice that the filter and amp envelopes are similarly tight and snappy, with a fast attack and a shortish release, as befits a poppy bass sound. The filter envelope reinforces the character of the amp envelope when they are this similar.

7 Play your Patch:

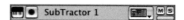
Enable the sequencer track for MIDI input so you can play the sound on your keyboard.

- You've programmed a bouncy, '80s synth bass. Go to the sequencer, make sure you have the MIDI plug icon showing by the SubTractor track (click under the 'In' column), and play some low notes on your keyboard to hear it. If you don't have a keyboard attached, create a Matrix pattern sequencer and enter some notes to hear the sound. You may want to change Polyphony to '1' in the Polyphony display, as this is a monophonic Patch.

8 Save the Patch:

- Click on the floppy-disk icon to the right of the Patch display and Save the Patch. Name the sound '80sSynBas'.

Saving the Patch.

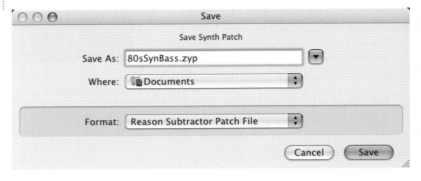

Now read on to learn more about the features you've just used.

The start of SubTractor sounds: the oscillators

SubTractor is a two-oscillator synth with noise generator, just like some of the most popular vintage analogues, such as the Sequential Circuits Pro One, the ARP Odyssey, the Korg MS20 and the Roland SH2, and modern, modelled 'Virtual Analogue' synths such as the Clavia Nord Lead and the Korg MS2000.

At its most basic, an oscillator is an electronic circuit that generates sound. In the same way that you excite oscillations in the air when you speak, producing sound, so this electronic circuit, when amplified, excites oscillations electronically. SubTractor copies the operation of this circuit in software.

Its two oscillators are identical and can both produce the same set of waveforms: select between Sawtooth, Square, Triangle, Sine and 28 'Wavetables' via the Waveform displays in both Osc 1 and Osc 2. There are good reasons for using both oscillators, but don't forget that you don't have to in order to create good sounds. Indeed, oscillator 2's default state is 'off' when you initialise a Patch.

The oscillator waveforms

Let's take a closer look at those oscillator waveforms, in the order that they appear in SubTractor. To hear them as you read about them, start by selecting the Init Patch from the Edit menu, move the Filter 1 Frequency slider to the top of its travel, 'opening up' the filter completely, so that you hear the full frequency range of the waveform, and choose the different waveforms in turn. Make sure you have the MIDI icon showing in the SubTractor track in the sequencer (click in the 'In' column next to the track name) and play a few notes on your keyboard with each.

A sine wave.

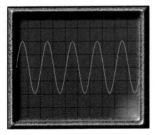

A triangle wave.

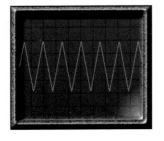

- The *Sine wave* is the simplest waveform an oscillator can produce, with a shape that actually resembles a wave. Sine waves have a soft, mellow, pure tone, non-piercing, with no harmonic 'overtones' at all. They work well for flute-type, airy, soft or delicate sounds.
- The *Triangle wave* has a jagged outline and a richer harmonic spectrum than the sine wave. It sounds something like a clarinet, but again is not piercing. Triangle waves are especially suitable for Patches with a 'pipe' or reed-instrument feel.

- The *Sawtooth wave* looks like its name – the sloping teeth on the edge of a saw. It's harmonically rich, having both odd and even harmonics, and has a bright, brassy, piercing sound. A reverse sawtooth waveform is termed a Ramp waveform. The sawtooth is the most useful for creating fuller Patches, including brassy, cutting and string-like sounds, and works well for bass sounds.
- The *Square wave*, which is a variety of Pulse wave, resembles the crenellated top of a castle wall. It contains only odd harmonics and has a characteristically synthetic, somewhat 'hollow' sound. Square waves are a good starting point for mellow, plucked sounds, hollow wind instrument-type sounds, pads (including ones with a string feel) and bass sounds.
- The 28 *Wavetables* would not be found on a real-world analogue synth, and in SubTractor are based on samples. They add a very useful degree of extra versatility and are good for hours of expermentation. As for which type of sound each provides a suitable basis for, the Reason Operation Manual gives a list of indications. These include Waveform 6, recommended for acoustic piano sounds; 10, for sub-bass sounds; 15 (bowed string instrument sounds, such as violins and cellos); 23, useful for mallet percussion such as marimbas; and 26, recommended for plucked, harp-like sounds. Don't take these indications as instructions, however, as it's all down to what you come up with while experimenting. For example, Waveform 29, recommended for metallic, bell-type sounds, makes good gritty electric piano/Clavinet sounds.

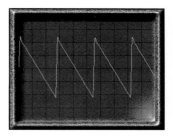

A sawtooth wave.

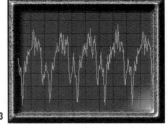

A square wave.

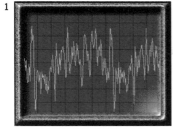

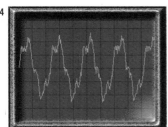

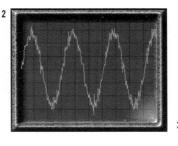

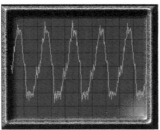

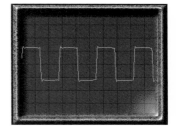

Pics 1–5:
A selection of the wavetable waveforms. *Waveforms displayed using the Scopion plug-in supplied with Steinberg's Cubase SX sequencer.*

Of course, since you have two samplers and a sample loop player in the Reason rack, you may never need to emulate real-world instruments specifically. The indications of what the different waveforms could be used for are simply guidelines. In any case, synthesis is a creative art in which you can make your own rules – to some extent, at least!

An obvious, but useful, thing to do when starting to program is to find Patches in the factory set that are something like the sound you want to cre-

Tip

Programming aid

While programming Patches, enter a simple repeating pattern of notes into a Matrix pattern sequencer linked to your SubTractor (or you could even play some notes or chords into the main sequencer). It's then easy to adjust parameters and hear instant results as the pattern plays. See the Matrix and sequencer chapters for info on using them.

ate and see which waveforms have been used as a basis for the Patch. But bear in mind that the choice of waveform is only one factor in the eventual sound of a Patch, especially since SubTractor offers so many facilities for radically altering the harmonic composition of the waveforms.

Oscillator tuning and its significance

Sounds made using both oscillators of a two-oscillator synth are often more than twice as powerful and interesting as sounds made with one oscillator. Why? Well, two waveforms at a time (which may have quite different characters) can be combined; the two oscillators may operate in different pitch registers; and if the oscillators are operating in the same register they can be 'detuned' against each other, for extra thickening effects. Tuning the two oscillators differently is a valuable option in programming good synth Patches, and can create various useful effects. The SubTractor oscillators are tuned via the Octave Display and the Semi(tone) and Cent Displays.

The Octave Display

The Octave display.

To the right of each oscillator Waveform display is the Octave display, where you can set the basic pitch range generated by the oscillators. A value range of 0–9, with a default of 4, is available. At the default setting, playing the 'A' above middle 'C' on an attached keyboard produces a pitch of 440Hz. Choosing a value of 5 shifts this up an octave (the same 'A' key on the keyboard will sound higher, being at 880Hz), and a value of 3 moves it down an octave (the same 'A' will sound lower, at 220Hz).

You'll quickly learn that this nine-octave range has limits. For example, if you select a value of 9, you'll eventually reach a point where the pitch is so high as to be almost inaudible, and finally a fixed pitch is reached (the oscillator is incapable of producing anything higher). At the lower extreme, at an Octave setting of 0, the oscillator will be producing a pitch so low that with some waveforms, you can hear discrete 'beats', which are the individual cycles of the waveform.

Notes at either extreme won't be of much immediate use to you, but they can be useful when using the FM and Ring Modulation options (more in a moment), for creating special effects or for adding texture to a Patch. This is because even if the sound produced by an oscillator is virtually inaudible it can still modulate another, and the modulation effect can be disproportionately large in comparison to the limited audibility of the sound.

The wide pitch range also provides plenty of options for customising SubTractor Patches to be playable in whichever key range is needed, and for creating Patches that have oscillators that are far apart in terms of central pitch, if desired.

The Semi Display

The Semi display.

As well as changing the oscillator's pitch range in octaves, you can also alter it in semitones – but only upwards. Do this via the Semi display, to the right of the Octave display, where you can raise the oscillator's pitch by up to an octave in semitone steps. If you need to tune downwards by a few semitones, first tune the oscillator down an octave with the Octave tuning control, then use the Semi display's 'up' arrow to get back to the required pitch.

The Cent display

This alters pitch in cents and is used for fine-tuning purposes. A cent is equal to 1/100th of a semitone, and this display offers a range of +/-50 cents. The Cent tuning control is used when slight 'detuning' of the oscillators is required.

The Cent display.

Oscillator balance

Balance the levels of the two oscillators relative to each other with the Mix knob in the Oscillator section. If the Mix knob is fully to the left, you'll hear only Osc 1, while turning it full right makes only Osc 2 sound. An equal balance of the two oscillators (knob centred) can be set quickly by Apple/Control-clicking the knob.

The Oscillator Mix knob.

Using Noise in your Patches

In addition to oscillators producing wave-forms, analogue synths often have a Noise Generator. Noise is indispensable for synthesising drum sounds and useful for adding attack and texture to other sounds. 'White' noise, the most common type pro-

The Noise Generator.

vided, is a mixture of all frequencies at equal amplitudes, or levels, and it sounds like AM radio static, wind noise, or surf. Pink noise has the lower frequencies boosted a little, and red noise is bassier still. The Noise Generator has three controls:

- *The Color control:* SubTractor's Noise Generator is more flexible than the equivalent device on many analogue synths, as it can produce variable noise, controlled by the Color knob; turned fully right, the output is white noise, while turning it left gradually enhances the lower-frequency elements, producing something more akin to pink and red noise. Turned full left, the output is a low rumble. Noise must be switched on if it's to be part of a Patch, by clicking on the Noise LED button, above, to light it.
- *The Level control:* Logically enough, this controls the level of the Noise output.
- *The Decay knob:* This tells the Noise Generator how long it should sound before fading out. The option is provided primarily because you might need just a short 'chiff' of noise at the start of the sound while attempting to synthesize flute-like timbres, for example, or some types of percussive sound.

Tip

Oscillator tuning

Obviously, tuning oscillators differently makes them each play a different pitch, giving the impression of two notes sounding even when you have only triggered one. So usually, if you are using anything other than a 'unison', with the oscillators tuned to the same pitch, you'll want to set musical intervals that work together. Tuning the oscillators an octave apart can produce rich and interesting effects. Another good interval to try is a fifth (seven semitones), especially for leads and some basses. A Perfect Fourth (five semitones) can work well depending on what you're playing, and tuning oscillators a major third apart (four semitones) approximates a trademark Detroit Techno sound, especially with fat, squelchy leads. Detuning oscillators in relation to each other by up to seven cents each is great for fattening a Patch with a subtle chorus effect. Don't go further, though, or you'll lose the pleasing, subtle thickness.

Tutorial

Create a kick and snare using Noise

Let's begin with the snare, which uses Noise to the greatest extent:

- Start with the Init Patch. Set a sine wave for Osc 1 and an octave setting of 3. Use a sine wave (or, alternatively, try a triangle wave) to provide a 'hit' of pitched sound which mimics the taut, tuned drumskin. If you want the drum to sound lower or higher, tune it appropriately with the Osc 1 tuning controls. Disable the

Oscillator 1 settings for Snare.

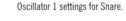

Noise settings for Snare.

Filter 1 and Filter Envelope settings for Snare.

'Keyboard Track' button, so that the sound does not change in pitch across the keyboard range.

- Turn on the Noise Generator by clicking its LED button. Set the Decay, Colour and Level knobs all to 127. This provides the burst of white noise that emulates the sound of the metal snare across the bottom of the real drum. Decay is set to full because the whole duration of the sound is noise; its contour will be tailored with the Amp Envelope. Set the Oscillator Mix knob to 90, because we want to hear more noise than pure waveform.
- Go to Filter 1 and set the Frequency slider to 94 and Resonance to 0. The Filter is fairly 'open' because we don't want to filter the white noise too much – we want some of those rattly, snare-like frequencies.
- Go the Filter Envelope and set A=24, D=40, S=0, R=40.
- Go to the Amp Envelope and set A=0, D=36, S=0, R=36. (Very fast attack, like a real drum, and moderately fast release, to simulate a fairly tight snare. If you lengthen the release slightly it gives the impression of a looser snare.)

Amp Envelope settings for Snare.

- You now have an analogue-style snare drum. Make sure you have the MIDI icon showing next to the SubTractor sequencer track name and play a note on the keyboard to hear the sound. Save it if you want to keep it.

Now for the kick drum:

- Create a new SubTractor for the kick if you would like to be able to play the snare and kick together in a pattern – remember, SubTractor is not multitimbral. Start with the Init Patch.
- Select a sine wave for Osc 1 and an octave setting of 1. This low sine provides a strong 'fundamental' frequency, giving the weight and body appropriate for a bass drum. Also try a triangle wave instead, to produce more of a subtly-pitched jungle-style kick. The sine gives more of a 'thump' to the sound, but the triangle is arguably more woody and authentic, and a bit easier to pick out. Disable keyboard tracking.
- Go to the Phase section of Oscillator 1 and click the LED next to the '-' sign, to light it. Turn the Phase knob fully right. This applies the maximum level of Phase Offset Modulation, in 'subtract' mode. POM thickens up this sound and adds the required complexity and presence.

Oscillator 1 settings for Bass Drum.

Noise settings for Bass Drum.

- Enable the Noise generator and set Decay to 40, Colour to 0 and Level to 98. Decay is fairly short because we only want a burst of noise at the start of the sound, to simulate the beater hitting the kick drum head. Setting colour to 0 produces a pink noise that has more bass energy. Move the control to the right (further towards white noise) if you want to add a more defined click to the attack.

- Go to Filter 1 and set the Frequency slider to 64. Select the LP12 filter type by clicking the LED next to its name.
- Go to the Filter Envelope section and set A=0, D=40, S=0, R=38. Turn the amount knob to 65.
- Go to the Amp Envelope and set A=0, D=34, S=0, R=40.
- Go to the Mod Envelope and set A=0, D=36, S=0, R=30. Set the Amount knob to 70 and make sure the Envelope destination is Oscillator 1. This creates a very fast pitch envelope, simulating the way the pitch of a kick drum will quickly slope off after the initial hit, and makes a big difference to the sound. Try it with and without the Mod Envelope to hear the difference.

Filter 1 and Filter Envelope settings for Bass Drum.

Amp Envelope settings for Bass Drum.

Mod Envelope settings for Bass Drum.

- That's the kick done. Save the sound if you want to keep it.

The only way you will be able to play these two sounds together easily from the keyboard, as if in a bass/snare drum pattern, is by triggering them from the ReDrum device. See the ReDrum chapter for instructions on how to make ReDrum trigger SubTractor synth sounds. Alternatively, record a simple drum pattern into the sequencer to hear the sounds play together.

Keyboard Tracking

The Keyboard Tracking switch for each oscillator sets whether the oscillator will produce different pitches in response to incoming pitch information – such as MIDI notes from a keyboard or pitch Control Voltages from the Matrix Pattern sequencer. If the switch is disengaged (not lit in red), the oscillator will only produce a single, fixed pitch. The primary purpose of disabling Keyboard Tracking (as we did in the drum Patches above) is to allow SubTractor to be used for synthesizing percussion sounds that should sound the same, and not change pitch, wherever they are played on the keyboard.

Introducing modulation

There are several easy and immediate ways of altering the basic waveforms produced by SubTractor's oscillators, and making them more dynamic, complex and

Info

What is modulation?

Modulation literally means alteration or adjustment, and in synthesis is just a jargon term for using something to change something else – for example, using an LFO to modulate the pitch of a sound in a cyclic fashion – making it go 'up and down' – and thus creating vibrato. Even an Envelope Generator could be thought of as a modulator, since it modulates, over time, the parameter to which it's assigned. The types of modulation available in synthesis include Amplitude modulation, where the volume of a sound is changed; Pitch modulation (as explained above); and Frequency modulation, where the mix of frequencies within a sound is changed. You can apply all these types of modulation, and more, within SubTractor.

The Phase Offset Modulation controls.

interesting as part of a synth Patch. One such method is 'Phase Offset Modulation', a novel technology not present on hardware analogue synths.

Phase Offset Modulation

POM creates a duplicate waveform of the same shape as the one being produced by a given oscillator and offsets the phase of the copy relative to the original. The offset waveform is then either subtracted from or multiplied by the original. A Mode button selects waveform subtraction, waveform multiplication or no phase modulation at all (so to switch off POM, set the Mode LED to '0'). The 'Phase' knob controls the amount of offset – the space between the two waveforms. This space can be modulated by the LFO, to add motion to the effect (more in a moment).

Pulse Width Modulation using POM

The classic synthesis technique of Pulse Width Modulation can be accomplished using the Phase Offset Modulation controls. PWM relies on the fact that the shape of a square wave (as mentioned earlier, a variety of pulse wave) can be altered so that it is 'up' for longer than it is 'down' (or vice versa), changing the harmonic content of the waveform. If this is done dynamically as the sound plays, the process is termed Pulse Width Modulation. POM produces a sound that's very similar to varying the pulse width of a square wave, the main difference being that the effect can be achieved with any of the oscillators' waveforms, not just the square wave. It sounds especially good with some of the more complex wavetable waveforms.

To create a Pulse Width Modulation effect, select 'Phase' as the destination for one of the LFOs or the Mod Envelope (different results will be obtained depending on whether you use the Multiply or Subtract mode set by the Mode switch). By the way, the Phase Offset of both oscillators will be modulated, if both are in use and have POM active.

The outcome, as the LFO or Mod Envelope works, will be a dynamic change in the phase offset that sounds very close in effect to PWM. In fact, applying POM to a sawtooth wave, and subtracting the duplicate from the main waveform using the '-' (subtract) mode, actually produces a pulse wave. If you modulate the width of this wave, you obviously hear Pulse Width Modulation.

Even without LFO or envelope modulation, POM is effective for fattening, thickening and giving more depth to a sound.

Info

Programming: A PWM-type sound

Create a rich, 'old-fashioned' PWM-style bass Patch as follows:
• Start with the Init Patch. Set a square wave on both oscillators (octave setting of 3 for Osc 1 and 2 for Osc 2).
• Set Amplitude EG Attack to 20 and Release to 45.
• Set the Phase knobs for the oscillators to values of 40 and 45.
• Make LFO1 output a triangle wave, and route it to modulating Phase.
• Set both LFO Rate and Amount to about 45.

• Set the Phase Mode switch for both oscillators to 'x' (multiply).

Play in the lower part of the keyboard. Swap Phase Mode between '0' (off) and 'x to hear how POM makes the sound almost 'sing'. You can set a very fast attack as an alternative, for a punch to the start of the sound. Also try sawtooth waves on both oscillators, for a very aggressive feel. Using the '-' (subtract) mode softens the sound.

Making the oscillators interact (1): Frequency Modulation

The FM knob.

Two special techniques increase the sonic variety of analogue synthesis by adding harmonics (overtones) that aren't in the original sound. Both require two oscillators as a minimum, and they make the oscillators interact rather than simply sounding at the same time.

The first technique, Frequency Modulation, configures two oscillators such that one is a 'carrier' and the other a modulator. The oscillator designated as the modulator is patched to the input of that designated as the carrier, so that the modulator waveform augments the mix of frequencies present in the carrier waveform. However, it is not just a case of adding the two waveforms together. The mix contains the carrier frequency, plus 'sum and difference' tones (see the explanation of Ring Modulation, below), and frequencies that are multiples of the modulator frequency. In complex waveforms (ie. waveforms other than sine waves), these 'sidebands' are generated for each overtone within the waveform, producing an even more harmonically complex output.

Frequency Modulation is applied with the FM knob to the right of the oscillator: in SubTractor, Oscillator 1's waveform is fixed as the carrier, while Osc 2's is the modulator. With the knob set fully left, no FM takes place, while turning it fully right applies maximum modulation.

When FM is being used, the oscillator Mix control should be fully to the left if all you want to hear is the sound of Osc 1 being modulated by Osc 2. If the knob is fully to the right, only the sound of Osc 2 will be heard – and since this oscillator is not being modulated by anything, only its unchanged output will be heard. You can hear a mix of the two by setting the knob to its centre position.

You can't do genuine, Yamaha-style FM synthesis, as found on the DX series of synths and the recent crop of FM softsynths, with SubTractor, as it only has two oscillators to combine, and you really need four as a minimum. Nevertheless, the FM knob can still help you create good approximations of distinctive FM timbres. There's a fine example sound in the Reason Operation manual. FM can add a feeling of edge and distortion to sounds where you want some grit, but is generally more controlled and less extreme than Ring Modulation – which we're just coming to now...

Making the oscillators interact (2): Ring Modulation

The Ring Mod switch.

This effect is applied with the Ring Mod switch to the right of the Osc 2 panel. Ring Modulation does its job by taking the frequencies output by two oscillators and both adding and subtracting them, producing the 'sum and difference' frequencies at the Ring Mod's output.

What is meant by 'sum and difference' frequencies? Well, if one oscillator is outputting a frequency of 100Hz and the other a frequency of 300Hz, the frequencies produced at the Ring Modulator's output will be 400Hz and 200Hz, the results of both adding the two original frequencies together and subtracting the smaller from the larger.

If the waveforms being output by the oscillators are simple – sine waves – not many sum and difference frequencies will be produced. If the waveforms are rich in harmonics, many frequencies will be summed and subtracted, and the resulting mix of frequencies may not be harmonically related. The result will probably be discordant and 'clangorous'. Ring Modulation is thus very useful for producing gong-like and bell-like timbres, which often have this discordant edge. However, that isn't why it's called 'ring' modulation – though it is quite a coincidence! Rather, the electronic circuits originally used to produce this type of modulation were composed of a ring of diodes.

As you might expect from the above, the effect of Ring Modulation is not dramatic with sine waves, nor if both oscillators (whatever waveform they're generating) are playing the same pitch, even in different registers (octave ranges). For example, if you ring-modulate two oscillators that are playing the same pitch and generating sine waves (no harmonics), the output will simply be the original pitch an octave higher: the two frequencies added together double the pitch, and one frequency subtracted from the other equals 'zero'. This does not mean that you shouldn't use Ring Modulation on sine waves, but the two oscillators producing the sines will have to be operating in different pitch registers if you are to hear any useful effect (see the Glockenspiel Patch in this section).

With all waveforms, the Ring Mod effect is much more pronounced if one of the oscillators has its pitch offset from the other. More variety is added by bringing in the FM and Phase Offset Modulation facilities.

A strength of ring modulation, as mentioned above, is simulating bell, gong and other metallic and percussive sounds, but it can be used subtly to add bite, fullness and depth to other types of sound, and for creating wonderfully weird special effects. The oscillator Mix knob should be turned fully right in order to hear just the ring-modulated sound.

Info

Programming: A realistic Glockenspiel using Ring Mod

Ring Modulation can create very discordant sounds – but you can also use it in a subtle way. Here's a very delicate glockenspiel, using simple sine waves tuned an octave apart, and Ring Mod.
- Start with the Init Patch. Turn on Osc 2. Select a sine for both oscillators, with an octave setting of 6 for Osc 1 and 7 for Osc 2 – it's a high, tinkly kind of sound.
- Turn the Osc Mix control fully right, set the amplitude envelope such that A=0, D=65, S=0 and R=65, and engage the Ring Mod button. Ring Mod immediately gives the sound just the right metallic edge.
- This Patch sounds most authentic played at middle C and above.
- Try programming a simple repeating pattern for this in the Matrix, for a minimalist feel.

Filters for sound sculpting

Analogue synthesis is also known as subtractive synthesis, because it takes as its starting point harmonically-rich waveforms and removes (or subtracts) parts of them to achieve the desired sound. You could compare the process to a sculptor starting to make a statue from a solid block of marble. Obviously, there's more material in the block than the sculptor needs, but a little or a lot of it can be chipped away to reveal the final shape of the statue.

The central tool in beginning to 'sculpt' one of these waveforms is the Filter, which removes (actually, attenuates or greatly reduces) frequencies from the waveform produced by the oscillator. Filter 1 is the more sophisticated of the pair offered by SubTractor, being a multi-mode device with a choice of five filter types, and controls for cutoff frequency, resonance and keyboard tracking. A dedicated Envelope Generator is also 'hardwired' to this filter – but EGs will be discussed in the next section.

Filter Frequency

The Frequency slider on both SubTractor filters determines the cutoff point at which the filter starts to work – the point above which unwanted frequencies are attenuated in the case of a Low Pass Filter, or below which they are attenuated in a High-Pass filter. So raising the cutoff frequency in a Low-Pass filter makes a sound brighter, as more high frequencies are allowed past, while raising it in a High-Pass filter makes the sound progressively more 'squeezed' and lacking in body as the lower frequencies are removed.

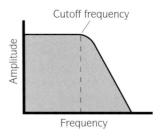

A Low-Pass Filter.

Choosing between filter types

The five filter types offered by Filter 1 are as follows:

*   *Low-Pass:* This type of filter attenuates all the frequencies above the selected cutoff frequency, leaving those below untouched – it allows the low frequencies to 'pass'. SubTractor offers two variants. The 24dB version provides the filter with a 'steep' roll-off curve, or slope, that is sometimes described as creating a punchy sound and is typical of classic analogue synths such as Moog's Minimoog. The 12dB Low-Pass filter has a gentler slope that leaves more of a waveform's original harmonics in the filtered sound, for a smoother effect in comparison to the 24dB option. Again, many classic instruments featured this type of filter, including Roland synths.Note that if the Frequency slider is right at the bottom of its travel with this type of filter, you'll hear no sound, as nothing at all can pass through the filter.

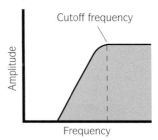

A High-Pass Filter.

*   *High-Pass:* This removes all the frequencies below the selected frequency, leaving those above untouched. The high frequencies 'pass'. The buzzy, nasal sound produced by a high-pass filter is good for creating sounds with an oboe-like, and in some cases a vocal, timbre. SubTractor's has a 12dB slope.
*   *Band-Pass:* Lets a range, or band, of frequencies through, removing those on either side. SubTractor's 12dB Band Pass filter offers two 'slopes', to cut off the frequencies above and below the band of frequencies to be allowed through. It manages this seemingly impossible job with one Frequency slider because when the Band-Pass filter type is selected, the Resonance slider functions as a 'bandwidth' control. As such, it determines the width of the frequency range around the central frequency that will be allowed to pass. The top and bottom of this range are the BPF's two cutoff frequencies, and the Resonance control moves them equally in relation to the central frequency; moving the Resonance control upwards narrows the band, and moving it down widens the band. This filter type has a slight nasal edge.

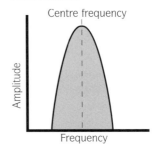

A Band-Pass Filter.

*   *Band-Reject (Notch):* Removes a range of frequencies, letting those on either side pass, and is essentially the opposite of a Band-Pass filter. As with the Band-Pass filter, the Resonance control determines the range of frequencies, around the value set by the Frequency slider, that are attenuated. Band-Reject filtering is not used often, as it has a very subtle effect, but it works well in combination with another filter – such as Filter 2, as explained below.

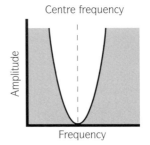

A Band-Reject Filter.

The small knob labelled 'Kbd' in this section controls keyboard scaling: turning this knob to the right causes the filter frequency to increase the further up the keyboard you play. The result is, with low-pass filters, that the sound becomes brighter as it becomes higher in pitch, which mimics the performance of many acoustic instruments.

Adding Filter 2

Filter 2 is a fixed 12dB Low-Pass device equipped with Frequency and Resonance sliders, an enable/disable LED switch (so it needn't be active if it's not doing anything in the current Patch) and a 'Link' switch. If you simply 'enable' Filter 2, it works serially with Filter 1 – ie, the output of Filter 1 is patched to Filter 2. Careful selection of cutoff frequencies, and filter type in Filter 1, can help create some interesting filter effects: for example, setting Filter 1 to High-Pass or Band-Pass and enabling Filter 2 (which is Low-Pass) allows you to produce formant or vowel-like effects; adding a little LFO-induced modulation can make SubTractor to appear to be almost speaking (nonsense, of course!)

Linking the Filters

The 'Link' switch creates a slightly different configuration (though the output of Filter 1 is still being passed through Filter 2). When the two filters are Linked, Filter 1's Frequency slider controls the frequency offset of Filter 2; whatever frequency has been set for Filter 2, in this mode, will be altered when you move Filter 1's Frequency slider. This linking has the effect of creating a 'super filter', with a 'slope' of up to 36dB and the added power of two resonance controls.

Filter Resonance

The Resonance (also known as 'Q') control accentuates the filter's cutoff frequency (and some frequencies in the immediate vicinity), most commonly in High-Pass and Low-Pass Filters but sometimes in Band-Pass and Band-Reject filters. The general result of increased resonance tends to be piercing and harsh, adding harmonic complexity to the sound and giving it a more cutting character.

The effect produced by the filter can be controlled over time – 'swept' in synth parlance – using an Envelope Generator (more in a minute). This causes a timbral swoop up or down to the cutoff frequency, and then a fade down or up from it – the famous filter sweep. You can go quite some way in synthesis just by mixing oscillators and modulating them with each other, but the end result won't necessarily have the harmonic interest over time that helps to keep the listener's interest; the filter, with filter EG, is a first step to adding that interest.

Envelope Generators for shape

Sounds, especially musical ones, have a shape or curve: a start, a middle, and an end. A sound may start sharply or have a slow attack, the middle portion may remain fairly constant or may swell, and the end may stop dead or tail off. With an analogue synthesizer, this change over time is simulated with amplitude (volume) Envelope Generators, or EGs. In their simplest form, they offer control over a sound's attack and its decay, though more commonly the envelope offers four stages:

The Filter Link switch.

- *Attack:* the Attack control of an EG controls how fast the sound reaches its maximum level. The attack for a percussion sound, which would reach its maximum level immediately, needs the Attack portion of its EG to be set to '0'. Longer Attack settings would cause a sound to fade in more gradually.

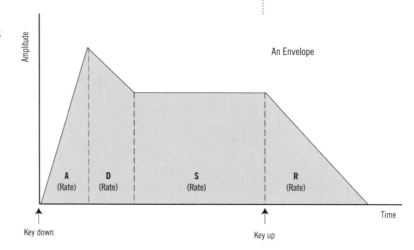

An Envelope

| A (Rate) | D (Rate) | S (Rate) | R (Rate) |

Amplitude

Time

Key down

Key up

- *Decay:* After the peak level has been attained, the sound starts to reduce in volume, and this phase is called the Decay. How long it lasts is set by the EG's Decay control.
- *Sustain:* The level to which the Decay portion of the envelope drops is determined by the Sustain parameter, and this level is held for as long as a key remains pressed, if you're controlling the synth with a keyboard.
- *Release:* The time taken for the sound's level to fade to silence after the key has been released is determined by the Release parameter of the EG.

An EG offering these four stages is termed an ADSR EG, and this is the type provided on SubTractor. As mentioned briefly in the filter section above, an EG can also be applied to a filter, so that the timbre of a sound, as well as its amplitude, changes over time.

The three SubTractor envelopes

Three Envelope Generators are available to SubTractor, which is a pretty good complement in terms of the average affordable classic analogue synth. Many budget instruments made do with just a single EG, which could be a big block to sophisticated sound construction. Two is standard – one for amplitude and one for the filter – so three is generous. One SubTractor EG is assigned to the amplitude, or volume, and another is assigned to Filter 1. The third EG is dubbed the Mod(ulation) Envelope, and is freely assignable to one of six 'destinations' – more on that in a moment.

The Amp (Amplitude) Envelope

Attack, Decay, Sustain and Release sliders are provided, creating a 'curve' that varies a sound's level over time, as explained earlier. EGs are often judged on the speed of their overall performance. Some synths are said to have sluggish EGs, even when their Attack is at its fastest setting and the rest of the envelope is set to produce a short overall curve. SubTractor's EGs are fast, like those on Roland's SH101, for example. Fast EGs are useful for producing Patches such as aggressive, clipped bass sounds that can cut through busy mixes.

The EG can also be set to produce a more leisurely curve: setting the Release parameter of the Amplitude Envelope to its full value creates an infi-

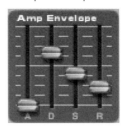

The Amplitude Envelope.

The Filter Envelope.

nite sound – it doesn't fade out when a key is released – and if you pull Release back a bit, the fade can still take up to 105 seconds. The Attack can also be set to take nearly a minute to fade in.

The Filter Envelope

Instead of controlling amplitude over time, the Filter EG controls changes to filter cutoff frequency, so that the filter allows more or less frequencies through ('opens' or 'closes') over time. If you manually move the SubTractor Filter Frequency slider up and down, the effect you hear is caused by the cut-off frequency being continuously changed. Setting a filter envelope simply allows this motion to be automated.

Fixed permanently to Filter 1, the Filter EG has two additional controls aside from its ADSR sliders:

- The *Amount* knob controls how strong an effect the envelope will have on the filter, by making the envelope open the filter more widely. Increasing the Amount value thus makes the envelope more pronounced. (However, if you have the cutoff Frequency slider set to maximum, increasing the value of the Amount knob will have no effect, as the filter is as 'open' as it can get and is already letting through as many frequencies as it can.)
- The Envelope *Invert* switch, with the upside-down envelope graphic, turns the envelope upside down; now instead of opening the filter, the envelope will close it over time. The effect of an inverted envelope is hard to describe, but it's an excellent option to have.

You may be thinking by now that Filter 2 doesn't have its own envelope generator, and you're right – but read on...

Info

Programming: Creating Filter Sweeps

The classic filter-sweep effect is quite easy to produce:
- Start by loading the SonderStrings Patch from the Pads folder in the SubTractor Patches folder in the factory ReFill (alternatively, load any old-fashioned type of smooth synth- string pad). Play a few notes or a chord to hear how it sounds – rather nice, but a bit tame.
- Now set Filter 1's frequency slider to 30 and Resonance to 75.
- In the Filter Envelope, set A=80, D=95, S=55, R=100 and Env Amount to 95.
- Play a few notes or a chord to hear the difference. If you play and hold for a moment and then release the keys, you'll hear the full effect as the envelope sweeps through, changing filter frequencies, which

are accented by the fairly high resonance setting.

The exact settings you need to create a filter sweep will vary with different Patches. If you're not hearing a result, turn up filter resonance to make the sweep effect stand out more, then tweak the filter envelope controls to make the envelope more pronounced, if needed. Conversely, if the sweep is giving your speakers or ears a hard time, turn down the resonance setting.

For a long sweep that continues to develop after you've released the keys, make sure that the Release parameter of the Amplitude Envelope is set moderately or quite high, as was the case with the SonderStrings Patch used in the example.

The Mod (Modulation) Envelope

The third EG has identical controls to the dedicated Filter 1 EG, but it can be be assigned to control one of six different parameters: the pitch of Osc 1 or Osc 2 (for varying pitch throughout the length of a sound); the Mix of the two oscillators; FM; Phase; or the cutoff frequency of Filter 2. That last option means that Filter 2 can have the same overall feature set as Filter 1, bar the variety of filter characteristics, and makes up for it not having a dedicated EG.

The Modulation Envelope.

Using the Modulation Envelope

Having a third, assignable EG gives you the power to control parameters that would not normally be controllable via an envelope, and adds even more flexibility to the SubTractor synth. For example, assigning the Mod EG to control the pitch of one of the oscillators can create siren-like swoops and other effects. It can also help to add a more natural feel to synth patches, especially those which might be broadly imitative of a 'real' instrument. Here's how.

Mod EG to pitch

Many real-world instruments naturally sound slightly out of tune on their attack, due to player variation or the physical properties of the instrument – woodwinds, for example, tend to blow slightly sharp. A small amount (a setting of 20 or less on the Amt knob) of a pitch EG (ie. the Mod EG routed to control the pitch of one of the oscillators) can mimic this effect if it is set to a very shallow curve. Suitable values might be something like A=5, D=15 S=0, R=0 – you want to produce a small, audible pitch blip that is nevertheless not too obvious, so experiment. Even on non-imitative patches this is quite a neat technique that gives a bit of extra interest to the attack of the sound.

Mod EG to Phase

Load the 'SaxSomething' Patch, again from the MonoSynths folder in the SubTractor Patches folder, and you can hear a similar technique being used. In this case, the programmer has assigned the Mod Envelope to control Phase Offset Modulation (rather than pitch) for the sound, with a shallow curve on the Envelope to make the blast of POM short. This creates a noisy, overblown front portion which greatly contributes to the realism of the Patch – think about the attack of a real sax. If you turn the Mod Envelope Amt control to the right, this effect is exaggerated. Turn the knob fully to the left, to remove the effect, and hear how badly it's missed! (Incidentally, notice how the programmer of this Patch has also assigned LFO2 to modulate POM very lightly, adding that bit more movement – almost a vibrato – to enliven the sound. More on LFOs in just a moment.)

Mod EG to Oscillator Mix

Assigning the Mod EG to control the oscillator Mix parameter allows you to move between the sounds of the two oscillators, giving an effect similar to the harmonic movement of simple wavetable synthesis. Here's a simple illustration:

- Initialise a SubTractor Patch, and switch on Osc 2.
- Set Osc 1 to produce a sawtooth waveform at an octave setting of 5.
- Set Osc 2 to output a square waveform with an octave setting of 3.

Info

Pitch EG on a brass Patch

An obvious use of a pitch EG effect, created by assigning an inverted Mod Envelope to Osc 2 pitch, can be heard in the Trumpoog synth-brass Patch from the MonoSynths folder in the SubTractor Patches folder of the factory Refill. Here, a fairly pronounced, but authentic, upwards swoop occurs at the start of every note played.

- Select 'Mix' as the destination in the Mod Envelope section.
- Set the Mod Envelope to A=0, D=90, S=63, R=0, and turn the Amount knob fully right.
- Go to the Amp Envelope section and set S=110.
- Now play a held note on your keyboard: first, you'll hear the low sound of Osc 2, which will gradually be joined by the higher sound of Osc 1 as the envelope makes the Mix of the oscillators change (to move instead from Osc 1 into a mix of Osc 1 and 2, invert the envelope with the invert envelope button). This kind of effect is particularly nice, with an appropriately programmed Patch, if you play and hold a chord (or the individual notes of a chord, one after another) until the second oscillator swells in, and perhaps treat the sound with some reverb or delay.

Try selecting FM as the Mod Envelope destination instead of oscillator Mix, turn the Mod Envelope amount to about 63 (or the FM effect will be far too grungy – and not in a good way!), and turn the Oscillator Mix control fully left, so that only the Frequency Modulated sound is heard. Listen to the complex, dynamic changes in the same sound, as the Mod Envelope alters the FM parameter, modifying the mixture of new frequencies created by the interaction of the two oscillators. Hold the note down for a long time to hear the full effect.

LFOs for movement

An essential part of analogue synthesis is the LFO, or Low Frequency Oscillator. The LFO is a modulator at whose heart is an oscillator that typically generates frequencies below the range of human hearing. When routed to another element of the synth, such as the main oscillator pitch or filter frequency, it modulates that parameter and causes it to vary. The result is vibrato (if pitch is modulated) and tremolo (if volume is modulated), effects which help add interest and movement to the otherwise static sound of the synth.

LFO1: The main SubTractor LFO

LFO1 features a list of waveforms the LFO can produce, and a list of destinations which it can be assigned to modulating.

How fast the LFO's cyclical modulation occurs (the speed of the pitch 'wobble', in the case of vibrato) is controlled by the Rate knob. The 'depth', or strength, of the effect (with vibrato, how extreme the pitch wobble is) is altered by the Amount knob.

The exact effect of LFO modulation is determined in part by the waveform the LFO is producing. SubTractor's LFO1 can generate:

- A triangle wave, which produces a vibrato effect when used to modulate the pitch of an oscillator, or a tremolo-like effect when it modulates Filter 1 Frequency.
- A square wave, which creates trill-like pitch variation with discrete steps when routed to Oscillator pitch.
- Sawtooth and inverted sawtooth waves, which create a sort of swooping siren effect, at their most extreme, especially when routed to oscillator pitch.
- A random waveform, and a 'soft random' waveform which sounds smoother. These approximate to what synthesists know as 'sample and

hold' waveforms. A Random waveform output produces a random series of voltages unrelated to any periodic waveform. It's ideal for modulating filter resonance, where ear-pleasing, unpredictable textural modulation can be added to a sound without compromising its pitch.

To hear the effects of different LFO waveforms for yourself:

- Start with the Init Patch. Set the Amount control in LFO1 to a value of 40. LFO1 defaults to generating a triangle wave controlling the Pitch of the two oscillators, so what you'll hear first when you play a note is an exaggerated pitch vibrato.
- Click on the LED switches for the different LFO waveforms in turn, then play a note to hear the pattern they impose on the pitch of the oscillators. Try turning the Rate knob, too, to increase or decrease the speed of the cyclic modulation.
- Try modulating the Filter Frequency. Click in the 'destination' column to select F. Frequency. Move through the waveforms again to see how different LFO waveforms affect the filter output. Turn the Amount knob to the right to make the effect more pronounced. Routing an LFO to control filter frequency is one of the most common and useful synthesis techniques, because it adds movement to a sound without affecting its pitch in any way.

Incidentally, both LFOs run constantly, but if you want to hear their effect you first have to route them to control a synth parameter.

The secondary LFO

Initially, LFO 2 looks as if it might be a simpler device than LFO1. In fact, it is merely different. Certainly, it only outputs a single waveform (a triangle), but even though it only has four destinations, to LFO 1's six, two of those are different from LFO1. In addition to Osc 1 and 2 and Phase, LFO 2 can be routed to Filter 2 Frequency and Amplitude. Both these options are worth having: just as both SubTractor's filters can have independent envelopes, if desired, so the filters can both be modulated by independent LFOs. It's useful to have Amplitude (ie. volume) as an LFO destination, too, for producing a true tremolo effect, as featured on many a classic electric piano sound on modern synths and samplers.

LFO 2's Rate and Amount controls operate as the same controls do in LFO 1, but it has two extra controls:

- The *Delay* control adds to the naturalness of the LFO's performance by allowing LFO modulation to be added gradually to a sound, fading it in rather as the player of an acoustic instrument would gradually add vibrato to a held note.
- The *Kbd (Keyboard Tracking)* knob, when turned to the right, causes the rate of LFO 2 to increase the higher on an attached keyboard you play. Again, this can add to the naturalness of a Patch if applied sympathetically, since a player of an acoustic instrument might tend to increase the rate of vibrato when reaching for higher notes. (You may not be trying to copy real-world instruments when you program, of course, but there may be times when you want synthetic textures to play the same kind of role in a track that a real instrument would play.)

Info

Programming Random LFO Modulation of Filter Frequency

For a rhythmic, bloopy sci-fi effect, try assigning a random LFO waveform to control filter frequency. To hear the effect, start with the Init Patch. Set the Filter 1 Resonance slider to maximum, select the first random waveform in the LFO 1 section, turn the Amount knob to full, and choose F. Frequency as the LFO1 destination. Play a note! This is especially useful now that you can easily synchronise LFO 1 to Song tempo, since V2 of Reason. Also try adding some timed delay to this kind of sound.

LFO2: a polyphonic LFO?

There is one important difference between the second LFO and the first: LFO 2 is technically 'polyphonic'. This has the effect of modulating every separate note played in SubTractor with its own LFO, which can give a Patch a subtle richness, especially when using SubTractor to play chords. LFO 1, on the other hand, produces a 'global' modulation that affects all notes being played in the same way. To illustrate the difference in sound quality produced by the monophonic LFO 1 and the polyphonic LFO 2, first try programming this slow-swell string pad:

- Choose a waveform: Start with the Init Patch. Select Waveform 15 for Oscillator 1, and an octave setting of 4.
- Apply POM: Set the Osc 1 Mode switch to '-' (sets POM subtraction mode) and the Phase knob to about 25.
- Set Filter Frequency and Resonance: Go to Filter 1 and set the Frequency slider to 55 and the Resonance slider to 45. Choose LP24 as the filter type.
- Create a Filter Envelope: Go to the Filter 1 Envelope and set it to A=85, D=105, S=105 and R=70. Set the Amt knob to 10.
- Create an Amp Envelope: Go to the Amp Envelope and set it to A=25, D=100, S=105 and R=75.
- Set the LFOs up for comparison: In LFO1 set a triangle waveform and a destination of Phase, with a setting of 42 on the Rate knob. In LFO2, choose a destination of Phase and a setting of 42 on the Rate knob.
- Hear the effect of the monophonic LFO1: turn the Amount control in LFO1 all the way up. Play and hold three or four notes of a chord, one right after another. Hold to hear a rather obvious and uninteresting global vibrato (almost a wah-wah effect) moving in the same direction on all notes in the chord. Now turn the Amount control all the way back to zero.
- Hear the effect of the polyphonic LFO2: Turn the Amount knob in LFO2 all the way to the right. Play and hold the same broken chord you just played a moment ago. You should hear a richer, subtle, chorused effect that's generally much more sophisticated, as the LFO produces a new pattern for each note.

If you assign LFO 2 to Filter 2 Frequency, dial in a high Amount, then play and hold broken chords, you'll hear the order of the notes you played reflected in the changing patterns of the modulated filter peaks.

Sync'ing LFO to Song tempo

Seasoned synth musicians know the compelling rhythmic effect created by synchronising the rate of LFO filter modulation with the tempo of a song. Now that we have Reason V2, Syncing LFO 1 to tempo is as easy as clicking on the 'Sync' button, to activate atutomatic sync. Try this with all sorts of tracks, especially faster tempo dance material.

The LFO 1 Sync button, introduced in Reason V2.

In earlier versions of Reason, there's no dedicated facility for syncing the LFO to Song tempo – but you can fake the effect very well by using the Matrix step sequencer. This technique is obviously useful for users of older versions of the software, but even if you have Reason V2.x, there are still advantages to the 'Matrix LFO' if you're prepared to do a bit of work. It also gives you some practice in using the Matrix as a control source for SubTractor; see the Matrix chapter for more on the 'Matrix LFO'.

Performance control parameters

Velocity Control

So far we've covered every step in the making of a synth Patch with SubTractor – from choosing oscillator waveforms and setting up filter and amplitude envelopes, to incorporating the modulation that makes Patches come alive. Now we come to one further way of introducing expression and feel into programmed sounds – and this time, it's the expression and feel that comes from actually playing and responding to the Patch in performance. It's all about velocity – how hard or softly you hit the keys, and how your instinctive playing touch will change the Patch you're using. (Of course, velocity can be provided by the gate level values of a Matrix sequencer pattern, instead of by your MIDI keyboard.)

The Velocity Control area consists of nine knobs. The setting of each of these knobs determines how velocity will alter the relevant synth parameter as you play – and you can use all of them at the same time, if you like. If the knob is set dead centre, velocity will have no effect – the parameter won't change no matter how hard or softly you play. (If a velocity knob has an active setting, the red LED above it will be lit, so you can see at a glance what is going on.) An occasional problem for newcomers is that they don't realise that no Patch (and this goes for the other devices too) will be velocity sensitive if there is no velocity response – notably amplitude – set up via these controls.

- *Amp(litude):* Affects how the volume of a Patch will respond to playing velocity. Moving the knob to the right sets up a 'positive' (and natural) relationship between velocity and volume – ie. the harder you hit the keys, the louder the Patch plays. Moving it to the left inverts that relationship so that hitting the keys hard makes the Patch get quieter.

- *FM:* Allows FM Amount to be increased or decreased as you play. Some common sense applies here: if you're not using FM, a negative setting of the FM velocity knob will have no effect, as you can't apply less than nothing. However, you can add FM to a Patch which doesn't have it 'programmed in', as you play, by using a positive setting of the FM velocity control.

- *M.Env (Modulation Envelope):* Controls the Modulation Envelope 'Amt' parameter, and thus makes any modulation envelope that has been set up sound more pronounced in response to velocity with positive settings of the knob, and less pronounced with negative settings.

- *Phase:* Allows Phase Offset Modulation Amount to be increased or decreased as you play. If POM has not been activated for the Patch (the POM mode is at 'o'), it can't be introduced via velocity, and if POM is only being used on one oscillator, the velocity knob will only affect its response for that oscillator. However, if both oscillators in a Patch are using POM, both their POM amounts will be altered, but the relative values of one parameter to the other remains the same, For example, if Osc 1's POM control is set to a value 20 higher than the POM control for Osc 2, then it'll be 20 higher any time the two parameters are altered via velocity.

- *Freq 2:* Makes velocity alter the cutoff frequency of Filter 2 – turn the knob to the left and a high velocity lowers the frequency, while turning it to the right makes high playing velocity raise the frequency.
- *F. Env:* Controls the Filter 1 Amt parameter, and thus makes Filter 1's envelope more pronounced in response to velocity with positive settings of the knob, and less pronounced with negative settings.
- *F. Dec:* Makes Filter 1's envelope's decay longer in response to high velocity with positive settings, or shorter with negative settings. This facility can produce a more subtle timbral effect on a sound than having velocity affecting the entire envelope, especially when you play slowly or gently.
- *Mix (Oscillator 1/2 mix):* Puts the oscillator Mix parameter under velocity control, so that one oscillator or another in a two-oscillator Patch can be made to dominate as you play harder or softer. Which oscillator will dominate is determined by giving the knob a positive or negative setting.
- *A. Atk (Amplitude Envelope Attack):* With positive settings, higher playing velocity makes the envelope attack slower, while negative settings make the attack faster in response to high velocities.

Info

Pitch-bend 'stepping'

Setting the pitch-bend range parameter towards its upper limit is one of the few things in Reason that will introduce quantisation artifacts into a parameter change – audible, discrete steps as the pitch-bend knob is moved. This is a problem with the majority of modern digital instruments, and it happens because the MIDI parameter in question – pitch-bend – has a fixed data range (in this case - 8192 to +8191), which it uses whether the bend in question is one semitone or 24 (two octaves). Thus, a slow bend with a semitone range will sound very smooth, with no stepping, but a 24-semitone bend will have very obvious stepping, because there is not really enough data available to properly describe all those steps with the same resolution. Luckily, the effect doesn't become really noticeable until you set the range to above 12 semitones, and you're unlikely to need this kind of figure very often. Synths usually come with the range of their pitch-bend wheel set to a usable two or three semitones.

Amplitude Envelope Attack provides a nice example of how to effectively use negative Velocity Control values. Starting with the Init Patch, set up the amplitude envelope with a slow attack (A=75 or so), and turn the Amplitude Attack Velocity Control knob fully left. Now, playing gently will produce a sound that has a slow attack – almost like bowing on a stringed instrument – while a harder playing style will cause the sound to have a more definite, staccato attack. This relationship would be very appropriate with many sounds.

If you now set positive Velocity Control amounts for Amplitude and Filter Envelope, the sound gets louder and brighter as its attack becomes more definite – and these three aspects of the sound co-operate to intensify the effect of high-velocity playing in a natural and sympathetic way, setting up behaviour which copies the way real instruments respond. You'll find your playing style will almost unconsciously adapt to take advantage of the expressive potential of these routings.

The pitch-bend and modulation wheels

No real synth would be released without pitch-bend and modulation wheels, so SubTractor has them too, even though they're just on-screen graphics. But you can grab and tweak them with your mouse, and tweaking the real ones on your MIDI controller keyboard will cause the virtual equivalents to move in response.

The pitch-bend wheel does one job: it bends the pitch of a SubTractor Patch up or down. With pitch-bend, you're able to add small or large expressive bends during a performance, in the same way that a string player, guitarist or singer might swoop up or down to a note. The numeric display and increment/decrement buttons adjacent to the wheel are used to indicate and change the its semitone 'range'. Set it to '1' and the wheel will apply a maximum of one semitone of bend, even when it is pushed to its full extent, in either direction – a semitone up if it's pushed fully forward, and a semitone down in the other direction. You can define a range of up to 24 semitones, using the up/down arrows next to the pitch-bend numeric display.

The modulation wheel is another common real-time performance control, and on most simple analogue synths it would have been fixed to LFO speed or filter frequency. The majority of modern instruments give you a choice of what to modulate using the mod wheel, and SubTractor is no exception. Like the Velocity Control section of SubTractor's front panel, the mod wheel is provided with a collection of knobs that can assign it to any or all of five parameters, each of which can provide a positive or negative response. The 'targets' for the Mod Wheel are Filter 1 Frequency, Filter 1 Resonance, LFO1 amount, Phase (POM, for both oscillators), and FM.

Key Mode and Portamento

SubTractor can be customised to respond to incoming note data in different ways, with the controls in the Key Mode and Portamento area. First up is the Mode switch, to select between 'Legato' and 'Retrigger' operations, which determine how Patches respond to being played from a MIDI controller.

- *Legato mode* is best demonstrated when playing monophonic sounds (set the Polyphony control to '1'). When you press and hold a key, any other key that you press thereafter will cause a pitch change, as you would expect, but won't retrigger the sound's envelope – there is no new attack, and the envelope started by the first note will continue. The lack of a new attack creates a smooth transition between the two notes – legato, in fact. This is excellent for smooth, fluid solo lines.
- *Retrigger Mode:* when this option is selected, the envelope re-starts for every new note played. Once again, this effect can be heard most easily when trying it out with a monophonic Patch, by playing the classic monosynth trill: play and hold one note, then rapidly play another one repeatedly to create the trill. With Legato mode, the trill is smooth, rather like an exaggerated vibrato, whereas Retrigger mode creates an effect more like a real trill on a piano, with each note having a defined attack.

Both Legato and Retrigger responses are available for polyphonic Patches, too, though Retrigger could be considered the norm for such Patches. If you choose Legato mode for a polyphonic Patch, you won't hear the effect of it until you've held down as many notes as the Patch's polyphony value; until then, every note triggers the envelope as normal. For example, if a Patch has four-voice polyphony and you select the Legato option, the envelopes will retrigger normally until you hold down a four-note chord; the next keys you press will not retrigger the envelopes, but carry on with the original envelope (as well as stealing notes from your four-voice chord).

Portamento

The choice between Legato and Retrigger operation becomes more meaningful when you have given a Patch a Portamento, or glide, setting. This is determined by the Portamento knob, and sets how long it takes to glide from one note to the next. Portamento can be used as an expressive aid, to swoop between notes in a tune or bassline; it's also an important part of Patches that seek to imitate the Roland TB303 Bassline bass synth. Portamento is inactive if the knob is set all the way to the left.

How Portamento produces 'gliding' during playing is governed by the Legato and Retrigger modes, especially in the case of monophonic Patches.

Select Retrigger and the Portamento glide will occur for every new note. Select Legato mode and the effect only happens when you play with a legato (as opposed to a 'staccato', or detached) 'touch' allowing you to control when Portamento will be applied as you play.

Portamento can also be used on polyphonic Patches; once again, in this case choosing Retrigger causes all played notes to swoop, while Legato mode only allows a swoop once your chosen 'polyphony-quota' of notes is already being played and you then play another note or notes. The swoop then moves up or down to the new note(s), stealing notes from the original chord. This can be a very pleasing effect for a closing chord in a track or section of a track, especially if you hold a chord and then swoop up to the same chord (or notes from within the chord) an octave higher.

Tutorial

Copying the TB303

Simulating a typical sound from Roland's perennially popular TB303 Bassline makes use of both the Legato trigger mode and Portamento.

- Start with the Init Patch. Select a sawtooth for Osc 1 ,with an octave setting of 3. You can also try this with a square wave and see which suits you best. Both sounds are quite characteristic of the 303, which only offered sawtooth and square waves.

Oscillator 1 settings for TB303 sound.

- Set the Polyphony parameter to 1, as the 303 is monophonic.
- Choose LP24 for Filter 1, since the 303's filter was technically 24db LP. A good starting point for cutoff frequency would be 44, and resonance 42.
- Set something like this for the Filter EG: A=6, D=44, S=65, R=20, Amount knob at 60. The TB303's envelope, which affected both filter and amplitude, was a two-knob affair (decay and envelope mod) which, due to the synth's circuitry, had an effect on the whole sound; all TB303 controls interacted in some way that's hard to replicate on other instruments. Leave the Amp Envelope controls as they are.
- In the Portamento/key mode section, select 'Legato' and set the Portamento knob to 70. This adds the typical TB303 'slide' effect when required.

Set key mode and Portamento.

- Now alter some of the Velocity Control knobs, so the sound responds more dynamically to velocity – mimicking the 'accent' feature of a genuine 303. Set Amp to about 4, F. Env to about 50, and F. Dec to -10. The last helps emulate a 303 'envelope mod' effect. Whack the SubTractor's level up so you can hear the sound really well.

Make the sound monophonic.

Filter 1 and Filter Envelope settings for TB303 sound.

Set up some velocity control.

- Now, from your MIDI keyboard, play a mix of staccato and legato notes, hitting the staccato notes harder; you'll hear the standard 303 biting attack, followed by a fairly typical slide effect.
- You can recreate the repetitive nature of a TB303 pattern by triggering this Patch from a Matrix. Start with a 16-step pattern, and mix and match obvious accents – high velocity settings in the Gate display – with the occasional tied note, to get something close to a TB303 in full flight. You can even ape a fairly standard TB303 composition technique by drawing in pitches at random in the display. Also try shifting the occasional note, especially one being treated to a slide, one octave up or down.

This kind of pattern in the Matrix will trigger the 303 sound in an authentic way. The crucial things are the mixture of high and low velocities and the tied notes that create the typical 'slide' effect.

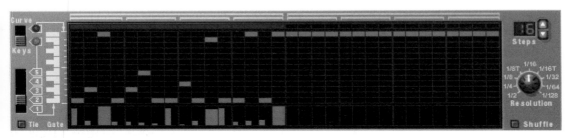

Note that the real 303 had a pitch range of about three octaves, and that it's not so much about 'bass' (though the TB303 could produce a very solid bottom end), as about lower-mid frequencies, with filter-excited accents. These settings are just a starting point. Customise them according to your idea of what the TB303 sound is. If you want more, Propellerhead will be happy to sell you two virtual TB303s (plus TR808 and 909 drum machines) in the shape of Rebirth!

Setting Polyphony

The polyphony control simply lets you define how many simultaneous notes SubTractor will be able to produce, between 1 and 99. Simple enough – but there are a few things to consider.

First of all, it's worth noting that there's nothing to stop you from giving all your Patches a polyphony value of 99. The value itself has no impact on your computer's CPU overhead, unless you actually play all 99 notes at once. Unused voices don't consume computing power. However, if you've programmed the amplitude envelope of a Patch to have a very long release setting, and polyphony is set to a very high number, you might find you're using more notes than might at first be apparent. Any notes that are still decaying after you've played them are using up polyphony, and hence CPU overhead, along with any notes that are currently being played.

It thus makes sense to set polyphony to just the number of voices you'll actually need for the part in question. (You will have to pay attention, though – if the note decays mentioned above can't play out because there is not enough polyphony for them, they will get cut off by 'note stealing', and it's for you to decide whether this decay truncation is audible in context, or not.)

However, in general, if a part – such as a bass line – only requires 1-note polyphony, just give the Patch that's playing it one note. In fact, if you're using the Matrix Pattern Sequencer, which is strictly monophonic, with a SubTractor, there's often no point in setting more than 1-note polyphony. And of course, there are certain performance effects – such as slurs and slides, as determined by the Key Mode parameters discussed above – that will only be possible if a Patch is strictly monophonic.

On the other hand, it may occasionally be desirable to select polyphonic operation for a Patch playing a monophonic line, precisely because it behaves differently than a strictly monophonic Patch. For example, a Matrix pattern (which is necessarily monophonic) playing a polyphonic voice with a noticeable sustain portion can give an impression of more going on than there actually is, due to the sustain of one note playing over the attack of the next, creating a sort of subtle harmony.

For polyphonic voices, try to stick to sane amounts of polyphony – four, eight, or sixteen – such as would be encountered during a normal performance. If you encounter note stealing (where earlier notes played are muted by later notes because their note 'slot' is required by the later note), it's simple enough to give SubTractor more voices.

Info

What affects CPU usage in SubTractor?

Most users should find that they have few problems with processor power, as Reason uses your computer's resources very efficiently. However, if you do encounter problems, perhaps with an older computer or a laptop, there are a few things to bear in mind regarding SubTractor.

- *Polyphony:* The number of notes actually being played by your SubTractor(s) has a bearing on CPU usage (rather than the amount of polyphony set in the Polyphony display). However, note decays may be using up polyphony unbeknownst

to you, as explained in the main text, so if appropriate set only the polyphony you know you require.

- *Oscillators:* Two-oscillator Patches use more power than single-oscillator Patches.
- *Filters:* Using one filter is more economical than using two – deactivate an unused filter; the 12dB filter type uses less power than the 24dB type.
- *Noise:* don't switch on the Noise generator if you're not using it.
- *POM:* Bear in mind that engaging POM doubles

the processing power required, so engaging it for both oscillators quadruples CPU usage for that SubTractor.

- *FM:* If you don't need FM, don't switch it on, and don't route a modulation source to it.

Also try engaging the Low Bandwidth button under the Patch Select display if your processor is struggling. This reduces high-frequency content somewhat and saves processor power. With, for example, bass Patches, the audible effect of this may be undetectable or negligible.

External Modulation via MIDI

In addition to being able to route velocity and mod wheel to a number of synthesis parameters, SubTractor also has a modulation area which allows you to route more esoteric MIDI data, originating from outside Reason, to its parameters. This section assigns any one of aftertouch, expression-pedal or breath-controller data to modulate up to four parameters, with positive or negative amounts, in a similar fashion to the Velocity Control and Mod Wheel assign sections. The four target parameters are Filter 1 Frequency, LFO Amount, Amplitude (volume), and FM Amount, each with a dedicated Amount knob.

As you'll read in the automation/remote control chapter, most Reason parameters can be easily set up to be governed by any incoming external MIDI Controller data, so you might wonder why you would need the external modulation controls with their fixed assignments. Well, one reason is that the settings made in the External Modulation panel are saved with a SubTractor Patch, where-as 'remote' MIDI mapping is only saved, less conveniently, at Song level.

In addition, data such as breath controller is transmitted by some special MIDI wind controllers, and musicians who play these instruments are used to having a simple way to route this data to performance parameters. It's also possible for non-wind players to buy dedicated 'breath controllers' (usually by Yamaha), though few instruments not built by Yamaha have the necessary input socket. (There are, however, a few third-party breath-controller-to-MIDI interfaces on the market.)

Aftertouch and expression-pedal data are fairly ubiquitous these days, with most modern synths being able to transmit them, though you may need an additional 'volume'-type foot pedal in order to transmit expression from your keyboard. Aftertouch is the MIDI controller that's transmitted as you press into the keys (adding extra feel) after a note has been played – hence the name. You may need to enable it on your keyboard if you want to transmit it to Reason. Usually, it's disabled as a default, since using it generates huge amounts of data which, in the early days of MIDI at least, proved a lit-tle overwhelming for some MIDI sequencers.

Patch layering with SubTractor

Occasionally, people complain that they can't make SubTractor sound as 'big' as they would like. Well, if you work on your programming skills, you can usually make sounds that are perfectly 'big' enough with SubTractor, but there is another way too. This technique can not only simulate a synth with more oscillators than SubTractor has, but also caters for those who like to set up 'layers' on their synth, for thick, complex, moving textures. It might at first seem as though there's no way to create such layers, and there is cer-tainly no way to control two or more SubTractors from one Matrix or one Reason sequencer track. The secret lies in the four MIDI buses of the Hardware Interface.

In the following example, we'll use four factory SubTractor Patches to cre-ate an ethereal piano/pad/bell layer, but you can, obviously, use the same steps with any sounds you like.

Tutorial

Ethereal piano layer using the MIDI buses

1 Set up the MIDI buses

- Start with an empty rack. Create a mixer and four SubTractors.
- Under the Edit menu, select 'Preferences'.
- In the dialogue box, select the Advanced MIDI page.
- Under the External Control heading, select your master keyboard as the MIDI input for each of Bus A to Bus D. Close the window.
- Back at the rack, go to the Hardware

Setting up the MIDI buses for the layer.

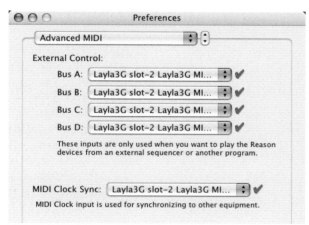

Bus A on the Hardware Interface routed
to Synth 1 of the layer.

Interface. Next to the 'Bus Select' label at the top, click on 'A' (Bus A)
- Go to Channel 1 on the Interface and click on the arrow next to the label.
From the pop-up, select 'Synth 1'.
- Now choose Bus B as you chose Bus A, and from the Channel 1 pop-up
select 'Synth 2'.
- Now choose Bus C and select Synth 3 from the Channel 1 pop-up.
- Now choose Bus D and select Synth 4 from the Channel 1 pop-up. When
you play your keyboard now, all four SubTractors will play at the same
time (playing the Init Patch, at the moment!) If you see a MIDI icon
anywhere in the sequencer track list, click on it to get rid of it.

2 Load the Patches for the layer
- In SubTractor 1, load 'Zaire' from the Pads folder in the SubTractor
Patches folder.
- In SubTractor 2, load 'Wurlitzer Piano' from the PolySynths folder.
- In SubTractor 3, load 'Zaire' again, as in the first step.
- In SubTractor 4, load 'Joshua Pad' from the Pads folder. Make a couple
of modifications to this Patch, as follows: Amp Envelope A=0, D=127,
S=60, R=72.

Load the four Patches.

3 Balance and pan the components of the layer
- Go to the mixer and set pan position for Synth 1 fully left with the Pan knob.
Adjust fader level to 86.
- Set fader level for the Synth 2
channel at 110.
- Set the Pan position full right for
Synth 3. Set fader level at 86.
- Set fader level for Synth 4 at 68.
- While you're at the mixer, create a
delay and a reverb and add just a
bit of each to every channel of the
layer (see the effects chapter for
how to set up effects with the

The four layers balanced and panned at the mixer.

mixer). This layer sounds pretty good without effects, but you know what
a bit of delay and reverb does!

4 Play and sequence the layer

- Play some laid-back chords on your MIDI keyboard. Not bad, eh? But how are we going to use that in a Song when there's no way to record a sequencer part for more than one device at a time?
- Select any one of the four SubTractor tracks in the sequencer. Click in the 'In' column to make the MIDI plug icon turn up.
- Engage record mode. Play the desired part.
- The part is only recorded to one track, so you now need to select the whole part in the sequencer window (draw a box around it with the selection tool) and use Apple/Control-G to 'group' the notes.
- Click the newly created Group to select it and Option/Control-drag downwards to the next track. This copies the whole performance. Do the same thing for the remaining two tracks of the layer.

The played part has been grouped and copied to the three other tracks.

- When you play back the Song, all four layers will be there as you played them.

Don't forget that you can layer sampler devices and Malströms, or mixtures of different devices, in the same way.

If you use this technique during Song creation, rather than as a real-time performance tool, you'll need to go to the Hardware Interface at the top of the rack and disconnect the routing that you've created between your master keyboard and the four synths in the layer, when you no longer need it for playing or recording. (Click the arrow next to the Channel label and choose 'Disconnect' from the pop-up.) Otherwise, you'll carry on playing the layer even when all you want to do is play or record a device that's linked to a sequencer track.

Extending the layering idea

There are further avenues for exploration with this layering technique. For example, you can experiment with the attack times of the amplitude envelopes for the different sounds – giving different layers different attack times will cause them to fade into the sound at different points when a note or chord is held. There's no way of assigning layers to groups of keys (for key splitting), but if you turn up the Filter 1 Keyboard Tracking knob on one layer, you can give something of the impression of the layer becoming gradually louder the higher up the keyboard you play; a similar effect can be managed by assigning negative or positive offsets to the 'Amplitude' knob in the Velocity section. And if it's a split you want in the final performance, manually edit out the notes that you don't want a particular layer to play in its copy of the performance in its main sequencer track.

There's even more fun to be had when you incorporate rhythmic or textural loops (via a sample playback device) into a layer, or if you use the CV and Gate system to arrange auto panning, tremolo and other dynamic modulation, as described elsewhere in this book, and incorporate in-line effects into the layer. Your imagination is the limit!

The rear panel

The audio output

The usual destination for the audio output of SubTractor is an audio input on the ReMix mixer, so that SubTractor can be heard and can be mixed as part of a track. This is the automatic audio connection Reason will make for you if you create a mixer, then a SubTractor. However, the new Malström device that's been introduced with Reason V2 has a pair of audio inputs, which opens up some new possibilities. See the Malström chapter for more. SubTractor's audio output can also, of course, be patched into an effect device (or chain of effects) for in-line (insert) processing of the synth's audio, or connected direct to the Hardware Interface.

The Sequencer Control Gate and CV inputs

These inputs are mainly for connecting a Matrix Pattern sequencer so that it can play a SubTractor sound. The CV (Control Voltage) sends note (pitch) information to SubTractor from the Matrix, while the Matrix Gate 'pulse' tells SubTractor when to play the note, how loudly to play it, and how long to hold it. (See chapter 4 for a fuller explanation of the Gate and CV system.) The correct connections are:

*   Note CV output of Matrix connected to Sequencer Control CV input of SubTractor.
*   Gate CV output of Matrix connected to Sequencer Control Gate Input of SubTractor.

These are the routings made when Reason auto-routes SubTractor and a Matrix for you, but you can, of course, make them manually.

If you wanted to trigger a SubTractor voice, perhaps a synthesized, analogue-style drum sound, with the ReDrum drum machine, only the Sequencer Control Gate input would be used, connected to a Gate Output of one of ReDrum's 10 drum-voice channels. You could thus have a SubTractor voice playing as part of a ReDrum drum pattern. Up to 10 SubTractors could be connected in this way, as in the 'Analogue Drum Sequencer.rns' Template Song provided with Reason.

There are also a couple of off-the-wall uses of these sockets, since Gate or CV outputs from any device can be connected to either of SubTractor's Sequencer Gate and CV inputs. Routing one SubTractor's LFO and Modulation Envelope CV outputs, for example, to another SubTractor's Sequencer Gate and CV inputs can create some very interesting sound effects.

The CV/Gate connections

SubTractor has probably the biggest range of CV and Gate sockets of any device in the Reason rack. You can do lots of fun things with these connections. See Chapter 4 for an explanation of the CV/Gate system and Chapter 19 for a chart giving suggested routings. The following tutorial also uses some of the rear-panel facilities.

Modulation tutorial

Rhythmic triggering of SubTractor envelopes (gated synth effect)

It's difficult to describe the great effects that can be achieved in this way, but the technique can be used to add rhythmic interest within a note, and can range from a subtle pulsing to a Shamenesque gated-synth effect – all achieved with the minimum of actual playing, as the triggers do most of the work for you. Work through this tutorial to get an idea of what's possible. It's a bit on the long side, but worth it for the results.

Starting rack for the gated synth effect.

- Make a new rack containing a

Make some changes to the factory Patch.

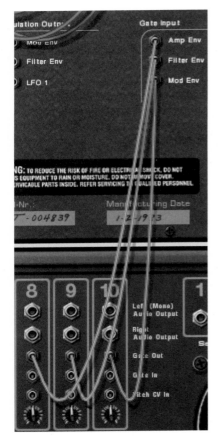

The ReDrum Gate Outs for channels 8-10 connected to the SubTractor Amp, Filter and Mod Envelope Gate Ins. ReDrum patterns will now trigger these envelopes. (Audio cables have been disconnected for clarity.)

mixer, a ReDrum drum machine and a SubTractor synth.

• Click in the SubTractor and select Techre Harp.zyp from inside the PolySynths Folder, in the SubTractor folder of the factory ReFill.

• Make some modifications to the Patch. Set Filter 1 Frequency to 90 and Resonance to 55. Go to the Filter Envelope and set Attack to 0 and Release to 50, with a 70 setting on the Amt knob. Go to the Amp Envelope and set Release to 45. These changes make the Patch work better with the triggering technique.

• Now flip the rack around with the Tab key. Click on the Gate Out socket of ReDrum channel 8. Drag the cable that appears to the Amp Envelope Gate input on SubTractor. Click on the Gate Out socket of ReDrum channel 9 and drag the cable that appears to the Filter Envelope Gate input on SubTractor. Finally, click on the Gate Out socket of ReDrum channel 10 and drag the cable to the Mod Envelope Gate input of SubTractor (see Fig 6.54).

• Flip the rack around to the front again. Select ReDrum drum channel 8 by clicking on its Select button and click on the following buttons in the row of square programming buttons: 1, 4, 7, 10, 13, 15. Alternatively, program your own pattern. It doesn't have to be complicated and could almost be random clicks, as it and the following two patterns will not trigger drums, but SubTractor's envelopes.

• Select channel 9 by clicking on its Select button and program a new pattern by clicking buttons 3, 6, 9, 12, 14, 16.

• Select channel 10 and program buttons 2, 6, 10, 14.

• Click on the Browse Sample button in Channel 1 of ReDrum and load a kick drum of your choice. Program a simple four-beat pattern by clicking on buttons 1, 5, 9, 13. (This is just for a rhythmic backbeat while you try out the gated synth effect.)

• Go to the main sequencer window at the bottom of the rack. Click in the In column of the SubTractor track to make the MIDI plug icon appear.

• If you try to play notes on your keyboard at this point, you won't hear anything. This is because normal note triggering is overridden when the envelope Gates are being used. You need to first click the 'Play' button on the sequencer, which makes the drum machine start playing and producing the Gate triggers. You'll hear the bass drum playing the simple pattern, and when you hold down a chord the rhythmic envelope triggering will begin.

Though you're just holding down a chord, with no rhythm in your playing, the chord is triggered in the rhythm of the first drum pattern you programmed earlier, on ReDrum channel 8. Other rhythmic interest is provided by the Filter envelope triggering in the second pattern we programmed, on channel 9, and the Modulation envelope triggering in the pattern programmed on channel 10. The result is instant rhythmic and tonal complexity that sounds as though much more is going on than is really the case!

Play different chords, and broken chords, and hold them, changing chords in response to what you hear, and you should soon get into it. Try playing lead lines, too. It's a very inspiring technique, so maybe set the sequencer in 'record', as you may well come up with some good stuff as you get carried away using it! Add some reverb and tempo-sync'd delay for even better effect.

Get ready to play.

Things to bear in mind:

- Different Patches will work, but if you want the Modulation envelope triggering, the Patch will have to include a Modulation envelope routing, and you may need to tweak the Amplitude and Filter envelopes too. You'll probably need a short attack and a medium release.
- If the Patch you choose really doesn't seem to trigger correctly with this technique, try setting the Decay mode instead of the Gate mode on the relevant ReDrum drum channel(s). You set this with the two-way switch next to the Length knob; Decay mode is the lower position. The Length knob allows you to adjust the length of the ReDrum gate pulse, so you can really tailor the pulse to what your SubTractor Patch requires.
- If you're triggering the Mod envelope, different results will be obtained depending on what the Mod envelope is routed to within the SubTractor Patch.
- You don't have to trigger all the SubTractor envelopes, though we've used all three in this example.
- We set up this example with drum patterns especially for envelope triggering, and only a bass drum playing as a rhythmic pulse. However, you can program a normal drum pattern and choose any drum channel from that to connect to a SubTractor Gate envelope input. Say your hi-hat on channel 6 is playing sixteenth notes: connect the Gate Out socket of that channel to the Sub's Amp Envelope Gate in and the chords and notes you hold on the keyboard will trigger in a sixteenth-note pattern that echoes the hi-hat perfectly. Now send the snare channel to the Sub's Filter envelope gate in and you'll get a reinforcing filter 'thwack' every time the snare hits. There are lots of other possibilities.
- Record your triggered chords and lead lines into the sequencer and then record manual tweaking of the Filter and Mod envelope parameters as automation data, for even more fun.
- Not only Gate Outs can be routed to the Gate Ins: it's equally possible to route Control Voltages (CVs) to these inputs. Experiment and you'll find that there are plenty of interesting textural and rhythmic effects to explore.

Some fast Patch creation and editing guidelines

As SubTractor is modelled on an analogue synth, most programming techniques evolved for analogue synths work with it. Dig out old books which give ideas and example patches and they can probably be adapted to SubTractor. In brief, though, here are some quick tweaks you can make to adapt Patches to your needs.

- A small group of synth parameters tend to have the most noticeable effects on synth Patches, so when you're quickly tweaking, home in on these first: amp envelope attack and release, filter cutoff and resonance, and possibly LFO speed and depth.

- Make Patches more snappy and responsive by setting a very short attack time for the Amp envelope. Longer, smoother fades are created with a long Amp envelope release time.
- Raising the cutoff frequency of Filter 1 (when it is set to one of the Low-Pass types) usually makes a Patch sharper and more cutting. Move the cutoff frequency down (with Low-Pass filters) to create a warmer, fuzzier edge
- Give a bass Patch a defined, percussive attack when you need it to really punch through, by 'layering' it with a ReDrum sound. This trick works if you're not using the Modulation Envelope for anything else. Take a cable from the Mod envelope's Modulation Output on the back of SubTractor to the Gate In of a voice channel in ReDrum. Have a kick drum loaded into that ReDrum channel. Make sure the Mod envelope has all its sliders set to '0'. This will cause the envelope to produce a 'blip' at its Modulation Output, rather than its standard CV curve. Now every time you play a note on SubTractor (whether via a pattern in the Matrix or in the main sequencer), it will trigger the bass drum sound in ReDrum. Tailor the bass drum to suit with ReDrum's channel sound controls.
- For atmospheric pads, try using an LFO set to a slow speed and routed to modulate filter cutoff, for evolving timbral movement on long-held chords.
- Every synth Patch in your track does not need to sound 'big' and impressive, so don't forget you can use single-oscillator Patches. Thinner, smaller sounds usually combine together better and help you avoid a soupy, ill-defined mix. Also contrast small sounds with big ones.
- Add weight to a bass sound with a sine wave. Create a bass sound with just one oscillator. Enable oscillator 2 and set it to a sine wave at the same octave setting or an octave higher than Osc 1. The sine's strong fundamental gives more depth to the sound without making the sound muddy or making it fill more space in the mix (sine waves have no harmonics).
- Syncing LFO movement to song tempo makes the rhythm of the track more compelling.
- For a fatter sound (especially with leads and basses based on sawtooth and square waves), choose the same waveform for both oscillators and detune one by up to +7 cents and the other by up to -7 cents. Slightly detuned sawtooth waves make good analogue string pads, with a little shallow modulation from the LFO routed to Phase. Filter out high frequencies to taste, for analogue-style warmth.
- For flowing, melodic lead lines, set 1-voice Polyphony and use the Legato play parameter, with Portamento set to around 50. Portamento with Legato mode is essential for certain solo lines – for example, if you're playing a solo with a flute-like sound, you probably wouldn't want envelope re-triggering on every note.
- Sounds can be made harder and more up-to-date with a touch of distortion from the Foldback Distortion device. A bit of distortion also helps to give an impression of greater loudness.
- For a modern dance bass sound, aim for a fast attack time, relatively fast release and quite a high filter resonance setting. Bass sounds that use

harmonically rich waveforms will tend to sound louder than those using purer waveforms. Try a fast filter envelope release time with these rich sounds, for extra definition in the attack and a thinner sustain that doesn't clutter the mix.

- When you can't be bothered creating a new sound, layer two or more different (or identical) factory presets using the 'SubTractor Stacking' method explained earlier in this chapter.
- Automate clicking the arrow keys next to the oscillator waveform display to get a sort of wave-sequencing effect as the oscillator waveforms change. This works best with the numbered waveforms.
- To speed up creation of specific types of sound, you could make a set of Patches that include your favourite and most often-used parameter settings, such as modulation assignments and suitable envelopes. Name them carefully, with a number scheme starting '01' – for example, '01 Basic Bass', 02 Basic Pad' and they'll appear at the top of the Browser list when you open the Patch Browser. Don't get too dependent on this kind of approach, though – often you get great sounds by starting from nothing and relying on accident.
- It's good for your programming skills to copy sounds from other synths. If you have an analogue synth, make patches on it and try to copy them using SubTractor. If not, you should be able to find lots of synth samples from various sources (see the NN19 chapter for some ideas). Load a synth sample into NN19 and use it to compare with your SubTractor efforts.

Basic Patches.

The ReDrum drum computer

The ReDrum drum computer offers the familiar programming interface of classic drum machines but with the sonic open-endedness that only a software beatbox can offer. Essentially uncomplicated in operation, it is nevertheless capable of producing results of great sophistication. It will provide the rhythmic backbone to your compositions if you choose to program your own drum parts, and can also be used to augment tracks built around sampled rhythm loops.

ReDrum is one of the three Reason devices that uses samples as its sonic raw material, and though this might at first seem restrictive, in fact it's one of the keys to this device's flexibility: any sound, whether percussive in nature or not, can be brought into ReDrum as a voice. You do not have to rely on the samples and kits provided with Reason: any AIFF or WAV sample, sample in a SoundFont or slice within a REX file, from any source, can be imported into ReDrum, which also opens up the possibility of using it with non-drum samples and with loops.

ReDrum basics

ReDrum is capable of playing 10 samples at one time. Kits of 10 samples – Patches – may be loaded 'all in one go' into its 10 voice channels, or you can instead load individual samples one at a time into each channel. You can edit kits by replacing individual samples in them, and ReDrum provides a range of editing facilities for changing the sound of kits.

Patterns of up to 64 steps can be programmed for ReDrum, using its built-in Pattern facilities. Patterns can then be chained in the desired order, as on a traditional hardware drum machine. Alternatively, play drum parts into the main sequencer, using ReDrum as a drum sound module. You're quite free to use more than one ReDrum device in a Song, if you're that much of a rhythm-programming virtuoso!

Creating a ReDrum device when there is already a ReMix mixer in the rack automatically links the ReDrum main stereo output to a channel of the mixer, so that you can hear ReDrum play. ReDrum's effect send system is also automatically linked to that of the mixer, so that you can use two of the effects assigned to the mixer on individual ReDrum voices. However, because ReDrum has individual audio outputs on its rear panel (like all the best drum machines!), you can also send any or all ReDrum voices to their own channel on a ReMix mixer, for more sophisticated effects and EQ treatment.

Other facilities on the ReDrum's rear panel take it far beyond the powers of real-world drum machines: the CV and Gate system offers numerous modulation and control possibilities. Add to this the fact that the movements of every control on ReDrum can be automated and you can see that rhythm programming need never be the same again for Reason users.

On your MIDI keyboard, MIDI notes 35–44 (the 10 chromatic notes upwards from bottom C on a 61-note keyboard) are permanently assigned to triggering ReDrum's 10 drum sound channels (note 35 to channel 1, 36 to channel 2, and so on). You can audition sounds from your keyboard, or by clicking the Sample Audition button in each channel, or via the Sample Browser window – more details later in this chapter.

Info

Keyboard Shortcuts

Apple/Control-B	Browse Patches
Apple/Control-X	Cut Pattern
Apple/Control-C	Copy Pattern
Apple/Control-V	Paste Pattern
Apple/Control-J	Shift Pattern Left
Apple/Control-K	Shift Pattern Right
Apple/Control-R	Randomise Pattern
Apple/Control-T	Alter Pattern
Shift-Click on Pattern Step Button	Enter 'Hard' dynamic value
Alt-Click on Pattern Step Button	Enter 'Soft' dynamic value
Apple/Control-click any control	Restores default value
Shift-click-hold on control	Access fine adjustment
MIDI keyboard notes C2-E3	Real-time drum sound muting
MIDI keyboard notes C4-E5	Real-time drum sound soloing

Get going with ReDrum

Load a kit (Patch)

Follow the usual procedure for loading Reason Patches, as outlined in Chapter 4, Basic Operations and Features.

Trigger some sounds

- Click on the audition button (the one with the arrow) at the top of channel 1. The sample assigned to that channel will sound once.
- Alternatively, go to the sequencer and make sure the MIDI plug icon is showing by the ReDrum sequencer track. (Click under the 'In' column if not).

- Press any key on your MIDI keyboard between C1 and the 'A' above that. The sounds in the kit will be triggered by the keys.

Actually programming drum Patterns will be discussed a little later in this chapter, after the parts of ReDrum, and what they do, are explained.

Guided tour

The ReDrum panel is divided into three main areas: the Patch Select area, the Drum Sound Channel area, and the Pattern Programming area.

The Patch load/save area

This is where Patches (drum kits) saved to your hard drive can be accessed (click on the folder icon) and saving operations initiated (click on the floppy-disk icon).

Patch select

Note the 'Channel 8&9 exclusive' button. When this is engaged, the sounds assigned to drum channels 8 and 9 (usually open and closed hi-hats) will never sound at the same time. This feature is recommended if you are programming a drum Pattern that is meant to sound realistic, as a human drummer could not physically hit an open hi-hat at the same time as a closed one (unless he or she had two hi-hats!). Using this button also creates the characteristic sound of an open hi-hat being 'choked' as it is quickly closed during the course of a Pattern.

The drum sound channels

The 10 channels in this area each correspond to an individual drum voice. Each channel features a sample-browser button with a folder icon (clicking on this button opens up the Sample Browser window) and sample-name display near the top. Not all channels have the same set of controls: all controls that are common to the 10 channels are explained first, then the special controls which differ between channels.

Drum sound channels

Common channel controls

Controls
common to all
channels.

Mute

Clicking the mute button for a drum channel prevents it from sounding.

Solo

Clicking the channel's solo button silences all other drum voices and leaves the solo'd one playing in isolation. You can use Mute and Solo for real-time drum mixing, bringing individual drums in and out of a Pattern as required. Real-time mutes and solos can be automated by recording their changes into the sequencer. (Mute and Solo can also be accessed from a MIDI keyboard; see the keyboard shortcuts at the start of this chapter.)

Sample Audition

Clicking the sample-audition button,which has an arrow icon, allows you to hear the channel's drum voice played without having to press a key on your MIDI keyboard (or, indeed, even have one attached).

Effect send knobs

S1 (Send 1) & S2 (Send 2) knobs control the level of signal sent from a drum voice channel to one or two effects processors; turning the knob pointer to the right increases the amount of effect – adding, for example, more reverb. The send knobs are normally used to let ReDrum access effects that are already connected to the mixer in the rack. As we'll discover when we look at ReDrum's rear panel, it has two 'Send Out' sockets (one each for S1 and S2). When you add a ReDrum module to a rack that already contains a ReMix mixer, these two sockets are automatically linked to two of the mixer's rear-panel 'Chaining Aux Send In' sockets. This allows ReDrum's two effect sends to feed the two effects connected to the mixer's first two effects send/return loops, as if ReDrum's sends were an extension of the mixer's send system. Each of ReDrum's 10 drum channels can thus have individual send levels to two effects.

Normally, if you wanted to process individual drum sounds with their own effects and levels, rather than applying the same ones globally to the ReDrum stereo mix, you would have to send those sounds, via individual outputs on the drum machine, to channels on your mixer, for processing there. This can certainly be done with ReDrum voices (again, see the section on rear-panel connections). However, if you're generally satisfied with the mix of sound being produced by ReDrum, but would just like to add a little reverb to the snare or a little delay to the hi-hats, say, you can do it conveniently from within ReDrum.

Pan Control

The Pan (Panoramic) pot sets the position of the individual voice in the stereo mix produced by the ReDrum module. Its purpose is to allow you to set up a good 'spread' of sounds from left to right in the stereo image. You can also use the Pan control to create special effects – for example, making one sound appear only in the left-hand speaker while the others play through the right, or (by using automation – see the automation chapter) make a hi-hat sound flip between left and right speakers.

Tip

Drum kit panning

Panning the individual instruments within a kit makes the sound picture more interesting and can also contribute to realism, if that's what you're going for. One good way is to visualise where a drummer's drums are situated in front of him or her. The bass drum is usually in the centre, so pan it accordingly. The snare is usually slightly offset, left or right, from the bass drum, so reflect this with pan position. Whatever side the snare is, the hi-hat will be a little further over from it on the same side. If a kit has one cymbal, try panning it opposite to the hi-hat. If there's more than one cymbal, pan one in the same, or slightly further in the same direction, as the hi-hat, and the other exactly opposite; pan any extra cymbals between those with the most extreme pan positions. Don't go over the top with extremely spaced-out panning, or the result will cease to be realistic.

Info

Mono or stereo?

ReDrum channels will load both mono and stereo samples. If the sample loaded into a channel is stereo, the LED between the two Send knobs lights up.

In the case of stereo samples, the Pan pot acts as a control to balance the left and right components of the sample.

Level and Velocity controls

The Level control alters the volume of the individual drum sound in the ReDrum mix, while the Velocity knob determines how a drum sound is affected by velocity information – whether generated by an external MIDI source or one of ReDrum's own Step programming buttons (which, as we'll soon learn, can transmit one of three levels of velocity).

If the Velocity knob is set to 12 o'clock – its accompanying 'LED' will be unlit – a sound's level is fixed to that set by the Level knob, and won't change at all in response to velocity. Move the Velocity knob to the right, and higher velocity levels will cause the drum sound to play louder, while lower velocities will produce a quieter sound. Moving the knob to the left reverses this relationship, so that high velocities produce quiet sounds and low velocities produce louder sounds.

The knob, in effect, is a velocity 'sensitivity' control: when it is in its central position, the sound is completely insensitive to velocity information. Turning it in either direction sets varying degrees of velocity sensitivity, according to the scheme explained above, and also makes the LED light up, so that you know that the sound is responding to velocity.

Obviously, there are occasions when you would not want a sample to have a velocity response – for example, if you're triggering loops or non-percussive samples with ReDrum, or (for authenticity) programming with samples of a drum machine that is not velocity sensitive. However, in general, varying velocities is an excellent way of introducing more expression and dynamism into a drum Pattern. Human drummers, after all, rarely hit a drum twice with exactly the same degree of force (and consequent volume). Even if you're not looking for realism in your programming, something like varying the velocities of alternate hits in a 16th-note hi-hat Pattern – for example, soft/medium, soft/medium – and so on, adds noticeable extra light and shade and helps avoid monotony.

Length knob

The length knob simply determines for how long a sample assigned to a sound channel will play. If you had loaded a sample with a long decay that should ideally be curtailed, for example, this would be the knob to use to temporarily 'edit' it, by turning to the left.

Decay/Gate switch

How the Length knob does its job depends on the position of the Decay/Gate switch. If this switch is in the 'down' position – Decay mode – a sound will decay naturally within its length as set by the Length knob. So you would get a shorter sound, but one with a natural sounding decay. With the switch in its 'up' position – Gate mode, with the 'square' graphic – the sound will play for the time set by the Length knob and then cut off dead, without a natural decay.

The Decay/Gate switch also affects how a drum voice plays when triggered from a MIDI keyboard (perhaps to be recorded into the main sequencer). If Decay mode is engaged, the sound will play for its set length no matter how long the keyboard key is held – even if the key is only briefly depressed. In Gated mode, the sound will play for only as long as the key is held down, or until its end point as set by the Length knob, whichever is the sooner.

Decay mode makes ReDrum sounds behave more as they would on a traditional drum machine (or as if played by a human drummer), where the entire sound is triggered every time, while Gate mode is perhaps more suited to working with non-percussive samples, or creating special effects. If you're using ReDrum to play back sound effects and rhythmic loops, the Gate option provides a little more control over how those samples will play back.

Bear in mind that if a sample loaded into ReDrum actually contains a loop point (causing it to play over and over when a note triggering the sample is held), setting the Length knob to maximum causes the sound to play continuously, even if you stop ReDrum's playback. This won't be a desirable effect in most cases, so just turn the Length knob back until the loop plays for as long as required.

Gate mode could be used with percussion samples to re-create the '80s gated drum effect, where the natural decay of a sound is cut off abruptly before it has finished playing, creating a tight, aggressive result.

There is an issue you may need to be aware of with the Decay/Gate switch when you use the 'Copy Pattern to Track' feature, but that will be covered later in this chapter.

The Select button
Clicking on a Select button chooses that channel's drum sound as the one which will be programmed by the 16 Step buttons below, during the process of Pattern creation. The Select buttons light when clicked, to show when a channel is activated for programming. Only one channel Select button at a time can be lit.

Special channel controls
The remaining ReDrum controls differ according to drum sound channel. This is probably because Propellerhead have in mind a scheme for mapping sounds to specific channels. When you open a drum kit from the factory bank, the drum sounds within it are automatically placed into channels 1-10. If the kit is a conventional rock-type kit, the bass drum is invariably assigned to channel 1, with the snare drum occupying channel 2. The toms map to channels 6 and 7, and the cymbal comes in on channel 10. Different editing parameters to suit these sounds have been provided on the respective channels.

Pitch knob
Eight of the 10 sound channels have a simple Pitch control knob, allowing a sample to be shifted in pitch by up to an octave in either direction. This is useful for drum tuning, special effects, or quickly matching the tempo or pitch of looped samples, if required. The exceptions are channels 6 and 7, which have a different control-set for pitch.

The pitch knob.

Channel 6 and 7 pitch controls
These channels offer four-knob control over pitch-bend effects. With these knobs set appropriately, sounds loaded into channels 6 and 7 will be 'bent' in pitch when triggered. If you don't want this to happen, just set the knobs to zero.

- *Bend:* The direction (up or down) and amount of pitch-bend is set by the Bend knob – left for a upward bend, right for an downward bend.
- *Pitch:* The ultimate pitch of a 'bent' note is set by the Pitch knob. This knob can also simply set the central pitch of the channel sample, as in the other channels, without any bending.
- *Rate:* The speed of a bend (how fast it goes from one extreme to another) is determined by the Rate knob.
- *Vel (Velocity):* This knob is associated with the Pitch knob and works in a similar way to the main velocity control discussed earlier, making the pitch-bend effects possible with channel 6 and 7 either sensitive or insensitive to velocity information (coming from a keyboard or programmed into a drum Pattern). With the knob in the 12 o'clock position, the pitch-bend effect won't change no matter how high the sound's velocity. Turning the knob to the right causes velocity to bend the sound down to the central pitch, while turning it right creates an upward bend; the actual amount of bend – the distance away from the central pitch that the bend starts – is determined by the velocity level. Higher velocity equals a bend that starts further away from the central pitch and is thus more extreme.

Channel 6 and 7 pitch controls

Tip

Easy pseudo-ethnic percussion effects

- Load House Kit 02 from the factory sound set, or load a couple of congas or something similar into ReDrum channels 6 and 7.
- Turn the pitch-bend Rate knob on channel 6 and 7 fully to the right or fully to the left, so no pitch-bend is applied to the sound. It simply plays back at the starting pitch of what would normally be the bend and doesn't swoop up or down.
- Now set some velocity sensitivity for the channels, by turning their 'Vel' knobs a little to the left or right. Both sound good, but

they create different effects. The sound will be best if you tune the congas down a bit, by turning the Pitch knobs to the left. If you do this, turn the Vel knobs right. If the sounds are tuned up (Pitch knob right), turn the Vel knobs left.
- Now program simple, complementary drum parts with varying velocities (use all three levels) for both channels. Try the following. (H=hard, M=Medium, S=Soft). Channel 6: Pad 1H , 4M, 7H, 9M, 12H, 15M. Channel 7: Pad 2M, 3S, 5S, 6M, 8M, 10S, 11M,

13M, 14S, 16M. You could alternatively program parts from the keyboard into the sequencer – then you can get a wider range of velocities into the part.
- Play the Pattern back. What happens is that a different drum pitch is produced by each velocity level. This sounds great with low-pitched Latin or ethnic-type percussion sounds.
- Turn the Bend knob in each channel slightly to the left and a swoop effect is created on each hit. This is great for simulating Talking Drums, tribal drums and Tabla effects.

These pitch-bend parameters can be used to create subtle or extreme swooping effects. However, they've probably been assigned to sound channels that favour tom sounds because the effect allows the natural bends that are appropriate to standard and roto toms to be created, as well as facilitating '70s/'80s disco 'syn tom' sounds. Velocity-controlled bends can be used to emulate tabla-like percussion, too.

Sample Start Offset Controls
The final pair of knobs in ReDrum sound channels 3-5 and 8-9 govern a velocity-controllable sample-start offset option.

- *Start:* This knob alters the start point of samples, in the same way that their end point can be altered by the Length knob. For example, a sample with an aggressive attack portion can be transformed into a different sound entirely by moving its start point past the aggressive attack, using the Start knob. Turn the knob clockwise to move the start point further into the sample and cut off more of its front portion.

- *Vel:* The Velocity knob applies a negative or positive offset to the effect according to velocity, so that playing a sound with a lower or higher velocity causes the start point to change dynamically. This effect, used even subtly, is very good for adding sonic diversity to a drum Pattern. The two knobs can also be used to enhance the realism and interest of your drum programming, perhaps to cause the main attack of a sound to be heard only when it's being 'hit' the hardest (ie. has a high velocity value).

Sample start offset

Tone Controls

Channels 1–2 and 10 each have a pair of knobs dedicated to tone control.

- *Tone:* Makes a sound more or less bright, by boosting or cutting high-frequency content. Turning the knob right makes the sound brighter, while turning it left makes it duller.
- *Vel:* The strength of this effect can be changed under velocity control, courtesy of the 'Vel' knob. By adjusting both parameters, you can cause a sound to become brighter in response to higher velocities, as a real drum would, or duller in response to lower velocities. Again, this is a useful aid in programming diverse and involving drum Patterns. Note that if your computer tends to struggle with Reason Song playback, avoiding using these features saves processing power.

Tone controls for channels 1–2 and 10

The Pattern Programming area

This is the business end of ReDrum, where you can create drum Patterns in 'step time' with the kits you've loaded.

Pattern Programming area.

Step Buttons

The 16 buttons running along the bottom of the ReDrum panel are the crucial section of the Pattern area. Each Step button corresponds to a step in the drum Pattern. You program a part separately for each drum sound you want in your Pattern, as follows:

- Choose a drum voice channel by clicking on its Select button.
- Click on the desired Step buttons, to light them and assign the drum voice on the selected channel to those steps in the Pattern.
- After an individual drum part (say, a bass drum) has been programmed, click on another channel's Select button to change to programming that drum's part with the Step buttons. Find more detail in the Tutorial elsewhere in this chapter.

In this way, a complete Pattern can be built up in single-drum passes.

Dynamic Switch.

Flam switch/value knob

Programming via the Step buttons can be done either while the Pattern is stopped or when it's playing back. Obviously, the advantage of entering drum hits during playback is that you can hear immediately how well they work in the Pattern. You'll notice that LEDs above the Step buttons light rapidly as the Pattern plays back, visually marking off its steps.

Cancelling steps and clearing Patterns

Any incorrect steps can be cancelled simply by clicking on the Step button again. An entire selected Pattern can be cleared from ReDrum by using 'Clear Pattern' in the Edit menu. You can also completely 'initialise' a ReDrum, by choosing 'Initialize Patch' from the Edit menu or a device context menu. This clears all samples and sets controls to their default values.

Dynamic Switch

One of three levels of velocity (approximating how hard the drum has been 'hit') can be assigned to a pad via the three-way Dynamic switch. Simply choose Soft, Medium or Hard with the switch before you click on the required Step button.

You can tell at a glance which velocity has been assigned to a Step button by its colour when lit: the darker the colour, the higher the velocity. If a step has already been programmed, you can still change its velocity, by choosing the dynamic value you want, then clicking on the Step button again.

Flam Switch and Value Knob

A flam is an expression or accent effect used by drummers, whereby the stick is allowed to bounce after a hit, causing two hits to sound in rapid succession.

You can program flams in ReDrum by engaging the Flam switch before programming a given step with the Step buttons, and setting the desired time between the two drum hits with the Flam value knob. It's easy to see which steps in a Pattern have been 'flammed', as the LEDs above them stay fully lit. Flams can also be entered manually for each step of a drum voice, by clicking the LED above each step; this turns the flam on or off for each step.

Steps Display and Edit Steps Switch

The Steps display sets how long a ReDrum Pattern will be, between one and 64 steps. The required number of steps is set by the up/down arrows next to the Steps numeric display. Even after you've programmed a Pattern with a given number of steps, you can set a different number of steps for the Pattern. Adding steps will result in silent steps playing at the end of the Pattern, while taking them away will result in the Pattern being cut off short, with the final steps not playing. The steps are still there if you do this, though, and will play back as before if you change the step number back to what it was.

Obviously, there are only 16 Step buttons for programming, so we need some way to make those 16 buttons program as many as 64 steps. This is where the Edit Steps switch comes in.

Steps display/edit steps switch

Program your first bank of 16 steps with the switch set to 1-16, then flip it to 17-32 for the next 16, 33-48 for the next 16, and so on. Being able to access a Pattern of up to 64 steps allows you to create an entire 4/4 bar with 64th-note resolution in one Pattern; some hardware drum machines would require you to chain two or more Patterns to create a similar effect.

Resolution Knob

When you create a ReDrum device from scratch, its 16 Step buttons default to generating events that are a 16th-note long – or enough 16th-notes to fill one bar in a 4/4 time signature. It's simple to change this note resolution with the Resolution knob, which provides nine values between a 128th note (very short indeed) and a half note (equivalent to eight 16th notes), including two 'triplet' values (where three notes play in the time that would normally be occupied by two). 1/8T divides each quarter note into three and gives a jazz/blues feel, while 1/16T divides each eighth note into three. The latter is useful for some contemporary dance styles. A Pattern written with 128th-note resolution will speed by eight times faster than one written with 16th notes.

Resolution knob

The resolution setting is global for a whole Pattern: if you need 32nd notes to write one drum part, then every other part in the ReDrum Pattern will also have to be written with 32nd notes, so give some thought to what note value is most appropriate for the Pattern you want to program before starting to program it. Though you can create longer note values by using smaller note values as building blocks, you cannot make smaller notes out of longer ones – the building blocks can't be split, so the resolution you choose should be that of the shortest note values the Pattern will require.

Bank and Pattern buttons

As we mentioned earlier, ReDrum Patterns can be up to 64 steps long. Not a bad length – but there's much more to come, because up to 32 separate Patterns per Song can be programmed and swapped between with the numbered/lettered Pattern buttons. Four Pattern banks (A-D) are accessed with the lettered Bank buttons:

Bank buttons

There are eight Patterns in each bank, accessed by the numbered Pattern buttons: Patterns are thus named A1, A2, A3 and so on, up to D8.

Pattern buttons

To select a new Pattern 'slot', simply choose a bank with one of the four lettered buttons and a Pattern slot inside that bank with one of the eight numbered buttons. Patterns can be selected manually, 'on the fly', with these buttons as ReDrum plays, allowing you to swap between them to hear different sequences of Patterns.

This manual Pattern selection can be automated in the main sequencer, by recording changes as you make them in real time. Computer keyboard keys or MIDI messages can be assigned to select Banks and Patterns, making this process even easier. (See the automation/remote control chapter.) Pattern changes may also be automated by drawing them directly into the sequencer. (See the sequencer chapter.) Complex chains of Patterns can thus be built up for a whole Song.

Above the numbered Pattern buttons is yet another button labelled 'Pattern'. This is the Pattern Mute switch, which mutes or unmutes ReDrum's audio output without interrupting actual Pattern playback. You can automate switching this button on and off to create Pattern breaks when making a drum track.

Enable Pattern Section

Enable Pattern Section

This button is usually lit, but if you disengage it (by clicking on it) all Pattern playback is disabled (as opposed to muted) and ReDrum may be used as a drum sound module, to be accessed by Reason's main sequencer or an external sequencer.

Shuffle switch

Shuffle switch

Engages the Shuffle parameter, which automatically adds a syncopated, 'triplet' feel, often referred to as 'swing', to the Pattern. The amount of Shuffle added is controlled by the value of the Pattern Shuffle knob at the far right of the Transport bar. If you find yourself tweaking the Transport Pattern Shuffle knob and not hearing any results, you probably haven't clicked the Shuffle switch in ReDrum to actually indicate that you want Shuffle to be applied to your Pattern.

Run button

Run button

To start ReDrum playing independently of any other devices you may have in the rack, just click its Run button. Clicking Run again stops playback. If you want to hear all your rack devices, including ReDrum, playing back together, use the Play button in the Transport bar, and any devices that are not muted will sound.

Using ReDrum

Changing Kits and Creating Custom Kits

The Reason factory ReFill includes a variety of kits in different styles. They are loaded into ReDrum using the patch-selection method common to all the sound-making devices, which is outlined in Chapter 4. Loading a new kit replaces any kit already present.

But aside from loading entire new kits, you can also create custom kits, where the kit is built up from individual samples of your choice. When a ReDrum device is created, it is empty. To load individual sounds:

- Click on the folder icon at the top right of one of the drum channels. This brings up the Sample Browser window.
- Use the magnifying glass icon to find the factory ReFill and then open any folder that has samples in it which you would like to try as ReDrum sounds.
- Double-click on the desired sample to load it into the selected drum channel.
- You can also click on the sample-name display in each channel. If no samples have yet been loaded into ReDrum, this will give you the option to 'Open (sample) Browser'. If a sample is already loaded into the channel, you should see a list of alternative samples to choose from.

> **Tip**
>
> **Autoplay Auditioning**
>
> Don't forget that there's a handy 'Autoplay' audition feature in the Sample Browser window, making it easy to choose between samples without first having to load them into ReDrum. Tick the 'Autoplay' check box, and thereafter simply highlighting a file name in the file list causes it to play. If you have a big list to check out, scroll through it with the up/down arrow keys on your computer keyboard, for rapid, mouse-free auditioning.

Even factory samples intended for use with the samplers can be loaded if you think you have a use for them. However, if you would like to stick with drums for the moment, the ReDrum Drum Kits folder contains a folder full of single drum-hit samples called Xclusive Sounds – Sorted. Here you'll find folders full of bass and snare drums, claps, hi-hats and other percussion.

It's also worth remembering that individual slices from within ReCycled REX files (which would normally be loaded into the Dr:Rex device) can also be loaded into a ReDrum voice slot. Drum loops are ideal material for turning into REX loops, and individual slices are quite likely to be discrete drum hits – perfect for ReDrum. The process allows you to easily isolate hits from any loop, so great drum sounds could be assembled from a number of sources, to create the kit of your dreams and create new patterns with the ReDrum traditional drum machine programming method. Load the slices by navigating to your REX loop folder via the Sample Browser in each ReDrum channel, and double clicking on a REX loop. The loop then 'opens' as though it is a folder, and you can double-click on one slice to load into the channel. This option isn't available on pre-V2 Reason.

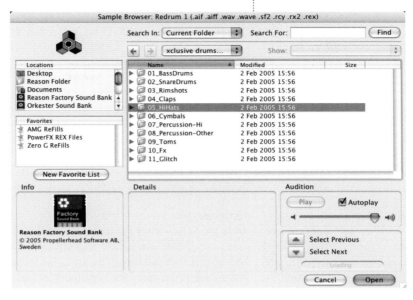

Load individual samples into drum channels with the Sample Browser.

In future you might find that although you're happy with most of the sounds in a given kit, the snare is all wrong, or perhaps you need a tambourine and your chosen kit doesn't have one. To replace one sound in a kit with a preferred alternative, just follow the procedure outlined above for loading individual sounds, afterwards saving the new kit under a new name.

Using 'Remove Sample', from the Edit menu, takes any loaded sample out of the selected channel, but you probably will rarely want to do this, as loading a new sample into a channel replaces the old one anyway. However, you may want to use 'Remove Sample' if you're 'Publishing' a Reason Song for posting on one of the Reason web sites. If you've only used four out of 10 sounds in a ReDrum kit, clearing the unused ones should help to reduce the file size.

Saving Kits
If you've created a kit you like, or have made edits to the sounds in a factory set, you can save it as a Patch. Find the procedure for saving in Chapter 4, Basic Operations and Features.

Saving Patterns
Patterns are not saved separately in ReDrum, but as part of a Song. Even if the Pattern is the only thing in the Song, the only way to save it is as a Song. Choose 'Save As' from the file menu.

Copying Patterns
Patterns may be copied between different Pattern memory slots, perhaps to speed up the process of creating 'variation' drum parts. Select the Pattern to be copied (by clicking on the required Bank and Pattern buttons – for example, A3); choose Copy from the Edit menu, or use Apple/Control-C; select a Pattern slot in which to copy the Pattern, by clicking the required destination Bank and Pattern buttons (for example, B1); Paste the Pattern into the new slot by using the Paste command from the Edit menu or Apple/Control V.

Info

Tempo

There's no tempo control in ReDrum, as the tempo for ReDrum Patterns is set in the Transport bar. Whatever tempo is set there applies to the whole Song.

You can copy Patterns between Songs by using the procedure above. Have the source and destination Songs both open, and copy and paste between them.

Bringing your own samples into ReDrum

It's very easy to import your own WAV or AIFF samples into ReDrum. You can also import SoundFonts and REX loop slices since Reason V2. The sample files should be saved in a folder on your hard drive. Follow the procedure given earlier for loading individual drum sounds, but navigate to this folder from within the Sample Browser. Double-click on the desired sample to load it into ReDrum. There appears to be no limit (other than computer RAM) on the length of samples to be loaded into ReDrum.

Pattern manipulation facilities in the Edit menu

Once a Pattern has been created, there are a number of ways of creating variations on it, that require you to simply make a selection from the Edit menu. These options may help you get out of a creative rut by suggesting new rhythmic possibilities, or by producing drum parts and Patterns that you would not otherwise have thought of. Note that keyboard shortcuts, listed at the beginning of this chapter, are available for the Pattern-level operations below.

Edit menu Pattern manipulation operations.

Shift Pattern Left and Shift Pattern Right

First of all, it's possible to shift an entire Pattern left or right by one step at a time. If, for example, you shift the Pattern one step to the right, a bass drum event that was previously on step one will now sound on step two. The final step in the Pattern, if active, would rotate around to step one.

Shift Drum Left and Shift Drum Right

Individual drum parts within a Pattern can also be shifted left or right, one step at a time. The drum part to be shifted is chosen by pressing its channel 'Select' button. Shifting the parts played by individual drum voices within a Pattern is a particularly good (and easy) way to add variation.

Randomise Pattern

Choosing 'Randomise' from the Edit menu causes Pattern steps to be automatically programmed for all drum voices. Randomise Pattern can thus be used even where no Pattern has yet been programmed. You will probably want to load a drum kit, though the process still works without a kit loaded.

As one might expect, the results are truly random, and can be rather chaotic. However, random Patterns can be rather compelling, and unusual or interesting Patterns often appear out of the randomness – just keep repeating the operation (no need to Undo in between repeats) until you hear something you like. If you're not a natural drum programmer, it's a useful feature. Practioners of jungle, drum and bass, and other contemporary dance styles, especially, could find inspiration here.

You might also glean something usable from a Randomised Pattern by muting some of its parts (use the 'M' mute buttons at the top of drum channels), leaving the more successful ones playing. Don't forget, also, that you can modify parts of a Randomised Pattern if you like only some of it. (Also consider randomised Patterns if you're using ReDrum's Gate Outputs to affect parameters on other devices, as explained later in this chapter.)

Randomise Drum

Randomise can be applied to individual drum parts as well as whole Patterns. Click a channel's 'Select' button, then activate the randomising process.

Alter Pattern

For slightly less chaotic variations than those provided by the Randomise function, select the required Pattern and choose Alter Pattern from the Edit menu. This process works on data that has already been written into the Pattern beforehand; unlike Randomise, Alter doesn't create data when applied. It rather modifies the current Pattern by re-ordering the notes in each drum part. No new events, dynamics or flams are added: the notes that are already in each part, with their dynamic and flam assignments intact, are simply reorganised. Altered Patterns are nearly as unpredictable as ones produced by the Randomise function, but are seldom as wackily busy!

Alter Pattern, like Alter Drum, below, is destructive of the Pattern it works on, so if you want to keep the unchanged original Pattern, copy it into another Pattern slot first, using the method described earlier.

Alter Drum

This process does the same as Alter Pattern, but for only the currently selected drum voice. As with Alter Pattern, an Altered Drum part has the same number of hits as the original part, placed in a different order.

Tutorial

Programming a drum Pattern with ReDrum

The basic procedure for programming a drum Pattern is straightforward. There's an example Pattern in the steps that follow, which you can input to play around with, but if you're already used to drum programming, of course you don't have to use it. Just program your own parts, following the operational instructions. Start with an empty rack, as described in Chapter 3, and create a mixer, then a ReDrum.

1 Select a Kit

- Load a drumkit, as described in Chapter 4. If you would like to follow our tutorial example, use DubLab BrushKit1 from the Brush Kits folder in the ReDrum Drum Kits folder (factory ReFill).

2 Set Pattern length and resolution

- Set the number of steps you would like in the Pattern by clicking on the arrows beside the Steps numeric display, or dragging in the display.
- Now choose the required note resolution with the resolution knob. If you are following our example Pattern, set Pattern length to 16 and resolution to 1/16.

3 Program Pattern 1

- Choose the first drum you want to program by clicking on the Select switch of its drum channel, to light the switch.

Info

Automating ReDrum controls

Every knob and switch on ReDrum, as with all the Reason devices, can have its movements recorded into the Reason sequencer for automation purposes or controlled remotely via the Remote system. This makes real-time sound-tweaking very easy and immediate to reproduce. As your drum Pattern plays back, you can move the pan control from left to right for auto-panning, tweak the tone controls for 'tone-sweeping', and introduce pitch effects by spontaneously altering pitch parameters. Even the simplest drum Patterns can be transformed into something far more complex and involving in this way.

You can see from the Keyboard Shortcuts at the start of the chapter that drums can also be muted and solo'd in real time using certain MIDI keyboard keys. Not only is this a good tool for live performance (on-the-fly drum mixing), the mutes and solos can also be recorded into the sequencer, like any other control movements, for the production of spontaneous drum mixes. See the automation/remote control chapter for details of recording automation. Automation recording is also covered in a more basic fashion in the Pattern programming tutorial elsewhere in this chapter.

Choose Pattern slot A1 for the first Pattern.

- Select a Pattern 'slot' by clicking on the A bank button and the '1' Pattern button, if this is not already selected.
- For our example, start with the Bass drum channel (channel 1). Program bass drum hits by clicking the Pattern buttons shown in the screen below. Where you see an 'H', set the Dynamic switch to Hard before clicking on the step. An 'M' denotes a Medium Dynamic, and an 'S' a Soft dynamic. You can alternatively (and more conveniently) leave the Dynamic switch in the Medium position, Shift-Click to enter a 'Hard' dynamic value, Alt-Click for a 'Soft' dynamic, and just click as normal for a Medium.

Pattern 1, Bass drum part.

- When the bass drum has been programmed, switch to programming the Snare, by clicking on the channel 2 Select switch and entering the hits shown below.

Pattern 1, Snare part.

- Repeat the procedure for the open hi-hat part (channel 8).

Pattern 1, Open Hi-hat part.

- Click the Run button to hear the Pattern and check that it sounds right. Click Run again to stop playback.

4 Save the Song

- Now it's a good idea to save the Song, if you haven't already. As you may have read, this is the only way you can save the drum Pattern. Choose 'Save As' from the File menu and give the Song a suitable name (something like 'Fast Guide Drum Demo', perhaps) in the file-saving dialogue, and navigate to the folder that you would like to save the Song in, or create a new folder.

5 Program Pattern 2

You wouldn't normally hear the same drum Pattern all the way through a track, so our example doesn't stay the same either. Having two Patterns will also allow you to get some practice in switching between Patterns on the fly, and also in 'chaining' them together in the main sequencer. If you're not following our example Pattern, program a second one of your own, using the instructions below. You might like to base the second Pattern on the first, by copying the first Pattern into a new Pattern 'slot', using the method described earlier in this chapter, and then modifying it.

- If you're following our example Pattern, you'll need to modify the factory kit, by replacing two of its individual sounds with ones from Reason's drum sample collection. First, we'll load the two new sounds into the current kit. Since the sounds assigned to channel 3 and channel 4 in this particular kit are not needed for the Pattern, we'll use their channels for the new sounds.
- Click on the 'Browse Sample' button (with folder icon) near the top of channel 3. From the Sample Browser window that appears, click the 'Find All ReFills' magnifying glass icon from the top right and choose the Reason Factory Sound Bank. Go ReDrum Drum Kits > Xclusive Drums – Sorted > 04 Claps > Clp-xtc7.wav. Double-click on the file name to load the handclap into channel 3 of ReDrum.
- Now click on the 'Browse Sample' button of channel 4. Go Xclusive Drums – Sorted > 07 Percussion – Hi> Tmb-xtc6.wav. Load the tambourine into channel 4.
- With Pattern A1 still selected in ReDrum, use Apple/Control-C to copy the Pattern.
- Click on the Pattern Selection button numbered 2, to select Pattern 'slot' A2. The button lights to show the Pattern is now in use. Use Apple/Control-V to Paste Pattern A1, which you've just copied, into slot A2.
- Input extra drum parts in the copied Pattern. First choose channel 3 by clicking on its Select button and input the following handclap hits.

Pattern 2, Handclaps part

- Now choose channel 4 and input the following tambourine hits.

Tambourine part

- Click 'Run' to check that the Pattern plays back and sounds right. Stop playback.

6 Switch between the Patterns

If all has gone well so far, you should now have a 16-step Pattern 1 and a 16-step Pattern 2 with added handclap and tambourine. Now you can try switching between the two while ReDrum plays back.

- Select Pattern 1 with the numbered Pattern selection button and click the Run key to start playback.
- When Pattern 1 has played through once or twice, select Pattern 2 with its key and hear playback switch to that Pattern. With 16-step Pattern, if you select a new Pattern while a Pattern is playing, ReDrum will switch to playing the new Pattern as soon as the current Pattern has played through. With 32-step Patterns, selecting the new Pattern at any time during the second half of the currently-playing Pattern starts the new one after the current one has played through to its end.

Incidentally, a tempo of 100bpm, which you set in the Transport bar, suits the example Patterns, which are adapted from the PC Publishing drum machine programming book Beat It! by Joe and Pauly Ortiz of Heavenly Media Productions.

7 'Chain' the Patterns in the sequencer

Now we need some way of making the Pattern changes permanent, so we're going to create a chain of Pattern changes, on the fly, as ReDrum plays, by recording the changes into the sequencer.

The ReDrum track in the main sequencer ready for recording.

- Find the ReDrum track in the main sequencer. This will have been created automatically when you created the ReDrum device. If, for some reason, you've deleted the ReDrum sequencer track, Create another.
- Click in the 'In' column by the ReDrum name in the track list, to make a MIDI plug icon appear, signifying that the track is ready for recording data.
- Ensure that the first Pattern you would like to appear in your chain (for our example, Pattern A1) is selected in ReDrum.
- Click the red Record button in the transport bar, then the Play button. Alternatively, use Apple/Control-Return, then the Space bar. You'll hear Pattern A1 playing. Allow it to play for as many repetitions as desired. If you're working with our example, let it play through twice.
- Towards the end of the second repetition, click on Pattern A2's Pattern Select button. When Pattern 1 has finished playing, Pattern 2 will start to play, and the change of Pattern will have been recorded into the sequencer track.

The automated Pattern keys.

- Repeat the last step, but select Pattern 1 instead of Pattern 2. Change between the two Patterns as many times as you like. When you want to stop, click the Stop button in the transport bar, or hit the Return key, twice, to return to zero. Press Play in the transport or hit the Space bar to hear the Pattern chain play back.

You'll notice that the Pattern keys on the ReDrum panel now have a green box drawn around them. This indicates that the controls in that area have been automated.

You can see the chain of Pattern changes recorded into the sequencer by viewing the Pattern Lane for the ReDrum track, and also edit them there.

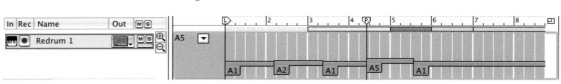

A chain of ReDrum Patterns in the Pattern Lane of the ReDrum track.

Pattern changes for ReDrum can also be programmed into the sequencer without this on-the-fly process, by drawing them directly into a Pattern Lane. See the sequencer chapter for more on drawing and editing Pattern chains.

Using ReDrum as a sound module

ReDrum can easily be used as a drum 'sound module' – you don't have to use its Pattern-programming facilities. Drum parts can be created in the main sequencer using ReDrum sounds, and external software and hardware sequencers can use ReDrum as a 'soft synth'. Below we run through the process for recording a drum part in the sequencer, first without a 'playback loop' set, then with a loop set.

Recording drum parts with the main sequencer

First, you need a kit loaded into ReDrum and a ReDrum track in the main sequencer.

1. Make the ReDrum track ready for MIDI Input

- Click in the 'In' column of the ReDrum track to make the keyboard icon appear.

2. Try triggering ReDrum sounds from your keyboard

- Play a few notes on your keyboard or controller – MIDI notes 35-44 (the 10 chromatic notes upwards from bottom C on a 61-note keyboard) are permanently assigned to triggering ReDrum's 10 drum sound channels. Any note outside this range won't make a sound.
- If you're using a MIDI drum controller, you'll have to use the controller's own editing facilities to assign the note numbers given above to your pads, since the note assignments can't be modified inside ReDrum.

3. Set up to record the drum part

When you're confident that the ReDrum sounds are triggering correctly, it's time to record a part. The full sequencing process is described elsewhere in the book, but here are the basics to allow you to record some drums.

- First, set the required tempo and time signature in the Transport bar.
- Decide if you need a click to play along with; if so, enable the Click button in the Transport and adjust the volume to suit with the Level knob. You can, of course, play along with a Dr:rex or NN19 loop, or a Reason Song, instead.
- Click on the 'Quantise Notes During Recording' button in the Toolbar at the top of the sequencer window (the one to the right of the button with a magnet icon in the screen below). This quantises as you play, making sure that the timing is tight. If you prefer to rely on your own timing, don't bother with this step. You can quantise afterwards, if necessary.

4. Record the part

- Press the red Record button in the transport bar, followed by the play button, or use Apple/Control-Return, followed by the Space bar. Recording starts immediately. Let the click play for a couple of bars if you need a count-in.
- Play a basic bass and snare part on your MIDI drum controller, if used, or perform the part by hitting the keyboard keys that trigger the sounds you want.
- When you've recorded as much as you want, click stop in the transport twice, or press Return twice, to stop and return to zero.

Setting up recording loops

The method of recording just described is fine if you plan to record an entire drum part in one go – if you're a real drummer using MIDI pads – but most

Setting up loop points in the sequencer for recording a two-bar section of drums.

of us would probably rather work in sections. To do this, you'll need to use the sequencer's loop facility. Looping a drum part while recording also allows you to gradually add different parts as the section cycles around, which is

what most non-drummers prefer. To record a two-bar section of drums:

- Set up loop points in the sequencer. This can be done in the transport bar by setting the Left locator number to '1' and the right locator number to '3', or you can drag the Left and Right locators (topped by 'L' and 'R' flags) to the correct positions in the sequencer Arrange View display.
- Engage the 'Loop On/Off' button in the Transport.
- Initiate recording. Bars one and two will now loop continuously until you stop recording.

To record a further section after the first one:

- Set the left locator where the first section ended and a right one wherever you want the second section to end.
- Drag the Position marker (topped with a 'P' flag) to the same place as the Left marker.
- Now enter record. Just these bars will now loop while recording. When you've finished, stop and return the playing position to zero.
- To play back both sections, first disengage the Loop On/Off button. Now play back.

Why record drums into the sequencer?

Recording drum parts in this way isn't necessarily better than using ReDrum's Pattern method; it's just different. One advantage of recording drum parts into the main sequencer is that the sequencer's editing, note manipulation and quantisation tools can be used. Musicians who have drumming experience will probably also find that they can record a drum part live with more human 'feel'.

In addition, if the drum sounds are played from a MIDI controller that transmits velocity information, velocity will be applied as a natural consequence of playing style (how hard you hit the keys!), rather than having to be applied manually in three levels, as is necessary when programming from ReDrum. The full MIDI velocity range (0-127) is available to drum parts when they are played in via a velocity-sensitive controller.

Using ReDrum as a sound module with external sequencers

It's quite possible to play ReDrum sounds via an external sequencer, either hardware or software, or from another sequencer application running on the same computer as Reason. See the chapter on running Reason alongside other software or hardware for more information.

Info

ReDrum and General MIDI

While ReDrum might appear at first to offer vague General MIDI compatibility in its note assignments, this is not actually the case. Nor is it possible for the user to create a kit that will be 100% GM.

There are two problems. First of all, there simply aren't enough drum voices within ReDrum to recreate a full, standard GM kit – that would require over 80 voices. And even attempting to replicate a basic drum kit – a GM kit includes many Latin percussion sounds – would be difficult. A basic kit for GM purposes might include three or four toms, three hi-hat states, and several cymbals, in addition to kick and snare, which could add up to around 18 drum voices.

The other problem is ReDrum's fixed MIDI note-to-drum sound channel assignments, which mean that you can't even remap the device's 10 voices to a completely stripped-down GM kit, and GM drum notes that fall outside this range can't be accommodated – for example, cymbals in a standard GM kit .

So if you plan to import Standard MIDI Files that utilise GM drums into Reason, or you have GM-compatible software or hardware drum modules in your studio that you'd like to be played by a MIDI File exported from Reason, it'll be up to you to edit the drum parts (or external drum assignments) accordingly. Alternatively, you could create a General MIDI kit in NN19 or NNXT, where you can have the correct number of drum voices and map them to the right keys. Find a great GM drum kit made in this way, by Psylux, at www.psylux.com/reason. It loads into both NN19 and NNXT.

The 'Copy Pattern To Track' Feature

The two main ways of creating ReDrum Patterns – programming in step time with ReDrum's own Pattern facilities and recording into the sequencer – have already been discussed, and both have their advantages. But the best of both ReDrum worlds, arguably, is available via 'Copy Pattern To Track', found under the Edit menu. This command copies the currently selected ReDrum Pattern to a track in the sequencer, so that it may then be manipulated by the sequencer's editing facilities.

- Decide which sequencer track to copy the Pattern to (usually the ReDrum track) and click its In column to make the MIDI plug icon appear.
- Set the Left and Right locators around the area you want the Pattern copied to. The Pattern will be copied such that it fills the space between the locators. If the locators are set eight bars apart and the Pattern being copied is 16 steps long (ie. one bar), eight repetitions of that Pattern will be copied into the sequencer track.
- Choose 'Copy Pattern to Track' from the Edit menu.

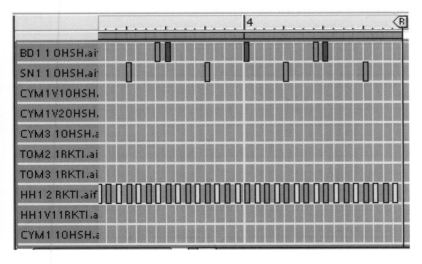

A ReDrum Pattern copied to a sequencer track. It now shows up as notes, in both the Drum Lane (shown here) and the Key Lane.

You can use this facility to build up a drum arrangement, by copying Patterns where you want them to occur in your Song. (Alternatively, look at 'Convert Pattern Track to Notes', below.) If you want to copy another Pattern into the same track, to follow the first, make sure to move the Left and Right locators to the position where you want the new Pattern copied. Otherwise it will paste on top of the first Pattern and both will play back together. Also remember to switch off the 'Enable Pattern Section' button in ReDrum when you have Copied Pattern to Track, or the Pattern will play back both from ReDrum and from the main sequencer, and you'll have two sets of drums going.

'Copy Pattern To Track' can be an ideal way of, for example, establishing a basic drum groove (say, bass and snare) for a whole song, which may then be embellished with extra parts played live from the keyboard.

The 'Convert Pattern Track To Notes' feature

This feature is similar to 'Copy Pattern To Track', but is available from within the main sequencer, under the Edit menu, rather than from ReDrum itself. It works on a Pattern chain that you have automated in the sequencer. If you've automated a chain, as explained earlier in this chapter, the Pattern changes are recorded into a sequencer track, and using 'Convert Pattern Track to Notes' on this track turns the chained ReDrum Patterns into notes in the sequencer. The whole Song's ReDrum part will thus be available for editing as notes in the main sequencer. One side-effect of this process is that ReDrum's 'Enable Pattern Section' and 'Pattern' buttons are disengaged automatically.

The other good reason for using this feature is if you would like to save a Song as a MIDI File, for playback on other MIDI File-compatible equipment. When you create a MIDI File from within Reason, only the data in the main sequencer is saved. You will thus have to get Pattern-based parts of the Song (ReDrum and Matrix Patterns) into the main sequencer to have them included in the MIDI File.

A potential issue

Both the 'Copy Pattern To Track' and 'Convert Pattern Track to Notes' features are extremely useful, but some users experience a particular problem with them in some circumstances.

The issue manifests itself as follows. A ReDrum Pattern including a sound of fairly long duration (such as a cymbal crash with a long decay, or a non-drum sample) that has a setting of 'Gate' on the Decay/Gate switch for its drum channel, is sent to the sequencer as notes. When the Pattern is played back from the sequencer, the long sound is 'cut off' short every time it occurs, and will not play out as it did before. This, obviously, changes the character of the Pattern.

When a sound is set to 'Gate' mode in ReDrum, its length is governed by the setting of the 'Length' knob – it plays for that length of time, then cuts off dead. You might want to set up a sound like this because you don't wish the sound to play with its original length or natural decay. But when a Pattern is sent to the sequencer as notes, the process uses a fixed, short note value for every hit in the Pattern. This short note then triggers the previously long sound, and because Gate is set on the Decay/Gate switch, the sound is only allowed to play for as long as that short trigger note before cutting off – the

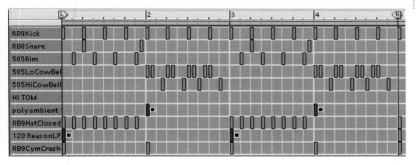

When you 'Copy Pattern to Track', every hit in the ReDrum Pattern becomes a short MIDI note that then triggers the relevant ReDrum sound. But if the sound is a long one and is set to 'Gate' in ReDrum, it will only play for as long as the short MIDI trigger note and then 'gate off'.

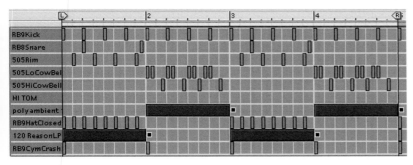

One answer is to identify the problem notes in the sequencer, shift-click on them to select them all, and drag the handle of one note to lengthen them all. If the notes are all on one 'line', you can quickly draw a rectangle around them with the Selection tool to select all, then do the same.

process basically ignores the setting of the Length knob.

You can get around this in two ways: either setting long sounds in ReDrum to 'Decay' instead of 'Gate', and putting up with the resulting slight difference in character; or going into the sequencer and editing the length of every note that triggers the problem sound – basically, lengthening the notes so that they play the sound as you want it. You can do this either in the Key Lane or the Drum Lane.

About Note values and time signatures

As you may know, or will discover from the chapter on Reason's main sequencer, Reason has a fully variable, but global, time signature. However, making this setting on the Transport bar has no immediate effect on Pattern-based devices such as ReDrum: if you decide your song should be in 7/8 or 11/16, ReDrum doesn't suddenly start operating in that time signature. Its default Pattern is still made up of sixteen 16th notes, effectively a 4/4 bar (four quarter notes to the bar), so if you want something other than this, you have to help the device along a little, to bring it into line with the main time signature. By using ReDrum's Steps and Step Resolution parameters it's possible to create the effect of virtually any time signature you like, for every Pattern, for example a global time signature of 7/8 would require ReDrum to have 7-step Patterns with 8th-note resolution or 14-step Patterns with 16th-note resolution.

An extension of this idea would allow you to overcome, in a small way, Reason's lack of a time signature track. You'd use ReDrum as a 'master time signature generator': create Patterns that have different step-lengths and resolutions, to give the effect of different time signatures, and chain them in the ReDrum sequencer track. Inserting the occasional 7/8 bar in an otherwise 4/4 Song, or alternating 4/4 and 3/4 bars thus becomes relatively straightforward, but be aware that Pattern changes won't necessarily be on the sequencer bar lines any more, Include a sound that works as a metronome in the ReDrum kit, creating a 'click' with it, and you can ignore Reason's overall time-signature and click parameters when building up the track.

The rear panel

Audio connections

Stereo Audio Outputs: The main stereo audio output pair of sockets are usually linked to one input channel of the Remix mixer, so that you can actually hear the ReDrum's output.

Aux Send Outputs

Next to the stereo audio output pair are the two output sockets for ReDrum's auxiliary (effects) send system.

If Reason has done automatic patching for you and there is a mixer in the rack, these are linked to the first two of the ReMix mixer's 'Chaining Aux Send In' sockets. However, you can manually link to the other two ReMix aux sends if you want to – or, indeed, any two of the four. (See the explanation of send linking in the section earlier in this chapter that describes the Send controls in the Drum Sound Channel area.) If there is no mixer in the rack, these sockets are not linked to anything.

Channel Audio Outputs

The remaining sockets are divided into ten vertical strips, one for each drum voice channel, just like the front panel of ReDrum. At the top of each strip is a stereo audio output pair, which is just like the individual output on a hardware drum machine or synth.

Sending ReDrum sounds to their own mixer channels

If you patch a lead into one or both of a drum channel's audio outputs, the sound assigned to that channel will be removed from ReDrum's main mix, and can be sent instead to its own mixer channel. There it can be processed with mixer channel EQ and all the mixer's send effects – useful if one sound requires extreme or drastic processing that you wouldn't want to apply to a whole kit. The procedure is given in full in Chapter 5, ReMix.

Removing a sound from the ReDrum mix in this way also allows you to process the sound with one or more Reason effects patched 'in line' between the sound's output and a mixer input. See the effects chapter for more.

ReDrum channel 3 (bottom of screen) patched to its own mixer channel.

Tip

Easy drum layering using gate ins and outs

You can't copy Pattern parts between drum channels in ReDrum, which is a bit inconvenient if you are one of those people who like to layer up two or more drum sounds playing the same part. You can get around this limitation by connecting the Gate Out of the source channel playing the part you want to double, to the Gate In of the target channel. The part now plays on both sounds, because the hits on the first channel are sent from the Gate Out and trigger the sounds on the second channel via that channel's Gate In. Any number of channels can be linked in this way, chaining channels Gate In-Gate Out. (See figure below.)

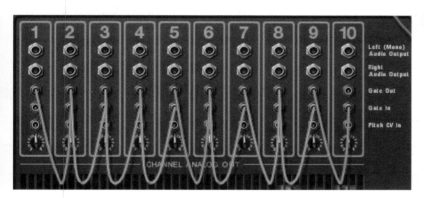

Connect the Gate Out of one channel to the Gate In of another, to make the first channel's part also play on the sound assigned to the second channel. All these channels will play the part programmed for the first.

Gate Outputs and Inputs

Whenever a step plays in a ReDrum Pattern, or a ReDrum voice is played from the main sequencer, it creates a 'Gate' pulse which triggers a drum sound (again, see Chapter 4 for more information on the Gate and CV system). The same pulse is also output via a Gate Out socket on the back panel, and has its length controlled by the Decay/Gate setting for the channel in question.

You can send that Gate pulse to trigger parameters on any device that has a Gate Input – other ReDrums, SubTractor, Malström, NN19, NNXT, Dr:rex, and the ECF42 Envelope Controlled Filter. The ability to set the length of the Gate pulse is a useful feature that allows you to customise the gate pulse to suit the sound being triggered. A normal ReDrum gate pulse is very short indeed, and usually causes just a quick blip to sound when triggering SubTractor or NN19.

Changing the Decay/Gate setting to 'Gate' and altering its length helps the triggered synth or sampler to produce a sound with more of its own character. See Chapter 21 for a chart giving some suggested Gate routings.

Advanced uses of Gate Ins and Outs

If you're simply programming drum Patterns in ReDrum, to play ReDrum sounds, you don't really have a use for the Gate sockets. It's when you want to do more interesting things that these sockets come into their own.

ReDrum Patterns triggering synth-drum voices

Gate pulses from each ReDrum Gate Out could be used to trigger the voices of up to 10 SubTractor modules programmed to create synthesized, analogue-style drum sounds. In fact, one of the templates supplied by Propellerhead with Reason is a rack configured in just this way – ReDrum triggering 10 SubTractor modules. The process is simple. (The SubTractor chapter has ideas on programming your own analogue drum sounds.)

- Create up to 10 SubTractors and load each with a percussion Patch.
- Link the Gate output of a ReDrum channel to the Sequencer Control Gate Input of one of the SubTractors
- Continue linking ReDrum channels with SubTractors in the same way.
- Now parts programmed in the ReDrum channels will play SubTractor analogue drum sounds.

A ReDrum Gate Out connected to a SubTractor synth to trigger 'analogue' drum sounds.

Rhythmic triggering of synth envelopes

Another possibility is connecting a Gate Out on ReDrum to a Gate In on any other device, for rhythmic triggering of various parameters – whichever ones are suitable to be controlled by that incoming trigger. Parameters that may be controlled in this way include the envelope generators of the SubTractor synth. The SubTractor chapter explains this technique fully – though it's not confined to use only with SubTractor; other devices have EGs too!

Trigger ReDrum via its Gate Inputs

Just as ReDrum's Gate outputs allow you to trigger parameters on other devices with ReDrum gate pulses, so you can trigger a ReDrum voice from another device (or even from another drum voice inside the same ReDrum).

Gate Outputs from the Matrix Pattern Sequencer or Dr:rex could be patched to ReDrum Gate Inputs, to provide an alternative source of rhythmic Patterns for ReDrum voices. Dr:rex, for example, has a Slice Gate output, from which a pulse is sent for every MIDI note that triggers a loop 'slice'. If you patch this to the ReDrum Gate Input of a drum channel playing a percussion sound, the sound will echo the rhythm of the sliced REX loop perfectly. Try a hi-hat, tambourine or even a cowbell for this.

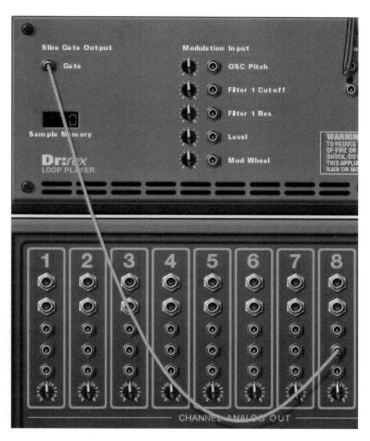

A Dr:rex Slice Gate Output connected to a ReDrum channel Gate Input, thus triggering the ReDrum sound on that channel.

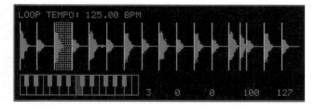

The ReDrum sound triggers in the rhythm of the slices in the REX loop.

Pitch CV Inputs

With the Pitch CV input socket, a 'control voltage' generated by another Reason device can be used to affect the pitch of a ReDrum voice. Connect the desired CV output of the other device to the Pitch CV In of a ReDrum channel. The 'Note' and 'Curve' CV outputs of the Matrix Pattern Sequencer are suitable, as are the Modulation Outputs of the SubTractor, NN19 and Dr:rex.

This facility opens up a wide area for exploration, by allowing the pitch of a percussion sound to be varied in subtle or extreme ways to add more interest to a Pattern. Applications such as mimicking tuned percussion – agogos, bongos, or African slit drums, perhaps – come to mind (providing you have the samples, that is!). Bear in mind that a drum voice being modulated by an external CV via its Pitch CV Input will still need to be triggered, either from a Pattern written within ReDrum itself or from some other trigger source in the Reason rack. Without the trigger impulse, the voice channel will not sound.

Using ReDrum as a simple sample mapper

Some Reason users have discovered that bringing loops and one-shot samples into ReDrum, as an alternative to NN19 or NNXT, is a quick, easy and fuss-free way of getting samples into the program. Samples loaded in this way can be instantly triggered from a keyboard, and can be sent to mixer channels for individual processing. Just load the samples you want to use, one by one, into ReDrum's drum voice channels, as explained earlier in the chapter.

As mentioned earlier, ReDrum voices are mapped to MIDI notes 35-44 (the 10 chromatic notes upwards from bottom C on a 61-note keyboard, or the C two octaves below middle C). The samples loaded into ReDrum can now be triggered, and recorded into the sequencer, by playing those notes on the keyboard. All the data for the various sample triggers will be recorded onto one track. (However, if you wanted MIDI notes for triggering the separate samples to be recorded on their own tracks, you could assign the ReDrum to multiple sequencer tracks and prime each of these tracks in turn, to record the triggers for one sample at a time.

You could, of course, also program Patterns in ReDrum that trigger non-drum samples, or use a combination of both methods, since ReDrum can be played by its Pattern system and a sequencer track simultaneously.

The ReDrum 'synth'

An extension of the idea of using ReDrum as a sample-playback device is to also connect the audio out of every ReDrum channel to the audio in of an ECF42 Envelope-Controlled Filter, and every ReDrum channel's Gate Output to the corresponding ECF42 Envelope Gate Input.

The combination of each ReDrum voice's basic envelope controls and the ECF42 creates what is, in effect, a simple, independent synth – the effect is heightened by triggering the filter section in the ECF from each ReDrum voice, just as would happen on a 'proper' synth. In fact, this is one significant advantage of triggering multiple samples from within ReDrum over key-grouping the same collection within NN19: NN19 has one filter with which to treat all samples currrently assigned to it, while the arrangement just described provides an independent, albeit slightly more basic, filter for each ReDrum voice. Of course, NNXT gives you independent filter settings per sample, but still the 'ReDrum Synth' is a fun thing to set up! Try it with drum sounds or with loop or melodic samples. See the effects chapter for step-by-step instons.

The NN-19 Sampler

Though the legend on the panel of the NN19 says 'Digital Sampler', NN19 is not actually a sampler at all – it's a sample player. NN19 can't record samples, but acts as a playback engine, mapper and sound processor for samples you load into it from the factory bank or external sources of your own. You can use it for playing back the phrases and rhythm breaks necessary for creating loop-based music, as well as instrument multisamples.

If used in the latter way, NN-19 can function as an additional synth within Reason. After all, many modern digital synths use multisampled waveforms as the basis of their sounds, providing synthesis facilities to tailor them – which is just what NN-19 does. Aside from the inability to actually sample, NN-19 does lack a few of the facilities you would hope to find in a fully-specified studio sampler, but it is quick and easy to use (and you can turn to the deluxe NN-XT sampler when you need a facility NN-19 does not have).

As you won't fail to have noticed, Reason doesn't allow direct audio recording into the program, and NN-19 is one of the main ways of compensating for this fact (as are NN-XT and potentially Dr:rex). With care, it can be used to play back sampled vocals, for example, for an entire song, though you will need other software to use alongside Reason. In fact, "extra software" is a recurring theme as we discuss NN-19, because arguably you'll need some additional bits and bobs (which needn't cost you much, if anything) if you're to have the maximum fun and use from NN-19.

NN-19 basics

NN-19 offers up to 99 notes of polyphony (plays up to 99 notes at one time). It's technically not multitimbral, as it can't produce different sounds at the same time on different MIDI channels, but it does allow you to spread many different samples across the MIDI key range. (And for multi-NN-19 perofrmances, just add more examples to your rack!) NN-19 accepts samples in AIFF and WAV formats, mono or stereo, at any sample rate and most bit depths, plus (since V2) SoundFont samples, REX files and slices from REX files. Other formats, perhaps from sample CDs, can't be loaded without first converting them with external software. See the section on using sample CDs later in this chapter. Obviously, patches from the new NN-XT can't be loaded since the new device is much more complicated, but individual samples from NN-XT Patches can be loaded and used to create an NN-19 patch.

Up to 127 separate samples can be loaded into one NN-19 device, one for each note of the MIDI note range, and there appears to be no limit on sample length other than the RAM of your computer. NN-19 can automatically map samples across a keyboard for you, but since it doesn't have editing capabilities you will ideally need to have edited the samples externally (or be using commercial, ready-edited samples) and set any internal loop points you require – NN-19 recognises loop points present within the sample. Basic looping, as in instructing the sample to play repeatedly end to end (a playback loop), is available within NN-19, but there are no other looping facilities.

Before you ask, NN-19 doesn't support velocity crossfading or velocity switching for sample layering; it has just one layer, for a start. Go to NN-XT for this. On the upside, samples can be processed in NN-19 as though they are synth sounds, with a very good set of synthesis facilities including envelopes, a filter and an LFO.

Info	
Keyboard shortcuts	
Apple/Control B	Browse Patches
Option/Alt-click on Keyboard Display	Audition sample
Option/Alt click above keyzone strip	Creates new keyzone
Apple/Control-click any control	Restores original value for Patch
Shift-click-hold on control	Accesses fine adjustment

Background to sampling

If you're a newcomer to sampling, or have never come across a simple explanation of the technology, it's probably a good idea to read this section, as it will help you understand more about samples, and later how NN-19 works, and what it can and can't do. If you already have enough sampling knowledge, you might prefer to skip on to the 'Guided Tour'.

What's a sample?

To go right back to basics, a sample is a digital recording of a sound. Sampling can be compared to movie photography. A film camera captures successive still 'frames' of whatever it is filming, and these frames are played back rapidly, one after another, to reproduce the movement of the original scene. Sampling does the same thing with sound, taking static digital snapshots of the sound at a given instant, and then playing them back to recreate the original.

What governs sample quality?

The quality of a sampled sound depends, amongst other things, on how many digital snapshots of the original sound are taken per second. If a sample is recorded at a sample 'rate' of 44.1kHz, for example, this means that 44,100 samples of it were taken every second. The result (as long as various other criteria are satisfied) should be a good-quality sample. Obviously, if you were to sample at say, 5kHz, the result would not be so good, as 5000 samples per second couldn't produce such a faithful representation of the original waveform. It would be rather like comparing cinema-quality film (24 frames per second) with the video output provided by the average webcam.

The other major factor in how accurately a sample reproduces the original sound is what's called 'bit depth'. Returning to the moving picture analogy used above, where sample rate refers to how many 'frames' (samples) are taken per second, bit depth refers to the amount of detail recorded for each of the frames. Each sample is described by the recording device in terms of digital 'bits', which make up 'words'. The more bits to a word, the more detailed and faithful the reproduction of that sample.

It should be noted that though the best fidelity is achieved with high sample rates and bit depths, the use of lower rates and lesser bit depths has been championed by experimental and dance musicians. Initially this may have been because young musicians only had access to older, cheaper sampling technology, which offered lower bit depths and sampling rates, plus limited sample RAM capacity (samples taken at lower rates/depths need less RAM). However, the sound quality lent by less-than-ideal samples is now actively sought, and musicians in various genres will now actually prefer to deliberately mess up a high-quality sample to give it the required crunch and grunge.

The beauty of a digital sample is that once it's recorded, you can process and manipulate it at will, software tools allowing. Such processing will have no harmful effect on the sample, unless that's what you want; but if you work on copies of the original sample file, you'll always be able to return to your starting point. Sample-like manipulation was achieved in pre-digital days using recordings on analogue tape; virtually any effect desired required the laborious copying and recopying of the original audio, each process moving a generation further away from the original audio in terms of fidelity and noise. There are few such problems when working with digital samples.

Do I need sample-editing software?

Sample-editing software (external to Reason) will enable you to trim silence, clicks or other unwanted elements from samples that you would like to use; increase their volume, if they are too quiet; reverse them; and permanently change their pitch. Some software allows a sample's length to be 'stretched' without affecting its pitch, or its pitch to be changed without affecting its length. This fairly recent development in digital audio gets around the general rule that making a sample shorter also makes it higher in pitch, as it is speeded up, and lengthening the sample drops its pitch. 'Timestretching' allows you to match samples that are the wrong tempo, length or key, to other samples, so that they can be used in the same track. This is a different method of making samples change speed to fit together than is used by ReCyle and Dr:rex, and is more suitable for non-rhythmic audio that can't easily be chopped into slices.

You should also be able to apply a 'loop' to the sample using external software. One example of looping would be to make a whole sample repeat in an end-to-end fashion. Another would be the addition of a loop to the middle or end portion of an instrumental sample – a single note from a guitar, violin or whatever – so that you'll be able to play tunes with it without the sample stopping dead (because it was too short) when you hold a key too long or play it too high. The loop allows the natural attack of the sample to sound and adds an artificial sustain, by cycling a portion of the natural sustain, to increase the sample's length.

What's multisampling?

Of course, any sound, once sampled and loaded into a sampler or sample player (such as NN-19), can be used to play tunes – the early days of sampling were rife with fairly poor novelty records involving singing sheep and dogs. However, it becomes evident quite soon that most samples can't be played at pitches that are far removed from their central pitch; they sound unnatural and occasionally comical – the phrases 'Mickey Mouse' and 'Darth Vader' can be used to describe the undesirable effects of samples played too high or too low in relation to their basic pitch. You may want this kind of effect, but if you don't, a technique called 'multisampling' is employed: if the sampler or sampling software allows it, several samples of the same sound at different pitches are mapped to different MIDI notes, or ranges of MIDI notes (keygroups or keyzones), so that transposition either doesn't take place when you play the sound, or only occurs over small ranges – the average sound can usually manage a few semitones of transposition before becoming too 'artificial'.

Ideally, one sample would be made for every note in the MIDI range (or the range you need in the final multisample), but this would require a lot of RAM on the part of the sampler, and a lot of time on the part of the samplist to actually record and edit the samples in the first place. By using 'compromise' multisampling, a smaller group of samples can be made to 'stretch' across the full keyboard range without too many ill-effects, making what is often referred to as a key 'map'. You can make such keymaps with NN-19, given suitable source samples to begin with.

Samples, and more

The technology to record, manipulate and play back digital samples is actually pretty phenomenal, and would have been rocket science not too long ago. But musicians want more, and the technology has obliged: practically all hardware and software sampling devices allow edited, looped and keymapped samples to be processed by a signal path that emulates that of a traditional analogue synthesizer. Facilities on offer can be as basic as a simple envelope generator, so that a sample's volume can change over time in a more natural fashion, or can run to resonant filters, LFOs, portamento, real-time parameter modulation and more. Reason owners really score in this area: not only does NN-19 have great sound-sculpting facilities within itself, but you can also call upon the powers of many of the other devices in the rack to enhance your samples.

Get going with NN-19

The 'Browse Sample' button.

Load a sample

When you create an NN-19, it's empty and you'll need to load a sample or Patch into it. Here we're going to load just a single sample.

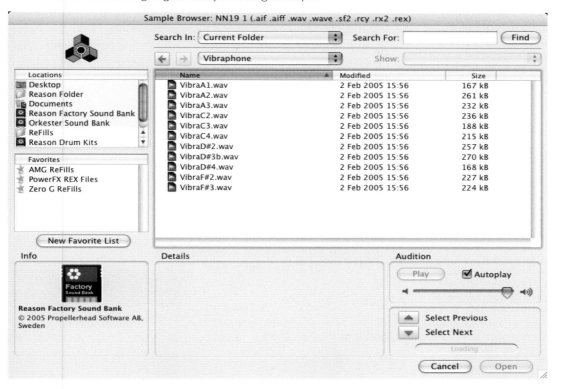

- Click on the blue folder button above the keyboard display to access the Sample Browser window.
- Navigate to a sample folder and select a sample you would like to load. Double-click on the file name or select 'Open'.
- The sample loads into NN-19, and you should see its file name appear under the keyboard display. If there is already pitch information in the sample file the sample will automatically be assigned by NN-19 to the key that corresponds to this pitch. If the sample has no such information within it, NN-19 will assign its Root Key to note C3 on the keyboard, where it will generally play back at its correct pitch. Whatever Root Key has been assigned to the sample, it shows as a highlighted note in the keyboard display. If you would like to change the MIDI note that will play back the sample at its correct pitch (give it a new Root Key), click on the note you want to change to in the keyboard display, or use the Root Key knob underneath the display to set the note.

The Sample Browser.

The sample loaded into NN-19. You can see its name in the display above the Sample knob. The 'Root Key' has been automatically assigned as note C3 on the keyboard.

- If the sample is a rhythmic one, such as a drum loop, you may not need it to respond to pitch, so you can switch off Keyboard Tracking, using the Kbd Track button in the Oscillator section. This will allow the sample to be played anywhere on the keyboard and not change pitch. Again, if a sample plays back at the wrong pitch when you have done this, change its Root Key as above.
- You should now be able to trigger the sample from your MIDI keyboard (make sure the MIDI plug icon is showing in the NN-19 sequencer track, by clicking in the 'In' column), use it as part of a sequence in the main sequencer, or even trigger it from the Matrix step sequencer.

In this example, you were able to use your MIDI keyboard to play the sample pretty much immediately because NN-19 automatically assigns the first sample you load to a 'keyzone' for playback. A sample won't play back unless it has first been assigned to a keyzone on the keyboard (which could be as small as one key or as large as the entire MIDI note range).

At this point, NN-19 considers the first sample's keyzone to be the whole keyboard; you can see this from the keyzone display strip across the top of the keyboard, which is solid pale blue, indicating a single keyzone. How the MIDI key range can be divided up into lots more keyzones, so that a sample can be assigned to each, will be discussed later. Until you or Reason creates keyzones, only one sample can be triggered from the keyboard.

Now that you can load and trigger a single sample, read on to learn more about NN-19's facilities.

Patch Load/Save

Guided tour

The Patch Load/Save Area

Load Patches into NN-19 and initiate saving operations, as usual, in the Patch area to the top left of the panel. (See Chapter 4, Basic Operations, for how to load and save Patches.) An NN-19 Patch consists of a sample or collection of samples, arranged in a keymap, together with its NN-19 panel settings. You can load Patches from the factory ReFill and other ReFills, as well as your own Patches when you have created them from groups of samples – more later.

The Keyboard Display

This is the central area for loading individual samples and organising them into a keymap, by assigning them to zones on the keyboard. You can also edit keymaps here.

Five octaves of keyboard are shown in the display, but it's possible to view another three octaves below and a little over two octaves above this range, so that you can assign and customise samples across the full MIDI note

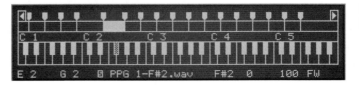

Keyboard display.

range. View the extra keyboard range by clicking the arrows located at the left and right of the display. If you don't have a MIDI keyboard connected to Reason, Option/Alt-click on keys in the keyboard display to hear samples play (if any are loaded). Also see Chapter 2 for details of software utilities that make your computer keyboard function like a MIDI keyboard.

To the top left of the keyboard display is the Sample Browser button. This works like the Patch Browser facility in NN-19 and other devices, except that instead of Patches, you're browsing individual samples. These can be located anywhere on any fixed or removable hard drive or CD-ROM that can be accessed by your computer.

The Keyzone Display

Above the keyboard display is a horizontal strip called the keyzone display. This runs the full length of the keyboard and is used for mapping samples onto the required keys, creating keyzones. Multiple keyzones spread across a keyboard make a keymap.

Keyzone display

The Sample Properties area

Beneath the keyboard in the display is the sample properties area. When a keyzone is highlighted (by clicking on it in the keyzone display, or by pressing a relevant MIDI keyboard key if 'Select keyzone via MIDI' is active), the properties of the sample assigned to that keyzone are shown in the properties area. The text in this area – and therefore the properties of the sample or keyzone – can be modified by the seven knobs under the keyboard display.

Sample properties area

- *Low Key:* Sets the lowest key boundary of the keyzone – the lowest note in the zone that will trigger the sample assigned to that zone.
- *High Key:* Sets the highest key boundary of the keyzone. Note that keyzones cannot overlap each other.
- *Sample:* Scrolls through the names of the samples currently loaded into NN-19, whether they have been 'keymapped' or not. You can load multiple samples one by one into NN-19, but make sure you turn the Sample knob so that the display reads **no sample** before loading each. Otherwise the new sample will overwrite the last one loaded.
- *Root Key:* Sets the Root Key of the sample (see Info box elsewhere in this chapter for more on the Root Key).
- *Tune:* Provides +/-50 cents of fine-tuning per sample (a cent equals 1/100th of a semitone), to allow you to tune individual samples in a keymap against each other.

- *Level:*. Lets you balance the relative volume of samples in a keymap.
- *Loop:* Sets whether a sample will loop on playback. Setting 'no loop' means that the sample will simply play once when triggered, and then stop until triggered again. Setting a 'Fwd' loop makes the sample play repeatedly end to end in a forwards direction, as long as a key is held or for the duration of the Amp Envelope curve. The 'Fwd/Bwd' option plays the sample once in a forwards direction, then immediately plays it backwards, and so on, continuously as above. If you load a sample that has been looped in an external editor, NN-19 automatically sets the Loop control to 'Fwd'.

Above the keyboard are two square LED buttons.

- *'Select keyzone via MIDI':* When this is active, you'll see a keyzone (and its central Root Key) highlighted in the display each time you play a MIDI note. You can select keyzones for editing in this way.
- *Solo Sample:* Isolates the currently selected sample, making it playable over the entire note range, even when it has been keyzoned as part of a keymap. 'Solo Sample' only works if 'Select keyzone via MIDI' is not active. It can be handy for checking how far up and down the pitch range a sample is suitable to use – how far in each direction you can play a single sample before it sounds too weird or unusable. You can also use 'Solo Sample' to determine which note plays back a sample at its correct pitch (by triggering it from successive keys), if the samples have already been automapped and are not all playing back correctly from their assigned keyzones.

Select keyzone and solo sample

The Synthesis Facilities

Once you've loaded and mapped the samples you'd like to work with, NN-19 effectively becomes a synthesizer, and the remaining signal path and panel controls are essentially those of a synth. They allow you to extensively customise samples to your own taste, changing their tonal qualities, creating new envelope shapes for them, applying modulation via an LFO, and so on. The one difference is that rather than applying these sound-shaping facilities to waveforms, as in SubTractor, you apply them to samples. Try them with all sorts of samples, not just instrument sounds, for cutting-edge weirdness.

Do note that the settings of the synthesis controls apply to all the samples that are part of a keymap. They are not independent per sample, which makes perfect sense for a group of samples (say, of a piano) which are meant to represent a single instrument when played, but is not ideal if you have a lot of unrelated samples loaded into NN-19 for triggering at different points in a track. However, if you need to treat individual samples with their own settings, just load each sample into its own NN-19, or use NN-XT in Reason V2, as this new device allows separate settings per sample.

The Oscillator Controls

Of course, NN-19 doesn't really have 'oscillators', producing waveforms like a synth – oscillators within NN-19, in effect, are the samples you have loaded, which you can

Tip

Transpose to make new sounds

Shift samples up or down out of their normal range to produce new sounds. For example, an amazing, authentic-sounding recorder sound was created from an old sample of blowing across the top of a large bottle. It was shifted up three octaves and looped in an audio editor. Also try triggering a rhythm loop at the same time as a copy of itself that you've transposed up an octave. It will be running twice as fast as the original but with the same feel, and the transposition lends an effect that can be interesting.

treat as though they were waveforms. Indeed, if you loaded a sample of a sine wave, you could mould and sculpt it with NN-19's synth section just as you could a sine wave in a real synth. Let's have a look at those 'oscillator' controls.

Oscillator controls

- *Sample Start knob:* This lets you change the playback start point of the sample, moving it further into the sample if needed. You might want to do this if a sample is too loud in its attack, or contains some undesirable element, such as a click or noise. Moving the sample start point past the place where the click occurs could save you from having to re-edit the sample in your wave editor and re-import it without the click. The Sample Start feature can also be used purely as a creative tool, since it allows a single sample to be used to create a different sound in different Patches; for example, removing the attack from a guitar sample produces a much more mellow, synth-like sound. This parameter can also be dynamically controlled, so that (for example) triggering it harder from your keyboard causes the attack to sound, while lower velocities (softer playing) start the sound further into the waveform, past the attack. If you're using real instrument sounds which you want to seem realistic, this method simulates how real instruments can behave. Harder playing causes the attack of a plucked guitar string, for example, to be very obvious, while sounding the string gently greatly minimises the attack. Also try this method for cutting a word or more off a vocal sample (or a chunk off a sampled loop), so that high velocities trigger the whole sample (for example) and lower ones take off the first word (or more). Do note that this parameter seems not to take account of sample length, which is a bit of a shame; for example, setting the start point as far 'in' as you can may completely overshoot the end of short samples, but may only get a short distance into a long sample.
- *Tuning controls:* The Oct control transposes samples as much as four octaves up or four octaves down, in octave steps, while the Semi control transposes by up to an octave, in semitone steps (upwards only; to tune down a few semitones, tune an octave down with the Oct control and then up to the required pitch with the Semi knob). The Fine knob is a fine-tuning control, providing a +/-50 cent tuning range. With these controls you can bring out-of-tune samples into line with your track, or transpose them for weird effects, but bear in mind that all the samples in the current Patch (keymap) will be affected equally by their settings. To tune individual samples in a keymap, use the Tune control under the Keyboard display.
- *Envelope Amount:* The labelling of this control may mislead you as to its purpose; it doesn't explicitly tell you which envelope is being referenced or to what end. In fact, it causes the Filter envelope (more in a minute) to also work as a Pitch envelope (at the same time as being used for normal Filter envelope purposes), causing the pitch of a Patch to vary over time. A positive or negative 'amount', affecting the direction of the pitch change, can be set. It's certainly useful to have Pitch envelope control, but it's a shame that it has to be slightly compromised by sharing the Filter's envelope. In practice, though, the small amounts of pitch variation you might add to a sound using an envelope will often work well if the Filter is using the same envelope as well – the filter-envelope curve reinforces the pitch envelope.

Tip

Sample auditioning

Don't forget that you can audition samples from the Sample Browser window, to save loading them just to see if they're what you want. Tick the Autoplay check box when the Sample Browser window comes up. Highlighting a file name in the file list now makes the sample play. If you have a big list to samples to audition, scroll through them with the up/down computer keyboard keys. Autoplay doesn't work with very long samples.

Tip

Keep loops in sync

If you're working with loops, it's generally more successful to keep re-triggering the loop from the sequencer (once a bar, or as appropriate) rather than setting the sample to keep looping end-to-end in NN-19 using the Loop knob. If you do this, the loop will probably eventually drift out of sync with the rest of your track.

• *Keyboard Tracking switch:* Here you can fix whether or not NN-19 will transpose its samples in response to incoming MIDI note data (from a keyboard, for example). Disengaging it effectively causes the sample or samples to play back at a fixed pitch, no matter what MIDI note is transmitted. This is useful for sound effect samples, loops and drum sounds, whose pitch you don't want to change. Disable keyboard tracking and you'll be able to trigger such samples from anywhere on the keyboard. Keyboard Tracking will need to be switched on if you're playing a conventional instrument multisample.

The Filter

Filter

NN-19's single, resonant, multi-mode filter is identical in specification to the SubTractor synth's Filter 1. Rather than removing frequencies from a harmonically rich waveform (or pair of waveforms), though, it's applying the same 'sound-sculpting' process to whatever sampled audio you've imported into NN-19. Unlike the filter on SubTractor, NN-19's can be switched out of the signal path if desired. The Filter has its own envelope, to the right of the main Filter section, and a Keyboard Tracking control. Refer to the SubTractor chapter for more detail.

The Envelopes

Envelopes allow aspects of a sound to be varied over time, in stages, according to the settings of the Attack, Decay, Sustain and Release sliders (see the SubTractor chapter for more detail on envelopes).

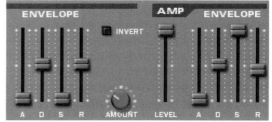

Envelopes

Tip

Filtered build-up

A popular effect, when a track opens with a naked rhythm loop, is to create a feeling of building by starting with the filter Frequency slider right down, so hardly any frequencies get through, then automate opening the filter gradually over a few bars, so the rhythm loop thickens up and gains presence bit by bit.

• *Amplitude Envelope:* Controls changes in level (volume or amplitude) over time. Use the Amp envelope to tailor such things as how fast or slow the attack of samples within a Patch will be, how loud the sound is when it comes in, and how long it takes to fade out after a key is released.
• *Level Slider:* This is the overall volume control for NN-19.
• *Filter Envelope:* Governs the opening and closing of the filter, in effect altering the filter frequency, and hence the texture of the sound, over time. The filter EG, of course, is the key to creating classic filter-sweep effects, in conjunction with fairly high filter resonance settings. A string pad sample is a good sound to demonstrate a filter sweep, but many other sounds work too. Create a slow filter envelope for your sample, set the frequency slider quite low, resonance quite high, and a fairly high envelope Amount (exact settings vary according to the sample). The resonance setting will make it easier to hear the sweep effect, but if the result is too harsh on your speakers, turn down resonance. See the filter sweep example in the SubTractor chapter for step-by-step directions. Create more unusual and ear-catching filter-sweep

effects by using the 'Invert' switch to flip the shape of the envelope upside down. This needs careful setting of the Frequency slider and the filter envelope controls if you are to hear a defined result. The important things are to turn up filter (cutoff) frequency and adjust the attack of the filter envelope upwards. With a normal envelope, the shape of the sweep starts at the point set by the filter frequency and goes up into a curve. Inverting the envelope makes the sweep start from the same point but then move into a downward curve. If filter frequency is set quite low, the downward curve has nowhere to go and you won't hear much effect. Raising filter frequency gives room for the downward sweep to occur. From this you can also work out why it's important to set a low filter frequency for a normal, upwards filter sweep, so that the curve has lots of room to sweep up.

- *Amount knob:* This control sets how strong an effect the envelope will have on the filter (lower amounts for subtle application of the envelope, higher amounts for obvious envelope effects).

The LFO

As explained in the SubTractor chapter, the Low Frequency Oscillator makes no audible sound but can be used to 'modulate' other sounds, adding movement and variety through effects such as vibrato (pitch modulation) and tremolo (volume modulation). The NN-19 LFO has the same number of waveform options as the LFO in SubTractor (triangle, up and down sawtooth, square, random and soft random), which each produce a different 'shape' of modulation effect.

The LFO can be set to modulate 'oscillator' (ie. sample) pitch, filter frequency, and pan, using the 'Dest' switch. Routing the LFO to pan allows you to gradually move a sound back and forth across the stereo field, the speed of the movement dependent on the setting of the LFO Rate control. LFO panning can be very pleasing with various sounds, even producing a Leslie-type rotating speaker feel. The Amount control sets the depth of the LFO effect. As an example, when modulating pitch with the LFO, low settings of the Amount knob cause very slight undulations in pitch, while high Amount settings cause deep, pronounced pitch variations.

From the front panel of NN-19 it is not possible to set the LFO to modulate level, to produce tremolo. However, all is not lost, as this can be done via the sockets on the back panel.

LFO Sync

As with other LFO-equipped devices, since Reason V2 NN-19's LFO can be sync'd to Song tempo, by clicking the Sync button in the LFO section. When Sync is enabled, the LFO Rate knob chooses from a range of note length subdivisions – the Tool Tip displays the selected time division.

The Performance controls

NN-19 features a number of performance controls, which route various synth parameters or incoming MIDI data to other parameters, to further increase the expressive potential of samples.

LFO

Velocity Controls

Incoming velocity data, from a MIDI controller, the main sequencer or the Matrix, can be set to have an effect on certain NN-19 sound parameters. The Filter Envelope amount can be changed by velocity, as can Filter Envelope decay, Amplitude (volume), amplitude envelope attack and sample start –

any or all. Use positive values of the knobs in this area to make higher velocity levels (harder playing) create more change, and negative values for the opposite effect – playing more softly creates more of the desired effect.

Velocity controls

The obvious example is assigning velocity to amplitude in a positive amount, so that playing harder makes the sound louder, but you could also use velocity to control the brightness of a sound, by assigning it to affect the filter envelope amount. Use velocity to control both amplitude and the filter envelope and you can create a fair simulation of how real instruments behave when hit or struck more forcefully – they get louder, but they also get brighter, as more of their natural harmonics are excited by harder playing. (Don't set the filter frequency slider too high if you want to do this. If the filter is already almost or fully open, velocity will have little or no effect.)

Set velocity to alter sample start point and you could make, say, the attack of a plucked guitar sample come through fully with high velocities and not sound as much (or at all) with lower velocities. This kind of technique helps with 'real' instrument samples, but try it with all kinds of samples. You'll probably have to fiddle with the velocity routing knobs and the Sample Start knob to get the best from this idea, but it's worth the trouble. As an example:

• Load factory Patch NYLONGTR from the Guitar folder in the NN-19 sampler Patches folder in the factory ReFill.
• Set the F.Env knob in the Velocity section to 25, the Amp knob to 20, the S.Start knob to -50, and the Sample Start knob in the Oscillator section to 70.
• Play the sound softly from your keyboard, and then really hit it hard to hear the difference. This is very effective when the Patch is played in a guitar-like 'picking' pattern with varying velocities. You could try this idea with the acoustic guitar picking pattern in the Matrix chapter.

In case you were wondering, there's a reason why we set the Sample Start knob to a negative value. If you set a positive value, higher incoming velocities would cause the sample start point to move further into the sample, losing more of the attack the harder you play. That's not appropriate for this example, since we wanted to make the sound softer, with a less obvious attack, at low velocities. The negative value thus means that lower velocities cause the sample start point to move further into the sample. Higher velocities have the opposite effect, so that the full attack comes through when you're playing hard.

Mod wheel controls

Mod Wheel controls

The modulation wheel can be made to alter any or all of filter frequency, filter resonance, filter envelope decay, amplitude and

LFO depth, in varying positive and negative amounts, with the five knobs in the Mod Wheel section.

MIDI Controls

An incoming MIDI stream (from a keyboard, for example) may include after-touch, expression pedal and breath controller data, and any one of these can be assigned to modulate up to three parameters of NN-19, with positive or negative amounts. The three target parameters are Filter frequency, LFO depth, and Amplitude (volume), each with a dedicated amount knob.

MIDI controls

Key Modes

NN-19, like SubTractor, can be customised to respond to how you play. The SubTractor chapter has full details of the options. The two available play modes, which determine how samples respond to being played from a MIDI controller, are Legato and Retrigger; select between them with the Mode switch.

Key modes

Portamento

Portamento, or 'glide', is controlled by this knob; turning it to the right sets how long the glide between notes takes, with the longest glide time set when the knob is fully to the right. See the SubTractor chapter for more on Portamento.

Portamento knob

The Spread Control

Spread is a 'playback' parameter, specified only for NN-19 and NN-XT, that essentially creates a stereo spread of samples, from left to right. The high notes on the keyboard are panned right, and the notes in between are placed equally in the stereo field between the two extremes. The Spread control itself governs the strength of the effect, so that when it's full on, the lowest sample in a multisample will be panned hard left, and the highest hard right.

Spread control

Three types of spread are available, via the Mode switch next to the Spread knob:

- *Key mode* shifts the pan position gradually from left to right the higher up on the keyboard you play.
- *Key 2 mode* shifts the pan position from left to right for each consecutive higher note you play, in eight steps, and then repeats the eight-step cycle as you continue to play further up the keyboard.
- *Jump mode* alternates the pan position of each note from left to right.

Spread is great for adding some nice stereo movement to piano parts especially, and adds realism to acoustic piano parts.

Using NN-19

Automatic sample mapping with 'Automap Samples'

The quickest way of loading multiple samples and creating an automatic keymap for them is 'Automap Samples'. This is useful if either you know you want to use a group of samples together in one NN-19 (perhaps they comprise an instrument multisample), or you want to load several unrelated samples and have them automatically mapped so that you can audition them from your MIDI keyboard.

For this example, let's say you have a group of samples of piano notes on your hard drive, recorded and edited by you, with each assigned a root key in your audio editor. Alternatively, you might be loading a well-constructed multisample set from a sample CD-ROM.

Load the group of samples.

- Open the Sample Browser.
- Load the group of samples by highlighting them all in the Sample Browser window and selecting 'Open'. NN-19 loads the lot, but assigns only the first to a keyzone – the entire keyboard at this point. The others stay in memory awaiting keymapping.
- Choose 'Automap Samples' from the Edit menu or a context menu.

Select 'Automap Samples'.

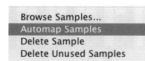

NN-19 instantly splits the existing keyzone into many keyzones and assigns each sample to a separate one. It calculates the size of the keyzones by dividing the number of keys between each sample into two, and assigning half the range to each sample. The sample's Root Key is always in the centre of its keyzone. The samples can now be triggered from your MIDI keyboard.

The samples loaded and Automapped.
The different keyzones are indicated by
the divisions in the keyzone display.

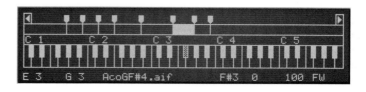

There may be occasions when you think you're loading samples that contain embedded pitch information, but they still play incorrectly after the 'Automap' process. In our experience, this can happen with sampled synth sounds, particularly those with heavy use of filter. In less severe cases, the pitch detection might place a note an octave higher or lower than you know it should be, though if a sample is more harmonically ambiguous, as a result of filter usage, it might be fourth or fifth out, in a different octave register. If the sample is your own, you could, of course, take care of the problem in your sample editor, but if it's a third-party sample, or you don't have an audio editor, you'll have to manually tweak the Root Key and use the 'Automap Samples' process again.

This collection of eight samples didn't Automap properly. The first one was mapped to a keyzone extending up to C3, with the other seven squashed into the subsequent semitones.

Editing the Automap

If you're lucky or well organised, the samples you've loaded will have pitch information embedded in them, and the Automap will be perfect, with samples assigned to appropriate Root Keys that will play them back untransposed, and sample keyzones spaced out properly across the keyboard for easy triggering.

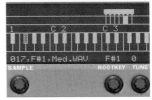

If, however, the group of samples does not have any embedded pitch data, selecting 'Automap Samples' will simply assign them to one keyboard note each, in semitones up from C3. There will be no attempt to rationalise tuning, so all samples will have C3 as their root pitch, which means that only a sample that was recorded at that pitch and actually assigned by chance to C3 on the keyboard will play back correctly. All the others will progressively sound a semitone higher.

Select each sample and give it the correct Root Key with the Root Key knob.

Instrumental Multisamples

If this happens to you when you've loaded a collection of individual instrumental samples, you'll need to give NN-19 a nudge. Select each sample's keyzone, by clicking it in the keyzone display, and change its Root Key to the correct note to play back the sample untransposed. (See the 'What's the Root Key?' box elsewhere in this chapter if you don't understand the whole Root Key idea – it's a very common area of confusion.) This should be relatively straightforward if the name of the sample includes some indication of root pitch – Guitar E2, for example – which should be the case with most third-party samples.

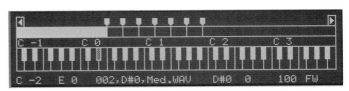

The result after assigning Root Keys and automapping again.

Now select 'Automap' again: NN-19 will use the new Root Keys to create the keymap, with samples nicely spaced and ready for playing.

Loops and breaks

If you've loaded a collection of loop or break samples, you have two choices. The simplest solution, if you won't be needing to change the samples' pitch across the keyboard, is to disable Keyboard Tracking in the Oscillator section. This way, all samples should play back at their original pitch no matter what key is playing them. (However, in some cases when Keyboard Tracking is disabled the samples do not play back at their correct pitches; we find samples sometimes inexplicably go 'out' by about four semitones. This is a known Reason bug. If it affects all the samples you have loaded equally, tweak the pitch controls in NN-19's Oscillator section to get the whole lot back to where you think it should be.)

You could alternatively disable Keyboard Tracking and use Automapping again, to create a better-spaced keymap: scroll through the loaded loops and breaks using the Sample knob, giving them Root Keys that will result in a well-spaced map. If you've loaded four or five sound effects or loops, you could assign the Root Key of each to the note 'C' in different octaves (C2, C3, C4, and C5, for example), or consecutive white notes. Now when you choose 'Automap Samples', NN-19 will use the new Root Keys to create the keymap. Don't forget to then save the mapped samples as a Patch. If you'd like to be able to transpose the samples after Automapping, re-enable Keyboard Tracking. The Root Key, which will be at the centre of each sample's keyzone, will play back each sample at its correct pitch, with a little transposition room to the left or right in the keyzone.

You can manually edit keyzones at any time by changing the lowest and highest keys of the zone using the Low Key and High Key knobs under the display, or by dragging the zone's handles in the zone strip above the keyboard, to enlarge or reduce the zone.

Deleting keyzones

You might find you have too many keyzones. To delete one, select it and choose 'Delete Key Zone' from the Edit menu.

Rearranging keyzones

You can't 'move keyzones about' in the keymap. If you need to reassign samples to different keyzones, you have to select the keyzone you want the sample on and scroll with the Sample knob to the sample name you want on that keyzone. The sample is now reassigned to that keyzone.

Loading samples individually and mapping them manually

If you want to load several samples one at a time into NN-19 (as you might if you're deciding which samples work well together), the procedure is different. Use the Sample Browser to open the sample you want to load. The sample will be assigned to NN-19's entire note range, as explained at the start of the chapter. You may now want to load another sample.

- First, select 'Split Key Zone' from the NN-19 Context Menu or Edit Menu. This will divide the whole MIDI note range into two keyzones; D#3 will be the top note of the lower zone and E3 will be the bottom note of the higher zone. Alternatively, Option/Alt-click above the zone strip to make a handle appear. This also splits the keyzone, at the key above which you have clicked.

If you're loading samples that do not need to change pitch across the keyboard, such as breaks and loops, just disabling Keyboard Tracking will mean that you can trigger them easily from the keyboard.

Change the size of keyzones by dragging the handles.

Option/Alt-click in the keyzone display to make a new keyzone you can load a second sample into. Option/Alt-clicking again splits the zone again, giving you a further zone – and so on.

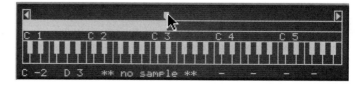

0• Click in the new keyzone you've created, to select it, and open your next sample. (If you load a new sample without splitting the keyzone, the previous sample will be overwritten. Having said this, you may load in samples without a keyzone if you rotate the Sample knob until the display reads **no sample**, as explained earlier, and load the new sample. The loaded sample will then have no keyzone and will have to be assigned to one if it is to be triggered from the keyboard.)

• If you have more samples to load, select one of the two keyzones, by clicking in the keyzone strip, and split it again, then load the sample you need. Proceed in this way. Edit the manual map afterwards, if necessary.

A keymap 'template'

The other thing you can do to make life easier when loading and mapping samples is to create an empty keymap 'template', so that every sample you load in can be assigned immediately to its own keyzone. By making a template, you can build up a keyboard map gradually as you decide which samples you would like as part of your NN-19 Patch. All you need to do is follow the steps above for loading individual samples, but don't load any samples – just create multiple zones. Now save the Patch – give it a name such as 'NN-19 Keymap Template' – wherever you save your Patches. Every time you want to create a new Patch from unrelated samples, you can open this Patch to give yourself a start. Even better, save it as part of your default Song (see Chapter 4).

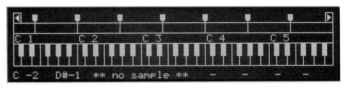

A keyzone 'template'.

To load a sample into one of the keyzones in the template, you only need to highlight the zone before loading. If you decide you don't want one of the samples you've loaded, load another into the same zone and overwrite the original sample, or choose 'Delete Sample' from the Edit menu or Context menu. You will probably still need to edit the zones once you've loaded in the required number of samples.

> ### Tip
> **Clearing unused samples**
>
> Once you've finalised a keymap for your NN-19 Patch, you might find that there are some samples left over, loaded but not assigned to keyzones. You don't want them sitting around using up RAM, so use 'Delete Unused Samples' from the Edit or Context menus to quickly remove any samples that haven't been assigned to keyzones.

Info

A Fast Guide: Newbie corner

If you're completely new to the workings of a sampler such as NN-19 (and at the risk of a bit of repetition), here's a potted explanation of the very basics of loading samples into NN-19 so you can use them in your Reason Songs. Let's assume for the moment that the samples are loops and breaks – ideally of the same tempo – and/or one-shots. Make sure your MIDI keyboard is properly connected and set up (see Chapter 2).

• Open Sample Browser, highlight all desired samples (up to 127!) and load.
• Use 'Automap Samples' from Edit menu to map samples to keys. The samples should then be triggerable from a MIDI keyboard,

via the notes that have been assigned to them by the Automap process.
• Disable Keyboard Tracking (so the loops/breaks will not change pitch when triggered across the keyboard). If any of the samples play back at the wrong pitch when triggered, change their Root Key (see Root Key info box elsewhere in this chapter). Edit automatic sample map if necessary, by changing Low Key and High Key of each keyzone with the dedicated knobs, or dragging the little blue handles in the zone strip above keyboard graphic in display, to extend or reduce keyzones.
• Enable NN-19 sequencer track for MIDI input

(click 'In' column next to track name; MIDI plug icon should appear).
• Engage Recording. Trigger samples with keyboard notes they have been assigned to, at desired positions as Song plays through. If you don't have a keyboard attached, draw a trigger note in sequencer display wherever you need one.

Find the detail for these procedures elsewhere in this chapter, and note that not all this procedure is suitable if you are loading instrumental multisamples. There are various alternatives and refinements to this process.

Using a sampler device for 'real' songs

As you'll have no doubt realised, Reason has no facility for recording audio of any kind. If you want to use real-world audio, such as the vocal performance for a song, alongside a Reason backing track, there are three solutions:

- Sync Reason to another application that does allow audio recording (this is dealt with towards the end of the book).
- Export sections of your Reason Song to disk (see the ReMix chapter) and load them into an audio application for re-sequencing, then record new audio alongside the imported Reason bits.
- Digitise the audio and load it into a Reason sample-playback device for triggering inside a Reason Song.

Of course, the last solution also requires that you have another application to enable you to record audio. This could be a MIDI + Audio sequencer, or it could be a simpler program, such as a basic audio editor or a sample sequencer that allows audio recording. In either case, if you're ultimately planning on the last method you still need to sync Reason to the recording program (or load exported Reason audio into it) so that the audio (say, a vocal performance or guitar part) you're recording will play in time with the Reason Song.

Why would you want to import your audio into Reason rather than simply leaving it in a parallel audio application? Well, perhaps your computer isn't powerful enough to reliably run both programs simultaneously, or perhaps you just prefer the idea of finishing your work in your favourite software – Reason!

Some practical guidelines

Working with long-form audio, such as vocals, in Reason requires planning. We wouldn't recommend recording the entire vocal performance for a song and importing it straight into NN-19 (or NN-XT), since this wouldn't leave you with much flexibility and there might be a tendency for the sample to drift in relation to the rest of the Song. Instead, we've chopped performances into sections – by line, for example – loaded the sections into individual NN-19 keyzones, and triggered them as they were needed in the Song. This approach leaves you free to re-arrange the performance, and also makes sure that nothing drifts out of sync.

When dividing vocals (for example), we don't usually cut exactly to the first word of every line or section; rather, we cut to the nearest beat or bar line before the first word in the sample (within the audio sequencing software that we use to record the vocals). This way, we can trigger the sample exactly on the beat and be sure that we won't miss any nuances in the performances. Very few vocalists sing exactly on the beat, and trying to work out where to trigger a fluid, extemporised performance so that original feel isn't lost can be a frustrating experience!

Sourcing samples

Samples suitable for use with NN-19 can come from many sources. First, and most obviously, there are quite a few in the factory ReFill you get free when you buy Reason. Second, there are many Internet sites where you can find samples to buy, and also freebies. Third, the world seems to be overflowing with sample CDs – free ones stuck to magazines and commercial ones you can buy. Fourth, and probably the most interesting, you can make your own

---

Tip

Reversing Samples

NN-19 doesn't specifically allow you to play sounds backwards. But you can fake reversing a sample by making its NN-19 loop setting (with the Loop knob under the keyboard display) FW-BW and setting a sample start point of 127 (with the Sample Start knob). The sample will play back reversed, but if you keep the key held down it will then play back forwards too. Avoid that by triggering the sample repeatedly at the correct intervals via the sequencer, so that it doesn't play through.

samples, either from records (bearing in mind copyright considerations) or by sampling the sounds around you.

Where to find free and commercial samples

The 'net is positively groaning with samples. Use a search engine to come up with more than you can possibly cope with, or (more conveniently) see Appendix 1 for a ready-made list of Internet sources of samples.

Recording your own samples

This book isn't the place to go into sampling techniques, but if you would like to get into recording your own 'real world' (as opposed to 'off record') samples, the essentials are as follows:

- A hardware sampler or sampling/audio recording software.
- A decent mic (if you plan on recording 'real' sounds and not just loops), preferably a condenser for the very best results.
- A good-quality soundcard and a preamp or 'recording channel'-type device.

A 'phantom power' source will also be required if you choose a condenser mic, but phantom power may be supplied either by the soundcard (if it is a studio-quality one) or external recording hardware, or by the 'recording channel'.

Using sample CDs

Ripping audio

One problem with audio sample CDs for Reason owners is that there's no way of getting their contents into the program without a 'file-extraction' stage, since Reason has no direct audio input capability. You will need additional software for this task.

To get the samples into Reason you'll need to 'rip' the audio off the CD with a suitable program (see the lists in Appendix 1), save it as WAV or AIFF, and load into NN-19 or NN-XT. Some audio editors offer a short-cut to creating multiple samples from a collection of separate hits that may make up a track on a sample CD, once the track has been 'ripped'. For example, DSound Pro for the Mac has an auto-extract function that turns hits separated by silence on a sample-CD track into individual sample files. And if you own Propellerhead's ReCycle, you can load a similar ripped sample CD track, have ReCycle 'slice' it for you, and Export the individual slices of a file (samples off the CD track) from the program as WAVs or AIFFs. In Reason V3.x, all sample devices now load REX (ReCycled) loops, in total or in individual Slices, without any WAV/AIFF export first.

Get Reloaded

If you visit Propellerhead's website and have created a user account you'll be able to download a handy utility called Reload, specially for converting Akai S1000 and S3000 formatted disks into more accessible media formats.

Info

Separate outputs

NN-19 does not have separate outputs, which you may well want if you would like to send individual samples to their own mixer channels for processing and mixing. If you need this facility, either create a separate NN-19 for every sample you want to send separately to the mixer, load your samples into NNXT (which does have separate outs) if you have Reason V2, or load them into ReDrum, whose 10 voice channels all have their own output.

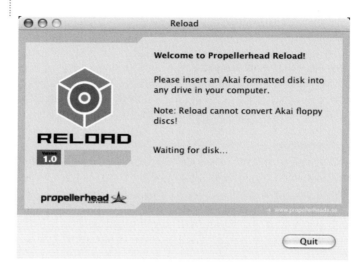

Reload can :

- convert an entire Akai disk into NN-XT Patch files and their associated samples, complete with names, key mapping and parameter settings.
- convert an entire Akai disk into a single ReFill file containing all the converted data, which saves considerable disk space without any loss of quality.

The samples created in the conversion can also be loaded into other Reason devices such as Redrum and NN-19. If you want to convert straight to a ReFill,
ReFill Packer version 2.4.0 or later must be installed on your computer. Reload works on CDs and removable disks - but not floppy disks.

Converting formats

Sample CD-ROMs, too, are not always plain sailing for Reason users. Many such CD-ROMs come in proprietary sampler formats, such as the very widespread Akai format, so these have to be converted into a format that Reason will accept (format conversion is also required for some samples you might find on the Internet).

Loop points in sample Programs (Akai-speak for multisamples) should be preserved after format conversion, but the Programs will have to be re-mapped across the keyboard. However, if a multisample that you have for-mat-converted was created properly by the producer of the CD-ROM, and the samples within it have embedded pitch information, mapping the multi-sample into NN-19 should be as simple as loading the converted samples and selecting 'Automap Samples' from the Edit menu.The good news is that most sound banks and sample collections now come with or are available with Reason-formatted files.

Editing and Looping Samples

If the samples you plan to bring in need editing, or are unlooped and you want to loop them, you will also need an audio editor of some kind. Some programs do a variety of tasks, including ripping, audio recording, editing and looping, so choosing one of these is obviously a tidy solution to many of the issues around bringing good samples into NN-19.

The most sophisticated applications will not necessarily be free (though they are often quite inexpensive). Fortunately, there are a variety of good freeware or shareware audio tools available for both Mac and PC. A list is given in Appendix 1. These include editors that will generally allow you to record your own mono or stereo samples, at a variety of sample rates and bit depths, via your computer's audio hardware or an external audio interface; trim and loop samples; apply processes such as normalising, timestretching, reversing and EQ; and save samples in WAV or AIFF format. You'll also get a large waveform display, with zooming capabilities to allow very precise editing and even spot removal of noise such as clicks and pops. Some soundcards come with free versions of commercial audio programs, so if you're shopping for a new soundcard you might want to bear that in mind and target your choice.

MIDI + Audio sequencers

Another software option for recording audio, that can then be imported into Reason, is one of the MIDI + Audio sequencers or sample-sequencer applications. If you already have one of these, such as Steinberg Cubase, Apple Logic, Digidesign Pro Tools LE, MOTU Digital Performer, or Cakewalk, you will be able to record audio with that, trim it to suit and export it as a WAV or AIFF file for loading into NN-19. However, you won't be able to set loop points properly with an audio sequencer.

There are very low-cost versions of some of these packages: for example, Steinberg Cubase LE and Logic Fun. Digidesign's Pro Tools Free (as the name implies) is free, well-featured and very useful. However in most cases these have been discontinued for some time and will not run on OS X, and are problematic on Windows XP. Some controller keyboards, such as ones discussed in the automation/remote control chapter come with a free MIDI + Audio application, so you might like to bear that in mind if you're shopping.

The rear panel

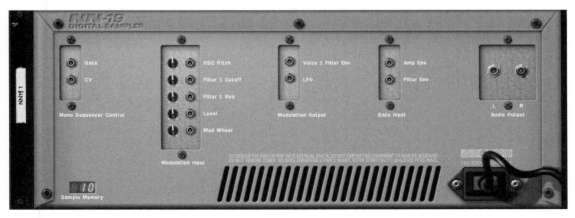

Audio outputs

The usual destination for the stereo audio output of NN-19 is an audio input on the ReMix mixer. This is the automatic audio connection Reason will usually make for you. However, Malström has a pair of audio inputs, which opens up some new possibilities. See the Malström chapter for more. The NN-19 audio output can also, of course, be patched into an effect device (or chain of effects) for in-line processing of NN-19's audio, or directly to the Hardware Interface.

The Sequencer Control Gate and CV inputs

These inputs are for connecting a Matrix Pattern sequencer to trigger NN-19 samples. The correct connections are:

- Note CV output of Matrix connected to Sequencer Control CV input of NN-19.
- Gate CV output of Matrix connected to Sequencer Control Gate Input of NN-19.

These are the routings made when Reason auto-routes NN-19 and a Matrix for you, but you can, of course, make them manually.

The other CV/Gate connections

NN-19 has a standard set of Modulation CV inputs and outputs, plus Amp and Filter Envelope Gate inputs. See Chapter 21 for a chart giving some suggested ways of connecting these sockets to others in the rack.

Info

Sample copyright

Be aware that not all samples that you will find on the Internet will be copyright free. If the samples you find are loops or breaks taken from old records (or if you take your own samples from records), you are legally obliged to obtain clearance for their use from the copyright holder. In practice, if you're just creating tracks at home for your own amusement, with these samples, you won't need copyright clearance. However, if the tracks are for commercial release, you will.

Dr:rex sample loop player

Dr:rex is dedicated to the playback and manipulation of sampled loops saved in a special format, the REX format, created by Propellerhead for their ReCycle software. The ability to use this format compensates to an extent for the fact that it is not possible to do conventional sampler 'timestretching' inside Reason, as the REX format allows loops and breaks of different tempos and pitches to be used together with ease in the same composition.

Although you will probably get the most fun from Dr:rex if you already own ReCycle and can thus prepare REX files of your own material, it is not difficult to find third-party REX files in various styles, to load into Dr:rex. Many REX loops come with the Reason factory ReFill, commercial REX files are readily available, and ReCycle owners often provide their own loops free to fellow users.

Dr:rex doesn't stop at playing back REX files: as well as allowing you to change their pitch and tempo, it enables you to treat REX loops via a full set of synthesis facilities, to subtly or radically change their character. Many other Reason functions are also available to REX loops, allowing them to integrate seamlessly into Reason Songs.

An introduction to ReCycle and REX loops

ReCycle's reason for existence is to allow audio files, in a variety of formats, to be divided into 'slices', automatically or manually. Slice points would tend to fall on rhythmically significant points in the audio file (such as the individual drum hits in a sampled percussion part). It's this slicing process that allows a ReCycle file to have its tempo changed without a change in pitch, and its pitch changed without changing tempo. No 'timestretching' is done (which, incidentally, means that if you shift the pitch of a REX loop far enough, you will still get 'chipmunking' and other standard sampling side-effects). Rather, slicing an audio file actually divides it into sections, all of which retain their same rhythmic relationship at any tempo. If a loop needs to be slower, its slices are simply played back with longer gaps between them, while to speed it up, the gaps will be reduced.

A suite of tools is offered by ReCycle for manipulating slice points and customising the way the final loop will play back. Some of these tools, usefully, allow the user to compensate for the inevitable gaps that will appear between slices when a REX file is played back very slowly.

A rhythmic loop sliced up in ReCycle.

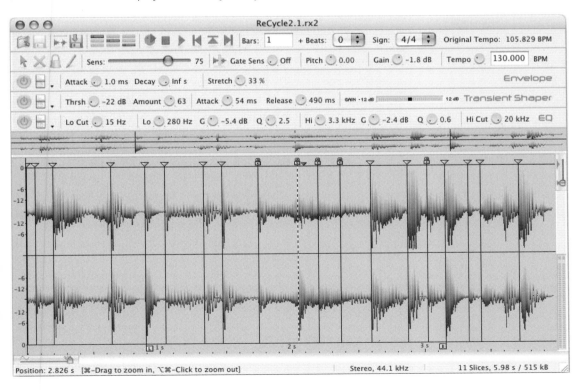

In general, ReCycle is best at working with strictly rhythmic material – drum parts, single-voice bass lines, and so on – but it is capable of processing much more. Reason's factory ReFill includes a handful of electric piano and guitar riffs, and a few synth-pad parts, for example. It's also quite possible to ReCycle sampled vocal parts, though the software's automatic slicing option doesn't tend to work well in these cases: it's necessary to insert the slice points manually at the starts of important words or syllables.

Part of a lead vocal processed with ReCycle. The slice points were largely inserted manually – vocals typically do not have the defined peaks and breaks that allow the automatic slicing process to work so well with rhythm loops. However, doing the job manually doesn't take as long as you might think.

You can consider sub-dividing a lead vocal into sections – individual lines, for example – and assigning each to its own D:rex. (The Dr:rex devices themselves could be routed to a submixer that's patched to the Song's main mixer — see the ReMix chapter for more on submixing.) It's fiddly, but the effort is worth it, as you're then free to change the tempo of Reason Songs that feature REX lead vocals, for example, in a way that isn't possible with vocal samples loaded into NN19 or NNXT.

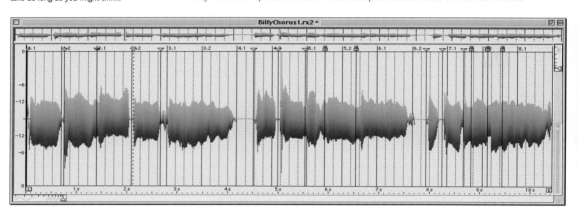

Dr:rex basics

Each Dr:rex can play back one REX file at a time. If you had three REX loops you wanted to use together in Reason, you would thus need three Dr:rexs in your rack. Loops created with ReCycle v2.x can be mono or stereo; earlier versions were mono only, but Dr:rex loads both types. The .rex, .rcy (PC ReCycle) and .rex2 file formats are all recognised.

Each REX loop can be composed of up to 99 slices and is a maximum of five minutes long. Every slice in the loop has a corresponding MIDI note that triggers it, meaning that you can play the slices from a MIDI keyboard, put them into a track in the sequencer, change their order, to make the loop sound different, and apply MIDI editing operations to them.

Aside from the controls in Dr:rex that allow you to work directly on the loop's constituent slices, you also have a filter and filter envelope, an LFO, an amplitude envelope and a simple modulation section with which to work wonders on REX files. Not forgetting the rear panel, where CV and Gate sockets allow you to do things with loops that can't be done anywhere but inside Reason.

Get going with Dr:rex

We're going to load a REX loop and use some of the Dr:rex controls on it. After this quickstart tutorial, these features and controls will be discussed in more detail.

- Create a ReMix device, if you don't already have one in the rack, then a Dr:rex.
- Use Apple-B/Control-B to bring up the REX File Browser.
- Click on the magnifying glass icon at the top of the dialogue box, to 'Find All ReFills'. Go Reason Factory Soundbank> 'Music Loops'> Variable Tempo'> 'Downtempo Loops'> 090_VinylRhodes. Double-click the file name to load the loop. Alternatively, load any melodic REX loop you happen to have.
- Click the 'Select Slice via MIDI' button, to light it.
- Now click the Preview button to hear the loop play back continuously. You can see a highlight move across the display as the different slices in the loop play back (this highlight would not appear if we hadn't clicked the 'Select Slice via MIDI' button, though the loop would, of course, still

Load the REX loop.

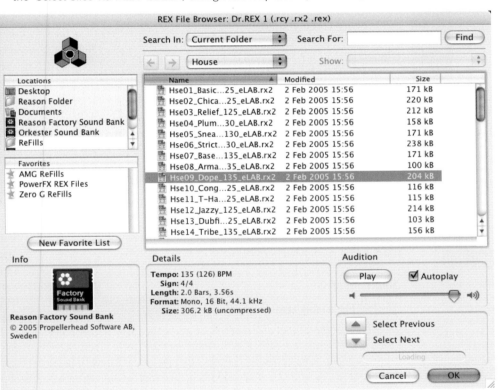

The loop loaded into Dr:rex.

play back). The loop will be playing back at the overall tempo set for the Song in the Transport bar, even though it says 'Loop Tempo 90bpm' in the waveform display. Set the Transport tempo to 90bpm to match the loop, if you are using our factory example.

- We'll transpose the loop in real time. While the loop is playing back, click a few notes on the small keyboard display under the waveform (the Transpose Keyboard), one by one. You can hear that the loop transposes according to the key you've clicked, but its tempo remains the same. Click the Preview button to stop playback. You can see from this how a melodic loop could be transposed up and down to make the basis for a whole Song.

- Now we'll get an idea of what can be done with individual slices. Click on any one of the slices in the loop to 'select' it. A highlight rectangle should appear over it. Turn the Pitch knob under the display until the number above it reads '7'.

- Click the Preview button again. As the loop plays back, when it gets to the slice you previously highlighted, you should hear that the pitch of that slice has been raised (by seven semitones). Obviously, this doesn't sound that wonderful with this loop, but you get an idea of the possibilities for changing loops! Stop playback.

- Pitch changing is not all you can do with a slice. Click any slice to highlight it, then go to the Level knob under the display and and set it to a value of '0'. Click the Preview button. The slice whose volume you've just turned down to nothing has dropped out of the loop. Well, actually it's still there – you just can't hear it with a volume of '0'!

- You can also change the Decay (length) of a slice, and give it a Pan position in the left-right stereo image. Experiment with these knobs, on slices of your choice.

Select a Slice (note the highlight rectangle) and raise its pitch by seven semitones with the Pitch knob.

The loop is not permanently changed by any of these operations, by the way! You can set the knobs under the display back to their original values for the modified slices, or just re-load the same loop to reset the knobs to their original states.

Guided tour

The REX file loading area

This is the equivalent of the Sample loading area in NN19, NNXT and ReDrum. Clicking the Browse Loop button with the folder icon, using Apple/Control-B, or choosing 'Browse ReCycle/REX files' from the Edit menu or a contextual menu gives you access to the REX File Browser, which you can use to navigate to the factory ReFill REX files or any other REX files on your hard drive. (Note that samples in other formats cannot be loaded into Dr:rex.)

File loading area.

The Waveform Display

Sliced Waveform

When a REX file is loaded into Dr:rex, it appears in the waveform display. Those familiar with ReCycle will recognise the appearance of a 'sliced' waveform, which looks like a series of signal peaks separated by vertical lines. The peaks are the main beats or rhythmic peaks of the loop – in a drum loop,

individual drum hits – while the lines are
the slice marks. It is possible to select
individual slices in the display, in order to
edit their tuning and so on, as we did in
the tutorial example above.

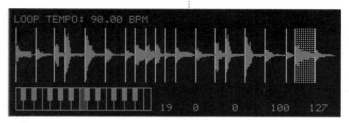

Stereo REX loops can, of course, be
loaded, but you only see a single mixed
left/right waveform in the display. This
makes no difference to the user, since

Waveform display.

everything done to the waveform is applied equally to the left and right sides
of it.

Waveform Tempo

The text immediately above the waveform in the display always shows the
loop's original tempo. But when a loop is loaded into Dr:rex it will always play
back at the current Song tempo, which is set in the Transport bar. This means
that if you use multiple REX loops in a Song, they should always fit each
other, and fit with the rest of the Song, in terms of tempo.

The Transpose Keyboard

This is where REX loops start to be fun. While the REX loop is playing back (either
because you have clicked the Preview key or have sent the loop's MIDI notes to
the sequencer to play back from there), clicking on the keys of the Transpose
Keyboard (or turning the Transpose knob under the display) transposes the loop
in real time, up or down one octave in semitone steps. The process can be automated: Transpose Keyboard clicks and Transpose knob tweaks can be recorded
into a Dr:rex track in the sequencer.

Transpose Keyboard.

Remember that you're transposing, not playing actual note pitches: just
because you click an E-flat on the Transpose Keyboard, that doesn't necessarily mean the pitch the loop plays is an E-flat. The original, un-transposed
pitch of the loop is played by the 'C' note in the middle of the Transpose
Keyboard. Clicking a C# will transpose by a semitone whether the original
pitch of the slice is a C or not – and so on.

A single melodic loop could, via transposition, be made to work over the
entire course of a longer piece. One of our favourite applications of this technique
is to create an arpeggio-like Pattern with other Reason devices – SubTractor
being played by a Matrix Pattern, for example – bounce it to disk as an audio file,
process the file with ReCycle and then load it into Dr:rex. Reason lacks an arpeggiator, and this technique almost makes up for it, since transpositions of the REX
loop arpeggio pattern can be made and recorded in real time, just as if you were
changing the chords being rhythmically broken by an arpeggiator. (The idea is
explained more fully later in this chapter.) We also use automated transposition
to change the pitch of other melodic material, making one loop work for a whole
track. Bass lines, especially, work well.

The Slice parameter knobs

Beneath the waveform display are six knobs, including the Transpose knob
which we've just discussed. These are used for firstly selecting individual

slices within a loop (the Slice knob does this) and secondly applying certain offset parameters to each of them – each slice can have its own set of four offset parameter values. The setting of each knob is shown in the waveform display immediately above the knobs. Note that these values apply to the currently loaded loop only: if you load a new REX loop, the parameters will be reset to their default values.

Slice parameter knobs.

Slice
Turning this knob scrolls through each slice in the loop, in turn. A selected slice is highlighted with a pale rectangle – see the screen in the tutorial example at the start of the chapter. You can also select slices in the waveform display by clicking on them, and this is rather easier than using the Slice knob. Once you've selected a slice, you can do various things with it, using the remaining knobs.

Pitch
Sets a pitch offset of up to 50 semitones above or below the slice's original pitch. Via this knob, you can change the pitch of each slice relative to the others – tuning parts of the loop, for example, to fit with what is happening in other tracks in the same composition, or re-pitching drums in a drum loop.

Pan
Lets you set a position in the stereo field for each slice. If the loop is mono, this helps to create some stereo interest, as you can pan the slices progressively across the stereo image. Also try setting alternate left/right pan positions for the alternate slices in a loop, so it bounces across the stereo image. If the loop is already stereo, the pan knob behaves as a balance control. So if a particular slice has audio in the left channel and none in the right, panning all the way to the right will make the slice, effectively, silent.

Level
Lets you set an independent volume for each slice.

Decay
Effectively a simple envelope control, the decay knob lets you shorten the length of each slice, giving you another way of customising how the loop sounds . Its default is 127, the maximum value.

Select Slice via MIDI
If this button is activated, pressing certain keys on your MIDI keyboard steps through the slices in the loop, one by one, just like turning the Slice knob (you'll also hear the slice play). The first slice of the REX loop is always

---

Info

Slice Auditioning

When you hold down Option/Alt and move the mouse pointer over the Waveform Display, the pointer takes on the shape of a speaker, indicating that the slices in the loop can be auditioned by clicking on them.

mapped to key C1 on the keyboard, and successive semitones from there trigger successive slices in the loop. As you step through the slices with the keyboard, you'll see them highlight in the display.

Select Slice via MIDI.

Preview button

Click to hear the loop play back continuously. This is not something you can automate or record into the sequencer, by the way! It's purely an audition feature that also lets you try out the effect of real-time transposing of the loop.

Preview button.

'To Track' button

This is one you'll be using a lot. Clicking the 'To Track' button sends the MIDI notes that trigger each slice of the current loop to a track of the Reason sequencer. (It's usually best if you send the notes to the Dr:rex track, obviously.)

- Highlight the desired sequencer track name, by clicking on it.
- Set the left and right sequencer locators around the area where you want the loop notes to go. The loop's-worth of notes will repeat automatically to fill the space between the locators when they are sent 'to track'. So if you want a REX drum loop to repeat for eight bars, even though the loop itself is only two bars long, set the locators around an eight-bar section in the Dr:rex track in the sequencer.
- Click the 'To Track' button. The notes should appear in the track. Each repetition of the loop will be automatically 'grouped', so that it can be cut, copied and pasted as one entity if desired.

To Track button.

See the sequencer chapter for details on positioning locators, editing, and so on.

Note that when you've sent the notes to the sequencer in this way, all the operations mentioned above still work on the loop in Dr:rex – all you've done is allow the sequencer to trigger the loop for you so that you can begin building a track with it. Real-time transposing using the Transpose Keyboard or a MIDI keyboard still works on the loop, and you can automate this – this will be coverered in more detail later in the chapter.

If you load a different loop into Dr:rex when you've already sent the MIDI notes for the previously loaded loop 'To Track', the slices of the new loop will be triggered by the MIDI notes for the old loop, when you play back from the sequencer. This won't be right, of course, but it could be interesting! You'll get new sounds (the slices of the new loop) being triggered in the rhythmic pattern of the previous loop. Whether this works or not depends partly on how well the number of slices in the two loops match up, but with drum loops this can be like changing kits for a pre-programmed drum pattern.

Sending a REX loop 'To Track'. The MIDI notes that trigger the Slices of the loop are copied into a sequencer track.

Info

'To track' or not 'To track'?

It's not compulsory to use the 'To Track' facility: you could just as easily trigger loop slices in real time from your master keyboard, recording the hits into the sequencer, or draw the hits into the note or REX lane in the sequencer's Edit View. This is a good way of re-using the original elements of a REX file.

The synthesis controls

Dr:rex's synthesis controls are very similar to those of NN19, which are themselves a cut-down version of the ones SubTractor has. If you need more info on synthesis in general, it's a good idea to read the relevant parts of the SubTractor chapter. But rather than sending you off to other chapters for basic descriptions of the synthesis controls Dr:rex has in common with other devices, here's a quick run through.

The Oscillator section

Oscillator section

Obviously, Dr:rex does not have an oscillator, in the sense that a synth does. What passes for the Dr:rex oscillator is the REX loop loaded into the device, which you can modify with a trio of pitch-related controls. The first two of these controls allow you to tune the whole REX loop.

- *The Octave knob* has an 8-octave range – four octaves up and four down ('normal', unshifted pitch can be restored at a value of '4').
- *The Oscillator Fine tune knob* has a range of +/-50 cents.

Don't confuse the above with the Pitch knob, which tunes individual slices in a loop, or the Transpose functions, which are really performance/track-building aids. The oscillator pitch controls simply adjust the pitch of the entire loop. The Fine tune knob is obviously useful for tweaking a loop to be in tune with other loops and samples you may be using in a track, but what about the Octave knob? Why would you need an eight-octave range? Well, try it out with a few loops and you'll see. Bass loops, for example, can be made into interesting high-pitched accent patterns, and, in general, extreme pitch-shifts on a loop are excellent for sound-design work or introducing a weird feel into your tracks.

The Envelope Amount knob

This may need some special explanation. With its slightly simplified synthesis controls (when compared to the synth devices), Dr:rex doesn't have a dedicated pitch envelope for controlling the pitch of a sound over time. What the Envelope Amount knob does is cause the Filter Envelope (more in a minute) to also work as a Pitch Envelope, and that then causes the pitch of slices within a loop to vary over time. The small amounts of pitch variation you might add to a sound using an envelope will often work well if the Filter is using the same envelope as well – the filter-envelope curve reinforces the pitch envelope.

The Envelope Amount knob has a positive and negative value range; with a positive Envelope Amount, pitch goes up and then down again, while a negative amount moves pitch in the opposite direction – down and then up. If you don't want any pitch enveloping to occur alongside the filter enveloping, just leave this knob at its centre position. By the way, if the Filter has been switched off (see below), the Filter Envelope controls can be used to set up just a pitch envelope.

The Filter

Dr:rex's single, resonant, multi-mode filter is identical to SubTractor's Filter 1. Rather than removing frequencies from a harmonically rich waveform, though, as in the case of a synth, it's applying the same 'sound-sculpting' process to whatever loop you've loaded into Dr:rex. Unlike the filter on SubTractor, Dr:rex's can be switched out of the signal path if desired, using the switch next to the 'Filter' label. More detail on filters can be found in the SubTractor chapter.

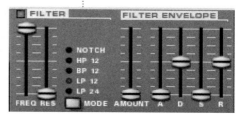

Filter and Filter Envelope

Filter Envelope

Governs the opening and closing of the filter, in effect altering the filter frequency, and hence the texture of the sound, over time. The filter envelope will have the most audible effect if you set the Frequency slider low and raise the Resonance and Envelope Amount controls.

In the case of Dr:rex, the filter is triggered anew (starts its action all over again) by every slice in a loop, which might mean that there isn't enough time for classic filter effects, such as filter sweeps, to develop. However, the effect of the envelope being triggered by slices – especially if the filter has been set to a high resonance – is rather like that achieved by triggering the filter externally, from a rhythmic source, and can be very effective. If the Filter as a whole is switched out, by the way, the Filter Envelope will have no effect, unless you are using it as a pitch envelope, as mentioned above.

The LFO

The Low Frequency Oscillator makes no audible sound but can be used to 'modulate' other sounds, adding movement and variety through effects such as vibrato (pitch modulation) and tremolo (volume modulation).

- *LFO waveforms:* Dr:rex's LFO has the same number of waveform options as the LFO in SubTractor (triangle, up and down sawtooth, square, random and soft random), which each produce a different 'shape' of modulation effect.
- *LFO 'destinations':* The LFO can be set to modulate 'oscillator' (ie. loop) Pitch, Filter Frequency, and Pan, using the 'Dest' (destination) switch.
- *Amount control:* This sets the depth of the LFO effect. As an example, when modulating pitch with the LFO, low settings of the Amount knob cause very slight undulations in pitch, while high Amount settings cause deep, pronounced pitch variations. If the Amount knob is set to '0', you won't hear any LFO action.
- *Sync button:* Click this to make the movement of the LFO sync to Song tempo. Unbeatable for rhythmic and ambient material alike.

LFO

Using the LFO

Choosing pitch as an LFO destination in Dr:rex can produce some useful effects, especially when the LFO is set to sync to Song tempo. Individual slices can be made to change pitch semi-randomly.

Routing the LFO to pan allows you to gradually move a loop back and forth across the stereo field. The speed of the movement depends on the setting of the LFO Rate control, and the pattern of panning differs according to the LFO waveform you've selected. For example, the square wave makes a definite repeating left-right swap, while the triangle does a gradual 'fading' pan from left to right and back. Click the Sync button for tempo-sync'd panning. You can set up very sophisticated, varying panning effects by doing nothing more than choosing different LFO waveforms – try automating the changing of waveforms to produce different patterns in different parts of a track.

From the front panel of Dr:rex it is not possible to set the LFO to modulate level, to produce tremolo. However, this can be done via the patch sockets on the back panel (more on that later in this chapter). Try the LFO modulating level with a percussion loop, for interesting 'compression-type' pumping effects.

Amplitude Envelope.

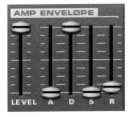

The Amplitude Envelope

This controls changes in level (volume or amplitude) over time. The standard ADSR Amp envelope is triggered by each slice in a loop, which means that it affects every slice of the loop separately and you canuse it to tailor the slices:

- *Attack:* Define how fast or slow the attack of slices within a REX loop are.
- *Decay:* After the peak level set by the Attack slider has been reached, the sound starts to reduce in volume; how long this reduction takes is set by the Decay slider.
- *Sustain:* This slider sets the level to which the Decay portion of the envelope drops; this level is held, in effect, for the length of a slice.
- *Release:* The time taken for the slice's level to fade to silence, before the next slice is triggered.

In practice, the effect of the Release portion of the amplitude envelope won't really be heard, since slices, especially in percussive loops, tend to follow on so quickly. For the same reason, altering the Decay and Sustain portions will tend to have much the same audible effect, of determining how long a slice will sound.

This relationship changes slightly if a slow attack has been programmed, with Decay and Sustain becoming more like their equivalents in the NN19 or SubTractor amp envelopes. The Dr:rex envelope also behaves more traditionally if the REX loop has long slices that you're triggering manually, to allow the envelope's development to be heard, which is especially useful if you're triggering individual samples polyphonically. (By the way, if slices seem to be cut short when you're triggering them manually from the keyboard, increase the Release value to let each slice play out for its full length.)

Level slider

The level slider next to the Amp Envelope controls serves as an overall volume control for Dr:rex. Usually, it's best to have this up full and adjust the device playback level via its ReMix mixer channel.

The Velocity controls

Incoming velocity data, from a MIDI controller or the main sequencer, can be set to have an effect on certain Dr:rex sound parameters. The Filter Envelope amount can be changed by velocity, as can Filter Envelope decay and Amplitude (volume) – any or all. Use positive values of the knobs in this area to make higher velocity levels (harder playing) create more change, and negative values for the opposite effect – playing more softly creates more of the desired effect. See the SubTractor chapter for more on using the Velocity controls in general.

Setting polyphony

Dr:rex's maximum polyphony is 99 notes, just like NN19 and SubTractor. This might seem odd for a device that's designed for playing loops. It's true

Velocity controls.

that most of the time 1-voice polyphony will do, but if you have a sliced-up drum loop, for example, you might actually like to play the individual slices as if they were part of a 'multisample' made up of separate drum samples – or re-program the MIDI trigger notes in the sequencer likewise. This could well result in more than one slice being triggered on a given beat, and this wouldn't be possible if you couldn't increase Dr:rex's polyphony value. When a Dr:rex is created, it defaults to 6-note polyphony, and this is probably a pretty sensible value for most occasions.

Polyphony display

Pitch-bend and Modulation wheels

The pitch-bend wheel bends the pitch of a REX loop up or down. With pitch-bend, you're able to add small or large expressive bends during a performance. Moving the pitch-bend wheel on an attached MIDI keyboard causes the on-screen wheel to move and pitch-bend to be applied to the loop during playback. The accompanying numeric display and increment/decrement buttons are used to indicate and change the semitone 'range' of the pitch-bend wheel.

Pitch-bend and mod

The Modulation Wheel is another common real-time performance control. In Dr:rex it may be assigned to control any or all of Filter Frequency, Filter Resonance, and Filter Envelope Decay, in positive or negative amounts.

Info

Saving REX files as MIDI Files

There may be time when you'd like to trigger the loop loaded into a Dr:rex device via MIDI, from another sequencer. The occasion might arise when you're using Reason as a virtual sound module and don't plan to work with any of its native sequencing facilities. Propellerhead have provided a simple, but useful answer: just select 'Export REX as MIDI File' from Reason's File menu, and you can save a little MIDI file containing just the triggers for the loop currently loaded into Dr:rex anywhere you like on your hard drive, for importing into your other sequencer.

REX loops can be saved as MIDI data.

The rear panel

Audio outputs

Dr:rex's stereo audio output can be connected to a ReMix mixer input channel (as it will be if Reason makes an automatic connection for you); to the
input of an effects device, for in-line effects processing; or to a pair of inputs
on the Hardware Interface. Malström has a pair of audio inputs, which opens
up some new possibilities. See the Malström chapter for more.

The CV inputs and outputs

As with the other devices, there is much potential in real-panel modulation
routings. See Chapter 4 for an explanation of the CV/Gate system and
Chapter 21 for some suggested CV and Gate routings.

The Gate Inputs

Dr:rex has two Gate Inputs, for the Amp Envelope and the Filter Envelope.
The effect of connecting a ReDrum voice channel Gate Out to a Dr:rex Gate
In, for example, will be to impose the rhythmic pattern being played by the
ReDrum channel upon the REX loop. In fact, the events in a Dr:rex sequencer
track which would normally trigger the slices in a loop no longer have any
effect on the Amp or Filter Envelopes if the Envelopes are being triggered
from another device. The result of external triggering of the Amp Envelope is
particularly noticeable and interesting: slices will only be heard if they coincide with an incoming trigger or occur during the time it takes for the envelope curve to complete its cycle. Triggering the Dr:rex Filter Envelope externally introduces rhythmic timbral changes to a loop, independently of the
main slice pattern.

You can also connect CV Outputs to Gate Inputs. For example, set up
LFO1 in a SubTractor to generate a square wave that's synchronised to Song
tempo (V2) with a 16th-note resolution. Now connect that LFO's Modulation
CV output to the Amp Envelope Gate input of Dr:rex; the effect will depend
on the loop, but a pseudo-random triggering of the amp envelope should
ensue, creating a different rhythmic pattern from the slices in the loop.

Slice Gate output

This outputs a Gate signal for each triggered slice in the REX loop. You could
route this trigger to a drum voice in ReDrum, so that the drum voice fires in
time with the Dr:rex slices.

If you're working with a bass guitar or bass synth REX loop, for example, try connecting the Dr:rex Slice Gate out to the Gate In of a channel in ReDrum playing a bass drum. This can get your rhythm section off to a nice, tight start: the bass Slices cause the bass drum to trigger in exactly the same rhythm, which can be very effective and compelling with the right loop – it needs to be quite sparse and running at a moderate to slow tempo. An alternative is triggering something like a ReDrum hi-hat via the Slice Gate output, which works better with faster or busier loops.

Note that when the REX loop has been sent 'to track', the MIDI trigger notes have a fixed velocity, and this velocity also affects the Gate pulse being sent from the Slice Gate output. If you're triggering a drum sound with the Slice Gate output, this can make the drum sound trigger rather too loudly. You can fix this by either going to the Dr:rex sequencer track and altering the velocity of the slice MIDI notes, or turning down the volume of the drum sound within ReDrum. Simply turning down the volume doesn't sort out the fixed velocity issue; you might prefer that the triggered drum sound respond to varying velocities since it sounds more interesting, or there might be a parameter within the drum voice channel that has a velocity controlled-element – including, depending on the channel, sample start time, tone or pitch bend. Thus it's probably better to alter the slice note velocities.

Dr:rex Slice Gate pulses could also be routed to any other device's Gate Input, so that the rhythm of the slices can be imposed on the other device. For example, if you send the slice Gates to SubTractor's Filter Envelope Gate Input, you cause the Filter Envelope to re-trigger in time with the REX loop slices, creating a useful subliminal emphasis of the rhythm.

Using Dr:rex

Saving your work
There is no such thing as a Dr:rex 'patch'; saving your Dr:rex work (the REX file and associated panel settings) is as part of a Song. (Choose 'Save As' under the File menu).

Copying loops
If you've changed a REX loop in Dr:rex and you'd like to use it with its changes in another Song, the way to do it is to copy the whole Dr:rex device, with the loop, from one song to another. Choose 'Copy Device' from the Edit menu or a contextual menu.

Use the synthesis controls on a rhythm loop
Working with the synthesis controls lets you radically alter the character of the individual drum hits in a loop, potentially changing them from thunderous crashes to nothing more than rhythmic clicks, and stages in between – great for making loops more original to you. Here's a quick example, using the amp envelope, the filter and filter envelope, and the LFO:

- Create a Dr:rex device if you don't already have one in the rack. Load the 'Hse06_strictly_130' loop from the House folder in the Dr:rex Drum Loops folder of the factory ReFill. (Alternatively, use another drum loop,

but expect to tweak the settings given below, for best effect.)
- Click the Preview button to hear this standard House beat play back.
- Make sure the filter type is selected as LP12. Set the filter Frequency slider to 45 and Resonance to 70.
- Set the Filter Envelope Amount to 95, then the envelope sliders as follows: A=0, Decay=20, Sustain=0 and Release=50.
- In the LFO section, enable sync by clicking on the Sync button (if you have V2), choose the first Random waveform (second from bottom of the list), and set the Rate knob to 1/4 (leave the mouse pointer over the rate knob until a Tool Tip appears, then you can get the value right). Set the Amount knob to 127. Select 'Filter' as the LFO destination.
- In the Amp Envelope, set A=10, D=70, Sustain=0, Release=65.
- Click the Preview button again to hear the modified loop play back. You should be able to hear the difference. This is just an example. Experiment!

The Dr:rex synthesis control settings for the modified example drum loop.

What can I do after 'To Track'?

When you've used the 'To Track' function, as explained earlier, and the MIDI notes for your loop are in the sequencer, that's not the end of the fun – in fact, it could be just the start of it! You can now work with those notes in the sequencer as though they were any other MIDI data, changing the playback of the loop slices without affecting the loop itself at all.

Viewing the slice triggers in the sequencer

You'll be able to see the loop trigger notes quite well enough in the sequencer's Arrange View if you only want to cut, copy and paste entire repetitions of the loop to arrange them into a track. The automatic grouping that Reason does with each loop repetition will help with this.

You can view the notes much more closely in the sequencer's Edit mode (access this by using Shift-Tab or clicking the button at the far left of the Toolbar). What you will see in front of you for the highlighted sequencer track is the special REX lane, which displays the REX slice triggers in a different way from the usual Key lane.

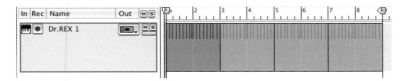

A REX loop sent to a sequencer track, using the 'To Track' facility. Here the MIDI note triggers are displayed in the sequencer Arrange View.

The advantage of the REX lane for displaying the MIDI notes that trigger a loop is that it shows a list of slice numbers on the vertical axis, rather than a keyboard diagram. The vertical list has 99 entries, one for each of the potential maximum number of slices in a REX file. Individual slices can be easily auditioned in the sequencer: leave your mouse pointer hovering for a second or two and it will turn into a speaker icon; now you can audition simply by clicking the slice numbers (or the keyboard graphic's keys, if you're using the sequencer Key lane to view slices).

REX slices are velocity sensitive, too, so the sequencer's velocity lane comes into use when editing a Dr:rex part.

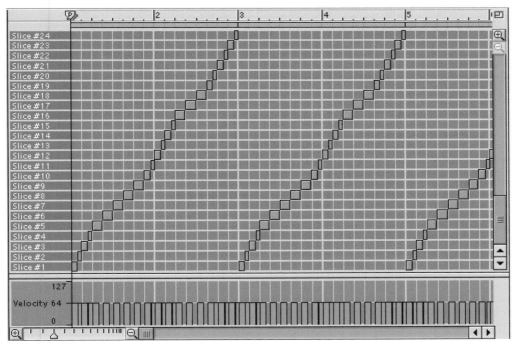

The same loop viewed in the REX Lane (Edit View), with the Velocity lane beneath.

If you prefer to view the slice triggers as normal MIDI notes, just access the Key lane for that track, by clicking the Key Lane button on the Toolbar, which has the keyboard icon.

Building up a track in the sequencer
For those who are not experienced in sequencer use, here's a quick run-through of the first steps you could take to create a track. See the sequencer chapter for more detail.

At the most basic level, assuming you don't want to make any changes to the order of the loop slices, but just want to use loops in their entirety, starting to build up a track based around several loops inthe sequencer is straightforward:

- Use 'To Track' for each Dr:rex device, to send the notes that trigger the slices in each loop to their own sequencer tracks, where you have set the left and right locators around the section you want to fill with the loop. It's probably easiest to just send four bars or so of each loop. Now you can audition all the REX files you've sent to track at the same time, by hitting the Play button on the Transport bar, or pressing the computer Space bar; engaging the 'Loop' button, also in the Transport bar, makes the four bars play continuously. Press the Space bar again to stop playback.
- Copy the Grouped notes that trigger the slices and place them wherever you would like each REX loop to play. Highlight a Group by clicking it, and option/control-dragging it to a new location (this places a copy of the original Group in the new location).

Building up a track with REX loops.

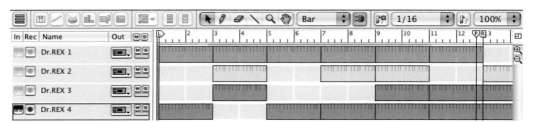

- For any section where you don't want a particular loop playing, either leave the track area blank, highlight the Group at that point and delete it, or automate a mute of that Dr:rex mixer channel, as discussed in the automation/remote control chapter.
- Now you can add extra parts using the other devices.

Automating loop transposing with a melodic loop

As mentioned earlier, melodic REX loops, such as short bass phrases, piano or keyboard licks, pad chord patterns, and so on, can be used to form the foundation of a whole track. You can extend the usefulness of a suitable loop by transposing it multiple times to create a 'chord progression'.

Once you've sent a chunk of loop MIDI triggers to the sequencer (using 'To Track'), you can try out various transpositions in real time just by playing back the track and clicking the Transpose Keyboard, or perhaps using the MIDI keyboard notes that transpose a REX loop (see Keyboard Shortcuts elsewhere in this chapter).

The next stage is to actually automate this transposition, recording your movements into the sequencer track. (Assume you've sent your loop's MIDI notes 'To Track' already.)

- Click in the 'In' column of the Dr:rex track in the sequencer to make the MIDI icon appear. Make sure you are in Overdub mode, not Replace mode (check the Overdub/Replace switch in the Transport bar). If you only want to hear the REX track, and not any other parts of the Song, as you transpose, you can solo the REX track by Option/Alt-clicking in the 'M' (Mute) column next to its sequencer track name.

- Click the red record button in the sequencer, then the play button (or use Apple/Control-Return, then the Space bar). Record mode is now engaged and the REX loop should be playing back.
- Click the keys of the Transpose Keyboard or press the relevant keys on your MIDI keyboard to transpose the loop up and down as desired. Transposition takes effect immediately you do this, so you can transpose even single notes on the fly if you're fairly alert. When you're finished, stop recording and return the playing position to zero. Then you can play back to hear what you've done.

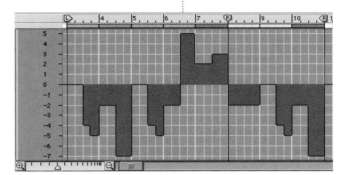

This is the 'Transpose' sequencer controller lane for a bass line REX loop that has been transposed up and down to make a new bass line. Transposition data can be recorded into the lane as keys on the Dr:rex Transpose Keyboard are clicked in real time, but in this example the transposition data was drawn in. The end result should be pretty much the same either way, but drawing can be more precise.

Re-ordering the slice triggers

If you want to depart further from the original composition of a loop, how about re-ordering its slices, so that they play back differently? You can do this in various ways:

- 'On the fly' re-sequencing: Don't use 'To Track' on the loop, but instead trigger the loop slices in real time from your master keyboard (just as if they were part of a multisample in NN19 or NNXT), while recording the triggering into the sequencer. Resequencing REX loop slices in this way can be effective with many different kinds of audio. For example, REX drum loops are typically sliced at each drum hit, and once you know which MIDI notes trigger the different hits, you can play them from the keyboard as if they are individual drum samples, creating a completely new drum part from the original hits. Then you can quantize or groove quantize them in the sequencer. It's possible to get a really good, slightly unnatural feel from this idea.

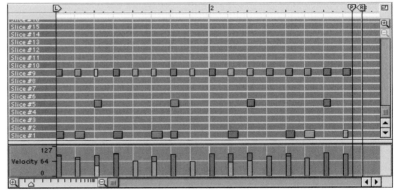

The slices of this REX drum loop were re-ordered into a new drum pattern by triggering them live from the keyboard while recording into the sequencer.

- The same goes for melodic loops, though the effect tends to be rather more random, since a loop won't necessarily be made of enough individual notes to re-sequence lots of new melodies. The technique can be particularly striking if you've ReCycled a lead vocal of some kind, slicing the vocal at the beginning of words or syllables. Try playing back the words or syllables at random from the keyboard.
- Re-ordering with sequencer edit functions: Use 'To Track' on the loop, then once it's in the sequencer, delete slices as required, copy slices or sections of the loop, and generally alter the order of the slices. One thing to try with percussion loops is highlighting the whole loop, then option/control-dragging it one or two beats to the right, creating a copy

with a different start time. You may get doubles, which can be deleted selectively if any don't work. Any bits that work particularly well can be copied and repeated, and you can apply Quantize and/or Groove Quantize to the new data. Make sure you have 'Snap to Grid' active in the sequencer, so you can drag to exact note subdivisions.

Even simply dragging a copy of the loop MIDI notes a bit to the right and upwards (or perhaps downwards if you're only copying a section of the loop) creates a different feel from a loop, making new fills and breaks. Here one copy was dragged twelve sixteenths later and another three sixteenths back and four slices up. The result sounds much more sophisticated, at a cost of very little effort.

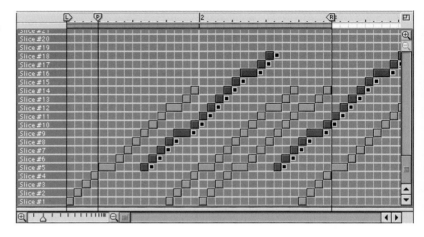

- Applying 'Alter Notes': The 'Change Events' dialogue (under the Edit menu) includes the 'Alter Notes' command, which randomises events and their locations. Try this on whole or partial sets of REX loop triggers in the sequencer. If you keep the percentage low to medium, the results are more immediately usable, but you can keep clicking 'Change Events' until you get something you like (Undo if you go a stage too far). Randomising slices in this way is worth trying with vocals or speech loops. The 'Scale Tempo' function, in the same dialogue, can be applied to a loop for a quick way of making it play back at, say, twice or half speed.

The Change Events dialogue.

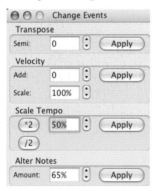

Using 'Alter Notes' on REX loop MIDI triggers in the sequencer. The slices that play the original loop are on the left, with the 'altered' notes on the right. You don't always have to alter them this much!

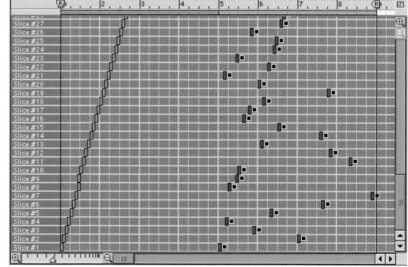

The 'Dr:rex arpeggiator'

Reason doesn't have that classic device for rhythmically breaking up chords, an arpeggiator. Some techniques which allow you to simulate arpeggio-like patterns are discussed in the Matrix chapter, but Dr:rex offers another method.

To get the most out of this technique, you'll need to be a ReCycle user, since the technique requires you to make some of your own samples to turn into REX loops. However, you may well find suitable, ready-REX'd material on dedicated sample CDs and web sites.

Basically, the procedure involves creating simple broken chord patterns with Reason devices (the Patterns provided in the Matrix chapter would be a good bet), bouncing them to disk as audio, ReCycling them and re-importing the loops into a Dr:rex device. Then the loops can be transposed to suit in real time.

- Choose or create a sound suitable for arpeggiating, in one of the synth or sampler devices.
- Connect a Matrix Pattern Sequencer to the device you've selected, and draw in a Pattern of notes that make up a broken chord. A Pattern based on root notes and fifths is probably best for a first attempt – C and G, for example – played across two or more octaves if you like. You might try alternating Cs and Gs going upwards in consecutive octaves, and perhaps coming down again, to fill up a 16-step Matrix Pattern (with eighth-note or 16th-note resolution).

A suitable arpeggio Pattern in the Matrix, triggering a SubTractor synth sound. As the Pattern extends across two octaves, you can't see all of it, but what's missing is only the top 'G' in the four-note Pattern.

- Now set a one-bar loop in the sequencer.
- From the File menu, select 'Export Loop as Audio File'; make sure only the Pattern you've just created is playing, with any effects you require, by deleting other devices, or by muting them in the mixer, or by soloing the instrument that's playing your Pattern.
- Load the resulting audio file into ReCycle, and have ReCycle automatically slice it for you. Set the loop's length, to fix its base tempo, and save. You might like to normalise the file before saving, as well as reducing it to mono, as long as the loop doesn't contain any important stereo information.
- In Reason, create a Dr:rex device, and load the loop you've just created into it.
- Set up a suitable loop length in the sequencer – say 16 bars – and click the 'To Track' button to send the MIDI notes to the Dr:rex sequencer track.

- To get a true arpeggiated effect, change the pitch of the pattern to suit the changing chords of a Song, clicking on the Transpose Keyboard in the waveform display as the loop is playing back. Sounds good, doesn't it? Decide what chords you need, and record the transposition changes to the Dr:rex track; you could alternatively draw the changes in manually in the track's Transpose controller lane.

The arpeggio Pattern sliced in ReCycle.

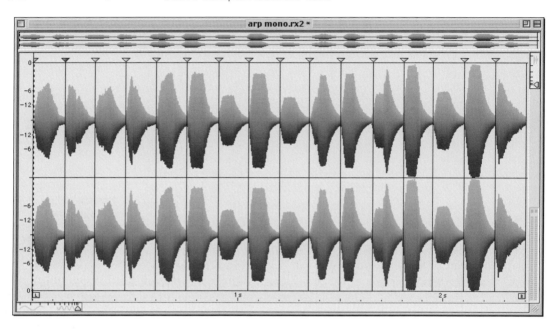

Load the ReCycled arpeggio back into Dr:rex and transpose up and down to suit, using the Transpose keyboard or drawing transpositions in the sequencer.

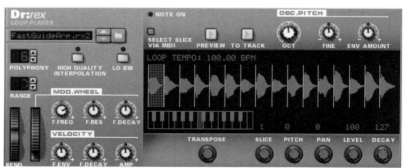

Once you've made a collection of ReCycled arpeggio patterns, you can load them in and play with them in almost the same spontaneous way as if you were playing an arpeggiator for real. If you like this technique, you could create a library folder for saving sampled arpeggio patterns, to use any time you need the effect; make sure the REX loop's file name contains a reference to the loop's key, or create all your arpeggio sample loops in C. Fifths or other neutral intervals are best, so that transposition has less chance of causing dissonances against the Song's main harmony. If you want more complex patterns, create minor and major (and even diminished, augmented and so on) versions of them. Use multiple Dr:rex devices if you need major and minor arpeggios in the same Song.

The REX 'multisample'

Something you might like to try is to create Reason sampler Patches of sounds from any hardware and software synths you own, allowing them to be used easily inside Reason. The conventional way of doing this would be to record multiple single samples of the sound, played at different pitches, trim their start and end points, save them as individual WAVs or AIFFs , load them into NN19 or NNXT and keymap them. But there is another way, if you own ReCycle.

Create a file in an audio recording program that is just a set of synth notes with a bit of silence between each, and save it as a WAV or AIFF. Recording could be done, for example, in a MIDI + Audio sequencer, such as Cubase or Pro Tools LE. This way, you could create a MIDI track to play the synth notes, and play back the MIDI track while recording the synth's output onto an audio track. If you use this technique to create a multisample from a software synth in Cubase VST, it's not even necessary to record its output to an audio track: Cubase includes the outputs of soft synths in the audio file created by its faster-than-realtime 'Export Audio' option.

A MIDI performance of chromatic notes set to play a VST Instrument in Cubase VST, which can be exported as an audio file for processing by ReCycle.

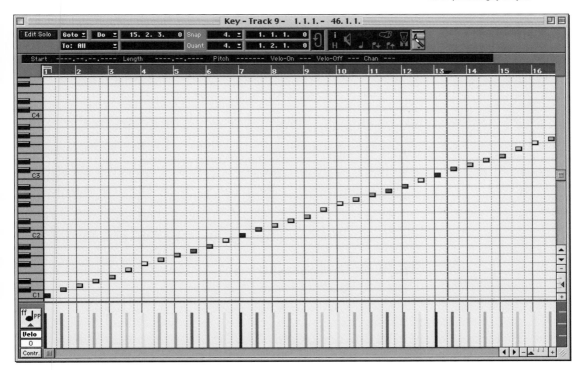

If you're bemoaning the fact that you can't easily use VST Instruments with Reason, this is a partial solution: create a chromatic multisample of the VSTi patch you'd like to use, ReCycle it, and load it into NNXT or NN19. The individual slices won't be looped, but you could just make sure that each note that forms part of the final audio file is long enough (and of course you can now set loops in NNXT...).

Load the file from the recording program into ReCycle and let the program slice the file at the peaks for you. Then load the REX file into Dr:rex and you can trigger those notes instantly, like a 'multisample'. Make sure to record consecutive chromatic notes for as many octaves as you need, starting at a 'C'. This way, the ReCycled version of the audio file will be split such that the notes on your master keyboard trigger slices at the right pitch in Dr:rex – REX slices are automatically mapped starting with C1 on the keyboard.

Since Reason V2, REX files can now be loaded into NN19 and NNXT, where they will be automatically mapped to MIDI keys for instant playback. In this case, the method above works as a quick way of making a conventional multisample. Did we say 'quick?' We should have said 'blindingly, astoundingly quick'! In addition, individual slices from within a REX loop can be loaded into both devices.

The Malström Graintable synth

This device was one of the most significant additions to Reason in its V2 update: a dramatic and gritty-sounding synth using a new synthesis method created especially for Reason. SubTractor is undeniably a great analogue-style instrument, but in a real-world studio you'd ideally have access to synths offering radically different characters. Malström, being based on a technology Propellerhead have called 'Graintable' synthesis, fills this need in the Reason studio. It's capable of producing incredibly impressive, sometimes atonal, timbres, and has amazing potential for evolving, moving textures and atmospheres.

Info	
Keyboard Shortcuts	
Apple/Control B	Browse Patches
Apple/Control-click any control	Restores original value for Patch
Shift-click-hold on control	Access fine adjustment

What is Graintable synthesis?

Before one can understand what Graintable synthesis is, it's probably necessary to know something about the two digital synthesis methods that have been combined to create it: Wavetable synthesis and Granular synthesis.

Essentially, granular synthesis divides sound into very small segments of discrete audio – grains, typically less than 100 milliseconds in length – each of which has its own frequency, harmonic spectrum and envelope. These events are then combined, layered or spliced to form a sound. Wavetable synthesis, at its simplest, organises a collection of single-cycle waveforms or short samples into a 'lookup' table, the whole or any part of which the synthesis system can access during the sound-making process, looping different waves, playing them back at different speeds (to change pitch) or sweeping through sections of the table to create timbral change.

Graintable synthesis, Propellerhead's merging of these two established technologies, takes as its starting point a sampled sound which is 'pre-processed using an extremely academic and complex method'. This process divides the sample into a table of periodic waveforms – grains – which happen to recreate the original sample when played back with no modification.

But of course it goes much further than that. The processing also frees the sample from certain constraints: the table can be played back at any speed without a change in pitch, it can be played back at any pitch on the keyboard without changing playback speed or adding unwanted artifacts, and individual grains can be isolated and looped, becoming the basis for Malström patches. In the case of the more complicated graintables, each individual grain may have its own distinct timbre, which helps to provide vastly more raw sonic material than the 82 Graintables would at first lead you to believe is available. The source material for sound creation is actually equal to all the grains of all the Graintables. It's hard to say how many grains this is, because the Graintables do not all have the same number of grains in them, but it's a lot!

The Graintable's playback can also be started from any point, which also has an influence on the texture of the sound produced. Further processing lets you alter the harmonic spectra of the graintable. And of course, the rest of the synth signal path and modulators can be brought into play to create a patch the likes of which can't be made with any other Reason device, and probably few other software or hardware instruments. Luckily for us, the signal path is effectively that of an analogue synth: if you can program SubTractor, or any other analogue synth, you should be able to effectively program Malström, once you've become familiar with how to manipulate Graintables. But if you don't have analogue synth programming experience, you should really read the SubTractor chapter, for some necessary background, before going on with this chapter.

The Malström signal path

You can follow the Malström signal path as easily as that of SubTractor. You get:

- Two graintable-based oscillators, each with a set of graintable manipulation tools.
- One ADSR envelope for each oscillator.
- One 'Shaper' distortion module and two filters, with comprehensive routing from the oscillators and between each other.
- A single filter envelope for the whole sound.
- Two tempo-syncable modulators – rather like LFOs with a wide range of unusual waveforms – each routable to a range of significant parameters.
- Mod wheel and incoming velocity routing panel, for real-time, performance-related modulation of a number of Malström parameters.
- Portamento, Polyphony and Legato mode controls.

Tip

Safety Zone

Something you may notice when you start playing with Malström is that it is capable of generating resonances that can be quite hard on the speakers (and ears). Simply keeping a COMP01 compressor, with a 3:1 ratio, patched in line with Malström's output makes a huge difference. The synth still sounds great and powerful, but you won't unexpectedly get that 'leaning back from the speakers' effect if the filter happens to do something piercing.

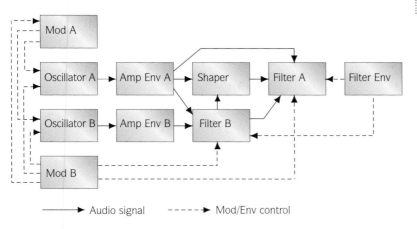

A diagrammatic representation of the Malström signal path.

———▶ Audio signal   -----▶ Mod/Env control

Malström basics

Malström is up to 16-note polyphonic, and, like SubTractor, is a monotimbral synth – that is, produces one sound at a time. You will thus need a Malström for every different Malström sound you wish to put in a Song. It may be triggered from the Matrix sequencer or ReDrum (Malström comes with a bank of drum sounds), as well as being sequenced in the main sequencer.

Seven factory sound banks covering various categories of sounds are provided, and you can, of course, program your own sounds, based on the factory preset graintables. As with every other Reason device (apart from NNXT), practically all Malström parameters can be remote controlled and automated. The synth also features a comprehensive range of CV and Gate connections (some of which are more flexible than the equivalents on other devices), on its back panel.

Beyond its novel synthesis system, Malström has one major difference from other Reason devices: a break in its signal path. The back panel offers an audio output after each of the oscillators, and an audio input to each of the filters. This amazingly simple innovation allows you to patch effects into a Malström patch's signal path and then apply filtering to the processed result, or better still, route the audio from any Reason device to one or both of Malström's filters.

Guided tour

The Patch Load/Save area

Load Patches and initiate saving operations, as usual, in the Patch area to the top left of the panel. (See Chapter 4 for details.)

Patch load/save

Oscillators A and B

The two oscillators feature an identical range of controls, and differ only in their routing to the Shaper and Filter sections (more shortly). Like the oscillators in SubTractor, these are the sound-generating heart of Malström. In this case, though, rather than a simulation of an analogue waveform, the oscillators each play a graintable. A few of the 82 graintables are actually essentially samples of analogue waveforms, one or two of which sound identical to those on SubTractor!

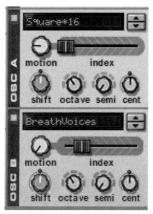

Oscillators A and B

Both oscillators can be active in a Malström patch, but since a single graintable can be used as the basis of a dense, complex patch on its own, you might not use both at all times. Hence each oscillator is equipped with an 'enable' button; if you do create a patch with just one oscillator, disabling the other will save CPU power.

Info

The Graintables

- *6 Bass:* AcidBass; ChorusBass; FMBass; PickBass; ThumbBass; WetBass.
- *10 FX:* Analogue Feedback; Drip; Flies; Gamenoise; GhostChord; MetalCans; OuterSpace; PinkNoise; ResonantNoise; Thunder.
- *5 Guitar:* AcousticGuitarSlap; AcousticGuitar; FuzzHarmonics; LoTwang; WahWah.
- *3 Misc:* Hammond; Strings; Tampura.
- *5 Perc:* AnvilHammer; Chime; FingerCymbal; Tabla; TubeSlap.
- *22 Synth:* 303Loop; AdditiveWave1-3; AmbientChord 1 and 2; Arpeggio 1 and 2; BlurbFlies; DXSuspense; FM1-4; Juno; RandomFilter; SpectralSweep; Sweeper; SweepingSaw; SweepingSquare; VocoderBands; VocoderSwirl.
- *11 Voice:* AngelChoir; Breath; BreathVoices; Elektronik; FemaleChoir; FemaleFalsetto; FormantSaw; JewsHarp; MaleChoir; Throat; TibetanMonks.

- *10 Wave:* PWM; Sawtooth; Sawtooth*16; Sawtooth*4; Sine; Square; Square*16; Square*4; Triangle; VSWaves.
- *10 Wind:* Bottle; BrokenBrass; Didgeridoo; Flute; FluteAttack; PlasticPipe; Recorder; Saxophone; Trumpet; Xaphoon.

As you may be able to tell from the names, some of the tables are imitative and some are impressionistic. The Wave Graintables are basically standard analogue-style waveforms, which you can use as you would use them in SubTractor. Where you see an asterisk in the 'Wave' Graintable names, this indicates a layered wave – ie. four square waves or 16 sawtooth waves. And 'what's a xaphoon?', you're asking. Good question: it's a compact, single-reed wind instrument invented a couple of decades ago by Hawaii resident Brian Wittman (visit http://www.xaphoon.com/ if you want to know more!).

Graintables themselves are selected, in the usual Reason way, via the Graintable name display in each oscillator. The remainder of the oscillator section is devoted to controls that govern how the graintable plays back.

- *Index:* This slider sets the point in the graintable – the 'Index Point' – at which playback starts. If the Index slider is set fully to the left, the Index Point will be the first grain of the graintable. With the slider set in the middle of its travel, playback would start from the middle of the graintable, which would play to its end, then flip back to the start and loop according to its fixed 'motion' pattern (see next control for details of motion patterns). If you start at the end of a Graintable – the final Index Point – the table simply loops from that point, flipping back to the beginning of the graintable, or playing immediately backwards, depending on its motion pattern.
- *Motion:* Once the graintable starting point has been set by the Index slider, the speed of movement through the Graintable is determined by the Motion knob. The middle position (12 o'clock) is the table's default speed, while turning the knob to the left slows it down and turning it right speeds it up. The audible effect, in the more complex Graintables, is similar to speeding up a rhythmic sample loop. With the Graintable 'Voice:Breath', changing the Motion parameter moves from a disturbing slow, heavy-breathing effect to a mad panting when Motion is faster.

Exactly how the motion from one Index point to another occurs depends upon the current graintable's 'motion pattern' – a definition of how the table behaves when it is looped. Graintables can either play repeatedly forwards, or forwards/backwards/forwards (and so on). Users can't alter this motion, and there's no quick way to figure out which graintables come with which pattern, beyond auditioning all 82.

Note that if the Motion knob is turned all the way to the left, motion ceases, and the initial 'grain', as set by the Index slider, plays continuously, producing a static, looped waveform. Although this can have the deadness of a perfectly-looped but very small sample (and a looping grain is a very small sample), it may well be a useful starting point for synthesis. It might be a tiny grain, but the Shift parameter (more in a moment), modulation and filtering can still be used effectively on it during patch creation – suitable grains become much more lively! Incidentally, when Motion is stopped, you canmove through the individual grains in the table, to assess them, with the Index slider.

- *Shift:* This knob has a negative and positive range, left and right of its default centre position. The parameter it controls is probably one of the most central to the potential of Graintable synthesis, yet it is probably the trickiest to explain. This is what Propellerhead say: 'The Shift knob changes the timbre of the sound (the formant spectrum). What it actually does is change the pitch of a segment up or down by resampling. However, since the pitch you hear is independent of the actual pitch of the graintable, pitch-shifting a segment instead means that more or less of the segment waveform will be played back, resulting in a change of harmonic content and timbre.'

The description isn't really explicit enough, but a little investigation reveals the following. You can get a feel for what Shift does by moving the Shift knob slowly, with a simple Graintable (such as 'Wave:Sine') loaded into an Oscillator. Play and hold a note, and as you move the Shift knob to the right, through the positive Shift range, you hear a stepping through a harmonic series of pitches for the note being played (see the 'Shift Exercise' box for more). The 'Shift' gradually and smoothly moves from harmonic to harmonic (to seven harmonics above the pitch of the played note with the knob fully right), rather like trying to slowly overblow on a flute and catching the stages between the lower and higher, overblown, sound. In fact, if you move the Shift knob rapidly to the right with the Sine graintable selected, it sounds a lot like a flute being overblown.

Technically, what appears to be happening is the creation/boosting of individual harmonics, caused by the resynthesized pitch-shifting of individual grains. The more complex the graintable, the less easy it is to pick out the harmonics by ear. If you move the knob quickly, and even on a sine wave, the effect is remarkably similar to oscillator sync on an analogue synth – what is a gentle stroll through overtones in the slow example above positively screams when Shift is moved, or modulated, quickly. A hard edge also becomes pronounced when the parameter is tweaked on a complex waveform. Turning the knob to the left appears to attenuate upper harmonics.

In practice, you probably don't need to know exactly what Shift is doing once you get used to the *sound* of what it is doing and come to appreciate what you can do with it. In many ways, it's like having another, specialised, filter. Use it with a static setting to change the sound and harmonic content of the graintable (as a starting point for a new Patch), or modulate it as you would any other parameter, for startling or subtle timbral movement.

- *Pitch:* The central pitch of an oscillator is controlled by three knobs, just as specified on SubTractor. The Octave knob sets the main register of the oscillator. An eight-octave range is offered, calibrated 0-8, with '4' as the central, default value. At this value, the 'A' above middle 'C' produces a pitch of 440Hz. The Semi knob functions in a similar way to the same parameter on SubTractor, offering an offset tuning range of 0-12 semitones, in semitone steps and an upward direction only (to transpose down by a few semitones, adjust the Octave knob down an octave, and then transpose up with the Semi knob). Finally, the Cent control provides fine-tuning in the range of +/-50 cents – ie. plus or minus half a semitone in single-cent steps. As with SubTractor, the Cent tuning control lets you easily detune Malström's oscillators, for thickening effects.

The Amplitude Envelopes

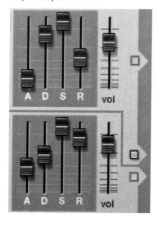

Amp Envelopes

Ordinarily, one would discuss all of a synth's envelopes in a section of their own. But Propellerhead have taken the quite advanced decision of giving each oscillator its own Amplitude Envelope, in the Oscillator section.

Both envelopes are standard ADSR (Attack, Decay, Sustain, Release) types, for controlling the output volume of each oscillator over time (see Chapter 6 for more detail). With its own envelope, each oscillator can have an independent volume curve, adding extra movement and sonic interest to two-oscillator Patches. For example, one oscillator could have a relatively fast, sharp envelope, while the other could fade in, and then fade out, slowly. Particularly interesting is the effect you can create by setting up the oscillators with independent envelopes, routing each to its own filter, and then using the filter 'Spread' knob to pan the two sounds left and right.

Each oscillator also has a Volume slider, which controls its output level before routing to the Shaper and/or Filter(s). You can thus balance the relative levels of the two oscillators in a Patch.

The Routing buttons

These (unlabelled) buttons to the right of the oscillators govern the routing of the oscillators' audio outputs to the Shaper and two Filters. The 'arrow' cut-outs on the green panel-graphics next to the routing buttons help you see where signals can be sent on from the oscillators (as does the green arrow between Filter A and the Shaper).

Routing buttons

- *Oscillator A* has two routing buttons, the topmost sending the oscillator output to the Shaper module and/or Filter A. If the Shaper is disabled, the signal passes straight to Filter A (which can also be turned on or off). The second button looks, at first sight, as though it belongs to Oscillator B, but in fact the green dividing line between the two oscillators does place it within the Oscillator A section. This button sends the output of Oscillator A to Filter B. Routing Oscillator A in this way results in parallel processing of its output by both filters, plus the Shaper if enabled.
- *Oscillator B* has just one routing switch, to pass its output to Filter B. Because Filter B has a routing switch of its own (more on this when filters are discussed), the Oscillator B signal can be passed to the Shaper and/or Filter A after passing through Filter B. As mentioned in the previous paragraph, if the Shaper is disabled, signal passes straight to Filter A. This means that it's possible to route Oscillator B's signal through both filters, and the Shaper if desired, in a serial configuration.

The routing options offered by these few switches can become quite complex. For example, Oscillator A can, as noted, be processed at the same time, in parallel, by both Filters A and B. But because the output of Filter B can itself be routed to the Shaper and/or Filter A, Oscillator A's signal has the potential to pass through Filter A (and/or the Shaper) twice: once directly and once via Filter B.

The basic Oscillator-Filter routing paths:

- Oscillator A -> Shaper -> Filter A
- Oscillator A -> Filter B -> Shaper -> Filter A
- Oscillator A -> Filter B
- Oscillator B -> Filter B
- Oscillator B -> Filter B -> Shaper -> Filter A

The Shaper

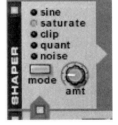

Shaper

This optional module, which can be switched into the signal path just before Filter A, is described as a 'waveshaper', and it does alter a waveform's shape in a non-linear fashion, adding harmonics and creating a more complex sound. In real terms, though, 'waveshaping' could be seen as a fancy word for distortion! Exactly how the waveform is 'shaped' is determined by one of five 'modes'.

- *Sine:* Supposedly creates a 'round, smooth' distortion. In practice, this very much depends on what you put through it. Probably best to apply in moderate amounts, though little tends to happen until the Amount knob is at or just beyond halfway through its travel.
- *Saturate:* Emulates somewhat the effect of overdriven analogue electronics, fattening a signal in a similar way to an overdriven guitar combo.
- *Clip:* An obvious 'digital' clipping is applied to the signal, flattening the peaks of its waveform.
- *Quant:* Utilises bit-reduction – data quantisation – to produce a characteristically grungy sound; as the Amount knob moves to the right, you hear more noise added to, and resolution removed from, the signal. If

crunchy 8-bit sound is your thing, this is the mode for you!

- *Noise:* This last option isn't strictly a shaper; it adds gradually more noise to a signal, until, with the Amount knob fully right, noise is all you can hear. The Shaper now behaves like a noise generator; the volume contour of the noise is shaped by the Amplitude Envelope of the oscillator that's passing through the Shaper.

  The Amount knob in this area governs how much shaping takes place. While each 'mode' has a distinctive edge, when the Amount knob is turned full right, you'll often be hard-pressed to tell the difference between them.

Note that the effect created by the Shaper can depend on the input signal; the more complex the audio (such as the more dynamic graintables, and REX loops being processed by Malström, for example), the more noticeable the effect.

The filters

Malström's filters A and B are identical in all respects, with the same range of filter types and the same controls.

Filter A

Filter types

The filter types available are 12dB Low-Pass, 12dB Band-Pass (not, as the manual states, High-Pass), Comb+ , Comb-, and AM . Sonically, the first two of these have much in common with the equivalents in SubTractor. Making the same filter and filter envelope settings on both devices, and choosing a waveform/Graintable such as square, sawtooth or triangle (identical in sound on both synths) produces a sound that has the same character and is almost identical, but for two things. The Malström filter sounds as though it has a wider range and more top end, and Malström's output is hotter than SubTractor's. See Chapter 6 for a description of these first two standard analogue filter types. The filter types that differ from what is available elsewhere in Reason are discussed below.

Filter B

- *Comb+ and Comb–:* Not only do no other Reason devices feature comb filtering, but very few other synths offer it as an option. A comb filter as specified here is a short delay line with adjustable feedback. Its unusually resonant processing occurs as a result of an input signal being delayed and fed back to the input of the filter. In the process, some frequencies are amplified and others are nulled; a plot of the comb filter in action would reveal the amplified frequencies as a series of harmonically related peaks. The plot looks just like a comb, hence the filter's name. The peaks translate to, often dramatic, timbral change.

  Without modulation, the comb filter effect can be hollow or ringing and rather like a static phaser. Add a filter envelope or modulation, and the filter comes to life, albeit with a sound quality rather like phasing or flanging, which isn't surprising given that the comb filter is a specialised delay line. Within Malström, the filter Frequency knob adjusts a comb filter's delay time; maximum delay, counter-intuitively set fully left, is about 30ms. The Resonance control adjusts the delay's feedback, which alters the shape and size of the resonating peaks. With the Resonance knob set fully right, and the Frequency knob set fully left, the effect is of a highly resonant and very strange reverb with a short decay. It can actually add sustain and decay to a patch that has a very short amplitude envelope setting – a result which can sound more natural than a genuine envelope, and adds an unusual sense of space to a patch. Old-fashioned short delay effects are also possible, and something like oscillator sync can also be produced.

The difference between the positive and negative comb filter options is that the negative version introduces a bass cut into the filtering process; the result is a little less resonant.

- *AM:* This 'Amplitude Modulation' type isn't so much a filter as a ring modulator – it produces the sum and difference tones of two input frequencies. One is the output of the oscillator in question, and the other is a built-in sine-wave generator, the frequency of which is controlled by the filter's Frequency knob. The filter Resonance knob governs the balance between unmodulated and modulated signal.

Filter controls

- *Frequency knob:* With standard analogue filters, the Frequency control determines the 'cutoff' point at which the filter begins to work – the point above which unwanted frequencies are attenuated in the case of a Low-Pass Filter. In the case of Malström's filters, the Frequency control operates just like this for the 'LP12' filter type, but has different functions for the other filter types. These functions are explained in the 'Filter Type' section above.
- *Resonance knob:* The Resonance control in a standard filter accentuates the filter's cutoff frequency (and some frequencies in the immediate vicinity), giving the sound a more rich and cutting character. In Malström, the function of this knob, again, depends on the currently-selected filter type. It's a standard resonance control (as just described) for the 'LP12' type, and a bandwidth control for the 'BP12' type. Its function in comb and AM filters is explained in the 'Filter Type' section above.
- *Kbd button:* Engages Keyboard Tracking. In SubTractor, NN19 and NNXT, keyboard tracking is set by a variable knob. On Malström, it's engaged with a button. The effect is the same, in that the frequency of the filter will change according to where you play on the keyboard, but in Malström there's no control over the extent of the change. Engage the button, and playing notes higher up on the keyboard will cause the filter frequency to increase, brightening the sound if a low-pass filter type is selected.
- *Env button:* If engaged, this button makes the filter respond to the settings of the filter envelope, varying its frequency over time. Since there's only one filter envelope for both filters, this button (in each of Filter A and B) means that you need not apply the envelope to both (though, of course, you can if you want to).

Filter Envelope

As mentioned above, Filters A and B share a single envelope, which is a bit of a shame. There isn't even a subsidiary envelope – such as the Mod Envelope built into SubTractor – that could be made to serve as an extra filter envelope. It seems that space was at such a premium on the Malström front panel that something had to give – so only one filter envelope. In prac-

Filter envelope

Filter Spread

tice, this one is just like the filter envelope on SubTractor: standard ADSR, with an Amount knob to control the depth of the contour, and an 'invert' switch to flip the direction of the curve.

The Filter Spread control

Essentially, when you're using the Filters in a parallel configuration, turning this knob to the right gradually pans the output of Filter A to the left and the output of Filter B to the right. It might sound like a simple enough idea, but heard in the context of the right Malström patch it has a brilliant effect. Be aware that there is no point in using the Spread control in serial filter configurations (everything gets panned to the left). However, if just the Shaper is patched into Filter A, a stereo result will still be produced.

The Modulators

Where other Reason devices have LFO(s), Malström has two Modulators – A and B. They are identical in terms of basic function, but each have a different collection of potential destination parameters that they can modulate. (Remember that the modulator imposes its own character on the modulated parameter, so different modulators can create radically varying effects in their target.)

What makes the Modulators so different from the average LFO is the choice of waveforms they offer for modulating Malström parameters. Certainly, you have the standard waveforms, such as Sine, Triangle, Sawtooth and Square, just like a normal LFO. But then Propellerhead go much further, offering over 25 extra advanced rhythmic 'waveforms' that create interesting modulations, full of potential. Indeed, 'waveform' hardly does it as a description for these.

Mod A and Mod B

The 'regular pattern' modulator curves that can be so useful for simulating arpeggiator effects.

As you'll read a few times during the course of this book, there's no arpeggiator in Reason (though there are various ways of faking one). Malström provides yet another way, because a handful of the Modulator waveforms behave just like arpeggiator patterns when routed to controlling Oscillator Pitch.

Modulator 'Waveforms'

Both Modulators are equipped with a 'curve' selector window; drag up or down in it with your mouse to select a modulation curve, or use the up/down buttons to step through the list. The curves are numbered if you have Tool Tips enabled, but not named; the graphic in the display usually gives a visual indication of what the curve will do as a modulator.

The non-standard curves fall into roughly four categories:

- *Regular pattern:* Curves 21 to 27 (you will need the Tool Tip to see the numbers for these curves) can be used to create arpeggio-like patterns when oscillator pitch is the Modulator's destination (and they create similar effects

when routed to parameters such as Filter Frequency and oscillator Shift).
How 'in-tune' the pattern is depends on how far left or right the target knob
is turned. For example, if Mod A Pitch is turned fully right for Curve 23, the
pattern rises in octave steps for three octaves and comes back down again;
likewise Curve 24 rises roughly in intervals of a fourth over a three octave
range and comes down again. (With the Pitch knob turned fully right, the
patterns go down for three octaves, and up again.)

Use these curves for something of a random modulation effect.

- *Semi-random pattern:* The graphics that appear in the Curve Display for Curves 6,7, and 28 appear to be random, but in practice the curves are not – they produce a repeating pattern, albeit quite a long one.
- *Envelope-like curve:* These include blips, forward and reverse swoops, and so on. They can be used, very effectively, for unusual envelope effects, especially when routed to pitch (and with the Modulator set to 'One Shot' mode, so the Curve doesn't loop), since there is no pitch envelope on Malström. Check out numbers 9-12 and 18-20.
- *Special effect:* Various strange wibbles are produced by 13-17, some of which are almost special envelope curves. Waves 29 and 30 produce the kind of effect you'd normally have to create by manually tweaking the Modulator rate knob – one produces a series of pulses, each of which is faster than the last, while the other is the opposite, starting with fast pulses, each successive pulse being slower than the last. Again, effective in 'One Shot' mode.

An easy way to unusual envelope effects is via these modulator curves and others like them.

Modulator Targets

The selection of modulation Targets differs from the LFOs on SubTractor, NN19 and Dr:rex. On these other devices, the LFO can be routed, from the front panel at least, to one parameter only. With Malström, the Modulator can be routed to several parameters, via bipolar Target knobs which can be used simultaneously. Turning the knob to the right, from the central position, adds increasing amounts of modulation to the target parameter; turning the knob to the left sends increasing amounts of inverted modulation waveform to the target – a curve that moves upwards with a knob turned to the right moves downwards with it turned to the left.

Each Modulator is also equipped with an A/B selector; this switch is used to decide which Oscillator and/or Filter parameters the Modulator should act upon; the choice is A, B or both. This choice is made for all Target controls in a Modulator; if A is selected for Modulator A, for example, its Curve will modulate up to three parameters on Oscillator A, leaving the same parameters on Oscillator B unmodulated.

Sci-fi effects and vintage synth-like oddness are available from the special effect-type modulator curves.

Mod A Targets
- *Pitch:* Oscillator A and/or B pitch.
- *Index:* Oscillator A and/or B Index start position.
- *Shift:* Oscillator A and/or B Shift parameter – modulates an Oscillator's harmonic content.

Mod B Targets
- *Motion:* Oscillator A and/or B Motion Pattern speed.
- *Level:* Oscillator A and/or B output level.
- *Filter:* Filter A and/or B cutoff frequency.

- *Mod A:* Controls the depth of modulation produced by Mod A; produces a particularly complex Modulation pattern.

Other Modulator controls
- *Rate:* Sets the speed of the Modulator's Curve. Can operate independently of or in sync with a Song's tempo, just like the LFOs on other Reason devices.
- *Sync:* Engage this button to sync a Modulator to Song Tempo; the Rate knob will select from a wide range of note sub-divisions.
- *1-Shot:* Engaging this causes the selected curve to play through once only, rather than loop continuously. This is a good option for some of the more unusual envelope-like and special effect Curves, and is great for creating interesting attack portions to a sound with the minimum of hassle. Choosing Curve 15 or 18, for example, adds a very defined attack 'blip', a bit like a pizzicato string pluck with the right sound. Engaging 1-Shot mode also means that you can hear exactly what a given Curve does as a modulator – choose a Curve, hold down a note, and you'll hear one instance of the curve's action.

The Play Parameters

Pitch-bend and Modulation wheels
See the SubTractor chapter for details on the use of pitch-bend and modulation wheels. What is notable about Malström's pitch-bend wheel is that it exhibits practically none of the 'stepping' you can hear with the pitch wheels of other devices: even on a 24-semitone bend, it's smooth all the way up and down, no matter how slowly you move it.

Mod wheel destinations

The Modulation wheel can be directed to control up to four parameters, each via a bipolar knob. As with the Modulation Targets, there's an A/B selector with which to select whether the available parameters of either or both Oscillators, Modulators or Filters will be changed by moving the mod wheel. The Mod wheel targets are as follows:

- *Index* of Oscillator A and/or B
- *Shift* of Oscillator A and/or B
- *Filter Frequency* of Filter A and/or B
- *Modulation* (amount) for Mod A and/or B

Velocity controls
Incoming MIDI velocity can be routed to modulate, in response to your playing, up to six Malström parameters. You can read more about Velocity control in the SubTractor chapter.

All control knobs are bipolar, sending positive parameter offsets in response to higher velocity levels when the knobs are turned to the right, and negative offsets in response to higher velocity when turned to the left. For example, playing harder causes oscillator level to increase with positive settings of the level Velocity knobs, or decrease with negative settings (this would be the 'natural' relationship between velocity and Patch response).

Velocity control targets are Osc A level (Lvl A); Osc B level (Lvl B); Filter

Envelope (F. Env); Amplitude Envelope Attack (Atk) for Osc A and/or B; Shift for Osc A and/or B; Modulation Amount (Mod) for Modulator A and/or B. The last three targets have a switch to select one or other, or both, of the possible targets.

Velocity destinations

Portamento

This control simply determines the rate of 'glide' between notes. It works for both monophonic and polyponic patches, and has none of the performance-related options of SubTractor.

Legato

Enabling this button forces the Malström patch to be monophonic, no matter what the polyphony setting is. There is no polyphonic legato option, as there is with SubTractor. When you play with a legato touch and this function engaged, pitch changes are smooth, with no retriggering of envelopes; play non-legato to trigger the envelopes every time. The only concession to polyphony is that if the polyphony parameter is set to more than '1', when you play non-legato all notes decay away naturally to the set polyphonic limit. It is never possible to play chords in this mode, though.

    See the SubTractor chapter for an explanation of how it is possible to use up more notes of polyphony than you are aware of. As with other devices, though, unused notes of polyphony on Malström do not consume CPU resources.

Level control/Audio output level meter

The final control on the front panel is a simple output-level knob, with bargraph level meter. No other Reason sound-making device has such a meter, and it may well be there because there is so much potential for harsh, hyper-resonant noise from Malström. If the meter is banging into the red, it's probably as well to turn down the output level knob, though it's usually better to keep device level controls up full and adjust relative levels at the mixer. In the case of Malström, the device itself can overload at high levels and with certain sounds, and simply turning it right down at the mixer is not really sufficient.

Level control/output meter

The rear panel

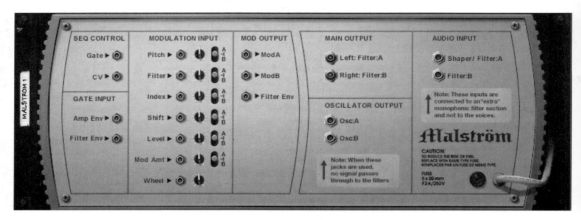

The audio outputs

Left/Right main audio outs

Malström has two audio outputs. These can be connected to an audio input on the ReMix mixer, so that Malström can be heard and can be mixed as part of a track. This is the automatic audio connection Reason will make for you if you create a mixer, then a Malström. The audio output can also, of course, be patched into an effect device (or chain of effects) for 'insert' processing of Malström's audio.

You will notice that the audio outs are labelled Left/Filter A and Right/Filter B. This may give the impression that Malström is a stereo synth, but strictly speaking it is not. When the two filters have been used in parallel and the 'Spread' control is set full right, so that Filter A is panned hard left and Filter B is panned hard right, the signal that has passed through Filter A comes out of the Left output and the signal that has passed through Filter B comes out of the Right one. You can thus create the impression of a stereo output in the right circumstances. (Note that if the filters have been disabled and both oscillators are in use, the Spread control can be used to pan the signals of Oscillator A and B left and right respectively, to be sent from the outputs in the same way.)

If you move the Spread control towards the left, the two filter output signals gradually pan towards the centre; with the Spread knob fully left, output is mono, and both filters are set to dead centre. Also, in patches involving serial filter routing, the output is strictly mono. Then you can use either the Left or Right output – there's no absolute need to use both.

Oscillator A and B outs

These are direct audio outputs for each Oscillator. The break in the signal path comes after the Amplitude Envelope and before the Filter section. More on the audio outs in the 'Using Malström' section later in this chapter.

The audio inputs

Malström is unique amongst the Reason sound-making devices in having a pair of audio inputs – one linked to the Shaper/Filter A and the other to Filter B. This extends Malström's usefulness in the rack even further, allowing the new synth to be used almost as a signal processor.

Signals sent to the Malström's Audio Ins do not actually go to the synth's main filters. They go instead to two auxiliary monophonic filters (the main filters are polyphonic) that operate in parallel with the main filters, and share their settings, but behave slightly differently.

The Sequencer Control Gate and CV Inputs
Triggering Malström sounds with a Matrix

- Note CV output of Matrix connected to Sequencer Control CV input of Malström.
- Gate CV output of Matrix connected to Sequencer Control Gate Input of Malström.

To trigger Malström sounds with a ReDrum, connect the Gate Out of a ReDrum voice channel to the Malström Sequencer Control Gate In. In all respects, the Sequencer Control Gate and CV inputs behave as their equivalents in SubTractor.

The CV/Gate connections
Malström has nearly as many CV and Gate sockets as SubTractor, and again they offer lots of potential for weird and useful noise. See Chapter 4 for an explanation of the CV/Gate system, if you need one, and Chapter 21 for a chart giving suggested routings.

One difference between Malström and the other sound-making devices is that a single Modulation CV can be routed to more than one target parameter on Malström, if the parameter has a rear-panel A/B switch. In these cases, the Modulation CV can be sent to the parameter in question on one or both of the oscillators, filters or modulators, depending on the setting of the switch.

Using Malström

Fast editing
Making quick tweaks to sounds in an analogue synth would often involve parameters such as Amplitude Envelope attack and release, to help make a sound start and finish as needed; Filter Envelope attack and release, to tailor its timbral evolution over its length as set by the Amp Envelope; and Filter Frequency and Resonance, to make the sound brighter or duller, and more or less cutting. You might also alter (or add) LFO modulation of a parameter such as Filter Frequency or oscillator pitch, to create more movement in the sound.

You can do most of the above when tweaking a Malström sound, with one or two qualifications.

- If you find that modifying the Amplitude Envelope attack of a preset does not get the sound to start as you want it to, check whether the Patch uses the Motion parameter. If a slow Motion speed has been set, this can create the feel of a slow attack that you won't be able to get rid of with the Amp Env attack control alone; you may also have to make the Motion speed faster.

• The attacks of some Malström factory sounds are created by the more unusual Modulator curves; if there is an attack you can't seem to modify sufficiently, look at the current Modulator curve, see if the attack is coming from there, and change the curve if necessary.

Graintable parameter tweaks

Then there are the very Malström-specific edits you can make:

• *Modulate Shift:* Where you might add some LFO modulation of Filter Frequency in a conventional synth (which you can do here too, with the Modulators), also or alternatively try modulating the Shift parameter (with a low amount) for added timbral interest. For subtle effect, use one of the classic analogue-style Modulator waveforms, but for a more sophisticated or strongly rhythmic feel choose one of the unusual curves.
• *Change Motion speed:* Altering the speed of motion through a graintable gives a different character in graintables that have timbral movement. Some graintables, however ('Wave:Sine', for example), don't change much or at all from start to end, and tweaking Motion on those won't do anything.
• *Choose a new Index point:* Tweak the Index slider for alterations in tone, with the same qualifications as above. If the graintable has little or no movement, changing the Index point won't have much effect. But especially in the graintables that have a very strong and evolving character ('FormantSaw', for example), moving the Index point right into the table could help you change its character significantly and make it more unique to you.
• *Stop Motion altogether:* Full left on the Motion knob fixes on a single grain (which one determined by the position of the Index slider) and then you have more scope to impose your character, rather than allowing that of the graintable to be imposed on you. Then work with all the synth's powers, apart from Index and Motion, to create a new timbre.
• *Increase or reduce Shift:* Radically or subtly, this also changes the character of the graintable, enabling the creation of timbres for very different purposes.

Combine these ways of changing graintables and you can see you have a lot of scope for individual sound design. Add filtering, other modulation possibilities, conventional enveloping, the Shaper, and the fact that you can layer two oscillators that may each be producing a very complex sound, and the possibilities are staggering.

Program a Patch

Here's a programming example to get you started if you're feeling daunted by what Malström has to offer. It's really intended to illustrate how you might use some of the facilities, but the sound produced is quite usable in itself, and unlike what you would produce with SubTractor. This is a two-oscillator Patch, producin a pad-like sound with a warm bottom end and a sparkly top end. If you listen to the selected graintables before proceeding with the rest of the patch, you'll notice when you're finished that they don't have much in common with the programmed Patch, which shows how you can move beyond the sound of the basic graintables. Incidentally, if a parameter isn't mentioned, leave it as it is. Use Tool Tips to help you set values.

- Make sure you have a mixer in your rack. Create a Malström, or choose the Init Patch (from the Edit or Context menu) if you already have one in your rack.

- *Make Osc A settings.* Choose the 'Voice:AngelChoir' graintable. Set Shift to 12; this makes the 'voice' sound higher and more ethereal. For the Osc 1 amp envelope, set A=50, D=90, S=10, R=70. Enable the top Osc 1 routing button; this sends the oscillator signal through the Shaper (disabled in this Patch) to Filter A.

Oscillator A and B settings.

- *Make Osc B settings.* Enable Osc B with its button. Select the 'Misc:Hammond' graintable. Set Index to 45 (this starts the Hammond organ graintable playing at a point past the attack, where the sound has a more pure quality with the following Motion setting); set Motion to -42 (slows down the graintable playback, eliminating the typical Hammond vibrato and creating a bell-like tone); set Octave to 6 (to make the bell-like tone higher); and Shift to -18 (takes some top edge off the sound). At the Osc B envelope, set A=10, D=52, S=127, R= 72. Enable the routing button, to send the sound to Filter B.

Left and below: Filter A and B settings.

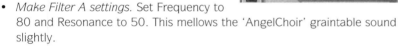

- *Make Filter A settings.* Set Frequency to 80 and Resonance to 50. This mellows the 'AngelChoir' graintable sound slightly.

- *Make Filter B settings.* Select Comb-. Set Frequency to 86 and Resonance to 30. Using comb filtering on the 'Hammond-bell' tone adds a more resonant depth than the straight low-pass filter. It also takes a little more 'ring' off Oscillator B and responds well to the subtle modulation added by Mod B in a moment.

Filter envelope settings.

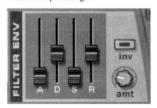

- *Make filter envelope settings.* A=0, D=53, S=0, R=53, Amount 30.

- *Make Mod A and B settings.* On Mod A, select Curve 19. Set Rate to 46 and Shift to 28. Set the A/B switch to 'A' only. On Mod B, select Curve 20. Set Rate to 48 and Filter to 32. The Modulators were set up to provide timbral movement in the Patch; 'Shift' is modulated only on Oscillator A because the effect becomes too obvious when modulated on both Oscillators. (Osc B has Filter Frequency modulation.) The selected curves offer subtly different but complementary parameter movements.

Left: Mod A and B settings.

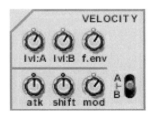

- *Create some Velocity response.* Set the Lvl A, Lvl B, Filter Env and Mod knobs in the Velocity section all to 14. These values make the Patch get slightly louder, brighter and more modulated in response to harder playing on the keyboard. Set the knobs higher to make these effects more intense with harder playing.

Velocity settings.

Figure 10.11
Spread the filter outputs for some stereo width.

- Spread the filter outputs. Finally, turn the Spread control towards the right (around 95 sounds good) to gradually spread the outputs from Filters A and B left and right, adding space and left-right separation to the Patch. Try this pad with delicate chordal playing and single notes, and slap on a bit of the essential reverb and delay!

Using the 'stepped' Modulator waveforms

Instant arpeggiator

This works because the stepped waveforms modulate the pitch of the oscillator in a way that echoes their own shape.

- Choose any waveform (graintable) you like in Oscillator A. One of the less abstract varieties would be a good first choice.
- In Mod A, select Curve 23 or 24.
- Turn Mod A's Pitch knob fully left.
- Enable Mod A's Sync button and choose a rate of 1/4, 1/8 or 1/16.
- Play a note on your keyboard: instant arpeggio!

  Also try Shift as a destination, or Filter frequency on Mod B. It's possible to play chords, though obviously the whole chord will be arpeggiated en masse rather than broken up – this isn't a real arpeggiator after all. Interesting effects can be created if you play broken chords, since each note will generate its own pattern.

Malström's audio input and stepped Modulator waveforms also provide an opportunity for applying arpeggio-like effects to other sound-making devices. Simply connect the audio output of the other device to a Malström audio input and route Modulator B to 'Filter'. There are a number of issues to bear in mind. First of all, it's best if the external sampler or SubTractor Patch is quite rich and sustaining – 'Melstrings', from NN19's Synth and Keyboard folder in the factory ReFill, works well, for example. Also, you need quite a high resonance value on the Malström filter, which should have a mid-range frequency value. Modulator B's Filter target knob is best at about +40 or -40; try out Modulator Curves 21-26; and as in the first example, above, engage the Sync button. Be prepared for the source patch to lose some of its character, as the resonant Malström filter provides most of the interest, and play around with various settings – it can be a very satisfying effect.

Stepped waveform lead lines

Another little trick using the stepped waveforms is really good for lead lines – if prog-rock ever has a serious revival, this'll be useful! It's most effective when applied to synth waveform graintables, such as the three sawtooth varieties.

  In Modulator A, choose Modulation Curve 23 (try 24, too, which produces a different result). Set the modulation rate not too fast – a value of about 30-40 is best (don't sync to Song tempo). Turn the Mod A Shift Target knob fully right. Select 'Wave:Sawtooth' or 'Wave:Sawtooth*4' in Oscillator A and create an amplitude envelope with Attack at about 35 and Release at about 60. Engage the Legato button. Now, if you play a legato lead line (not taking your fingers off the keys between notes), you'll find that what you're playing shifts in register as you play, as if it was an octave higher; keep playing legato and at some point it'll shift another octave. Play non-legato, and the sound is back in its normal range; it'll only shift if you hold a note or play legato. This sounds very reminiscent of an effect prog-rock keyboard players used to create with pitch-bend or oscillator sync, and is especially effective if you play fast.

Mod A and Oscillator A settings for pitch-stepped lead lines. Also make sure to activate the Legato button.

Using the audio ins and outs
The possibilities offered by the combination of post-oscillator audio outs and pre-filter audio ins extend the potential for patch creation with Malström and the scope for sound design within the whole Reason rack. Here are a few things you might try:

Send oscillator output to the mixer
A very simple idea is routing the signal from either oscillator straight to its own mixer channel, without filtering. This might seem like a strange move, but complex sounds can be created just by manipulating Malström's Graintables (the Modulation and Play parameter options are still available), leaving the Shaper and Filter sections free for processing audio from other devices. (You may notice that some of the Malström factory presets don't bother with filtering at all.)

Send oscillator output back to Malström inputs
Another simple patch would route the audio from Malström's Oscillators back to its audio inputs. This seems like an even stranger move, but you will actually produce a different sound like this, since you'll be using the parallel, 'extra' monophonic filters rather than the full polyphonic versions offered in the main signal path. (The envelopes of the 'extra' filters work in single-trigger mode: the envelope triggers when you play a note, but if you hold that note, notes that you play subsequently will not retrigger the envelope. The filter envelope in the main signal path works with multiple triggering; every new note, unless you've engaged 'Legato', triggers the envelope.) Sending an oscillator signal to the Shaper via the 'back door' (the Shaper/Filter A audio input) creates a different result, too: all the notes you play will be treated as a block, rather than individually, which makes the Shaper's distortion effects behave more as they would with, say, a guitar being processed by a distortion pedal, creating a denser sound.

An extension of the last patching idea is to place some effects between the oscillator outs and the filter ins, bringing a new meaning to the term 'insert effect'. You could patch in a single delay or distortion device, or a whole chain of effects, before repatching to the filters. The effect-enriched Malström sound would then be able to go through the filters, offering yet another set of sonic possibilities that would differ according to the particular effect or effect chain being used.

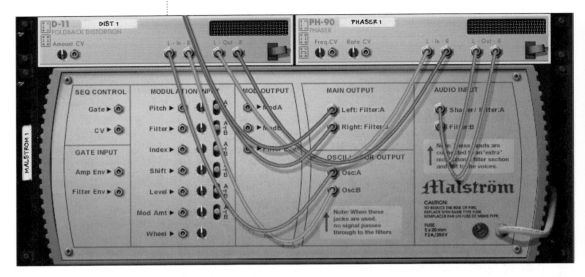

The rear-panel patching necessary to treat Malström's oscillator outputs with effects, then send the effected sound back into the filters. Very interesting possibilities...

Malström as a signal processor

This way you can add filtering (and Shaping) the Malström way to other devices. The external audio is processed by Malström's 'extra' filter(s) and mixed with the main Malström audio, if any is present. (Of course, there may not be any if you are using the synth only as a signal processor for another device.)

The small problem with this idea is that the Malström Filter Envelope (in common with all envelopes) won't work without being triggered. If you simply patch the output from a SubTractor, for example, to a Malström audio input, the filter will basically be working as a sort of resonant tone control – fine, if that's all you want. Filter frequency movement can be added courtesy of Malström's Modulators, but if you want the particular sweeping effect of an envelope, you'll need to find some way of triggering it.

If the device you'd like to process has a Gate output, triggering the Malström Filter Envelope is easy. Imagine you want to process a single ReDrum voice: patch the audio out of the ReDrum channel to a Malström audio in, and the Gate output of the ReDrum channel to the Malström's Filter Envelope Gate in. Now, when ReDrum is running, the ReDrum voice Gate out triggers the Malström Filter Envelope and the drum voice can be processed with the full force of Malström's versatile filter (as well as gaining access to the Shaper if you've plugged into the Shaper/Filter A input). Something similar can be achieved for REX loops with the Dr:rex Slice Gate out.

Where the device has no Gate output, the situation is different, but a result is still possible. It's not possible to trigger Malström's own envelope without a Gate, but a CV from an external envelope can be sent to sweep Malström's filter frequency just as its own envelope would sweep it. Imagine you want to process a SubTractor with the Malström:

- Patch the audio out from SubTractor to one of Malström's audio ins.
- Click on SubTractor's Mod Env out and drag a cable to Malström's Filter Modulation CV input; turn the trim pot fully right.

- Flip back to the front of SubTractor, and create a Mod envelope curve that will make the filter sweep you want in Malström.
- Playing notes on SubTractor will trigger SubTractor's Mod Envelope, sending CV values from the Mod Env out that will create a filter sweep with Malström's filter.

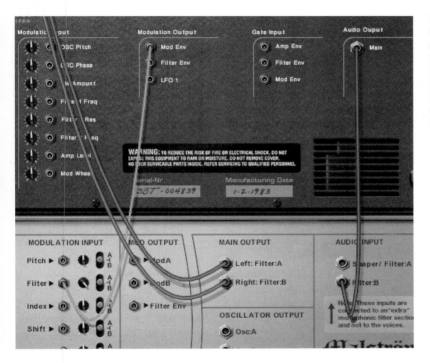

Processing a SubTractor sound with Malström's filter. Setting up the required envelope shape using SubTractor's Mod Envelope and then connecting its Mod Envelope CV out to Malström's Filter Modulation CV in means you can use Malström's filter without having to figure out a way of triggering its Filter Envelope.

To get a similar effect with NN19 or Dr:rex, you'd have to use their Amp or Filter Envelope Modulation CV outs.

Mix Malström and external audio

Just because you want to use Malström to process another device, that doesn't mean you don't get to use the same synth for playing a Patch. You can play a single-oscillator Malström patch going through one filter while processing a loop produced by Dr:rex, for example, via the other filter. If you stick to using both filters in parallel, you can still create the pseudo-stereo filter effect with the Malström's Spread control: the Malström-filtered oscillator would go out of one output and the filtered external audio would go out of the other. You could then route these outputs to their own mixer channels, for individual control on a mix.

The NN-XT Sampler

Like NN19, the NN-XT mega sampler does not actually sample, but functions as a playback engine, mapper and sound processor for samples loaded into it. It can be used for any kind of samples – instrumental or loop/phrase – but it has sophisticated facilities that take it beyond the capabilities of NN19 and make it particularly suitable for instrumental samples. In playback terms, NN-XT is certainly the equal of any hardware sampler, even top-end studio devices, and opens up new vistas of performance expressiveness for sample use within Reason.

NN-XT basics

If you don't know much about sampling, it would be best to read the 'Background to Sampling' section in the NN-19 chapter before going on with this chapter.

As mentioned above, NN-XT is a sample player. It accepts samples in AIFF and WAV formats, mono or stereo, at any sample rate and most bit depths. It also loads sounds in the SoundFont format developed by sampler and synth manufacturer Emu. SoundFonts are just standard WAV samples processed through a special editor program that makes them usable as multisample patches by compatible software and soundcards. A huge number of free and commercial SoundFonts is available on the Internet. NN-XT can load both entire SoundFont 'presets' (which you can think of as multisamples), via the Reason Patch Browser, and individual samples from within the preset, via the Sample Browser. NN-XT also accepts entire REX files (again, via the Patch Browser), and will load individual slices from REX files (you've guessed it – from the Sample Browser). You may also load NN19 Patches and samples. Other sample formats need converting with external software before they can be used in NN-XT; Propellerhead's own ReLoad is one, and there's a list of other software possibilities in Appendix 1.

There is no practical limit, beyond your computer's RAM, on how many samples NN-XT can load. Each and every sample loaded can have its own independent synth parameter settings (as opposed to NN19's global parameters for all loaded samples). With 16 individual mono audio outputs (or eight stereo outputs) on NN-XT's rear panel, you'll be able to route selected samples or groups of samples to ReMix mixer input channels for mixing and processing.

NN-XT is up to 99-note polyphonic, and isn't strictly 'multitimbral'. However, it is possible to set up 'key splits' of different sounds or groups of sounds, and route each to its own rear-panel audio output, creating the effect of different sounds being produced simultaneously by the same device.

The automatic sample-mapping facilities of NN19 are greatly improved upon in NN-XT, and the new device is capable of deriving the root pitch of almost any sample – without that information necessarily being embedded in the sample file – via pitch detection. It can then assign multiple samples to correct keygroups across the keyboard. This simple two-step procedure is speedy, producing a perfect keymap almost every time. NN-XT also allows you to set a loop point inside a sample, for on-board looping of both rhythmic and instrument-note samples without recourse to an external audio editor.

One of NN-XT's chief innovations (for Reason) is the ability to 'layer' samples, allowing several to be mapped to the same keyboard keys and played at the same time. Layered samples may also be 'split' with reference to velocity, so that a given sample in a layer only sounds when the keyboard keys receive a certain level of velocity. Layers may also be 'crossfaded' to smooth the transitions between velocity-split samples, for a more natural sound.

Info

Keyboard Shortcuts

Apple/Control-B	Browse Patches
Apple/Control-A	Select all Zones
Apple/Control-C	Copy Zones
Apple/Control-V	Paste Zones
Option/Alt click above keyzone strip	Creates new keyzone
Apple/Control-click any control	Restores original value for Patch
Shift-click-hold on control	Accesses fine adjustment
Option/Alt-click sample in sample column	Audition sample at root pitch only, without synth parameters
Option/Alt-click note in keyboard display	Audition sample at relative pitch denoted by key, together with all synth parameters

Get going with NN-XT

Load some samples and make them into a Patch

This process works for almost any pitched instrumental samples. In this example, we'll map a set of NN19 Grand Piano samples:

- Create an NN-XT. Click on the 'Load Sample' folder icon at the top left of the main display to open the Sample Browser and navigate to 'Grand Piano' in the Piano folder of the NN19 folder in the Factory Sound Bank ReFill.
- Highlight all the samples in the Grand Piano folder, by pressing Apple/Control-A on your computer keyboard, and click 'Open' to load all the samples into NN-XT.
- What you'll see is a list of sample names to the left of the display and a set of 'key zones' to the right of the sample names. Each of the zones at this point have a range of C1-C6, which you can see by referring to the keyboard graphic above. Leave the Zones highlighted, or press Apple/Control-A on your computer keyboard to highlight them if they've become de-selected.

The Grand Piano samples just loaded into NN-XT.

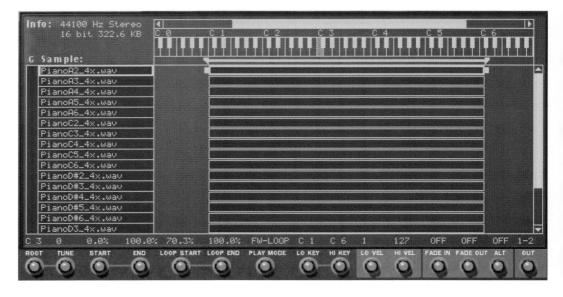

- Select 'Set Root Notes from Pitch Detection' from the Edit or Context menu. You'll see a progresss bar as Reason detects the pitch of each sample.
- When that's done, select 'Automap Zones' from the Edit or Context menus. What you see now is a descending diagonal series of zones across the display, as each selected sample from top to bottom of the Sample Area is assigned to a zone, left to right. You should now have a correctly tuned multisample Patch with all individual samples evenly spread across the keyboard with appropriate key ranges.

This is what the display looks like when the samples' pitches have been detected and each sample has been automatically mapped to a set of keys (zone) on the keyboard.

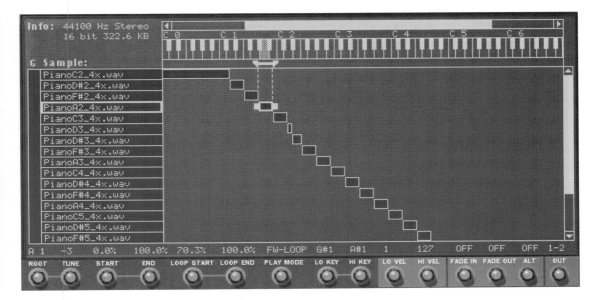

- Play notes from your keyboard now and you'll hear a reasonable approximation of a piano. All you need to do now is tweak the synth parameters – mainly the Amplitude Envelope – to make it sound more realistic. Save the Patch if you want to keep it.

Later in the chapter semi-manual keymapping is covered, which is required for non-pitched samples, and creating a layered Patch with velocity crossfading.

Guided tour

NN-XT is split into two components: the Main Panel and the Remote Editor. The Main Panel is used for loading Patches and making global offsets of a small set of parameters that apply to all samples in a Patch. Individual sample parameters are manipulated in the much larger Remote Editor.

NN-XT is unique in that it can be displayed in the rack in three ways. The large Remote Editor can be 'folded' away or displayed in full using a clickable arrow in its upper right-hand corner. This leaves just the Main Panel and its offset controls visible, and is the best option when you don't need the precise editing options offered by the Editor. The Main Panel itself can be folded to fill just a single rack space; this option also hides the Remote Editor even if it was fully visible before folding.

The main panel

The Patch load/save area

Access NN-XT Patches stored on any drive attached to your computer via the Patch Load/Save buttons to the left of the LCD display, and save your own edited Patches, using standard Browser and Save windows. You can also load NN19 Patches, ReCycled REX loops and SoundFonts via this area. (See Chapter 4 for Patch- and sample-loading details.)

Global editing controls

Anyone not planning to use original sample material may need to go no further than the Main Panel. Once a Patch has been loaded, the six knobs here provide 'offsets' to significant synth parameters for every sample or sample Group in the Patch, allowing Patches to be rapidly tailored to fit with the user's composition.

Positive or negative offsets of the following parameters can be made:

- *Filter Frequency:* Quickly brighten or darken a Patch, by changing how much of its high-frequency or low-frequency content is filtered out (in the case of the most commonly used low-pass and high-pass filter types).
- *Filter Resonance:* Make a Patch more cutting, hard-edged and resonant by boosting the frequencies around the filter cutoff frequency. Likewise, go in the opposite direction to soften an already-resonant Patch somewhat.
- *Amplitude Envelope Attack, Decay and Release:* Tailor the sound's essential contour over time with these three controls.
- *Mod Envelope Decay:* This knob offers the only way to add automation or remote control to NN-XT's Mod Envelope. Thus an envelope describing a filter sweep (when the Mod Envelope is assigned to Filter frequency) can be altered to a certain extent in real time via this knob, if desired.

The tweaks made here are 'non-destructive' offsets, in that they don't permanently alter the Patch. Their settings are, however, saved as part of a Patch.

You'll notice before long that the knobs, wheels and global volume control on the Main Panel are the only controls in NN-XT that can be automated or set up for remote control via a hardware controller or other method. These controls are therefore one of the main routes to introducing real-time variations into NN-XT sounds.

Pitch-bend/Mod wheels and External Control

- The *Pitch-bend* wheel behaves as normal, reflecting the movements of your keyboard's pitch-bend wheel (if you have a keyboard attached) and bending the pitch of the sound smoothly up or down, through a range of up to 24 semitones, which is set on the Remote Editor panel. Pitch-bend range is set per-sample, though the action of the wheel affects an entire Patch. In the case of an instrument multisample Patch you would normally want to give all the constituent samples

Wheels

of the Patch the same pitch-bend range. However, you can be more adventurous with this facility, creating different pitch-bend effects for each sample in a Patch with one movement of the pitch-bend wheel.

- As an example of how this idea could be used, imagine a Patch containing three layered samples of a synth sound or waveform. Set the pitch-bend range of the first layer to 12 semitones, the second to 7 and the third to 3. Now when you play a note (say a 'C') on the keyboard (necessarily playing the three layers at the same time) and move the pitch-bend wheel upwards to the full extent of its travel, the three samples move smoothly up to end on a three-note chord, as the tops of their pitch-bend ranges are different. (In the case of the 'C', we get a C-minor chord, first inversion.) This sounds very neat, takes very little trouble, and is a great performance trick. Note that if you turn the pitch-bend wheel fully in the opposite direction as you hold down the note you get a major chord. Starting on the same 'C' produces F-major.

- The Modulation wheel (labelled 'W') is also similar to that on other Reason devices, save that the destinations to which it can be routed are selected in the Remote Editor for each sample, rather than for the device as a whole. Six destinations are available: Filter Frequency; Filter Resonance; LFO1 Rate; LFO1 Amount; Mod Envelope Decay; and Mod Envelope Level. Since these destinations can be different for the different samples in a Patch, you can achieve complex modulation effects with one movement of the wheel. Try setting some of the samples in a synth-type Patch to be modulated by a tempo-synced LFO generating a sawtooth or square waveform and bringing in the modulation to taste with the Mod wheel, for an instant rhythmic boost to (or basis for) a track.

- The 'X' wheel is allied to NN-XT's 'External Control' system. As with SubTractor and NN19, the aftertouch, expression pedal and breath controller data that can be part of a MIDI stream may be routed to modulate NN-XT synth parameters. NN-XT does this in a slightly different way to those other devices, though. You can still assign Aftertouch, Expression or Breath Controller data coming in from your MIDI controller device to up to six modulation destinations (the same ones as for the Modulation wheel). However, if your MIDI controller does not generate one or any of these types of data, you can alternatively use wheel X to generate them instead, so that you don't lose out on modulators over Reason users with more sophisticated keyboards.

Info

Why are so few NN-XT parameters automatable?

Only the controls on NN-XT's Main Panel can be automated or remote-controlled. None of the synthesis or other parameters offered by the Remote Editor are accessible in these ways. While regrettable, this is quite understandable. There is the potential to fill an NN-XT patch with a huge number of samples, each of which can have individual settings of a screen full of synthesis parameters. Every parameter for every sample (and there are more than 70 parameters available on the Remote Editor) would potentially need a MIDI controller message assigned to it, so that it could be automated or remotely controlled. There simply wouldn't be enough MIDI controllers available with the Reason remote control/automation system as it is currently configured.

Master Volume control

Governs the overall level of all samples within a patch. It's automatable, and can be controlled via MIDI.

The Remote Editor panel

Load Sample

Click the folder icon at top left of the central 'LCD' to access the Sample browser. You can load one sample, or highlight many samples in a folder and load them simultaneously. From the browser, you'll be able to load AIFF and WAV files, plus individual slices from within a REX loop or individual samples from within a SoundFont.

The Key Map display

The Key Map Display is the imposing central 'LCD' display of the Remote Editor and is where you can organise samples into a Patch. It is sub-divided into several distinct areas.

Key Map display

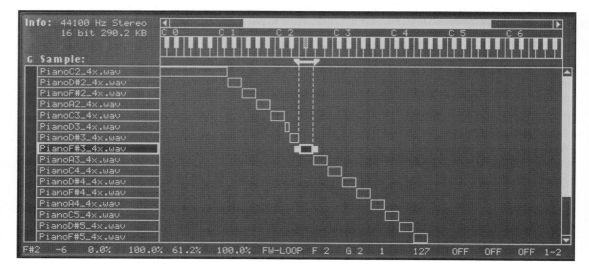

The Sample Area

As samples are loaded, sample names appear in a scrollable list, the Sample Area, down the left-hand side of the Key Map display. Clicking on a single sample name in this list highlights it for editing. It turns dark blue and gains a heavy outline. Now it has what Propellerhead call the 'Edit Focus'. Any changes you make to synthesis parameters in the Remote Editor will apply to this sample, as will any changes you make to the sample-specific controls under the Key Map display – such as root note, loop points, key range, and so on.

Selecting Multiple Samples

Multiple samples in the Sample Area can be selected at the same time, in one of four ways:

- Use Apple/Control-A: This selects all the loaded samples, which highlight in dark blue.
- Draw a selection rectangle in the Key Range area (more in a moment): This can be used to select all or some of the loaded samples.
- Shift-click sample names: Selects multiple samples, which do not have to be contiguous.
- Click in the 'Group' column (more in a moment): This selects all the samples in a Group.

Now changes to synthesis parameters will affect all the selected samples – sensible if you are working on an instrument or vocal multisample Patch and you want all the samples within it to have a consistent tone.

Sample Area

The darker-coloured samples have been selected.

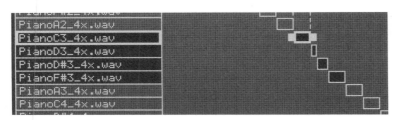

Edit Focus when multiple samples are selected

In this case, the Edit Focus situation changes. When multiple samples are selected, altering NN-XT synthesis parameters affects all the selected samples, as mentioned above. However, the main sample – as opposed to synthesis – parameters, such as loop points, can only be altered for one sample at a time, even if multiple samples are selected. In this case, Edit Focus allows you to define which single sample will be affected by those sample-parameter changes. By default, when multiple samples are selected, the final one selected will have the Focus, but this can be changed.

The top sample here has Edit Focus, shown by a heavy outline.

Imagine you've loaded a handful of samples which make up a piano multisample, and have selected them all so that you can change their Amplitude Envelope Release (a synthesis parameter). Having done that, you notice that one of the samples in the group is a little out of tune and you want to fix it using the Tune knob (accessing a sample parameter) under the display. You can't do this without giving the problem sample Edit Focus. Click on that sample once. The group of samples remains highlighted in dark blue but the sample you've clicked on also gains the heavy outline, showing that it has Edit Focus. Now when you change the Tune knob only the sample in Focus will be altered.

Loading samples via the Sample Area

Double-clicking on a sample in the sample-name column calls up the Sample Browser and is an alternative to loading samples via the Sample Load area or using 'Browse Sample' from the contextual menu. However, if you load a new sample in this way, it will overwrite the sample that's already loaded into that location in the column.

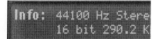

The Info area.

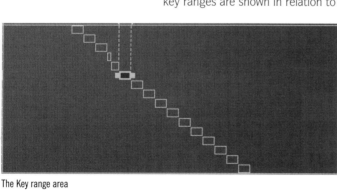

The Key range area

The Keyboard area

This provides a visual representation of the 127-strong MIDI note range. The combination of the Keyboard area and the Key Range area below it allows you to graphically see what samples are mapped to what keyzones across a MIDI keyboard. Scroll bars above the keyboard allow you to access the extremes of the range, as there isn't enough space to show all 127 notes in the display; you can see about seven octaves worth at one time.

It also possible to see the Root Note of the currently selected sample (the MIDI note that plays the sample back at its untransposed pitch) in the Keyboard Area: each time a keyzone is selected in the Key Range area, its Root Note shows as a shaded note on the graphic keyboard.

The keyboard area. You can see the root note of this sample as a shaded key.

The Info area

Top left of the Key Map display is a space offering a few lines of data regarding the currently selected sample – the one that's 'in focus'. You can thus see its sample rate, bit depth, size and stereo/mono status at a glance.

The Key Range area

This is the biggest space within the Key Map display, and shows graphically the key ranges – ranges of MIDI notes – which will play each sample. As with NN19, key ranges are shown in relation to the graphic keyboard discussed above. If you load a set of samples that have not yet been assigned to zones on the keyboard, all you will see is a set of dark-blue bars, each corresponding to a sample name, and each spanning the key range C1-C6, in the Key Range area. As you map the samples (or ask NN-XT to map them automatically for you), the lengths and positions of the blue bars change to reflect the MIDI notes that will now play back the mapped samples.

Semi-manual sample mapping

Most of the time, you'llprobably use the efficient automatic mapping routine described near the start of this chapter, but this will not work on rhythm loops, sound effects, hits and other unpitched samples. Instead:

- Load the sample or samples you'd like to use in your Patch.
- Set the Root Note for each sample with the Root knob under the display. Make sure the sample has Edit Focus before you set its Root note.
- Select 'Automap Zones' from the Edit or Context menus.

The notes you choose as Root Notes in this situation depend on the result you'd like. With just a few samples, you might select consecutive 'C's; doing this gives each sample a Zone offering six or seven notes of transposition above and below the Root Note. With more samples, you could select consecutive ascending Cs and Gs, which would provide a few notes of transposition. If what you want is consecutive white (or black and white) notes to trigger each sample, simply set these consecutive notes as each consecutive sample's Root Note. Using 'Automap Zones' then assigns each sample to a key zone made up of just one note.

Sample keyzones can also be set manually, in one of two ways:

- Select the sample, by clicking on its name or Zone bar, then use the 'Low Key' and 'High Key' knobs under the display to set the lowest and highest notes you want in the Zone – say, C3 and G3.
- Select the sample as above and click and drag the handle at either end of its Zone bar (or at either end of the 'Tab Bar' directly under the keyboard – more in a moment), so that the Zone encompasses the notes you want, with reference to the Keyboard display above.

Keyzone operations
Moving

As well as being enlarged or reduced in size, keyzones can also be moved to a different part of the keyboard, simply by grabbing with the mouse and moving left or right in the Key Range area. Dragging a zone automatically changes its Root Note, shown by a shaded key on the Keyboard display.

Duplicating

Selecting 'Duplicate Zone' from the Edit or context menu makes an exact duplicate of a zone (or zones) and places it immediately below the original in the list: the sample assigned to the original zone, plus all its sample and synth parameters will be duplicated. This is a useful trick if you'd like to make a layered Patch out of the same sample but with variations on the original's settings.

Adding

The 'Add Zone' operation creates an empty keyzone in the Key Map Display, and an empty entry in the sample list (the text 'No Sample' appears in the list entry). You can resize and move the keyzone just as a normal one, and even adjust all its Synth Parameters. This seems to be a feature without purpose, but it could be handy if you wanted to create a multi-zone template Patch, with keyzones ready set, into which you could load samples for auditioning. It can also come in handy to have an empty zone if you'd like to initialise all the synth parameters in an existing layer; just highlight the empty zone and the one you'd like to initialise, and select 'Copy Parameters to Selected Zones' from the Edit or Context Menus.

Deleting

Delete a selected zone by hitting the backspace key or selecting the Delete option from the Edit or Context menus. This removes the zone and the sample assigned to it. You may remove a sample from within a zone (leaving the zone where it is) via 'Remove Sample' from the Edit or Context menu.

Sorting

If you've made a messy-looking key map, as a result of creating zones manually, the 'Sort Zones by Note' operation, accessed via the Edit and Context Menus, arranges the zones tidily, as if they had been automapped. Sample zones are arranged from the top down – zones with lower key ranges are at the top, and those with higher key ranges are towards the bottom. You can also 'Sort Zones by Velocity'. With this option, samples or Groups that are played by lower velocities appear lower in the display, and those played by higher velocities appear higher in the display.

Lock Root Keys

The lock root keys button

The fact that a sample's Root Note moves with its keyzone means that if you actually want the effect of the sample being played far from its correct pitch (for example, to create the kind of 'munchkinised' vocal that's currently popular), you won't be able to easily achieve it – at least, not unless you use the 'Lock Root Keys' button above the display. Click this button when the sample in question has the Edit Focus and its Root Note will stay put as you move key zones. The practical result is to change the timbre of the sample when it's played back in its given key range.

One more thing to watch out for is that part of the Pitch Detection routine also corrects sample pitches. Where this has happened, the sample's Tune Sample Parameter reads something other than '0'. Often, though, NN-XT gets it wrong, and the sample is dragged badly out of tune. The problem should be immediately audible, so click on the 'Select Zone Via MIDI' button, play through the multisample until the out of tune sample(s) are highlighted, and manually return the tuning parameter to '0' for the affected sample(s). That said, a multisampled layer that has samples that are slightly out of tune can produce a natural, realistic texture.

The Tab Bar

This is a thin strip just below the Keyboard Area that makes it easy to see the key range of the currently selected sample, even in a very busy display.

Select a key zone, and a connection, consisting of a dotted line from either end of the zone, appears between it and the Tab bar. The key zone is also highlighted in the Tab bar itself. Dragging the highlighted area in the Tab bar has the same effect as dragging the zone itself: dragging on the handle at either end edits the high and low keys of the zone, while dragging the whole highlighted area in the Tab Bar moves the corresponding key zone and changes its root key.

The Tab bar

When 'Select Keyzone via MIDI' is activated (more in a moment), pressing a key on your MIDI keyboard also causes the Tab Bar to reflect the selected keyzone.

The Group area

This is the official name for the column labelled 'G' to the left of the Sample List. Samples in NN-XT can be 'Grouped' so that synthesis parameters (and a handful of sample parameters) can be applied to them all equally. While it's possible to achieve the same result by highlighting multiple samples or zones, once sam-

Tip

Pitch-detection pitfalls

Not all samples respond to NN-XT's Pitch Detection routine correctly. Harmonically rich samples and synth samples with lots of resonance are often problematic. However, wrongly-detected pitches tend to be an octave out one way or the other. (The offending samples usually stick out a mile: you'll see layers where none should be.) If this happens, use the 'Solo Sample' button to isolate each sample in turn, to discover which is in the wrong register. Often, the sample's name will be helpful: if it's called something like 'EPiano C5' and its root pitch has been detected as C6, clearly there's a problem. Some collections of samples may be numbered sequentially – EPiano 1, Epiano 2 and so on – so, again, if any numbers are out of sequence, wrongly-detected samples can be easily spotted. Give the sample Edit Focus, manually adjust its root pitch, using the Root Key knob under the display, go through the Automap Samples routine one more time, and all should be well.

ples are Grouped selecting them is a one-click process: just click in the 'G' column next to the Sample List. Grouping is essential for the samples that make up each layer in a multi-layered Patch, for example, since it makes it easy to give all the samples in the Group the same Synth Parameter values, ensuring that it retains a coherent tonal quality, envelope contour, and so on. In addition, when you group a set of samples that is to form a layer, the Group gets a much tidier appearance in the Key Range area, such that it looks like a layer and you can immediately see clearly how its samples are assigned to keyboard zones.

The group area

Grouping samples

- Select the desired samples (contiguous or non-contiguous) by Shift-clicking on them in the Sample List or Key Map Display.
- Then choose 'Group Selected Zones' from the Edit or Context Menus.

By default, as you load samples into NN-XT they make up a group of their own, until you tell NN-XT otherwise. Even if you only have one sample loaded, this is seen as a Group all by itself. Grouped samples are visually distinguished in the Group Area, being marked off by horizontal dividing lines that stretch across the keymap display.

Groups and Edit Focus

When a Group is selected for editing, one sample in that Group (the first) still has the 'Edit Focus' and will be the only one affected by changes to sample (as opposed to synthesis) parameters. However, Edit Focus can be given to any other sample in that Group simply by clicking on it.

Removing samples from a Group

Samples can be removed from a Group by simply clicking and dragging the sample out of the Group. This has no effect on how a Patch plays back, but the removed sample will no longer be affected by edits made to its former Group.

Solo Sample

This button behaves just as the equivalent in NN19 – see that device's chapter for more.

The Solo Sample button

Select keyzone via MIDI

Again, this button behaves like the equivalent in NN19; when it's active, you'll see each Key Zone (and its central Root Key) highlighted in the display each time you play a note on your MIDI keyboard. You can select keyzones for editing in this way – even for samples that are velocity split. However, only the Zone set to respond to your last-played velocity level is selected in this case.

Select Keyzone button

<table>
<tr><td colspan="2">Info</td></tr>
<tr><td>

The Edit and Context menus have a Reload Samples option which allows you to quickly reload one or several samples into the slots which they already occupy. While this might initially seem fairly pointless, it can be quite useful. Reloading a sample causes the first nine sample parameters –

</td><td>

the ones that can only be applied to one sample at a time – to reset. It might get you out of a jam if you find you've gone several parameter tweaks too far, or if you've Duplicated a zone whose synth settings and sample you'd like to re-use, but you want to change its sample parameters.

</td></tr>
</table>

Tip
Warning! Make sure that a sample isn't highlighted, or 'in focus', when loading samples into NN-XT. If a sample is in focus, the new sample will overwrite it.

The Sample Parameter knobs

Ranged immediately beneath the Key Map Display is a row of sample-specific parameter knobs. The current values of these knobs can be seen immediately above them in the bottom part of the display. Changing the settings of the knobs alters the properties of the selected sample or samples.

There are two kinds of sample parameter: those which can only be applied to one sample at a time (shown on a dark background), and those which can be applied to multiple samples, just like the synth parameters (shown on a lighter panel). The 'single adjustment' parameters applicable to only one sample at a time are:

The single adjustment sample parameters can be altered for only one sample at a time.

- *Root:* Sets the MIDI note which plays the sample back at its original, untransposed pitch.
- *Tune:* Provides a +/-50 cent tuning control, which should be used to match the tuning of samples to each other and a central tuning reference. For special tuning effects in the context of a Patch, use the three tuning controls – which include a Fine Tune control – amongst the synth parameters.
- *Start and End:* Use these knobs to set playback start and end point offsets for the sample, perhaps moving the start point into a sample to cut off an unwanted attack or a silent portion, for example. Start and End points are shown in the display as percentages, to one decimal place. However, the Tool Tip that appears when you tweak these knobs shows values in 'frames' – individual samples, in other words – and if you press the Shift key on your computer keyboard while changing Start and End points, you can increment/decrement in single frames (samples). This is obviously a more accurate way to set Start and End Points, which may be placed anywhere in a sample, all the way to its last 'frame'.
- *Loop Start and End:* These two knobs mean that we can now loop samples within Reason. It has always been possible to loop a sample end to end for playback, but now loop points can be set inside a sample. This feature is doubly useful if you don't yet have a sample editor but are collecting instrumental multisamples from the internet: as you may have noticed, often these are not looped.

As with Start and End parameters, Loop Start and End are shown as a percentage of the sample in the display, but expressed in frames (samples) in the Tool Tip. Later in this chapter, you'll find a walk through of the process of setting a loop in an instrument sample, and some guidelines for producing loops in NN-XT.
- *Play Mode:* Determines whether or not a sample will loop on playback, and what kind of loop will be used. If a sample has loop points defined, or you've set a loop in NN-XT with the Loop Start and End parameters, it's this region that will be looped. Otherwise, the whole sample loops, end to end. The five playback modes are:

Info

NN-XT knobs

As you get into using NN-XT, you may notice something odd: when you alter knob settings, the knobs appear to keep moving even if you've reached one extreme or other of their travel. This is because NN-XT's knobs mimic rotary 'data encoders' rather than normal 'potentiometers'. In the real world, rotary encoders are sometimes specified on digital equipment that needs to make a limited number of controls access many parameters; a digital mixer, for example, might have one channel's worth of rotary encoders that are used to edit the parameters of many channels. Using rotary encoders means that the designers don't have to worry that the user might have the knobs in the wrong position when changing channels, as the value of the control for any given channel is indicated (as with layers in NN-XT), by an LED display of some kind.

- *Forward:* Plays the sample once from the start to the end, then stops. This is the mode to set if you don't want the sample to loop at all.
- *Forward-Loop:* Plays the sample and then repeats the loop section; the loop will carry on playing after the key triggering it has been released. How long it continues depends on the setting of the Release parameter of the Amplitude Envelope. Forward-Loop is the normal mode for most instrumental samples.
- *Forward-Backward:* Plays the sample and then repeats the loop section alternately forward and backward; this mode responds to the setting of the Amplitude Envelope in the same way as the Forward-Loop option. A Forward-Backward loop can be used to create a more natural result with instrument sample loops in some instances where a forward loop is buzzy or clicky. It's best if you have an editor that lets you work with and refine alternating loops – not all will – since just selecting this option in NN-XT will usually introduce more clicks. Tweaking the Loop Start and End parameters can occasionally help.
- *Forward-Sustain:* Works like Forward-Loop except that the looped section only repeats when a key is held down, playing to the end of the sample when you release the key. If the sample has no specific loop set up – it loops end to end – it loops for as long as a key is held down and stops dead when the key is released.
- *Backward:* Plays the sample once, in reverse, without looping.
- *Low Key and High Key:* These knobs set the MIDI note number of the lowest and highest keys – the Zone – that will play a sample. Use for manually mapping samples across the keyboard and for adjusting keyzones.

The remaining Sample Parameter knobs are of the 'multiple adjustment' variety, and can be changed for two or more selected samples or Groups. The first four of these controls are key in setting up velocity-split Patches.

The multiple adjustment sample parameters can be changed simultaneously for two or more selected samples or Groups.

- *Low Velocity and High Velocity:* As the Low Key and High Key parameters determine which range of notes play a sample, so the Low and Velocity parameters determine the velocity range that will trigger each sample/zone or layer in a Patch, so that your playing touch will bring in different sounds depending on how hard you play. Velocity-switched layers would typically be samples of the same instrument made at different dynamic levels, such as a softly-played and a more aggressively-played piano. You might set the a low velocity range (say 1-60) to trigger the soft samples, and a high velocity range (61-127) to trigger the aggressive samples. Now when you play the Patch, a velocity of up to 60 will cause the soft sample to come through, and you won't hear the aggressive sample, but if you play with a velocity louder than 61 it's the aggressive sample that will be triggered, and the soft sample won't sound. Other samples in the Patch would have their low and high velocities set so that they came in and out at appropriate velocity levels. Velocity zones can overlap, so that two samples or layers will sound together during the overlap. In addition, the overlap can be made to 'crossfade' – see the next entry.
- *Fade In and Fade Out:* These controls allow you to manually set up smooth transitions between overlapping velocity zones, by 'crossfading' those zones – the overlapping velocity ranges fade in to or out from their

nominal value. Fade In is calibrated as 'Off', then 1-127, with 127 being the top of the MIDI velocity range; Fade Out is calibrated 'Off', then 127-1, with 1 being the bottom of the MIDI range. Crossfading doesn't have to be used just for fading between layers; it can also be used to gradually fade in a layer over another layer that has a full velocity range.

There's an even easier way to set up crossfading, that saves you from having to fine-tune the fade-in and fade-out values for every layer, since NN-XT has an automatic routine. Set up overlapping velocity zones for as many zones as you'd like to crossfade, select all those zones, and choose 'Create Velocity Crossfades' from the Edit or Context Menus. The Fade In and Out values are set automatically, and this is usually very successful. However, you can modify the values, with the Fade In and Fade Out knobs, if the automatic crossfade has not produced the exact effect you're after.

- *Alt:* This neat option lets you define a set of related samples or layers – two or three variations of the same snare hit, for example – that will randomly alternate on playback. Though using this option does consume more RAM, the result should be a more natural sound; after all, if you play a real instrument, no two consecutive notes will ever be exactly alike, due to variations in playing touch and instrument response. The Alt feature allows you to simulate this unpredictability to some extent. Samples to be alternated should occupy the same key and velocity ranges. Highlight all the required samples or layers and turn on the 'Alt' knob; now, when you play notes within that key/velocity range, NN-XT will play back the selected samples or layers at random.
- *Out:* This knob allows a selected sample or group of samples to be sent from NN-XT via its own audio output, directly to the mixer or through an effect device or chain of effect devices first. The knob scrolls through NN-XT's eight pairs of stereo outputs. Individual mono samples can be routed by using the Pan control (found amongst the synth parameter Sample Output controls, discussed below) to pan the sample hard left or hard right – meaning that the eight stereo outs can effectively be used as 16 mono outs, or a combination of stereo and mono outs. The separate output facility is ideal for use with drum/percussion-based

Info

Submixing saves power

The most obvious use for velocity splitting is creating multisampled layers of instrumental samples made at different dynamic levels. Most instruments sound very different played softly than played aggressively, and while it's possible to imitate this variation in dynamics to some extent using a single multisample and synthesis parameters, a more convincing result is produced if you can create a multisample at each of several significant playing levels – one very quiet multisample, one moderately loud, one at a 'normal' level, and one fortissimo, for example – and assign them to different velocity ranges. This technique uses much more RAM, and takes more sampling

and sample editing time, but for some Patches the results are worth it.

Velocity splitting is all well and good, but transitions between velocity zones can sound noticeably abrupt, as the switch from a moderate to a loud sample occurs, for example. One answer is to apply crossfading around the zone boundaries, so that a little of an upper layer fades gradually in at the transition boundary as the lower layer fades out. Two samples are playing at this point, and there is an impact on CPU overhead (since more polyphony is being used), but the effect should be of a more natural move from zone to zone. You can apply the technique to many instruments; for example,

velocity-split three snare hits, with a crossfade between each – one a light tap, the next a moderate hit and finally a full-on whack. As you play consecutive notes with more velocity, the tap fades into the moderate sample, which in turn fades into the whack. The technique can also be used more creatively than imitatively, allowing impressionistic and expressive layers to be set up; for example, a classic layer in sample-based instruments is piano and strings. Crossfade the two layers so that the piano plays alone at low velocities while the strings come in when you play more forcefully. The variations are endless.

Patches, so that individual percussion voices can be routed to their own mixer channels, or insert effects, for specialised effect and EQ processing, and/or mix balancing; a more effectiv e drum mix can be created in this way. In addition, Patches that are made up of a series of distinct sample types separated into keygroups, such as might be the case if you were using one NN-XT to simulate a multitimbral setup (for example, a keyboard split featuring bass, piano and pad on different keyzones), could have each keyzone routed to its own output, again for individual mixing and processing.

The Synthesis Parameters

The Amplitude Envelope

We've discussed ADSR (Attack, Decay, Sustain, Release) envelopes else-where in this book – see the SubTractor chapter for the detail. In the main, NN-XT's envelopes, including the Amplitude Envelope, function in a similar way to the envelopes on other Reason devices, allowing the shape or timbre of a sound over time to be defined. However, in NN-XT three extra features are offered over the usual ADSR shape.

Amplitude envelope

- *Hold:* An additional Hold stage between the Attack and Decay envelope stages controls how long the envelope stays at the Attack level before moving to the Decay portion of the curve.
- *Delay:* The Delay parameter allows up to 10 seconds of delay between a note-on event and the envelope firing up to let audio pass through. Note that the triggering of the sample itself isn't delayed, so if you delay the envelope for too long on a short non-looping sample, you'll hear nothing! However, careful use of the Delay parameter, on the Amp envelope especially, can allow complex wave-sequencing-type effects to be created, where different layers in a Patch can be made to 'come in' over time. Low values of this parameter can also simply add texture to a Patch.
- The *Key to Decay* parameter is rather like keyboard tracking for the envelope's Decay value. Turning the knob to the right causes the Decay value to be increased the higher up the keyboard you play, while turning it to the left lowers the value the higher up you play. There is no effect with the knob set in the middle position.

The Mod Envelope

There is no dedicated filter envelope in NN-XT. Instead, there's a Mod Envelope, which can be routed to filter frequency and/or pitch, via a pair of dedicated knobs, to allow the timbre and pitch of a sample or group of sam-ples to change over time. Otherwise, the Mod Envelope is equipped with the same facilities as the Amp Envelope discussed above.

Mod envelope

NN-XT's Envelope stages are not calibrated in arbitrary value ranges, as with other Reason envelopes. A, H, D and R are all calibrated in seconds, while S is calibrated in dBs (this stage governs level rather than time, remem-ber) with a maximum level of 0dB. A and H have a range of 'off' or 0.3ms to 50 seconds, while D and R range from 1ms to 200.2 seconds.

Filter

The Filter

The filter implementation on NN-XT is similar to that that of the other Reason sound-making devices, though it also offers a (Low-Pass) LP6 option, offering a 6dB filter response that is rather more subtle than the other examples. There are also differences in how the Frequency and Resonance parameters are calibrated. Frequency is calibrated, logically enough, in Hz (8.2Hz to 28.2kHz), and the Resonance parameter is calibrated as a percentage.

NN-XT's approach to filter keyboard tracking is also different to that of other devices. The control is calibrated in cents – 100ths of a semitone – per key and the parameter itself is bipolar. With most filters, you'd have a unipolar parameter: turning the control in one direction would cause the filter frequency to increase the further up the keyboard you play, so that (with Low-Pass filters) the sound became brighter as it became higher in pitch. The bipolar option lets you reverse that relationship (a sound filtered with a low-pass type becomes duller higher up the keyboard), by turning the knob left. Fully left is the knob's default position: here, tracking is turned off. With this knob at its central position, filter frequency remains constant across the keyboard.

Note that if a filter isn't needed for a particular sample or Group, disabling it (with the On/Ofvf switch) saves a little CPU overhead.

The LFOs

LFO1

LFO1 is roughly equivalent to the main LFO offered by SubTractor, providing the same six modulating waveforms: triangle, square, sawtooth, inverted sawtooth, random waveform, and a 'soft random' waveform. Additional facilities include a delay parameter and a key sync feature.

LFO1

- *Rate:* Sets the speed of the LFO; if the LFO is free running, its 'oscillation' speed is calibrated in Herz (0.03 to 110Hz). If Tempo Sync is chosen, via the Sync switch, this knob selects a time division (between 16/4 and 1/32).
- *Destinations:* LFO1 can be routed to up to three destinations, each set by a dedicated knob: pitch (with modulation amount calibrated from -2400 to +2400 cents), filter frequency and level. All three knobs are bipolar. Turning them to the right, from the central position, adds increasing amounts of modulation to the target parameter; turning the knob to the left sends increasing amounts of inverted modulation waveform to the target. A curve that moves upwards with a knob turned to the right moves downwards with it turned to the left.
- *Mode:* This three-way switch selects where LFO1 derives its speed information from; the choices are free running, tempo sync and Group rate. The first two are specific to the LFO for an individual sample; choose the Group rate if you've Grouped samples – say as a multisampled instrument layer – together and would prefer to have the LFOs for all samples running at the same speed. Of course, the free-running speed or tempo-sync sub-division could be selected for all samples in a Group anyway, but selecting the Group Rate option means you don't even have to ensure that all samples in a Group are selected before making changes to LFO rate.
- *Delay:* It's possible to set up to 10 seconds of delay before LFO

modulation fades in after a note has been played. This is useful as a special effect, and for emulating how musicians gradually introduce performance variations such as vibrato on acoustic instruments.

- *Key Sync:* Forces the LFO waveform to start afresh whenever a new note is played, making the LFO more or less polyphonic – a different LFO pattern, at the set speed, is initiated for every new note played and held. If this switch is disabled, the LFO is free-running, and every note that you add to a held chord will be modulated with the same LFO pattern as the other notes.

LFO2

LFO2 is an altogether simpler device, but is always polyphonic (key sync'd by default). It cannot be tempo-sync'd and generates one waveform (a triangle). Available modulation destinations are Pan and Pitch, and up to 10 seconds of delay after a note-on message can be defined before modulation sets in.

LFO2

The Pitch Controls

These controls set the tuning of each sample in relation to other samples, as well as how samples respond to the pitch-bend wheel.

Pitch controls

- *Sample-tuning controls:* Octave (+/-5 octave), Semitone (+/-12 semitones) and Fine tuning (+/-50 cents) parameters. Choose the 'Fine' control for creating detuning effects, rather than the 'Tune' control amongst the Sample Parameters; the latter should be used solely for setting a sample's absolute pitch. NN-XT is unique, in Reason terms, in having a positive and negative value for its semitone tuning parameter; this helps to make tuning samples rather more convenient than on other devices. Use the Octave parameter to create doubled octave effects, or to force a sample to play outside its normal range without messing around with Root Keys in the Key Range Display.
- *Pitch-bend range:* Samples can be set to bend by up to 24 semitones when the pitch-bend wheel is moved; this value can be set independently for each sample (or layer) if desired, allowing you to 'bend' into a chord from a single note.
- *Keyboard Tracking:* This unusual option essentially allows you to customise the intervals between the keys on your keyboard. Normally, the interval between each consecutive black and white key would be a semitone. But altering Keyboard Tracking allows you to increase this interval to as much as an octave, or to as little as 1 cent – a hundredth of a semitone. This means that, with care, certain alternate tuning systems could be used in NN-XT (for example, quarter tone intervals are available if this parameter is set to 50). Even if you're not interesting in alternate tuning systems, this parameter could assist in producing ethnic-sounding tuned percussion and drum Patches. A value of '0' for the Keyboard Tracking knob fixes a sample's pitch so that the same pitch is generated no matter what key you play. This is a good option to have when creating a drum kit, or adding rhythmic loops and sound effects to a Patch: it won't matter where they're played on the keyboard, since they'll always play the same pitch. At the knob's central, default position, the interval between keys is 100 cents (or one semitone), which is what you will normally want.

Sample output controls

The Sample Output controls

- *Level:* Sets the volume level of the selected sample or Group. Allows you to balance the relative samples in a layer, or layers in a Patch, against each other.
- *Pan:* Sets the position in the stereo field of the selected sample or Group; if a given sample is stereo, Pan adjusts left-right balance. When working with a Patch that has several layers, you'll often find it worthwhile to give each layer its own pan position, creating a satisfying stereo spread. The result will be much more lush and involving, and you'll also be able to hear each layer more distinctly if it has its own place in the stereo field. In conjunction with the 'Out' Sample Parameter discussed earlier, the Pan knob also allows you to route individual (mono) samples to their own audio outputs.
- *Spread and Spread Mode:* See the NN19 chapter for an explanation of these controls, which allow you to create a variety of stereo panning effects with one sample or Group.

The Velocity Controls

Velocity Controls

These knobs allow you to make selected aspects of a sample or Group respond to the velocity information provided by your playing touch on the keyboard, notes in the main sequencer, or parts programmed into the Matrix Pattern Sequencer. Any or all of five parameters can be set to be affected by velocity: Filter frequency; Level (you must have some response set via this control if you want the sample or Group to be sensitive to playing velocity); Mod Envelope Decay; Amp Envelope Attack; and Sample Start. See the SubTractor chapter for more.

Even if you are using velocity splitting or crossfading on your NN-XT Patches, you should pay attention to the Velocity Controls. A sample or layer may be set to come in at a certain velocity, but its lev el should still be under velocity control, so that it works with your playing to produce a truly convincing result. You can also use velocity control creatively, by setting the separate layers in a Patch to behave differently with different velocity-control settings.

The Modulation Controls

Modulation controls

Each sample in an NN-XT Patch may have its own pitch-bend value, to respond to the device's global pitchbend wheel. In the same way, each sample may use a range of modulation-wheel routing parameters, which govern how the global mod wheels affect each sample. There are six destinations, each accessible via a bipolar knob: Filter Frequency; Filter Resonance; Mod Envelope decay; LFO1 Amount; LFO1 Rate; and Level.

Any or all can be used. Typical uses would be to route the mod wheel to filter frequency, so that you can 'play' a filter sweep, or to LFO1 amount, so that you can control the amount of LFO modulation as you play.

Each of the destination knobs has a pair of buttons, labelled W and X, next to it, which correspond to the two mod wheels in the Main Panel. Click the W button next to any destination parameter knob, for example, to make movements of the W wheel alter that parameter. The W and X wheels can be enabled simultaneously for each knob, if desired. Because wheel X is tied into the External Control system, as discussed in the Main Panel section above, enabling the X switch for a modulation parameter also routes the selected External Control source (aftertouch, breath controller or expression pedal, selected in the Main Panel) to that parameter. To sum up, if wheel W is enabled, the main mod wheel (W) will alter a given parameter, and if wheel X is selected, the second mod wheel and/or the External Control source will alter the parameter.

The Group parameter controls

These parameters apply only to Grouped samples (though, as discussed elsewhere in this chapter, if you've only one sample loaded it is seen by NN-XT as a Group in its own right). They're ideal for Grouped samples that make up a layer in themselves. A Group is selected by clicking in the 'G' column next to the sample list.

Group controls

- *Key Poly:* Set the polyphony of a Group, between 1 and 99 notes, via this two-digit display. NN-XT polyphony is rather more flexible than this parameter might indicate. This average hardware sampler has a fixed polyphony that is always divided by the number of simultaneous samples being triggered at any one time: for example, a 32-note polyphonic hardware sampler with which you are playing a four-sample layer will only be able to offer eight-note polyphony, as four layers are sounding at the same time. With NN-XT, if you set polyphony for a Group to eight notes, you will always be able to get eight notes – even if that Group is made up of layered zones, so that playing one note actually triggers two or more samples. A four-layer Group with polyphony set to 8 could actually play a maximum of 32 samples, but unlike the hardware sampler, you could increase polyphony for each Group or add more layers. The only possible limitation is your computer's RAM and CPU.
- *Legato/Retrig:* This two-state key-mode switch determines how a Group responds to being played from a MIDI controller, or a part recorded into the main sequencer. See the SubTractor chapter for details on Legato and Retrig modes.
- *Portamento:* Portamento, or 'glide', is controlled by this knob; turning it to the right sets how long the glide between notes takes, with the longest glide time set when the knob is fully to the right. See the SubTractor chapter for more details.
- *LFO1 Rate:* This sets the speed of modulation for LFO1 in a Group which has its LFO mode set to 'Group', as discussed in the section on LFOs earlier in this chapter.

Tip

Copying parameters between keyzones

It's easy to copy synth parameters from one zone to another or several other zones. Simply highlight all the zones that you'd like to copy the settings to, and the zone with the desired (source) settings. Make sure the source zone has Edit Focus, as explained elsewhere in this chapter, and select 'Copy Parameters to Selected Zones' from the Edit Menu. This also works for copying settings from one Group of samples to other Groups.

Tip

Conflicting parameters

NN-XT is a powerful sample-manipulation device, with many parameters. Each sample, individually or as part of a Group, can be given its own set of parameter values; selecting a sample immediately changes the parameter values on screen to those of the selected sample. But what if you select several samples – perhaps to adjust the various synthesis parameters for all those samples at one go – and want to make sure that you don't change certain individual parameters that are important to specific samples?

Enter a simple and neat solution: if you select two or more sample zones, and an 'M' appears next to any parameters (it stands for 'Multiple'), this indicates that the flagged parameter has different settings in the highlighted zones. If you adjust the parameter now, it'll change for all selected samples, but overwrite a value for a particular sample that you'd like to keep. The 'M' flag simply lets you know not to alter that parameter; if you'd like to alter an 'M'-flagged parameter for all other samples that you've highlighted, you'll need to deselect the sample

that you don't want to change.

Incidentally, when the parameters of selected samples are different, the settings you see on the NN-XT panel are those of the sample that currently has Edit Focus.

'Multiple' indicators

The rear panel

Audio outs

NN-XT has 16 individual audio outputs, arranged as eight pairs. The first pair doubles as the main stereo out. These two outputs, labelled 1/L and 2R, are the ones automatically connected to the mixer when an NN-XT is created. The other outputs are not connected automatically, but if you click and drag from an odd-numbered socket (3, say), its even-numbered partner (4) comes with it, which is helpful when routing stereo audio out of NN-XT.

Note that it is not possible to customise the scribble-strip naming for NN-XT individual outs on the ReMix mixer input channels; they're denoted as (for example) 'NN-XT1 3-4' (for outputs 3 and 4 of the first NN-XT in the rack) or 'NN-XT1 Output 3' (for a mono channel).

The Sequencer Control Gate and CV inputs

Triggering NN-XT sounds with a Matrix

- Note CV output of Matrix connected to Sequencer Control CV input of NN-XT.
- Gate CV output of Matrix connected to Sequencer Control Gate Input of NN-XT.

These are the connections made when Reason auto-routes NN-XT and a Matrix for you, but you can of course make them manually. An NN-XT Patch can also be triggered by a ReDrum channel gate output connected to the NN-XT Sequencer Control gate input.

The other CV/Gate connections

NN-XT has a standard set of Modulation CV inputs, plus Amp and Mod Envelope Gate inputs. See Chapter 21 for a chart giving some suggested ways of connecting these sockets to others in the rack. Note that NN-XT does not have CV outputs, for the same reasons that it does not allow automation of every control. There can be many samples in an NN-XT Patch, and each sample has its own set of synthesis parameters – potentially requiring a huge and impractical array of CV outputs.

Using NN-XT

Create a layered Patch

Layering as a technique is full of potential, and is especially welcome in NN-XT since it isn't available to other Reason devices without juggling MIDI busses and multiple devices. Create a layered Patch as follows:

- Load a set of samples which you would like to form a layer.
- Map the samples appropriately across the keyboard (as explained elsewhere in this chapter).
- Group the 'layer'.
- Load other sets of samples and proceed as above for each set. (If you happen to load several sets of samples (intended as several layers) one after another and then do the mapping procedure on the whole lot, the samples will map and play back correctly, but they'll look messy on screen and will not be divided neatly into separate areas of the display.)
- When you play the resulting Patch from your keyboard, the layers will sound together. This may be as far as you need to go if you only need a 'massed' Patch. If not, you can refine the Patch by setting different layers to play only at certain velocities (velocity splitting), or velocity crossfading between layers, as explained in the next technique.

A Patch made of two layers. Each layer has been grouped, as you can see from the dividing line in the display.

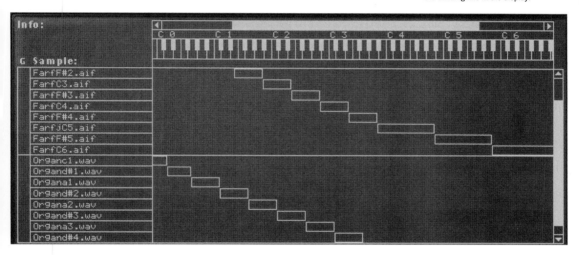

If you're creating a Patch with more than two or three layers, you'll probably find it helps to have two NN-XTs available. In one, assemble a single layer, perfecting its keyzones, sample parameters and appropriate synth parameters, then use the Copy and Paste Zones functions to copy it into the other NN-XT, where you'll be compiling the finished Patch. This technique makes it easier to focus on a layer without having to scroll through what could be a very busy Key Map Display, populated with loads of sample zones.

Create an 'instant' layered Patch

A time-honoured quick way of making a layered Patch is to take keygrouped sets of samples from existing Patches and layer them to create a new Patch. This is one of the easiest ways of creating more complex, rich and interesting Patches with NN-XT. You must have two NN-XTs open here – one with which to compile your composite Patch and the other in which to load the Patches (one at a time, obviously) whose layers you'd like to borrow. Let's try an example.

- Create two NN-XTs.
- Load the Grand Piano Patch from the NN-XT Sample Patches folder in the factory Refill into the first NN-XT.
- Load the VNS+VCS+BSS (Violins/Cellos/Basses) Patch from String Combinations/Strings/Orkester.
- Unfold the Remote Editor, and press Apple/Control-A on your computer keyboard to select all the samples in that Patch, and Apple/Control-C to copy them. There are three layers to this Patch, each already conveniently Grouped.
- Return to the first NN-XT, and use Apple/Control-V to paste the layers just copied.
- That's it: play the first NN-XT and you have a rather fine layer of piano and massed strings (the latter in silky 24-bit quality).

Then velocity-crossfade the layers

Using the example above, we'll create a velocity crossfade.

- Select the three layers that make up the strings part of the Patch, by clicking in the Groups column next to the sample names, holding Shift on your computer keyboard so that you'll be able to select them all.
- Change the Low Velocity parameter to 60.
- Play the Patch: playing softly triggers just the piano; playing harder makes the strings join the piano.
- Now select the three string layers again
- Change the Fade In parameter to 90.
- The difference is subtle: playing softly will produce just the piano as before, but playing louder will cause the strings to begin fading in once your velocity is over 60. The strings will reach their full volume as the incoming velocity passes 90.
- A little reverb and delay makes this Patch sound even nicer. Don't forget to save it if you want to keep it.

Tip

Keyzone appearance

The appearance of keyzones provides information as to their status in a Patch. If a zone is shaded with a striped pattern, this shows that it shares a key-range with another zone but plays in a different velocity range – ie. is part of a velocity-split Patch.

Part of the piano/strings layer. The striped fill in the keyzone 'bars' shows that these samples have had a velocity range other than 1-127 set for them.

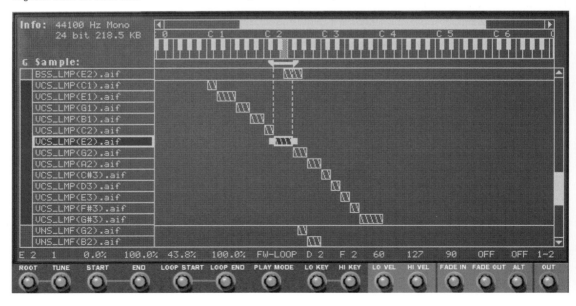

Sample looping in NN-XT

While it is best to use an external sample editor if you plan to loop a lot of individual instrumental samples, there may be times when it's convenient to set a quick loop point inside NN-XT. Alternatively, you may find yourself without an editor program at some time, in which case a grasp of NN-XT's Loop Start and End parameters would be useful.

NN-XT, of course, does not allow you to see the waveform of the sample you want to loop. Fortunately, loops can be refined by ear – and used to be in the earlier days of sampling, with just a numerical readout to help, before samplers got such good graphic looping displays and sampling software came along. One tip while you're setting a loop point is to play a note, then press and hold your keyboard's sustain pedal. You can change loop parameters (along with many others) and hear the results while the note is being held, getting around the need for three hands!

Rhythmic/drum samples

There is a good argument for not bothering to loop these. With such a sample, simply ensure that its Sample Start parameter is properly set so that there is no dead space at the start, which would throw it out of sync when played back end to end, and that the Sample End point is set so that there is a neat finish at the end of the final beat of the phrase. Then retrigger the loop from within the main sequencer or via the Matrix, as often as you require it to sound. This will ensure that it never drifts out of sync with your track.

However, there may be times when you need to give a rhythmic sample a loop – for example, you might want to have a phrase start from its beginning, play to a certain point and then loop a section in the middle. You might also like the effect of the sample looping and fading out with a long release on the Amp Envelope as it loops.

To loop a sample end-to-end, select the FW-Loop Play Mode option, and trigger the sample from your keyboard. The start of the loop is the beginning of the sample, so you don't need to set a start point. If the loop clicks, set a Loop End point slightly in from the end of the sample, in case there's some dead air there. You need to ensure that the loop is as near to click-free as you can get it, and that you haven't compromised the sample's tempo. You may also need to 'edit' out the extra beat that some drum loops contain.

Looping a section within the sample can be more tricky; keep moving the Loop Start point until you find the beginning of the section you want to loop, then adjust the Loop End parameter until it falls in the right place. You might be able to use the Tool Tip sample-length value; if you know a sample is three bars long and it just happens to be 90000 frames, then chances are if you move your Sample Start point to around 40000 frames and the Sample End to around 70000 frames, you'll be close to looping the second bar of the sample.

Instrumental samples

There are a few guidelines you can use to help you set a good loop point in an instrumental sample, such as a synth pad sample you've found on the Internet. Such samples are often not looped, which is fine if the sample is long enough. However, if you want the ability to play really long notes without wor-

Tip

Velocity splitting vs crossfading

Though the example given in this chapter ultimately velocity-crossfades the layers in a Patch, you don't have to do this. Especially in the case of instrumental samples that are meant to emulate real instruments, some people prefer to achieve a natural-sounding velocity split simply by using more layers at different dynamic levels. Obviously, switchover points between layers will be less obtrusive if each layer has only a slightly different dynamic level than the last. You can emulate a real instrument's response more smoothly with six layers of dynamics than with three, for example.

rying about running out of sample, looping a section of the sound will allow it to sustain indefinitely and make it much more usable. Start with the FW-Loop Play Mode selected.

The Loop Start and Loop End knobs allow you to set a real loop inside NN-XT. Using Tool Tips and your ears, it's possible to be quite precise.

- Don't put the Loop Start point too near the beginning of the sample, especially if the sample has a definite attack. You need to find a point in the sample, probably during the 'sustain' portion, where its state is as steady as possible, in terms of level, modulation and other aspects of the sound. Try a Loop Start point of around 50% to begin with. Bear in mind that if a sample does not really have a 'steady state', you will probably need to set quite a short loop.

- Change the Loop Start point value up and down a little to hear what happens; you'll very probably hear a click or bump every time the sample reaches the Loop Start point, and as you move the Start Point about the character of the bump or click should change, as the points where the two states of the sample (pre-loop and post-loop) join. What you're actually looking for is a 'zero-crossing' where the two sides of the sample are as alike as possible. While changing the Start point, you may find that the click or bump becomes softer and less aggressive as you approach a suitable position.

- When you hear soft, rather than hard, bumps/clicks, or a sort of 'wobble' in the sound rather than a click, switch to making fine parameter changes. Do this by pressing Shift while changing the loop point, so that you see single-sample increments or decrements in the Tool Tip. You might get lucky and locate a smooth loop point quickly; you'll know if you've succeeded because the sample will apparently play forever, as you hold a key down, with no undesirable artifacts. If not, you may have to try again with a new Start point, or settle for a loop point that is merely least obtrusive. Bear in mind that if the sample is to end up in a layer with others, a less-than-perfect loop point may not be too problematic. Lowering the filter frequency (with filter set to low pass) can sometimes disguise an obvious loop point.

- Sometimes it may be possible to avoid setting a Loop End point: the sample will loop from the Loop Start point to the end of the sound and then back to the loop start, and so on. This may sound OK. However, if the sample naturally ends mid-cycle, you'll never get a smooth join, and in this case you will need to set a suitable Loop End point, moving back in from the end of the sample a bit and using the guidelines above again.

Remember that Reason has ten levels of undo, so if you have a loop that's nearly OK, and you make a change that ruins it, just undo. You can go ten steps past the 'nearly OK' loop and still return to it.

There are some little tricks that may help you find that perfect loop. For example, play the sample an octave or two lower while refining your loop. This lets you hear more precisely what's going on in a rhythmic loop, particularly, and can also help isolate loop problems in instrumental samples. Also try the opposite: instrumental samples often reveal bad loops when played an octave or two above their normal pitch. What might be a quiet warble at normal pitch can produce an annoying buzz two octaves above. If you fix or minimise the buzz at the higher pitch, the loop should play back even better in its normal range.

You can also try to place a loop in a tonally bright section of the sample – providing this isn't near the beginning, of course – as a loop glitch is often harder to hear in a bright sound. Beware of making a loop too short: you'll know you've gone too far when the loop starts playing weird pitches. In fact, often a bad loop will not only buzz or click but will also be out of tune with the rest of the sample. This can indicate a mismatching phase in the waveform.

One final point: if you do use the loop feature within NN-XT, remember that you're not actually looping the original sample, just its usage in NN-XT. Of course, if you save a Patch with a looped sample in it, it'll still be looped when you load the Patch into NN-XT again. If you take your time in deciding what sample editor to get, and carry on looping within NN-XT, you might like to collect the looped samples into one Patch, so that you don't have to loop any of them again next time you want to use them: use the Copy Zone function to move a newly looped sample to a central loop-collection Patch. Then, if you want such and such a sample for use in another Patch, you don't have to remember where it is, since it'll be collected in one place. Use the 'Solo Sample' button to audition individual samples in the loop-collection Patch.

A few ideas

- NN-XT is ideal for creating strange, ethereal, evolving pad Patches of the type you'll find on popular sample CDs. Set up multiple sample Groups as layers, bearing in mind that you can mix sounds derived from electronic sources, such as synths, with samples of traditional instruments. Selected layers could also be treated with effects by sending them from an NN-XT audio output to a mixer channel (to use 'send' effects), or via an insert effect or chain of insert effects, such as distortion or flange. Since each layer (Group) can have its own LFO setting, try routing LFO1 to Level and setting a different (slow) rate for each layer, to create the impression of different layers coming to the fore in turn; add a long delay setting for LFO1 and the modulation will fade in slowly. Set a long, slow attack on the amplitude envelope for one or more layers, to bring it/them in later than the others. One or more layers might also benefit from a slow filter sweep controlled by the Mod Envelope. Also consider routing LFO2 to pan for selected layers, to add a moving, spatial dimension to the pad. Other ideas include using LFO1 to slowly modulate the filter frequency on one or more layers, creating a pulsing effect; setting a long delay for LFO1 would make the pulsing fade in gradually. Also try adding textural or rhythmic samples as a layer, but at a really low, almost subliminal level; set pitch keyboard tracking for any rhythmic layer to '0', so that the texture or rhythm doesn't change pitch as you play the Patch.
- Try mixing a sound with a reversed version of itself – this is particularly good with rhythmic samples. If you don't have a sample editor, load a sample into NN-XT twice; set one to play forward (FW), and the other to play backwards (BW). Neither loops, so you'll have to retrigger to get a

Tip

Copying zones between NN-XTs

Selected keyzones, individually or en masse, can be copied and pasted between NN-XTs, complete with all Synth Parameter data, just by using the normal copy and paste edit commands. This would allow you to copy the zones that make up a whole Patch loaded into one NN-XT and paste them into an NN-XT that has another Patch already loaded into it, creating an instant layer between the two. This is a much faster way of building layered Patches than loading individual samples into an existing Patch and editing them to recreate the effect of the desired layer. There's more detail on the procedure elsewhere in this chapter.

continuous effect. The alternative is to use the FW-BW loop on the layered sample, which doesn't produce exactly the same result; every other loop will be forwards.

- Create NN-XT Patches from SubTractor or Malström waveforms. Doing this allows you to create layers of SubTractor- and Malström -based sounds within one device, and also to access NN-XT's slightly better-specified LFO1. Simply set up a very short loop – a 16th-note or 8th-note long – in the sequencer that triggers the desired device playing the desired note. Use 'Export Loop as Audio File' from the File Menu, in effect saving a short sample to your hard drive (repeat with different notes if you'd like a multisample). Load the sample into NN-XT and use it as the basis for synthesis. If you've bounced a relatively simple waveform, such as a triangle, sawtooth, square or sine, with no filtering, modulation, envelope or effects, you'll even be able to easily loop the sample once loaded into NN-XT. If the synth sound you're bouncing proves to be tricky to loop, bounce a longer version – adjust the note length in the Matrix and the transport bar left and right loop markers accordingly. Creating a layered (or dual-oscillator) effect, using one sample twice, is easy: once you've created the loop and some basic settings for one sample, select it and choose 'Duplicate Zones' from the Edit or Context menus. You can now detune, pan and otherwise customise the second version to create a varied layered Patch.
- The FW-BW Play Mode is a useful effect in its own right, especially for special effects with rhythmic loops.
- The FW-Sustain loop is great for catching and looping a section in the middle of a sample – a few beats of a drum loop or one or two words of some sampled speech – which can be looped as required, by holding a key on your MIDI keyboard down, before allowing the rest of the sample to play out.
- Real drums tend to rise in pitch as they are hit harder. There's no way to route velocity to pitch in NN-XT, but you can easily simulate the same effect. Load one sample two or three times, and assign each to the same key range, but to different velocity ranges. Now tune the samples that are set to respond to higher velocity values a little sharp – say 10 cents for the middle sample and 20 cents for the higher-velocity sample. The result will be a drum sound going slightly sharp as you 'hit' it harder.
- Load two versions of a sample – one dry and one lightly or heavily processed, say with distortion, EQ or reverb. Assign them to different velocity layers so that playing harder causes the heavily processed sample to play. You could alternatively assign the two samples to an 'Alt' group, so that the processed sample plays at random. A similar result could be achieved by assigning the same sample to two different velocity layers (or an 'Alt' group), and routing one out of NN-XT via its own individual output, to be processed by a chain of Reason effects. The first idea is probably best for percussion samples, while the second could be used by any kind of sample (or sample Group), since you wouldn't need individually processed (and looped!) versions of each of the multisamples being layered.

- Layer two examples of the same sample and tune one slightly up and the other slightly down (less than +/-10 cents, or the result might sound out of tune) for instant thickening and/or chorusing. Pan the two samples left and right, to produce a satisfying stereo spread. This is one way of getting a pseudo-stereo result from a mono sample.
- Route Mod Wheel/Aftertouch to level, filter frequency and/or LFO1 Amount for different layers in a Patch, to fade them in or to bring in different effects as you wiggle the wheel or apply aftertouch; particularly effective if you bring in sync'd LFO effects, especially slow, subtle ones.
- If you've created a big, multi-layered texture of a Patch (as might result from the ideas in the first tip, above), and you know you'll only need a few notes of a given length at a couple of pitches, export those notes to your hard drive; reload them into another NN-XT, and trigger the notes in your song. This could save RAM and CPU overhead if the Patch was very complex and sample-heavy.
- If you've made samples of audio from a cassette or some other noisy source (of course, it's your own material on which you hold the copyright...) and aren't able to clean them up elsewhere, you can use NN-XT's Low-Pass Filter to reduce hiss; the gentle 6dB variant is particularly effective for this.
- Create a sound that combines the attack of one sample – either a short, percussive sample or the front end of a longer sample you've 'trimmed' with the sample Start and End knobs – with the sustain of another; use the amp envelope decay and adjust its attack setting to make the second sample fade in under the attack sample. This is a simulation of the synthesis method offered by some mid-'80s commercial synths.
- If you've got a sample of some vinyl crackle – or can sample some yourself – loop a long section and layer it with another loop, or a whole song, to add that 'just off the record' vibe.

Info

The multitimbral NN-XT

NN-XT is not a multitimbral instrument, but if you set up different samples on their own keyzones you can use it in a similar way. For example, map a basic drum kit to the lower octave of the keyboard, a bass sample to the next octave or two, and a pad to a couple of octaves above that. Assign that NN-XT to three separate tracks in the main sequencer, re-naming each to reflect the instrument assigned to it. Now if you record within the range for each instrument keyzone, you'll have independent parts. The different instruments can even be sent to their own ReMix channel for processing and mixing. The advantage of this idea is that you only need one NN-XT loaded into your rack, which not only makes your rack less busy but also puts less strain on your CPU than installing one NN-XT per instrument. A drawback is that there is only one set of pitch-bend and mod wheels for the whole Patch, and using a wheel would affect all instruments in the 'multitimbral' Patch. Still, it's possible to customise how each instrument responds to the wheels, so that you don't produce any unwanted results.

The Combinator

What is the Combinator?

The Combinator isn't an instrument or an effect – it's a sort of a 'shell' into which you place any Combination of other things. What it does is gives you a tremendous amount of new flexibility to use the modules you already have. It's sort of a microcosm of a Reason rack, in the sense that you can do all the things you'd normally do with a rack full of modules, only inside a contained 'wrapper' module. It saves and loads patches so you can instantly recall any Combination of instruments, effects, mappings or pattern devices. The way to add devices to a Combi is to click in the space at the bottom of it, causing the red insertion line to appear. When this is lit, any device you create will be created inside the Combi. You can drag and drop devices from anywhere in the rack into a Combi by dragging their handles - the parts attached to the rack - into the Combi. When you do this, their original patch connections to the main mixer remain intact. Either manually re-patch them or do the following. As you drag the devices into the Combi, hold the shift key and they will be re-routed to inside the Combi. If you hold option (Mac) or alt (PC) as you drag the devices, they are copied rather than moved. You can drag devices within a Combi to re-order them, and the Combinator itself can be moved around the rack like any device. Combining multiple devices is as simples as multiple selecting them (by holding the shift key) and selecting Edit > Combine. To remove one or more devices from a Combi, choose the device and select Edit > UnCombine or Edit > Delete Device.

A look at the controls

A default Combinator is an empty mini-rack. Use the file load button or click on the name field to open a browser.

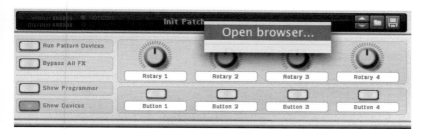

Browse patches from the Combi window

Click inside the space at the base of the unit and a red line appears. Now, any devices you create will be placed inside the Combi until you click outside of the area. If you're going to build an instrument or instrument / effect Combi it's best to start with a Line Mixer for the purposes of submixing. Note that the pitch bend and mod wheels send data to every instrument device within a Combi.

The buttons and knobs have their functions assigned from inside the Programmer window.

The programmable Combi buttons

The control buttons act as follows:

Run Pattern Devices causes any pattern-based devices like the ReDrum or Matrix within a Combi to run independently of the main sequencer. This is great for live performance as you can run an entire song from within a single Combi by carefully planning the playback order of patterns. With the button deactivated, the patterns will only play when you start the main sequencer.

Bypass All FX does what it says on the label, bypassing every single effect device in the Combi, whether attached as send or insert.

Show devices within a Combi

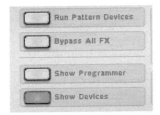

Show Programmer / Show Devices expand or contract the Combinator to reveal or hide its various elements.

Around the back

Notice that there are separate ports for connections inside and outside of the Combinator. At its simplest, a Combi would contain some devices which would be automatically routed to the From Devices ports, and on through the Combi Output ports to the main mixer. If you were using the Combi as an effects chain, it would need an In signal, which would come in the opposite direction, through Combi Input to To Devices. The Combi input ports are only usable in an effect Combi. There are also Gate and CV ins for sequencer control (say from a Matrix) and Modulation Input CV controls for each of the four rotary controllers. To help manage routing you can show and hide the different Combi windows from the rear panel as well.

Picture com 4 The rear panel connections

Info

It's important to create a line mixer or even a ReMix as your first step when making a Combi. If you just start to add instruments, only the first instrument will have its outputs sent to the main mixer. If you create a mixer and then add the instruments, their outputs are routed to that mixer, and the summed output is sent to the main mixer. Basically if you don't do this, you'll only hear the output of the first instrument you create!

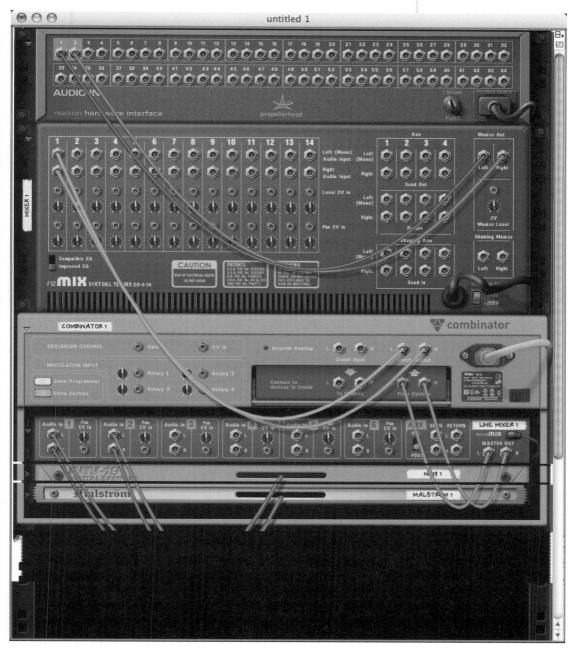

A clear example of simple routing in the Combinator. Trace the signal from the modules via the Line Mixer, Combinator and ReMix.

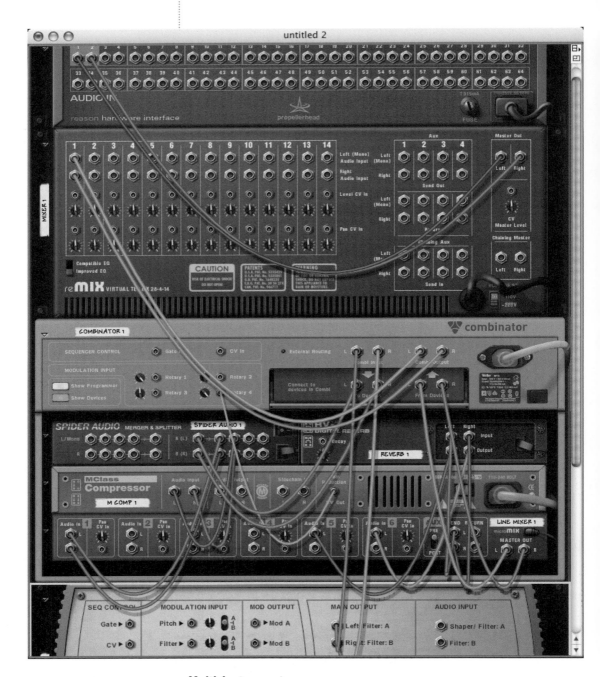

An effect Combi, showing a synth routed through a multi-effect and on to the mixer.

Multi-instruments

One thing the Combinator is good at is making huge sounds. By layering up multiple instruments and effects within a single Combi you can play them all at the same time. Layering sounds up in this way it's much easier to create new and massive patches, as big as your CPU will allow. You can for example create lush orchestral sounds by layering up pianos, strings, reverbs and

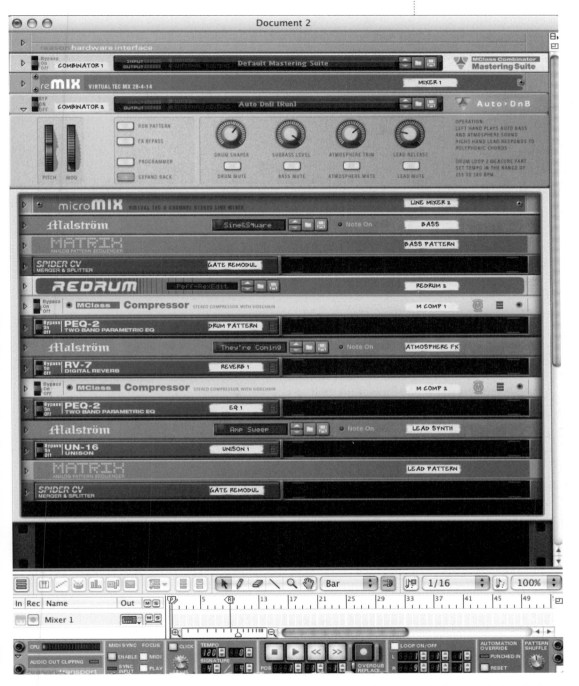

horns all into a single Combi. Or, mix different synth modules and effects to create complex electronic sounds. Remember that a Combinator has a single MIDI track, and that your master keyboard will play every module inside it at once. Modules within Combis can't have their own sequencer tracks, although you can attach Matrix sequencers to them.

Create very complex layered instruments and manage them easily

For really cool sounds, you can add pattern devices to a Combi. So, by adding a Matrix or a ReDrum and pressing the Run Pattern Devices button, the sequence will play, but only when you press keys. Otherwise it won't make any sound. The sound will also be synced to tempo! This is an excellent way of playing arpeggiated sounds and being sure they will stay in time. It also makes you look like a real pro!

Use pattern devices within a Combi and you can play sequences independently of the main sequencer

In this way, using a couple of control surfaces or keyboards you could do an entire performance without having any data in the main sequencer at all. By further customising the Combi and mapping some pads or keys to mutes, pattern changes and so on you can play an entire track, plus variations, from within one Combinator. Remember that each Matrix can store four banks each of eight patterns so there are 32 possible pattern variations within each one. And then remember also that you can have a number of people with controllers locked to separate Combinators, and the vast possibilities for live performance become apparent.

The Programmer window

The way to manage Combis is by using the programmer window. Press the Show Programmer and Show Devices buttons on the Combinator. For each device within a Combi you can assign the four knobs and buttons on the front of the Combinator to perform a different task. Do this by opening the Programmer window, selecting the module you wish to control and then selecting from the list of available controls for rotary knobs 1-4 and buttons 1'-4'. This is incredibly useful because it means you can make one control do several things at the same time. For example, assigning rotary 1 to control cutoff knobs on four synths will create a sort of master cutoff control, letting you move them all at once. In another example, a button could be made to control multiple effect on/off buttons, letting you punch groups of effects in or out at the same time. Right-click or control-click on the various Mod routing menus in the Programmer to assign controls. What's available depends on what modules you have loaded. Use the Device list on the left of the window to assign parameters to the different devices.

Map control devices to a Combinator and get control over the modules within it

The programmer window lets you customise the actions of the front panel controls

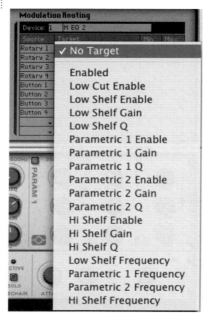

Manually rename the controls after you assign parameters to them

Extra options

For maximum control, the last two rows in the Source column of the mod routing window are freely assignable. The first eight are tied to the eight controls on the front of the Combinator, but the last two aren't. By clicking in these blank fields and choosing one of the eight controls plus a destination parameter, you could have one control affecting up to three parameters on the same device. For example, a Rotary knob might control pitch, cutoff and LFO amount on a Subtractor. When you moved the control you would get a really drastic change in the sound – far more so than you could do using a single Subtractor knob. Using the min and max boxes for each control, you can specify a minimum and maximum value for the control. For example, you may want a knob only to go as far as 100 rather than all the way to the default 127. Buttons tend to simply switch things on or off. In this case, they will have a minimum of 0 (off) and a maximum of 1 or 127 (on). Some parameters involve steps rather than simply on or off. For example, a Subtractor OSC 1 Wave control has a minimum of 1 and a maximum of 31, as there are 31 possible waveforms. In these cases, pressing the control button will cycle through the presets.

CV control

Any CV connections you make within a Combi are saved within the Combi patch. This also applies to any CV connections between a device within the

Combi and the Combinator itself. For example, a Matrix or ReDrum hooked up to the CV inputs on the back of the Combinator.

Split and layer

An easy way to split instruments over the keyboard is to open the Combi Programmer window and for each instrument, define a key range. This sec-tion is contextual, so you get a different view depending on which instrument you select. Drag the key range slider for each instrument to set its boundaries. Remember, only instruments can be split, not effects. In a typical example you might want, say, a double bass and a ride cymbal to occupy the same range

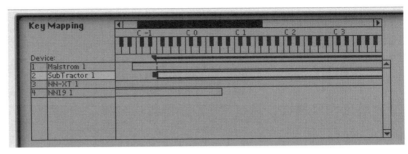

of keys in the bass, then a piano in the mid and a trumpet at the top. This would be simple to set up using the key range sliders and would give you a full band at your fingertips over a normal MIDI keyboard range.

You can use the keyboard to audition selected instrument devices by pressing Option (Mac) or Alt (Windows) and clicking on the keys. This is really useful for playing live. You may for example want to put a bass at the bottom end, piano in the middle and drums at the top of the keyboard. Easy to do by splitting the keyboard into zones. There are some great preset Combis included in Reason to try out.

When a Combi is set up with multiple instruments and overlapping key ranges, you might want to find another way of controlling when they come in. By using velocity ranges you could do this. Imagine you wanted a piano and string sound, but you only wanted the strings to sound when you played the keys hard, and when you played softly you just wanted the piano. Simply select an instrument from the Device list and click in the Velocity Range Hi and Lo boxes, dragging the mouse up or down until you find the point at which you want the sounds to trigger. Once set, the device will only be triggered by notes within that velocity range.

Define key ranges to split sounds over the keyboard.

Assign control parameters for the devices within the Combi to the front panel buttons and knobs.

Directing MIDI focus to devices within a Combi.

Tip

Although by default MIDI input is sent to all devices in a Combi, you can direct MIDI to any individual device in a Combi just like any other device in the rack. The devices in a Combi are shown below the Combinator device on the Out menu, in the same order as in the Combi.

Ways of creating Combis

- Drag any module into the Combinator's rack
- Click inside the Insertion area (with the red line) and use the Create menu or right click and choose Create a device.
- Select one or mode devices in the rack and choose Edit > Combine
- Drag a device from inside one Combinator to another!
- Use Edit > Copy Device, click inside the Combi and choose Edit > Paste Device.

A new look

The Combinator is the only module in Reason which can have its appearance altered by a user. With the Combinator selected, choose Edit > Select Backdrop. You can use any file you want but it must be in .jpg format and must have the dimensions 754x138 pixels. You can't edit the buttons or knobs, just the 'skin' of the Combi. To remove a backdrop choose Edit > Remove Backdrop. The Combi Backdrops folder is included inside the Template Documents folder in Reason's program folder and provides some .PSD and .jpg formatted files which make a good starting point for customising your own.

Selecting a Combi backdrop.

Getting started with the Combinator

Here's a walkthrough that will help you get a grip on this particularly handy module. Create a new project with a single Combinator and a ReMix mixer. One of the most common uses for this new device is to build complex instruments. Click inside the empty space at the bottom of the Combinator. You'll see it turn red.

With this selected, any instruments you create will be placed inside the Combinator. However, it only has stereo outputs so it's generally worth creating a Line Mixer to submix the contents of the Combi. Select Create > Line Mixer 6:2. Then add a Subtractor and an NN-19. Spin the rack round by pressing tab and you'll see Reason has auto-routed them into the mixer, and the mixer to the Combinator.

A red line means any devices you create will be placed in the Combi.

Load some patches. Try a synth pad in the Subtractor and a piano in the NN-19. Play the keys and you'll hear you're playing both sounds at once. Alter the levels using either the volume controls on the modules, or better still, the gain controls on the Line Mixer.

Using a Line Mixer to sub-mix within a Combi.

Try backing the pad sound off a little. With the NN-19 selected, choose Create > DDl-1 to add a delay to the piano. Reduce the dry-wet control to eliminate the latency in the piano sound.

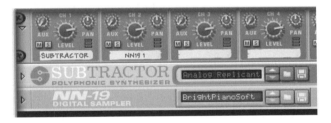

The Line Mixer front panel.

Repeat the process to add an RV-7000 reverb, but this time do it with the Line Mixer selected. The reverb is added as a send on the mixer, and so raising the aux controls for channels 1 and 2 will apply some reverb to the sounds. What you should have by now is a fairly full-sounding patch. Now, imagine you wanted a bass as well, but to be able to split the sounds across the keyboard and play them all at once. Clicking in the empty space at the bottom of the Combinator again, choose Add > NN-19 and load a bass patch. Anything will do, but a double bass works particularly well. At first, all three sounds will trigger together, which isn't much use here. Press the Show Programmer button on the Combinator's front panel. Now select the second sampler – the one with the bass loaded – and locate the box that says Key Range Lo : Hi. Click and hold in the Hi box, and drag the mouse downwards. You'll see the top split point of that sampler moving down the keyboard. You could also have scrolled up the keys to find it.

Setting key ranges for split and layered multi-instruments.

If you lower the split point of the bass to C2, it gives you a good range to play with. However the other instruments are also still playing in that range, so select them in the Programmer window and raise their lower split points to the note above C2, in the same way you lowered the bass split

Combis can contain pattern devices, run
independently of the main sequencer.

Tip

Some Combis contain lots of
modules and samples, and so
take a while to load. A more
efficient way of browsing a library
of Combis is to select Create >
Create Device by browsing
patches. This shows you the
contents of a Combi and lets you
play it before committing to add it
to the rack.

Browsing for Combis.

point. You will find now that everything below C2 plays the bass and everything above it plays the piano pad. This is really useful for playing live.
Remember this is all happening within a single Combinator, and that you can
add as many instruments as you like and layer and split them over the keyboard in this way to create some really huge sounds.

When you're happy with the sound it's worth saving it in the normal way by
using the save button. You can also put pattern devices in a Combi. Try adding
a Matrix attached to a synth to this Combi and drawing in some note data. If you
press Run Pattern Devices on the front panel of the Combinator, it will play the
Matrix. This happens independently of the main sequencer, but in sync with it.

The soundbanks that are supplied with Reason contain some really good pre-
configured Combinator patches, split into easy-to-search categories. Some of
them are incredibly complex and contain multiple pattern devices, but it's simple
to modify them to suit your needs and then re-save them under a new file name.
This saves you an awful lot of initial work in building patches. The Combinator is
also available in the form of an MClass mastering suite – all the available effects
chained together in a ready-made Combi. It's best inserted between the Main
mixer and the hardware interface, to ensure that it is applied to the whole mix.
See the MClass chapter for more on this.

TIP

Since Combinator patches are actually very
small in size, they're ideal to share with others.
Remember that any sample-based devices you use
will require the samples they have loaded to be
present on any system you open them on. Many
third party companies are producing Combi
patches and ReFills to download for free or for a
small fee. They're a great way to expand your
sound library, and someone else has done all the
hard work!

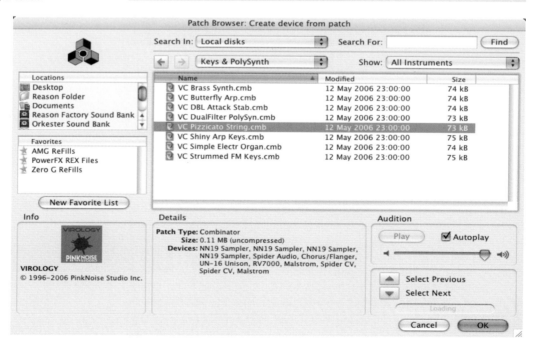

The Matrix Step Sequencer

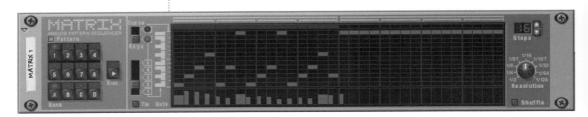

It seems that no matter where you turn there are secret weapons in Reason. Such is the Matrix, an analogue-style step sequencer that not only allows the creation of musical sequences, but also has a multitude of applications in the control and modulation of other Reason devices.

Despite its usefulness, the Matrix may be one of Reason's least well-known devices, perhaps in part because many users, especially younger ones, don't have personal experience of the analogue step sequencers with which the Matrix shares its approach, and partly because the method of using it is not as immediately obvious as some of the other devices. If you're one of the peo-

ple who hasn't yet exploited the powers of this great control and composition tool, it's well worth the effort to learn.

What's step sequencing?

In its very simplest form, what is a sequencer? It's a device for allowing a series of notes and timing intervals to be specified, which are then triggered on an attached sound source for automated playback. For a sequencer to meet these requirements, there is no actual need for the notes and timing intervals to be entered into it via a real-time performance – the method most commonly used by modern MIDI sequencers. The sequence can instead be built up one event at a time, simply by specifying what pitch should occur on each 'step' of the sequence, how long each step should be (or the resolution of all steps), and how many steps there will be in a sequence. Rests can even be incorporated by specifying steps where no event will play.

Whether built into a synth or supplied as stand-alone units, the original analogue step sequencers from the 1960s onwards performed these tasks via an automated stream of control voltages (usually providing pitch information) and gate pulses (providing note 'triggers'). These sequencers could play short melodies on, or control other parameters of, an analogue synth.

The CV values were determined by a row of knobs (or in some cases sliders), with each knob being equivalent to one step of the sequence. Simple units might have just one row of, say, eight knobs, making an eight-step sequence possible, but more sophisticated devices would be equipped with three rows of up to 16 steps each. The CVs produced by each row could be used to play notes on three separate synth voices, or play a monophonic musical line with one row, as the other two rows controlled other parameters, to add more expression to the performance.

In fundamental respects, the Matrix Pattern Sequencer is similar to its analogue forebears. It's a monophonic device that makes no sound of its own (it must be connected to a sound-making device) and outputs up to three 'Control Voltages' per sequence step: one for note data, one for trigger data (which also includes velocity information), and one generic 'curve' CV that produces an equivalent to MIDI controller data. All three control voltages, the latter two especially, can be deployed to control various parameters on other devices in the Reason rack, just like the outputs of a true analogue step sequencer. However, the Matrix has been optimised to suit a software step-sequencing implementation.

Instead of knobs we have the grid, on which the steps, pitches and triggers are entered and displayed. Instead of turning a step knob to set a pitch, you click a step rectangle in the grid. Instead of a trigger being automatically generated for each step (as with the analogue step sequncers), we enter a trigger event on every step where we want a note to sound.

Matrix basics

Each Matrix controls one sound source and sequences a monophonic musical line. Up to 32 Patterns can be programmed into each Matrix, and each Pattern can be up to 32 steps long, with step resolution variable over a wide range. Patterns can be freely chained into Song-length sequences, using the facilities of the main sequencer.

When you create a Matrix, if you first click in the sound-making device that you would like to control with it, Reason will automatically make the necessary connections between the two devices for you. If you need to manually connect a Matrix to a synth (or sampler) device, Tab to the back of the rack and patch the Note CV Output of the Matrix to the Sequencer Control CV Input of the synth. Then connect the Gate CV Output of the Matrix to the Sequencer Control Gate Input of the synth. The sound-making device should, of course, have audio connections to the mixer.

Get going with the Matrix

In this example, we'll program a simple 32-step 'picking' Pattern to be played by an NN19 acoustic guitar Patch. Then we'll transform it into a 12-string acoustic with some copying and transposing.

- Starting with an empty rack, create a ReMix mixer, an NN19 sampler and a Matrix. Reason automatically does the necessary automatic routing between the three devices for you.

Starting rack for the Matrix example.

- Go to the Transport bar and set a tempo of 100bpm in the Tempo display.
- In the NN19, load ACGUITAR.smp from the Guitar Folder in the NN19 Sample Patches folder of the factory ReFill, or any other nice acoustic guitar sample Patch you have. (See Chapter 4 for details of patch loading.)
- In the Matrix, set the Steps value to 32 and switch the Resolution knob under it to 1/8.
- Enter the Pattern you see in the screen below. The note rectangles in the upper part of the display are entered simply by clicking in the correct rectangle of the grid. To enter the 'Gate' bars in the lower part of the display that cause each note to play, click the Tie button to the left of the

Set Steps to 32 and Resolution to 1/16.

display, then click and drag the mouse across the gate display area.
(Creating 'tied' note triggers like this allows the notes of the Pattern to
sustain more naturally and not cut off abruptly.) Note that screens are
'reversed out' for clarity.

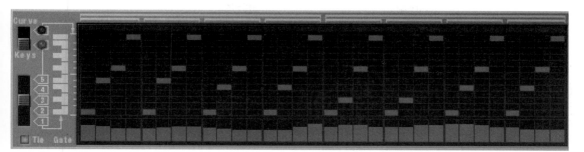

The heights of the bars, which also define the velocity of the note they
sit beneath, do not have to be all the same – in fact, it's better if they're
all slightly different, as we're copying guitar picking. You can change the
height of these bars (and thus the velocity of the notes) if you like, by
clicking on one and dragging up or down. Click the Matrix Run button to
hear the Pattern play. Click Run again to stop.

Guitar picking Pattern, first step. Enter
the notes in the top note grid and the
Gate bars in the lower part of the screen.
Use the keyboard display to help you
place notes.

- Create a second NN19 and load the same acoustic guitar patch.
- Create a second Matrix. Click in the first Matrix and use Apple/Control-C
  . This copies the current Pattern, which should be the one you've just
  programmed.
- Click in the second Matrix and use Apple/Control-V to paste your Pattern
  into the second Matrix.

Grab a Gate bar
with the mouse
and drag up or
down to change
velocity of the
note directly
above.

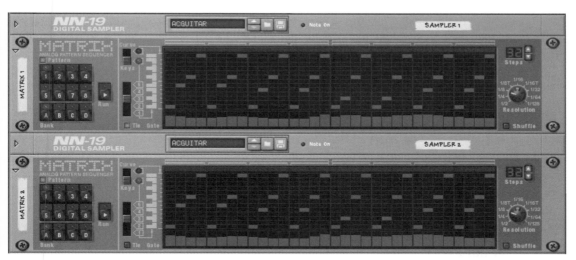

- Still in the second Matrix, use Apple/Control-U to shift the whole Pattern
  up one rectangle (one semitone) in the display. Do this eleven times
  more, shifting the Pattern up by one octave in total. The transposed

Create a second NN19 with the same
patch, and a second Matrix. Copy the
Pattern from the first Matrix into the
second.

Pattern simulates the higher-pitched second set of strings on a 12-string guitar.

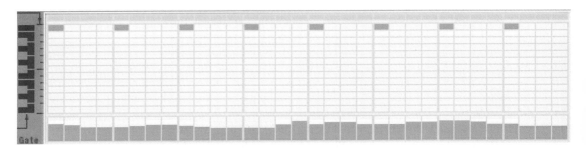

The same Pattern in the second Matrix, transposed up by one octave. If you move the five-way switch to the left of the display up to the '4' position, this shifts the whole display up an octave and you'll be able to see the rest of the notes in the transposed Pattern.

• Click the Play button in the Transport bar and both Patterns will play back together, sounding like a finger-picked 12-string acoustic. It sounds even better if you add some reverb or delay (see the ReMix chapter for how to use effects with the mixer). Save the Song (see Chapter 4 for saving details).

Guided tour

The Pattern Window

Most of the Matrix's front panel is occupied by the Pattern Window, which is divided into two parts. This is where you program a Pattern. When you've finished and you click the Run button (or the Play button in the Transport bar), the Pattern will play back repeatedly, end to end, until you stop it. Don't forget that to hear a Pattern play back, you need to have the Matrix connected to a sound-making device, such as a SubTractor synth or NN19 sampler.

The Note Grid

The Note Grid is a 32-step x 12-note matrix on which note data is programmed. Steps are on the horizontal axis, while pitches are on the vertical. To help you place pitches more easily, to the left of the grid is a one octave C-C keyboard display which can be transposed up or down to encompass a five-octave range; choose the range you would like with the five-way switch to the left of the keyboard. The centre position of this switch is '3', and you have an extra range of two octaves up and two down. If you need to input a Pattern that goes beyond one octave in the display, use the switch to display the next octave up or down.

Matrix Note Grid.

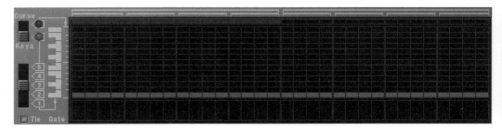

Notes are programmed by clicking in the grid display at the desired step and pitch. You will notice that every step already has a note on it by default – the long line of red-shaded boxes across the display at C3. When you click to enter a note, what you're actually doing is moving the one that is already on that step to the position you need. If you click on a different pitch at the same step, the shaded box will move to the new position. You can only enter one note per step, obviously. Clicking on a box in the grid makes a useful highlight appear, running from the box you have clicked to the keyboard display, for easy note reference.

The Gate (Trigger) Strip

The Gate (Trigger) Strip, immediately beneath the Note Grid, is where Gate (trigger) events – vertical bars with variable height – are inserted, by clicking and drawing with the mouse. Adding a Gate event on a step tells any note also on the same step that it should play. Any step without a Gate event will not sound, even though it has a note on it. Matrix Gates also incorporate velocity information, telling a note how hard or softly to play. The higher the Gate bar you draw, the more velocity is generated. To remove a Gate event that you've entered, just drag the bar down as far as you can, until it disappears.

Trigger strip

The Tie Switch

This switch, to the left of the Gate display, simply doubles the length of a Gate event, making the bar twice as fat and allowing tied (and slurred) note pairs to be created – there will be no separate 'attack' for the second note, so it will lengthen the note and make it sound as though it is continuous. Next to the Tie switch in the accompanying picture you can see such a 'tied' event. You could even program one note to play non-stop for the whole Pattern – just insert tied Gates for every step. To create tied Gates, either click the Tie switch on before drawing the trigger, or use the keyboard shortcut (Shift-draw) that toggles 'Tie' on and off.

Tie switch

Showing a 'Curve CV' in the display

The Curve/Keys switch, to the left of the display, generally defaults to the 'Keys' position, where notes are shown as explained above. However, if you switch it to the 'Curve' position, the display changes to one suitable for entering values for the so-called 'Curve CV'. Any notes you have programmed do not disappear when you switch to the Curve CV display – they'll still be there when you go back to 'Keys' mode.

The Curve/Keys switch.

The Curve CV basically provides an easy way to control, from the Matrix, any Reason device parameters that have a rear-panel CV input – such as filter frequency on a SubTractor synth, for example. Just connect the Matrix's Curve CV output to the desired CV input on the desired device.

The 'curve', described by the 32 possible steps in a Matrix Pattern, is drawn in manually, using the mouse, with the value on each step corresponding to a change in a parameter value on any connected device. Just as the height of the trigger bars in the Trigger Strip corresponds to their velocity, the height of the bars you create in the Curve CV display corresponds to the parameter value they send out.

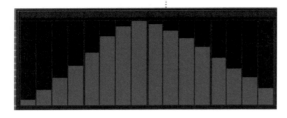

A 16-step CV curve drawn into the Matrix Curve display to control a selected device parameter. The short bars correspond to low parameter values and the tall ones to high values.

The shortest bar you could draw in the display would correspond to a parameter value of 1, and the tallest to a value of 127 (this range, of course, is the parameter value range of most Reason devices). In the case of the filter frequency example, a very short bar would send out a value of 2 or 3 to the SubTractor filter, and the setting of the filter at that time would increase by that amount; a bar with a height 'worth' 10 would increase the filter frequency setting by 10 – and so on.

The object of the exercise is to draw in a Pattern of bars that alters the destination parameter in the way you want – and because the Matrix runs in sync with Song tempo, the parameter changes will be made rhythmically. A real 'curve' Pattern could be made to 'open up' a filter and then close it again, creating a filter-sweep effect (see the SubTractor chapter, if you're not familiar with sound synthesis). However, you don't have to draw an actual curve – you could just as easily draw an alternating Pattern of tall and short bars, if that creates the effect you want. If you're drawing a curve or ramp, remember that Shift-drawing lets you easily create a smooth line.

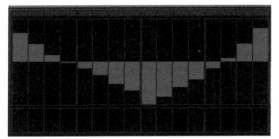

A bi-polar control curve.

The sequence of parameter value changes is output as the Matrix plays, via a dedicated socket on the rear panel, alongside – and independent of – any pitch and trigger information it might also be transmitting.

'Bipolar' parameters, which have both positive and negative values, such as the Pan control on ReMix mixer input channels, can also be controlled by the Matrix Curve CV. A switch on the Matrix's back panel selects the bipolar option. When it is selected, a horizontal line, representing a value of '0', bisects the display. In this case, the curve you draw will be centred on that line and will go above and below it – indicating, in the case of a pan control, automated movements to the left or right ; how far left or right is determined by the length of the bars. With this option, dynamic, moving pan effects can be created alongside a normal, note-based Matrix Pattern.

The Steps display

This display, to the right of the Pattern Window, is where you set the number of steps you would like in your Pattern – anything between 1 and 32. Alter the number with the up/down arrows, or click the number in the display and drag up or down. A red highlight across the top of the Note Grid shows how many steps have been set for the Pattern. The number of steps can be changed at any time, even when you've already programmed notes and gates for the Pattern. When you lengthen a Pattern, empty steps are simply added to the end of it. Shortening a Pattern doesn't delete notes you have already programmed – it just prevents the Pattern from playing them.

Steps display

The Step Resolution Knob

Step Resolution knob

Set how long each step in the Pattern will last with this knob. Musical divisions of half-note, quarter-note, eighth-note, eighth-note triplet, 16th-note, 16th triplet, 32nd-note, 64th-note and 128th-note are available. If you choose the quarter-note resolution, every step in the sequence will be a quarter note long.

The note resolution chosen for the Pattern affects how long the Pattern lasts and how fast it will seem to play: a 16-step Pattern with 16th-note resolution will last for one 4/4 bar, as will a 32-step Pattern with 32nd-note resolution. A 32-step Pattern with half-note resolution will last for 16 bars. At the furthest extreme, a 32-step Pattern with 128th-note resolution would only last the duration of a single quarter-note!

You should also consider the shortest length of notes you might want in your Pattern before making a choice of note resolution. If you choose eighth-note resolution, for example, you'll be able to create larger note values by tying eighth-note steps – for example, tie two for a quarter-note – but you won't be able to make smaller note values, if you need to program something using, say, 16th-notes.

The Bank and Pattern buttons

Each Matrix has 32 Pattern memories, arranged as four banks (A-D) of eight Patterns (1-8), so you can create 32 Patterns in one Matrix. Patterns are named with their Bank and Pattern – for example, A1. Each Pattern can have its own independent Step Resolution and number of Steps, and its own Shuffle on/off status.

To select a memory slot to program a Pattern into, choose a bank and a Pattern by clicking on the appropriate buttons. Red LEDs on the buttons light to tell you which Pattern is currently selected. Patterns can be selected manually, 'on the fly', with these buttons as the Matrix plays, allowing you to swap between them to hear different sequences of Patterns.

This manual Pattern selection can be automated in the main sequencer, by recording changes as you make them in real time. Pattern changes may also be automated by drawing them directly into the main sequencer. Complex chains of Patterns can thus be built up for a whole Song. Pattern chaining is covered later in this chapter.

The Shuffle switch

This switch engages the Shuffle parameter, which automatically adds a syncopated, 'triplet' feel, often referred to as 'swing', to the Pattern. It actually works by delaying all sixteenth notes that fall in between eighth notes. The amount of Shuffle added is controlled by the value of the Pattern Shuffle knob at the far right of the Transport bar.

If you find yourself tweaking the Pattern Shuffle knob and not hearing any results, you probably haven't clicked the Shuffle switch in the Matrix to actually indicate that you want Shuffle to be applied to your Pattern. Note that if you have a ReDrum Pattern running that has Shuffle activated, any Matrix Pattern also running will probably also need Shuffle, or the general effect could be rather odd.

The Pattern Mute switch

This switch mutes or unmutes the currently playing Pattern without interrupting its playback – the Pattern is still running, but you can't hear it.

Tip

Changing modulation speed

If you've created a Matrix just to control another device with the Curve CV, you can use the Step Resolution knob to alter the speed of the modulation the Matrix is providing. For example, if you've created a bipolar curve to control the pan position of a ReMix mixer channel, setting a higher step-resolution value will cause the left-right panning to increase in rate. If your Matrix is producing notes/gates and a Curve CV, however, you won't be able to adjust the rate of the Curve CV in this way without affecting the note/gate data too.

Bank/Pattern buttons

Shuffle switch

Pattern Mute switch

Run button

The Run button

This sets the Matrix playing without you having to run the whole Reason Song, which is obviously useful during Pattern creation. Click the Run button again to stop playback. To play back the Matrix and the rest of the Song together, use the Play button in the Transport bar, or the Space bar on the computer keyboard.

Using the Matrix

Cutting, Copying and Pasting Patterns

Patterns can be cut, copied and pasted between Matrix Pattern memories using the cut/copy/paste Pattern items from the Edit menu or the usual keyboard shortcuts. Select the desired source Pattern memory, use cut or copy, select the destination Pattern memory, and paste.

You can also cut or copy Pattern data between Matrixes in the same rack, and between separate Songs. To copy between Matrixes in different Songs, have both Songs open and proceed as above.

Chaining Patterns

When you've programmed two or more Matrix Patterns for different parts of a Song, you're going to want to arrange them into the right order, with the right number of repetitions of each. You can do this by creating a Pattern chain, where changes from one Pattern to another are recorded into a track of the main sequencer. The method described here works 'on the fly', as the Matrix plays, and is pretty much the same as the method for chaining ReDrum Patterns, if you are familiar with that. Obviously, you need more than one Pattern programmed into your Matrix.

- Find the Matrix track in the main sequencer. This track should have been created automatically when you created the Matrix device, but if you find you don't have a Matrix track, create one.
- Click to the left of the Matrix name in the track list, to make a MIDI plug icon appear, signifying that the track is ready for recording data.
- The Matrix should be right in front of you, as you have selected its sequencer track. Ensure that the first Pattern you would like in your chain is selected.
- Click the red Record button in the transport bar, then the Play button (or use Apple/Control-Return then the Space bar). You'll hear the Pattern playing. Allow it to play for as many repetitions as desired.
- Towards the end of the final repetition you want, select your next Pattern, with the Matrix's Bank and Pattern buttons. When the current Pattern has finished playing, the next one you selected will start to play, and the change of Pattern will have been recorded into the sequencer track.
- Change between the two Patterns as many times as you like, or add others in the same way. When you've finished, stop playback and return to zero. Start playback again to hear the Pattern chain reproduced. If you find you don't like the chain you've recorded, doing the procedure again will overwrite it with a new chain. Alternatively, edit the chain in the sequencer (more in a moment).

Incidentally, if you find you want a few bars where no Matrix Patterns are play-ing, an easy way of achieving this is to select a Pattern that has no data in it, wherever you want a break. Try Pattern D8, the 32nd memory in the Matrix!

An alternative way is to automate switching the red 'Pattern' LED button on and off as you are recording, which mutes playback: the current Pattern's data isn't output, but the Pattern carries on running in the background. Be aware that when you click the Pattern button off or on, the change does not take effect until the beginning of the next bar of the Reason Song.

You'll notice that the Bank and Pattern buttons on the Matrix now have a pink box drawn around them. This indicates that the controls in that area have been automated. The automation/remote control chapter explains how you can assign Pattern changes to keys on your computer keyboard, or to MIDI messages, such as notes on a MIDI keyboard.

You can see the chain of Pattern changes you've recorded into the sequencer by viewing the Pattern Lane for the Matrix track, and edit the changes there. See the sequencer chapter for more.

Yet another way of arranging Matrix Patterns so that they come in where you want them throughout a Song is to use 'Copy Pattern to Track' to send Patterns to a track of the main sequencer (more in a moment). You can then cut, copy, paste and edit them with conventional linear sequencer facilities. As with many operations in Reason, there are several ways of achieving the same result!

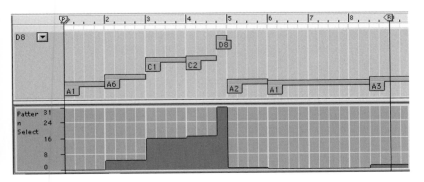

An automated Pattern chain viewed in the sequencer Pattern Lane. Note Pattern D8 (no data in it) being used to create a Pattern break.

Other ways of creating Pattern chains

Pattern changes for the Matrix can also be programmed into the sequencer with-out the on-the-fly process described above, by drawing them directly into the Matrix's Pattern Lane. Chaining Patterns on-the-fly during playback is great for experimenting with Pattern order, and encouraging 'happy accidents', but draw-ing Pattern changes into the sequencer is an excellent method if you already have a strong idea of the order you want for your Matrix Patterns.

Manually drawing Pattern changes also lets you make changes mid-Pattern – you can have just half a Pattern play if you like, whereas the on-the-fly method always waits until the current Pattern has finished playing before responding to a change you may have made. The method for drawing and editing Pattern chains is described in the sequencer chapter.

Interestingly, Pattern changes, and Pattern Mute button switching, can also be drawn and edited in the Controller lane for the Matrix's sequencer track. You may sometimes find this method better than using the Pattern

Lane. See the automation/remote control chapter for a trick to make Pattern-chain creation quicker and easier.

The 'Copy Pattern to Track' facility

This Edit menu option converts a selected Pattern to notes on a track of the main sequencer. Velocity values for the notes are taken from the velocity information in the Pattern's trigger events. Any Curve CV programmed for that Pattern does not convert (but see the sequencer chapter for a way to preserve the Curve CV of a copied Pattern).

There may be times when you will want to do more editing and development on a Pattern than is possible with the Matrix, and on these occasions it's useful to 'send' the Pattern to the main sequencer, where so much more can be done with it. You may also need this feature if you plan to make your Song into a MIDI file, as only data that's in the main sequencer is saved as part of a Reason MIDI file.

With the desired Pattern selected in the Matrix:

- Locate the main sequencer, and the track for the device that is currently assigned to the Matrix. If you have a SubTractor connected to the Matrix, that SubTractor's sequencer track is the one you need. Alternatively, you can select another device's track, to have the Matrix Pattern played by that. (There isn't much point in copying the Pattern to the Matrix sequencer track, since the Matrix itself produces no sound. If you do Copy to the Matrix track, you'll just have to change its destination device anyway.)
- Set the left and right locators around the section of the track where you want the Matrix Pattern copied (see the sequencer chapter for full instructions on using the sequencer).
- Select 'Copy Pattern to Track' from the Edit menu; click 'OK' in the alert box that appears, since you do want "to create data on a track that plays another device than the one selected". The Pattern will be automatically copied into the sequencer track, as many times as necessary to fill the space between the locators. If you want to copy another Pattern into the same track, to follow the first (perhaps they're verse and chorus bass line Patterns, for example, which should be on the same sequencer track), make sure you move the Left and Right markers around the location where you want the new Pattern copied. Otherwise it will paste on top of the first Pattern and both will play back simultaneously. (Incidentally, the other way to end up with multiple Matrix Patterns sketching out a Song structure on the same sequencer track is to first 'chain' them, then use the 'Convert Pattern Track to Notes' facility in the sequencer. More on this procedure in a moment.)
- Now that the Matrix's Pattern is safely copied to a main sequencer track, you'll probably want to either delete the Matrix from the rack or disconnect it from the synth it is connected to – otherwise two copies of the same Pattern data will play at the same time. If you're using the method described in the sequencer chapter for preserving any Curve CV

The alert box you'll see when you copy a Matrix Pattern to a non-Matrix sequencer track.

You are about to create data on a track that plays another device than the one selected. To continue, press OK. Otherwise click Cancel, select another track and try again.

Cancel　OK

that the Pattern has, you won't want to delete the Matrix, only reconnect it in the way explained there.

Convert Pattern Track to Notes

If you have a chain of Patterns set up in the sequencer, as described earlier, you can use the 'Convert Pattern Track to Notes' feature in the main sequencer to instantly send the notes of the Matrix Patterns in their correct order to a sequencer track, where they can be edited and processed more easily. This feature is very similar to 'Copy Pattern to Track', explained above, except that it works on a whole Pattern chain rather than individual Patterns. As with the 'Copy Pattern...' facility, you might need 'Convert Pattern Track...' if you want to save your Reason Song as a MIDI File, as only data in the main sequencer is included. This operation will only work on the Matrix's sequencer track, so you'll have to subsequently assign whatever instrument was being played by the Matrix to the track. Note also that this process deletes the Pattern chain (and turns Pattern selection on the Matrix off), so if for any reason you think you might need the chain, you should make a copy of the track and run the Convert process on the copy.

Pattern manipulation facilities in the Edit menu

Once a Pattern has been created, there are a number of easy ways of changing it. All the following functions can be applied to a Pattern in real time, as it plays back, if desired. Unfortunately, none of them can be automated.

| Shift Pattern Left |
| Shift Pattern Right |
| Shift Pattern Up |
| Shift Pattern Down |
| Randomize Pattern |
| Alter Pattern |

Pattern manipulation options available in the Edit menu or Matrix Context menu.

Shift Pattern up/down

This facility shifts a whole Pattern up or down by one semitone at a time – basically, transposing it. You can access this function (and the others explained below) from the Edit menu, but the easiest way to use it is with Apple/Control-U, which shifts up, or Apple/Control-D, which shifts down. Just use the command repeatedly to shift by the required number of semitones. There's no need to select any data in the display: as long as the Matrix is highlighted, these key commands will work on the current Pattern.

Use these facilities, for example:

- When you've changed the key of a whole Song and you need to transpose a Matrix Pattern to match.
- When you want to double a Pattern with the same thing playing an octave higher or lower on a different sound (copy the Pattern to another Matrix connected to another synth and shift it up or down an octave). This can sound very effective.
- When you want to create a parallel harmony part for a Pattern already programmed (copy the Pattern to another Matrix and shift by a suitable interval, such as a fourth or fifth – five or seven semitones respectively).

The Curve CV is not affected by the Shift Pattern Up/Down feature.

Shift Pattern Left/Right

A whole Pattern can be shifted left or right by one step at a time using Apple/Control-J (left) or Apple/Control-K (right). A note which appeared on step 32 of a 32-step Pattern would 'shove over' and appear on Step 1 if the Pattern was shifted one step to the right. This facility has uses in creating music with a repetitive, textural feel; where several Patterns are running together, shifting some or all left or right can create an interesting pseudo-polyrhythmic effect. Since the Curve CV is affected by the Shift operation, controller information can be similarly changed in real time, and this may be generally more useful than shifting note Patterns.

A Matrix Pattern (original in screen 1) shifted eight steps to the right (screen 2).

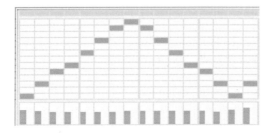 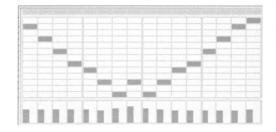

Randomise Pattern

The Randomise Pattern function can be used even where no Pattern has yet been programmed. Choosing 'Randomise' from the Edit menu, or using Apple/Control-R, causes random notes, gates and Curve CV values to be automatically programmed into the current Pattern. The Step resolution and number of steps are retained. The Randomise process overwrites data that is already in the Pattern, so before you begin it, it might be wise to select a new Pattern memory slot, if the current one contains a Pattern you wish to keep. Alternatively, save the Song. (If not, there are the usual 10 levels of Undo.)

The problem with Randomise Pattern is that it operates across the Matrix's full five-octave range, so the Patterns it produces are completely unlike anything a musician would normally program, and frankly fairly unusable. However, you can run the process repeatedly, increasing the chances of it producing a usable result. You might alternatively find that a random Pattern produces fragments of melody that are worth developing. Using the 'Copy Pattern to Track' function from the Edit menu or a Context menu (see explanation earlier in this section), you may convert the Matrix Pattern to notes on a main sequencer track and then use the main sequencer's editing facilities to delete unwanted notes, leaving the best bits for development. You might also like to try applying a Randomised Curve CV to some device parameters – it could at least lead to an effect that you might never otherwise have achieved!

Alter Pattern

This is a rather more useful facility than Randomise, as it takes the note, gate and Curve CV values that have already been programmed into the currently selected Pattern and swaps them about. The result often still sounds as though it is related to the source Pattern, and thus is potentially useful for creating variation Patterns that complement the original. You can Alter repeatedly until you get something you like. As with Randomise, this function overwrites the existing Pattern, so you may want to work on a copy.

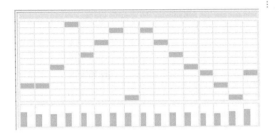

The first screen in Figure 12.12 modified with the 'Alter Pattern' function.

The other useful application of a Matrix 'library' would be to store a set of Curve CV Patterns that produce different effects, to save you drawing them anew each time you need one.

Info

What musical tasks is the Matrix good for?

By its nature, the Matrix is ideal for producing rhythmically precise, tight music that depends to some extent on repetition. Dance music, in all its factions, is well-suited to Matrix-style Pattern-based composition. Likewise, classic electronic music – think Tangerine Dream – is also a good bet. Of course, any kind of music can be created, providing you're prepared to think in blocks of up to 32 steps; just plan and break down phrases accordingly. The wide range of resolutions opens up some interesting avenues for exploration, too, especially when using Matrix as a source of control data rather than notes; Patterns of half-note or 128th-note resolution can produce remarkable results, with gradual evolution at one extreme and a blur of events at the other.

The rear panel

The Curve CV output

Any controller values programmed into the Curve CV display are output via this socket, which can be connected to the CV or Gate inputs on any other device in the rack, to alter suitable parameters. You're not guaranteed a good result from all of them, but all are worth experimenting with. The results, in any case, will also depend on the Curve you've programmed.

Curve CV output.

Recommended places to connect this output include synth Filter Frequency and Resonance Modulation inputs (see later in the chapter for a technique to copy LFO modulation of filter frequency), FM Amount and Oscillator Phase Modulation inputs, and envelope Gate inputs. Also experiment with DDL1 Delay Feedback and Pan CV inputs, and other CV inputs of the effect devices. ReMix pan and level CV inputs are worthy too. Later, you can discover how to create mixer auto-pan with the Curve CV.

Note CV output.

The Note CV output

The pitches programmed into a Matrix Pattern are sent out of the Note CV output as control voltages. Normally, this output is connected to the Sequencer Control CV inputs at the rear of sound-making devices, but it could be connected to any other CV or Gate input in the rack. The results of using the Note CV in this way may not always be predictable, but it's definitely worth trying.

Quick Idea

Something that works very well is connecting the Matrix Note CV output to the Pitch CV Input on a ReDrum drum voice channel which has a drum part programmed for it and a suitable voice loaded. Note data sent from the Matrix will then affect the pitch of the ReDrum voice on that channel. If you use a tom, tuned African drum sample or tuned Latin percussion, the pitch variations in the drum sound are very effective, and can create the impression of a programmed ethnic drum part. It works well with cowbells too.

You'll need to draw notes in the Matrix display (these can be orderly or quite random) over a wide pitch range in order for there to be a variation in drum pitch. For some reason, notes that are less than about four or five semitones apart don't seem to have much effect on it. Also be sure to tweak the drum voice's rear-panel CV trim pot to suit the effect.

Gate CV output.

The Gate CV Output

The Gate data drawn in the lower part of the Matrix Pattern display is output here; it provides the all-important trigger without which the Note CV would produce no sound at all. It's not enough to connect just the Note CV output of the Matrix device to a SubTractor or NN19 in order for that device to make a noise: it also needs trigger information, sent from the Gate CV output.

The Gate CV can also be used to produce rhythmic triggers for routing to any Gate or CV jack in the Reason rack. The many potential destinations include the separate Gate inputs for SubTractor's three envelope generators (for adding rhythmic interest to held sounds), and any of the drum voices in a ReDrum kit.

The Bipolar/Unipolar switch.

The Bipolar/Unipolar switch

When a Matrix is created it defaults to a Unipolar curve for the Curve CV display. This type of curve is most suitable for controlling parameters which have a positive value range (1-127). To control parameters with a value range that is negative and positive, such as pan position – -64 to +64 representing full left and full right – you need the ability to draw a bipolar curve, with a centre axis representing a value of '0', as mentioned earlier in this chapter. Switching to Bipolar changes the display to make this possible.

Some ways of using the Curve CV

Creating auto-panning

With a simple note Pattern programmed in the Matrix, we're going to create 'curves' to control mixer channel pan position. The effect will be to pan the notes of the Pattern (played by a SubTractor synth connected to the mixer channel), in three different ways.

You need at least a ReMix mixer, a Matrix and a SubTractor synth in your rack. The SubTractor audio output must be routed to the audio input of a ReMix channel.

- First, ensure that that the Matrix is connected to a SubTractor synth for sequencer control (Matrix Note CV out connected to SubTractor Sequencer Control CV in; Matrix Gate CV out connected to SubTractor Sequencer Control Gate In).
- Now connect the Matrix Curve CV output to the Pan CV Input of the mixer channel the SubTractor is routed to. This means that the Matrix can send messages to the mixer that will affect the pan position of the SubTractor mixer channel.
- While you are at the rear of the rack, set the Matrix to Bipolar operation.

- Back at the front of the Matrix, input a 16-step, 16th-note Pattern – just put a note on each of the first 16 steps. The tune doesn't really matter, as it's only there to illustrate the panning effect, but a sound with a short decay and a tempo of about 100bpm will allow you to hear the effect most clearly. Then copy this Pattern and paste it into memory locations A2 and A3, following the instructions for copying Patterns given earlier in the chapter.

The Matrix, SubTractor and ReMix connected correctly for Matrix panning of the SubTractor notes going through channel one.

Pattern A1 Curve data.

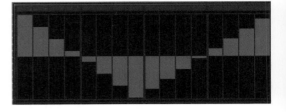

- Now switch to 'Curve' mode, using the 'Keys/Curve' switch. You are now looking at the Curve CV display. Select Pattern A1 and input the data you see in the screen below. It does not have to be exact, but should be something like it.
- Select Pattern A2 and program the second screen of data into that. Do the same with Pattern A3 and the data in the third screen.

Left: Pattern A2 Curve data.

Right: Pattern A3 Curve data.

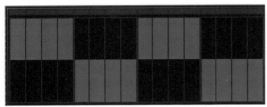

- Select Pattern A1 again, and click the Matrix's Run switch to set the Pattern playing. What you will hear over your speakers or in your headphones is the notes in the Pattern gradually panning from right to left, and back to the right again.
- Select Pattern A2. What you hear now is the first beat of the Pattern (four steps) in the right-hand speaker, the next beat in the left speaker, and so on – basically, panning on every beat.
- Select Pattern A3. You'll hear the individual notes of the Pattern swap rapidly between right and left speakers – panning on every step.

Obviously, because the step number and step resolution must be the same within one Pattern, a Pattern's Curve CV has to have the same settings as its notes – if the main note Pattern has 16 16th-note steps, the Curve CV has to have 16 16th-note steps. But if you would like settings for a Curve CV that are different from those for the note Pattern, you can set up another Matrix just to provide the Curve CV.

Just create a second Matrix and connect its Curve CV output to the mixer channel Pan CV (the first Matrix is connected to only the SubTractor if you do it this way). Create, for example, a longer, slower and more gradual pan curve, like the one in the screen below, using a 32-step Pattern length. This one has 32 steps for panning the 16-step note Pattern produced by the first Matrix.

A 32-step Pan curve. This pans more gradually.

The examples we've given here control pan position for the sound-making device being controlled by a Matrix, but you can, of course, do the same thing for a device being played by the main sequencer.

Faking a Sync'd LFO

Seasoned synth musicians know the brilliant rhythmic effect created by synchronising the rate of LFO filter modulation with the tempo of a song. This is usually done by routing incoming MIDI clock to the LFO, overriding its speed or rate control and locking the peaks in the LFO's movement to a rhythmic sub-division of the incoming MIDI tempo information – 16th-notes or 8th-notes, for example.

Since Reason V2, the LFOs of synths and sample playback devices have been sync'able to song tempo – just click the Sync button. Even so, the 'Matrix LFO' which discussed here, and which was the only way to create this effect in earlye versions of Reason, has a couple of its own advantages, not least of which is the ability to set a completely different value for each step of a curve Pattern.

How does it work? Well, the peaks in the LFO's waveform mentioned above can be simulated by sending controller data to Subtractor from the Matrix, with the rhythmic effect provided by the Matrix's event 'steps'. In effect, a controller value producing a filter change is sent to SubTractor on each step of a Matrix Pattern, and because the Matrix automatically syncs to Reason's Song tempo, the filter changes are sync'd to the Song's tempo too. The effect is very similar to the real thing.

- Create a mixer, then a SubTractor. Starting from the Sub's Init patch, set Filter 1 Frequency to 30 and Resonance to around 65. You can use any sound you like when you get used to the technique, obviously – this is just for illustration.
- Create a Matrix. If you don't already have a Matrix in the rack, the new one will automatically connect its Note CV and Gate outputs to your SubTractor. At this point it's better if this doesn't happen, so click inside the Matrix and choose 'Disconnect Device' from the Edit menu. Alternatively, hold down Shift while creating the Matrix, to create it with no connections.
- Now we need to set the Matrix to control Subtractor Filter Frequency. Tab to the back of the rack. Connect the Matrix's Curve CV output to the SubTractor's Filter 1 Frequency Modulation input. (Incidentally, the knob next to the Filter 1 Frequency socket governs the depth of the modulation applied to Filter 1 Frequency. Tweak this knob to make the filter modulation more subtle or more pronounced.)
- Tab back to the front panel. We now need to input a random controller curve Pattern into the Matrix, to emulate an LFO effect that would be created by a Random waveform. Select the 'Curve' option with the Curve/Key button. In the 'Steps' display, select an odd number of Pattern Steps – 19, 23, 31, or whatever (we'll tell you why in a moment). Now input a random controller value on each step. See the screen below for an example. Now the Matrix will generate a control voltage, to alter Subtractor's filter frequency, for every step.

Tip

The Matrix for anyone

If you're not a person who finds it easy to plan and execute a Matrix tune, there's nothing wrong with inputting notes pretty much at random, adding some Gate events, and seeing what comes out. Don't forget that you can drag the mouse along the Matrix grid to create a lot of notes (or Gates) in one go. As the Pattern plays back, alter notes that don't work, or add and take away Gates to change the rhythm, until you have something you like. In the SubTractor chapter there's a patch to program that emulates a TB303 Bassline synth, with an explanation of how to use semi-random Matrix input to achieve something authentic-sounding.

Matrix Curve CV output connected to SubTractor's Filter 1 Frequency CV input.

Input a random series of values in the CV display. This emulates a 'random' LFO waveform modulating filter frequency.

• Now to try out the effect. Go to the main sequencer and ensure that the track assigned to SubTractor has the MIDI socket in its MIDI In column, by clicking to the left of the track name. Now you can play it from your MIDI keyboard. Hit play in the Transport, to start the Matrix playing its 'LFO' Pattern, and play some rhythmic held chords. You should hear the characteristic sound of Sample & Hold or Random LFO. Increase Song tempo in the Transport and the filter will modulate at a faster rate – when you are working in context of a Song, the 'Matrix LFO' rate will thus always follow your Song tempo. You can also achieve the effect of different LFO rates by changing the Step Resolution in the Matrix.

We suggested creating a Matrix Curve Pattern with an odd number of steps to ensure that the random effect doesn't become predictable. This is most relevant when you have a note Pattern playing on one Matrix and you're setting up a second Matrix with a Curve CV to affect that Pattern. If you chose 16 steps for the Matrix generating the notes and 16 steps for the Matrix generating the Curve CV, the same controller value/note pairs would come around regularly. Choose 17 steps for the Curve Matrix, and it'll take quite a few repetitions before identical combinations of controller step and note coincide.

A Curve CV Pattern to emulate an LFO 'square wave' modulating Filter Frequency.

You can simulate other 'LFO' waveforms with this technique too. For example, to create the straight 'up and down' Pattern provided by an LFO square wave modulating SubTractor's filter, for example, follow all the instructions above, but input a CV Pattern, as illustrated in the screen below, of alternating full and 50% values. It's OK for the Pattern to be an even number of steps here, since what you're after is a regular pulse.

Advantages of the Matrix LFO

This 'Matrix LFO' method is actually more flexible than simply sync'ing an LFO to MIDI clock. First of all, the 'LFO waveform' created by the Matrix will always start at the right place; with the real thing, there can sometimes be a chance that you'll start playing in the middle of a waveform cycle, and that there will be a slight delay before the desired modulation starts.

Secondly, you have complete control, within the context of the Matrix controller display, over the value of each step of the 'LFO'; indeed, you can actually create rhythmic LFO Patterns, to really underline the feel of your track, which you certainly can't with the real thing.

And lastly, you have a much wider range of rhythmic note values than the average MIDI-Clockable LFO – you can choose from the full range of the Matrix's resolution, from a half-note up to a 128th-note.

Arpeggios with the Matrix

As you'll have read elsewhere in this book, Reason (sadly) doesn't have an arpeggiator. Luckily, however, there are a couple of ways to mimic the effect of this classic device – one of which is described in the Dr:rex chapter. Arpeggio-like effects are possible, too, with some of the advanced modulation waveforms available in V2's new the Malström graintable synth. The Matrix can also be used to achieve the desired effect.

- Decide which sort of arpeggiation Pattern or Patterns you'd like to use in your music, work out how they break up the average chord, and decide on what sort of chord shapes you'd like to work with. If you have access to an arpeggiator elsewhere in your studio, built into a hardware synth, software instrument or another sequencing package (Cubase, for example, has an arpeggiator module), you can play with these and analyse their output.
- Now reduce the Patterns to the notes of a chord based on C, and draw the notes into a Matrix Pattern.
- Copy the Pattern and paste it into an empty Pattern location in the same Matrix.
- Using the 'Shift Pattern up/down' functions in the Edit menu, transpose the Pattern up or down. Do this on multiple copies, transposing the Pattern to suit the chords that you're using in the Song. Note that you may also have to change individual steps within transposed Patterns to make them play in tune with a given chord – thirds will be a particular issue; they'll need to be switched from major to minor and vice versa.
- Now chain the Patterns, in the Matrix's sequencer track, to create the effect of a real arpeggiator, changing chords in response to your Song's harmonic structure.

You could, of course, save one or several Matrixes that are loaded with these Patterns as a library Song, so that you don't have to keep creating them from scratch. Just load the Song, and copy the Pattern you need to a Matrix in the Song you're working on, transposing further copies to match the new work's chord scheme.

Here, for you to play around with, are a collection of typical arpeggiation Patterns – you could produce many, many more. All the example Patterns have been kept within the one octave range of the Matrix note grid display (they are all based around a 'C' chord) but feel free to increase Pattern lengths and input the same notes in the next octave as well. Use any step resolution that suits you. Arpeggios usually sound great with a bit of timed delay, too.

Real-time Matrix transposing from the keyboard

One thing that's a bit sad about creating arpeggio Patterns with the Matrix is that it's not possible to transpose the Patterns in real time from the key-

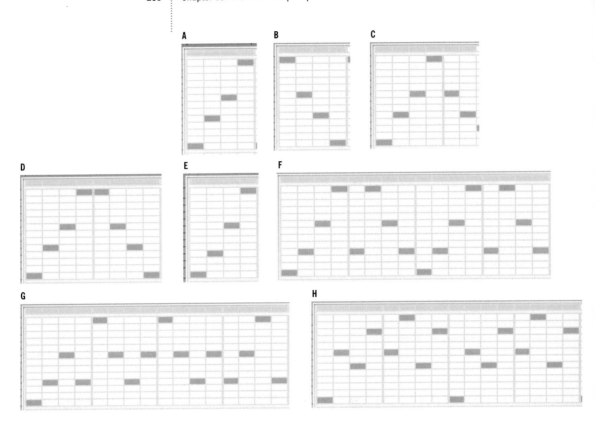

A Four-step 'up' arpeggio (major). Screens 'reversed out' for clarity.

B Four-step 'down' arpeggio (major).

C Six-step 'up/down' arpeggio (major).

D Eight-step 'up/down' arpeggio (major).

E Four-step 'up' arpeggio (minor). To produce a minor 'upward' arpeggio from the major ones above, you simply drop the second step by one semitone, as in this example. If the arpeggio is going 'down', drop the fourth step by a semitone.

F 16-step up/down arpeggio (minor). The fifth step and the thirteenth step can alternatively be programmed one octave above the E-flat they play in this screen. Just flip the octave switch up one position, showing the next octave of notes, and program the E-flat there.

G 16-step minor Pattern. You can make this a major Pattern by turning all the E-flats into 'E's (raise by one semitone).

H 16-step Pattern that's neither major nor minor (though it has a minor 7th in it!).

board, in the same way that you can with Dr:rex when you've prepared an arpeggio loop.

However, a fantastic solution to this conundrum can be found on the Internet, at the Pegasus web site (http://home.t-online.de/home/pegasus-wtal/). Pegasus (Peter Gaydos) very kindly agreed to his idea being explained in this book. Thanks, Peter! More Reason material can be found on his web site too – it's well worth a visit.

In general, the technique allows you to transpose, in real time, a pattern being generated by the Matrix; that pattern could be the notes that describe an arpeggio, or any other notes.

- Create a SubTractor and a Matrix and flip to the back panel.
- Route a cable from the Matrix Note CV socket to the SubTractor Oscillator Pitch Modulation Input, and turn its trim pot fully right.
- Route the Matrix Gate CV to the SubTractor Amp Level Modulation Input; you may find that the Amp Level input's trim pot will need to be turned fully right, too.
- Create a pattern in the Matrix.
- Ensure that the MIDI socket appears in the 'In' column for the SubTractor's main sequencer track, then press play on the transport bar, or use the Matrix's Run button to engage playback. You'll hear nothing until you play your keyboard to trigger the SubTractor.
- Play your keyboard. Even now you may hear nothing: because you're manipulating the pitch of SubTractor via the rear-panel modulation input, the oscillator pitch settings on the front panel are all out of whack. Everything will probably be transposed far too high, so you'll need to bring the octave setting in SubTractor down to '0', '1' or '2'. You may also find it worthwhile to program your Matrix parts in the lower registers to give you more flexibility when programming the SubTractor. Almost no factory Patches will work with this technique unless you transpose them down, and maybe do extra tweaking too.
- Once your performance becomes audible, what you'll be hearing is a Matrix pattern which transposes in response to the notes that you play on the keyboard. You can even play chords, which play with the same

The rear panel patching to set up Matrix transposing of a sound-making device (in this case, SubTractor) via your MIDI keyboard.

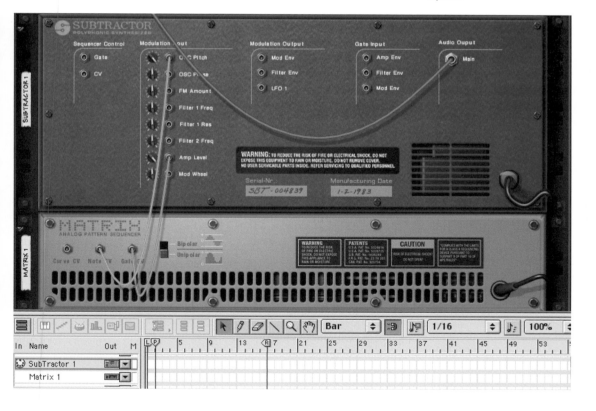

rhythm and pitch relationships as the pattern. Having said that, the technique is most effective with harmonically neutral arpeggiator-like patterns and similar material. Whatever you program, you'll hear nothing at all unless you play from your keyboard. This tells SubTractor what notes to play, and triggers the envelopes; the actual rhythm of your performance and the melodic relationship between the notes being generated and transposed is determined by the Matrix.

Expanding the technique

There are a number of ways to expand on this technique: for example, routing the Matrix Gate CV output to the SubTractor Amp Env Gate In produces a slightly different result. Experiment with other SubTractor Gate Ins, and also play around with the trim pot values; you'll hear some distinctly non-equal tempered intervals if the Pitch Modulation Input trim pot is set to anything other than its maximum value, but this can be rather interesting in its own right.

A performance as described above could even be recorded to a sequencer track. If you're feeling particularly adventurous, it's also possible to route your master keyboard to all four of Reason's 'Advanced MIDI' External Control buses and, via the Hardware Interface, play four SubTractors (or other devices; this technique works with all sound making devices, bar ReDrum and Dr:rex) via four Matrixes set up as described above, to create a transposable 'instant track'. (All four Patterns transpose at the same time via your keyboard input, which is great when you have four different Matrix patterns going at the same time.) You could even record the whole lot to the sequencer, too. Recording such a multi-device performance (as well as using the four MIDI buses mentioned above) is discussed in the SubTractor chapter.

Effects

The virtual representation of an electronic music studio would be unthinkable without a little audio icing. Artificial effects have been an essential feature of music for many years, and are now an integral part of the creative process. Indeed, most electronic musicians would find themselves lost without effects – timed delays increasing the

interest and complexity of arpeggios and drum patterns, gentle chorus on an electric piano, grungy distortion on a menacing lead line, echoing ambience around a string pad... Effects help synth sounds and samples come to life.

Effects basics

Reason's effects come in the shape of nine 'half-rack' modules, each providing one treatment or process: reverb, digital delay, distortion, envelope-controlled filtering, chorus/flange, phase, compression, unison and parametric EQ. Two further, full-rack, devices provide sophisticated reverb processing and distortion effects respectively.

Apart from the full-size reverb and distortion devices, each effect has a fairly simple set of controls, but can be connected into chains of pretty much any length (depending on computer power), to create multi-effects configurations. Effects, whether singly or in chains or Combis, can be used either in mixer send/return loops, to treat several sound sources at the same time, or 'in-line' with devices, treating just that device ('insert' processing is achieved in this way). However, though you could use all of the effects devices in both these ways, there are generally accepted music-production rules for which ones should be used in which configuration. That will be discussed shortly.

Like all other Reason devices, the parameters of the effect devices are fully automatable, via the sequencer, and all but the compressor have CV connections to allow one or more parameters to be controlled by other devices in the rack. This opens up even more creative possibilities.

The MClass modules are of course also effects in Reason, but as they are intended largely for mastering they are dealt with in a separate chapter. In truth you can use any effect in any way or combination, but for the sake of simplicity they are dealt with separately here.

Get going with the effects

Create some send/return effects

If you're not familiar with how effects are used in the Auxiliary (aux), or effect sends and returns of a mixer, it's a good idea to read the section called 'The Auxiliary Send/Return System' in the ReMix chapter.

- Create an empty rack as explained in the first step of the Tutorials chapter.
- Create a ReMix mixer, an RV7 Reverb and a DDL1 Delay. Reason automatically connects the output of the RV7 to Auxiliary Return 1 on the mixer, and the output of the DDL1 to Auxiliary Return 2. You can see this on the front panel of the mixer by looking at the scribble strips in the Return section, top right corner of ReMix. You can see it on the rear panel by hitting the Tab key to reveal the cable connections. Also note, in the screen below, how Aux sends 1 and 2 have been automatically connected to the Left (mono) inputs of the RV7 and DDL1, to allow the mixer send controls to 'tap' signal from any connected sound sources and route it to the two effects devices.
- Set the wet/dry balance knob on the front of both the RV7 and the DDL1 to fully 'wet' – that is, all the way to the right.

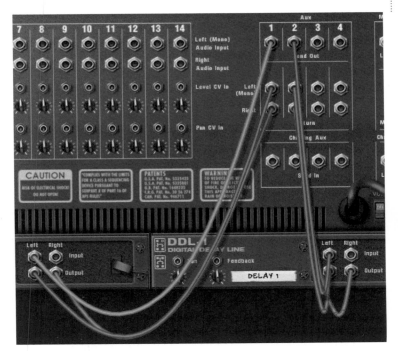

A reverb and a delay connected to the mixer as send effects.

Set the wet/dry balance knob fully wet.

Use the Aux knobs to set how much effect you would like to hear.

- The Reverb and Delay effects are now available to process signal going through any of the mixer channels. How much effect is applied to each channel is set by the red Aux 1 and 2 knobs in each ReMix channel strip. If you don't want a particular send effect applied to a particular channel, just set the appropriate Aux knob in that channel to zero.
- If you would like to hear the send system in action, create a SubTractor synth. Reason automatically connects this to mixer channel 1, and also automatically creates a sequencer track for it.
- Load a sound into SubTractor, make sure the keyboard icon is showing next to the Sub's sequencer track name, and play a few notes on the keyboard. You should hear a 'dry' synth, with no effects applied. Now move the Aux 1 red knob in mixer channel 1 to the right. This increases the send level to the reverb and makes the reverb audible. Play a couple more notes to hear the reverb on the synth notes, and add more reverb if you like, by turning the Aux 1 knob further to the right. Turn it fully left to remove the reverb effect and do the same procedure with the Aux 2 control, to hear delay applied to your synth sound.

If you were to turn the rack around and connect the output of SubTractor to the input of ReMix channel 2 rather than channel 1, you would get the same results from tweaking the Aux 1 and 2 controls on that channel – the effects are available equally, via the sends, to all 14 mixer channels.

Create an 'insert' (in-line) effect

An 'insert' effect is connected directly to one sound source and only treats that sound source. If you're starting with an empty rack, add a ReMix and a

Tip

A short cut

If you want to preview or audition an effect without actually loading an effect module into the rack, you can do so from the Browser. Reason will actually load the unit temporarily in the background, but only keep it if you click OK. Anything that's playing or any notes you press will sound through the effect you're auditioning, depending on how you have the rack connected. This is a great way to go through multiple effects to find what works.

SubTractor, as described above, then do the following:

- Click on the SubTractor, then create an effect – a DDL1 delay, say. Clicking the sound source before creating the effect tells Reason that you want the effect to be connected in-line with that sound source. Now if you flip round to the back panel, by hitting the Tab key on your computer keyboard, you'll see that the SubTractor's output has been patched to the input of the DDL1 and the DDL1 output has been patched to the mixer input previously used by the SubTractor. The DDL1 has been placed between the SubTractor and the mixer channel.

A DDL1 connected to a SubTractor as an in-line or insert effect.

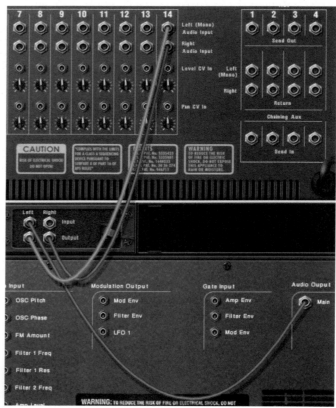

Since you don't have an Aux send control to set the balance between 'wet' and 'dry' (processed and unprocessed) signal with an insert effect, you use the 'Wet/Dry' control on its front panel.

- Play a few SubTractor notes on your keyboard: its sounds are now treated with whatever delay setting the DDL1 has. Adjust the DDL1's wet/dry control to 64 (50/50 wet/dry), or whatever value produces your preferred balance between untreated and treated signal.

A

Signal tapped off from every channel and sent, in varying amounts, to effect device

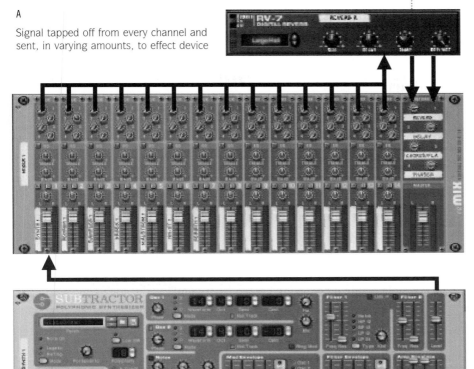

Effected signal returns to mixer. Amount of effect in mix set by return controls

Sound source connected to mixer input. Sources connected to every input can take advantage of the send/return effect.

The difference between send and insert effects. (See overleaf for picture B.)

B

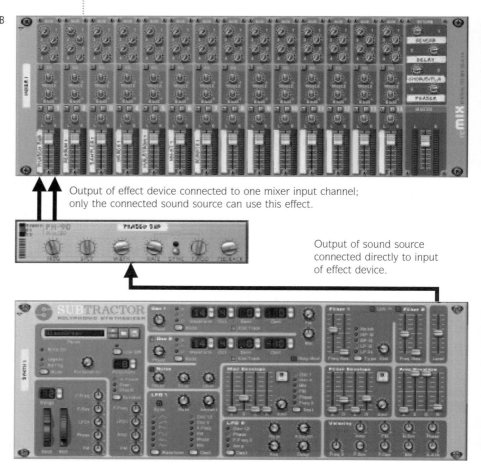

Output of effect device connected to one mixer input channel;
only the connected sound source can use this effect.

Output of sound source
connected directly to input
of effect device.

Chaining effects

Two or more effects, whether used in a send/return system or in an in-line
configuration, can be linked into a chain, for multi-effect processing. Making
a chain is very easy:

- Click the effect device you wish to begin with, then create another effect
  device. It will be automatically connected after the first.
- To add another effect at any point in a chain, click on an effect device to
  select it and then create a new device. The new device is inserted after
  the selected one. For example, if you had a chain of compressor-
  distortion-flanger, clicking on the distortion effect and then creating a
  delay would insert the delay between the distortion and the flanger.

When you're making a chain of effects devices, you can put each new effect
wherever you want it in the chain, but bear in mind that the order of a chain
makes a difference to the final sound, as explained later in this chapter.

If you delete a device from a chain, or from an in-line connection – for
example, removing a reverb patched in-line between an NN19 and a mixer

channel – the two devices either side of the 'break' are automatically re-connected. The NN19 would then be directly connected to the mixer.

Automatic effects patching logic

Though you're free to connect effects devices in any way you like, Reason offers a number of automatic routings. Some of them operate by default, without any specific action on your part, and some can be directed by you. For example, clicking on a sound-making device, to select it, and then creating an effect, tells the program that you want that effect connected 'in-line' with that device. Clicking on a mixer before creating an effects device tells Reason to connect that device to an available send/return loop on the mixer. This will happen for the first four devices created, since the mixer has four loops. If your rack has a mixer and one or more sound-making devices, you need to highlight the mixer first for this automatic send/return linking to occur – or Reason may think you want the effects connected to the sound-makers. After the four loops are full, the automatic patching rules change.

Reason always attempts to connect effects in a logical way for you, but if you don't want the connections it has made you can always choose 'Disconnect Device' from the Edit menu or a Context menu. Alternatively, create devices while holding down Shift to make them with no automatic connections at all; you can then do the necessary patching yourself.

It's very difficult to explain the auto-patching rules without making the reader more confused than before – and actually, you will probably manage perfectly well without knowing exactly why Reason is doing what it is doing – but a few things may be worth bearing in mind. One is that when you create a second mixer for your rack, its four aux sends are automatically connected by Reason to the aux send/return system of the first mixer, so that the second mixer has access to the same set of effects as the first. When you now add more effects to the rack, they can't be connected to the second mixer, because its loops are effectively in use. If you disconnect the aux-system linking between the two mixers, subsequent effects can then be auto-connected to the send/return loops of the second mixer, just as they were with the first. However, you'll need to highlight the second mixer for this to occur.

Also, if you want to create an effect chain to use in an aux send/return loop, you'll have to patch it manually for the first two devices in the chain. Once you have made at least a two-device chain connected to a loop, however, Reason 'knows' you want a chain and when you make a new effect device with the final effect device in that chain highlighted, it will auto-connect the new device to the end of the chain for you. Another thing worth knowing is that you can't get an automatic connection between an individual ReDrum drum voice and an effect, though you can between ReDrum's main stereo output and the effect. You have to patch the former manually.

Effects vs Processors

As explained in the ReMix chapter, not all of the effect devices should really be used via the send/return system. The rules on signal processing that usually pertain in the studio make a distinction between 'effects' and 'processors'.

The first four effects created can be automatically patched into the mixer's four send/return loops.

Tip

Saving processor power

If your computer is short of power, always try to use effects via the mixer send/return loops, rather than 'in-line' as inserts, as this way a handful of effects can treat as many sound sources as you like. You can have up to four effects (or effects chains) in send/return loops on a mixer, so with careful use of the aux controls quite different treatments can be set up for different sound sources. Use Line Mixers to boost the send effect capability of the main mixer.

- Effects: With true effects – for example, delay, reverb, chorus – the final sound relies on a combination of the effected (wet) sound and the un-effected (dry) sound, the balance being set by whoever's doing the mix.
- Processors: These – primarily EQ, filtering and dynamics processors such as compressors – are designed to process an entire signal and to present the listener with only the processed signal, rather than a mix of processed and unprocessed signal. If you have EQ'd a problem sound, for example, you don't usually want the un-EQ'd sound mixed with the EQ'd version, undermining the work you've done.

How it works in Reason

The colour coding of the Reason half-rack effect devices reflects the effect/processor division to some extent: the red devices are mostly effects and the silver ones are designed as processors. The scheme is upset some-what by the red colouring of the PEQ2 equaliser, and that's before we even examine the classic blue of the RV7000 reverb, or the '70s creaminess of the Scream 4 distortion unit!

Since the mixer send/return system is primarily for mixing effected and dry sound, the general practice is not to use processors in it. Processors would normally be used instead in mixer 'insert points', which provide a method of treating the sound going through one mixer channel only, and treating the entire sound. However, we don't have insert points in the Reason mixer, so we can instead create 'insert' configurations (as in the examples above) for treating the entire output of a single sound source. To copy the 'correct' use of processors in the studio, one would set up the processor devices only in 'insert' configurations.

The devices designed to be used as 'processors' – ie. only in 'insert' configurations – in Reason.

The true 'effect' devices can be used either way:

- In insert configurations, their Dry/Wet control sets the balance between processed and unprocessed signal.
- In send/return configurations, the Dry/Wet control should be set fully 'wet' and the balance created with the mixer aux send control (and ReMix master auxiliary return controls) .

In Reason, there are ambiguities, however: the chorus, for example, has no Dry/Wet control. If it is used in-line, the balance between dry and effected signal is pre-set, while if it is used in a mixer send/return loop, the return con-trol in ReMix's master section sets the balance. And while one would perhaps

consider Phaser an 'effect', in Reason it's configured as an 'insert' processor, and thus has no Dry/Wet balance control. This is logical in a way, since phasing usually treats an entire sound, with no 'dry' component. Nevertheless, you may find that Reason's Phaser also functions well as a send effect, though if you use it like this there may be additional complications on a mix due to the absence of a Dry/Wet control.

In the final analysis, Reason does not actually prevent you from using the processors 'incorrectly', and if you find applications for them in this way, good luck. It's as well to know the accepted rules and the reasons for them, even if you then decide to ignore them!

The devices designed to be used as effects in Reason – ie. in the mixer send/return system or as inserts.

Guided tour

Common controls
Before examining the individual effects devices, let's have a look at the features that the devices have in common (this holds true for the more advanced RV7000 and Scream 4 devices). First, on the front panel:

- Power/Bypass switch: Selects the operational state of the effect device; 'Bypass' allows 'dry' signal to pass through the device unprocessed, and is therefore perfect for switching between the dry and effected sound so that you can compare the two while tailoring effect or processing treatments. 'On' engages the effect for normal operation, and 'Off' disables the unit entirely – not even unprocessed audio passes through.

Power/Bypass switch

- Input Meter: This bargraph meter provides a visual indication that audio is coming into the device, and at what level. However, don't panic if the meter goes into the red, since the effects devices are, according to Propellerhead, incapable of being overloaded and clipping. The meter basically just lets you know that signal is present. If the output of an effect appears to be overloading, simply turn its mixer channel or aux return down.

Input meter

- Audio inputs and outputs: On the rear panel of all devices are left and right audio input sockets and left and right audio output sockets. Depending on the device, these jacks will offer mono, dual mono/true stereo, and/or mono-to-stereo processing. The routing options that produce these results are illustrated on the rear panel of each device by two or three graphic flowcharts. The options available will be discussed as each device is introduced.

Audio Ins and Outs

- CV inputs: All effect devices, except the COMP01 compressor, also have one or several CV control options on the rear panel – again, these will be discussed in due course.

CV inputs

Info

Fine knob adjustments

Remember you can access fine control of device knobs by holding down Shift as you operate the knob. This may be especially useful with the small changes you often need to make to effects parameters.

As with the ReMix mixer channels, effect devices auto-sense whether what you are connecting to them is mono or stereo, and the appropriate automatic connection is made. You don't have to think in advance about creating a purely mono chain of effects for a SubTractor synth, for example. However, if an RV7 (stereo reverb) is placed at the end of a mono effects chain, it will also be connected in mono – just its left output will be connected to a ReMix input, so you will probably want to manually connect the right output as well, to restore the reverb's stereo operation.

RV7000 Advanced Reverb

- Stereo in/Stereo out (true stereo operation), Mono In/Stereo out
- Insert or Send/Return operation

Reverb (short for reverberation) is probably the most widely used artificial effect there is. It's integral to recorded music because it simulates what happens to sound in the real world, giving the impression of a genuine acoustic space that recorded music can otherwise lack, or making sounds seem to occur in a different place from that where they were recorded. Reverb allows completely artificial sounds (such as electronic synth timbres) to seem as if they exist in a real space.

In the real world, every sound is reflected back from the multiple surfaces around us, the echoes arriving at the ears after the original sound has occurred, coming from different directions, and taking a finite time to die away. All these aspects of the reverberation of the sound give the brain information about the source of the sound and the size of the space we are in.

The three main stages in the development of reverberation are pre-delay, which is the time taken between the original sound reaching the nearest reflective surface and bouncing back to the listener (this will be longer in a larger space where the sound has a long way to go before hitting a wall or other surface and reflecting back); early reflections, which are the first, spaced-out echoes returning to the listener; and, finally, the complex later reverb caused by the combination of multiple reflections bouncing back and forth until they lose so much energy that they die away – or decay. As the reflections decay, the loss of energy manifests itself not only as a reduction in volume, but also as a reduction in the high-frequency content of the successive echoes.

Reason offers two reverb processors – the advanced RV7000, introduced with V2.5, and the original, but less well-specified and less CPU hungry, RV7. The RV7000 is equivalent to many stand-alone reverb plug-ins, and has a sophisticated design and sound. It also functions in true stereo, which means that the input signal is not mixed to mono before processing. Processers that do mix the input produce an artificial stereo reverb output that's mixed with the original, unmixed stereo input, to simulate a stereo effect. The RV7000's approach is much more realistic an natural.

Its approach to editing is also different from that of the other effects: it features a collapsible remote programmer, similar to that offered by the NNXT advanced sampler. This approach echoes that taken by a handful of professional rack-mounting studio reverb units. Unlike all but one other effect, the RV7000 also allows patches to be saved an loaded; a huge library of presets is included in the supplied ReFills.

Reverb algorithms

There are nine reverb algorithms – or types – at the heart of the RV7000. Each simulates a specific type of space, and can be modified by up to seven different parameters; the parameter set is different for each alogorithm. The parameter controls are arranged around a central graph-like display, which handily illustrates the effect of the reverb you're creating – this takes the form of decay level, and density, over time. An eighth control selects the algorithm itself. You'll see, after a quick scan down the following list, that more traditional space simuations are joined by non-'real' algorithms, the logic of which is explained as they arise.

- Small Space: Perfect for emulating the sound of a small room, or even smaller spaces such as booths and cabinets.
- Room: More of a traditional room simulator, this algorithm works with slightly larger virtual spaces.
- Hall: Larger still, not surprisingly, think of this algorithm as simulating the average church hall or similar facility.
- Arena: A really big space can be created with this algorithm, as you might expect, an emulation helped by separate pre-delay for left, right and centre reverb processing.
- Plate: The distinctive sound of the classic electro-mechanical approach to creating reverb effects – transducers fixed to large sheets of metal – is offered with this algorithm. It's great for vocals, not so great for drums due to an inherent splashiness.
- Spring: The budget electro-mechanical approach to adding space to audio featured actual springs; can be found even today in guitar amplifiers. Not great for drums due to boinginess.
- Echo: A tempo-syncable echo effect rather than a reverb per se . Good for special effects due to the way the echo repeats diffuse.
- Multi Tap: More delay rather than reverb, and again tempo-sync'd/ Four different delays make up this algorithm, with full control over delay, level and pan position. This and previous algorithm offer true stereo delay effects, which the DDL1 (more later) can't without extra work.
- Reverse: Artificially creates the sound of a reverb tail playing backwards, an effect classically achieved by playing tapes backwards! The effect here

is less artificial than with some simulations since the input is actually sampled, treated, and then played at the end of the reverse effect.

RV7000 Controls

There are broadly two sets of controls: those of the remote programmer, which change from algorithm to algorithm, and those of the main panel which can be accessed when the remote programmer is not visible. (Incidentally, the programmer is enable by clicking the little arrow next to the socket labelled 'Remote Programmer'; an animation of a cable starts, and the programmer expands below). In addition, the remote programmer offers three sets of parameters. First of all, there's the main parameter set, plus separate displays used for editing EQ (a two-band EQ appears after the reverb) and setting up the 'gate'. The distinctive sound of gated reverb effects was popular in the 80s, with an obvious cutoff applied to the reverb's decay. The RV7000's implementation can be used rather more creatively than the original effect might lead you to believe.

The controls on the main panel allow broad sweeps to be made to whatever settings have been made in the remote programmer.

- EQ Enable: Allows the EQ to be switched in or out of circuit.
- Gate Enable: Lets you try and effect both with and without the gated treatment.
- Decay: Controls reverb length, or delay feedback with echo/delay algorithms.
- HF Damp: Controls how quickly the high frequencies decay as the reverb itself decays. Use to quickly add warmth to a reverb sound
- Hi EQ: Simply put, this control makes the overall reverb more or less bright.
- Dry/Wet: Balances the input and treated signals.

The controls available within each algorithm take a little more discussion. Some parameters are common to several algorithms. Most have no more than seven, though plate has just two, and Multitap actually has 16, though 12 of those are duplicated parameters for each of the four taps.

- Size (Small Space, Room, Hall, Arena): Determines the size of the emulated space. The top value of this parameter ranges from 9.7m for Small Space to 59.9m for Arena.
- Room Shape (Small Space, Room, Hall): Four different room shapes, which aren't revealed by Propellerhead, determine the character of the reverb.
- Modulation Amount (Small Space, Room, Hall): How much the reverb will be randomly modulated; helps produce a more natural sound, and can be used for special effects.
- Diffusion (Room, Hall, Arena, Spring, Echo, Multi Tap): Contributes to the density of the reverb sound, Low settings make it possible to hear discrete reverb bounces, almost as echoes, whilst higher settings become more smeared and indistinct in texture. With the Echo and Multi Tap algorithms, this parameter adds more repeats around the main delays, for a more smeared effect.
- Early Reflection -> Late (Room, Hall): Sets the length of time between an overall treatment's early reflections and the main reverb tail.
- Early Reflection Level (Room, Hall): Sets the level of early reflections; 0 is

the normal value, but higher values are useful for crating special effects.

- Low Frequency Damp (Small Space, Plate, Spring, Multi-tap): Provides control over the decay of low frequencies in the processed signal. Damping down the lowe frequencies creates a less boomy, intrusive sound.
- Predelay (Small Space, Room, Hall, Plate, Echo): Controls the time between the input and the processed signals; controlling predelay helps add definition to treated signals.
- Tempo Sync (Echo, Multi Tap, Reverse): Enables tempo sync to those algorithms that offer it. Echo, delay or length values can be entered in terms of note sub-divisions.

The remaining parameters are specific to the given algorithms.

- Small Space, Wall Irregularity: co   ntrols the position of the virtual walls, with higher values adding more surfaces and angles, creating more complex resonances.
- Arena, Left/right/mono delay: set the times for left, right and centre predelays in this large reverb algorithm.
- Arena, Stereo/mono level: adjusts the levels of the delay times.
- Spring, Length: controls the length of the virtual spring – it can be up to 1m long.
- Spring, Dispersion frequency: controls the frequency of the initial 'boing' produced when a spring creates its reverb effect.
- Spring, Stereo on/off: makes this a stereo or mono spring reverb line.
- Echo, time: Sets the echo value, up to 2000ms.
- Echo, Spread: Adjusted in concert with the Diffusion parameter, turns this algorithm into more of a primitive reverb processor. It provides control over the ghosted echoes produced by Diffusion.
- Multitap, Edit Select: Chooses whether one of the four taps or repeat time are to be edited by the remaining knobs.
- Multitap, Tap Delay/Level/Pan: Each of this algorithms has its own set of parameters; the delay parameter has a maximum value of 2000ms.
- Multitap, Repeat Time: Sets the time between each repeat of the whole collection of multitaps. The number of repeats is controlled by the main panel's Decay control.
- Reverse, Length: sets the time from when the input signal enters the RV7000 to the it being played back; during this time, you'll hear the reversed version of the signal.
- Reverse, Density: controls the apparent thickness of the effect. Low values actually produce more of a reverse delay effect rather than the true reverse reverb sound.
- Reverse, Dry/Wet: Adjusts balance between delayed input source and the reversed effect that leads up to it.

EQ and gate parameters

In addition to the main reverb parameters, RV7000 has dedicated EQ and gate parameters, using the same central display of the remote programmer and switched by the little column of Edit Mode button/LED combinations to the lower left of the programmer.

Info

Set the Reverse algorithm's Density parameter to 50% saves CPU overhead with no adverse effects on the process. Though some input signals may benefit from higher Density values, its worth using this as your normal upper limit , especially in busy session.

Info

ReMix's new pre-fade option for its auxiliary send four is perfect for the RV7000's Reverse algorithm. When using this effect, enable the pre-fade option, wire up an RV7000 via the aux 4 loop, and turn the main channel fader for a source being treated all the way down. This way, you'll hear just reversed audio with no intrusions from the original, right way round, audio.

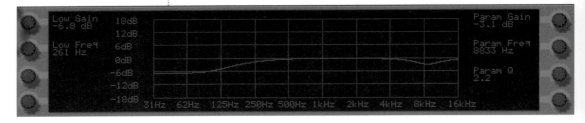

RV7000 EQ edit display

EQ

- Low Gain: Governs the amount of cut or boost of the low-shelving filter.
- Low Frequency: Sets the frequency below which the Low Gaincontrol is applied.
- Parametric Gain: The amount of cut or boost for the parametric EQ.
- Parametric Frequency: Sets the center frequency of the parametric EQ.
- the level should be decreased or increased.
- Parametric Q: Controls the bandwidth of the centre frequency. With lower values, a wider range frequencer around the centre are affected.

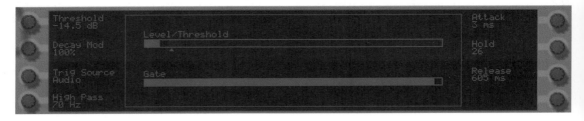

RV7000 gate edit display

Gate

Threshold: When Trig Source is set to 'Audio', this parameter determines the audio signal level which opens the gate. Low values will allow almost any sound to trigger the gate, while high values will require really loud sounds to be input before triggering occurs.

Decay Modulation: Controls how decay time is lowered as the gate closes after triggering. Careful use of this parameter lets you eliminate the effect of previously treated tails being audible with newly triggered sounds.

Trigger Source: Tells the gate if its to be tigerred via audio or MIDI/CV.

High Pass: Lets you set a frequency below which sounds won't trigger the gate, when Trigger Source is set to 'audio'.

Attack: Sets the legth of time between a trigger being detected and the gate opening.

Hold: When the Trigger Source is audio, use this parameter to conrol how quickly the gate closes after being triggered.

Release: The length of time taken to close the gate, after the Hold time has elapsed.

Mono or stereo?

As you'll realise as you read through this chapter, the RV7000 is the only true stereo processing device in the Reason rack. Some other devices are able to process left and right channels discretely (if not fully independen- dently), and others mix the stereo input to mono, or take a mono input, and create a fake stereo process. Note that the RV7000, though it can, if you wish, be used as a mono in/stereo out processor (or, if you're particularly perverse, a mono in/mono out device).

Mono Signals
When treating mono signals, a lead is fed to the left input only, and a stereo reverb effect is produced from that input.

Stereo Signals
The left and right channels of a stereo signal are treated independently, with a mix of dry and treated signal appearing at the output. No summing of the input is involved.

RV7000 rear panel

The CV Inputs
Three parameters can be controlled by Reason's CV System. Reverb decay or echo/delay feedback can be controlled by one, HF damp another and the third is a trigger for the RV7000 Gate option. With this last input, the length of gate signal governs the length of gated reverb.

Reverb applications and considerations
How much?
Reverb is generally best used in moderation. Long reverb decays clutter up a mix very quickly, leaving less space for the parts you want to hear. Use low send amounts if the reverb has a long decay, or keep to shortish decays, unless you have a sparse section where you want to create a specific 'large' ambience. Longer reverbs are often more effective on monophonic sound sources. If you must use a reverb with a long decay on a busy mix, don't 'send' everything in the mix to it: leave parts – particularly rhythmically important ones – with no send level set to that particular reverb.

Reverb on Drums
Watch out with adding reverb to bass drums; the effect may be boomy and excessively resonant, creating a muddy feel in the low end. Gated reverb can be useful on snare drums (and possibly bass drums), as there is no reverb 'tail' to compromise definition and separation.

Reverb and 'distance'
Vocals are the obvious choice for reverb processing, but note that long reverbs will have the effect of distancing a lead vocal in the mix. Indeed, any sounds that are heavily reverb'd will seem further back in the mix, while those

with no reverb, or just a short one, will seem closer to the listener. You can use these facts to help create front-to-back perspective in your mix, just as panning creates left-to-right perspective. An RV7000 dedicated to processing a vocal could have a pre-delay of 100ms or so, to add distance and add definition.

Different reverbs on different parts

Also differentiate parts from each other with reverb – for example, you could treat backing vocals, which don't need to be heard as clearly as lead vocals, with longer reverb (which also gives an ethereal feel), and lead parts with shorter, in-your-face reverb. You might also remember the less power-hungry RV7 when running multiple reverbs!

Dry = Modern

Contemporary production uses far less reverb than in the past; a dryer, up-front sound is generally more fashionable for pop music than a heavily reverbed one.

The RV7 Reverb

RV7 front

- Mono -In/Stereo Out, Stereo in/Stereo out (with internal summing before reverb process)
- Insert or Send/Return operation

See the RV7000 device overview for a look at the basics of reverb – the data is valid for Reason's original reverb, the RV7. Having talked about the RV7000 in such glowing terms, you might wonder why the RV7 is still around. Three reasons. First, Propellerhead are keen to maintain backwards compatibility, so that files created in early versions of Reason will always be loadable in later versions. Second, RV7 uses a lot less computer processing power than RV7000, and might be a better choice when the latter's sound quality isn't so needed. And third, some of us just like the sound of the RV7! I know it's often been moaned about, but it does have a character of its own, and as you'll read in this section, it's a rewarding challenge trying to get it to sound good.

Reverb algorithms

The RV7 offers a number of reverb 'types' which are meant to simulate the characteristics of different acoustic spaces.

- Hall: A "fairly large" hall, according to Propellerhead's description, with a "smooth" characteristic.
- Large Hall: A larger hall with, as you may expect from the above, an obvious pre-delay. You can hear this as a gap between the sound being reverb'd and the very first echo being produced.

- Hall 2: Offering a "brighter attack" than the other Hall.
- Large Room: A large room with hard surfaces giving clear early reflections.
- Medium Room: A medium-sized room with "semi-hard" walls.
- Small Room: Recommended for "drum-booth"-type reverbs.
- Gated: Produces a reverb with an abrupt cut-off, an effect which became popular in the 1980s.
- Low-Density: With this reverb type it's possible to hear the individual delays within the reverb. The reverb tail tends to accentuate certain frequencies present in the original sound, often with pleasant results. This special effect is recommended for pad-type sounds, but can work well on other material – even percussion in the right circumstances. If your computer is struggling, switching to this reverb type might help, as it requires less processing power than the other types.
- Stereo Echoes: Not a reverb as such, but more of a ping-pong delay, with the echoes bouncing back and forth between the left and right sides of your stereo mix.
- Pan Room: Similar to 'Stereo Echoes', though the softer attacks of the delays give the impression of echoing around a furnished room. This algorithm's delays fade into a reverb-like tail, while those produced by 'Stereo Echoes' remain pretty much separate.

RV7 controls
Each reverb algorithm can be adjusted with a set of simple parameters:

- Size: This parameter allows you to change the apparent size of any of the rooms. At the 12 o'clock position of the Size knob, the 'space' is at its preset size for the algorithm. Turning the knob left makes the space smaller; turning right makes it larger. In the case of the Stereo Echoes and Pan Room types, 'Size' controls the delay time. Although this parameter can be changed in real time, and automated, you should be aware that moving the knob actually mutes RV7's output (dry input signal included), cutting off any reverb tail that might be fading.
- Decay: Alters the length of time over which the reverb 'tail' dies away after the sound has stopped. If this knob is turned fully right – to a value of 127 – the decay gives the impression of never fully dying away, creating an infinite reverb effect. In fact, just for interest, an experiment achieved a decay time of nearly 30 minutes, but by the time this particular reverb died away it wasn't so much a reverb tail as a very quiet metallic drone! At the 12 o'clock position, the decay is at its preset length for the algorithm's room size. Turning the Decay knob left or right shortens or lengthens the decay, respectively. This parameter does not function for the 'Gate' algorithm, and it works more or less as a feedback control for the Stereo Delay and Pan Room algorithms.
- Damp: Reduces the high-frequency content of the reverb. Reducing HF content of reverb reflections usually creates a more natural-sounding and less obtrusive reverb.
- Dry/Wet: Adjusts the balance between the unprocessed input signal and the reverb effect; it should be set to 'wet' – fully right – if the reverb is being used in a send/return loop, because the mixer channel supplies the fully dry signal, which is balanced, via the aux return control, with the

wet signal coming from the reverb. If the reverb is used as an 'insert' effect, you can set your preferred balance between treated and untreated signal with the Dry/Wet knob.

Mono or stereo?

You can process both mono and stereo inputs with the RV7, but the reverb produced in both cases will be stereo.

Mono signals

When processing a mono signal, the RV7 creates a stereo output from a mono input by producing different patterns of reflections for the left and right channels. The signal is still mono; it is the reverb that comes out in stereo.

Stereo signals

When processing a stereo signal, the RV7 'sums' the two sides of the stereo input to mono for processing, and then proceeds as for a mono signal, finally outputting the reverb in stereo. In this it differs from a true stereo device, which would process both sides of the stereo signal independently, with no summing.

However, don't worry that your stereo signal itself will emerge from the RV7 in mono; the stereo signal is passed through the device intact, and mixed with the pseudo-stereo reverb if the Dry/Wet control on the front panel is adjusted appropriately. The effect is of a fully-stereo process, though there is a slight compromise in the reverb effect itself, in that any stereo 'imaging' in the original input will be missing from the reverb'd version of that input. This is a compromise found in many budget and mid-price hardware reverb or multi-effects units, and is not a major cause for complaint. (Check the 'advanced' effect ideas at the end of this chapter for a way of creating an 'approaching stereo' reverb.)

Note that you could, if you wished, use the RV7 as a mono in/mono out device (by connecting only the left in and out of the device), but that the reverb effect would not be as convincing or pleasing as if it were in its normal stereo mode.

RV7 back

The CV input

Just one RV7 parameter is controllable by CV input – decay time. One idea for using this is connecting a SubTractor LFO1 Mod output to it, to put the reverb decay under LFO control. This can be effective with drum patterns where, if you tweak a bit, you can get the effect of one hit being noticeably reverbed and the next hardly at all, and so on. Also try subtle LFO modulation of reverb decay on laid-back solo or chordal parts – perhaps piano – for a bit more light and shade. Use the first sample & hold waveform on the Sub's LFO1 for a properly random effect.

Alternatively, use the Matrix's Curve CV output connected to the CV input on the RV7. Create your own bipolar pattern of controller changes to alter reverb decay in time with the track. (See the Matrix chapter for more.)

Reverb applications and considerations

The comments made on the use of reverb in the RV7000 hold true for the RV7, perhaps even more so since RV7 is not as high powered or sophisticated. Less is always more with 'budget' reverbs!

DDL1 front

DDL1 Digital Delay

- Mono In/Stereo Out, Stereo In/Stereo Out (with internal summing before delay process), Mono In/Mono Out
- Insert or Send/Return operation

Delay essentially provides simple echoes – repeats – of the input signal. Digital delay is the hi-tech descendant of tape-loop echo, and is as ubiquitous and, these days, almost as essential as reverb – probably more important if you create exclusively synth-based instrumental material. It's easy to use, applicable to a wide range of sound sources, and very versatile. Indeed, the temporal manipulation of sound offered by controlling artificial delays is at the heart of a whole family of effects. Basic delays are offered by Reason's DDL1, while variant 'time-domain' treatments are offered by the CF101 and PH90, which will be discussed shortly.

DDL1 controls

- Unit: This parameter determines whether the DDL1 will create delays in terms of milliseconds (or ms, thousandths of a second) or tempo-synchronised 'Steps'. If you want your delay repeats to lock into Song tempo, use the Steps unit mode.
- Delay Time: Sets delay time – the time between the input sound and when the first delay repeat is heard. As you may have gathered from the 'unit' switch, this interval can be defined in milliseconds or in terms of 'Steps' – divisions of a beat. When delay time is specified in ms, any value between 1 and 2000ms (two seconds) can be set. If it is set in Steps, the value of each step depends on the Step length parameter – see the next entry. (Just as a matter of interest, switching between the MS and Steps 'Units' modes will show you the actual delay time for a given Step value at the current Song tempo.)
- Step Length: Sets the length of the steps when the DDL1 is operating in Steps mode. The options available are a 16th note or an eighth-note triplet. With the former, the tempo-related steps produced by the delay will be multiples of 16th notes, whereas with the latter, steps will be multiples of an eighth-note triplet, suitable for music with a definite swing or triplet feel.The rule is that the lower the Step Length setting, the faster the delay repeats will seem to occur. With a Step Length of 1/16, a delay time of '1' means that the time between the input sound and the first

delay repeat will be a 16th-note, and that subsequent repeats will occur at 16th-note intervals (assuming some Feedback has been set – see next control). A delay time of '2' creates delay repeats at intervals of two 16th-notes – an eighth note. At a Step Length of 16, delay repeats will occur a whole note (sixteen 16ths) apart. With Step Length set to 1/8T, the delay time is specified in eighth note triplets: a value of '1' equals one eighth-note triplet, '2' adds another eighth-note triplet to the delay time, and so on. In this instance, a whole note of delay time is reached at a value of 12 – a whole note being equal to 12 eighth-note triplets. It is possible to use values higher than 12, to create delay times longer than a whole note, but only if a Song's tempo is much faster than 120bpm (at which tempo a whole note lasts for 2000ms, the longest delay possible).

- Feedback: This control determines the number of delay repeats, by sending the delayed signal back to the input and through the delay process again, creating delays upon delays. How long it takes for the delays to cease building up is determined by the setting of the Feedback knob. Move the knob full left and you get one repeat of the input signal; move it fully right and the same repeat will keep recurring, infinitely.
- Pan: Sets the pan position of the delayed signal if the DDL1's output is connected in stereo. If 'Pan' is set dead centre – a value of 64 – exactly the same delayed audio is routed to both left and right outputs. This control has no effect on any stereo audio that might be passing through the DDL1: that audio remains in stereo, with no panning.
- Dry/Wet: As with the reverb device, above, this adjusts the balance between the unprocessed input signal and the delay effect; it should be set to 'wet' – fully right – if the delay is being used in a mixer send/return loop. If the delay is used as an in-line effect, set the balance of treated and untreated signal with this control.Note that when you first create a DDL1, the Dry/Wet control defaults to 100% Wet and you only hear the delayed signal. In an insert configuration, this may make it sound to hi-tech newcomers as though the signal being processed has suddenly fallen out of sync with the track. Just turn the knob back towards the left until your dry signal comes through in the desired amount.

Mono or stereo?

The DDL1's input and output routing works in a similar way to that on the RV7, in that the unit can be configured to process mono or stereo signals. There is one big difference: while the DDL1 can process both mono and stereo inputs, its effected output is always mono, in spite of the stereo out connections. This is contrary to what you might think is being indicated by the routing diagram on the rear panel: the two icons show mono-to-stereo operation or stereo summed to mono with a processed stereo output. The one concession to stereo operation is that the front-panel Pan knob can position the processed signal between the left and right outputs.

If the audio being processed is stereo, it'll remain in stereo at the DDL1 outputs, assuming the Dry/Wet mix control is set correctly, but the delays will always be mono. One happy side-effect of this routing anomaly is that the DDL1 is perfectly capable of working as a purely mono processor, such as might be desirable in a multi-effect chain being applied to, say, the mono output of a SubTractor synth. This option isn't indicated by the routing icons on the delay device's back panel. For mono use, connect jacks to the left input and left output, which is the standard operating procedure for mono audio within Reason.

True stereo delay processing will be discussed later, using Reason's flexible patching system and multiple DDL1s.

DDL1 back

The CV inputs

Two DDL1 parameters are available for external control via Reason's CV system: pan and feedback. Both can be used to add interesting variations to a delay effect. For example, pan can be controlled by an LFO output on a SubTractor or a Curve CV from a Matrix, to produce auto-panned delays, even if the delay is patched to an aux return in the mixer or is a part of an effect chain.

The effect of feedback being controlled over time is harder to explain than do – you can get an idea by tweaking the control manually while some audio is being delayed – but is well worth experimenting with. Try linking the Delay Feedback CV input to a SubTractor LFO1 Mod Out to alter delay feedback randomly. The LFO's sample and hold waveforms are perhaps best for truly random effects. On a drum pattern, this has the effect of varying between, for example, lots of delay repeats one second, then none, then a few, then lots again, increasing the interest of the part.

Quick 'jungle' drum effects

Also try this variation on the above, with a drum pattern, for some easy jungly effects. Basically, a SubTractor LFO is going to be used to randomly modulate Delay Feedback, with the delay applied to selected ReDrum voices.

- Start with a mixer. Create a DDL1 with the mixer selected, so the delay will be linked into one of the mixer's send/return loops.
- Add a SubTractor synth, and connect its LFO1 Mod Out to the DDL1's Feedback CV In jack, at the rear; turn the trim pot fully right. Make sure the LFO is outputting a random waveform (one of the bottom two in the list of LFO waveforms on the Sub front panel).
- Return to the front of the rack, set the DDL1's feedback control to the 12 o'clock position, and input a delay time of between 40ms and 60ms (this will vary depending on your pattern and the effect you prefer, but the key is to keep delay time fairly low).
- Create a ReDrum, connected as normal to a mixer. Load a Kit and create a drum pattern.
- On selected drum voice channels, turn up the send control that corresponds to the DDL1 send/return loop on the mixer. For example, if a snare is on channel 2 of the ReDrum and the DDL1 is patched into send/return loop 1 on the mixer, you would turn up

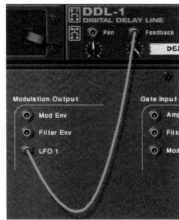

Connecting the SubTractor to the DDL1.

The front-panel settings for the DDL1.

Turn up the relevant send control on the ReDrum channels where you want the drums processed with the random delay.

drum channel 2's 'Send 1' knob. A value of about 80 or 90 should produce a good result. You could process just a couple of drum voices in this way – snare and hi-hat, for example – but it also works very well with larger numbers of voices.

• You'll hear random fast, blurred, pseudo-rolls of varying lengths for all drum voices that are being processed by the DDL1, with different rolls triggered on different beats. Quite jungly, especially at faster tempos.

Experiment with LFO waveforms and speeds, and as an alternative modulation source for the Feedback CV input, try connecting the Curve CV output of a Matrix device, and draw a random curve in the device's display. You may find that shorter columns are more effective – they're equal to lower, less extreme feedback values – interspersed with occasional peaks. Randomness is enhanced by selecting the 1/8th note resolution and an odd pattern length, such as 29 or 31 steps.

If these ideas produce a more extreme result than you would want throughout an entire track, copy the drum pattern to another ReDrum pattern slot, edit the copy to have all effect sends at zero and switch between it and the delayed pattern as required.

Delay applications and considerations

Drums and rhythmic parts: Delay is incredibly effective with rhythmic material such as drum parts and repetitive synth parts (perhaps sequenced with the Matrix), especially if matched to Song tempo. Delay creates extra rhythms not present in the original part, adds complexity, and helps a groove to move along.

Ambient material: Delay is also very good with ambient material, particularly if used to build up complex patterns of overlapping echoes.

Guitar parts and vocals: The adaptable delay can also be suitable for guitar parts and vocals, where it creates a different effect to reverb. A slap-back echo (short delay of around 50-200ms, no Feedback), for example, immediately creates a '50s kind of feel, as it was much used on pop music of the 1950s and early 1960s.

Timed delays: Steps mode provides an instant path to rhythmic, timed delays which lock to a Song's tempo. Try eighth-note and sixteenth-note repeats (that's a Step value of 2 or 1 respectively), with a moderate amount of feedback – up to about 60 – for instant gratification on arpeggiator-like synth patterns and individual drum voices in a ReDrum pattern. In general, timed delays are great when used on synth sounds that are short, thin and spiky, though they can work really well on more developing sounds too, adding textural interest.

There's an awful lot you can do with the DDL1, probably the most versatile effect in the Reason rack. Later in this chapter there are some ideas to be going on with.

CF101 Chorus/Flanger

• Mono In/Stereo out, Stereo In/Stereo Out, Mono In/Mono Out
• Insert or Send/Return operation

Once upon a time, effects such as chorus, flanging and phasing (see next device) would have been produced by a digital delay equipped with some specific extra controls. The popularity of these effects has led to the development of specialised units that are still delays at heart, but are specially optimised.

Chorus, so named because it is meant to give the impression of more than one instrument playing at the same time, is based around delay. However, it is also called a 'modulation' effect, because its characteristic sound is produced by LFO modulation of those delays. Flanging uses even shorter modulated delays than chorus, with more obvious modulation amounts and high feedback (positive and negative) values to produce a more exaggerated effect. The CF101 is designed to produce both chorus and flange effects.

CF101 controls

- Delay: Sets the delay time for the effect; shorter times, towards the left, are used for flanging effects, while chorusing is produced as you move this knob towards the right. The maximum delay time is 20ms.
- Feedback: Just as with the DDL1 digital delay, this control feeds back the delays to the input to increase their intensity, adding to the depth of the effect being produced. The negative and positive values available to this parameter tend to accentuate different frequency ranges within the input signal. The more extreme effects produced by turning feedback fully left or fully right are typical of flanging, while chorus effects benefit from settings around the middle range.
- LFO Rate: The LFO built into the CF101 is used to modulate the device's delay time, which causes the sweeping, moving sound expected from chorus and flanging. The Rate knob controls the speed of the LFO and thus the speed of the 'swoosh'.
- LFO Modulation Amount: Just like the 'Amount' parameter on the LFOs of Reason's sound-making devices, this parameter governs the depth of the modulation. Setting it to '0' disables the LFO.
- Send Mode: The CF101 is the only effect in the rack with a switch for setting send or in-line operation. No mix control is provided: in in-line mode, the balance of wet and dry signal is preset at an equal mix, while in send mode (LED lit) the balance is determined by the mixer aux return level. Note that if the CF101 is set to operate as a 'send' effect while it is actually being used as an insert effect (Reason does not prevent you from doing this), its output is more of a weird – and potentially atmospheric – pitch modulation/vibrato effect. This happens because much of the chorus/flange effect depends on the mix of dry and effected signal, and enabling 'send' mode sets an effected-only output.

Mono or stereo?

The CF101 is essentially a stereo processor, though paradoxically the classic stereo 'moving' chorus effect only happens with a mono input and stereo output (and only when the LFO is engaged). The stereo effect is created by sending a straight processed signal to the left output and an inverted version of the processed signal to the right.

The device can also produce a chorus effect in mono, on a mono signal, using just the left input and left output. Stereo devices connected to the CF101 are provided with independent processing of the left and right signals, with no mixing – in fact, two-channel, rather than stereo, chorusing. Both channels are effectively mono, and there is no 'stereoization' of the two output channels.

CF101 back

The CV inputs

Two parameters can be controlled by Reason's CV system – Delay Time and LFO Rate. Seriously bizarre (and pretty much indescribable) effects can be produced by connecting the modulation outputs (Mod Envelope, Filter Envelope and LFO1) of a SubTractor synth to the CF101's CV inputs. Experiment with envelope shapes for the best effect. It might also be useful to control Delay time with a unipolar Matrix curve, for rhythmic stuttering effects.

Chorus and flanging applications

Both chorus and flanging can be used to enliven a variety of sounds. Chorus is a particularly versatile effect.

Guitar

Strummed acoustic guitar parts are given extra sparkle with some chorus (and maybe a touch of reverb), and it also works with electric guitars.

String parts

Try subtle chorus on synth strings and sampled ensemble orchestral string parts, for an extra-wide, majestic feel, and on melodic synth parts.

Bass

Certainly experiment with using a little chorus on bass, particularly fretless bass samples.

Flanging

This stronger treatment also suits guitars, and even possibly vocals if you're looking for a '60s feel. You can even get some neat effects with flanging on drum patterns, especially in a breakdown section. Try it on any sound source, but beware of creating an over-gimmicky effect.

Chorus + Reverb

A pair of CF101s with an RV7 reverb can create a lovely Mellotron-ish vibe for ensemble string samples. The Hall reverb setting provides a suitably elegant space, while the CF101s provide a bit of pitch modulation that (kind of) simulates the 'wow' and instability of a Mellotron tape. (As you may know, the Mellotron was a very early, analogue tape-based 'sampler'.)

Hook up mixer aux send 1 to the left RV7 input.

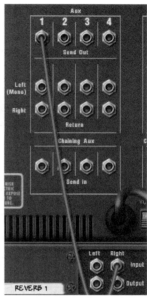

- Start with a mixer. Create an RV7 with Shift held down, to disable automatic routing. Connect aux send 1 of the mixer to the left input of the RV7.
- Create a CF101 with Shift held down. Make front-panel settings of Delay = 105; Feedback = 23; Rate = 48; Mod Amount = 92.

Chorus settings.

- Now copy the entire CF101 (Copy Device, under Edit or Context menu) and Paste into the rack next to the first one. You can change the panel settings of the second CF101 very slightly, if you like, for a bit more complexity.
- Tab to the back of the rack and connect the left output of the reverb to the left input of one CF101 and the right output of the reverb to the left input of the other CF101. Connect the outputs of the CF101s to mixer input channels 13 and 14.
- Back at the front, on the mixer, pan one chorus hard left and the other hard right.

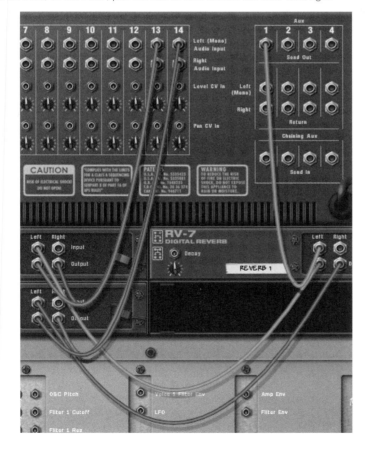

The CF101s connected to the RV7 and routed to the mixer.

Info

Copying effect settings

Where you want two or more effect devices with the same or almost the same settings, just copy and paste the desired device using the Edit menu or a Context menu.

- Use the Hall reverb with no modifications on the RV7; the Dry/Wet control should be fully wet.
- Create an NN19, which should be automatically connected to mixer channel 1. Load the BIGSTRINGS Patch (inside NN19 Strings folder) from the original Reason factory set.
- Turn up aux send knob 1 on mixer channel 1. A good level is about 12 o'clock. Play some lush, slow chords.
- It's up to you whether you choose Send or Insert mode on the CF101s – there is a difference in the sound, as in Insert mode the chorus and reverb mix, while in Send mode they don't.

PH90 Phaser

PH90 front

- Mono In/Mono Out, Mono In/Stereo Out, Stereo In/Stereo Out
- Insert operation

Phasing is a swirling effect treatment created by using a very short delay to introduce phase shifts between source and treated signal. These shifts cause momentary cancellations and reinforcements in the frequency spectra of the source signal over time, the result being the characteristic swirling the effect is known for.

Reason's PH90 phaser has been configured exclusively as an insert effect and is not meant to be used via the send/return system. This is, according to Propellerhead, a four-stage phaser, which means that there are four 'notches' in the device's frequency response curve. If the phaser's frequency is altered, manually or via its LFO, the notches move in parallel over the frequency spectrum. Control is provided over the distance between the notches, as well as their width.

PH90 controls
- Frequency: Sets the frequency of the PH90's first notch.
- Split: Starting from the Frequency just set, this determines the remaining three notch frequencies – it sets the distance between each notch, starting from the base notch frequency.
- Width: Sets the width of each notch, changing the character of the phasing effect. Higher width values make the sound more hollow.
- LFO Rate: Sets the speed of the LFO, which modulates the phaser's frequency.
- LFO Frequency Modulation: Sets the depth of LFO effect. As with the CF101, giving this parameter a value of '0' has a special effect: it creates a "static, formant-like sound", which is enhanced with the addition of feedback.
- Feedback: In the case of the PH90, this parameter behaves rather like a filter's resonance control, with the feeding back of the processed signal to the inputs adding harmonics and changing the tone of the phasing effect.

Mono or stereo?
Just like the CF101, the PH90 is essentially a stereo processor, though a 'moving' phasing effect only occurs with mono input and stereo output (and

only when the LFO is engaged). The stereo effect is created by sending a straight processed signal to the left output and an inverted version of the processed signal to the right.

The device can also produce phasing in mono, on a mono signal, using just the left input and left output. Stereo devices connected to the PH90 are provided with independent processing of the left and right signals, with no mixing – in fact, two channel, rather than stereo, phasing. Both channels are effectively mono, and there is no 'stereoization' of the two output channels.

PH90 back

The CV Inputs

Two PH90 parameters can be controlled by Reason's CV system – Frequency and LFO rate. Great effects on held chordal parts, played on a pad/string synth sound or sample, can be obtained by connecting a SubTractor (or any other) LFO Modulation output to the PH90's Frequency CV Input. As the LFO is modifying the Frequency of the first Phaser notch, you hear the sweep of it moving and changing through the sound, with the other three notches changing behind it. Connecting a synth Envelope Modulation Output to the Frequency CV in produces a similar effect, but you can make the sweep evolve for longer, by setting a slow envelope. You'll need to experiment with settings to suit the sound being used, obviously. Note that the PH90's Frequency Modulation knob can be set to zero, if you like, when you are modulating Frequency externally.

Phaser applications

Phasing is particularly useful for pad sounds, guitars, electric pianos, even vocals in the right circumstances, lending a spacey, psychedelic quality for special effects, and adding a 'luminous' aura to sounds if used subtly. It can be very dramatic with chordal playing on rich sounds such as orchestral and organ-type pads (you can achieve something like a rotating speaker effect on organ patches with careful use of phasing). Try it generally on sounds that could do with fattening and lifting.

D11 Foldback Distortion

D11 Front

- Mono In/Mono Out, Stereo In/Stereo Out
- Insert operation

Distortion, once the bane of recording engineers, is now seen by many as a creative tool to be embraced and manipulated. There's nothing better for adding an edge to a tame sound, or making something already quite mean or aggressive even more so. Reason's distortion processor, the D11, couldn't be simpler in operation.

D11 controls

- Amount: Simply sets the amount of distortion to be applied to the input signal
- Foldback: Determines the type of distortion to be applied. This is a variable control that moves from gentle 'saturation' at one extreme to a severe 'clipping' distortion at the other.

The two in/out pairs function independently. A single input can be processed in mono, or two inputs (dual mono or stereo) can be processed with their independence maintained. There is no internal mixing for this effect, which is designed for insert use. Both sides of the stereo input are treated to exactly the same process.

D11 back

The CV input

The Amount parameter can be controlled by a CV. This would allow the input to be varied between more and less distorted in a dynamic way during performance – controlled, for example, via a Filter Envelope CV Modulation output from a sound-making device. This sounds good if you set a strong, noticeable filter envelope.

Distortion applications

For dark or aggressive contemporary-sounding basses, try some distortion. Then there's the obvious cliché of distortion to add weight and power to sustained lead-guitar samples and lead synth sounds. You may find drum voices enhanced by a touch of D11 distortion in the right track; kicks take on a pitched, jungly feel, for example, and extra character is added to any contemporary hard-edged dance drum pattern. There's not much versatility to be squeezed out of the D11 for this application – it'll give you one 'sound' and one 'sound' only – but it's a sound that's worth having.

If connected in a chain of other effects, the D11 can be used just to add a little saturated warmth to the proceedings. For some reason, a setting of 64 (dead centre, and the default when the device is created) on the 'Foldback' knob seems to be the best one for a variety of different sounds!

ECF42 Envelope-Controlled Filter

ECF42 front

- Mono In/Mono Out, Stereo In/Stereo Out
- In-line operation

Take out the voltage-controlled filter from SubTractor, and it would be, more or less, the ECF42. You can find more detail about how filtering works in the SubTractor chapter, but briefly a filter removes (actually, attenuates or greatly reduces) selected frequencies from a waveform, changing its sound, while the envelope allows the filtering effect to develop over time, introducing a feeling of movement and variation into the filtered sound.

ECF42 controls

- Mode: The ECF42 offers three filter types: 24dB/octave low-pass, 12dB/octave low-pass and 12dB/octave band-pass. A low-pass filter removes all the frequencies above the selected one, leaving those below untouched – it allows the low frequencies to 'pass'. A band-pass filter lets a range, or band, of frequencies pass, removing those on either side. The dB/octave figure describes the 'slope' of the filter, or how severely it attenuates the filtered frequencies. A slope of 12dB/octave is gentler than one of 24dB/octave, leaving more of the original harmonics in the sound for a smoother effect, in comparison to a steeper filter slope.
- Frequency: The Frequency parameter sets the cutoff point at which the filter starts to work – the point above which unwanted frequencies are attenuated in the case of a low-pass Filter. Raising the cutoff frequency makes a sound brighter, as more high frequencies are allowed past. Lowering it makes a sound warmer and duller as the high frequencies are reduced.
- Resonance: The Resonance control accentuates the frequencies around the filter's cutoff point, adding a progressively more piercing, edgy and synth-like character to the sound as Resonance is increased. When the band-pass option has been selected, the resonance control alters the upper and lower limits of the band of frequencies around the centre frequency.
- Gate LED: Flashes whenever the envelope generator is triggered, either by a trigger pulse arriving at the Gate input on the rear panel or via MIDI.
- Envelope Attack, Decay, Sustain and Release: These are the controls that set the envelope governing the action of the filter over time. The envelope basically varies filter cutoff frequency, so that the filter allows more or less frequencies through ('opens' or 'closes') over time. The Attack control governs how quickly the envelope begins to open up the filter after a trigger has been received. Once the envelope has reached its maximum value (opened the filter as far as allowed to by the setting of the Envelope Amount parameter), the Decay parameter sets how long the envelope takes to get to the next stage; this stage is the Sustain level, the filter frequency that will be maintained for as long as the trigger is being applied. Once the trigger stops, the Release parameter determines how long it will take for the filter frequency to return to its start value. The sound can thus continue to develop even after the trigger has ceased.
- Envelope Amount: Governs how strong an effect the envelope will have on the filter frequency. Low amounts cause a shallow envelope, and high amounts create the most extreme change.

- Velocity: The ECF10's ADSR envelope generator has to be triggered externally – without the envelope being triggered, the device is simply a fixed filter – via a 'Gate' input socket at the rear. This control governs how strongly the Envelope Amount parameter will react to any velocity data contained in the trigger signal, allowing envelope action to intensify the effect of the filter in response to increased velocity.

Mono or stereo?

The ECF42 can operate as a mono device, or as a dual mono/stereo device. It can happily process a stereo signal, but there is no internal mixing so both left and right channels are processed independently. There is no mix control since the filter is offering 'processing' rather than an effect.

ECF24 back

The CV inputs

Frequency, Resonance and Envelope Decay can be controlled via the CV system, while the filter's envelope can be triggered via a Gate input. Any Gate Output in the Reason rack – such as that provided by the Matrix, Dr:rex or ReDrum drum voice channels – can be used to trigger the ECF42's envelope.

Filter applications

Fixed filtering

The ECF42 may be used on any sound, submix or even entire mix. You can use it as a fixed filter, with no envelope control over filter frequency, just by passing a signal through it and not triggering its envelope in any way – it becomes a kind of equaliser when employed like this. Movement may alternatively be introduced into the input signal by altering the ECF's CV-controllable parameters with other devices in the rack.

Envelope-controlled filtering

If you would like to use the built-in envelope control of the filter, it is important to note that, unlike the envelopes on a synth, the ECF's envelope needs an external trigger to operate – more on that in a moment. Using the ECF like this makes it possible to add dynamic VCF-type signal processing to Reason devices that lack built-in filtering – mainly ReDrum – or extra filters to devices that already have them, such as SubTractor and NN19.

Filtering with ReDrum

Using ECF42 filtering with ReDrum expands its sonic potential even further, infinitely increasing the range of weird, effective and useful sounds you can get from it.

The method for adding ECF42 filtering to a ReDrum voice is straightforward.

The fact that each ReDrum channel has a Gate output means that triggering the ECF's envelope is one cable connection away, and the combination of ReDrum voice – which can be anything from a simple mono drum hit to a long stereo, looped sample – and ECF42 essentially creates a mini-synth. What we have to do is make the ECF treat the audio output from a drum voice, while at the same time making the drum voice's Gate Out trigger the ECF's envelope.

We'll presume you have a ReMix in your rack, and that you've created a ReDrum that is connected to a ReMix input channel. Load a drum kit, or load individual samples into some of the drum voice channels.

- Create an ECF42 while holding down Shift, disabling automatic connections.
- Choose a ReDrum channel, tab to the rear panel, click on the audio out socket of the channel and drag the cable that appears to the input of the ECF42.
- Click on the ECF42's output and drag the cable that appears to a ReMix input.
- In the same ReDrum channel we started with, click on the Gate Out socket and drag the cable to the ECF42's Gate In socket.

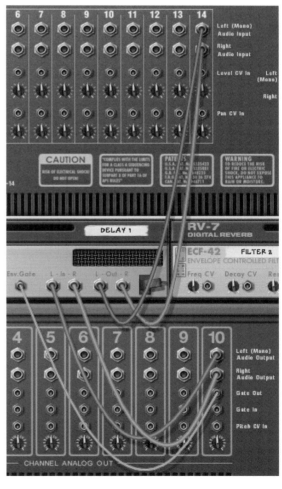

A ReDrum channel set up with ECF42 filtering. The channel is now a simple synth.

- Create a drum pattern on the ReDrum, including a part for the voice that's being processed by the ECF42. You can switch between treated and untreated audio by clicking the 'Bypass' button on the ECF's front panel, allowing you to hear its effect. Tweak the ECF42's controls to hear what you can do to the drum voice. If there isn't much audible effect, turn the Frequency parameter to the left, lowering filter cutoff frequency, so that the envelope movement starts from a lower point and is thus more obvious. Turn the Resonance control to the right (increasing Resonance, so you can hear the filter frequency changes better), and do likewise with the Envelope Amount knob. Experiment with the Envelope controls.
- Computer power allowing, you could give every ReDrum voice its own ECF42 filter.

Propellerhead point out that the ECF42 is also ideal for using with a Pattern-based device such as the Matrix or ReDrum, to create 'pattern-controlled' filter and envelope effects. ReBirth RB338 owners will know what's going on here: a simple, preset pattern-controlled filter is a key part of ReBirth, providing rhythmic, textural activity superimposed on ReBirth sounds. In Reason, though, the pattern and the filter are completely under the user's control, so that you can define the rhythm of the pattern and how it affects the filter's response. The technique is described in detail in the Reason Operation Manual.

COMP01 Compressor/Limiter

COMP01 front

- Mono In/Mono Out, Stereo In/Stereo Out
- In-line operation

A compressor basically provides automated control over the level of an audio signal, resulting in a more even, controlled sound with loud peaks reduced and quieter parts increased in level. Compression subjectively increases the loudness and 'punch' of a signal or track, while at the same time reducing its dynamic range, and is very widely used in modern music. As well as helping to produce the kind of powerful sound we're used to from pop music these days, compression also prevents distortion due to signal overload on peaks, when used properly.

COMP01 controls
- Ratio: Determines exactly how much compression, or gain reduction, is applied to the signal. At a ratio of 1:1, no compression is applied; at 2:1, if signal input level increases by 2dB, a level change of only 1dB appears at the compressor output; at 16:1, which is a pretty severe ratio ('limiting', really), for every 16dB of input level increase the output level increases by only 1dB.
- Threshold: Sets the level below which signals are not affected by the compressor. If you wanted compression only to kick in to control loud peaks, you would set the threshold so that the compressor only began operating once the signal level was nearing that of the loud peaks.
- Attack: Sets how quickly the compressor responds to signals that have reached the threshold level. If Attack time is set too short, you may lose the very start of important sounds, such as the attack of percussion sounds, as they are rapidly pulled down in level. If it is set too long, however, there is the risk of uncontrolled peaks sneaking through and causing momentary distortion before the compressor begins to act.
- Release: Sets how quickly the compressor ceases to act after the signal has fallen back below the threshold. A very fast release time may result in 'pumping', or audible gain changing, and one that is too slow could result in the compressor still working when a quieter sound (that doesn't need compression) occurs, reducing the sound's level still further. Setting the right release time thus helps to ensure that the compression sounds natural, with no bizarre level fluctuations. However, some people like the sense of urgency and power that can be conferred by 'pumping' – it's all down to taste and application.
- Gain reduction meter: Shows how much gain reduction is being applied to your signal, or how much its level has increased due to the combination of compression and auto make-up gain. (The last compensates for the fact that when loud sounds are 'pulled back' the overall impression may be of a quieter signal, by boosting overall level.)

Mono or stereo?

The COMP01 can operate in mono or in true stereo; that is, if you input a stereo signal for processing, both left and right components are treated independently with no internal mixing.

COMP01 back

Compressor applications

You can use the COMP01 for processing mono signals, such as vocal and instrumental samples, synth sounds and individual drums; stereo submixes, such as entire rhythm sections; and complete stereo mixes. Though it is quite a simple device, Reason 'power users' make much use of the COMP01 to increase the impact and presence of their mixes. Most would maintain that compression is essential to dance tracks, and that a final mix should be compressed – connect a COMP01 between the stereo output of your main mixer and the Hardware Interface.

Setting up is largely a matter of working by ear. One of the keys to using the COMP01 successfully seems to be to make very small parameter adjustments and then listen for the effect; if necessary, make another small adjustment, check again, and proceed in this way.

PEQ2 2-band parametric EQ

PEQ2 front

- Mono In/Mono Out, Stereo In/Stereo Out
- In-line operation

Although the ReMix mixer is equipped with two-band EQ on each channel, there are times when something more precise on the equalisation front is desirable. Enter the PEQ2 two-band parametric equaliser.

The parametric equaliser is so called because the important EQ parameters – Frequency, Q (or bandwidth) and Gain – are under the control of the user. The two bands of EQ on each ReMix channel are fixed frequency and fixed bandwith, with 24dB cut or boost. By contrast, the two bands provided on the PEQ2 have a wide, fully variable frequency range, variable gain (which cuts or boosts the desired frequency), and variable bandwidth (the range of frequencies around the selected central value to which the gain parameter will be applied). These controls allow you to focus on one or two frequencies (or frequency bands) of your choice, and cut or boost them for creative effect or as a corrective processing tool.

While the PEQ2 is a two-band device, both bands (dubbed A and B) don't have to be active. If you only need to process one frequency, disable the other band with the provided switch; it saves a little CPU overhead.

PEQ2 controls

- EQ curve display: Provides a graphic representation of the frequency response curve created by the equalisation process. As you turn the gain control up or down, you'll see the curve move up or down from the central axis, showing the effect of boosting or cutting the selected centre frequency. The width of the peaks or troughs in the frequency response curve indicates the bandwidth set by the Q control. If both frequency bands are being used, the curve will show two peaks and/or troughs. Across the bottom of the display, a range of frequency values, in 10 divisions from 31Hz to 16kHz, is provided, to give you a rough idea of what centre frequency you're aiming for; to the right of the display, a vertical gauge provides a quick visual guide to the amount of cut or boost being applied. The centre line is marked 0dB, and the upper and lower limits are +18dB and -18dB respectively.
- Channel B Engage switch: Turns on the 'B' frequency band.
- Frequency: Sets the centre frequency of the EQ band, in a range going from 31Hz at the lower end to 16kHz at the upper.
- Q: Determines the width of the band of frequencies around the centre frequency that will be affected by the Gain control. At high values, producing a narrow bandwith, a very small range of frequencies will be cut or boosted. Lower values will increase the width of the range to be treated, though not all frequencies will be affected equally. The effect of the gain control becomes less pronounced towards each edge of the bandwidth range, as illustrated by the curve that appears in the EQ display.
- Gain: Offers 18dB of cut or boost.

Mono or stereo?

The PEQ can operate in mono or in true stereo; that is, if you input a stereo signal for processing, both left and right components are treated independently with no internal mixing.

PEQ2 back

The CV inputs

CV control is provided over the frequency of both bands, which takes the PEQ2 even further into the area of creative processing; dynamically changing the frequency in a random or planned fashion, by connecting a Modulation CV output from a sound-making device to its CV Input, creates swept filter effects.

EQ applications

Shaping individual sounds

For example, if a sound seems a little dull, and it can't be made brighter at source, it should be possible to find, and boost, a suitable frequency within it that increases brightness. Likewise, you can cut frequency ranges to reduce unwanted components of a sound.

If you're not familiar with parametric EQs, you might be wondering exactly how you use one to do these jobs. Well, imagine a bass synth sample that's swamping the bottom end of your mix. Patch the sound through a PEQ2, turn up the Gain control (to, say 20-30) and move the Frequency knob slowly to the left (into the lower-frequency end of the spectrum) until you hear the problem frequency becoming even worse. Stop right there. Go back to the Gain knob and turn it to the left, cutting (reducing gain) at that frequency until the over-bassy sound is tamed. Where the problem frequency is at the upper end of the frequency range, you would search for it by turning the frequency knob to the right.

Increasing the 'Q' setting makes your display 'pointer' thinner and sharper, and allows you to home in on smaller ranges of frequencies. If you're searching for a particular frequency (say, 200Hz), you've a better chance of locating it fairly accurately with a really skinny display 'pointer'. The easiest thing is to set the Gain knob for maximum cut – fully left – and the Q knob fully right. This turns the frequency curve into a precise, downward-pointing arrow that allows you to more easily select a frequency from those along the bottom of the display. Then cut or boost as desired, first changing the Q setting to suit, when you have located the right frequency area.

Creating a 'pointer' to find EQ frequencies more easily.

Chain two or more PEQ2s to access more EQ bands. Plan your tweaks carefully, though, and make sure you're not doing something with one EQ that negates or is negated by the second, such as cutting a frequency with the first PEQ2 in a chain that you then try to boost with the next.

EQ'ing effects

Also use the PEQ2 for damping down unwanted frequencies in an aux send/return effect treatment such as a reverb. You can place a PEQ2 between the reverb and the mixer aux return to create a more sophisticated high-cut – damping – control than that provided on the reverb. Cutting in the vicinity of 8-9kHz is a good starting point.

Mix EQ

Another main application of the PEQ2 is overall EQing of a stereo mix to improve its tonal balance. However, you should generally try to get your sounds right at source rather than relying on EQ to sort out everything in the mix. Choose samples and loops carefully, and edit synth patches to make them work better with other sounds.

When you do come to EQ, it is often better to cut than boost, though sometimes you will need to boost individual sounds. Apart from the fact that the ear is generally more tolerant of EQ cut than boost, which may be perceived as unnatural-sounding, cutting helps to produce a cleaner mix and make space for other parts to be heard. The aim is to share out the frequency spectrum between the parts of the mix, to give each its own space.

One technique that can be very helpful when EQing a mix is 'notching'. You can do this with principal parts in your mix that you feel need attention. If you're having trouble with an important sound not having the correct prominence in the mix, due to conflict with other sounds that are in the same frequency range, don't just keep boosting its EQ. A better idea is to try to process the less important, conflicting sounds, to cut some of the frequencies they share with the sound you need to highlight. This works well with acoustic guitar parts that fight with vocals.

The technique for determining the best frequency to cut is similar to the example of parametric EQ use above.

- Patch a PEQ2 in line with the device producing the important sound.
- Turn up the Gain control, and sweep the frequency control until you hear a really heightened version of the sound; you're aiming for the main frequencies that define the sound, and at the right spot the sound will seem louder and clearer.
- Make a note of this setting – it won't be an actual frequency value, remember, but a parameter value of between 0 and 127.
- Return the gain control to '0', bypass the PEQ2, or remove it from the rack.
- Now patch PEQ2s in line with the sound sources that are conflicting with the important sound, locate the frequency you just noted down, on all of them, and apply as much cut – by turning the gain knob to the left – as is necessary to make the desired sound more prominent in the mix and the mix begin to sound less muddy. Experiment with the Q control to find the bandwidth that works best.

Don't neglect panning, in tandem with EQ, to create separation in a mix, especially where two sounds are fighting for the same area in the frequency spectrum and you can't easily separate them with EQ. Pan them to different places in the stereo image, as well as doing what you can with EQ.

To use EQ as a mix 'finishing' tool, try placing a PEQ2 between the stereo out of your main mixer and the inputs of the hardware interface, then using it to boost slightly at the low- and high-frequency ends of the spectrum. Keep the boost gentle by using a wide bandwidth – that is, Q knob left. This boost compensates for the psychoacoustic fact that the human ear is more sensitive to mid frequencies, hearing them more easily, and less sensitive at the lower and higher ends. Boosting the extremes thus allows them to 'catch up' a bit and be heard more clearly.

If you like, you can connect another PEQ2 before the first and set it to cut slightly in the mid-range (maintain that wide bandwidth setting!), reinforcing the effect of the second EQ boosting at the extremes, though you may be happy enough with just the 'boost' EQ. The combination of the two EQs copies the 'smile' EQ curve as used in club PA systems.

This kind of EQ curve may help increase the loudness and clarity of your mixes.

The exact areas where you boost and cut may vary slightly according to your mix, and do remember that we are only talking about moderate amounts of both. You don't want to create a completely artificial sound picture. The mid-range cut, in particular, has to be done carefully, because a lot of important sounds exist in this area – female vocals tend to, for example. Top off this EQ configuration with a COMP01 set for overall mix compression, and even a DDL1 set for stereo width enhancement (see later in this chapter), if you like. The improvement in the power, clarity, loudness and polish of your mix should be worthwhile.

Tip

A few useful EQ frequency ranges

Bass Drum: Most of the energy of a kick drum resides below 200Hz, though working around 80Hz boosts depth and thump. The click or attack can be emphasised at 2-6kHz.

Snare Drum: Snares have energy in the range 200Hz-10kHz. For a fatter sound, boost in 2-300Hz range. The 'snap' of the snare can be emphasised at around 5kHz.

Hi-hats: Emphasise 'sizzle' in the 8-12kHz range.

Bass guitar: Increase bottom and fullness by

boosting at 60-80Hz. Increase attack between 800 and 1.1kHz. Also try this on synth basses.

Vocals: Add presence by boosting at around 5kHz. Reduce sibilance by cutting between 7 and 11kHz (use a narrow bandwidth and search around for just the right area, to avoid a detrimental dulling effect). Reduce 'nasal' quality by cutting at around 500Hz-1kHz, but watch you don't take too much body out of the sound.

In general, boost between 20 and 200Hz for punch and power; try to avoid boosting between 200Hz and 1kHz (the low-mid where the ear is

quite sensitive), as this can create a sound that is tiring to listen to; boost moderately in the 1kHz-5kHz range for extra definition and brightness, but beware of introducing a tinny quality; add sparkle in the 5-16kHz range. When you're searching for the right area to boost, use the first part of the technique for 'notching', explained elsewhere in this section, but don't switch to gain reduction when you've found it. Set quite a wide Q and move the gain 'bump' around in the display (keeping to the right general area) by tweaking the Frequency knob, until the sound is most pleasing to you.

The UN16 Unison

- Mono In/Stereo out, Stereo In/Stereo Out, Mono In/Mono Out
- Insert or Send/Return operation

This strange little device was introduced with Reason's V2.5 update, and matches the red set of existing half-rack effect devices. It offers 'thickening' effects somewhat similar to a chorus, though without controllable modulation, by detuning the input signal with four, eight or sixteen copies of itself. The detuned voices are spread across a stereo field, wtih no control over spread, beyond the psychoacoutic effect achieved by increasing the detuning amount. Though there is no modulation of the signal, as is the case with a chorus or phaser device, some feeling of movement in the processed signal is produced due to the cancellation effect of the detuned *s, and the random way in which the extra voices are generated.

Subtle width and movement can be added to mono audio – such as the output from the mono-only SubTractor synth – though if the effect is used to extremes, the input signal tends to become very blurred and rather out of tune. But, of course, this is exactly the effect you might want!

UN16 controls

Voice Count
A switch that selects 4, 8 or 16 detuned voices .

Detune

Sets the amount of detuning produced by the generated voices. Due to the psycho-acoustices of the effect, this can appear to be functioning as a speed control, too.

Wet/Dry

Adjusts the balance between the unprocessed input signal and the Unison effect; it should be set to 'wet' – fully right – if the device is being used in a send/return loop, because the mixer channel supplies the fully dry signal, which is balanced, via the aux return control, with the wet signal coming from the UN16. If the Unison is used as an 'insert' effect, you can set your preferred balance between treated and untreated signal with the Dry/Wet knob.

Mono or stereo?

Think of UN16's 'stereo in/stereo out' option as a dual mono and you won't be far off the truth. As with the CF101 and PH90, a true stereo signal, with full fat results, is only produced with 'mono in' operation. The effect also work in mono if you simply patch one lead to the UN16 left input and one from its left output.

UN16 back panel

CV Inputs

CV control boils down to an input that allows you to control the Detune parameter; the mount of this external control is governed by a depth value knob.

Unison applications

Specific applications for UN16 are surprisingly hard to come up with. It's a simple device, and effective (pardon the pun) in its own way, yet has no obvious hardware equivalent beyond certain simple guitar effect pedals. It certainly can be used to add life to troublesome mono material, and even though the detuning isn't extreme as such (though the overall effect can be), guitar samples and guitar-like patches take on a 12-string feel. Sample-based and synth bass patches can also benefit from this pseudo-chorus, producing an effect rather similar a simple old-fashioned chorus pedal. Bung samples through it, too, especially if they're mono: instant stereo presence and fattening without the mix becoming cluttered. With the Width control to minimum, an lively airiness is produced. Finally, individual mono drum samples, from the individual outs of ReDrum or NNXT, can also be spiced up with UN16: try processing hand claps, snares and cymbals and hear the feeling of space you get, even if you pan the result away from dead centre.

As mentioned above, SubTractor is an ideal input for UN16. Despite SubTractor being mono, I often have stabs at creating synth pad sounds with it, but without something extra the result just doesn't have the enveloping feel of the genuine article. For this, you need stereo, and a UN16 patched across the SubTractor output is often just the effect needed to give the resulting sound an extra boost. It has a Leslie-ish feel that suits pads (and organ patches, of course) that the phaser and chorus/flanger devices don't have.

In fact, if Reason's CF101 chorus/flanger or PH90 phaser devices doesn't quite provide what you're after during a given session, then patch in the UN16 – the shimmery chorus of its more subtle settings may do the job.

Be warned that the cancellation-type effect generated by the interaction of the generated voices can result in some attenuation of the input signal – just turn it up on the target ReMix channel! In addition, the feeling of 'width' produced by lower values of Detune may be lost if you check your mixes in mono; sounds processed in this way may also appear attenuated when auditioned in mono.

The Scream 4 Sound Destruction Unit

Scream 4 front panel

- Mono In/Mono Out, Stereo In/Stereo Out
- In-line operation

The D11 Foldback Distortion, introduced earlier in this section, was part of the Reason's original device lineup. It's also been something of a poor relation, though not one that wouldn't necessarily be invited to parties. With V2.5 of Reason, however, Propellerhead revealed to the world that they knew how to make a real distortion processor, in the shape of the Scream 4 Sound Destruction Unit. D11 is capable of a couple, or at best a very limited range, of sounds; the full-sized Scream 4 is infinitely variable and infinitely pleasing. If you like your distortion, you'll love Scream 4.

Inspired by processors that are aimed more at the guitar market, in terms of design, knob shapes, colour scheme and sound, Scream 4 nevertheless adds an analogue-like warmth to anything that's processed by it. And some of the processing algorithms wouldn't be found on a typical guitar effects device. Most settings are based around a series of analogue processing simulations, but the designers being Propellerheads, the remaining options are in the same vein, but aggresively digital in their distortion. Subtlety, too, can be massaged from Scream 4, adding warmth and fuzziness to parts or mixes in almost the same manner as hardware devices such as enhancers and valve compressors.'

Control Set

It might be a single processing device, but Scream 4's signal path is divided roughly into five sections, though the manual and front panel suggest three: input gain (the Damage Control knob); the Damage Type selection area, where a basic algorithm is selected and two parameters control the overal distortion effect; an EQ section, which despite being labelled 'Cut' offers an effective three fixed bands that can be boosted as well as cut; the Body section, which models the 'space' that the effect appears in, rather like a speaker cabinet simulator but moreso; and, finally, a master volume control.

Scream 4 Damage

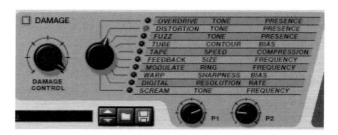

Damage

Let's start again, in more detail. From the left, Damage can be enabled or disabled with a little button, and the Damage Control (or input gain) set. Then you select your Damage type – the distortion algorithm – and tweak one or two of the parameters that each is supplied with, arranged in a handy matrix, using the P1 and P2 knobs at the bottom of the parameter matrix. The algorithms and their two parameters are as follows:

- Overdrive: an analogue-style, crunchy, dynamic overdrive effect – very responsive to your playing style, or the changes of level in input signal. P1 controls the basic tone – turning it produces a brighter effect – and P2 controls presence by boosting high mid-range frequencies before the distortion effect.
- Distortion: a denser, thicker version of Overdrive, with more of a compressed, levelling effect. P1 controls tone and P2 presence, as with Overdrive.
- Fuzz: is a classic sound that produces a bright distortion at low 'Damage Control' settings up to out of control shredding at higher input gains. Again, P1 and P2 control tone and presence respectively.
- Tube: any analogue-style simulation is going to have a tube algorithm, and Scream 4 is no exception. Expect warmth at low settings, morphing to levelling and distortion at higher P1/P2 values. P1 controls contour – described as a sort of high pass filter that changes the tone and character of the effect – and P2 controls bias. This changes the symmetry of the distortion by boosting or cutting harmonics in the same way as a real tube amp circuit.
- Tape: this is a strange algorithm, but a good one, simulating the clipping and compression of analogue tape being driven to its limit; it has a feel rather like keeping the meters in the red when recording to tape. P1 controls tape speed (higher frequencies are vut the slower the speed), and P2 controls compression amount, or ratio.
- Feedback: exactly what it says on the tin. Typical feedback is produced by holding your eelctric guitar next to an amp turned up to 11, or by placing a mic right next to a speaker that's being used to monitor that mix. Scream 4's is just as hard to control as the real thing, but very

satisfying when that control is mastered. Be careful with the Damage Control knob. P1 controls size, or the distance between the source and its feeding back echo, and P2 controls frequency, or which overtones will be made more obvious in the feedback howl.

- Modulate: think ring modulation, though here a signal is filtered and compressed before being multiplied with itself, and then distorted. Rather resonant and rather clangorous. P1 controls 'ring', the resonance of the filter, and P2 controls the filter frequency. Higher frequencies equal a more piercing effect.

- Warp: more distorted modulation, this effect distorts and multiplies the input signal with itself. P1 controls sharpness, ranging from soft, compressed distortion to a sharper sound, richer in harmonics. An effect of multiplying a signal with itself is that the fundamental pitch is removed from the signal, leaving overtones only. P2, labelled Bias, adds the fundamental back to the processed signal.

- Digital: not to be found on many guitar processors, this is a bit- and sample-rate reduction algorithm. It seems that the noisy, crunchy convertors on older digital gear is a sound to be nostalgic about! P1 controls bit rate, and P2 controls sample rate.

- Scream: a fuzz-like effect with bandpass filter that offers high resonance and gain settings, in line with a distortion effect. Capable of convincing 'wah wah' effects underontrol of the dynamics of the input signal. P1 controls tone, and P2 controls filter frequency.

Cut

Here, 18dB of cut or boost can be applied to low, mid and high frequency bands. It's equipped with its own on/off switch, so can be easily removed from the signal path if not required or for fine-tuning a treatment in a 'modular' fashion.

Body

Like the Damage and Cut sections, this can be added to or taken out of the signal path by a switch. It's a tricky concept to describe, being of the 'you'll know what's going on when you listen to it' variety. So, have a play. In the meantime, here goes.

All sound has a place in space, whether its the room you're sitting in now or the speaker cabinet that a guitar might be amplified by. The size, shape and wall coverings all have an effect on the resonances of the sound that bounces around back to your ears. That's what the Body' section of Scream 4 is working with: room or space resonances – the interaction of reflected waveforsm that multiply and cancel each other – though pushed a little further than that. This is a Reason process, after all.

Essentially, it creates the space and resonances that Scream 4's effect appears in; the manual suggests that Body parameters could emulate the sound of a particular speaker cabinet, but its much more dynamic than that: an envelope follower, controlled by the 'Auto' parameter adds auto wah and fixed flange effects, so that the space resonances have movement and feel as they're being modulated. The user selects one of five body types (though

Scream 4
Cut

Scream 4 Body

Info

The envelope follower in Scream 4 monitors the level of the processed signal, and creates an on-the-fly envelope in response to that changing level. This is then routed to the Scale parameter, inducing comb filter and flanging type effects due to the changes in 'room' resonance.

they come with no descriptions), and can then control the size of the space (Scale) and its resonance (Reso). The Auto knob controls how much effect the envelope follower has on the Scale parameter.

Mono or Stereo?

Scream 4 can operate in mono or in stereo; if you input a stereo signal for processing, both left and right components are treated independently with no internal mixing, but with both sides treated to identical processes. One could, theoretically, process two completely different mono signals as no mixing is involved, though the differing levels of the two signals might have undesired effects on the level-dependent elements of the circuitry. You wouldn't be able to change parameters for left and right channels, either.

Scream 4 rear panel

CV Inputs

Scream 4 is more like a sound-making device than the other effects devices in the way that it has a good array of CV inputs – and, unusually, a single CV output. Damage Control, the two algorithm parameter knobs (P1 and P2) and the Body section's Scale parameter can be placed under CV control. The CV output comes from Auto parameter's envelope follower, and lets you add a a CV signal that's controlled by the 'playing' characteristics of any device to a parameter of any other.

Distortion applications and considerations

Distortion is largely an effect of taste; you'll know if its too extreme or not extreme enough. Generally, it should still be possible to make ouf what the source signal is doing musically, and the Cut and Body sections should be used thoughtfully so as not to create a sound that completely dominates, in terms of level and frequency ranges, the rest of the mix. Unless that is what you want. Process drums with Scream 4, and even the most lightweight kit can be made as heavily industrial as you want! Always experiment.

The important parameters to pay attention to initially are in the Damage section. Small tweaks of Damage Control can produce big effects. In fact, keep this parameter to its lower settings, and you'll find that the remaining Damage parameters can be used to quite subtle effect. Even so, when using Scream 4 as a mix 'sweetener' between your main ReMix and the Hardware Interface, it would probably be best to focus on algorithms that aren't aiming to destroy the input signal! Try Tape and Tube first, working with lower values on the P1/P2 controls. The Cut section can then be engaged and its sliders moved ever so slightly to add high frequency or bottom end enhancement – getting the hang of this can be very satsfying, adding a presence to

Reason mixes that are tricky in any other way. Cutting the mid and hi frequencies, for example, while boosting the bass can add a real dub-like heaviness to a mix.

The Body section can be brought into play, too, but is harder to control; avoid the Auto parameter and its envelope follower as auto wah may not be something you'll want to hear across a whole mix. But as a performance-enhancing tool, it's rather good, and solo'ing with Scream 4 sensing your platying dynamics is satisfying and inspiring. Too bad we can't yet treat audio from the outside world – more guitarists might join the Reason universe to access Scream 4!

Effect order in chains

Reason effects are designed just as much for linking as for single use, allowing you to indulge in multi-effects processing to a practically infinite degree. The creation of multi-effect chains, whether for insert processing or use in the mixer's send/return loops, is simple, and their content is entirely up to you. You can patch what you like where you like. However, there are certain broad conventions – not really rules, since they're regularly subverted – concerning what sort of effect goes where in a chain.

The general principle is to put signal processing – EQ, compression, filter, distortion – earlier in the chain, followed by delay, followed by phaser or chorus, followed by reverb. But if patching them in a different order gives you a sound you like, by all means do it. A good case could be made for swapping delay and phaser/chorus, and it's not unheard of to put chorus after a reverb, to create a swirl in the reverb. Try all sorts of orders and you'll soon get an idea of what works.

In a multi-effect 'insert' chain, you may want to think twice before inputting a stereo signal into a DDL1, as its output is always mono. If your putative chain is processing a stereo signal, or has become stereo at some point in the chain, and you want a delay effect, perhaps you should use two DDL1s. Patch them in mono between the left and right sides of the stereo chain. This will allow you to set different delay times for each side (or just the same if you like) and maintain full stereo integrity.

Also consider the different effects that may be created by your choice of insert or send operation: for example, using delay plus reverb as an insert chain will result in each delay repeat getting its own little 'halo' of reverb, while if you use the delay and reverb as send effects only the original sound is reverbed, as the delayed repeats of the sound are routed to their own aux return on the mixer and have no contact with the reverb at all.

Reason 3 users will be able to use the Combinator to create complex effects chains rather than having to save Songs containing pre-built ones. In this case, the Combinator acts as a microcosm of a whole project. Into it you can place any combination of devices you like and save and load patches instantly. So you could for example create a great effects chain for processing vocals, or compressing drums, and use it multiple times in different projects without having to copy or paste anything.

On the rear panel of the Combinator are simple ports for connecting all the devices within the Combi, and the Combinator to the "outside world", which generally means on to the main mixer.

For much more on this, see the chapter dedicated to the Combinator.

Effect 'presets'

None of the half rack effects and processing devices are equipped with the facility to save and load patches. When you have an effect configuration you like, you either save it with the Song it was created for (then hope to remember where it was if you would like to use it in the future) or also save it separately as a Song with a name that describes it. You could make a separate folder on your hard drive just for effect configurations (and chains).

Another idea is to save one Song containing many effects configurations, chains and settings, treating the Song as a library. You can then copy and paste the required effect devices or chains into new Songs when you want them. Devices would obviously have to have descriptive names, such as 'Best Vocal Reverb', and chains would have to be named such that the group of devices was recognisable as a chain. If you copy devices at the same time (by selecting them all and then copying), their interconnections go with them when they are pasted elsewhere.

To quickly distinguish between sets of devices that belong together, consider placing a 'folded' device (say, a ReBirth Input machine) between each set. Create these 'spacer' devices while holding down Shift, so that you don't get any unwanted connections. Then name each spacer device to indicate the chain that is coming next in the rack.

An 'effects library' Song.

More advanced effect techniques

There are many ways of using the Reason effects, and Reason users constantly come up with ingenious ideas for combining them, sometimes to do jobs they were probably never designed for! It would probably take a book to explore the possibilities thoroughly, but here are just a few ideas for using some of the effects in a more advanced way.

Inspiration can also be found on the Internet Reason forums, where people sometimes post their latest methods, and by looking at how effects have been used in Songs posted by other Reason users. Expert practitioners sometimes devote sections of their own web sites to passing on their power effects ideas. See Appendix 1 for some web sites to try. It's also worth noting that many of the effect techniques given in recording books (especially older recording books) should be reproducible using the Reason effects.

'Parallel' effect processing

So far, only serial processing has been discussed – plugging a Reason sound-making device or ReMix auxiliary send into one effect, and then patching the output of that effect to the input of another effect, and so on until a (serial) chain producing the desired effect is created.

Parallel processing would take the sound-making device's output or mixer aux send and process it with two or more effects or effect chains in parallel. The texture produced would be quite different from that of using the same effects serially. Imagine a sound being processed by delay and chorus: in a serial chain, the delays would be chorused. If the effects were used in parallel, each effect would be applied separately to the input signal, which would be chorused on one side and delayed on the other: the chorus and delay would never affect each other's action. It's hard to explain how this sounds, but to these ears the effect can be a lot nicer! As will be explain shortly, parallel processing also offers extra opportunities for automated effects implementation.

Creating a 'splitter' box

Working with parallel processing configurations is now a straightforward process with V2.5's Spider audio merger/splitters. Simply plug the audio out of the source device or ReMix aux send into one Spider Audio splitter circuit, and route up to four split Spider Audio outs to as many parallel effects chains as you like.

But it's also possible to achieve a similar result with other devices – and users with a pre 2.5 version of Reason might find the technique useful. This technique is retained for readers without the latest version, and because using a DDL1 (or CF101 Chorus/Flanger) as a splitter offers the potential for more creative processing, by adding parameter tweaks to the split signals.

This technique exploits the fact that although the DDL1 is a mono processor, it always routes a mono input to both of its outputs. If you switch the DDL1 to 'bypass' mode (click the Bypass switch to its topmost position) no effect is produced, but an exact copy of the input signal is routed to two outputs.

The difference between serial and parallel effect processing.

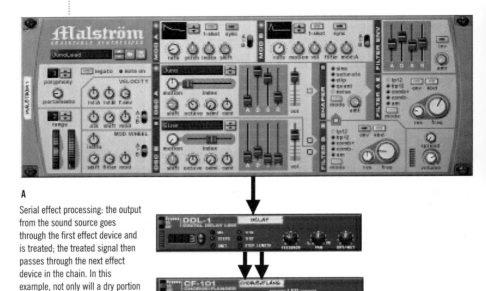

A

Serial effect processing: the output from the sound source goes through the first effect device and is treated; the treated signal then passes through the next effect device in the chain. In this example, not only will a dry portion of the synth sound be treated by the chorus device, a delayed portion will also be treated, resulting in chorused delays.

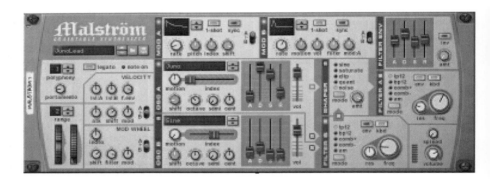

B

Parallel effect processing: the output from the sound source is split into two separate signals. Each is then processed, in parallel, by its own independent effect device. The two effects do not interact with each other and the delayed signal is never chorused.

The sound source audio output should be connected to the splitter DDL1's audio input. Both the splitter's outputs can now be routed to different effect devices or effect chains. The output from the effect device at the end of each chain should then be routed to its own mixer channel. As long as the mixer channel for each chain is unmuted, you'll be hearing the effect of parallel effect processing. (Whenever you use a DDL1 as a splitter box, you might like to name it 'Splitter', so you don't confuse it with any other DDL1s that are actually creating effects.)

Setting up a sound source connected to a DDL1 in 'splitter' mode (Bypassed). Each DDL1 output is then connected to a separate effect device. This configuration processes the signal separately with delay and chorus.

Instant effect-chain switching

You can also use this technique in a different way: to swap instantly between two different effect chains being used on the same input signal. Just mute and unmute the chains' respective mixer channels – and this process, of course, can be automated. The two chains could be drastically different. You could swap, say, from a heavy, aggressive chain using distortion one moment to a delicate, haunting sound using chorus and reverb the next. Guitarists are used to creating parallel chains of effects and switching between them on stage; this makes a similar idea possible in your Reason studio.

There may be instances where the tendency of this technique to cut off dead the decays of one effect chain, when you swap to the other, is not desirable – though, of course, the effect of the sudden abrupt transition may be just what you need. If it's not, there is a solution.

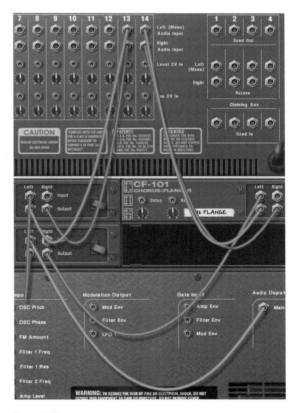

- Instead of putting the DDL1 'splitter' into bypass mode, turn it 'On', set its Delay time to 1ms (the minimum value in MS mode), and turn the Feedback control to minimum.
- Turn the Dry/Wet balance control to fully 'wet'. There will now be a 1ms delay on the input signal, which should be undetectable for virtually all purposes.
- Because the output is now a treated signal, it can be panned between left and right – with the pan control – and this panning can be automated in the main sequencer; switching

Figure 14.22
The rear-panel connections for the 'splitter' setup.

from fully left to fully right and back again has the effect of turning one chain off and the other on, but with each effect channel at the mixer having a chance to die away naturally. This switching from left to right is easy enough to automate in the main sequencer's controller lane editor, since you can draw in a curve describing full left followed by full right operation as easily as if it were just a switch parameter.

The 'splitter' DDL1 settings you'll need to be able to switch effect chains without one cutting off the decay of the other.

The possibilities don't end with two parallel chains: each output of the splitter could itself be routed to another splitter. For example, adding two 'splitter' DDL1s to a DDL1 that's already functioning as a splitter would provide you with four parallel chains.

Creating multiple chains of effects will have an impact on your computer's CPU overhead, and you'll also require more mixer channels to handle the extra returns. You'll have to juggle the musical possibilities against any impact on your computer system.

'Approaching stereo' reverb

As mentioned earlier in the chapter, the RV7 sums a stereo input to mono before creating a pseudo-stereo reverb for it. The following was developed while trying to create something approaching a true stereo reverb, and which might still be valid for readers without access to the RV7000 true stereo reverb intoduced in V2.5. It also uses less CPU overhead than an RV7000. In the process, it seems that for some reason the configuration improves the sound of the RV7 reverb – several blind testings appear to confirm this! Try it and see what you think. It's suitable for stereo audio such as sub-mixes from a ReMix, stereo samples of backing vocals, loops, and even mono lead vocals.

You may notice that during this procedure a stereo effect send/return loop is constructed from two standard ReMix aux loops. This is because there's little point in connecting a stereo reverb to a mono send/return system such as that of the ReMix mixer. However, the consequence of this is that every time you want to change the send level to the reverb, you'll have to move two aux send knobs, instead of just one, as you'll discover during the creation of this effect. Of course, V2.5 has stereo aux sends, if you decide to try this technique in the later versions of Reason. You may use any reverb setting you like as long as it is the same for both RV7s.

- Create a mixer, if your rack doesn't already have one, and two RV7s. Make sure the connections from mixer aux sends 1 and 2 have been automatically made to each RV7 left input.
- Connections will also have been made from each device's stereo out to the aux returns at the back of the mixer. Disconnect these and instead connect the RV7 outputs to one mixer channel each. For convenience, we route to channels 13 and 14.

- Now pan one RV7 mixer channel full left and the other full right; this might seem counter-intuitive, but stick with it. You now have what is essentially a stereo reverb created from the left side of one RV7 and the right side of the other. Ensure that whenever you change a parameter on one RV7, you make the same change on the other.

- Create an NN19 device (it'll be automatically patched to input 1 if nothing apart from the reverbs are in your rack) and load a patch to try the reverb with – perhaps Grand Piano or Grand PianoSoft from the factory ReFill. Set the NN19 'Spread' control to about 12 o'clock or higher. This creates a convincing left-to-right stereo spread of the multisamples in the piano patch.

Pan the RV7 mixer channels left and right.

First stage of the 'stereo reverb'. Mixer aux sends are connected to the inputs of the two RV7s, and the RV7 outs are patched into mixer channels.

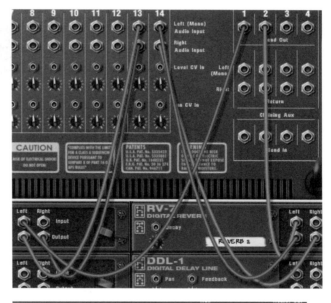

- In order to process any stereo device (including NN19) properly with the stereo reverb, it's necessary to connect the device's left and right outputs to their own mixer channels. The NN19's left output is already connected to mixer channel 1; go to the back of the rack, disconnect the right output and connect it to the left channel of mixer input 2. Pan mixer channel 1 full left and channel 2 full right; ensure the level controls for both channels have the same value.

- Now turn up aux send 1 on mixer channel 1 (the left-hand side of your stereo NN19 piano) and aux send 2 on channel 2 (the right-hand side). Set the same send level for both.

Right: The outputs of the stereo sound source (in this case NN19) each have to be connected to their own mixer channel. (Other connections have been omitted from the picture for clarity.)

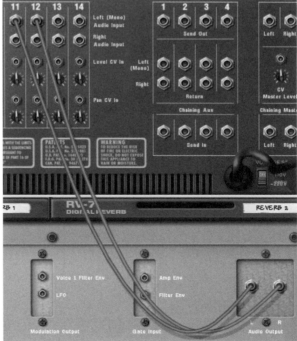

Control the level of the reverb from one aux send knob on each channel – aux 1 on one channel and aux 2 on the other.

Tip

Though the delay/echo algorithms in RV7000 work in true stereo, you might like to try this stereo delay processing trick, that's really simple in Reason V2.5 or 3. Simply patch one DDL1 to the left socket of a ReMix aux send and another DDL1 to the right socket. Patch one output from each to the left and right aux returns. There: instant stereo delay processing!

Play some notes, and you'll hear not only a stereo piano performance but a fair simulation of a real stereo reverb.

As mentioned above, this stereo reverb can be used on mono sound sources, such as SubTractor, with minor operational changes. The trick is to control send level with aux sends 1 and 2 on the one mixer channel that the mono source is going through, and pay attention to panning. If the SubTractor is panned dead centre, both sends should have the same value, but if you pan the synth to the left you should turn down some of send 2 – the one feeding the right-hand side of the stereo send . The further left you pan, the more send 2 should be turned down. The same goes for panning right, except that you should turn down send 1. This helps to simulate the correct behaviour of a genuine stereo aux send.

'PianoVerb'
Something else you can add to the above technique, which you may ind improves it further, is your own pre-delay for the reverb, using a pair of DDL1s. This makes a really nice reverb that seems to suit mellow pianos.

The obvious thing to do for creating pre-delay would be to place the delays before the reverbs, but you can alternatively place the delays after the reverbs. This makes a degree of sense, in that the input signal hits the RV7, the reverb is produced, and then there's a delay before you hear it. The dry signal, meanwhile goes through un-delayed, so that there is a gap between hearing it and hearing the start of the delayed reverb – a pre-delay!

Using this order in the chain seems to give audibly better results, with an increased sense of space and definition. The sometimes annoyingly ringy and metallic tail of the RV7 reverb is also smoothed, smudged, and generally made more acceptable, allowing you to use slightly longer decay times than you otherwise might. Again, try some emotive chordal playing with the factory ReFill Grand Piano or soft Grand, or any decent piano sample, and this effect configuration. To create this effect, start with the 'Approaching Stereo' reverb:

* Create two DDL1s while holding down Shift.
* Flip to the back of the rack. Click and hold the cables that are currently connected to the outputs of the first RV7 and drag them to the outputs of the first DDL1; click the cables connected to the outputs of the second RV7 , and drag them to the outputs of the second DDL1.
* Connect the outputs of the first RV7 to the inputs of the first DDL1, and make the same connections between the second RV7 and DDL1.
* Set both RV7s as follows: Algorithm – Hall; Size – 26; Decay – 34; Damp – 50.
* Set both DDL1s to a delay time of 60ms, no Feedback.
* Add a little more high-frequency damping by enabling the EQ for each reverb channel in the mixer, and setting Treble amount to -14.

Delay ideas
Delay, the basis of all the other effects, in one way or another, provides many possibilities for creating interesting treatments. Some are offered below. However, one or two of these ideas will require the 'splitting' technique discussed in the 'Parallel effect processing' section above. Note that where a technique is a bit involved, you're asked to start with an empty rack, just for

the sake of clarity. If you already know what you're doing with Reason's effects, though, you may not find that necessary.

Highlighting single events

One technique that can be effective (but in moderation, or it can be a bit cheesy) is adding delay repeats only to a single word or vocal phrase here or there, or even an individual drum hit (especially snare) for emphasis. You might know this kind of treatment as a 'dub echo' effect.

With the delay connected to an aux send/return loop, wait for the word or phrase you want to treat as the track plays back, and just before it occurs, turn the delay aux send control to full. Turn it back down again right after the word or phrase. You can automate this via a track in the sequencer for the mixer. Create a track, assign it to the mixer, make sure the MIDI plug icon is showing next to the mixer track, then go into record and tweak the aux send control. (See the automation chapter for more details on automating controls.)

Stereo width enhancement

This technique enhances the perceived width of stereo audio. It could be used to add width to the output of a stereo device such as NN19 or ReDrum, or a sub-mix within a Song, or to widen the stereo image of a final Song mix.

- Connect the left output of a stereo device or mix to the left input of a ReMix channel – say channel 1. The effect is probably more obvious on a mix.
- Connect the right output of the device or mix to a DDL1 set to a delay time of up to 20mS, and connect the left output of the DDL1 to the left input of ReMix channel 2.
- Pan the channels left and right respectively, and you'll hear stereo that appears to move beyond your speakers.

There will probably be mono compatibility issues, so go carefully if this is likely to be a problem for you. It might be advantageous to separate any bass sounds: sledgehammer stereo width enhancement such s this can occasionally lead to blurring in the bass. Bass generally lacks stereo information, but if a particular sound has a lot of higher overtones, width enhancement can add a pleasant phasey spread. Adding different width enhancements to different parts of your mix could help stop things getting smudgy.

Creating really long delays

There may be times when 2000mS, the DDL1's maximum delay time, isn't long enough for an effect you might be after. Really long delays can be useful for creating pseudo-random textures, created by echos appearing long after the delayed audio itself has finished playing. There are plenty of sound design opportunities to be exploited by incorporating four-second, six-second or even longer delays into the process; the textures created by purely abstract sounds repeating regularly over a period of time can be really compelling. Long delay times can also be used to create '70s-style tape delay effects that produce the impression of a second performer playing along, in round-like fashion, with whatever you're playing or sequencing in Reason.

Extending delay times in Reason is simple: just chain DDL1s to get the maximum delay time you require. If you set the Wet/Dry control of every DDL1 in a chain to fully 'wet', what you'll get out of the last device in the chain is a delay that's equal to the sum of the delay times produced by the devices in the chain. So if you connect eight DDL1s the maximum delay time will be 16 seconds.

In the example below we'll create a chain of four DDL1s, producing an aggregate delay of eight seconds, to be patched in a ReMix aux send/return loop. To hear the delay, you'll need a sound-making device connected to the same ReMix. When you've done the following steps, turn up the aux send 1 control on the device channel and play a few notes on your keyboard.

- Starting from an empty rack, create a ReMix.
- Now create four DDL1s, with the Shift key held down to disable automatic connection.
- Hit the Tab key to flip to the back of the rack. Drag a lead from the left output of the first DDL1 to the left input of the second; hold down Shift while doing this, so that the right audio connection isn't also made by Reason. Make the same connection between DDL two and three, and then between DDL three and four.
- When all four DDL1s are connected, plug a lead from the ReMix's Aux

The rear-panel routing for connecting four DDL1s to make one long delay time.

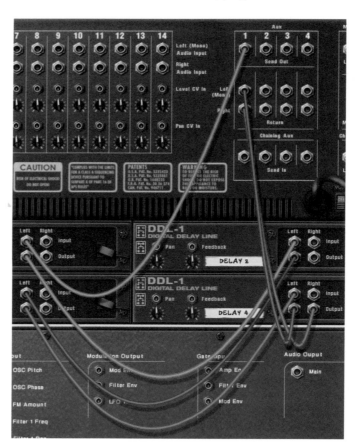

Send Out 1 to the left input of the first DDL1 in the chain, and connect the left-right output pair of the last delay in the chain to Aux Return 1.

- You now have a chain of four delays; set the wet/dry control of each DDL1 to completely wet and the feedback control fully left. Set the delay time for each DDL1 to 2000mS to achieve an eight-second delay from the chain.

Identical front-panel settings for all four DDL1s.

- Adding more delays to the chain is simple. Highlight any DDL1 in the chain (except the last one) and create a new DDL1. Reason will automatically patch it into the chain correctly, in mono. Just make sure that any new DDL1 added has its Dry/Wet control turned to fully wet and that, initially at least, the Feedback control is fully left, at minimum.

You may want to experiment with Feedback, to add repeats within each DDL1's delay, but be careful if you do: anything more than a very modest amount of feedback on one or two of the delays can cause an out-of-control, distorted avalanche of delays, potentially damaging speakers and/or ears!

Deluxe multitap delay

Chaining DDL1s also opens up the possibility of a deluxe, highly controllable 'multi-tap' delay, with each DDL1 in a chain producing one 'tap'. The advantages of this kind of extravagant setup include the ability to set an independent delay time for each and every tap, allowing you to construct more interesting, complex delay patterns, generating counter-rhythms to the rhythm of the input signal. You can even alter level, pan and EQ for each tap independently, perhaps making the taps fade out convincingly towards the end of the chain, or increasing and reducing tap level to create dynamic interest.

It's possible to achieve this effect because, as mentioned earlier, the DDL1 has two outputs, which each pass the delay effect in parallel. In the chain described in the 'Creating long delays' section above, the left output of each DDL1 is patched to the left input of the next device in the chain. But because the same delayed signal also appears at the right output of each DDL1, this secondary output can be routed to its own mixer input.

The output from each delay sent to the mixer makes a separate 'tap' in the multi-tap delay, rather than joining with the outputs of the others to create one long delay, like the example above. Of course, the long delay is still created, as the left outputs of the DDL1s are still connected to each other, and will still emerge at the end of the chain, but it will just sound like another 'tap' in the multi-tap effect. One point worth remembering is that the tap produced by each device in the chain is delayed from the previous tap, not the main input signal.

Again, to hear the effect, you'll obviously also need a sound-making device connected to the mixer. After setting up the effect, turn up the aux send 1 control on the device's mixer channel and play a few notes on your keyboard, or record a simple part into the sequencer.

• Create a chain with as many DDL1s as you think you need, using the instructions in the 'Creating really long delays' section. In order to make this demonstration easier to handle, though, you might like to keep the chain down to the four devices of the last example. Keep Feedback on each device set to zero for now.

• Now patch the right output of each DDL1 in the chain to its own ReMix channel (connect the leads to the left mixer channel input in each case).

Rear-panel routing for multi-tap delay.

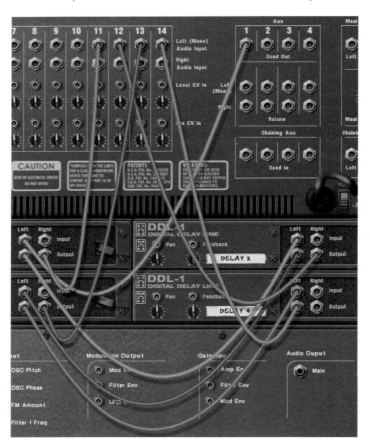

• As this is a multitap delay we're creating, you probably won't want each DDL1 set to its maximum delay time, as we did in the previous 'long delay' example. Set the delays to different step values, so that when you start a track and apply the effect you'll hear a rhythmic delay pattern. You can regulate the pattern according to the number of steps you set for each DDL1. Patterns of this type create a very Kraftwerk vibe if you use the right type of synth sound or sample.

• Pan the first DDL1 mixer channel hard left and the last one hard right. Give the others pan positions that create a good spread between the two extremes. You don't have to do this panning step, but the effect sounds nicer if you do.

The fun thing about this is creating different delay patterns by inputting a different Step value on each DDL1.

This technique sounds great with eight DDL1s processing arpeggiated chords played on a short, harp-like synth patch. You can even set the Steps unit number on each DDL1 so that as the delay repeats pan across the stereo image they appear to become faster: simply set fewer steps on each successive device. Try 16 steps on the first DDL1, 15 on the second, 14 on the third, and so on, down to 9 steps for the eighth DDL1.

A subtle extra dimension can be added to this idea by using the treble EQ control in each mixer delay channel to take some top-end off each delay 'tap'. Cut the treble progressively, starting with a little off the first delay channel, then a bit more off the next, and so on, until the last 'tap' has as much treble cut as possible. This softens and dulls the repeats, rather as they would soften and dull if going through a tape delay.

It's easy to see how mixer channels could get used up in a configuration such as this, so perhaps be prepared to give over a ReMix mixer just for this effect; see the ReMix chapter for details on using multiple ReMixes together.

Send-based delay feedback

The Feedback control on the DDL1 – indeed, any delay processor – controls how much of the delayed signal is fed back into the delay process, thus producing the effect of more repeats of the audio being treated. But there's another, old-fashioned, way of doing the same thing. It sounds rather different, and very effective. What you need to do is actually create a feedback loop, by sending the delayed audio physically back to the input of the DDL1 it's just come from. This is done via a channel on the mixer.

The DDL1 patched into the mixer for send-based feedback.

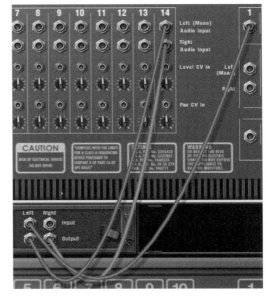

• Start with an empty rack. Create a mixer and a ReDrum. Then create a DDL1, while holding down Shift. Leave the delay Step setting at 3, but set Feedback to zero.
• At the back of the rack, connect the mixer's aux send out 1 to the DDL1's left input and the output of the DDL1 to mixer channel 14.
• Load a drum kit into ReDrum and create a simple pattern (or even Randomize a pattern) so you can hear the effect. Turn up the aux send 1 control on the hi-hat or snare voice channel in ReDrum. Set the pattern playing.

346 Chapter 14: Effects

- Begin turning up the aux send 1 control on mixer channel 14. Only turn it up a little bit at first – there's a point at which the feedback will go out of control, and then you'll get genuine feedback of an unpleasant kind, so do be careful. As you advance the send control towards the critical 'out of control' point, the repeats take on an increasingly metallic, filtered character, which sounds great.

Try automating increasing the channel send level almost to the critical point, where the repeats are getting really mad, and then pulling back from the brink by turning the send control back. This creates a great feeling of building urgency. Also experiment with adding a little genuine feedback in the DDL1 itself, as this adds a 'phased' feel to the repeats, as well as enabling you to get the 'filtered' sound at less extreme settings.

The MClass Effects

Introduced in Reason 3, the MClass effects are a suite of four new effect devices, available individually or as a Combi, which seek to help you get a better overall sound out of Reason. They do this by processing the summed output of the project – usually sitting between the main mixer and the Hardware Interface – to increase the volume and dynamic range of the sound. They are much more similar in style to professional studio mastering hardware effects than typical plugins. One problem with earlier versions of Reason

was that final mixes tended to be a bit flat and lifeless. ReWiring Reason into Cubase, Pro Tools or Sonar et al. could help to fix this by processing the output through some special plugins, but it's nice that Reason is now able to do it all in-house.

What is mastering?

Put simply, mastering is the process of tweaking a mixed track so that it has the greatest possible dynamic range, and is as consistently close to 0db as possible without clipping. It is also the process of taking a collection of tracks – an album, for example, and treating all the tracks so that they have similar sonic and dynamic characteristics. In other words, so that they sound like they all belong on the same record. Finally, good mastering will make a track sound good on any medium, from a top-end hi-fi to a boombox or a car stereo, all of which have wildly different electronics and speakers. Mastering is in many cases the difference between tracks that sound good and tracks that sound great. If you have ever wondered why your tracks sound quiet and lifeless compared to commercial CDs despite being normalized, it's because they employ experienced mastering engineers to squeeze every last bit of dynamic range and loudness out of commercially produced music.

Traditionally, tracks would be mixed, laid down to CD or DAT and then taken to a mastering facility where they would be processed as individual stereo files. In Reason the process is slightly different, in that you sort of have to do everything at once. The signal is still being generated by Reason's modules as it passes through the effects and the mixer, then the MClass effects and finally through the Hardware Interface out to a stereo file on your computer, or a hardware recorder like a CD or DAT machine. One benefit of doing things this way is that you can mix your tracks while taking account of the mastering processing. Frequently, mastering will dramatically affect a mix. For example, there could be just the right amount of bass in your original mix, but far too little once the mastering processors "rein in" the bottom end in the course of creating a more balanced signal. Of course you can tweak the MClass effects to compensate for this, but it helps to be aware of how they are changing the sound.

So technically the MClass effects aren't mastering in the conventional sense of the word, but what they are doing is making the overall sound much bigger, punchier and more balanced, and that's what mastering aims to do. As for creating a consistent sound for a number of tracks, the best approach is to set up a Mastering Combi, save it and then re-use it with minor tweaks for each track of the album.

General tips for mastering

Don't spend ages mixing a track and then stick a Mastering Combi in at the end – you'll probably have to re-balance everything because the Combi will change the sound and require you to tweak many of the channels again. A better idea is to have a good rough mix going on, then insert the Mastering Combi and perform all the final fader and EQ tweaks, knowing that the sound you're hearing will be the sound you end up with.

Don't monitor at very high volumes. It gives a false impression of the overall level of a track. By all means test mixes at high and low volumes, but most listening should be at a sensible level. In fact monitoring at very low levels will give you a whole new perspective on the balance of your track. Neither Reason nor your monitors should be pushed to full volume. Keep an eye on the level meters – especially the master fader – to make sure there isn't loads of clipping. You can get away with the odd red light – digital meters are extremely accurate but the odd red doesn't mean it's clipping, unless you can hear it with your own ears.

Don't make tracks too busy if you can possibly avoid it. Having space in a mix and not letting lots of instruments fight for the same space in the same frequency range makes mixing and mastering a lot easier. Trying to separate out a bass and a bass drum, or a piano and a synth in the same range can be tricky. Also remember that it doesn't really matter if an instrument sounds strange when you solo it up, as long as it sounds good when the whole mix is playing. Mixing and mastering is about symphony – an overall balance, and not letting anything dominate too much.

Test your masters on different systems. What sounds good on your speakers might sound bad on someone's hi-fi. If it does, make a note of what was wrong – e.g. too much bass – and come back to Reason to fix it. You should be aiming for a consistent but powerful sound.

Don't be afraid to try presets with names that may at first sound totally unsuitable. For example, loading up a hip hop mastering preset over an orchestral track. Sometimes it will sound terrible, but other times it will lend a totally unexpected feel to a track which you hadn't even though of trying.

Mastering Combis

The easiest way to use the MClass effects is in Combi form, as the Combinator makes it simple to build or tweak complex effects chains as well as controlling them from the buttons and knobs on the front panel. There's also the added bonus that patches can be instantly saved and recalled for use in different projects. Choosing Create > Combinator with the Hardware Interface selected will insert the Combi between the Mixer and the output, making sure the whole signal from the mixer is processed. Because of Reason's modular design you could of course insert any number of Mastering Combis anywhere in the rack, although this is by far the most effective way of processing a track.

Tip

There's nothing to stop you using more than one Mastering Combi in a rack. However, be careful not to overdo it and apply too much effect, which can leave your track sounding over-produced.

A Mastering Combi

The Factory Sound Bank contains a folder of handy Mastering patches to get you started. As always, the Browser will display a breakdown of what's contained within each one, and you can load and audition them from the Browser while the track plays, letting you see if a preset is going to be wildly unsuitable or quite useful.

The preset mastering patches have parameters pre-mapped to the rotary controls on the front panel of the Combinator so it's easy to quickly tweak important aspects of the sound. To edit in more detail you can simply click the Show Devices button to make the Combi reveal what's inside it.

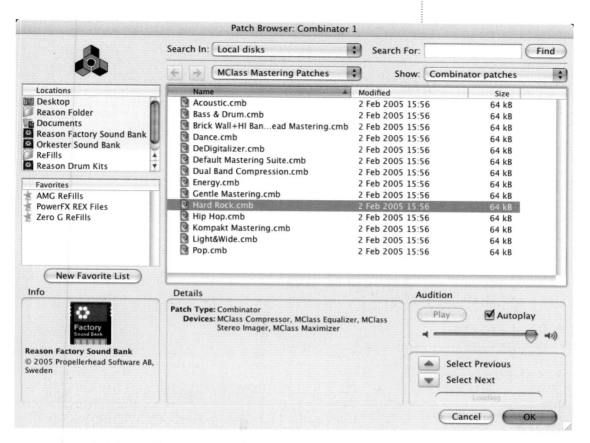

(Above) Preset Mastering Combi patches

(Left) The shortcut control buttons

The programmer window

One of the Combinator's most useful features is the programmer window which lets you assign any parameters from the modules inside a Combi to the buttons and knobs on the Combinator's front panel for quick access. The Mastering presets have the most useful parameters ready mapped, but you can always edit them or if you're building your own, set them up for yourself. Here's a look at how it's done in the hip hop preset on the Factory Sound Bank.

The Combi contains four MClass modules in a chain. The four rotary knobs are assigned but the buttons are not by default. In the device list on the left of the programmer window you choose which device you're viewing the properties for. The routing window on the right will change depending on which you select. Here you can see compressor 1 has rotary 1 assigned to input gain. If you move rotary 1 you'll see the control on the compressor move too.

Assigning parameters in the
Combinator's programmer window

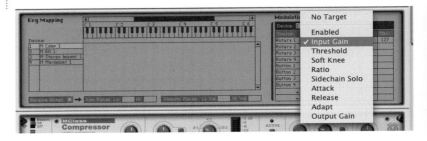

The Stereo Images has no rotary controls assigned, so you could try deselecting one of the EQ rotaries to free up a button then assigning that rotary to a parameter for the Stereo Imager. You can in fact assign a rotary or a button to multiple controls on multiple modules, although this can get confusing unless you really want one control to change several things at once.

Different devices have different assignable parameters`

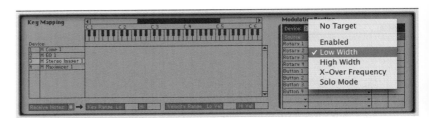

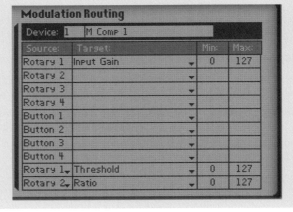

The MClass effect devices

You can use the MClass effects either as a Combi effect chain, or individually in a project. It's easy also to add further devices to existing Combis, or build your own.

The MClass Equalizer

EQ is crucial to both mixing and mastering. Treating the whole mix with EQ helps to iron out any discrepancies such as hissy top end or boomy bass. Mids, which can often disappear a bit into a mix, can also be brought out with EQ. The MClass Equalizer has two independent, fully parametric bands along with high and low shelving bands and also a lo cut switch. The separate bands are ordered from left to right, starting with the lowest and ending with the highest. Each of the bands can be independently switched on or off using its red switch at the top left corner. Changes which you make are reflected in the graphic waveform on the left, which helps a lot in seeing which frequencies you're boosting or cutting. You can't drag the waveform using the mouse, only the rotary knobs.

The EQ graphic display

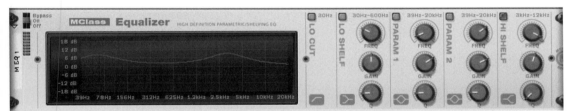

The Lo cut control will remove any frequencies below 30Hz, which will eliminate any rumble. Low frequency rumble can make a mix sound bad.

The parametric EQ 1 and 2 controls operate independently and affect the sound differently depending on how you set them up. The Frequency controls set at which frequency the levels should be raiser or lowered, and the Gain knob determines by how much the frequencies should be altered. The Q control changes the width of the affected area around the frequency you have set. A higher Q value means a narrower frequency range. You can see how this works by moving the controls and watching the graphic display change.

Finally, the Lo and Hi shelf controls will boost or cut the bottom or top end based on the frequency, Q and gain settings you enter. This is good for fixing a boomy bass or a top end which is too quiet or too loud. The Q knob controls the slope of the shelving curve. Try playing with it to see how it affects the sound.

The MClass Stereo Imager

This module addresses a longstanding issue with Reason. That is, an apparent lack of real stereo width in exported tracks, leading to a "lifeless" effect compared to other recorded material. The Stereo Imager splits the signal into two bands – hi and lo frequencies, allowing you to cut or boost both independently. The idea is that you will probably need to tighten up the bottom end of the signal by narrowing the Lo Band towards the "mono" setting, and

MClass Stereo Imager

Tip

If you set the Solo switch to 'Lo' and the Separate output switch to 'Hi', the Stereo Imager will operate as a basic crossover filter, delivering the Lo band signal from the main output and the Hi band signal from the Separate out.

at the same time boost the Hi Band towards the "wide" setting to open up the top end.

The Lo and Hi Band controls let you make either band more mono)to the left) or more stereo (to the right). A centered knob means no change from the original signal. The LED meters show you how much the signal is being widened or narrowed by. The X-Over control in the middle sets the frequency at which lo and hi frequencies are separated. You can tweak this if your track is particularly muddy in the bottom end or lacking sparkle at the top to ensure more or less of each frequency band is tightened or widened. Finally, the solo section lets you audition each band separately, which is useful when you're fiddling with the X-Over knob to see where the frequency split is occurring.

The MClass Compressor

Compression is crucial to achieving a balanced sound, as it prevents peaks from jumping out of the mix whilst at the same time making elements of a track sit more comfortably with each other. The MClass Compressor is a single band compressor suitable for a range of compression applications. When applied to a mix, generally you should use moderate amounts of compression with a relatively gentle attack. Electronic music like techno and trance calls for harder, more "pumped" compression effects to fatten up the bottom end.

MClass Compressor

Controls

The Input Gain knob sets the drive level. That is, how much input the Compressor receives. It works together with the Threshold control, which decides at what level compression will start to be applied. With the input level below the Threshold you set, no compression is applied. As soon as the level is reached, the compression kicks in. The lower the Threshold, the sooner the compression is applied and therefore the more compression is applied overall. A very low Threshold and a high input gain setting will make for an overly compressed sound.

The Ratio knob lets you set how much gain reduction is applied to the signal which passes the Threshold. 1:1 means no reduction, 4:1 means greater reduction and so on.

The Soft Knee button, when pressed, ensures that compression is applied gradually and not immediately, for more musical results. At higher compression ratios, when the compression kicks in the effect can sound artificial and very obvious. Using Soft Knee makes the effect more gentle.

Attack and Release are important for controlling how the compressor behaves. Attack determines how quickly the compressor acts on a signal which passes the Threshold. A low setting means the signal is immediately compressed. A higher setting allows more signal through before compression kicks in. Release is the opposite, governing how long it takes for the compressor to die away after the signal drops back below the Threshold. A low setting here produces heavily pumped compression. The Adapt Release button differentiates between short and long peaks. Finally the Output Gain knob controls the output gain and can be used to compensate for the gain reduction caused by compression.

The compressor also supports sidechaining, which lets you activate compression based on specific frequencies. This is handy for tasks like de-essing. For example, by attaching an equalized signal to the Compressor's sidechain inputs you can make the compression more or less responsive to a specific frequency range. By mixing an equalized signal with an unprocessed version of the same signal using a Spider audio splitter, activating the Solo sidechain setting on the Compressor and identifying the problem frequencies you can make the Compressor sensitive to specific frequencies. See the Reason manual for a practical example of this.

The MClass Maximizer

The last but by no means least of the MClass effects is the Maximizer. Essentially this is a limiter – a device which raises the loudness of a mix without distorting or clipping. It is crucial to boosting the overall perceived volume of your track, and is best used in a Combi between the Mixer and Hardware Interface. Monitor the effect and the overall volume of the song using the level meters. Peak mode displays a faster response to peaks and VU mode displays average levels.

The MClass Maximizer

Controls

Input Gain controls the amount of signal passing into the Maximizer and Output Gain the signal passing out. Output should usually be set to zero. The Limiter section can be switched on or off, although you'll probably always have it on. The Attack and release controls, like the Compressor, determine how quickly limiting is applied and how long before the limiter lets the sound pass through without affecting it. Here. There are three buttons, Fast, Slow and Auto. If in doubt, the Auto setting makes Reason adapt to the material automatically.

The Look Ahead control causes the Maximizer to analyze the signal it's about to receive and check for peaks up to 4ms ahead of what's currently playing. The idea is that if it detects any it is able to adapt its gain reduction accordingly and rein in the peaks without any obvious jerky compression effects. It's a good idea to leave this on.

The Soft Clip control works by adding a warm sounding distortion the peaks in the sound. It also acts as a "brick wall" limiter, ensuring no signal over 0db passes through. Use the Soft Clip Amount knob to adjust the tonal characteristics of the soft clip effect.

Of course all these modules work together to affect the finished sound of your music. Making changes in one will affect the way the others respond, so mastering really is a balancing act. The Presets are an excellent starting point, and in many cases will just need tweaking rather than radically altering to give you a great sound. If you want to see just how much the Mastering effects are adding to your music, try temporarily bypassing them and you'll see much of the life, energy and sparke disappear until you re-activate them.

As good as the MClass effects are, you may still want to import your mixes into another software package and experiment with other mastering tools, or indeed take them to a professional mastering facility. At the end of the day whatever works best for you is the right thing to go with. Reason may do you proud, or you may find that another option for adding that finished sparkle is what does it for you. Either way, it's nice to have the option to do it in Reason.

The BV512 Vocoder

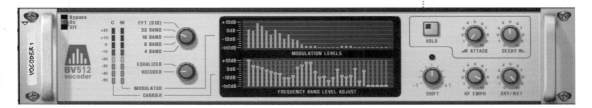

From its inception as a research tool at Bell Labs in the 1930s, the vocoder has remained an important part of the electronic musician's sonic arsenal, and thus a logical extension of the Reason rack. Whether stolid studio-bound musique concréte in the 50s, classical crossover courtesy of Wendy Carlos in the late 60s, or what some might term pop music hell in the 70s, the vocoder has had a place. It seems never to have gone truly out of fashion, and even now, is a recognisable and valid part of many contemporary music styles. Daft Punk is just one name from the last few years who have used the tool, their slightly ironic take on futuristic retro sounds. You'll know the sound: it's a bit steam driven, with the other-worldly, breathy effect of a machine speaking or singing. Many classic BBC theme tunes produced by the late Radiophonic Workshop feature vocoding, and the device can be heard on tracks by Pink Floyd, ELO, Laurie Anderson and Devo.

So what was, and is, a vocoder? First of all, its an acronym, though whether the source phrase is VOice EnCODER or Voice Operated reCOrDER is open to some debate. Its developer, one Homer Dudley, didn't mean to create a musical effect, but a tool to help with research into reduced bandwidth speech transmission over long-distance phone lines. (Dudley was also behind an uncanny keyboard-controlled speech synthesizer called the voder.) The effect can be heard on movie soundtracks over the next few years – including Disney cartoons! – in more of a sound design context. But a meeting between Dudley and electronic music pioneer Werner Meyer-Eppler, then the Director of Phonetics at Bonn University, after the war led the vocoder towards more musical settings. Meyer-Eppler, a major inspiration for the coming German Electronische Musik movement, and his use of the vocoder influenced , and established it as a musical tool.

The device was actually called a parallel bandpass vocoder, which gives us a few clues as to how it does its job. It enables the tonal character of one sound to be imposed on another. In most past cases, a speaking or singing human voice would be imposed on a sustained synth sound. The words, timbre and texture comes from the voice, but the pitch (which could be a monophonic line or chords) come from the synth. Technically, the voice is called the modulator in the process, and is continually analysed by a bank of filters. The synth, dubbed the carrier, also passes through a bank of filters, but the level of each band in this bank changes in response to the output from the analysic filter bank. The spectral – and thus timbral – characteristics of the modulator filter bank are duplicated in the carrier bank and thus applied to the carrier signal. With speech, you'll hear words spoken by the carrier, which can be quite weird. Two points: the more filter bands a vocoder is equipped with (classic examples tend to have 12 bands or more), the more accurate the result; and the modulator doesn't need to be in tune in any way since only its spectral characteristics are being nicked by the filter banks.

BV512 basics

Propellerhead's interpretation of the vocoder, the BV512, initially appears to be a bit of a conundrum. It's one of the better-specified examples to be found in software, with a maximum 0f 32 band vocoding and a 512-band fast fourier transform (FFT) option (more soon). It is also lacking the one thing that nearly every other vocoder has: a real world audio input. The effect tends to be real time, with people singing live as they play an integral or external keyboard to produce the carrier pitch. Reason currently has no audio input capabilities, but the BV512 can do everything else just fine. There's also the quetion of whether a vocoder is an effect or an instrument. It certainly processes audio, but the way in which it interacts with audio is different, becoming part of a performance, or patch if you like. It also has options for playing the frequency bands form a MIDI keyboard, which adds to the fuzziness.

If you want the classic singing synth effect, play back samples of speech from an NN19, NNXT or Dr:Rex with a SubTractor or Malström as carrier. But the beauty of this device is that any sound can be a modulator and any sound can be a carrier. there are no fixed assignments, and no internal sound source. So, should you wish to impose the sound of a distorted indistrial drum kit onto a gentle ethereal pad, then go right ahead.

Details are on their way, but it's worth knowing that Propellerhead have gone that extra mile again with the BV512: powerful vocoder it might be, but flick a switch and it becomes a precise equaliser, with four, eight, 16 or 32 steep, fixed frequency low pass filter bands – again with a 512-band FFT option. In this mode, only the carrier input is used; the modulator is ignored. The frequency bands aren't quoted by Propellerhead – use your ear – but with this tool, you'll be able to slice your audio very precisely indeed whether you're working with EQ for corrective or creative purposes. Examples will arise, but lets just mention that you can cut out everything in the audio signal except the rhythmic hiss of hi hats or the dull rumbling thump of a kick drum.

Try this

To get a feel for the classic vocoded effect, let's have an example. There's no ideal way with Reason, since there isn't much ready-made material of a vocal nature. So, start with your empty rack. Add an NN19 sampler and a Matrix

BV512 vocoding demo

pattern sequencer, ensuring their gate and CV connections are linked. Into the NN19, load the FemaleAHH patch from the Voice folder in the the Reason Factory Sound Bank's NN19 Sampler Patches collection.

Now, program a part in the Matrix sequencer; the example just used repeating 'C' notes for all 16 steps. You might like to play with the NN19 patch's polyphony and amplitude envelope settings to make it sound a little more natural.

Now load a Dr:Rex, and from the Browse Loop button, surf through Music Loops to Variable Tempo, to Downtempo Loops. there are some nice impressionistic pad textures here; the example used 100_DreamPad_mlp_eLAB. Ensuring that the Dr:Rex's track is selected in the sequencer, press the 'To Track' button, to enable this loop to play back when you hit Play on the sequencer transport. You might like to change the song's tmepo to 100bpm, to suite 100bpm loop we've just loaded.

The next step is to load a BV512 into the rack. Flip the rack to the rear, and eliminate any automatic connections, unless they happen to be correct! The correct connections for the first part of the example are to route the output from the Dr:Rex to the carrier input on the vocoder, then connect the left output of the NN16 to the modulator input.

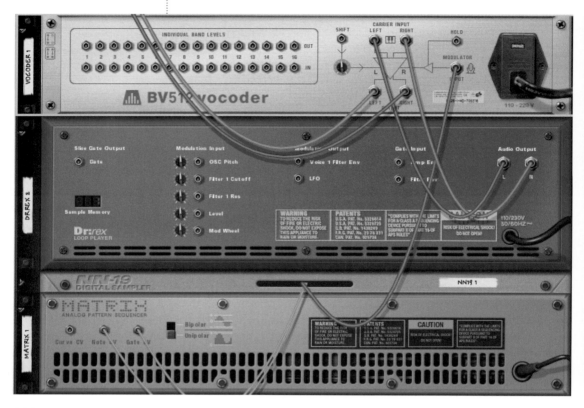

BV512 vocoding demo rear panel

All being well, pressing play on the sequencer will let you hear the pad riff taking on some vocal-like texture, as well as the voice part's rhythm, though the pitch will be that of the REX loop. You'll be able to hear the sound of the Dr:Rex – the carrier – by popping the BV512 into bypass, and the modulating NN16 voices by shifting the Dry/Wet control to fully dry. You might find that the effect is more pronounced if you select the four band option. Further timbral changes can be made by selecting different numbers of bands and 'drawing' slider changes in the lower half of the central display, and moving the Shift parameter.

For a different take on the effect, stop playback, go to the back panel again, and swap the connections, so that the NN19 is carrier and Dr:Rex modulator. Not quite as good, but a step towards using the BV512 in unusual ways where you're free to choose which audio is modulator and which carrier.

Then try this

Just add a ReDrum or Dr:Rex to your rack, and then a vocoder. If the wiring hasn't happened already, go the rear and patch the stereo out from your device of choice to the modulator inputs of the vocoder. Now, back at the front load a drum kit and create a pattern (if you've selected the ReDrum), or load a drum-based rhythmic loop from the factory ReFill into Dr:Rex. (Make sure you 'To Track' the loop so that it'll play back when you press play.)

After telling the BV512 to be an equalizer, select 32-band or FFT mode (though this mode does induce a small delay that'll be obvious with drums), and hit play on the sequencer. You'll just hear drums. Grad the mouse, and click and sweep across the lower part of the BV512's display, moving all the little fades to zero – the bottom of their travel. You'll hear nothing. Now carefully raise individual sliders, or groups of sliders, and hear what happens. You'll gradually hear low frequencies build up to the kick part of the drum pattern as you raise sliders from the left, and the hi hat as you raise sliders from the right. A little practice, and you'll discover which sliders help you isolate which frequency bands more effectively.

This technique can be expanded, to really isolate frequency bands in mixes or samples – dance-oriented devices have similar tools that allow DJs to isolate bits of tracks so that they can be more easily matched and remixed on the fly.

Guided tour

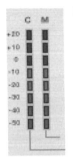

BV512 level meters

Bypass switch
As with the effects devices, the BV512 has a bypass switch. When the device is functioning as a vocoder, In bypass mode, the carrier signal passes unscathed while the modulator is muted in bypass mode; if it's an equaliser, you can use the switch to A/B treated and untreated audio. 'Off' switches the device off entirely.

Level meters
Tri-coloured bar graphs, labelled C and M, which monitor the level of the carrier and modulator signals respectively.

Band switch
Select the number of bands used for processing, in either vocoder or EQ mode. The options are four, eight, sixteen, 32 and FFT. The last, fast fourier transform, mode is a 1024-point process that's not based on bandpass filters at all, though it does represent 512 frequency bands. It's best suited to speech or vocals, were very clear results, with good intelligibility is produced, at the expense of a little (20mS) processing delay. This delay makes FFT mode unsutiable for time-dependent audio such as drums and so on.

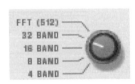

BV512 band switch

Equalizer/vocoder switch
Simply switches between vocoder and equaliser modes.

EQ/vocoder switch

Modulation level display
This is the upper part of the central display, and shows the spectrum of the modulator as a dynamic, moving display.

Modulation level display

Frequency band level adjust
The lower part of the central display provides control over the level of all filter bands – there are four, eight, sixteen or 32 sliders depending on the mode you've chosen. Moving them accentutates or attenuates a

Frequency band level adjust

given frequency band – and as we'll discover, each slider can be automated. This changes the output vocoded sound, or curs/boost frequencies in EQ mode. If you're using the FFT option, you don't all of a sudden get 512 frequency sliders to play with! Rather, each slider/band represents several frequency bands, and bars to the right control inbcreasing numbers of bands due to the FFT frequency ranges being distributed in a linear fashion over the whole frequency range.

Hold button

Hold button

Enabling this button freezes the current filter setting, disabling the modulator signal and filtering the carrier with the settings as indicated by the 'frozen' display. Hold is also automatically turned off when you stop the sequencer, and has no function in EQ mode.

Attack

Attack knob

Only available in vocoder mode, this parameters works on all envelope followers at once. A value of zero causes the vocoder to respond as fast it can – the most desireable option, most of the time. Altering the attack creates a less defined effect, good for creating pad-line sounds.

Decay

Decay knob

Only available in vocoder mode, and again controls the decay time – how quickly a filter band level drops – for all the envelope followers.

Shift

Shift knob

The carrier filter frequencies can be shifted up or down with this control, which changes the character of the vocoded or EQ'd sound, rather as if one was working with the carrier's formants. Automate or tweak in real time for unusual sweeping effects.

High Frequency Emphasis

HF Emphasis knob

A carrier signal's high frequencies can be boosted with this control, contributing to a clearer vocoded sound. Especially useful when a carrier is lacking in brightness. Only functions in Vocoder mode.

Dry/Wet

Dry/Wet knob

Turn fully to 'wet' to hear just vocoder sound. Any other position mixes in some of the modulator signal. Only available in vocoder moder.

The rear panel

Audio inputs

There are three audio inputs in all. The carrier inputs take the fom of a stereo pair, though a mono signal can be modulator if its plugged into the left input. If you do have a mono modulator, the vocoded output will also be in mono.. In equalizer mode, the carrier input is route to the EQ section. The thrid input is the sole modulator socket; its mono only, and has no function when the BV512 is in EQ mode.

Rear panel

Audio outputs

There's just one stereo output pair, and this can be routed where you like, a with any other Reason device: it's own ReMix channel or in-line effects, for example. It carries either a mix between the vocoded audio and the modulator signal (balanced by the Dry/Wet fornt panel control), or EQ's audio in equalizer mode.

CV inputs and outputs

The BV512 has rather a lot of CV ins and outs due to the fact that there are no fewer than 16 of each dedicated to individual band levels alone. CV levels generated by the vocoder's envelope followers are output by the top row; these signals are further shaped by the front panel Attack and Decay controls. Send these to any available CV destination in the Reason rack for filter, pan, level andother modulations that echo what's happening in the vocoder, often in a subtle manner. External CVs can be routed to the individual bandpass filters, controlling their level rather than the envelope followers. Your vocoder would then be using control voltages as modulators rather than audio. Interestingly, the top row can be patched to the bottom row, so that the envelope followers don't necessarily control the frequency band it's normally hard-wired to. There aren't enough CV ins and outs to accommodate 32 bands – let alone 512! – so each pair controls or generates CVs from groups of frequencies. If your chosen operating mode has less thanh 16 bands, then only the requisite number of CV connections will be active.

In addition, there's a Shift CV input, with trim pot, so that this useful parameter can be automated or modulated from elswehere in the rack.

Gate inputs

There's just one gate input here, controlling the Hold parameter. Triggered frequency freezes can produce interesting rhythmic textures – route gate outs from ReDrum voice channels, or from the Matrix.

Going further

Because everything is just a mouse, or a MIDI controller away, real time control of BV512 functions is not only easy but begging to be exploited. The repatching possible on the back panel also helps subvert what we usually expect a vocoder to be. Unexpected spectral changes and sweeps are a few virtual patch cables away.

Vocoders tend to be honds on real time processors, and while that's not strictly possible with the BV512, there is one real time aspect: create a sequencer track, assign the BV512 as that track's output and make it active for MIDI playing. Now use your master keyboard to play the mod gain amount for up to 32 bandsremote control. The action starts at MIDI note 36 (C two octaves below middle C), and goes up chromatically. The harder you play, the higher the level of the 'triggered' filter band.

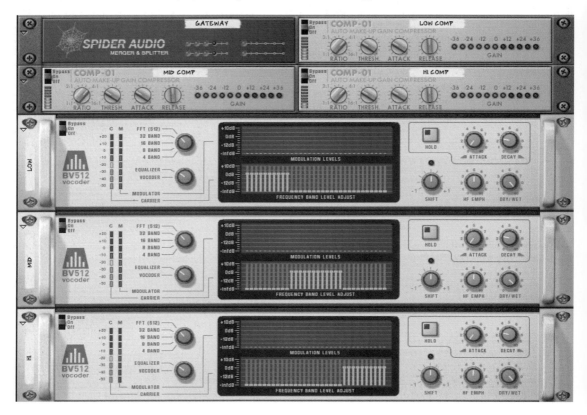

Multiband front panel

If you're excited by the possibilities offered by the 512's equalizer mode, then have a visit to Propellerhead's web site. One their many on-line tutorials stretches this mode to the limite. Mastering has always been a something Reason users would like to do within their favourite sotfware, but the tools aren't really up to it – until now. The technique in question uses a Spider Audio, a BV512 in EQ mode and a handful of COMP01 compressors to create a multi-band compressor. In this way three separate frequency bands of your mix or any bit of audio in the rack can be compressed separately, just as if you were using an expensive add-on plug-in or external hardware.

You'll need to add one Spider Audio, three BV512s and three COMP01s. Route the audio from your main ReMix to the Spider's splitter circuit, and route three of the outputs to one BV512 each. Patch the output of each 512 to a COMP01, and then send the COMP01 outputs to the Spider Audio's merge ciruit. The merged output should go to the connections 1 and 2 (the main stereo out) on the Hardware Interface. Now, label each 512/COMP01 pair something like Low, Mid and High so you can keep track of what's going on from the front panel – the mass of cablinge makes it busy at the back, but it's just a rack of hardware at the front!

Multiband rear panel

First, makes sure all three BV512s are set to Equalizer mode, and that the FFT option is selected. Now, for the BV512 labelled 'Low', move all but the bottom ten sliders to zero – the bottom of their travel. With the Mid unit, move all but the middle twelve to zero, and for the High equalizer, leave only the top ten sliders active. You can leave the COMP01s as they are right now, and have a listen to your mix. A/B'ing may be a little tricky, but you will hear a difference. Play with the COMP controls to compress the different bands differently, and also play with the frequency levels on each 'band' of our virtual multiband compressor. You might also like to play with different bands of frequencies, and even make a four-band processor! it's all very complicated, but minimising all the units being used can make the rack look less busy. And of course, you can download a little RNS file from www.propellerheads.se that contains all the routings ready made: just highlight and cut and paste the setup to any song where you'd like to use it – or make it a permanent part of your default song. Have all the BVs and COMP01s bypassed until you're ready to mix, though, so you don't get a false impression of the mix while its in progress.

Using just one BV512 as a mix processor is valid, too: in FFT mode especially, you'll find that tweaking the upper frequency band controls may help to bring out a vocal or solo instrument in an otherwise muddy mix, and the lower bands will certainly help add depth, kick and presence. The mid bands are probably best avoided on mixes until you've got a handle on what's going on sonically, expect perhaps for cutting mid bands on a mix that's a bit 'honky'.

But remember that although speech and a synth pad might be the classic modulator/carrier pairing, in Reason anything can modulate anything. There are no input level controls, though, so be prepared to manage most audio distortion issues from the source devices. Beyond that, carry on vocoding!

Spiders

Many longstanding Reason users felt that early versions of the software lacked one simple, but really desirable, feature: a way to route a CV or gate output to more than one destination. In classical modular analogue synthesis, this would be quite a common facility, especially in larger systems, using the so-called 'mult'(iple) module. This module would simply offer several jack sockets wired together so that one gate or CV could be easily routed to multiple destinations, to trigger multiple envelopes, play several oscillators from one keyboard or sequencer, or route modulation CVs to more than one target. A simple module perhaps, but one that opened up many opportunities for creative sound design.

With Reason V2.5, the situation changed. The software's flexible gate and CV interconnection system becomes even moreso thanks to a new device dubbed Spider. And that's not all: Spider not only provides gate and CV splitting capabilities, but Propellerhead have designed it to merge control signals. It doesn't stop there, either, since Spider is actually the overall name for two modules, and the second splits and merges audio signals. You just have to know that these modules, as simple as they seem, are going to be the inspiration for a lot of fun and creativity.

Both Spider CV and Spider Audio are simple devices in concept, and simple in design. Each takes up just half a Reason rack space, has flow charts and a few activity LEDs on their front panels, with all connections taking place at the rear. If the merging and splitting offered by one Spider isn't enough, then chain them. Doing so incurs no delays, and there is little impact on your CPU overheads whether you use one or several Spiders in a Reason session.

Spider CV

Spider's splitting capabilities enable it to allow one Matrix step sequencer to play up to three SubTractors Malströms, NN19s and/or NNXTs. The Spider CV offers two splitting circuits, each of which takes a CV or gate input and mults it to

three outputs. Use Split A and Split B, as they're labelled, to route CVs and gates respectively to multiple sound sources. But of course, any gate or CV can be multed in this way, so that modulation CVs can be routed to destinations across several devices and gates can be set to trigger sounds or other effects in synchrony. Now, whenever you want to create tempo-sync'd effects, you'll be able to apply them from one central CV source, whether that's an LFO or Matrix modulation curve or any other source. Just set one LFO, for example, rather than having to edit the LFO on several devices.

Additionally, each circuit has a fourth, inverted, output, a subtle difference which adds even more to the creative potential – an inverted LFO moves in the opposite way to its standard cousin. Similar patches could have, say, filter cutoff being modulated in opposite directions from one LFO. This could be an LFO on one of the two devices (most devices have an LFO CV output), a free-running LFO on a device that's not being used for audio, or a Matrix CV curve creating pattern-style modulation. The resulting texture can have more interest and movement than basic layering of LFOs, and impression that can be enhanced by panning opposite swoop effects to panned left and right, and adding different effect treatments.

Merging of up to four gate and/or CV sources to one destination might initially seem a little harder to come to terms with, but why not? In practice, this slightly esoteric option will provide you with the chance to create effects with CV-controlled parameters that are more unpredictably rhythmically than, say, with even a random LFO waveform. This is especially the case if the two LFO waveforms you're mixing are themselves are random (choose the sample and hold option if available). Mixing modulations sources – LFOs – can also produce more satisfyingly complex results, adding movement within a sound that wouldn't be otherwise possible. it certainly opens up modulation potential not available on most modern synths.

Merging modulation CVS with those destined to control notes on synth or sampler devices can also produce interesting, if often unpredictable results. Semi-random transpositions can be created, though in some cases the options are better suited to live performance, in spite of trouble necessary to control some on-screen elements with a mouse. For example, lets merge a bipolar Curve CV from one Matrix with a note CV generated by a second Matrix: for the merge input being used by the note CV generated by the second Matrix, turn its merge input amount knob on the back of the Spider CV fully right, and set the knob for the Matrix Curve CV merge input to 32. Set all Matrix curve steps to the central line, for no transposition. Experiment with a one step pattern first, and write a pattern in the second Matrix. Its Gate CV is patched the gate CV input of a Subtractor, Malström or NN19, say, and the merged CV from the Spider CV is routed to the Note CV input. As the pattern plays back, move the curve CV up and down; if you're careful, you'll hear semitone transpositions. Extend this by adding more steps to the curve CV Matrix, with a step resolution of 1/4 or 1/2, adjusting the transposition for each curve step.

Spider CV Facilities

There are no controls on the front panel of Spider CV.

• Signal Indicators for Merged CVs: The CV signals routed to the merge

circuit's inputs cause virtual LEDs to flash when
activity is present.

Spider CV rear panel

- Signal Indicators for Split CVs: Each of the two
  incoming CVs causes a virtual LED to flash
  when signal is present.
- Merging Connections: On the rear, four virtual jack sockets merge into
  one.
- Merging input trim pots: Each merging input connection is equipped with
  its own offset knob that controls the depth of the CV signal being
  merged.
- Splitting Connections: There are two splitting circuits, arranged as an
  input socket, three straight outputs and an inverted output.

Spider Audio

Being able to split and merge audio with a
dedicated device – both actions were sort of
possible if you got creative with pre-V2.5
effects devices – is a surprisingly useful
option. There will often be times when you'd

Spider audio front panel

like to mix the outputs of several devices where you'd rather not give up the
rack space and computer CPU overhead to a ReMix mixer. For example, if
you're using multiple Dr:Rex devices to play back a selection of related loops
– one bar each of a chord progression, say – it might be handy to be able to
sub-mix their outputs before routing them to ReMix. In normal circumstances, each Dr:Rex would take up its own mixer channel, and you'd have
to set up level, EQ and effects settings multiple times – in most circumstances, these setting should probably be the same for related audio. Submix them with a Spider Audio, route its single output to one ReMix channel,
and you can control the sound of the aggregate Dr:Rex collection as if it were
a single device. This simple device saves your rack space, CPU overhead, and
mouse time all in one half rack package.

Anywhere that you might like to route audio – whether that's effects,
Combis, ReMix, Malström's audio ins or the BV512 vocoder – may benefit
from having audio mixed before routing, either for convenience or creativity.

Splitting audio has its uses, as illustrated in the effect devices chapter.
Take one mono, two mono or one stereo input, and route it to as many as
four different effects chains – or vocoders! – for some complex parallel processing. A mono input, such as generated by SubTractor, is automatically
routed to left and right outs of the splitting circuit. If you input two mono signals, they'll be split to two independent chains of four mono outs. With
Reason's automation system, it would be possible to switch instantly between
each chain, to create special effects and a more dynamic mix from fewer
musical elements. Of course, you could also remix the outputs from parallel
effects chains with the Spider Audio's merging circuit, if you didn't need the
automation option. As any guitarist will tell you, parallel effects sound different from the same processors in a normal chain.

Spider audio rear panel

Spider Audio Facilities

There are no controls on the front panel of Spider Audio

- Signal indicators for Merged Audio: Stereo virtual LED pairs flash when audio is present at the corresponding merging input.
- Signal Indicators for Split Audio: The audio being split causes the virtual input LED monitor to flash.
- Merging Connections: Four stereo pairs of virtual jacks are merged to one stereo output pair.
- Splitting Connections: Configured as two mono splitting circuits or a single stereo splitting circuit, labelled A (L) and B (R), two rows of jacks each offer one input routed to four output jacks.

The Sequencer

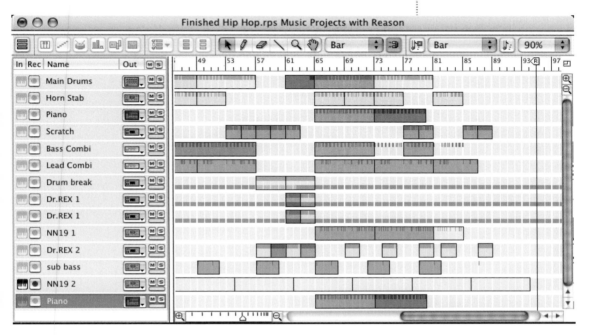

For many musicians, Reason's sequencer will be enough to ensure that, unless they need to record audio, there is no need to go outside the program for MIDI recording and arranging facilities. The sound sources in the Reason rack can be used to create sophisticated tracks with this device, and since it also provides the means to record and edit automation data, in many ways it's the hub of Reason activity.

Sequencer basics

For those not familiar with modern sequencers, their primary job is to let you build up a musical arrangement by recording tracks of MIDI performances, allow those tracks to be played back together, to make a 'multitrack' sequence, and provide facilities for editing pretty much every aspect of the tracks. This would include notes (to correct playing errors or make a performance sound different), timing (to 'quantise' sloppily-played notes so that their timing is tightened, or creatively alter playback timing), velocity and other MIDI controllers. The sequencer also allows tracks to be cut into sections, which can be moved or copied elsewhere for rapid re-arranging.

The sequencer window in its 'rack' position.

Reason's sequencer is functionally similar to other professional MIDI sequencers, except that it doesn't transmit MIDI data outside the system (it controls only the devices in the Reason rack), and has a reduced feature set

Info

Keyboard Shortcuts

Option/Alt-click 'M' column in track list Solo track

Toggles
Apple/Control-1 Toggle small/no sequencer display
Apple/Control-2 Toggle small/full sequencer display
Shift+Tab or Apple/Control-E Toggle Arrange/Edit view
Apple/Alt Toggle Selection/Pencil tool

Event editing
Apple/Control-G Group selected events
Apple/Control-U Ungroup selected events
Shift-draw/resize Group Disable snap of Group end
Shift-move notes/Groups Constrain to horizontal or vertical
Apple/Control-K Quantise selected notes
Option/Control+ move data Copy data instead of moving it

Controller viewing
Option/Alt-click device control Show controller lane in Edit View
Option/Alt-click Lane button in Edit View Show selected lane only (hide others)

Locators
Option/Control-click in ruler Set Left Locator position
Command/Alt-click in ruler Set Right Locator position
Shift-click in ruler Set End Marker position

Magnify tool
Option/Control-click with Magnify tool Zooms out instead of in
Shift-click with Magnify tool Restricts zooming to the horizontal

For sequencer-transport shortcuts, see the Transport Shortcuts box later in the chapter.

---

in comparison with the major MIDI + Audio sequencing packages, such as Cubase, Logic and Sonar, making it rather easier to use. It offers as many tracks as you want and will automatically create a sequencer track for every new sound-making device and Matrix pattern sequencer you add to the rack. You can of course add tracks of your own – for example, if you need to automate ReMix mixer parameters, you create a sequencer track for the mixer, into which automation data for mixer parameters is recorded.

The sequencer is presented in two different views: the Arrange view, where you can see an entire arrangement with all its constituent tracks at the same time; and the Edit view, where you may examine and edit one track at a time in detail. Different 'zoom' levels are available to let you display the data at a size that best suits your purpose.

The sequencer window can occupy as much or as little space on your screen as you like: drag it up or down in the rack to reveal more or less of it (you can hide it behind the Transport

Sequencer Track for Scratch Sequencer Track
Create Device by Browsing Patches...
Combinator
Mixer 14:2 Line Mixer 6:2
SubTractor Analog Synthesizer Malstrom Graintable Synthesizer NN19 Digital Sampler NN–XT Advanced Sampler Dr.REX Loop Player Redrum Drum Computer
MClass Mastering Suite Combi MClass Equalizer MClass Stereo Imager MClass Compressor MClass Maximizer
RV7000 Advanced Reverb Scream 4 Distortion BV512 Digital Vocoder
RV-7 Digital Reverb DDL-1 Digital Delay Line D-11 Foldback Distortion ECF-42 Envelope Controlled Filter CF-101 Chorus/Flanger PH-90 Phaser UN-16 Unison COMP-01 Compressor/Limiter PEQ-2 Two Band Parametric EQ
Spider Audio Merger & Splitter Spider CV Merger & Splitter
Matrix Pattern Sequencer ReBirth Input Machine

Device context menus have a 'Create Sequencer Track' option.

if you like) or use Apple/Control-2 to make it fill the screen. It's also possible to tear off the sequencer window completely (using the 'Detach Sequencer Window' command under the Windows menu, or the 'Detach Sequencer' Button) and display it in a different position on the screen, or even on another monitor altogether. The sequencer window can also be resized to fill your whole screen (drag the edge to enlarge, as you would any other window, or use standard maximise/minimise methods).

Some basic operations

Creating a track

When you create a sound-making device, a sequencer track should be automatically made for it. If you need to create an additional track, use 'Sequencer Track' under the Create menu or 'Create Sequencer Track' from a sequencer Context menu (Control/right mouse-click in the sequencer). If you do it the latter way, you will have to assign the track to the desired device by clicking on the arrow in the Track list to summon a device pop-up. An option in each device's Context menu, labelled 'Create Sequencer Track for...', creates a specific track which you don't have to assign, for that device.

Deleting a track

Select the track name and hit backspace on the computer keyboard. You may also use 'Delete' in the Context menu or the Edit menu. If a device is assigned to the track, you will see a dialogue asking if you want to delete the device as well as the track. You may delete both, or just delete the track and keep the device.

Re-ordering tracks

Click on the track name and drag the track to wherever you want it in the track list. Move multiple tracks by shift-clicking them and dragging en masse.

Recording into a track

See the MIDI recording tutorial later in this chapter.

Editing MIDI parts

See 'Some typical editing examples' later in this chapter.

Guided tour

The Transport Bar

The Transport bar is a permanent part of the Reason rack – it can't be removed – and has facilities that are used by all the devices in the rack. However, it is probably used the most by the sequencer. It offers the following:

Transport controls and Locator position display

- *Transport controls:* Play (arrow), Stop (square), forward Fast Wind and reverse Fast Wind (double arrow) controls, and a red Record button, are provided. Use these to initiate recording (press Record, then Play), stop recording, and navigate through Songs. Alternatively, use the transport keyboard shortcuts.

- *Locator Position Display:* This 3-segment 'POS' display shows, in bars, beats and 16th notes, where the sequencer's Position cursor is currently located within a Song. A location of 3 3 2, for example, would mean that the Position cursor was at bar 3, beat 3, second sixteenth note of that beat. The calibration of this display does not change with sequencer grid resolution. As well as dragging the cursor in the sequencer display to set a new position, you can also enter numerical values into the 'POS' display (by double-clicking and entering a value in the pop up that appears, or by dragging the number with your mouse) to send the cursor to a new location. Wherever the Position Locator is, that's where the Song will play back from.
- *Click button and Level control:* The Click button enables a metronome click, to aid timing while playing. One click per beat, with an accent on the downbeat, is heard as the Song plays back. The Level control changes the volume of the click.

Click button and Level control knob

- *Tempo Display:* Set Song tempo with the arrows next to this display, or click in the display and drag up or down to change the value. Tempo range is 1 to 999.999 beats per minute. Reason does not have a tempo map facility, so you won't easily be able to change tempo within a Song, unless you sync the sequencer as a slave to another sequencer that does have a tempo map facility. Slaving to another sequencer is discussed in the chapter that covers using Reason with other software and instruments. Also look for a workaround later in the chapter that allows you to create the impression of a tempo change.

Tempo/time signature

- *Time Signature Display:* Time signatures of between 1/2 and 16/16 can be set via this display. Any value between 1 and 16 is available for the first figure (the 2 in 2/4, for example), but only values of 2, 4, 8 and 16 are available for the second. Time signature is set globally for the Song – it is not changeable per bar, for example.
- *Overdub/Replace switch:* Sets recording mode to Overdub, in which new material recorded as a sequencer loop cycles is simply added to the older material on the same track; or Replace, in which the older material is replaced by the new material. Obviously, you'll want to be careful with Replace mode, to avoid losing material you want.
- *Loop On/Off button:* Enables the recording/playback loop, whose boundaries are set by the Left and Right Locators in the sequencer display. Setting a loop allows you to easily work on one section of a Song.
- *Loop Position Display:* This display has a Left and a Right row of digits, showing (respectively) the positions of the Left and Right Locators, in terms of bars, beats and sixteenth-notes, as with the Position cursor. Change values in these displays to move the Locators, as an alternative to dragging them in the display, or using the keyboard shortcuts listed near the start of the chapter.

Loop button and loop position

- *Automation Override Section:* This area comes into play when controls on a device have been automated. As a Song is being played back and

Automation override section

automation moves are being reproduced on the automated device, the automated controls may still be grabbed and moved, overriding the recorded automation data. This is especially useful in 'live' operation, where you may wish to make spontaneous changes during Song playback. The red 'Punched In' LED lights if recorded automation is overridden in this way. Normal (recorded) automation operation can be resumed by clicking the 'Reset' button. See the automation chapter for more.

Pattern shuffle control

• *Pattern Shuffle Control:* As mentioned in the ReDrum and Matrix chapters, this knob sets the amount of 'Shuffle' feel to be applied to Patterns on these devices. In the sequencer, it is used in conjunction with the Shuffle Quantize option, to set the amount of Shuffle applied to selected data.

• *MIDI Sync:* Click this button if Reason is to be sync'd with an external MIDI device such as a sequencer or drum machine. When Reason is sync'd in this way, the Play button in the Transport bar does not function. Play must be initiated from the other device (the Master), since Reason always operates as the Slave when sync'd externally. The green LED flashes when sync information is being received. (See the chapter on using Reason with other software and instruments for more.)

Midi sync and focus

• *Focus:* The two buttons labelled MIDI and Play in the Focus section are used to determine how multiple simultaneously-open Reason Songs behave. If MIDI Sync is not enabled, the top Song always has 'MIDI Focus' – it's the one that will be addressed by your master keyboard and edited by your hardware controller box, if one is connected. If, however, you are using MIDI Sync, enabling both MIDI and Play Focus in a Song causes all incoming MIDI data and sync to be sent to that Song even if it's not the topmost open file.

It is also possible, when sync'ing to MIDI clock, to give one Song MIDI Focus and another Play Focus. In this case, the Song with MIDI Focus can be played and controlled by your MIDI hardware, and the Song with Play Focus will play back in response to incoming MIDI sync. Thus, you can have two instances of Reason playing at the same time, albeit with one functioning as a sound module only – a facility that could potentially be useful when using Reason in a live situation: the Song being sync'd would be like a backing track, while the other Song could be jammed and improvised with in real time over the top. At one time it was planned that Reason would have more live-specific features, and the 'Focus' options are left over from those early developments. Note that enabling MIDI Sync on one Song enables it on all open Songs, and that enabling MIDI and Play Focus in one Song disables them in all others.

Maximum visibility in the rack can be attained by 'folding' the Transport, using the small arrow between the two rack screws on its left-hand side. This comes in handy when you start editing NNXT patches.

The rewind/forward wind controls do not work as you might expect from other sequencers. Keys 7 and 8 on the numeric keypad wind through the Song one bar at a time. If this is during playback, you will hear the winding occur. The Num Lock and '=' keys wind fast if the key is held down for two seconds, but playback continues as normal until you have reached the new desired playback point and released the key, whereupon playback goes from the new point.

Info

Sequencer Transport Shortcuts

Numeric Keypad		Main Keyboard	
Key	Function	Key	Function
Enter	Play	Space Bar	Play/Stop
'0'	Stop/return to zero (press twice for the latter)	Return	Stop/return to zero (press twice for the latter)
'*'	Engages Record mode. Press Enter to record	Apple/Control + Return	Engages Record mode. Press Space bar to
Num Lock	Rewind		record.
'='	Fast forward	Apple/Control + M	Toggles metronome click on/off
'/'	Turn loop on/off		
'1'	Go to loop start		
'2'	Go to loop end		
'7'	Go to previous bar/rewind (press repeatedly/hold)		
'8'	Go to next bar/forward wind (press repeatedly/hold)		
'+'	Increase tempo value		
'-'	Reduce tempo value		

The Arrange View

The Arrange View (see screen shot at the start of this chapter) allows you to get an overview of all the tracks in your arrangement and is divided into three distinct areas: on the left is the Track list; the track data-display grid is to the right of this; and running across the top of the screen is the Tool Bar where most operations and tools can be accessed. You can record material in either the Arrange or Edit view, but the Arrange view is likely to be the most convenient place for this.

The Track List

Each line in the Track List refers to one Reason device and comprises four columns:

The 'In' column

This is where you must click to enable MIDI input, and therefore MIDI recording, for the device assigned to that track.

Where this MIDI input comes from is determined by what you have previously set in the Control Surfaces preferences dialogue box, under Preferences in the Edit menu. Reason will automatically read from the specified Master keyboard you have connected for inputting notes into the sequencer.

Clicking in the 'In' column causes a keyboard icon to light, and until this icon appears the track will not be ready to accept input from your MIDI keyboard. This is therefore the first thing to check if you don't hear anything when you play a note.

The 'In' column also provides a way to see whether Reason is receiving MIDI data from your keyboard: with the keyboard icon showing, play some notes, and if all is well a small green meter under the M and S buttons will show activity. If the keyboard icon is showing and you can't get the meter to appear when you play, something is set incorrectly in Preferences, or there's an improper connection between your keyboard and the computer.

Track List

It's only possible to make the keyboard icon appear on one track at a time, because you can only record MIDI notes on one track at a time.

The Rec column

New in V3, this column indicates not that the track is record enabled, but that automation is record enabled for the track. The keyboard icon, which can only be active on one track at once, shows that MIDI notes will be recorded on that track. However the Rec button can be activated for multiple tracks. This means that parameter changes (not note data) can be recorded on all those tracks which are Record enabled. There are many applications for this. For example, if you're recording in a loop and want to tweak the controls of many modules without stopping and re-focusing MIDI, just record enable several tracks and as you play back, use the mouse or a control surface to make the changes. This helps you keep a vibe going without having to keep stopping.

Another use is through Remote. With a number of control surfaces connected and locked to various devices (see Remote section of Setup chapter), a number of people can record parameter changes and trigger Combinator patterns in realtime, all from the same project. So although you can't record multiple keyboard performances in realtime, you can record one (the master) plus many other hands-on changes from different people.

The Name column

Shows the name of the device assigned to that track – for example, Redrum 1 or Dr:rex 1 if the device is the first of its type added to the rack. If there is already a device of the same type in the rack, Reason will add a '2' to the device sequencer track name when a new device is made. When you create a sequencer track yourself from the Create menu or the sequencer Context menu, the track will be called 'New track' and will need assigning to a device (see next entry). Device Context menus also let you create a specific new track for the device.

Any track name may be changed by double-clicking it to bring up a pop-up, where you can type in a new name of up to 30 characters (but note that device 'scribble strips' can only accommodate 16 characters). When you change the name on a track that was created automatically by Reason (for all sound making devices) or was created by you using the Context menu for a specific device, this change is reflected in the name on the 'scribble-strip' of the assigned device. Likewise, if you change the name on a sound-making device for which Reason automatically made a sequencer track, the track name changes to reflect your new device name.

This relationship between custom device names and track names does not exist in the case of sequencer tracks you create yourself with any method other than the device-specific Context menu: if you want the device name and the track name to be the same in this case, you have to change both yourself.

The Out column

When a track has a device assigned to it, an icon of that device shows in the Out column next to the track name. The arrow next to the icon is where you must click if you want to assign that track to a different device. Clicking the arrow summons a pop-up containing a list of the names of every device currently in the rack, including mixers and effects.

You can select a new device for that track from the pop-up (if, for example, you want to hear the track played by a different instrument), or choose 'Disconnect'. The latter option means that the track will not play or control any device.

The 'M' (Mute) column

Click in the 'M' column to silence a track, stopping it from sounding when an arrangement is played back. Muting in this way only works for note data that has been recorded into the sequencer, not pattern chains that have been recorded to automate playback of ReDrum or Matrix patterns.

You can also 'solo' one or more tracks (make it/them play back alone, with the other tracks of the arrangement muted) here. Simply press the "S" button for the track. You can solo and mute non-sequential tracks. To un-mute or un-solo all tracks which are currently being affected, use the M and S buttons at the top of the entire column.

The Track Data Display

This area is where you will actually see the data that has been recorded into a track. Pitch is represented on the vertical axis and time on the horizontal. Data is colour-coded: in the Arrange View, notes display as small red vertical lines; pattern chains from the Matrix or Redrum show as thick horizontal bars in yellow; and controller data appears as horizontal blue bars. Note 'Groups' (more in a moment) show as colour-coded panels.

Across the top of the track data area is the ruler, which is marked out in terms of bars and beats, and helps you to keep track of where you are within a Song. You will also notice four thin vertical lines crossing the display, each topped with a small flag.

- *The Position cursor*, topped with a 'P' flag, moves across the track display as a Reason song plays. You can move the Position cursor manually by dragging its flag with the mouse, or changing its location in the 'POS' numeric display in the Transport bar. Pause the Position cursor in the midst of a song when you would like to stop by clicking the Transport Stop button. Return the Position cursor to the start of a Song (when the Song is not playing) by clicking the Stop button once or twice more. (There are also keyboard shortcuts for these actions; see box elsewhere in this chapter.) Note that the Position cursor can sometimes obscure one of the other locators, so if you think you've lost one, move the Position cursor and see if there's anything hiding under it!
- *The Left and Right locators*, topped with L and R flags, define Left and Right playback boundaries to make a loop. If, for example, you wished to set up a two-bar loop to play back repeatedly and help you record a new part, you would set the Left locator to the 'in' point, where you wanted the loop to begin, and position the Right locator at the 'out' point. The loop is only effective if the Loop On/Off button in the Transport bar is engaged. Move these locators by dragging, entering values into the POS display, or using Option/Control-clicking in the ruler to set the left locator and Command/Alt-clicking in the ruler to set the right one.
- *The End marker*, with an 'E' flag, shows the end of a Song. This information is used by the 'Export Song as Audio File' command to

Track assignment pop-up

Disconnect
MClass Mastering Suite Combi
M Comp 1
M EQ 1
M Stereo Imager 1
M Maximizer 1
Mixer 1
RV7000 3
M Comp 2
Main Drums
EQ 1
Scream 1
Horn Stab
RV7000 1
Piano
M Comp 1
RV7000 2
✓ Scratch
Bass Combi
Line Mixer 2
Delay 1

Seq mute and solo

Arrange data display

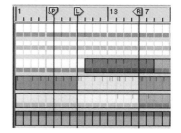

Tip

Fast rack navigation

Clicking on a sequencer track name automatically puts the device assigned to that track in front of you in the rack, which is a quick way of getting to a device if you want to edit it. An alternative is to Control/right-click in any device and select a new device from the 'Go To...' pop-up choice in the Context menu. The latter will only take you to a device that the selected device is connected to, either via audio or CV connection.

define what the end of the Song is considered to be. You may continue to record beyond the End marker, but if you then Export the Song, only its content up to the End marker will be exported. Move the end marker by dragging it or Shift-clicking in the ruler to set a new position for it.

The Zoom controls

Zoom controls, which look like magnifying glasses, are provided across the bottom of the track data display for zooming in and out on the horizontal scale, and in the top right-hand corner of the display for zooming vertically. Zoom in, making the data display larger, with the '+' control and out, making it smaller, with the '-' control.

The horizontal zoom function also has a slider, which you can drag to change zoom resolution; clicking in the slider area takes you instantly to a given zoom level. Zoom levels can be set independently for the Arrange and the Edit view.

Magnify Tool

Introduced in V2 of Reason was the magnifying tool, which will be discussed later in this chapter.

The Tool Bar in the Arrange View

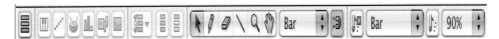

Not all the tools in the Tool Bar will be available to you in the Arrange View. The ones that are only relevant to the Edit View are greyed out while you use the Arrange View. Switch between the Arrange and Edit Views by clicking on the combined Arrange/Edit buttons to the far left of the Tool Bar (this toggles between Arrange and Edit Views), or – more conveniently – by using Shift-Tab on the computer keyboard to toggle the two Views.

The Selection tool

Choosing the Selection Tool allows you to select events in the track display area, so that you can edit or otherwise process them. Click on individual events, or draw a box (a 'selection rectangle') around several events, to select them.

Data highlight in grey when selected. Once highlighted, the events can be moved, cut or copied, and pasted. (Also see 'Selection and Snap to Grid', below.)

Drawing a selection rectangle to select events.

- *Move:* Select events and drag to the required location.
- *Cut:* Select events and use Apple/Control-X.
- *Copy:* Select events and drag while holding down the Option/Control key to copy to another location, on the same or a different track. Alternatively, select events

---

Zoom controls

Info

Cursor 'Follow'

In normal operation, the Position cursor follows the Song position as it plays back. You can disable this 'following' by using Apple/Control-F, or unchecking 'Follow Song' in the Options menu. If you find the cursor isn't moving along with Song position, you may have accidentally disabled 'Follow'.

Info

Automatic sequencer tracks

You can prevent Reason making a sequencer track for every new device you create by holding down Option (Mac) or Alt (PC) when you create the device. Do this if you know you won't need a sequencer track for the device – perhaps it's a pattern-based device whose own pattern-recording facilities you plan to use. Sequencer tracks are not automatically created for mixers and effects, but you can get an automatic track for these devices if you hold down Option or Alt when creating the device. In effect, Option/Alt reverses the usual relationship between devices and automatic sequencer tracks.

and use Apple/Control-C , to copy, then click in the ruler where you would like the data to appear and choose Apple/Control-V to paste. The latter method only pastes data within the same track from which it was copied.

- *Paste:* Click in the ruler at the location where you want to paste the data and use Apple/Control-V, or choose Paste from the Edit menu. This method pastes data only into the same track from which it was cut.
- *To select data across multiple tracks:* Click and drag down or up to encompass the desired tracks.
- *To select non-contiguous data:* Select the first event or events you require, highlighting them, then hold down the Shift key on your computer keyboard and select other data elsewhere on screen: it, too, will become highlighted, and you'll be able to drag, cut or copy the unconnected chunks as if they were one, even across tracks.

Selection and Snap to Grid

The selection rectangle can be 'quantised' to the current 'snap' value, if the tool bar's 'Snap to Grid' option is enabled. This makes it easy to select data in exact amounts. For example, if Snap to Grid is set to 'Bar', data will be selected to the nearest bar. You don't even have to drag the mouse to select the required area if Snap to Grid is active: just clicking in the display causes the bar (or whatever) to be selected. See 'The Snap Value pop-up' in a moment for setting Snap values.

Constraining selections

When you're using the Selection tool to move or copy data – whether to another point in the same track or to another track entirely – shift-dragging 'constrains' movement to the horizontal or vertical. This is useful if, for example, you would like to move a group of notes to another track, but want them to appear at the exact same bar and beat location.

Grouping Data

Data can also be 'Grouped', a helpful option which causes all the selected data to be treated as if it were one entity for the purposes of moving and editing.

To Group Select the required events with the Selection tool and use Apple/Control-G from the computer keyboard, or choose 'Group' from the Edit menu. (Alternatively, for contiguous data, draw a selection rectangle around the data with the Pencil tool to Group automatically.)

To Ungroup: Use Apple/Control-U, or choose 'Ungroup' from the Edit menu, to Ungroup the data.

The length of Groups may be changed by clicking and dragging the handle that appears when the Group is selected. Groups can only contain contiguous data from one track; a multi-track Group is not possible. You'll notice that Groups are colour-coded by the sequencer, but unfortunately the user has no control over how the colours are allocated.

The Pencil tool

Choose the Pencil tool and your mouse pointer becomes a pencil. In the Arrange View, the Pencil tool makes Grouping of contiguous data on the same track easier. Simply drawing a selection rectangle around the required

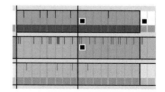

This data has been 'grouped'.

data with the pencil tool automatically groups that data. The Pencil tool quantises its actions in response to the current Snap value, if Snap to Grid is activated, just like the Selection Tool, for precise and easy Grouping. You can toggle between the Selection and Pencil Tools by pressing Apple/Alt on your computer keyboard.

The Erase Tool

As you might expect, this tool is the opposite of the Pencil tool – it lets you easily erase data rather than drawing it.

To erase single events: Select the tool, and click on the unwanted event. It disappears.

To erase multiple events: Draw a selection rectangle around the unwanted events; a shaded box appears around them and the events disappear when you release the mouse button.

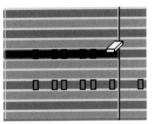

Note that if Snap to Grid is enabled, all identical events within the current Snap value (within the bar if Snap is set to 'Bar', for example) will be erased even if you just click on one of them. Snap also applies when selecting a group of events with the Eraser – the selection rectangle will snap to the currently set grid value. One neat graphic side-effect of using Snap to Grid whilst erasing is that a 'shadow' appears at the end of the Eraser and highlights the area to be erased.

Erasing events with Snap to Grid enabled (at Bar resolution in this example).

The Line Tool

This tool is really only usable in the Edit View (more later). It's selectable in the Arrange View, but all it does is mimic the function of the Selection Tool.

The Magnify Tool

The Magnify tool turns your mouse pointer into a magnifying glass with a 'plus' symbol in it. Both horizontal and vertical zoom are provided in one handy tool. Select it, and repeatedly clicking in the display zooms into the clicked area more precisely than with the fixed zoom controls. Drawing a rectangle around a section of data with the Magnify tool causes only that data to be magnified. There are 16 levels of zoom between this tool's maximum and minimum value.

To zoom out, Option/Control-click with the Magnify tool selected; the tool itself then shows a 'minus' sign in the magnifying glass. Zooming can be restricted to the horizontal plane by pressing Shift at the same time as zooming.

The Hand Tool

This tool has a simple but very useful job: it lets you click in the sequencer display and drag left/right and/or up/down for instant scrolling. It's a good alternative to using the scroll bar to the right and bottom of the display to locate events for scrutiny and editing, as had to be done before the Hand Tool was introduced in V2. Simply click and intuitively drag to where you want to be.

The Snap Value pop-up

This menu allows you to select the Snap resolution for the Arrange View. The selected value defines the grid resolution in the track data display. So if you select the 'Bar' Snap value, a pale grey vertical line appears in the display every bar, and if you select '1/16', a vertical line appears every 16th note. With the Snap to Grid button enabled, any selecting, moving or pasting that you do will snap (or, as the Operation Manual puts it, be "magnetic") to the selected value.

The Snap to Grid button

To make sure that any editing you do is snapped to the current Snap value, enable this button, which has an icon of a magnet. Disable it if you want to work 'freehand' and position data by ear or between grid positions.

The 'Quantize Notes During Recording' button

Selecting this button before playing means that quantizing, or automatic timing correction, will occur as you play from your MIDI keyboard into the sequencer. Whether or not you might want to do this will be discussed later in the chapter, when the issues around quantizing will be covered.

The Quantize Value pop-up

Sets the sub-division of the beat or bar to which mis-timed notes will be corrected if quantization is applied, during recording or as a post-recording process. Values between 'bar' (one bar) and 1/64 (one 64th of a note) are available. If 1/64 was selected, the quantized note would be moved to the nearest 64th note subdivision, giving very subtle quantization. By contrast, with a 1/4 note quantize value, every note would be moved much further, to the nearest quarter-note subdivision, which could potentially spoil the feel of the performance if it included shorter note values than a quarter note.

A common value to choose is 1/16, or 1/16T (sixteenth-note triplet), which will tend to suitably tighten most sloppy playing in pop idioms. If your playing is very out of time, you might try to apply a high value first (such as 1/64 or 1/32), and process with lower values in turn until you hear an accurate result. The usual 10 levels of Undo are available (select Undo from the Edit menu or use Apple/Control-U) if you feel you have gone too far.

Also found in the Quantize Value pop-up are the Groove Quantize options, Shuffle quantize and the 'User Groove' facility. More on these later in the chapter.

The Quantize Notes button

This button applies the quantize process to selected data after it has been recorded – as opposed to while it is being recorded; the latter is selected with the 'Quantize notes during recording' button.

To quantize after recording

- Select a whole track by clicking its name in the track list, or select a section of data within a track.
- Choose a quantize value (and a Quantize Percentage if desired)
- Click the Quantize Notes button or use Apple/Control-K.

If you don't like the result, Undo the operation and try another set of parameters.

The Quantization Percentage pop-up

It sometimes makes more musical sense to apply just a bit of quantization to a performance, so that the result does not sound too rigid. With this pop-up,

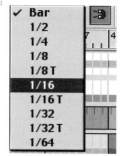

Snap to Grid and Snap Value

Tip

Holding down Shift while Snap to Grid is enabled allows you to alter the length of a note (drag with the Selection tool) while still having its start point snapped neatly to a grid position.

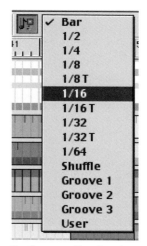

Quantize on record/quantize value

Quantize notes and Quant percentages

Tip

Mac mouse

If you're a Mac user, consider buying a mouse with a second button, like Apple's Mighty Mouse, and assigning this button to the 'Control' key. This makes tons of Reason operations (such as Control-clicking to summon context menus) quicker and easier. Mice with three buttons are even more useful!

you can select a weighting for the quantize process. At 100%, all notes that do not fall right on the beat subdivision currently selected will be moved forward or backward to the nearest subdivision to comply. Choose 50% and the offending notes will be moved only half of the distance between where they are now and the nearest subdivision, tightening up timing to some extent, but retaining some of the performance feel. Weightings of 90%, 75%, 25%, 10% and 5% are also available. If you're going to experiment with percentages, you need to Undo between each try. If you have already quantized at 100%, there is little point in then choosing 50% if you have not Undone, as the notes have already been moved as far as they can be.

Make a MIDI recording

If you've read the chapter this far, you should be getting familiar with the controls and functions needed to undertake a recording, so now it's safe to have a go. This tutorial takes you through the steps necessary for the creation of a simple drum, bass and piano composition. The sequencer's quantization facilities and some of its editing features are also used. Note that this tutorial asks you to record every part directly into the sequencer, for practice, although this is by no means the only way with Reason. (Chapter 3 has a Quickstart Tutorial that uses the sequencer and the other composing facilities of Reason, if you would like to try that.)

Before you do any MIDI recording, ensure your MIDI keyboard and your MIDI interface (if using a separate one) are connected correctly to your computer, as explained in Chapter 2. In the Reason MIDI Preferences (found under Preferences in the Edit menu), ensure that Sequencer Port is set to your MIDI keyboard and that the MIDI channel selected is the one on which your keyboard is transmitting. Again, Chapter 2 provides more on configuring your setup.

You may also want to set your keyboard, if it is a synth rather than a 'dumb' master keyboard, to 'Local Off', which disables its own sound generation. Alternatively, turn down the volume control on your synth so that you don't hear its own sounds when you play. The latter option may be more convenient.

- Start with an empty rack, as described in the first tutorial in Chapter 3.
- Create a Mixer, then a SubTractor synth, a ReDrum drum machine and an NN19 sampler. Load a bass Patch into SubTractor, a drumkit of your choice into ReDrum, and a piano Patch into NN19. See Chapter 4 for Patch-loading details.
- The sequencer should be showing the Arrange View. If it is not, click the Arrange/Edit button in the far left of the Tool Bar, or use Shift-Tab to toggle the two views. Create a two-bar loop by setting the left locator to the start of bar 3 and the right locator to the start of bar 5 (drag them, Option/Control-click in the ruler to set the Left locator and Command/Alt-click to set the right one, or use the POS display). Two bars have been left blank at the start because the sequencer does not have a count-in facility, so starting two bars in fakes a count-in.
- If the Loop On/Off button in the Transport is not lit, enable it by clicking on it, or by using the forward slash ('/') key on the numeric keypad.

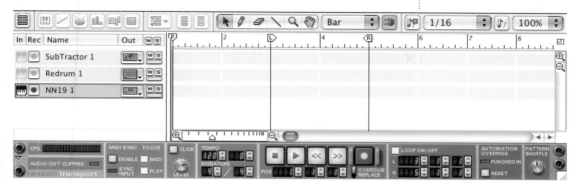

- Choose a tempo and time signature for your recording. If you want to keep it simple, leave the default 4/4 time signature in the Signature display in the Transport, and the default tempo of 120 beats per minute (bpm).
- Ensure the the Overdub/Replace switch in the Transport is set to Overdub. In this mode, you add to the material already recorded on each pass if you keep playing. This is generally safer than Replace mode, which replaces older material with new material.
- Since the first thing we'll be recording is a simple drum pattern, set the Quantize Value to 1/16 and click the 'Quantize Notes During Recording' button. This ensures spot-on timing for the drum hits.
- Enable the metronome click by clicking the Transport 'Click' button or using Apple/Control-M. Start playback (by clicking Play, hitting the Space bar, or using Enter on the numeric keypad) to check the click volume, and adjust if necessary using the Level knob under the Click button. Stop playback and return the playing position to zero, by clicking the Stop button twice, or twice hitting '0' on the numeric keypad or the Return key on the computer keyboard.
- Click the In column of the Track List next to Redrum 1, so that a MIDI plug icon appears. This signifies that the track is ready to accept MIDI input from your keyboard.

Set up a two-bar recording loop with the Left and Right locators.

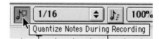

Set Quantize Value to 1/16 and enable 'Quantize Notes During Recording' with the button.

We've set a loop here because this is how many people begin a track, but you don't have to do this when you work by yourself. If you prefer to record long, extemporised performances and build an arrangement around these, just don't set a loop, or disable the Loop On/Off button in the transport.

If all these steps seem like a lot of bother, how about saving them in your default song, in which your preferred settings – such as a favourite set of devices, a count-in and starting loop, preferred recording mode and click level, are saved? See Chapter 4 for some other ideas, and for how to save a default song.

With the above preparations complete, it's time to actually record something.

Initiate Recording
Click the red Record button followed by the Play button; or press the numeric keypad 'star' key followed by the Enter key; or use Apple/Control-Return, followed by the space bar. The metronome will start.

Record the drum part

Wait though the two-bar count-in, then play two bars of a simple bass drum and snare drum part, with two keys on your MIDI keyboard. Redrum sounds are mapped to the 10 keys starting at C1 on your keyboard; the bass drum and snare drum are usually triggered by C1 and the adjacent C-sharp respectively. The two-bar loop will cycle around and you will be able to add to your recorded part on each pass if you want to. You may prefer, in fact, to play the bass drum part on one pass and the snare part on another, though you will probably get a better feel into the part if you can play both in the same pass.

The kick/snare drum part in the Arrange View.

Stop recording and assess the result

When you're satisfied, click the Stop button in the Transport, or press numeric keypad '0' or computer keyboard 'Return', two or three times, to stop recording and return the playing position to the start of the Song. If you would like to re-do the part, you can Undo; alternatively, you could click in the track data display, use Apple/Control-A to highlight all the notes, then delete using backspace on the computer keyboard. Later in this chapter we'll discuss how you can alternatively edit a part that has unsatisfactory sections in it.

Add a bassline

Click next to the SubTractor track in the 'In' column of the Track List, to make the MIDI plug icon appear. Now you can play the synth from your keyboard. Disable input quantization by clicking the 'Quantize Notes During Recording' button. Make sure the Position cursor is at the start of the Song. Enter record mode, as explained earlier, and play in a two-bar bassline as you listen back to the drum part. Stop recording and return the Position cursor to the start of the Song.

Decide whether to quantize the part

Quantize the bass part if necessary.

Since we didn't use 'input' quantizing during the recording of the bass part, there's a good chance that its timing is not perfect. If you feel it needs tightening up, decide on a quantize value from the Quantize Value pop-up, click on the Synth track name in the Track List, to select the whole track, then click the Quantize Notes button or use Apple/Control-K. (The Quantize functions are discussed in detail elsewhere in this chapter.)

Add some piano chords

Repeat the step above for the NN19 Sampler track, playing some simple piano chords instead of a bassline. Apply quantization after the part has been recorded, if you feel it's needed.

Save the Song

We're not quite finished with working on this demo piece, but it's a good time to save, as you wouldn't want to lose anything at this stage through an unforeseen crash. Go to the File menu and choose 'Save As'. Name the Song in the dialogue that comes up, choose or create a folder for it, and click Save.

Copy the parts to make a longer track

You've now recorded a sequencer composition, but to make it longer, we're going to copy the two existing bars and paste them at the end. We can also use the opportunity to create some note Groups. First set the Snap Value pop-up to 'Bar' and enable the 'Snap to Grid' button, so that all selecting and moving will be forced to the nearest bar division.

Click in the note display and use Apple/Control-A to select all the notes. Now use Apple/Control-G to Group them, so that the notes on each track are treated as one entity.

The three tracks of the composition before and after grouping.

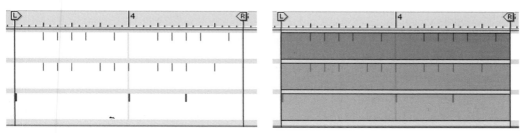

Each track's notes are highlighted in a block of colour, to show that they are grouped. Now select all three groups by Shift-clicking on each. To copy the notes, Option/Control-drag the whole section to the start of bar 5, copying it to the new location in the process.

Copy the two-bar composition to make a four-bar composition.

Drag the Right locator to the start of bar 7, so that when you play back, the new four-bar loop will play. Use Apple/Control-S to save the changes to the Song.

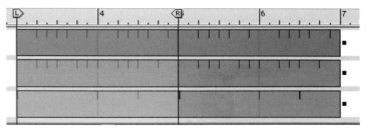

Note that you don't have to use Groups when you copy the two bars in the above step – you can simply use Apple/Control-A to select all the notes, then copy them to the new location as above. We just worked in the Grouping for some practice.

Save the Song again. Now you can add extra parts if you like, to develop the piece further.

More on quantizing

Groove quantize

Groove quantizing, which aims to impose a different rhythmic 'feel' on the quantized material than the one it currently has, has become very popular in recent years. Three groove quantization options – Groove 1, Groove 2 and Groove 3 – are available under the Quantize Value pop-up, plus a Shuffle quantize and an option to create a 'User groove'.

Propellerhead describe the preset groove options as "three different, slightly irregular patterns". You can hear what they are doing by first programming a drum pattern in the sequencer, or using 'Copy Pattern to

| Shuffle |
| Groove 1 |
| Groove 2 |
| Groove 3 |
| User |

The groove quantize options.

Tip

Find your way around

If you keep needing to jump to a particular location in a Song, use the Left and Right locators flexibly – turn the Loop button off and, say, set the Left marker to the middle eight and the Right marker to the last chorus. Use the 'Go to' marker shortcuts (1 and 2 on the numeric keypad) to jump to these locations instantly.

Track', under the Edit menu in ReDrum, to copy into the sequencer a pattern you've already programmed. Then select the events you want to quantize, choose one of the Groove options from the Quantize Value pop-up, and click the Quantize Notes button. Play back the pattern and listen for differences. Toggle between the quantized and un-quantized pattern using Apple/Control-Z (Undo) and either Apple/Control-Y (Redo) or Apple/Control-K (to re-quantize). Also try changing the Quantization percentage to alter the strength of the effect. Undo before trying the next groove quantize option.

The preset Grooves may be useful to you in loosening up the feel of a drum pattern, say (though they can be applied to a whole composition if desired): the only way to know is to try the Grooves in turn with your pattern or composition, adjusting the Quantization Percentage if needed. If it works, you'll soon know.

The effect of the very good Shuffle quantize option is governed by a combination of the Pattern Shuffle amount, set by the Pattern Shuffle knob in the Transport bar, and the Quantization Percentage value. A subtle, effective swing can be added to a part with a low percentage. High settings can produce a contemporary 'swing beat' feel, characterised by imposing a syncopated triplet rhythm on 16th-note patterns.

Creating a User Groove

This feature is very fast to use and potentially useful for giving different played and programmed parts the same feel, so that they will sit well together.

- Select a section of MIDI data whose feel you want to apply to other parts. Propellerhead recommend 1-2 bars of the wanted material, and we've found that this is probably the best amount to use.
- Choose 'Get User Groove' from the Edit menu or sequencer context menu. The program turns the rhythmic relationships in the selected data into a groove template, and the Quantize Value pop-up shows 'User'.
- Select the track or section of track you want to quantize and click the Quantize Notes button. The selected notes are quantized.

Creating a User groove is as easy as selecting a section of MIDI data and choosing 'Get User Groove'.

Get User Groove

Now, when User Groove is selected, quantizing will be to this template, providing other parts with something of the feel of the 'sampled' performance. Unfortunately, the User Groove template is temporary: it's not saved with the Song – though of course any parts whose feel you have changed with the User Groove will remain changed when the Song is saved.

Ideas for working with the User Groove include taking a drum pattern and using it to quantise another drum pattern/part, or a bassline or instrument part. If you are, or work with, a drummer who uses a MIDI kit, or you have a MIDI percussion controller, you could play a drum pattern live into the sequencer, derive a User Groove from that and quantise other parts to it. There are also a number of MIDI drum and instrument loop collections on the market featuring MIDI performances by top musicians, unquantised and therefore offering lots of 'human feel'. Files such as these could be imported into the sequencer and have User Grooves derived from them. For the most subtle effect with User Grooves, try a quantize percentage of 75 or 50.

REX loops for User Grooves

You can also derive a User groove from a REX loop. We don't exactly have the facility in Reason's sequencer to quantise MIDI data according to the feel of a sampled audio loop (which is available in some sequencers), only according to the feel of other MIDI data. However, since every loop in Dr:rex comes with a set of MIDI notes, to trigger the REX 'slices' (see the Dr:rex chapter for more), we can try something similar.

REX loops are sliced according to strong rhythmic peaks, and a MIDI note generated at each slice position. The MIDI notes therefore necessarily correspond, to an extent, with the timing of the loop. You can use these MIDI notes as the basis for a User Groove, after sending them to a sequencer track with Dr:rex's 'To Track' feature, and thus get the feel of an audio loop into other parts in the sequencer. Whether or not the effect is pleasing is down to the REX loop you choose and the other part(s) you quantize with the loop. A rather artificial (and sometimes lumpy) feel can pretty easily be introduced. At its most successful, the technique can be used to subtly move the notes in another part towards the feel of the REX loop, underlining the rhythm in a subliminal kind of way, but you should expect to experiment with the percentage setting, Here are the steps, if you would like to try it:

- Create a Dr:rex device, load the desired REX loop and send its MIDI notes to the Dr:rex sequencer track, using the 'To Track' button, as explained in the Dr:rex chapter.
- In the Arrange View, select all the REX notes on the Dr:rex sequencer track, then go up to the Edit menu and select 'Get User Groove'. 'User' should appear in the Quantize Value pop-up.
- Select the data to be quantized and click the Quantize Notes button, or use Apple/Control-K. If the effect is not what you're looking for, Undo, change the value in the Quantize Percentage pop-up, and re-quantize.

You might find it helps, after you have used the 'To Track' function, to home in on just a group of REX MIDI notes where there is most rhythmic activity, select those, and use only them as the basis for the User Groove.

To quantize or not to quantize?

Quantization is an extremely useful option, especially since most pop musicians are not formally trained, but you certainly don't have to use it all the time. If a freely-played part sounds good in context of the Song you're creating, leave it unquantized. You may find that the feel that makes it sound right will be spoiled even with carefully applied quantization.

Input quantizing, or quantizing during recording, should be approached with care. If you've played what you think was a good performance but the input quantizing you set has rendered it undesirably stiff on playback, you can't get back the original performance. You can safely use input quantize when you're recording a part that you know needs to be very regular, perhaps a drum pattern. But on the whole it's more sensible to leave quantizing until after the part has been recorded, when you will have much more flexibility to apply different types and levels until you get a result. By the way, still try to aim for good timing, if you can, as there is then more chance of the quantize process producing a satisfactory result.

Tip
Quantizing can create new material

Quantizing a part incorrectly, with too low a note resolution, can produce undesirably lumpy results, but it can also be used as a creative technique in its own right. By quantizing a part that has a sixteenth-note feel with a 1/8 quantize value, say, you make the smallest note value in that part an eighth note and radically change the part's feel. This can produce new rhythmic or melodic material, that will probably still fit into your arrangement, from an existing part. Just remember to do this with a copy of the original part!

Info

Copying sequence data between songs

Data from Reason's sequencer, including controller and pattern data as well as note data, can be pasted from one Song into another. You can cut or copy and paste sections of tracks, whole tracks, or several tracks at a time. If you select non-contiguous data, on one or several tracks, it will be pasted into the other Song with the same temporal relationships as it had in the original Song, starting from the location of the Position cursor.

Listen to a part before quantizing and try to ascertain the smallest note sub-division that's been used: if you've recorded a part with lots of 16th-note activity, setting the Quantize Value to 1/8 will produce a very unsatisfactory result. If you think you have used the correct Quantize value (say, 1/16), but the result sounds stilted, with too many notes that have been moved in the wrong direction, Undo and try a finer resolution – say 1/32 or 1/64. Notes that are pulled in the wrong direction with a 1/16 value may go in the right direction with a finer note resolution. If you still don't have quite the right result, try 1/16 again (but don't Undo between these two stages, as the effect will be cumulative).

Also experiment with the Quantization Percentage value, since this parameter can help to retain the feel of an otherwise sloppy performance while correcting note positions sufficiently. You can work on a copy of the note data if you feel more comfortable doing that, though there are 10 levels of Undo to offer some security.

If none of the quantize options fixes the part in the way you want, you have two options: play it again, or go in and manually move notes about to suit, in the Edit View. You may be able to combine light quantizing with manual editing of the odd uncooperative note, to get the result you're after.

Open the Song whose data you want to copy and the Song you want to copy it to, and select the required data in the 'source' Song. Use Apple/Control-C to copy it. Click in the other (destination) Song to bring it to the top. Move the Position cursor to where you would like the data. Use Apple/Control-V to paste it.

A new track is automatically created by the sequencer for each track's data that is pasted into the destination Song, so if you paste data from three tracks, three new tracks will be created for it. Data can't be pasted like this into an existing track of the destination Song, but it can, of course, be cut from the new track(s) created and pasted into whichever track you like.

The Edit View

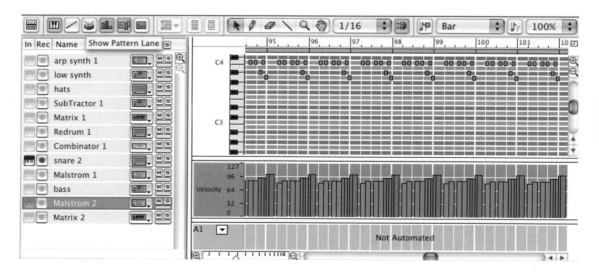

Now that you know something about how to record with the sequencer and use the Arrange View, you can move on to editing your work. As you would expect from its name, the Edit View's main purpose is to allow you to edit the musical and controller data that makes up your tracks, as well as seeing it in more detail. You view just one track at a time in the Edit View: select the track you want to edit, by clicking on its name in the Track List, then use Shift-Tab to enter the Edit View, or click the combined Edit/Arrange button.

Like the Arrange View, the Edit View is divided into three areas – Track List to the left, Data Display grid to the right, and a Tool Bar running across the top. There is one small addition: a narrow 'Group Strip' runs between the Data Display's ruler and the Data Display itself, allowing you to quickly see which data has been Grouped. Groups are indicated by coloured bars in the Strip. You can see one such Group Strip in the Edit View screen that heads up this section.

The Track List functions in just the same way in the Edit View as it does in the Arrange View – read the previous section for details. The differences for Edit View are in the other two elements. For a start, all the tools in the Tool Bar are available in Edit mode, with none greyed out. In addition, the grid can show six different types of data, in what are called Lanes. A vertical zoom is available for each Lane.

Info

How long is the Song?

There's no option to change Reason's ruler to display Song location in time instead of bars and beats. But if you want to know quickly how long a Song is, make sure the End marker is at the end of the Song, close the Song (make sure to save first), then start the process of openin g it again from the Song Browser. Select the Song in the Browser list, and on the right-hand side under information you'll see Length (in minutes and seconds), tempo and time signature for the Song.

The Edit View Lanes

Each track can show up to six Lanes, each defined in a different colour and displaying a different type of data. Not all Lanes will be relevant to any one device track. For example, there is little point in showing the Pattern lane (specific to ReDrum and Matrix) for a track that's assigned to a SubTractor synth, since this particular device can't respond to Pattern changes. Lanes within a track can be shown or hidden by clicking their Lane Selection button in the tool bar (more in a moment), but the order in which they appear in the track display is fixed. They may be resized by grabbing and dragging their top edge up or down.

Key Lane

In this lane (likely to be the one you use most often), notes appear as bars of varying lengths in a now-traditional 'piano roll' grid display. The vertical axis represents pitch and has a graphic of a piano keyboard to help you locate notes, while the horizontal axis represents time, in bars and beats.

Key Lane

Notes are shown in shades of red against a blue background. The darker the note colour, the higher the velocity of the note. Any MIDI note data for a given track can be seen in the Key Lane, whether it is notes you've played in from a MIDI keyboard, or the notes that correspond to Dr:rex 'slices' when the 'To Track' function in Dr:rex has been used.

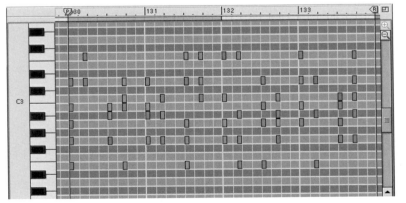

REX Lane

The REX lane is just another way of displaying note data – except that this time the notes are the MIDI events that trigger REX loop 'slices' (see the Dr:rex chapter for more). Instead of a keyboard graphic along the vertical axis, the REX lane has a list of slice numbers (1-99, the maximum number of slices in a loop being 99), while the horizontal axis represents time. When you have used the 'To Track' feature to send a REX loop's MIDI notes to a sequencer track, you can thus use the REX lane as an alternative to the Key lane, to see the slices laid out, and even move them about and re-order them to make the loop play differently.

REX lane

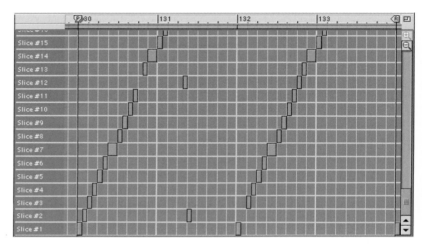

Drum Lane

Yet another way of displaying MIDI notes, this time the notes that trigger ReDrum voices. The drum lane uses a grid that's somewhat like the drum editors in other sequencing software, with 10 drum voice names listed in the vertical axis and time, once again, in the horizontal. Notes show as very short red bars. Interestingly, if you select the Drum Lane for a sequencer track that's assigned to an instrument other than ReDrum, the list consists of 128 entries – one for each of the 128-note MIDI range.

Drum Lane

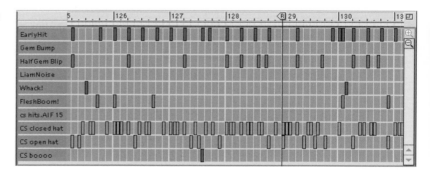

Velocity Lane

The velocity information recorded with MIDI notes is displayed here, as a series of vertical bars – the higher the bar, the higher the velocity value. The velocity bar for a note lines up with that note in the lane above. Velocity for a note (basically, how loud it

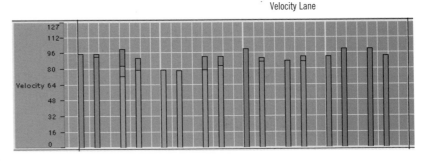

Velocity Lane

sounds) can be edited by grabbing the top of its bar and changing its height – drag up for higher velocity and a louder note, or down for lower velocity. Draw a line or curve in the velocity lane with your mouse to change many velocity values in one pass. You can't actually create a velocity event here, as you can create a note in the Key Lane by drawing with the Pencil tool: a velocity event is only created when a note event is created.

Pattern Lane

When you change patterns with ReDrum or the Matrix while the sequencer is in 'record' mode on the relevant track, those changes are recorded into the special Pattern Lane. On playback, the changes will automatically occur exactly as you recorded them. Of course, you can edit the changes in the Pattern Lane, and just as easily draw in changes manually from scratch. How to do this will be explained shortly.

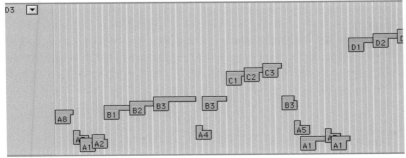

Tip

Editing velocity in multiple note clusters

In a busy track, especially a polyphonic performance with many notes falling on the same beats, it can be very hard to change the velocity of a specific note without changing that of notes that occur on the same beat. In this situation, select the note or notes whose velocity you want to change in the Key (or any other note-based) Lane, using the Selection tool; swap to the Pencil tool; hold down Shift and alter the length of the relevant velocity bar. Although several velocity bars may be sharing the same space, only the velocity data specific to the selected note or notes will be changed.

Controller Lane

The data for any automated parameters of your rack devices are recorded into the Controller Lane. This lane has 'sub-lanes', one for each controller available on the device in question. A ReMix mixer track, for example, will be able to display 159 sub-lanes, one for every controller (such as channel pan, level and mute for every input channel) that can be automated on the mixer.

You can display as many sub-lanes as you like for a track, but data will only appear in them for parameters that have been automated. For example, in the case of a SubTractor, if you had automated Filter Frequency, LFO Rate and FM Amount, you would see data in these three sub-lanes. Any other sub-lanes displayed would be empty except for the legend 'Not Automated'. Controller data can be edited here, and even drawn into the display. Note that though the viewing size of Controller sub-lanes can be changed with the zoom tools, it is not changed independently for each sub-lane – viewing one smaller or larger will mean that you view at that size all sub-lanes currently showing.

Controller Lane

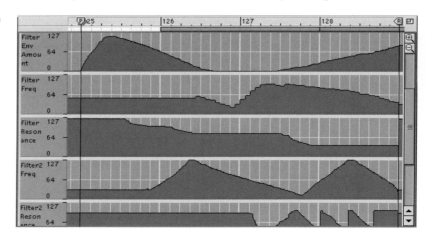

The Tool Bar in the Edit View

Lane Selection Buttons

Lane selection buttons

Each of the editing lanes can be shown, or hidden, by clicking on a dedicated button on the left of the Tool Bar. The six buttons (left to right, below) select the Key Lane, the REX Lane, the Drum Lane, the Velocity Lane, the Pattern Lane and the Controller Lane. Each features an icon that illustrates the Lane's function.

The Selection tool in the Edit View

The Selection tool behaves very much in the Edit View as it does in the Arrange View, except that in the Edit View you have easier control over individual notes. The Selection tool still allows you to Select notes or groups of notes so that they may be Moved, Copied and Pasted. It also resizes notes – grab and drag the handle at the end of the note. When notes have been selected in the Edit View, they may be quantized, just as in the Arrange View.

The Pencil tool in the Edit View

In the Edit View, the Pencil tool can undertake a number of extra event-creation tasks:

- *Drawing Notes:* In the Key, REX and Drum Lanes, the Pencil can be used to create new notes, with position and final length governed by the Snap value, if Snap to Grid is enabled. Click in the lane, hold down the mouse button, and drag the bar that appears to the required length.
- *Drawing and editing controller data:* In the Controller lanes, click and drag the pencil tool across the display to create controller data. As an example, drawing a deep curve in the Mod Wheel controller sub-lane for a SubTractor, NN19 or Dr:rex track would create a full sweep of the mod wheel, and a corresponding modulation change on the device, without

you having to touch the mod wheel itself at all. Use the Selection tool if you want to copy and paste controller data. (Later in this chapter controller drawing and editing is discussed in detail, with examples.)

- *Creating and editing Pattern changes:* click the arrow in the Pattern Lane to bring up a pop-up list of ReDrum or Matrix Pattern labels (A1-D8). Select a Pattern from the list and draw a line in the Pattern Lane. A bar will appear to indicate Pattern playback at that point. Make sure you have 'Snap to Grid' enabled when you do this, otherwise you could find yourself inserting Pattern changes at unexpected and inappropriate intervals.The length of the bar sets how long the Pattern will play for, depending on the grid resolution set in the Edit View, but once you have drawn in a bar, the pattern will continue to play until a new pattern occurs. Choose new Patterns and draw more lines to create a Pattern chain. Use the Selection tool to select groups of Patterns, which can be copied and pasted like any other data – useful for quickly building up the Pattern chain for a whole Song. Also see the Automation and Remote Control chapter for an alternative way of creating Pattern chains, using the Controller Lane.

Selecting a ReDrum or Matrix Pattern from the pop-up list in the Pattern Lane.

The Erase tool in the Edit View

Using the Erase tool in the Edit View, individual events can be erased by clicking on them, events within the current Snap resolution (within the bar if Snap Resolution is set to 'Bar') will be erased if just one event is clicked, and it's possible to draw a rectangle around a group of events to erase them all.

Be careful when erasing individual notes with Snap enabled – notes within the Snap resolution having the same pitch as the selected note will be erased; all others will be left alone. To Erase controller data, highlight a section of data with the Erase tool, either freehand or to the current Snap resolution. The controller value after erasure will be that of the controller at the start of the selection.

Drawing a Pattern change into the Pattern Lane.

The Line tool in the Edit View

Edit View is where the Line Tool comes into its own, allowing the drawing of completely straight lines in the Velocity and Controller Lanes. Smooth velocity ramps, fades or other controller moves can thus easily be created. For these and many other drawing purposes, the Line tool is preferable to the Pencil.

To use the Line tool, click where you want the line to start and move the mouse pointer to the desired line end point. Release the mouse button. The Line tool will create a perfectly straight line without 'Snap to Grid' being enabled; if Snap is enabled, however, it draws a straight line at the selected resolution. This may mean that the 'line' is actually a series of stepped parameter changes, an effect that's especially visible at coarser resolutions (1/2-note, 1/4-note or 1/8-note, for example).

You can create horizontal lines by Shift-drawing with the Line tool, which is ideal for creating a fixed parameter change at a given value over several beats or bars.

The Magnify tool in The Edit View

Exactly the same functionality is offered by the Magnify tool in the Edit View as in the Arrange View. Note that zooming is applied to all visible Lanes; it's not possible to zoom into just one. If the latter is what you want, hide all Lanes other than the one you wish to examine.

Tip

Selective velocity editing

There may be occasions when you need to adjust the velocity of several notes in a MIDI part that aren't contiguous – for example, all the snare hits in a ReDrum track. This is easy if you select all the snare 'notes' by drawing a selection rectangle around them with the Selection tool (or shift clicking individual notes if there aren't many to be changed) and then Shift-draw with the Line or Pencil tool across the velocity Lane, at the desired velocity level. This changes only the velocity for the selected notes, leaving all others unchanged.

The Hand tool in the Edit View

The Hand tool behaves in a similar way in the Edit View as it does in the Arrange View. The one slight difference is that vertical dragging – moving the Hand Tool up or down – can be achieved independently for each Lane. This is especially valuable in the Controller lane – dragging to a Sub-Lane you'd like to view or edit is rather easier than using the scroll bars to the right of the display, especially if you only have a little of the Controller lane showing. Scrolling can be restricted to the horizontal or vertical if you first press the Shift key. Only horizontal scrolling is permitted in the Velocity Lane.

The Controller Lane Tool Bar functions

Three extra functions become available in the Tool Bar when the Controller Lane is displayed. These functions allow you to easily view the controller sub-Lanes you want to see, and they are accessed by clicking on dedicated buttons.

Controllers button

- *Controllers:* Clicking this button brings up a menu listing every available controller for the device assigned to the sequencer track. Choosing one of the options on the menu makes a sub-lane appear for it in the Controller Lane. Any number of controllers may be selected. A tick next to a controller name in the menu means that the controller has already been selected. An asterisk next to the name means that automation data has already been recorded for that controller in that track.

Show Device Controllers

- *Show Device Controllers:* This is a quick way of making a sub-lane visible for every controller, rather than selecting them one at a time as above.

Show controllers in track

- *Show Controllers in Track:* Selecting this button shows a sub-lane for only those controllers that have been automated as part of the track – the most sensible viewing option for much of the time.

In Reason versions prior to V2, there is an extra 'Hide all controllers' button which hides all the sub-lanes in the Controller Lane. Since V2, this is no longer there, but the option to 'Hide all controllers' is available from the 'Controllers' button pop-up.

The 'Hide all controllers' option, in Reason V3.x.

Groups in the Edit View

You can create Groups in the Edit View, by drawing a selection rectangle around notes and using Apple/Control-G or choosing Group from the Edit menu, as in the Arrange View, but there is also another method . Simply clicking on one note with the pencil tool and using the Group command causes every note that also plays within the duration of that note to be grouped. It's also possible to shift-click on two or more notes – they don't have to be contiguous – use the Group command, and all notes that fall between the earliest and latest selected notes will be included in the Group.

The length of a Group will generally be that of the longest note selected, or will be equal to the space between the two furthest-apart, non-contiguous notes being Grouped. However, if Snap to Grid is enabled in the Tool Bar, a Group's end will jump to the current Snap value: for example, even if you click on a 64th note in the display and create a Group, the Group will be one bar long if Snap to Grid is set to 'bar'.

Groups set in the Arrange View carry over to the Edit View, and vice versa. The Group strip under the ruler in the Edit View shows coloured bars where Groups occur, to correspond with the colours given to Groups in the Arrange View.

Easy Grouping in the Edit View: select one note, Group, and every note that plays within the note's duration becomes part of the Group. Here just the higher 'C' was clicked, then the 'Group' command used.

The Change Events window

Choosing Change Events (available in both Edit and Arrange View) from the Edit menu brings up a window that allows you to apply a set of 'transformations' to selected MIDI data and to tempo. It's an excellent tool for musical experimentation.

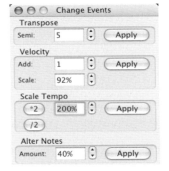

Left: Change Events window

In all cases, select the notes to be transformed, open the Change Events window, and enter the required values. Click 'Apply' to make the process work. This can even be done in real time, during playback. You can use Undo if you don't like the result, but it may be wise to work on copies of any parts that you'd like to retain in their original state.

Below A (and B overleaf) Transposing notes easily with the 'Change Events' Transpose option.

Transpose

Up to 127 semitones of upward or downward pitch change can be applied to note data. In Figure 15.18, the second group of notes has been transposed up by two semitones.

Velocity

A fixed velocity value can be added to or subtracted from the current velocity value of selected notes with the 'Add' option (the range is -127

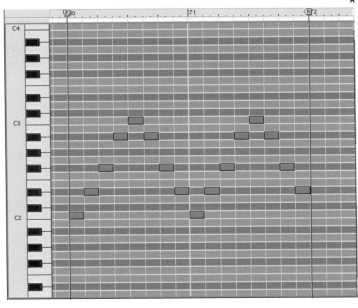

A

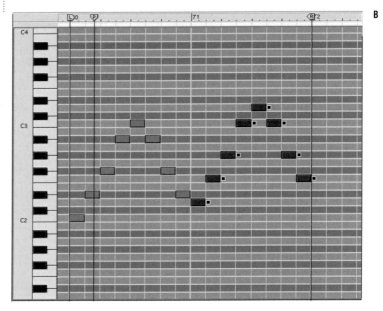

to +127). This is useful if you have, for example, played a part too quietly but are otherwise happy with its feel and dynamics. Adding a fixed amount to all the note velocities makes the performance sound louder, but preserves the dynamics as they are. The notes in the first screen of the figure below were played quietly. In the second screen a value of 65 has been added to all of them.

A and B
Using the 'Add' velocity option in Change Events to increase the velocity of each note by the same fixed amount.

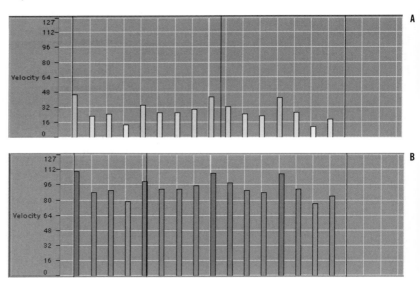

Velocities can also be 'Scaled' with a percentage value of between 1% and 800%. A value of 100% is equal to no change. Because the process makes percentage changes, rather than adding fixed amounts to existing levels, changes of more than 100% tend to increase the difference between lower and higher velocities, while values of less than 100% narrow the gaps.

As an example, if a note had a velocity of 100, scaling by 110% would add 10% to that value, making a velocity of 110. Doing the same thing with a velocity of 50 would add only 5, for a final velocity of 55, and a difference between the lower and higher velocities of 55. If you had simply added 10 to both velocities, the difference between the two would still be 50, so scaling has increased the difference between the two velocity levels. The second screen in B (right) shows the effects of scaling the notes in the first screen (the same one used in the 'Add' example above) by 150%.

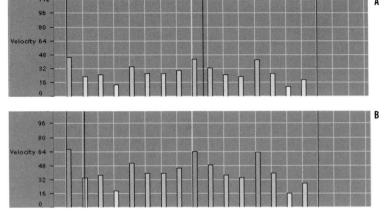

A and B
Increasing note velocity by using the 'Scale' function in 'Change Events'. This has the effect of increasing the difference between the lower and higher velocities.

The Reason Operation Manual notes that by using the 'Add' and 'Scale' velocity functions in tandem, it's possible to manipulate a performance's dynamics; the example given applies a percentage of less than 100, to narrow the gaps between low and high velocities, and then adds a fixed amount to the result, which has the audible effect of making the performance sound compressed, with lower velocities increased in level.

Scale Tempo

Contrary to what you might initially think, this parameter doesn't work on a Song's actual tempo. In fact, it works on the positions and lengths of selected notes and their relationships to each other, making them seem to play faster or slower by shortening or lengthening them and adjusting their positions by a percentage of between 1% and 800%. Two preset buttons provide helpful access to the double-time (+2) and half-time (/2) options most of us will usually want. A pattern of eighth notes will be turned into 16ths if the 'tempo' is scaled by 200%, or quarter notes if scaled by 50%. In the example shown in the figure A right and B overleaf, the pattern which previously occupied two bars has been scaled by 200%. It now plays in the space of one bar and sounds twice as fast.

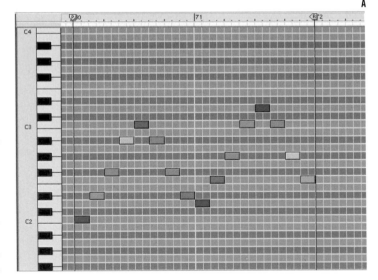

A (and B overleaf)
Using Scale Tempo at 200% to make a note pattern last half as long.

This process does open up some interesting possibilities – see the technique later in this chapter for faking tempo changes – and with careful marshalling of Scale percentages to process data on different tracks, you should be able to create true polyrhyth-

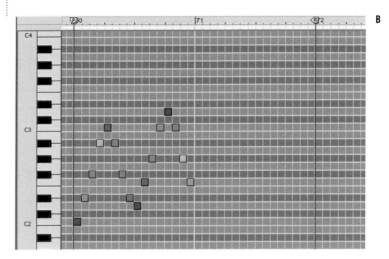
B

mic music. Even if you don't feel that adventurous, there's a wide range of new musical material available to you if you Scale notes by various amounts and then quantize the result to fit a Song's real tempo.

Alter Notes

Offers a pseudo-randomise feature, taking the pitches, lengths and velocities of all selected notes and redistributing these values to create new musical material. There is a percentage weighting, from 1% for little change, up to 100% for the most drastic change. The second screen (B opposite) shows the results of using Alter Notes with a value of 20% on the notes in the first screen.

A (and B opposite)
Applying 'Alter Notes' to randomly modify selected notes.

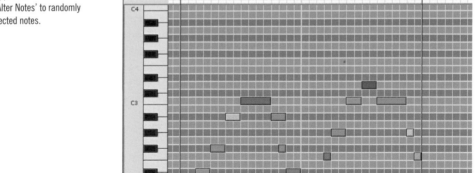
A

Alter Notes can produce useful variations if you experiment with it, and even if only a bar or two of usable material is generated, you can simply copy and paste that. Try using the process on a melody, pasting the altered version to another sequencer track and assigning it to a new sound on a different device, for an instant counter-melody that will probably work alongside

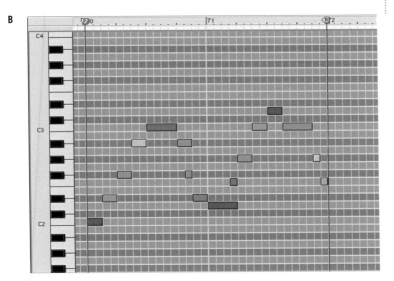

the original. The Alter operation is random and produces a different version every time it's used, even with the same source material and percentage setting, so it's worth doing repeatedly.

Other functions in the Edit menu

A set of additional editing features not mentioned so far can be found under the Edit menu:

- *Duplicate Track:* Makes an exact copy of a sequencer track, assigned to the same device as the original.
- *Insert/Remove Bars Between Locators:* Set the Left and Right locators around the desired number of bars; choose Insert Bars to insert that number of empty bars between the locators, pushing on subsequent material by that many bars. This is ideal for creating a break in a sequence where nothing should play. Choosing Remove Bars erases the desired number of bars and causes material before and after the locators to be butt-joined. Both operations work across all tracks.
- *Convert Pattern Track to Notes:* This operation works on a chain of Pattern changes for ReDrum or the Matrix that has been recorded into the sequencer. Clicking on the device name in the Track List and choosing this option from the Edit menu converts the data in every pattern in the chain into note and other data on the same sequencer track. When this operation is performed, Pattern selection on the device in question is disabled (so that Patterns do not play back simultaneously from the device and the sequencer) and the chain of Pattern changes in the Pattern Lane is erased. See the Matrix and ReDrum chapters for more on this feature.
- *Find Identical Groups:* Select a Group of notes in the Arrange View and choose this option in the Edit menu. All groups containing the same data will be highlighted. This feature works in the Edit View only if the Group has first been selected in the Arrange View.

Tip

Preserving a CV curve in a Converted Matrix Pattern track

When a Matrix pattern chain is converted to notes, using 'Convert Pattern Track to Notes' in the Edit menu, any controller CV curve that you had set up in the Matrix, to modulate a parameter on the attached synth while the Matrix also plays the notes of a pattern, does not convert with the notes. The controller curve might be a large part of the effect you need for the Matrix pattern, so you may well want to preserve it. The best way to do this is: duplicate the sequencer track that contains the Matrix pattern chain; convert one of the two identical Matrix tracks as usual; go to the Matrix device and flip around to the back panel, using Tab, and disconnect the cables attached to the Note and Gate CV sockets. The Matrix will now only be generating the controller curve, while the Pattern notes come from the converted sequencer track. This method also allows the Curve CV to be preserved in a Matrix Pattern that is copied to the main sequencer using the 'Copy Pattern to Track' function.

- *Clear Automation:* erases all automation data on the selected Controller sub-lane in the Edit View.

Some typical editing examples in the Edit View

The note-editing moves in the following examples are affected by the value set in the Snap Value pop-up, and will snap to exact bar or beat locations if Snap to Grid is selected.

Lengthening notes

This is something you'll often want to do, if you've played a bass line, say, and it's too staccato. It's the easiest thing in the world just to lengthen some of the notes to change the feel. In the Edit View, choose the Selection tool. Click on the note to select it. A handle appears at the edge of the note. Grab the handle and drag the note out to the required duration. To shorten the note, drag in the opposite direction.

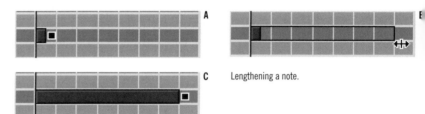

Lengthening a note.

To change the duration of several notes simultaneously (by the same amount), select all of them, then drag the handle of one.

Moving notes

The top note in the figure below is out of time with the others in the chord. To move it, select with the Selection tool, and drag to the right location.

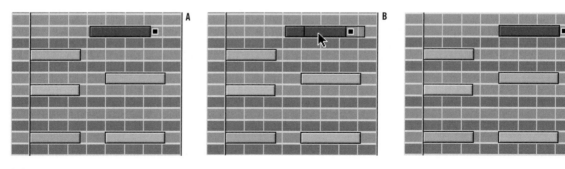

A–C
Moving notes.

Copying notes

Select the notes to be copied. Use Apple/Control-C to copy them. The cursor moves to the logical paste position for consecutive copies. Use Apple/Control-V to paste. To paste somewhere other than the automatic paste position, move the Position cursor before pasting.

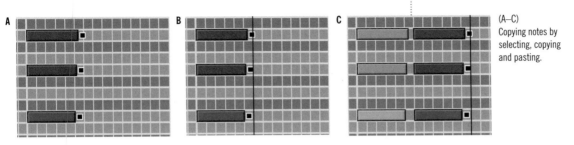

(A–C)
Copying notes by
selecting, copying
and pasting.

Alternatively, select the notes to be copied and option/control-drag to the new location, as in the figure below.

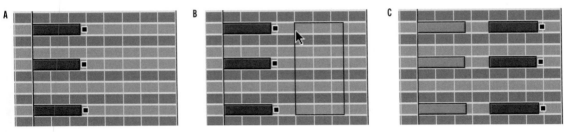

A–C
Copying notes by option/control-dragging
to the required location.

Quantizing selected notes

The first set of four notes in screen A below is perfectly in time. The second set is not and could benefit from quantizing. Select the notes to be quantized. Set the appropriate Quantize Value in the pop-up (in this case 1/8, as the pattern is an eighth-note pattern which we want to correct to the nearest eighth-note grid position). Now use Apple/Control-K (or click the Quantize Notes button). The notes are moved to the correct positions, as in screen B.

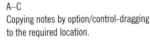

A and B
Select the notes that
are out of time,
choose a Quantize
value and quantize.
Inthe second screen,
the selected notes
have been quantized.

Drawing notes

Select the pencil tool. Click in the note display at the required pitch, and drag. Release the mouse button at the required note length.

A and B
Drawing notes into the Edit View with the
pencil tool.

A   B

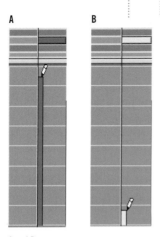

A and B
Making a note quieter by dragging its
velocity bar.

Editing note velocity

The velocity lane must be displayed by clicking its Lane-selection button in the Tool Bar. Select the pencil tool and click and drag the velocity bar of the note whose velocity you would like to edit – up for louder, down for quieter (as in the figure left). The note and velocity bar both change shade to reflect the change.

Creating crescendos

Select the Line tool. Click and hold near the bottom of the velocity bar for the note where you want the crescendo to start. Drag the mouse upwards across the subsequent bars to create the crescendo, as in the figure below. If you still have V1.x of Reason, use the Pencil tool.

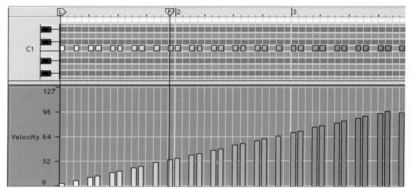

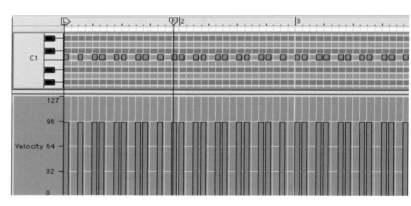

A–C
Drag the Line tool across the velocity
display to create a crescendo.

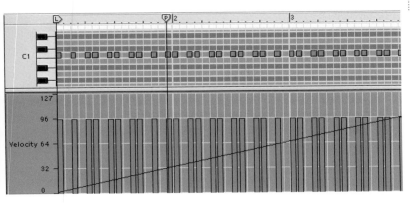

Editing and creating Controller data

Controller data recorded when controls and parameters of Reason devices are automated can easily be graphically edited in the controller lanes of the Edit View. Many musicians also like to draw in controller data, finding that this gives them more power over precisely how the controller will affect their sound, is sometimes more convenient than moving on-screen knobs with the mouse, and also gives rise to effects that might not have been created simply by recording control movements.

Before you can do any kind of controller work, you need to display the controller lanes you want to use, as explained earlier in the chapter. Note that the Snap value has an effect on controller editing and drawing; if Snap to Grid is active, drawing and editing moves will snap to the nearest grid division.

Controller editing

An example of a controller that may often need editing is Volume – perhaps when a mix fade-out, performed with the master fader in the mixer, is not smooth enough.

Clicking the 'Show Controllers in Track' button in the Edit View Tool Bar will display all the sub-lanes that are in use for the selected track. In this case it would be a mixer track. Alternatively, you can Option/Alt-click the device control in question to be shown the relevant controller Lane immediately. The figures below and overleaf show a fade, which was performed with a mixer fader, in the Volume sub-lane: you can see a plateau, representing the track's volume prior to the fade, then a downward slope, which is the fade itself. The slope is not particularly smooth, and there's a sudden drop at the very end.

With the Line tool, you can go right in and smooth out the slope, as shown in the last screen (B overleaf).

A (and B overleaf)
A bumpy Volume fade being smoothed ot in the Volume Controller sub-Lane.

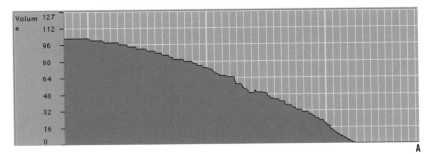

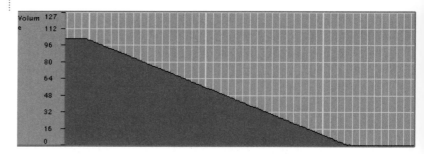

Controller drawing

Here are just a few ideas for what to do with controllers. These are literally the tip of a very big iceberg.

Pan

A mixer parameter that's easy to automate like this is pan. Setting a sound to flip between left and right in the stereo image is great for introducing movement and dynamism.

The pattern in the figure below was drawn into a Pan sub-lane with the Line tool, to move pan position from the centre axis into positive values (hard right at the highest values) then back towards the centre and down into negative values (eventually hard left), then back again. The ruler helps you make your panning data conform to bars and beats if needed. You don't have to laboriously draw lots of curves – controller data is just data like any other, and you can cut, copy and paste it. If you would like to pan a track left to right in a regular fashion for any period of time, just draw the curves necessary to pan left and right once, then copy and paste them. Use 'Clear Automation' from the Edit menu or the device's context menu if you find you've made a complete mess and want to start again.

A controller pattern in the Pan sub-lane that will result in pan moving from left to right twice.

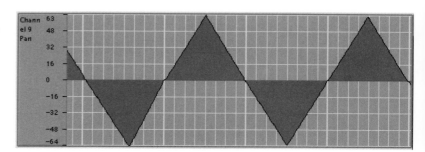

Mixer channel Mutes

The pattern of controller drawing in Figure 15.33 produces mixer-channel mutes. Each dark (blue) bar denotes the 'on' value for the mute; the thickness of the dark bar denotes how long the mute is working, while the space between the bars represents time when the mute is 'off'. The same kind of pattern would control any other 'switching' process, such as solo or EQ on/off.

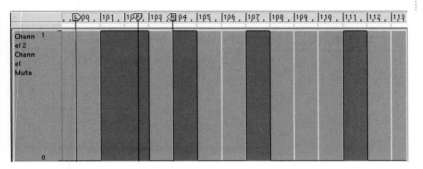

This controller pattern produces mixer mutes – dark bars are mute 'ons'.

Filter Frequency

The shape in the figure below, drawn with the Line tool, creates the characteristic timbral movement of a filter sweep on a SubTractor synth track, over about five bars. We start with filter frequency at a value of 64 (filter about halfway open) and gradually move up to fully open (a value of 127), then close the filter down again, to a value of less than 30. Copy and paste the curve to continue cyclic filter-sweeping – very ambient! Use the pencil tool if you want an actual 'curve', though the audible effect will be very similar either way.

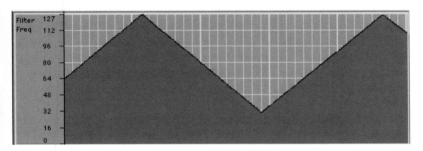

A filter frequency controller curve to create a filter sweep.

Importing and exporting MIDI files

The Reason sequencer can both import Standard MIDI Files (Types 0 and 1) and export Songs as Standard MIDI Files (Type 1).

Importing

- Under the File menu, select 'Import MIDI File'. A MIDI File Browser opens and you will be able to navigate to the folder where your MIDI File is saved. Click on the file name and Open the file.
- The MIDI File opens into the sequencer window. If the MIDI File is a Type 1 (multitrack) File, there will be a separate Reason track for each track in the MIDI file. If it's a Type 0 file (all data on one track), there will be a separate Reason track for each MIDI channel used in the MIDI track. Track names should come with the MIDI file, along with their original MIDI channel name, but there is a chance they will not. (In our experience, Controller data doesn't always come over as expected, either.)
- The tracks will not have assignments to Reason devices, so you'll need to

Tip

Some more shortcuts

Get to know and use the keyboard and numeric keypad shortcuts. This will make sequencer operation much faster and smoother, and save wear and tear on your mouse arm. The computer keyboard arrow keys can be used quite extensively for some jobs that would otherwise require the mouse. In the Track List, the up/down arrows step through entries; in the Arrange View the left/right arrows step sequentially through Groups in a track; in the Edit View the left/right arrows step sequentially through notes. Shift-arrowing steps through groups or notes, selecting them as you go.

create an appropriate rack and assign each track to the device and sound of your choice. Reason is not General MIDI-compatible, so if your MIDI file has a drum part that conforms to General MIDI mapping, you may have to make or modify a Reason drum kit so that it also conforms as far as possible to GM (see the ReDrum chapter for more on GM and drums inside Reason). You could alternatively move drum notes to new notes in the drum edit lane, so that they are played by the right sound in ReDrum.

• When you've adjusted the MIDI File to suit, save it in Reason as a Song.

Reason does not have a tempo map, so if there are tempo changes in the MIDI file, these will not translate. The tempo throughout the File when it is imported into Reason will be the first that occurs in the file.

You may experience small anomalies with MIDI File import from other sequencers. For example, MIDI Files saved in Cubase VST import into the Reason sequencer with two extra bars at the start of the file. These bars are Cubase's preset count-in, and since the Reason sequencer doesn't have a count-in, the extra bars seem to be part of the main body of the file when it is imported. If this happens, simply set the Left and Right markers around the two extra bars and use 'Remove bars between locators' from the Edit menu.

Exporting

MIDI files exported from Reason are of Type 1 (separate MIDI track for each track in Reason).

If the Song includes Patterns from ReDrum or the Matrix, these must be converted to notes in the sequencer, if they have not already been converted, before MIDI File export. This is because exporting as a MIDI File only includes data that is in the main sequencer. Use the 'Copy Pattern to Track' function under the Edit menu in the Redrum or Matrix, if a Pattern chain has not been automated in the sequencer, or 'Convert Pattern track to Notes' under the Edit menu in the sequencer, if a Pattern chain has been automated. If you don't do this step, parts of the Reason Song that are dependent on Pattern-based devices won't be saved as part of the MIDI File. (Remember that no sample data of any kind can be saved as part of a MIDI file, though REX sample loop MIDI slices, for REX loops that have been sent 'To Track', will be included.)

• Make sure the End marker is set where you want the Song to end.
• Select 'Export MIDI File' from the File menu.
• Name the file in the Export MIDI File dialogue. If you check 'Add Extension to File Name', the necessary .mid file extension will be added to the name for you.
• Choose a location and save the File.

Track names should be included in the File, but all the tracks will be set to MIDI channel 1. They will thus have to be re-set when the file is loaded into another sequencer.

Tip

Punch-in/out

There's no dedicated punch in/out facility in the Reason sequencer. One way to proceed if you need to re-do a section of a track that you performed live is to re-record the section with a record loop on another track of the sequencer, then copy the new bit and paste into the old track at the right place – basically, 'comp' sections together into a good track.

Advanced project: faking tempo changes

As you have probably gathered by now, Reason doesn't have a tempo map facility to allow you to change tempo throughout the course of a Song. A tempo map is literally that – a chart of the points during a Song at which you would like its tempo to change. It's especially useful for emulating the kind of speed variations that are typically introduced into music by real human people playing. For example, when a band plays a song, they'll change tempo spontaneously and unconsciously to produce an effect, getting faster towards and during a chorus, and slowing for quieter, more laid-back passages. Tempo mapping has lots of applications in film and TV music, too.

Perhaps the Reason sequencer will get this facility eventually, but in the meantime there is something you can do to introduce the impression of a tempo change, if not the reality. This technique is rather fiddly and long-winded – though it is easier to do than to explain – and in no way flexible enough to emulate a real tempo map (for that, you will need to sync Reason to an external sequencer that does have a tempo map, and if you have such a sequencer you should do that rather than go to all this trouble!). However, it does allow you to do things like speed up a chorus, as mentioned above, slow down an ambient section of a track, or do a sudden dramatic tempo change.

The drawback of the technique is that it basically screws up the relationship between the bars and beats intrinsic to the music and the bars and beats of Reason's ruler. For this reason, you should use it only when a Song is utterly finished and needs no further editing, and also that you work on a copy of the original song. It only works on MIDI note data, not on patterns from ReDrum or the Matrix, so convert these to notes in the sequencer first (use 'Copy Pattern to Track' from the device or 'Convert Pattern Track to Notes' in the sequencer) . It also won't work on tracks with sampled loops, except if they are REX loops. REX loops have MIDI notes to trigger their slices, and since this technique works on all MIDI notes, it will affect REX loops as it should.

The key to the whole idea is the Scale Tempo function in the Change Events window. What we are basically going to do is apply Scale Tempo to sections where we want the impression of a tempo change. If you've read the text earlier in the chapter about the Change Events window, you'll know that Scale Tempo works by changing note values and positions rather than actual tempo. It's probably a good idea to read that section now if you haven't yet.

The Scale Tempo problem

The important thing to realise is that because Scale Tempo actually moves notes along independently of proper ruler positions, when you apply the process to just a section of the Song its notes are moved relative to all the notes that occur thereafter. If Scale Tempo has been used to shorten the duration of the section (speeding up tempo), there will be a gap between the end of the Scaled section and the next notes, as you can see in the 'before' and 'after' screens of the figure. The first section in the second screen has been scaled.

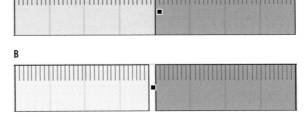

Tempo -scaling the first section to make it seem faster also makes it take up less space (because its note values are shortened) and introduces a gap between it and the next, unscaled section.

A and B
In the second screen, scaling to slow down the tempo has resulted in the section becoming longer, as the note values are increased. See the overlap area, where the scaled section now impinges on the following unscaled

If the duration of the section has been lengthened with Scale Tempo (slowing down tempo), some of the scaled notes will run over the top of the notes in the unscaled section. This is illustrated in the figure below: screen A shows the original (unscaled) version. In screen B, the first section has been scaled to slow it down, but this lengthens the space it occupies, and some of its notes now overlap the second, unscaled section.

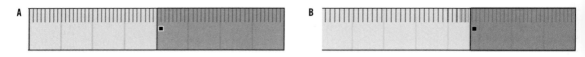

We therefore have to apply Scale Tempo from the point at which the tempo change is required, right to the end of the Song, so that all subsequent notes are pulled back or pushed on accordingly. In the next figure , the first section is not Scaled, while the subsequent ones are. This is the only way we can apply Scale Tempo to sections and avoid gaps or overlaps – we have to apply it from each point where a change is required, right to the end of the song, to change all notes after the tempo change equally. (Of course, the relationship of the scaled notes to the ruler will still be disrupted by the process, but there should be no audible effect to the listener.)

Apply Scale Tempo from the point where the tempo change is needed, right to the end of the Song, to avoid gaps or overlaps. Then apply the next change from where it is needed to the end of the Song – and so on.

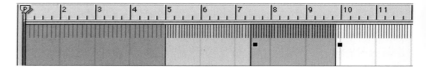

Obviously, then, you have to insert your tempo changes going from the beginning of the song onwards, and not jumping about here and there.

Do the Scale Tempo calculations

For the purposes of the tutorial, we're going to assume a Song at 120bpm whose two choruses we want to speed up to 125bpm, for a bit of subtle extra energy. We therefore need two Scale Tempo percentages: one to speed 120bpm to 125 for the choruses, and one to slow 125 back down to 120 after choruses. Remember that values over 100% increase tempo and values under 100% reduce it. We work out the Scale Tempo percentages before starting, as follows:

- Take the tempo that you want to change to (125bpm in our case) and divide it by the Song's current tempo (120bpm).
- Mutiply the result by 100. The result is 104.1667, which is the ideal Scale Tempo percentage to change 120bpm to 125bpm. We can't enter fractional percentages in the Change Events window, so round the figure up or down to the nearest whole number – 104%. Make a note of that number.
- Now do the calculation you need to take the speed back down after the choruses. Take the tempo that you want to change to (120 in this case), and divide it by the new current tempo (125). Multiply by 100. The result is 96, the Scale Tempo percentage that will slow 125bpm back down to 120bpm after choruses.

You could alternatively do the necessary calculations with a software studio calculator utility such as Bjoern Bojahr's Production Calculator (for Mac). This has a special loop-matching calculator that lets you easily work out tempo-matching percentages. See Appendix 1 for where to find it.

Mark out the Song

Because Scale Tempo moves notes along and affects their relationship with the sequencer ruler, we have to divide each track into Groups, which creates blocks of colour to provide a visual reference of where sections start and end.

- Have your finished Song open in the Arrange View.
- Decide what is the shortest section whose tempo you might want to change in your Song. It will become clearer later why this is necessary. For this tutorial, we'll assume it's four bars, because we're presuming the smallest section of Song we have is four bars – a four-bar intro and a couple of four-bar linking sections between chorus/verse transitions. (This technique is really too fiddly to use with sections shorter than a bar.)
- Select the first four-bar section of the Song, across all tracks, as in the screen above, by drawing a selection rectangle, then use Apple/Control-G. This creates separate four-bar groups on every track.
- Select and Group the next four bars of the song in the same way. Continue selecting and Grouping four-bar sections across all tracks for the rest of the Song. Each four-bar group is now coloured.
- Make a note – using pencil and paper – of where you want tempo changes, in terms of four-bar Groups, rather than bars and beats. We want tempo changes at the start and end of two choruses, so we make a note of the fact that the first chorus starts, perhaps, at the sixth four-bar group and the second chorus starts at the fifteenth four-bar group. The choruses are each sixteen bars (four four-bar groups) long.

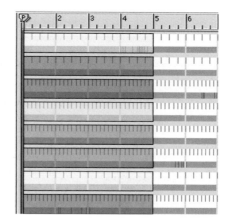

Marking the song out into sections (here it's four-bar sections) across all tracks and Grouping them to create a coloured reference. This will help with Song navigation when ruler positions are disrupted.

Apply Scale Tempo in stages

- Locate the first chorus – at the start of the sixth four-bar Group – and select from the start of it to the end of the Song.
- Open the Change Events window. In the Scale Tempo box, enter the first value from the calculation above – 104% for our example. Click Apply. This speeds up the tempo to 125bpm for the selected part of the Song.
- Now locate the very end of the chorus we just sped up, which is where the tempo needs to go back to its original value. Select from the chorus end to the end of the Song.
- In the Change Events window, enter the second calculation value into the Scale Tempo box. In our case, it's 96%. Click Apply. The tempo from that point to the end of the Song will be slowed back to 120bpm (or thereabouts), leaving the first chorus at 125bpm.
- Locate chorus 2, starting at Group 15, and select from the start of it to the end of the Song. In the Change Events window, enter the first calculation value again – 104% for our example. Click Apply. The whole

selection (which includes the second chorus) is speeded up to around 125bpm.

- To take the rest of the Song's tempo back down to around 120bpm again, select from the end of the second chorus (the start of Group 19) to the end of the Song. Use Scale Tempo on this selection, with the second calculation percentage – 96% for our example.

Some of you may be thinking now that since the results of the Scale Tempo calculations are sometimes fractional, and we can't enter fractional values into the window, there will be a gradual 'drift' away from the desired tempos as successive Scale Tempo operations are performed. This is true, but the effect is minimal with the handful of changes you would expect to want as a maximum in one Song – though it will be greater with larger individual tempo changes. But in general, if the tempo at the end of the Song is 121bpm instead of 120bpm, who is really going to notice? However, if you're bothered about this inaccuracy, it can be reduced by doing the following.

For each Scale Tempo calculation, take the rounded percentage that results from the calculation and convert it back to a bpm value: divide the rounded percentage by 100 and multiply by the 'current tempo' value used in the calculation described above. This provides you with the actual bpm value that was created during the Scale Tempo process, rather than the ideal tempo we were aiming for. Use that bpm value as the 'current tempo' for the next Scale Tempo calculation.

Using the same figures as in the example above, we got a rounded percentage of 104% to speed up 120bpm to 125bpm. If we divide this by 100 and multiply by 120, we get a bpm value of 124.8. This is the actual tempo the Scaling operation produced. Use this figure when you calculate the next Scale Tempo percentage. In our case, 120 divided by 124.8 times 100, which equals 96.15%.

It makes very little difference for only a couple of tempo changes (or small tempo changes), but by using the actual tempo produced by the Scaling operation as the basis for the next calculation, you can maintain greater accuracy over multiple tempo changes. Of course, each fractional percentage to be entered into the Scale Tempo box will still have to be rounded up or down.

You can modify these instructions for any tempos, or to do successive tempo-increasing operations rather than going back to a slower tempo in between. It's obviously quite easy, with this technique, to do a single, dramatic tempo change in the middle of a track, and then back to the original tempo. If you're very dedicated, though, or have lots of time to spare, you can even apply more gradual changes by working on shorter sections at a time.

Automation and remote control

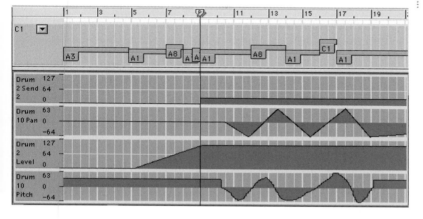

Automation data in the sequencer Controller Lane.

Automation is the term used to describe the process of recording the changes you make to controls (knobs, sliders, switches) in Reason, such that during playback your changes are reproduced exactly as you made them. It's an immensely useful function that allows you not only to create complicated mixes that would otherwise be very difficult (if not impossible) to execute with one pair of hands and a mouse, but also to make all manner of exciting things happen to sounds, samples and effects.

Automation is very simple to achieve in Reason: almost all controls are automatable, and your tweaks are simply recorded in the main sequencer, as if they were notes or any other data. You can even set up a hardware control surface (MIDI fader box), with its controls mapped to on-screen Reason controls, and make spontaneous, hands-on changes. The third method of automating controls is actually drawing controller data into a special lane of the sequencer – not as spontaneous as real-time automation, but very precise. Note that you can now record automation data for more than one device at a time in Reason if you are working 'on the fly', by recording your control tweaks into the sequencer – sometimes newcomers to the program don't immediately realise this.

Also in this chapter you'll read how to set up remote control of Reason, not only via the MIDI fader/knob boxes that give hands-on control of the program and via Remote, but also by assigning computer keyboard keys and/or MIDI keyboard keys to control Reason functions.

The Controller (automatable parameter) list you can access for each device in the sequencer Edit View. This is the Dr:rex list.

Amp Env Attack
Amp Env Decay
Amp Env Sustain
Amp Env Release
Master Level
Filter Env Attack
Filter Env Decay
Filter Env Sustain
Filter Env Release
Filter Env Amount
Filter On
Filter Freq
Filter Q
Filter Type
Osc Octave
Transpose
Osc Fine Tune
Osc Env Amount
LFO1 Rate
LFO1 Amount
LFO1 Wave
LFO1 Dest
Filter Freq Mod Wheel Amount
Filter Res Mod Wheel Amount
Filter Decay Mod Wheel Amount
Pitch Bend Range
Amp Vel Amount
Filter Env Vel Amount
Filter Decay Vel Amount
LFO Sync Enable
Mod Wheel
Pitch Wheel
Sustain Pedal

What can and can't be automated?

In general, you will be able to automate patch but not sample selection in most devices, nor some controls that do not have an effect on the sound. In addition, you can't automate the making of cable connections, nor movements of rear-panel Trim pots, on any device. The easiest way to see what you can automate for a given device is to go to its track in the sequencer (or create one if you don't have one yet), select Edit mode to access the Edit View, click the Show Controller Lane button in the Tool Bar, then click the Controllers button. A pop-up will appear with a list of all the controllers – ie. automatable parameters – available for that device. For example, doing this with an RV7 reverb brings up a list showing Enabled (this is the Bypass/On/Off switch), Size, Decay, Damping, Algorithm, and Dry/Wet balance, which can all be automated. Another method is to select a device and choose Options > Remote Override Edit Mode, which shows all automatable parameters for the device.

Recording automation

On-the-fly tweaking

This is the basic and most straightforward method of automation. As an example, let's imagine you want to automate moving a SubTractor's Filter Frequency slider up and down, to impose timbral changes on the SubTractor sound. (Just move controls or activate switches as you normally would, while automating them.) But the procedure is the same for any automatable control in Reason.

Obviously, you need to have a SubTractor part already recorded in the main sequencer. Also, before you do anything, make sure the 'Overdub/Replace' switch in the Transport bar is in the 'Overdub' position.

- Go to the sequencer track for SubTractor (or whatever device you are automating).
- Click in the 'In' column to the left of the sequencer track name to make the keyboard icon appear. The track is now ready to accept data.
- Click the red Record button, then the Play button in the Transport bar, or press Apple/Control-Return, then hit the Space bar. Your part should play back.
- When you reach the place where you want the control changes, grab the SubTractor Filter Frequency slider (or whichever control you're automating) and move it to get the effect you want. Keep tweaking for as long as you like. You may stop tweaking while the track is playing back, then start tweaking again if you like.
- When you've finished, click the Stop button in the Transport, or press the Return key, two or three times, to stop and return to zero. Click the Play button or hit the Space bar to hear the filter-swept part play back. The control you've automated will have a green box drawn around it, to indicate that it is automated. You can clear the recorded automation at any time by choosing 'Clear Automation' from the Context menu that pops up when you Control-click/Right-click on an automated parameter. (Clear Automation is available as both a Context menu option and an

The automated control will have a green box drawn around it.

Edit menu option when a Controller Lane is
highlighted in the main sequencer.)

This is what automation data looks like
in the sequencer Arrange View.

Do note that the position the control was in before you began
recording the automation is the position it will jump back to
as soon as you stop recording. In many circumstances you will thus probably want to
ensure that the automation changes you make lead you smoothly back to the 'base'
position of the control. This should avoid an abrupt change in timbre or level if there
is a note still playing when automation recording is stopped.

Recording more automation for the same control

If you find you want to change some of what you've done, locate the place
where you want to change, go into Record again, grab the control at the
appropriate point during playback and make new movements.

Be aware that as long as you continue playing back the Song in Record mode, the
old automation data is being overwritten by the new. Even when you stop moving the
control, if you're still playing back in Record mode the older data is being overwritten. You thus need to cease recording as quickly as possible if you want to preserve
subsequent automation data after the area you wanted to replace.

You can either:

- Press the space bar to stop recording, as soon as you've finished the new
  control movements, or
- Click the Reset button in the Transport bar. This immediately stops older
  automation data from being replaced by new. The advantage of this
  method is that you don't now have to stop playback of the Song, but can
  continue through it, recording new bits of automation for the control in
  question if you like, then Resetting after each new bit if you wish to
  preserve what comes after.

The automation
Reset button.

Having to mouse down and click the Reset button can leave a small gap in your
automation, though, where you're still in record but are not tweaking the control.
One way to reduce this is assigning control of the Reset button to a key on your
computer keyboard (which you can activate much faster than mousing down to
click the Reset button). Assigning computer keys to Reason functions is explained
later in this chapter, in the 'Remote Control' section.

Editing automation data in the sequencer

The alternative to going into Record mode to make changes to your automation
(controller) data is graphically editing the data in the controller sub-lane of the
sequencer (see 'Where can I draw in automation data?', later in this chapter).
The Sequencer chapter explains how controller data is actually edited.

Live tweaking of automated controls

Automation moves you have already recorded for a control can be overridden simply by grabbing the control and moving it during playback. As long
as you are not in 'record' mode in the sequencer, the automation data will
not be permanently affected – this just allows you to make changes, for
example, during live performance. As you move the automated control, the
'Punched In' indicator in the Transport bar lights, and from that point the

recorded automation for the control is disabled. You can re-activate it via the Reset button in the Transport. The recorded automation is also automatically reset when playback is stopped.

Automating other controls on the same device

To automate other controls on the same device, proceed as for automating the first control, as explained above, just move the new control instead. The sequencer will record the data into the relevant controller sub-lane in the same track. Automation data that has been recorded for other controls will not be affected. You can, of course, move different controls on the same device during one automation-recording 'pass'.

Note that it is also perfectly possible to swap devices while the sequencer is in 'record', by clicking the 'In' column for another device, to activate MIDI input, then tweaking controls on that device. So, for example, you could be tweaking SubTractor's controls, then (still while the sequence is playing back), click NN19's sequencer track 'In' column and switch to tweaking NN19's controls instead. This could all get a bit hectic, though, unless you set a section in the sequencer to loop and just work on that until you're happy.

It is possible in Reason 3 to light more than one record icon in the sequencer and thus activate automation recording for more than one device at a time. The keyboard icon denotes MIDI note input, and that can only be active on one channel at once. In order to record automation data for a secondary device, the MIDI controller must be set up as being 'with controls', as these are what Reason picks up and maps to the device. See 'Surface Locking' later in the chapter for more on this.

Drawing automation

Some people hardly use on-the-fly automation recording at all, preferring to draw data into the relevant controller sub-lanes of the sequencer. The effect on the device being automated is exactly the same as if the data had been recorded in real time, as explained above. The difference is that you don't get to hear the changes as you create them, in the same way. (Though, as it happens, you can draw controller data as a Song plays back, if you're so inclined!)

Drawing automation data is good in two ways. On the one hand, if you know exactly what you want it allows you to be very precise with controller values and

Mixer channel mutes drawn in the sequencer. Drawing in such data makes the control moves very precise.

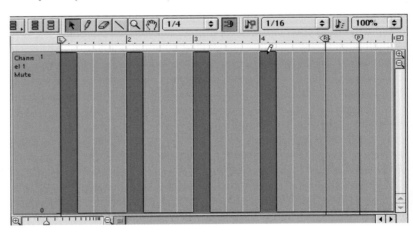

the exact locations of controller changes – especially with something like mixer mutes. You can also take your time and not have to worry about making a mess of things while in Record mode. On the other hand, if you have no idea at all what you want, it can be fun to play around, drawing in data semi-randomly and then listening to see if any interesting effects have been created.

Where can I draw automation data?

Every sequencer track is divided into Lanes, which you can choose to show or hide, and one of these is the Controller Lane (see the sequencer chapter for more). Every control that can be automated on each device has a 'sub-lane' in the Controller Lane. As an example, sub-lanes are available for level, pan, mute, solo, EQ, aux sends, and more, in the Controller Lane of a ReMix track.

To draw controller data to automate a control, you need to get to the relevant lane in the device's sequencer track. There are two quick ways:

- Option/Alt-click the control you want to automate.
- The sequencer instantly switches to the Edit View, the sequencer track for the device is highlighted, and a Controller sub-lane is revealed for the clicked control

or:

- Control/Right-click on the control you want to automate, to summon a Context menu.
- Choose 'Edit Automation' from the menu.

Choose 'Edit Automation' from a control Context menu and you'll be taken straight to the relevant controller lane in the sequencer.

If you want to 'see where you're going', so to speak, here's the longer way:

- Click the sequencer Mode button in the Toolbar to access the Edit View, if it's not currently showing.
- Click the Show Controller Lane button.
- Click the Controllers button in the Tool bar. A pop-up will appear with a list of all the controllers – ie. automatable parameters – available for the device, as illustrated earlier in this chapter.
- Scroll down the list and choose the desired control.

Sequencer Mode button.

Show Controller Lane button.

Controllers button.

When you've done one of these procedures, a blue sub-lane, labelled with the controller name, appears in the sequencer display. (If the parameter has not yet been automated, you'll see the legend 'Not Automated' in the lane.) Draw the desired pattern of controller data in the display with the Pencil tool and/or Line tool. It shows up in solid blue. When you play back the Song, the control (in our screen, pan position on ReMix channel 12) will be automated according to the data you drew in.

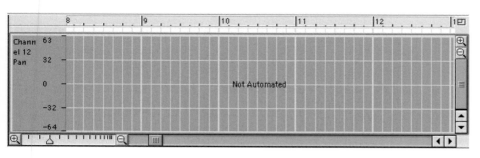

A 'not automated' Pan controller lane.

Some controller-drawing info

- The numbers on the X-axis (left-hand side) are the value range for that control (1-127). The sub-lane for controls that have bi-polar value ranges (such as pan, -64 to +63 – left to right) has a horizontal line across it, which data can go above and below.
- Different patterns of controller drawing result in different effects on device parameters. Some examples, including Pan, are given in the Sequencer chapter.
- The background grid represents time and can be set to different resolutions, just like the note display grid. The ruler is there at the top to help you place where you are in terms of bars.
- Controller drawing can be 'snapped to grid', just like note data, for very precise changes. Just choose your desired resolution and activate the 'Snap to Grid' button in the sequencer Tool bar. Sometimes you may not want this to happen, as it can create a 'stepped' effect. This wouldn't usually be desirable if you were wanting to create a smooth freehand curve.
- Controller data can be cut, copied and pasted just like note data, so you candraw just a little and copy it elsewhere in the track, if appropriate. You can also use the Scale Tempo operation in the Change Events dialogue (Edit menu) on automation data, to change the apparent speed of controller movements (such as filter sweeps, for example).
- In Reason version 2 and above, the Line tool makes it easy to draw smooth fades.
- It will probably help to display the Key Lane (where the notes have been recorded for the track) above the controller sub-lane where you're drawing data, so you can marry up the controller data with what's happening in the track.

The 'Snap to Grid' button and grid resolution pop-up.

Recording MIDI fader box moves

Probably the most fun way of automating Reason controls is via a MIDI hardware controller box. Assigning the physical controls of such a unit to alter on-screen controls of Reason devices removes the limitation of having to tweak with the mouse, allows you to alter two controls at the same time (or more if you have friends!) and makes the software devices feel like real instruments.

Before you can record automation with a MIDI controller box, you have to assign the controls on the MIDI box to the controls in Reason. This procedure is explained in a moment, in the Remote Control section. Using the MIDI controller box for automation once you have assigned its controls will also be dealt with.

Tip

What can I do with automation?

A major use of automation in Reason is to add real-time timbral and other tweaks after a track has been recorded, adding interest and variation to what might be quite simple material. Creative uses of this kind of automation are probably unlimited – for example, automating movements of the Filter | Frequency slider in the synth and sampler devices, for easy filter sweeping; pitch-bend and modulation wheels; tweaks of any other synthesis controls; ReDrum sound con trols, such as the channel Pitch knobs; movements of effect parameter knobs such as Reverb Decay, Delay Feedback and Pan, Chorus Feedback and | Mod Amount. 'Functional' uses of automation include automating pan position, mutes, solos, level changes and fades of ReMix mixer channels for Song mixdown; level, pan, mute and solo of individual drum voices in ReDrum; on-the-fly Pattern changes in ReDrum and the Matrix.

Automating Pattern chains in the Controller Lane

The usual method for automating Pattern changes in the Pattern-based devices is via the Pattern Lane in the main sequencer, where changes are recorded and may also be edited or drawn in (see the Sequencer chapter for more). If you are drawing

in Pattern changes, every time you need to change Pattern you have to click to summon a pop-up menu list, choose the desired Pattern, then draw it for the desired duration. An alternative is to use the Matrix/ReDrum sequencer track's 'Selected Pattern'

Controller sub-lane. Display the Pattern Lane above this controller sub-lane. When you draw data into the Controller sub-lane, a Pattern label will appear in the Pattern lane, and you'll see this Pattern label change according to the controller value you have drawn into the controller sub-lane. Dragging the controller data up or down changes Pattern, without you having to select a pop-up menu or choose anything. You know which Patterns are being selected by your controller drawing because you can refer to the Pattern Lane, above.

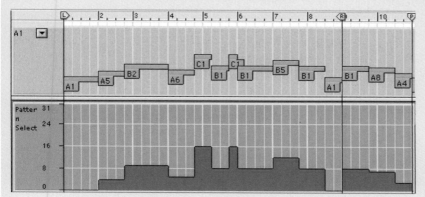

Easier Pattern chain automating in the 'Selected Pattern' Controller sub-lane.

Surface Locking

New in Reason 3, the Remote system is geared towards giving you greater hands-on control of your racks and projects. Setting up is explained earlier on, and once you have defined your various connected MIDI devices in Reason's preferences you can get to work building a multi-controller setup for spontaneous recording or live performance. This is actually much easier than it sounds thanks to the clever way in which Surface Locking works.

Using more than one MIDI controller in Reason 3

Remote – the basics

When you set up your main MIDI keyboard you can choose to make it the Master Keyboard. This is the sequencer input and the keyboard you will use to control Reason in normal operation. You can only record note data into Reason's sequencer on one track at a time, and it is the Master Keyboard which plays that note data. Whichever MIDI track has the keyboard icon lit will be receiving notes. However in Reason 3 with Remote, you can control other modules at the same time by locking subsequent controllers to them, and although you can't record note data for those other modules using secondary controllers, you can record all other automation data like faders, filters and patch selection.

Reason picks up what devices you have installed and assigns controls on modules to the controls on the hardware automatically. If you have an officially supported controller which appears as an option in the Preferences you'll get a totally optimized control mapping. If you are using a more generic controller Reason will make an educated guess and pick the most likely controls to map. For example, volume, filters and osc controls. By default, all connected controllers follow the Master Keyboard. That means that both keyboards will play a device at once. In this situation you can record note data from two or more keyboards at once because they are both playing on the same sequencer track. So for example with a big Combi or a piano loaded you could have one person playing the left hand from one keyboard and someone else playing the right hand. Both could be tweaking controls in realtime, and everything could be recorded. With two controllers sending data to one device, both will control various front panel controls, as determined by Reason until you manually remap them.

Locking Surfaces to Devices

A more popular use of Remote will be where several people want to play and control the same project at the same time. In this case, you will need to lock devices to modules in order to proceed. Although the Master keyboard will always play whatever you select in the rack or the sequencer, you can make additional controllers which you connect lock to specific devices, in which case they won't ever move unless you unlock them. The idea is that you can play one device and control another using separate controllers. One particularly useful suggestion is to lock a device to the main Mixer so that channel levels, mutes and solos are always at your fingertips as you play.

A 'control surface' really just means a MIDI input device, be it a simple keyboard or a fully-fledged MIDI controller like the Mackie Control.

There are several ways to lock a surface to a device in Reason's rack.

1. Select Options > Surface Locking. You will see a window displaying all the MIDI devices you have set up and a Lock To Device menu. By choosing a surface (not the Master Keyboard) you can assign it to a specific device.

That hardware controller will now be auto-mapped to the parameters on the front of the module you have just locked it to. If you select Options > Remote Override Edit Mode you will see a small padlock denoting that the module is locked to a surface.

> **Tip**
>
> The Master Keyboard can't be locked to a device unless you choose to "Use no Master Keyboard" in the Preferences.

Assigning a device to control a specific module in the rack

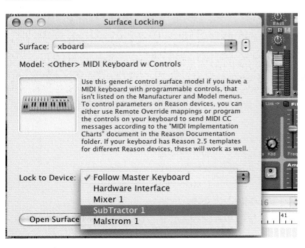

A module which has a control surface locked to it displays a padlock in Remote Mode

2. A much quicker way is to use the contextual menu. Simply control-click or right-click on a module and from the list of available controllers which appears, choose one. All the assignable surfaces you have set up will appear in this list. You can only lock one surface to one device at a time, but you can lock more than one surface to the same device. For example, to get comprehensive control over a mixer using several hardware controllers.

To unlock a surface from a device, you can either user the contextual menu to de-select the 'Lock To' option, or open the Surface Locking window and reset the surface's setting to 'Follow Master Keyboard'.

Use the contextual menu as an alternative way of locking devices together

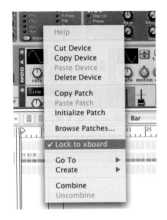

Recording with locked surfaces

If you select more than one red record button in the sequencer you will activate data (not note) recording for those tracks. Only the track with MIDI focus (the keyboard icon lit) will record note data, and it will be controlled by the Master keyboard. However, every other device will record any input from the mouse or from other MIDI control surfaces as automation data. This can be accessed and edited in the usual way. If you unlock a device or re-lock it to another module, Reason will remember any automation you have already recorded in the sequencer.

Remote override

Reason 3 comes with some excellent standard mapping for translating the controls on your MIDI surfaces on-the-fly to the parameters on whichever device you select in the rack. If like most people you have a MIDI surface which isn't specifically supported by Reason (which is most of them, as there are so many on the market), or you just want to take matters into your own hands, you can easily re-program the MIDI controls and the way your hardware talks to the software.

Reason shows you which parameters are standard mapped

Oscillator A Motion – Standard mapped to Roland RD700 SX : CC 92

How it works

If you select 'Remote Override Edit Mode' from the Options menu, all devices except the one you have selected are greyed out. The device will show a series of new icons – blue arrows and yellow knobs. The blue arrows denote parameters that can be mapped to a control on a control surface, and the yellow knobs show parameters which are already standard mapped by Reason. To be able to see which parameters are currently mapped for a

A parameter, double clicked, about to be re-assigned

device, you have to direct MIDI input to the sequencer track it is connected to by clicking on the Keyboard icon in the sequencer.

Once you have chosen the parameter you want to assign there are two ways of making it happen. The first is to double click on the arrow or knob, changing it into a rotating lightning bolt. If you then press a key or move a control on the relevant control surface, it will be mapped to that parameter.

The second method is to right-click / control-click on the arrow or knob and choose Edit Remote Override Mapping. This gives you a window which lets you input the controller in a different way. You can select a Surface from the menu, then one of the many CC or pedal controls available for that Surface. You can also manually input the name of a note.

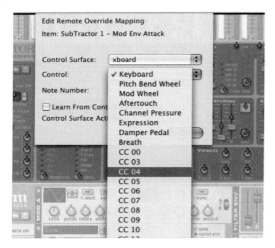

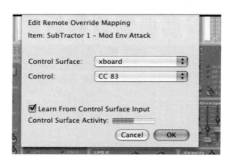

Make Reason auto-detect by moving the controller on your control surface

Manually specifying a MIDI controller channel to assign to a parameter on a module

For a quicker alternative, check the 'Learn from Control Surface Input' box and simply move the control or press the note yourself. Reason will detect the specific MIDI device and control for you.

Tip

Reason will warn you if your mapping conflicts with one you've already set. If you are trying to paste in the mappings into a device in the same project, a dialog appears to warn you. You then have the choice of cancelling the operation, or to move the existing overrides to the new device.

Reason will warn you if you try to assign a CC that's already used

Any overridden parameters will now show up as lightning bolts in the rack when in Remote Override Edit mode, even if the device in the rack doesn't have MIDI focus.

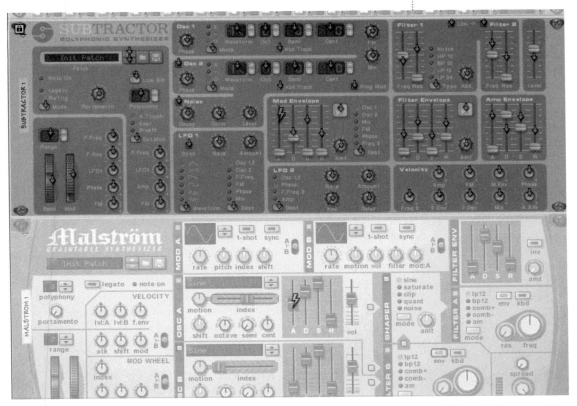

Overridden controls show up even if the device isn't selected

Quickly access the mapping window with the contextual menu

Tip

You don't have to be in Remote Override Edit Mode to quickly assign a controller. In normal view, simply right-click on a parameter and select Edit Remote Override Mapping, which takes you straight to the window.

Removing Remote Overrides can be done by selecting the parameter, right-clicking and choosing 'Clear Remote Override Mapping. Alternatively, select a device and choose Edit > Clear All Remote Override Mappings for Device. The same menu lets you copy and paste overrides between devices. Note that you must be in Remote Override Edit mode to see the clear, copy and paste overrides commands.

Clear, copy or paste remote overrides
using the Edit menu in Remote Override
Edit mode.

Additional Remote Overrides

Selecting Options > Additional Remote Overrides opens a window containing some handy extra commands which are useful in a live setting, or for continuous recording of different modules without stopping and starting. Some, like Undo and Redo are pretty self-explanatory. Map Undo to a key or a button and pressing it will undo the last action performed in Reason. The most unusual are the selection shortcuts. For example, assigning Target Previous / Next Track to two buttons on a control surface lets you move MIDI focus in Reason's sequencer up and down. Effectively, you can switch between instruments live without going near the computer. Incredibly useful for live performance. And Select Prev / Next Patch for Target Device lets you override the standard patch selection controls as auto-mapped by Reason. Use this if you prefer to always use specific buttons on your control surface for selecting patches. Assigning additional overrides from this window simply involves double clicking the name and choosing a button, key or knob to map it to, as before.

Further specialised assignable controls

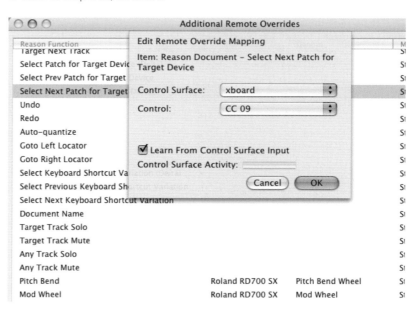

If you have created a particularly complex remote control setup you may want to save it as a template song, as remote setups that you create are saved with the song, not globally. Reason remembers its standard mappings on a global level.

Uses for Surface Locking

Surface locking is equally useful in a studio, recording or live performance situation. Here are a few examples.

1. In your studio, set up your main MIDI keyboard as the Master, then any other keyboards you have as secondary controllers. Lock the controllers to devices for which you have already recorded note data in the sequencer. Now as you play back whilst recording, you can manually tweak the controls of the locked modules and also record new data by assigning the master keyboard to different devices. With proper setup you could do this without having to touch the computer, which makes for a more organic composition experience.

2. In a live situation, replicate the setup from above. This time, using a powered USB hub, connect a number of surfaces and have different people controlling them. Although they can't directly play the modules they can control them, and there's a brilliant workaround involving pattern devices, especially the Combinator.

If you pre-prepare a track well, you can have different people contributing just as much to a live performance as the person playing the Master keyboard. The key is that pattern-based devices like the ReDrum and the Matrix can have their pattern selection buttons assigned to controls using the Remote Override method described above. So by assigning drum patterns 1 to 8 of a ReDrum to, say, the first 8 keys on a MIDI keyboard, the player can switch between them, triggering them at will as the song plays. The same applies to Matrix patterns. And because there are four banks of eight presets per module, the possibilities are huge.

Even better, with the Combinator you can use the same trick to control the assignable buttons and knobs on its front panel, as well as any of the modules within the Combi. So for example you use the Combi programmer window to assign a button to switch between Matrix patterns while the Matrix controls an NN-XT with multiple loops and samples loaded. Then when you move the control on the keyboard you have the power to switch between those different loops. Using the Combi means you can collect lots of controls together on its front panel for easier tweaking, rather than doing it using individual modules (see pic overleaf).

This process sounds much more complicated than it really is. Try it using one of the supplied 'Run' Combis (with pattern devices) from the Factory Sound Bank and you'll soon see how much fun it is. Any changes you make can be recorded so you can capture the perfect performance, or indeed iron out any mistakes later.

3. In a studio or live setting, lock a dedicated MIDI control surface to the ReMix Mixer for total control over levels, solo and mute as you play, without having to use the mouse. For this to be really effective you need a well-specified MIDI controller with enough faders and buttons to give you the level of control you want. .

Tip

Effects can be controlled remotely as well as instruments. Patch, preset and dry-wet can be assigned as well as many more.

Edit Remote Override Mapping

Item: Combinator 1 – Rotary 4

Control Surface: xboard

Control: CC 83

☑ Learn From Control Surface Input

Control Surface Activity:

Cancel   OK

Assign controls to trigger loops and patterns in a Combi for total creative freedom

Remote Control

Computer keyboard remote

You may be familiar with the useful computer keyboard shortcuts that are preset in Reason – such as the space bar for stopping and starting the sequencer – but you can also define extra keyboard keys to control functions of your choice, mentioned earlier in this chapter.

Check 'Enable Keyboard Remote' in the Options menu, then choose 'Edit Keyboard Remote' to show which controls can be remotely assigned.

✓ **Enable Keyboard Remote**
 Edit Keyboard Remote
 Clear All Keyboard Remote

- Under the Options menu, make sure 'Enable Keyboard Remote' is checked, or use Apple-G/Control-G to enable it.
- Select 'Edit Keyboard Remote' from the Options menu. In the device that's currently highlighted, yellow arrows will appear, pointing at all controls that are available to be assigned to computer keyboard keys.

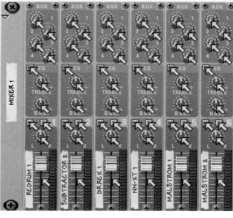

The available controls are shown by arrows.

- Alternatively, if you know the parameter you want to remotely control is available, use a Context menu: don't select Edit Keyboard Remote, but instead Control-click/right-click the control. This summons a pop-up where you can choose 'Edit Keyboard Remote'. (Then skip the next step, and go on to the subsequent one.)
- Click the control you want to assign to a key. The Keyboard Remote dialogue pops up.
- Press the keyboard key you want to use. The Key Received meter should show activity, and the name of the key you pressed is shown in the dialogue. Click OK and the key is assigned to that control.
- Continue as above for other keys if desired.
- When you're done with assigning, click 'OK'. You can change individual key assignments at any time by repeating the process above, or clear all the key assignments for a Song by selecting 'Clear All Keyboard Remote' from the Options menu.

The Keyboard Remote dialogue.

Which controls could I assign to the keyboard?

As keyboard keys act as on/off switches, you will probably not want to assign them to knobs and sliders, which need 'continous'-type control. If you do assign a key to a slider or knob, pressing that key toggles between the two extremes of the control's travel – which might be usable on the odd occasion! (In the case of 'multi-selector' buttons used for such things as selecting filter types and LFO destinations in SubTractor, pressing the computer keyboard key assigned to the button will cycle through the options.)

Mixer mutes and solos could be assigned to computer keys.

Computer keyboard keys are especially suitable for controls such as mutes and solos on the ReMix mixer. You could assign mutes to one row of keyboard keys and solos

to the next, for easy real-time performance mixing, for example. Shift-key combinations can be assigned if you run out of keys. Mixer mutes and solos are also preset in Reason to certain MIDI keyboard keys, but you may prefer to use computer keys – and if you run Reason on a laptop you may not always have a MIDI keyboard with you.

Note that not all keyboard keys can be assigned : for example, you can't assign any of the ones that are already preset by Propellerhead, including Numeric Keypad keys (see the Sequencer chapter for a list of these).

Saving remote control assignments

Unfortunately, specific remote assignments are only saved at Song level. There's no specific facility within Reason for 'remembering' preferred assignments.Thankfully the Remote system auto-maps a device's controls to modules' controls by default. The best thing to do with specific setups you've created is either save a Song which only has the relevant devices and their remote assignments in it, but nothing recorded into the sequencer, or save the same thing as part of your default Song, which opens every time you launch Reason. See Chapter 4 for details of saving a default Song.

Tip

Wot, no automation?

You may occasionally experience a small bug with automation, whereby when you open and play a Song its recorded automation doesn't play back, and it sounds as though the Song has not been automated. Quickly fast-forwarding through the Song and then returning to zero (press '0' on the numeric keypad or the Return key twice, or double-click the Stop button in the transport bar) resets the automation and makes the Song play back properly.

Reason and MIDI Control

Before going into the remote control of Reason via MIDI, here are a few words about what makes MIDI control possible in the first place, for those who are not yet up to speed with MIDI.

Although you don't have much occasion to use MIDI (the Musical Instrument Digital Interface) actually within Reason itself, the program has a 'MIDI specification' like all other MIDI devices and software. Part of the MIDI standard, which allows MIDI-equipped gear to communicate with other MIDI-equipped gear, involves 'MIDI Controllers'. Amongst other things, these messages allow parameters on one instrument or device to be altered by controls on another MIDI device. The MIDI standard specifies 128 of these MIDI Controllers, and it is up to the manufacturer of the equipment to decide which MIDI Controllers will be assigned to which parameters on their equipment.

Propellerhead have done just this with Reason: nearly every parameter on every Reason device, such as Amplitude Envelope Attack on SubTractor, channel level on ReMix, or delay feedback on a DDL1, has a MIDI Controller number assigned to it, and messages sent via MIDI to that Controller number will alter that parameter in Reason. For example, MIDI controller number 7 alters volume in Reason devices.

From this, it should be easy to see that if you have a way of sending a MIDII Controller message from outside the software, you will be able to alter Reason controls remotely. In recent years, as software instruments have become more widespread, hardware MIDI controller boxes – literally small tabletop units with a surface covered in knobs or faders and sometimes also switches – have become increasingly popular. The knobs or faders transmit MIDI Controller messages when they are moved, and these messages alter controls in the software instrument. Once you're set up, using a hardware controller unit with a software synth is like using a real-world synth with knobs on it.

How MIDI controller boxes work.

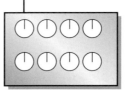

**MIDI Hardware
Controller**

The MIDI hardware controller knob is set up to transmit a specific MIDI controller message that the synth recognises as an instruction to alter one of its own controls – in this case, Filter B Frequency.

Remote control using a MIDI keyboard

MIDI control can be used to allow keys on your MIDI keyboard to alter Reason parameters. Reason comes with various functions already assigned to MIDI notes, so that pressing certain keys on your keyboard controls those functions. (MIDI Note 0 is C-2 (five octaves below middle C or C3), MIDI Note 60 is C3, and Note 127 is G8.) Note that any key on your keyboard can fire the gate trigger on both the RV7000 ECF42.

ReMix

White keys between MIDI Notes 0 and 23	Channels 1–14 Mute
White keys between MIDI Notes 24 and 47	Channels 1–14 Solo
White keys between MIDI Notes 48 and 71	Channels 1–14 EQ On/Off

ReDrum

All keys between MIDI Notes 36 and 45	Trigger drum channels 1–10
White keys beween MIDI Notes 48 and 64	Mute drum channels 1–10
White keys between MIDI Notes 72 and 88	Solo drum channels 1–10

Dr:rex

All keys between MIDI Notes 0 and 11	Transpose down 1 semitone per key
MIDI Note 12	Reset to original pitch
All keys between MIDI Notes 13 and 24	Transpose up 1 semitone per key
MIDI Note 26	Trigger entire loop
All keys between MIDI Notes 29 and 127	Trigger Slices 1–99

BV512

All keys between MIDI Notes 36 and 67	Mod Band Gain 1 to 32
MIDI Note 72	Hold

If you try to use some of these assignments, you may discover that they make use of some rather inconvenient MIDI keys; for example, the 72-note version of Korg's Trinity can't be transposed far enough to. take advantage of functions mapped to the lower end of the MIDI note range. Your keyboard may be more transposable!

The assignments listed above are fixed, so if your keyboard can't use some of them, you will have to go about things in a different way. Some MIDI hardware controllers have assignable buttons which can be set to send out Note Numbers via MIDI. It should thus be possible to set up the buttons to send MIDI notes that correspond to the wanted function – for example, ReMix channel mutes.

Alternatively, use the method described later in this chapter for MIDI Remote Mapping – but using your MIDI keyboard instead of a MIDI hardware controller box. This would tell Reason which keys (of your choice) on your MIDI keyboard should activate functions such as mutes, solos and so on.

Setting up a MIDI hardware controller

Obviously, you need a suitable MIDI controller unit. These usually have 16 knobs or faders, so you can assign 16 Reason controls to be altered by them,

---

> **Tip**
>
> **Keyboard control of Matrix and ReDrum Pattern changes**
>
> It's useful to set up computer keyboard keys or Control Surfaces (as explained elsewhere in this chapter) to switch Patterns in ReDrum and the Matrix, rather than mouse-clicking the Pattern buttons to change Patterns. Go into record mode in the sequencer and you can spontaneously swap between Patterns to build up a Song on the fly. Switching Patterns in this way would also be an option during live performance. You can also set MIDI keyboard keys to do the same job: assign a key of your choice to Pattern Bank selection, using the method described in 'Using MIDI Remote Mapping' and it and the three semitones above it will select the four Banks; assign a key to Pattern selection and it and the next seven semitones will select the eight Patterns in the current Bank. You might need to tape a few labels to your master keyboard to keep track, though!

and some work on a Bank system, whereby you can switch banks to assign additional sets of 16 controls. (See the section later in this chapter for more on MIDI hardware controllers.)

If you are using a standard MIDI setup – ie. MIDI controller keyboard and separate MIDI interface – the MIDI Out of your hardware controller box will have to be plugged into a MIDI In of the MIDI interface, which in turn is connected to your computer. If you have a USB keyboard with built-in MIDI interfacing, or a MIDI controller keyboard with a selection of knobs for controlling software parameters, or even a combined MIDI/audio interface and hardware control surface, consult the unit's manual for MIDI connection instructions.

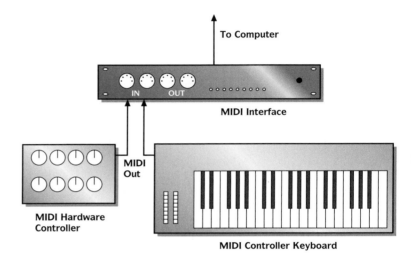

A basic MIDI controller setup.

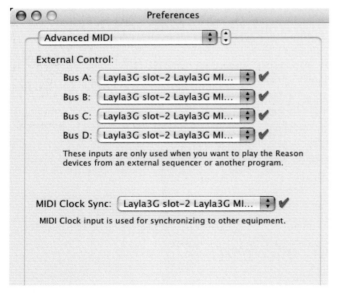

Selecting your controller as the 'Remote Control' MIDI input in the Advanced MIDI Preferences.

Using 'MIDI Remote Mapping'

Please note that the final part of this chapter, from here to the end, applies only to versions of Reason prior to 3. The Remote system was introduced to alleviate the complexity of external MIDI control and automation, and Surface Locking took things a step further. If you have a version of reason older than v3, or are interested in MIDI setup, read on. If you have v3, the Remote and Surface Locking sections will explain how to get the most out of automating and controlling your software.

The easiest way of setting up a hardware controller for remote control is Reason's MIDI Remote Mapping, found under the Options menu. With this method, you make Reason learn which controls on the MIDI box will alter its on-screen controls.

- Go to the Edit menu and select Preferences.
- Choose the 'Advanced MIDI' page.
- In the bottom part of the Advanced MIDI page, click the box next to 'Remote Control' and choose the MIDI input that your controller is connected to from the pop-up menu. It's best, if you have a multi-port MIDI interface, to reserve one MIDI input just for your MIDI controller. (If you have only a single-port MIDI interface there are issues you will need to address, which will be explained shortly.)
- Select the device in the rack – let's assume it's a ReMix mixer – that you want to control via the MIDI control surface, by clicking it.
- From the Options menu, select Edit MIDI Remote Mapping. Green arrows will appear on the ReMix device, pointing at all remote-controllable knobs, sliders and switches.
- Alternatively, if you know the control you want to assign is available for remote operation, use a contextual menu: don't select Edit MIDI Remote Mapping in the Options menu, but simply Control-click/right-click the control. This summons a dialogue box where you can choose 'Edit MIDI Remote Mapping'. (Then skip the very next step, and go straight to the 'Learn from MIDI' check box.)
- Click on a device control you want to assign to your MIDI box – say, a mixer fader – and the MIDI Remote dialogue box appears. The dialogue is waiting for you to tell it which MIDI controller message (sent from your hardware control surface) will alter that on-screen fader.
- Click the 'Learn from MIDI' check box and tweak the knob or slider on your MIDI controller box that you want to assign to that Reason mixer fader. The MIDI Received meter should register activity when you do this, and Reason now knows which MIDI controller message should change that parameter. Click OK and the assignment is made. Do the complete procedure for as many controls as desired.
- When you have made a successful assignment, the green arrow previously pointing to the control in question changes to a pale green box. When you are finished with assignments, you must go back to the Options menu and un-check 'Edit MIDI Remote Mapping'.

(Instead of using 'Learn from MIDI', you can, alternatively, manually key a MIDI controller number into the Controller window. For example, you may know that Knob 1 on your control surface transmits Controller 20. If you entered '20' as the Controller in the MIDI Remote dialogue, Knob 1 on your control surface would then alter the mixer fader.) 'The Clear All MIDI Remote mapping' command under the Options menu gets rid of the assignments you have set up if you want to start again.

Recording automation moves with 'MIDI Remote Mapping'

The Reason Operation manual states that automation recording is not possible with MIDI Remote Mapping. It actually is possible, and is usually quite straightforward:

- First, ensure your hardware controller is selected as the MIDI Input for the Remote Control buss, in Advanced MIDI Preferences. It's not

You can see which controls are available for remote operation by choosing 'Edit MIDI Remote Mapping' in Options.

The MIDI Remote dialogue. Check 'Learn from MIDI' and move the desired control on the hardware controller.

necessary to select the device for which you'll be recording controller data, but it is necessary to ensure that the device is assigned to a sequencer track.

- Click in the 'In' column to the left of the device's sequencer track name to make the MIDI plug icon appear. The track is now ready to accept data – in this case, MIDI controller data generated by your MIDI controller box.

- Engage 'record', and wiggle the MIDI controller box's knobs or faders; their on-screen counterparts should move in response.

- Stop and play back; you should see the same moves happening again.

The MIDI Remote Mapping system lets you create assignments between your controller box and more than one Reason device, within the same controller 'bank' on the MIDI box, or in a different bank. This is great for live performance, and when creating spur-of-the-moment changes during a live mix to DAT or CD. Unfortunately, it's still only possible to actually record changes for one device at a time – selected, as usual, by ensuring the MIDI socket is enabled in a Sequencer track's 'In' column. While recording movements for a device in this way, you'll still be able to control parameters on another device that have been assigned to your controller box, but these movements won't be recorded.

'Direct Controller' programming

MIDI Remote Mapping is the easiest method of setting up controller units, because the 'Learn from MIDI' mode saves a lot of trouble, and you can simply decide which controllers need to be assigned as and when you need them. It's also a good option for people with a preset-type MIDI controller box, such as the original Keyfax Phat Boy (whose controls always transmit the same, fixed controller messages). However, it is also slightly restricted in its flexibility. Why?

After setting up MIDI Remote Mapping as explained above, Reason has learned which controls on the MIDI controller box alter the Reason device controls for that Song. When you save the Song, the assignments are saved with it. But the MIDI controller box has learned nothing at all about Reason, and when you want to do the same thing again, in a new Song, you'll have to teach Reason which controls should do what, all over again. (The alternative is that you do the above procedure with a blank Song and save the Song as a Default, using it as a starting point next time.)

The other method of setting up a MIDI control surface – Direct Controller Programming – involves you manually telling each knob, fader and switch on the controller box to transmit the MIDI controller number necessary to alter a specific parameter in Reason. The controller numbers pre-set to Reason parameters are given in the Reason MIDI Implementation PDF that comes with the program.

This method takes longer and is more trouble, but when you have done it those control assignments are saved in the hardware controller itself. You create one profile, or set of profiles (one each for several devices, perhaps), and you'll be able to use them at any time in any Reason Song, since the profiles have been created in the hardware controller rather than within Reason,

Figure 18.23
You may be able to use the controls of an instrument you already own to alter Reason parameters.

Tip

Using your MIDI gear for remote control and automation

Many synths and workstations, and other MIDI devices are equipped with faders or knobs capable of generating MIDI data. If you don't have a dedicated MIDI control surface, these faders or knobs can be assigned to do the jobs discussed in this chapter. You can find out if your instrument's controls generate MIDI data by connecting a MIDI analyser to the output of the instrument, tweaking a control and seeing if anything registers on the analyser. The instrument manual may also tell you.

and the controller, rather than the Song, now 'knows' what should alter what.

You must have a programmable MIDI controller box to use Direct Controller Programming (not all controllers are programmable).

'Direct Programming' a hardware controller

You'll need the MIDI Implementation chart for Reason, provided as a PDF document when you install the program. The relevant parts are also supplied as an appendix to this book, which is easier than using the PDF. What you basically have to do now is customise the faders or knobs on your MIDI controller box to transmit MIDI controller messages corresponding to the controls you want to alter in Reason.

The exact procedure for telling the knobs or faders which MIDI controllers to transmit will differ from unit to unit. Broadly speaking, you will need to:

- Look up the MIDI Controller numbers for individual Reason device parameters, in turn, in the MIDI Implementation chart.
- Somewhere in the controller box's editing system, assign those numbers to be transmitted by knobs or faders on the controller box.

It may be necessary to input parameter ranges and other data, but the box's user manual should provide all the details. The best thing to do is make separate templates for controlling different devices – one for SubTractor, one for ReMix, one for ReDrum, and so on – saving them in different memories on your controller.

Fortunately, in the case of the Reason synth and sampler devices there is a good chance that if you create a template (or 'profile') that controls major parameters for one device, it will work for other devices. This is because

Propellerhead have assigned similar controls across different devices – for example, filter resonance and cutoff frequency, and amplitude envelope controls – to the same MIDI Controller numbers. The same controller that works for one of these parameters in SubTractor should also work for that parameter in NN19, Dr:rex, and so on. There will never be any conflicts, because it's only possible to address, and hence record controller movements for, one device at a time in this mode. (Note that no MIDI controller messages are available for ReMix aux send 4.)

We recommend that you check the manufacturer's web site before you do all this, in case they've already provided a suitable template, or templates, for use with Reason. If not, you'll have to refer to the controller box's manual for instructions on making the assignments. Luckily, some boxes – such as Philip Rees' C16 – can be configured using an on-screen computer editor, which is very handy.

Having created a controller template, get Reason working with the controller box:

• Make sure the controller box is connected to Reason via MIDI as explained earlier.
• Go to the Reason Edit menu and choose 'Preferences'.
• Choose the MIDI page.
• Select your MIDI controller box as the Sequencer Port input. (You may notice that this step differentiates Direct Controller Programming from MIDI Remote Mapping explained earlier; in the latter, the Remote Control port is selected as the MIDI controller's input.)

Some MIDI controller boxes come with a software front-end, like this one for the Philip Rees C16, which makes configuring them much easier.

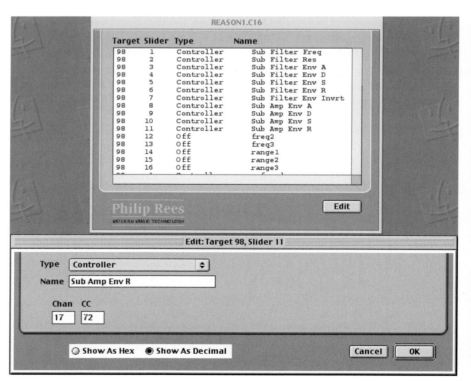

- In the sequencer, select the track assigned to the device you'd like to control.
- Click in the 'In' column to the left of the sequencer track name to make the MIDI plug icon appear. The track is now ready to accept data – in this case, MIDI controller data generated by your MIDI controller box. When you move controls on the box, the correct ones as assigned by you should also move on screen.

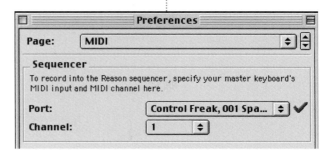

In MIDI Preferences, make sure the hardware controller is selected as the Sequencer Port.

Note that with this method of using a hardware controller you won't be able to play a Reason device from your master keyboard at the same time as using the MIDI controller box, since the software doesn't allow more than one MIDI instrument to be set to the Sequencer Port. There are a couple of hardware workarounds to this problem, though.

The first idea is to connect the MIDI Outs of your master keyboard and MIDI controller box to a MIDI 'merge box', and connect the merger's MIDI output to an input on your MIDI interface. Alternatively, patch the MIDI out of your master keyboard to the MIDI in of the controller box and the output of the controller box to your MIDI interface. Most hardware controllers allow this, merging the output from your keyboard with the controller movements before sending the mix of MIDI data to the MIDI Out port.

To record automation moves

Recording moves from your MIDI controller box using Reason's fixed MIDI assignments has a lot in common with the process of recording a standard MIDI performance from your keyboard.

- Make sure that your hardware controller is selected as the MIDI input for the sequencer port, in MIDI Preferences.
- If the device for which you're recording controller moves hasn't been assigned to a sequencer track, make that assignment now.
- Click in the 'In' column to the left of the sequencer track name to make the MIDI plug icon appear. The track is now ready to accept data – in this case, MIDI controller data generated by your MIDI controller box.
- Start recording, and wiggle the fader box's knobs or sliders; their on-screen counterparts will also move.
- Stop recording and play back; you'll see the movements you just recorded playing back.

With this method of automation, you'll have to ensure that there's a compatible template programmed in the hardware controller box for each device to be automated. You may need to select a different profile, and will certainly need to move the 'In' column MIDI icon to the relevant device track, each time you want to record automation for a different device.

Two ways of using a master keyboard and a 'direct controller'-programmed fader box at the same time with Reason.

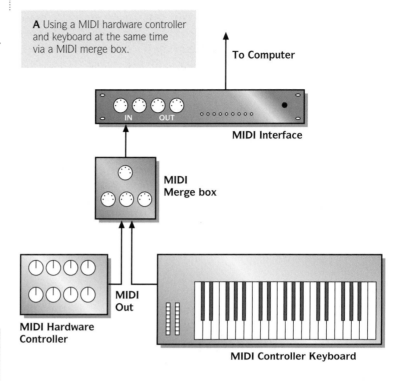

A Using a MIDI hardware controller and keyboard at the same time via a MIDI merge box.

To Computer

MIDI Interface

MIDI Merge box

MIDI Out

MIDI Hardware Controller

MIDI Controller Keyboard

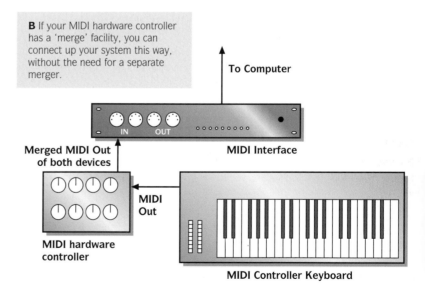

B If your MIDI hardware controller has a 'merge' facility, you can connect up your system this way, without the need for a separate merger.

To Computer

MIDI Interface

Merged MIDI Out of both devices

MIDI Out

MIDI hardware controller

MIDI Controller Keyboard

Potential problems with MIDI Remote Mapping

If you have a setup that gives you only one MIDI input to Reason (such as those with a single-port MIDI interface, to which is linked your master keyboard and a MIDI controller box), you may experience problems when trying to record automation movements with the controller box, if you have assigned the controls using MIDI Remote Mapping. The same problems could arise even if you simply want to be able to play a Reason device from a MIDI keyboard at the same time as tweaking Reason controls via a MIDI box.

With these systems, if you want to record automation data into the sequencer you need a sequencer MIDI input active, and if you want to use a MIDI controller box, via MIDI Remote Mapping, to actually create the automation moves, you need a Remote Control MIDI input also active. Both these MIDI inputs will be selected in Preferences, and any MIDI data that comes into your single MIDI port will be sent to both these Reason inputs. This can cause a conflict which may be revealed by more than one control in Reasonbeing changed when you move a control on your fader box.

Let's explain by example.

- Imagine Knob 1 on your controller box is preset by the manufacturer to send out controller number 7. In the MIDI specification (and in Reason), this is the Volume controller.
- You've done a MIDI Remote Mapping using Learn mode and have mapped that same knob to control filter cutoff frequency in NN19. You now want to record filter cutoff frequency changes, so you enable the MIDI icon on the NN19 track and go into record.
- When you move Knob 1, a Controller 7 (volume) message goes to the Remote Control Reason MIDI input , which 'knows' that you've assigned that Controller to filter cutoff in your MIDI Remote Mapping assignment. The message thus thus changes filter cutoff, as desired.
- The same Controller 7 message goes simultaneously to the sequencer MIDI input, which doesn't know about your MIDI Remote Mapping, but will respond to Reason's preset MIDI controller assignments – so the message changes NN19's volume too! Filter cutoff and volume are changed at the same time, by the one message from your controller box. Not what you will usually want. And this could happen multiple times with different pairs of controls.

Some solutions

Separate master keyboard and MIDI controller box

If you have this setup, there are two relatively simple answers to the problem:

- Set the sequencer MIDI Input in Reason to a different MIDI channel. You'll need the MIDI page, in Preferences, under the Edit menu. If you do this you will also have to set your master keyboard to transmit on that same channel, so that it can still act as the sequencer input device. Now any messages coming in on the hardware controller's MIDI channel will be ignored by the sequencer MIDI input.
- Alternatively, set the MIDI controller box to transmit on a different MIDI channel to the one set for the sequencer MIDI input.

If you're using any of the four 'External Control' MIDI buses (the ones that are routed through the hardware controller at the top of the Reason rack) for playing Reason devices externally, you'll also have to make sure that the hardware controller's MIDI channel is different from any MIDI channels being used via the buses.

Taking advantage of MIDI channels will also allow you to get more out of a preset MIDI controller box, as long as it has a MIDI channel switch. This way, the same collection of preset knob/fader assignments could provide up to 16 times as many control options when working with MIDI Remote Mapping.

All-in-one keyboard/MIDI controller

If you use a keyboard with a MIDI controller knob section, the solution is slightly different, and you may have to get your hands dirty in the operating system of your keyboard. You'll need to refer to the MIDI Implementation Chart PDF file that was provided when you installed Reason, and check out which MIDI Controllers have not been assigned to any Reason device parameters. Now configure your keyboard's MIDI knobs or sliders to transmit just these MIDI Controller numbers (as if you were doing Direct Controller programming, as explained earlier in this chapter). Then, use 'learn' mode to assign the faders or sliders to the parameters you'd like to tweak, via MIDI Remote Mapping (also explained earlier in this chapter).

There may be one further alternative, depending on your keyboard. The Midiman Oxygen 8, for example, lets you set a different MIDI channel for each of its eight knobs, as well as the MIDI Controller numbers to be transmitted, while having the keyboard itself transmit on a different MIDI channel.

Tip

Synth/sampler controls

If you just want to assign a few sound-device parameters to hardware controls, to help you make quick changes to the most significant parameters, the best ones in the synths and samplers are probably Amp Envelope attack and release; Filter Cutoff and Resonance; and possibly LFO rate and depth.

Reason with other software and instruments

R eason has been designed as a self-contained electronic music studio, but there are a few things it can't do alone – and there may well be occasions when you want it to integrate with other software you already have, or even with hardware you own.

One of the main ways of using Reason alongside some of the major MIDI + Audio sequencers which so many of us have is ReWire, the Propellerhead-designed communication protocol that many manufacturers have taken up for their software. If you use a package that is ReWire-compatible – and most up-to-date sequencing software is – you are obviously in the best situation for integrating that package with Reason. However, if your software isn't that co-operative, a certain level of communication can be achieved with more basic MIDI and audio patching.

When it comes to hardware, the situation is much more simple. You'll either be syncing Reason via MIDI clock to an external sequencing device or drum machine, or you'll be playing the devices in the Reason rack from an external keyboard or hardware sequencer (or even from sequencing software on another computer). How that works exactly will depend on your MIDI interface, but there's certainly a set of rules you can follow that should enable you to get a working setup going.

What is ReWire?

ReWire 2.0 (the latest implementation) is a PC and Mac system for transferring MIDI data and audio seamlessly between software applications running on one computer. It could be thought of as a multi-channel MIDI and audio cable between two programs. With ReWire, Reason audio outputs can be sent to another application, where they can use that application's mixing facilities and effects, and can be combined into a mix with material created in the other application. Up to 64 channels of audio can be routed out of Reason, via the Hardware Interface at the top of the rack, so it would be possible to route as little as just a complete stereo mix out of Reason, or as much as all the audio from many individual devices.

In terms of MIDI, ReWire 2.0 facilitates control of Reason devices from another application. When Cubase SX, for example, is ReWired to Reason, Reason devices appear in the 'Track Output' pop-up and can be assigned as sound sources for Cubase MIDI tracks. Any Reason device can thus be played, or controlled, from within Cubase, just as if it were a hardware instrument attached to your MIDI interface. Used in this way, Reason becomes a virtual rack of sound sources, and you don't even have to use Reason's sequencing facilities if you don't want to.

ReWired applications can also run together in perfect, sample-accurate

 Cubase SX   File   Edit   Project   Aud

✓ Not Connected

Layla3G MIDI Out

Reason Hardware Interface
Reason Mixer 1
Reason Main Drums
Reason Horn Stab
Reason Scream 1
Reason RV7000 1
Reason Piano
Reason RV7000 2
Reason M Comp 1
Reason Scratch
Reason Bass Combi
Reason Line Mixer 2
Reason Spider Audio 1
Reason Delay 1
Reason Delay 2
Reason SubTractor 1
Reason SubTractor 2
Reason SubTractor 3
Reason SubTractor 3 Copy
Reason Lead COmbi
Reason Line Mixer 2 Copy
Reason Spider Audio 1 Copy
Reason Delay 1 Copy
Reason Delay 2 Copy
Reason SubTractor 1 Copy
Reason SubTractor 2 Copy

ReWire 2 allows Reason devices to be
the sound source for tracks in another
ReWired sequencer application. Here you
can see Cubase SX's 'Track Output' pop-
up, showing that Cubase can use any of
the listed Reason devices.

synchronisation. In addition, activating the transport buttons on one ReWired program automatically controls all others, so you can freely move between programs and not have to worry about which one is 'master'.

Some software may only be compatible with the older ReWire 1, and all that will be possible is the sync'ing of transports and playback, and the routing of audio from Reason to the host. This, of course, is not a shabby option, but if you want to play and sequence Reason devices from within the host application, you'll have to resort to a workaround. Under MacOS 9.x, this would normally be OMS's IAC – Inter Application Communication – bus, and on the PC, you'd need a software widget such as Hubi's Loopback Device or Midi Ox's MIDI Yoke (both are available free on the internet). These options let you route MIDI from one application to another within one computer.

ReWire compatibility

Propellerhead divide ReWire-compatible applications into two classes: 'synth' (slave) applications and 'mixer' (host) applications. Reason is usually classed as a synth application, to be ReWired to a mixer application. However, when Reason is ReWired to ReBirth (via Reason's ReBirth Input Machine device), Reason would be classed as a mixer application, the only situation in which this is the case.

At the time of writing, the following 'mixer' applications are ReWire compatible; those that are ReWire 1 compatible support the transfer of audio and synchronise transports, but do not offer direct MIDI control of Reason devices from the 'host' application. If you're running older versions of software, perhaps under older operating systems, ReWire 1 compatability may be all you can achieve. The list of ReWire compatible software continues to grow, and the definitive list can be found at Propellerhead's web site.

• Ableton Live (ReWire 2)
• Adobe Audition (ReWire 2)
• Arkaos VJ (ReWire 2)
• Arturia Storm (ReWire 2)
• Cakewalk Sonar 2.0+ and Project5 (PC; ReWire 2)
• Cycling '74 MAX/MSP (ReWire 2)
• Digidesign Pro Tools 6.1+ (ReWire 2)
• Apple Logic family (Mac OS X; ReWire 2)
• Emagic Logic Audio, V4.7.3 - 5 (Windows & Mac OS 9; ReWire 1)
• Line6 GuitarPort (ReWire 2)
• Mackie Tracktion 1.5+ (ReWire 2)
• MOTU Digital Performer V4+ (MacOS X; ReWire 2)
• MOTU Digital Performer V2.7 and V3.x (MacOS 9; ReWire 1)
• Opcode Vision DSP (MacOS 9; ReWire 1)
• Opcode Studio Vision (MacOS 9; ReWire 1)
• Propellerhead Software Reason (ReWire 2; for ReBirth)
• ReFuse (ReWire 2)
• Sony Acid 4.0+ (PC; ReWire 2)
• Speedsoft VSampler (ReWire 2)
• Steinberg Cubase SX 1 or higher (ReWire 2)
• Steinberg Cubase SL 1 or higher (ReWire 2)
• Steinberg Cubase VST 5.1 (ReWire 2)

- Steinberg Nuendo 1.5+ (ReWire 2)
- Synapse Audio Software Orion (PC; ReWire 2)

The focus will be on procedures for the most widely-used MIDI + Audio sequencers. Obviously, neither of us owns all these MIDI + Audio sequencers, nor are we expert in the use of all of them. The information we supply regarding ReWire usage comes largely from the manufacturers of the sequencers, from Propellerhead themselves or from Propellerhead's US and UK distributor, M-Audio.

Installing ReWire

You don't have to install ReWire – its features are an integral part of Reason and it is taken care of when you install Reason, with the necessary software widget placed on your hard drive automatically.

General ReWire procedure

Launching applications

In general, whatever ReWire-compatible application you'd like to use with Reason, the launch procedure is: launch the host – 'mixer' – application, then launch Reason. This ensures that Reason is ReWired to the host software. What happens from this point depends on how the host integrates with ReWire and whether it's compatible with the original version of ReWire (which links transports and streams a maximum of 64 audio channels) or ReWire 2, the latest incarnation, which adds MIDI streaming and can handle up to 256 audio channels, though may still only handle 64. Usually, with the latest host software, activating Reason as a plug-in from within the host application causes Reason to launch automatically.

Quitting applications

Quitting order is the exact opposite of launch order: close down the slave applications, and then the host. The order of both launching and quitting is important; ReWire won't work if you don't observe it, and in some cases you can cause trouble for your computer.

As mentioned in the chapter where the ReBirth Input Machine is discussed, Propellerhead's ReBirth has to be run as a slave to the host application alongside Reason. You won't be able to ReWire Reason to the host, and then ReWire ReBirth to Reason, via the RIM. If there is any effects processing within Reason that's important to a ReBirth performance, you'll have to export it as audio and import that into the host application. Otherwise, you'll be able to sync the ReBirth performance, but not replicate the Reason processing.

Some users recommend that Reason not contain any MIDI data in its main sequencer if it is being ReWired, particularly if you're using Windows (this shouldn't stop you from using the Pattern-based devices). Personally, we've never encountered any problems when sync'ing a fully-sequenced Reason Song to Cubase via ReWire; the devices can still be played as normal, if required, and process individual Reason devices with Cubase plug-ins (on a Mac).

In Reason, make sure that there are no lit keyboard icons in the sequencer track list MIDI In column; otherwise, your master keyboard will play two devices at once – one via ReWire, and the other via the Reason sequencer track. You could of course disable the Sequencer Port MIDI In in Reason's

Info

Reason and VST plug-ins

One of the most common questions asked by prospective users of Reason is 'Can I use VST plug-ins with it?', and VST plug-in compatibility is also one of the most-requested features by existing users. Well, this facility within Reason looks unlikely to be coming any time soon, if ever, so your best bet is to run the program in conjunction with a sequencer that is VST-compatible, if you really want to use VST plug-ins.

Tip

Submixing saves power

Making use of ReMixes as submixers, as explained in the ReMix chapter, is probably a good idea if you're trying to route a very complex Reason session via ReWire to another audio program. For example, let's say you have a reasonably busy Reason session, with 14 devices, plus a ReDrum device providing 10 individual drum voice outputs. That's between 26 and 38 channels of audio to send via ReWire to the other app (the total depends on whether the devices are mono SubTractor or stereo NN19 or Dr:rex devices, and doesn't allow for the fact that ReDrum voices can be stereo, which would take the potential total to 48 audio channels!). A couple of submixers – one to submix the ReDrum sounds and another to submix the remaining devices – reduces that stream to two stereo channels, or four ReWire channels in all, which has to be more manageable, and leaves you with room to pick out just the Reason instruments that you really want to treat with signal processing on the host software.

basic MIDI Prefs, but disabling the MIDI icon is simpler and means you don't have to keep changing your prefs when using Reason in stand-alone mode.

Using Reason with ReWire applications

Steinberg Nuendo and Cubase SX

Cubase SX.

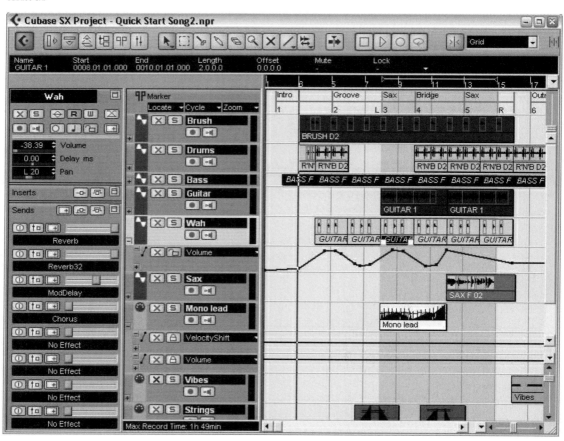

Nuendo is Steinberg's high-end audio workstation software. Many of its innovations have trickled down to Cubase SX, the company's successor to VST. Both support ReWire 2 (providing your soundcard is ASIO compatible), but Cubase SX is a Mac OSX- and Windows 2000/XP-only application. Nuendo needs to be V1.51 or higher to work with ReWire. Integrating Reason into either package is similar to doing the same job in VST.

- Open Nuendo or SX
- Open Reason.
- From the 'Devices' menu, select Reason.
- A ReWire window dedicated to Reason will pop up, and you enable Reason channels here, just as you would in VST. You have, as expected, up to 64 audio channels available.
- Devices in the Reason rack also become available in the MIDI Output pop-up menus for the MIDI tracks of both Nuendo and SX.

Both combinations – Reason/Nuendo or Reason/SX – offer full sync and cross-device transport control, and Reason audio will be included in any mixes to disk produced by either Steinberg program.

Steinberg Cubase VST

Running Reason with Cubase VST (on an older Mac or PC) should be quite

Steinberg's Cubase VST.

straightforward. First, make sure you have V5.1 or later of Cubase. Older versions only support ReWire 1.

- Open Cubase VST
- Open Reason.
- In Cubase, open the ReWire panel, from the Panels menu. This provides a list of all available audio channels from any ReWire-compatible software instrument you have installed on your computer.
- Enable the top two channels – labelled Reason Mix L and Reason Mix R. This routes the stereo mix from Reason into the Cubase mixer. A stereo input channel, coloured red, will be placed between the last of your mixer's audio input channels and the first of the mixer's Groups.
- Enable extra inputs in the panel to create extra ReWire input channels in the Cubase mixer. It's possible to enable up to 64 audio channels for Reason in this panel, with each corresponding to an audio output in Reason's Hardware Interface. (Inside Reason, audio is routed to a ReWire channel by connecting a device to the corresponding input on the Hardware Interface.)

The VST ReWire panel.

Two other things happen once you enable channels in the ReWire panel. First, the transport of either Cubase or Reason will control the playback of both programs; even loop points and tempo will be matched in the two applications. Second, because Cubase VST is ReWire 2 compatible, it's possible to select Reason devices from the track list in Cubase's Arrange window, and play them or record a performance with them.

Every device in the linked Reason Song appears as a destination in the 'Output' column in the Cubase track list – even the devices that don't respond to note data, such as the effects and mixer. This is so that you can automate the devices from within Cubase. When recording MIDI parts in Cubase that play Reason devices, make sure that your controller has been de-selected as the MIDI Input for the Sequencer Port in Reason's basic MIDI Preferences; alternatively, ensure that no MIDI Icons are visible in the MIDI In column of any sequencer tracks. Otherwise you'll be playing two instruments at once – one from within Cubase and one directly via Reason.

That's all there is to it: Reason parts appear in the mix exactly as expected when you 'Export Audio', to bounce a mix to your hard disk from within Cubase. At the end of your session, quit Reason, and then Cubase.

There may be times when you'd like to transfer your Reason audio into Cubase – perhaps your computer isn't up to the job of running a full Reason

Song alongside Cubase. While there isn't a way to record ReWire audio directly into Cubase audio tracks, there is a bounce-to-disk process which is almost as fast:

- With Reason rewired to Cubase, mute any unwanted parts in the Cubase track list.
- Set Cubase's loop markers such that there will be enough time in Cubase for the desired Reason audio to play out fully.
- Select 'Export Audio Tracks' from Cubase's File menu.
- In the Export Audio Tracks window, select a folder for the audio to be saved to, and tick 'Import to Pool', 'Import to Audio Track' and 'Export Between Locators'.
- Press Save, and in faster than real time, the audio from the ReWired Reason Song will be saved to Cubase's Audio Pool and loaded into a new audio track.

Of course, you can apply any Cubase effects, EQ or processing to the Reason audio during the bounce.

Tip

Cubase mono mix channel workaround

When you're ReWiring Reason to Cubase VST, note that, apart from the first two channels you send, all Reason's ReWire outputs will appear as individual mono channels in the VST mixer. If you're routing a stereo pair – from a Reason submixer or stereo device – two ReWire channels will be required, and two channels in the Cubase mixer. This might be a problem if you'd like to apply a VST plug-in effect to a stereo NNXT patch, say: you'd have to create one instance of the effect for each channel, rather than just creating a single stereo effect, and then you'd have to tweak two lots of parameters to keep the effect the same for both channels. Currently, there's no way to link two VST mixer channels for stereo operation, although the level fader and mute/solo buttons for two consecutive odd/even mixer channels can be controlled together by holding down Option/Alt on the computer keyboard while operating the control.

The best idea may be to route both sides of a stereo pair of ReWire channels to one of the VST mixer's eight stereo Groups. The routing option is available at the bottom of the VST mixer channel. Once routed to a Group, the Reason stereo audio can be processed by one set of insert effects, and have its level controlled by moving one fader.

Right
Two mono ReWire channels panned hard left and right, to bring a stereo signal from Reason into Cubase VST, are being routed to one of VST's Group channels, via the pop-up shown. This will make it easier to apply VST effects to, and change the level of, the Reason stereo audio.

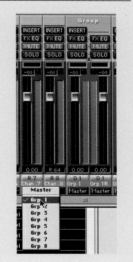

Apple/Emagic Logic

Older versions of the Logic family – marketed under the Emagic name – were only compatible with ReWire 1, from V4.71. The latest releases, from V6 and now available as the MacOS X-only Apple Logic, are ReWire 2 compatible. Reason launches easily from inside the program , with full audio and MIDI integration.

If you're still using a pre-ReWire 2 version of Logic, the start-up order is the same as for every other application:

- Open Logic.
- Open Reason.

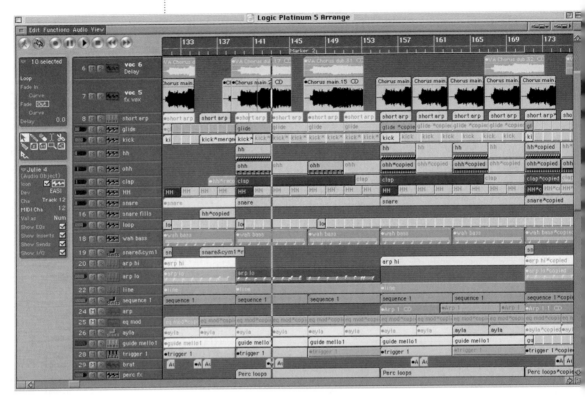

Logic Platinum.

- In Logic, select an audio track in the Arrange page.
- In the Track Parameters window on the left, click Channel. From the pop-up, select 'Instrument', and from the sub-menu select 'Others'.
- Yet another sub-menu appears, and it's from here that you can select ReWire channels from Reason.

This far, Reason will sync to Logic, and you'll hear a Reason performance coming in via the Logic mixer. Users who would like to play Reason devices from Logic MIDI tracks will need a special widget to route MIDI data from Logic to Reason. On the Mac, you'd use IAC (Inter Application Communication), which has to be selected as a custom option during OMS installation. On the PC, you have the choice of Hubi's Loopback Device from Hubert Winkler or MIDI Ox's MIDI Yoke. These options let you route up to four streams of MIDI data from Logic to Reason's External Control buses, and so to the Hardware Interface where individual MIDI channels on each bus can be routed to a device.

It has been noted (by Midiman, US and UK distributors for Reason) that Logic must be playing in order to trigger Reason as a rack of MIDI devices.

MOTU Digital Performer

V4 of Mark of The Unicorn's Mac-only Digital Performer is ReWire 2 compatible, and launches Reason easily, with full bussing of MIDI and audio. Older versions (from V2.72) were ReWire 1 only, so sync'd Reason and streamed its audio into

the DP mixer. If you're still working with the old system, you'll need FreeMIDI
1.45 or higher (FreeMIDI is MOTU's OMS-like MIDI communication protocol),
and OMS v2.3.7 or higher; you'll also need OMS's IAC drivers. Reason is not

Digital Performer.

directly compatible with FreeMIDI, but FreeMIDI can be made to be compatible
with OMS, which Reason does support.

- Put FreeMIDI into OMS compatibility mode, by ticking 'Use OMS when
  available' in Preferences inside the FreeMIDI application. Any future
  changes to your studio setup will have to be made in OMS. You'll also
  have make sure that OMS is set to 'Run MIDI In Background', via the
  OMS MIDI Setup window, accessible from the Edit menu, and also that
  Digital Performer itself is set to run in the background (this can be set in
  DP's preferences).
- Open Digital Performer.
- Open Reason.
- To hear Reason's output, create an Aux track in DP (do this from the
  'Add Track' menu accessible from DP's mini-menu). Assign Reason's
  Left/Right mix output to the track (DP Aux tracks are mono or stereo
  depending on what's routed to them). To record Reason audio to a DP
  audio track, create a mono or stereo audio track, and assign Reason
  outputs to it as required.

To route MIDI from a Digital Performer MIDI track:

- Set the MIDI track's output to an IAC Bus, and enable Record.

Tip

OMS doesn't exist on OS X. Use
the Audio MIDI Setup
application in the Applications >
Utilities folder to manage system-
wide in/out settings. CoreAudio
and CoreMIDI let the software
(Cubase, Logic) handle much of
the i/o preference setting, so you
won't need to do much beyond
making sure devices are visible in
Audio MIDI Setup.

- In Reason, set the same IAC Bus as the input for one of the software's four 'External Control' buses in Advanced MIDI preferences.
- In the rack, go to the Hardware Interface. Select the bus that you've just assigned to IAC; then, for any of the 16 MIDI channels, select a Reason device from the pop-up.
- Assign this MIDI channel to the DP MIDI track, and you'll be able to record a performance with the Reason device from within Digital Performer.

There have been some unusual artifacts reported when using ReWire with Reason and Digital Performer. The oddest is a sort of inverse latency where Reason's audio is ahead of DP's MIDI and audio data. This doesn't happen to everyone, though, and we've seen a fix reported that involves patching a DP delay plug-in into the Reason audio's patch, and delaying it enough so that it runs in sync with DP.

Cakewalk Sonar

V2 and higher of the Sonar PC-only MIDI + Audio sequencing software is now compatible with ReWire 2, offering full synchronisation, audio streaming from Reason into Sonar, and MIDI streaming from Sonar to Reason. Not only can you use DXi plug-ins within Sonar to treat Reason audio, but bouncing a Sonar mix to disk will include all Reason audio.

Cakewalk's Sonar.

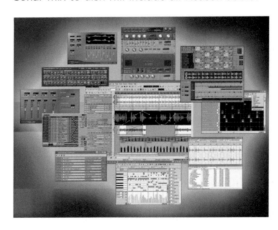

- Open Sonar.
- In Sonar's Synth Rack, from the Insert menu, select 'ReWire Device'.
- Click on the Properties icon to launch Reason.
- Decide what outputs from Reason you'd like to use. Sonar creates audio tracks to accommodate them.
- When routing an additional individual device from Reason, route its audio to an input or inputs on Reason's Hardware Interface, create another audio track in Sonar and select the Reason ReWire channel(s) that correspond to the device.

You can mix Reason audio alongside the rest of the Sonar session, or record its output to audio tracks.

To play Reason devices from Sonar via MIDI, create a MIDI track and set its output to 'Reason' and its 'MIDI Channel' to that of the desired Reason device – all available devices will appear in a pop-up. The selected Reason device can be played, and recorded with, just as if it were a real hardware synth or a soft synth running inside Sonar.

Using Reason with non-ReWire applications

If your MIDI + Audio application doesn't support ReWire, you're not so well off for using it with Reason, but it almost certainly can be done. There are two basic problems that you have to solve. First of all, you need to get MIDI from the non-ReWire application to Reason, either to play devices or to simply synchronise Reason playback via MIDI clock. (Reason can only ever be the 'slave', so you'll have to select an appropriate input for it to receive 'MIDI Clock Sync' in Advanced MIDI prefs, and enable MIDI Sync in the transport bar.) MIDI interconnection can almost certainly be achieved by OMS's / Audio MIDI Setup's IAC (Inter Application Communication) on the Mac or Hubi's Loopback Device/MIDI Ox's MIDI Yoke on the PC. There are links for downloading both these utilities at the Propellerhead web site.

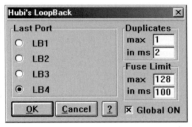

On the PC, you can use Hubi's Loopback Device (or the similar MIDI Yoke) to set up MIDI routing between non-ReWire apps and Reason.

Then you need to find a way to route audio from Reason into the non-ReWire application. This may be tricky, though not impossible. On the Mac, as described in our Digidesign ProTools LE example below, it's possible to use Sound Manager to route Reason audio out of the computer's own built-in audio hardware and back into your audio interface. There may be other solutions, for both Mac and PC, if you have more than one audio interface. It all depends on what drivers you have available and which can be used simultaneously.

Digidesign Pro Tools LE

The latest version of the ProTools family have ReWire capabilities built in. So anyone running V6.x under MacOS X or Windows XP will have no problems. Adding a ReWire plug-in to a PT session, choosing Reason, and enabling the desired audio inputs and MIDI channels is no problem. The process is the same as for any other plug-in and also opens Reason for you.

If you're still stuck on MacOS 9.x, then you'll be working with ReWire-less V5.x. Luckily, there are a couple of solutions to this problem . A less-than-ideal technique links PTLE's MIDI output to Reason via OMS's Inter Application Communication (IAC) buss. Audio is handled by passing Reason out of the Mac's built-in audio hardware, using Sound Manager, and into PTLE's audio hardware. If you're lucky enough to have a second soundcard, whether PCI, USB or FireWire, you may be able to adapt the technique as long as the card can be set to output Sound Manager audio; if the card has a digital output, all the better, since the digital out can be routed to Digi 001's digital input. Playing latency isn't too bad, and can be improved by enabling Low Latency Monitoring under PTLE's Operations menu.

* Open ProTools LE.
* Open Reason.

Tip

Software is constantly evolving so to keep up to date on exactly what is ReWire compatible, visit http://www.propellerheads.se/ technologies/rewire/

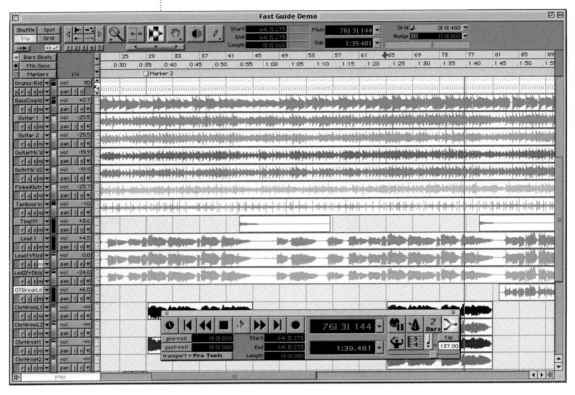

Pro Tools LE.

- If you want to just synchronise Reason's playback to PTLE, go to PTLE's 'MIDI Beat Clock' dialogue, under the MIDI menu. Select an IAC Bus by ticking in its box.
- In Reason, select the same IAC bus as the source for the MIDI Clock Sync pop-up in 'Advanced MIDI Preferences', and click the 'Enable' MIDI Sync button in Reason's transport bar. This will allow Reason to be controlled from PTLE's transport, and follow PTLE's tempo. The communication is not two-way; Reason is the 'slave'.
- To route Reason audio into PTLE, take a stereo lead from your Mac's audio output and plug it into two free inputs of your Digi 001 hardware. In your PTLE Session, create a stereo Aux input channel and set its input to correspond with the hardware ins just assigned to Reason.

So far, we've managed to sync Reason to PTLE and have its audio come into the PTLE mixer. There's no direct way to route individual device audio from Reason to PTLE (unless your second audio card, if you have one, allows it in some way), but it is possible to have a PTLE MIDI arrangement play Reason devices, as follows:

- Assign the MIDI outputs of the required MIDI tracks in PTLE to a MIDI channel on a spare IAC bus.
- In Reason, select the same IAC bus as the destination for one of the External Control buses in Advanced MIDI Preferences.
- In the Reason Hardware Interface, assign Reason devices to the desired

MIDI channels on that bus. PTLE will now be able to play the devices in Reason's rack.

You may need to adjust PTLE's Hardware Buffer Size and CPU Usage Limit, and also CPU Usage Limit, if you're plagued by crackling and other unwanted artefacts. By the way, if Reason is providing all the backing to a song, via its own sequencing system, we'd tend to bounce sections of the mix to disk as audio and load those files into PTLE (leaving it until the end, so we're close to a final mix). Then we wouldn't lose any audio quality, as a result of going out of the Mac's audio hardware, at all.

The elegant solution to the problem is available as a US$29 internet download. ReFuse, developed by Leigh Marble, lets you run up to 16 channels of Reason audio to Pro Tools and offers two-way linking of both applications' transport controls. OMS IAC would then be used to achieve MIDI sequencing of Reason devices from within PT. Check out http://www.refusesoftware.com for more. This option is good for V5.x PTLE running on MacOS 8.1 to 9.x.

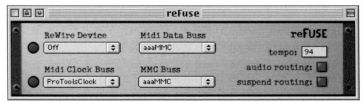

Leigh Marble's ReFuse offers Mac users of Digi's non-ReWire Pro Tools a solution to integrating the two applications more easily.

Reason as sound module with external sequencers

Not only can Reason be used as a virtual sound module, with or without ReWire, for software running on the same computer, it can also be used in this way with sequencers external to the computer. These could be stand-alone hardware sequencers or grooveboxes, sequencers built into a workstation synth or sampler, or even sequencing software running on another computer (perhaps even an ancient Atari ST; we sometimes do this).

Whatever your situation, you need some way to route MIDI data from the external sequencer to Reason's devices. Here's a simple example:

* Connect a MIDI Out from the external sequencer to a MIDI In of your MIDI interface.
* In Reason's Advanced MIDI preferences, select this MIDI In as the input used by External Control Bus A.
* In the Hardware Interface at the top of the rack, select Bus A.
* Now, for each of the 16 MIDI channels on Bus A, select a Reason device which you would like to control from the external sequencer.

If your external sequencer is equipped with multiple MIDI Outs and you would like to use them all, you'll need a MIDI interface with the same number of inputs. Of course, you won't be able to use more than four separate MIDI inputs, since that's the number of External Control buses in Reason; however, most stand-alone hardware sequencers have two MIDI Outs at most.

Once the external sequencer's MIDI Outs are connected to your MIDI interface's input ports, and you've configured the External Control buses, you need to work the Hardware Interface to tell Reason which MIDI channels on which bus will be playing which devices in the Rack.

Synchronising Reason to an external device

There may be occasions when you'd like to synchronise a Reason Song to an external sequenced performance. Again, the process is simple:

- Ensure that the MIDI Out which is transmitting MIDI Clock from the external device is connected to your MIDI interface. (Also ensure that the external device has been set to transmit MIDI Clock.)
- In Advanced MIDI preferences, select this device as the input for MIDI Clock Sync.
- Enable the MIDI Sync button in Reason's transport bar.

Now, when you start playback on the external sequencer, Reason should also play and follow its tempo. And remember: Reason cannot be a MIDI Clock 'master' (the source of MIDI clocking information); it can only be a slave (following MIDI clock from the master).

20 fast tips

1 Fold devices when you don't need their front panels. This saves a little CPU overhead, makes rack navigation faster and allows you to get a better overview of your rack, as more is visible on screen at the same time.

2 Use mixer aux loops for effects where possible. Not only is this more efficient in terms of processor power, it's quicker to set up, and you can use many permutations of the four effects available via the aux loops.

3 Get a hardware controller and set it up to allow you to do synth programming and mixing with real controls. Not only is it faster (once you've put in the time making the original control assignments), it's easier and more intuitive. Your controller may be natively supported by Reason, which is even better.

4 Make a really good default song to save you time and effort whenever you start a new project. See Chapter 4 for a list of the kind of things to include in it.

5 Get familiar with the device layering technique explained in Chapter 6. You'll be able to create big, unique new sounds fast and with the minimum of programming effort. Create some great Combis to achieve the same ends.

6 Create involving tracks quickly by automating control movements.

7 Use the Autoplay facility in the Sample Browsers to check sounds without loading them into a device. Take advantage of the new Browser's favourites and preview features.

8 Drag in numeric displays to change values quickly. Only use the spin controls (up/down arrows) if you need to increment/decrement by just one or two. Likewise, click directly on the LEDs next to Multi-mode selectors rather than repeatedly clicking the Mode button to cycle through the options.

9 Get to know the keyboard shortcuts intimately. The shortcuts you will probably use most are a handful of sequencer ones: Apple/Control-2, which toggles the 'rack' and 'maximised' sequencer window views (Apple/Control-1 toggles 'rack' view and no sequencer window at all);

Shift+ Tab, which toggles the sequencer Arrange and Edit views;
Apple/Alt, to toggle between the Selection and the Pencil tool; Tab to
toggle between the back and front of the rack; Apple/Control-K, which
quantises selected notes; Apple/Control-G, which groups parts for easy
moving and editing; and Option/Control drag, which is the most convenient way of copying parts. Have Snap to Grid enabled when you do the
last and the part will snap neatly into place. Standard keyboard shortcuts for such things as cut/copy/paste, and open/save file are also
essential.

10 Learn and use the sequencer Transport keyboard shortcuts. Using the
numeric keypad, you can boil down the recording process to '*' to
engage the Record button, Enter to play (starts recording), '0' twice to
stop recording and return to zero. Numeric keypad '1' and '2' go to
the loop start and end. The Space bar is alternatively very convenient
for starting and stopping playback. If your control surface is supported
natively under Remote, it may well have transport controls that you can
use without having to even touch the mouse.

11 Make sure you save your most often-used insert effect chains as
Combis, which can be instantly recalled and used again and again in the
same project. The same applies to multi-layered or split instruments.

12 Learn the easy ways to navigate the rack. Scroll up and down the rack
with the keyboard arrow keys and each device will be selected as you
pass it. This saves you mouse-clicking to select the desired device.
Alternatively, clicking on a device track name in the sequencer scrolls
the rack so the device is in front of you, ready-selected. A mouse with a
scroll wheel will save lots of time.

13 Don't forget the Change Events window for quick transposing of
notes/parts and easy editing of velocity.

14 Get ReCycle for treating your own loops to use in Dr:rex. This costs
money, but saves time in the long run, and helps you produce much
more original music, as you won't need to rely on other peoples' loops.
You can even export to disk loops of your own music you've made with
Reason, ReCycle them, and then load back into Dr:rex for further man-
gling. This saves on system resources too.

15 Make sure you use the favourites and locations sections of the browser
that Reason offers for quick access to your personal Songs, Patches and
samples. It takes minutes to do this but will save you lots of hard drive
navigating time in the future.

16 If you find yourself with folders packed full of device patches, samples
and REX loops, consider making your own ReFill, using ReFill Packer.
This will centralise all your Patches and samples as of the Packing date,
and the personal ReFill will show up amongst all ReFills when you select
the magnifying glass icon in a Browser window. ReFills offer the bonus
of storing your samples in 50% less space, using lossless data compression; you can then archive the originals and regain space on your hard

drive. Don't do this if you plan to swap Songs with anyone, since they would need your full ReFill in order to play your Songs back.

17 Quickly give Matrix Patterns twice the impact by copying the Matrix and the device it's triggering, and selecting a different patch on the copied sound-making device. Make sure you connect the audio out of the sound making device to the mixer (this can be done quickly by selecting 'Auto Route Device' from the context menu). It can be quite effective to pan the two versions hard left and right.

18 When you want to edit or draw automation for a device control, get to the right controller lane fast by simply Option/Alt-clicking the control. (The device must already have a sequencer track.) Don't forget that you can cut, copy and paste controller data to save drawing in lots of it.

19 Use ReMixes and Line mixers as submixers, as explained in the ReMix chapter, to help simplify complex mixes.

20 If you experience problems with your Reason set-up, or have a question on any aspect of its use, the best way to get fast assistance is probably from other Reason users via the main Reason forums on the internet, as listed in Appendix 1 of this book. Also search any question archives on the main Reason web sites, as someone may well have answered your question already.

A fast guide to CV/Gate routings

The table on pages 458 – 461 is intended to provide some help, for those not familiar with the CV and Gate system, regarding what effects can be produced by different interconnections. It is only a starting point, of course, since a vast range of effects can be produced, according to the settings of the 'source' parameter and the 'target' parameter. By 'source', we mean the CV or Gate output, while 'target' is the input or destination for that routing.

What do modulation routings actually do? Well, in short, they allow parameter movements on one device to be controlled by those on another. This can produce a very effective feeling of timbral and rhythmic unity in a composition.

However, some connections you can make are not intended to have an effect on the sound, per se, but rather to accomplish something else. For example, routing a Redrum Gate Out to the Gate in of the next channel makes the second channel fire in the same rhythm as the Gate pulses from the first , as explained in the ReDrum chapter, so you can easily layer drums playing the same part. Another example is Peter Gaydos' Matrix arpeggiator idea, explained in the Matrix chapter, where clever Gate and CV routing, coupled with the routing of incoming MIDI from your master keyboard, makes it possible to transpose Matrix Patterns in real time. The chart is not specifically designed to allow you to make those kind of imaginative leaps – that's down to your own ingenuity as you get used to the system.

The chart focuses on the effects produced by routing CV and Gate between devices, but another major use of the back-panel CV and Gate connections is to provide access to routings within one device that are not available from the front panel. For example, some of the sound-making devices do not have a pitch envelope, or the option to route an envelope to pitch from the front panel. However, these devices allow you to route any available envelope to Oscillator Pitch via the rear panel, so you can, after all, have a pitch EG.

Rear-panel routings also allow one modulator – say, a SubTractor Mod Envelope – to be sent to two destinations: perhaps to Phase via the hard-wiring on the front panel, and Oscillator Pitch via the rear-panel cable connections. Equally, one parameter can be affected by two modulators. Either way, the result is even more interesting sounds, with even more movement.

Things to bear in mind:

- The effectiveness of routings involving envelopes as the source modulator can depend on the shape of the source envelope itself, as well as the shape of the Amplitude Envelope on the target device. If the Amp Envelope is set to produce a very short sound, for example, the full effect of some source envelopes may not be heard.
- The effect of routings using an LFO as a source will differ according to the choice of source LFO waveform.
- You can regulate the effect of the modulation being set up with the rear-panel Input trim pot on the target parameter. If the effect is good but not strong enough, you may be able to increase its intensity by boosting the Input trim pot.
- In a 'normal' hardware modular system, you might not be able to patch gates to CVs and CVs to gates, or may not get a good result if you did. The virtual voltages inside Reason are such that this is not only possible but a big part of advanced synthesis and sound design inter-device modulation.
- Sequencer Control CVs and Gates, Matrix Curve CV outs, effects CV and Gate control and certain aspects of ReDrum routing are dealt with separately in the device-specific chapters.
- In some cases, routing a CV or Gate from a source parameter to a target parameter will override the normal function of the target parameter. This will often be desirable, such as when a Gate pattern produced by a ReDrum voice channel is triggering a SubTractor envelope at the same time as you're playing it from your MIDI keyboard: the rhythmic envelope triggering actually overrides the triggers produced by your keyboard. Even if you play your keyboard, you won't hear the filter envelope triggering unless the ReDrum is in play mode.
- All but one Malström Modulation CV inputs can be routed to one of two or both destinations.
- Experiment!

Tip

Devices as modulation sources

The beauty of the CV/gate system as implemented in Reason is that it almost gives synthesis facilities a life of their own, allowing them to go off and do their own thing to a certain extent. For example, you can think of any device's LFOs as independent modulation sources that you can use elsewhere – add a sound-making device to your rack just so that you can use its LFO . Say you could do with another LFO to modulate an NN19 or Dr Rex parameter, because their single LFO is already in use: just make a SubTractor (for

example) and connect its LFO CV output to the CV input of the parameter on the device you want to modulate. Similarly, if you'd like to make a free-running auto-pan effect, you can create a SubTractor and route its LFO to a mixer Pan CV Input. If a spare multi-waveform LFO could add useful modulation to one of the effects devices (via the CV inputs offered on all but one), do likewise. The addition of an extra device or two just for LFO modulation shouldn't add too much to your system load, since you won't be using any actual voices.

CV/Gate Routing Possibilities

	Envelope Outs	LFO/Mod Outs	Gate Outs (ReDrum)	Slice Out (Dr:rex)	Auto CV out (Scream 4)	Individual band level outs (BV512)
Oscillator Pitch CV In	Create pitch EG effect on target by changing pitch over time in response to envelope curve on source.	Vibrato-style pitch modulation of target. Rate according to source LFO, depth set by target CV trim pot.	Create rhythmic pulse effect on source in time with any ReDrum voice pattern. Effect is subtle, and varies in response to velocity levels assigned to Redrum pattern. steps. Change Length, Decay/Gate parameters of ReDrum voice channel for variation.	Worth experimenting with, but Slice gate pulse usually too short for strong, obvious effects.	Worth experimenting with, though level dependent changes in pitch would need to have low trim pot settings to keep results in tune.	Most parameters will respond to the CV generated by each enveloped follower in the Vocoder device, for timbral echoes of the processed sound elsewhere in the rack. Not likely to do much with gate inputs.
Oscillator Phase CV In (SubTractor)	Change in target phase mod over time echoing EG curve of source. Timbral sweep/swell, can be more subtle than filter sweep.	Rhythmic change in phase offset modulation of target in response to rate of source LFO and depth of target CV trim pot. Can sound like Pulsewidth modulation.	As above	As above	Changes in response to incoming level could be fruitfully routed to this parameter, potentially adding a more organic feel to the performance.	As above
FM Amount CV In	Change in strength of FM effect over time echoing EG curve of source. Can create dramatic, moving effects. Start with FM amount low on target.	Regular, rhythmic change in strength of FM effect on target, in response to rate of source LFO and depth of target CV trim pot.	As above	As above	As above	As above
Filter Cutoff Frequency CV In	Filter sweep on target produced by envelope curve of source. Classic filter sweep needs pronounced envelope.	Continous cyclic filter-sweeping on target, speed in response to source LFO rate, depth to target trim pot. With random waveforms, classic 'sample & hold' effects produced.	As above	As above	As above	As above
Filter Resonance CV In	Dynamic change of target resonance, echoing EG curve of source. Can produce distinctive, highly resonant, vocal-like and whistling effects with right EG curve.	Effective, regular, rhythmic resonant accent on target. Speed set by source LFO rate, depth by target trim pot.	As above	As above	As above	As above
Amp Level CV In	Creates amplitude EG effect (level varies over time) on target, echoing EG curve of source.	Tremolo-like amplitude modulation of target. Speed set by source LFO rate, depth set by target CV trim pot.	As above	As above	As above	As above
Mod Wheel CV In	Imposes source EG curve dynamically on parameter(s) assigned to target mod wheel. Allows single EG to modulate up to five parameters simultaneously. (No need to move Mod wheel.)	Cyclic modulation of up to five parameters assigned to Mod Wheel on target. Speed/Depth altered as above. Very complex/weird modulations possible.	As above	As above	As above	As above

	Envelope Outs	LFO/Mod Outs	Gate Outs (ReDrum)	Slice Out (Dr:rex)	Auto CV out (Scream 4)	Individual band level outs (BV512)
Index CV In (Malström)	Sweeps from one grain to next in graintable, echoing source EG curve. Can produce dramatic, evolving effects.	Regular move back and forth through grains in graintable. Speed set by source LFO rate. With 'Breath' graintable, produces 'panting', for example! Position of Index slider significant.	Can create dramatic, variable index triggering in time with Redrum voice pattern. Work on Redrum Length/Decay/Gate settings and step velocity for best effect.	As above	As above	As above
Shift CV In (Malström)	Sweeps Shift in shape of source EG. Dramatic alternative to filter sweep with many graintables, also weird speaking effects with vocal tables. Decent oscillator sync impressions with synth waveforms.	Regular, rhythmic change in harmonic spectrum of sound in response to rate/waveform of source Modulator. Can work well when also modulating this parameter with Malström's own Mod A, at a different rate.	Produces velocity sensitive blips in the Shift parameter in response to ReDrum voice pattern.	As above	As above	As above
Mod Amount CV In (Malström)	Sweeps Mod amount; depth of modulation increases and decreases in response to envelope shape. The right shape can add sophisticated delay to onset of modulation.	Modulates either or both of Malström's Modulators, in the same way that Mod A can be a target for Mod B. Can produce very complex modulation patterns.	Adds rhythmic impulse to Modulator's cycles, reducing audible depth of modulation at high trim pot settings. Work with Redrum's Length/Decay/Gate settings to tailor the effect.	As above (though perhaps a little more successful with this parameter)	As above	As above
LFO Rate CV In (NNxt)	Rather unusual and unpredictable cross-modulation effects as envelope tries to sweep LFO rate. Global for all LFOs in NNXT patch.	Creates interesting, complex LFO patterns. Global for all LFOs in NNXT Patch.	Interjects rhythmic emphases into LFO cycle, sometimes sounding like frequency or amplitude modulation. Adjust Redrum Length/Decay/Gate settings and step velocity for best effect.	As above	As above	As above
Pan CV In (ReMix, NNxt)	Causes target Pan to move in response to shape of source envelope, for dynamic left/right motion. Motion occurs on each source envelope trigger; more obvious with long Amp Env Release on target.	Strong left/right panning of target; speed of pan dependent on source LFO rate, width of pan determined by target CV trim pot.	Causes target pan to move left-right in response to velocity of individual drum voice Pattern steps. Subtle variation can be added by manipulating Length, Decay/Gate parameters of ReDrum voice channel.	As above	As above	As above
Envelope Gate Ins	Can in some cases usefully trigger other devices; slow attack on source EG creates slow or delayed attack on target device.	Trigger envelope of target at LFO rate of source.	Every gate pulse from source retriggers envelope on target. Use for rhythmic triggering of envelopes, eg in time with drum pattern. Works with or without drum sound. With Dr:rex Gate Ins, makes Slices play with rhythm of drum part.	Gate produced by every REX loop Slice retriggers envelope on target. Can produce very effective rhythmic triggering of envelopes in time with loop Slices.		As above

CV/Gate Routing Possibilities

	Envelope Outs	LFO/Mod Outs	Gate Outs (ReDrum)	Slice Out (Dr:rex)	Auto CV out (Scream 4)	Individual band level outs (BV512)
ReDrum Pitch CV In	Produces pitch EG effects, providing sample assigned to ReDrum voice channel is long enough (or envelope routed to it is fast enough). More sophisticated enveloping than provided by voice channel 7 and 8 pitch bend parameters	Lets you add vibrato effects to sample in ReDrum; particularly effective with longer samples, and if LFO is sync'd to Song tempo. Trim pot serves as LFO depth control.	Random pitch variations of drum voice in response to velocity. With trim pot low, can simulate how real drum pitch goes up slightly on stick impact.	As first entry in this column.	Worth trying; if the sample is right, could be very interesting in a 'talking drum' kind of way.	As above
Gate In (ReDrum)	Source EG triggers ReDrum sound. Try for adding percussive attack to sound of target, especially bass sound playing bass line.	Interesting cross-rhythms can be produced by triggering a drum voice via an LFO, especially with random LFO waveform.	Connecting Gate out to Gate in within same ReDrum makes source channel trigger target channel in same pattern for instant layering effects.	ReDrum sound triggers on every Slice of REX loop. Use to beef up REX loop with extra percussion - try hi-hat/cowbell samples loaded into ReDrum.	No effect	As above
Damage Control CV In (Scream 4)	Careful: worth trying, but wide envelope sweeps will cause distortion.	See left	Add rhythmic pulsing to process; a bit subtle but worth a try.	Slice pulse a bit too short for this purpose.	Effect already present in device, but could make preocess even more repsonsive to level.	As above
P1/P2CV Ins (Scream 4)	Add movement to Scream 4 process in response to envelope.	Add rhythmic or S&H modulation to algorithmoi parameters; makes Scream 4 effect that bit more versatile.	Subtle rhythmic pulse, worth a try.	As above	As above	As above
Scale CV In (Scream 4)	Control the auto wah/resonance effect of the Body section.	As left, but with rhythmic effect	As above	As above	As above	As above

	Envelope Outs	LFO/Mod Outs	Gate Outs (ReDrum)	Slice Out (Dr:rex)	Auto CV out (Scream 4)	Individual band level outs (BV512)
Detune CV In (UN16)	Sweep the detune effect over time.	Rhythmically pulse the detune effect, adding a little more movement to a moving effect.	As above	As above	Changes in response to incoming level could be fruitfully routed to this parameter, potentially adding a more organic feel to the performance.	As above
Shift CV In (BV512)	Create dynamic formant-like effects by moving the Shift parameter over time.	Create rhythmic formant-like effects by moving the Shift parameter in time with the Reason song.	As above	As above	As above	As above
Hold Trigger in (BV512)	No real effect	As left	Rhythmically control the 'stepped vocoder' effect produced by the equivalent front panel switch	As left	No real effect	As above
HF Damp CV In (RV7000)	As above	As above	As above	As above	As above	As above
Gate Trigger In (RV7000)	Worth a try; slow envelope can add a delay to the gated effect.	Interesting cross-rhythms can be produced by triggering the gate via an LFO, especially with random LFO waveform. Might be subtle, though!	Add real rhythmic impulse to gated reverb effect.	Good companion, especially when triggering a gated reverb that's processing the source Dr:Rex	No real effect	As above

Appendix 1
Reason websites, sounds and software resources

Web sites

The internet is such a fluid entity that any listing drawn from it is just a snapshot and likely to go out of date quite quickly. Sites come and go, have name changes, suffer from dead links and so on. Thus, be aware that the links listed here may not work. Sometimes, you'll be able to find the right place by searching on http://www.google.com. The sites featuring forums are likely to provide users with a very good idea of which are the best fan sites, which are run by the most knowledgeable Reason users, and which are the best sources of free ReFills.

Specific Reason content
www.freewebz.com/dorumalaia/: Free Reason ReFills.
www.getimo.de/linkpage2/html/index2.php: Audio info, tutorials, ReFills to download, links, dedicated Reason section.
www.peff.com: Lots of Reason and ReBirth-related stuff from expert Reasoner Peff (Kurt Kurasaki). Find various interesting Reason configurations to download; also a list of sources for ReFills.
www.propellerheads.se: Need we say more?
http://melodiefabriek.nl/: Dedicated Reason user site offering news, tips, tutorials, patches, reviews and links.
http://reason.fan.free.fr/: ReFills, patches, files, news, links and chat.
www.reasonfreaks.com/: Links, files, refills, message board, and more.
www.reasonstation.net: Next to the Props' own site, this is probably the biggest and most comprehensive Reason site, featuring active message boards for when you have problems, a Song board, tutorials and more.
www.simonmorton.freeserve.co.uk/cakewalk2reason.htm: Cakewalk users will appreciate this collection of Studioware panels for Cakewalk 6 or above, which allow you to control Reason and record your changes in Cakewalk, enabling Reason to be used as a sound module and sync to Cakewalk tempo.

General audio/recording/gear sites
www.audiomelody.com: Site covering free music and audio software, including downloads, reviews and tutorials.
www.dancetech.com: Extremely comprehensive site offering tons of reviews, gear info articles, instructional articles, tutorials, gear-specific features.

www.digido.com: Invaluable technical articles from revered mastering engineer Bob Katz.

http://www.harmony-central.com: Lots of news, message boards, user reviews, gear classifieds, all sorts of music technology resources including tutorials and documentation on this huge site.

http://www.hitsquad.com/smm: Loads of links to free and commercial synths, effects plugins and much more.

http://homerecording.com/bbs: Threaded boards covering wide variety of audio, software and home-recording topics.

http://homerecording.about.com/?once=true&: Decent site covering many aspects of home recording.

http://homerecording.com: A 'knowledge centre' for anyone interested in recording and mixing their own music.

www.kvraudio.com: Massive resource for everything plugin and ReFill-related

http://www.musicplayer.com: American general site covering Keyboard, Guitar Player and Bass Player magazines. Professionally moderated forums.

www.looperman.com: Electronic music resource including tutorials and samples.

http://machines.hyperreal.org: Music Machines synth review site.

www.macmusic.org: News, forums, info, all Mac music related.

www.midifarm.com: News and lots of MIDI articles.

www.musicianstechcentral.com: General audio, MIDI, synth and recording How-To articles, a tech Q&A, news, and lots more.

www.musictechmag.co.uk: Up to the minute news, reviews and technique for all aspects of music technnology

www.myspace.com: The best site for getting your music heard by a massive worldwide audience.

www.pc-publishing.com: Home of the UK's foremost publisher of music technology-related books.

www.proaudiorx.com: Lots of recording-related articles, links, and more.

www.prorec.com: Professional online recording magazine.

www.recordingwebsite.com: Equipment reviews, recording articles and advice, message board and chat room.

www.soniccontrol.com: Another one of those comprehensive all-round audio sites including news, FAQs, features, boards and user reviews.

www.sonicspot.com: Free software to download, message boards and articles.

www.sonicstate.com: Large, well-established site packed with an ever-increasing selection of users reviews, news and more. Also home to The Gas Station, a themed set of musicians' message boards, and Sonic Store, an online shop.

www.soundonsound.com: Web site of Europe's foremost hi-tech music magazine, offering up-to-date news, gear classifieds, forums, and free access to years worth of top-quality reviews, technical features and artist interviews (free access to articles over six months old). Inexpensive online electronic subscriptions covering the brand-new content also available. Home to the monthly Reason Notes column.

www.stompbox.co.uk: General musicians' site, with lots of features.
www.synthzone.com: All things synth and software.
www.tweakheadz.com: "Sample CDs, gear advice, secrets of MIDI and audio production." Check out this informative site for message boards, How-Tos, gear reviews, and beginner and advanced audio and MIDI articles.
www.usb-audio.com: Low-latency USB Audio drivers for various devices from Propagamma.

Free samples

Here are just some of the places you can find sample fodder for nothing. Also use search engines to turn up more.
www.analoguesamples.com: Packed with free samples of analogue synths and drum machines, most in WAV format. Also offers a monthly FTP service where for a small fee members can get access to all the site's samples via more convenient FTP, plus samples that are unique to the monthly service.
www.dancetech.com: Extensive range of free samples, as well as lots of other hi-tech music content. Reason forum
www.findsounds.com: Search engine for finding samples on the net.
http://hem.passagen.se/lej97/kalava: Small, mainly drum-orientated free WAV sample archive
www.samplearena.com: Free downloadable samples in a variety of formats including WAV. Also sample collections for sale on CD-ROM.
www.synthzone.com/sampling.htm: Great list of sites offering free samples in a variety of formats
www.modarchive.com/waveworld/: Collections of free WAV samples of synths, drum machines, and more.
http://bassandtrouble.com/sounds/wavs3000/wavs3000.htm: Small set of WAV samples including bass, drum and synth sounds.
http://www.dooleydrums.com/: Set of WAV-format drum loops played by owner of site, drummer with 20 years playing experience.
http://www.dogbeats.co.uk/: Free drum breaks, also copyright-free, in WAV format.
www.samplenet.co.uk: Over 3000 online samples, plus news and features.
http://www.top50wavsites.com/index.html: Top 50 WAV site links.
http://www.sound-planet.de: Links to free samples.
http://soundproz.com/: Free MP3-format samples, plus inexpensive sample CDs to buy.
http://www.samplez.de/index.php?id=8: German site (in German) offering lots of free MP3 samples in various categories.
http://s4u_site.tripod.com/samples.html: Lots of style-categorised samples in MP3 and WAV format. Also SoundFonts to download.
www.samplemania.org/: Moderate selection of WAV and AIFF samples.
www.modarchive.com/waveworld/: free drum samples, loops and instrumental samples in WAV format.
http://soundfx.com/freesoundfx1.htm: Free sound effects to download in WAV and AIFF format, if you don't mind giving them your email address.

Commercial samples

This list doesn't include every commercial sample site in the world, but it's a good start.

www.timespace.com: A leading UK supplier of a huge variety of quality sample CDs and CD-ROMs. You can also purchase sounds to download.

www.soundsonline.com: US-based sample-CD supplier, also with very good sample download service (search for sounds by type and bpm) from US$1 per sample.

www.bigfishaudio.com: Another large US-based supplier of sample CDs and CD-ROMs, also shipping overseas.

www.primesounds.com: Huge, professional archive of WAV and AIFF samples, organised into genre, including loops and full instrument multisamples. You need to subscribe to the site to download samples, but all can be previewed online. Cheapest subscription rate is equivalent to US$10 per month at time of writing.

www.platinumloops.com: Royalty-free loops and samples. Subscription site with two different levels of subscription.

www.sonomic.com: Vast online sample library (claimed to contain 200,000 sounds) in WAV and AIFF format, downloadable for cost of monthly subscription (from US$30 at time of writing) or can be purchased per sound (from $1.99 each).

Specific Reason content (ReFills, etc)

www.propellerheads.se: Find details of ReFills of all types at Propellerhead's own web site, including free user ReFills and commercial ones.

www.reasonrefills.com: Commercial ReFills from long-established UK sample CD producer AMG. Now offers what may be the largest range of ReFills.

www.electronisounds.com/: WAV-format sample CDs to buy, plus REX-format drum sample CDs.

www.lapjockey.com: Source for a new 'Flatpack' CD from UK developer Lapjockey, featuring a mix of rare analogue synth and classic drum machine sounds, plus modern and experimental synth kits. Contains samples, loops, patches and Song templates (featuring interesting cross-modulation patching and synthesized rhythm sequencing), and exploits the 24-bit capability of the software. Also featured are original patches for both SubTractor and Malström.

www.powerfx.com: Reason ReFill CDs.

PC Audio Software

Shareware/Freeware

Awave ACDR (www.fmjsoft.com): Audio ripping software. Available in time- and feature-limited shareware version and inexpensive commercial version.

Exact Audio Copy (www.ExactAudioCopy.de): Free audio ripping program.

MPEG DK GoWave (www.xaudio.de/pages/gowave.html): Free program that converts MP3s to WAVs, useful for MP3 samples you may find on the web.

Yamaha Tiny Wave Editor www.yamahasynth.com/down/index.htm: Comprehensive free audio editor including many editing, manipulation and looping tools, plus timestretching. Originally support material for the A-series samplers, but suitable for general audio editing. Loads and saves in AIFF and WAV formats.

www.audioattack.de/: Visit this site for links to several freeware audio editors for download.

http://audacity.sourceforge.net: Audacity for Mac, PC and Linux is a brilliant open-source multitrack audio recorder and editor.

Commercial

Adobe Audition www.adobe.com/products/audition/main.html: Cost-effective yet full-featured and widely-used audio editor with good format-conversion facilities.

Awave Studio (www.fmjsoft.com): Inexpensive general-purpose audio software offering lots of features, including format conversion (many formats), plus audio editing, batch conversion and crossfade looping. Supports DirectX plug-ins for file processing. Also consider the cheaper Awave Audio for format conversion. Limited shareware versions of both available for trying out.

CdXtract (www.cdxtract.com): Format-conversion software. A vast range of formats can be converted to other formats, including WAV and AIFF, and the software offers sample CD-browsing and databasing features, plus batch-conversion facilities.

EZ-Editor (www.ez-editor.com): Very inexpensive audio editor that offers editing tools, good looping features, and more.

Samplitude (www.samplitude.de): Family of three full-featured audio recording/editing programs, with entry-level Samplitude Master costing around 300 Euros. 90-day trial versions downloadable.

Sony Sound Forge (http://mediasoftware.sonypictures.com/): Powerful audio toolbox with wide range of features including full audio editing and audio ripping from CD.

Steinberg Wavelab (www.steinberg.net): Highly-respected and very comprehensive professional audio editing and mastering package. Also does CD burning, batch processing and sample editing and is compatible with a wide range of file formats, for format conversion.

Mac Audio Tools

Shareware/Freeware

CdXtract (www.cdxtract.com): Format-conversion software. A vast range of formats can be converted to other formats, including WAV and AIFF, and the software offers sample CD-browsing and databasing features, plus batch-conversion facilities.

D-SoundPro (www.d-soundpro.com): Possibly the king of Mac shareware editors, DSound Pro loads and saves in AIFF, SDII and WAV formats, has support for various sampler formats, offers sophisticated audio editing and sample extraction facilities, and has timestretching and a crossfade looping feature. More than worth the $39 shareware registration fee. Trial version available for download.

DSP-Quattro (www.dsp-quattro.com) Now marketed by i3, D-Sound Pro migrates to MacOS X and becomes even better! Not just an audio editor, but a VST instrument and plug-in host and playlist editor. Still marketed on line, Quattro costs 99 euros.

Prosoniq sonicWORX Basic (www.prosoniq.net): Free version of SonicWorx commercial audio editing package, for MacOS 9.

SoundHack (www.soundhack.com). Useful audio editor, with CD ripping option and some brilliant manipulation tools.

SndSampler (www.provide.net/~moorepower/ahg/sndsampler): Full-featured and respected shareware audio recorder/editor, does audio ripping, sound extraction/file conversion, and offers other interesting facilities.

SoundApp: Audio recording and editing program which also converts between many formats, including MP3 to WAV/AIFF.

Yamaha Tiny Wave Editor (www.yamahasynth.com): Comprehensive audio editor including many editing, manipulation and looping tools, plus timestretching. Originally support material for the A-series samplers, but suitable for general audio editing. Loads and saves in AIFF and WAV formats.

http://audacity.sourceforge.net: Audacity for Mac, PC and Linux is a brilliant open-source multitrack audio recorder and editor.

Commercial

BIAS Peak (www.bias-inc.com): Powerful audio editor offering comprehensive audio recording and wave editing features, timestretching, sample looping tools, reading and writing of multiple file formats. Also available in much cheaper LE version with many of the same features.

Gallery CD Studio (www.gallery.co.uk): Fast audio ripping from CD.

Prosoniq SonicWorx **(www.prosoniq.com)**: Professional $400 audio editor that also rips audio off CD. Also available in Artist version offering some of the same and some extra features, for $200.

TC Works Spark (www.tcworks.de): Family of full-featured, Mac-only audio editors with format conversion facilities. Entry-level versions very cost-effective; SparkME, for Mac OSX only, is a free download.

Sound Studio (http://www.felttip.com/products/soundstudio/) A simple and cheap yet fully featured audio recorder and editor for OS X.

Appendix 2
Further reading

Software/Computers

Propellerhead Reason Tips and Tricks: Hollin Jones, 2005 (PC Publishing)

Music Projects with Propellerhead Reason: Hollin Jones (PC Publishing, 2006)

The Fast Guide to Cubase SX V3: Simon Millward (PC Publishing)

PC Music – The Easy Guide: Robin Vincent (PC Publishing)

Reason in Der Praxis: Thomas Alker (PPV Medien). German-speaking readers may like to get hold of this. We don't really speak/read German ourselves (sorry!), but this book seems to be highly regarded by those who have read it.

Music Theory/Programming

The Musician's Guide to Reading & Writing Music: Dave Stewart (Backbeat UK)

Beat It! Serious Drum Patterns... : Joe and Pauly Ortiz (PC Publishing)

Synthesis

The Quick Guide to Analogue Synthesis: Ian Waugh (PC Publishing)

Sound Synthesis and Sampling: Martin Russ (Focal Press)

General Recording/Technology

Tips for Recording Musicians: John Harris (PC Publishing)

Home Recording Made Easy: Paul White (Sanctuary)

'Basic' series: Paul White (Sanctuary). Titles include Digital Recording, MIDI, Live Sound, Effects and Processors, VST Instruments, and Mixers

Recording and Production Techniques: Paul White (Sanctuary)

Practical Recording Techniques: Bruce and Jenny Bartlett (Focal Press)

Modern Recording Techniques: David M Huber and Robert E Runstein (Focal Press)

Magazines

MusicTech Magazine (www.musictechmag.co.uk). Excellent monthly resource for news, reviews, technique and knowledge of all kinds. Home to excellent Reason, Cubase, Logic and Sonar workshops.

Sound On Sound (www.soundonsound.com). Ongoing, detailed music technology and recording information in the shape of features, reviews and interviews.

Keyboard (www.keyboardonline.com): Well-established American title carries authoritative music technology and recording reviews, lab tests, features and interviews.

Electronic Musician (www.electronicmusician.com): Respected US title featuring wide range of music technology content.

Index